BY YUVAL NOAH HARARI

Sapiens

Homo Deus

21 Lessons for the 21st Century

Unstoppable Us

Nexus

Nexus

Nexus

A BRIEF HISTORY OF INFORMATION NETWORKS
FROM THE STONE AGE TO AI

Yuval Noah Harari

RANDOM HOUSE

NEW YORK

Published in the United States by Random House, an imprint and division of
Penguin Random House LLC, New York.

RANDOM HOUSE and the HOUSE colophon are registered trademarks of Penguin
Random House LLC.

Published in the United Kingdom by Fern Press, an imprint of Vintage,
a division of Penguin Random House UK.

Library of Congress Cataloging-in-Publication Data
Names: Harari, Yuval N., author.
Title: Nexus: a brief history of information networks from the Stone Age to AI /
Yuval Noah Harari.
Description: First edition. | New York: Random House, [2024] |
Includes bibliographical references and index.
Identifiers: LCCN 2024011713 (print) | LCCN 2024011714 (ebook) |
ISBN 9780593734223 (hardcover) | ISBN 9780593736814 |
ISBN 9780593734247 (ebook)
Subjects: LCSH: Information behavior—History. | Information networks—
History. | Information technology—History.
Classification: LCC ZA3075 .H375 2024 (print) |
LCC ZA3075 (ebook) | DDC 001.09—dc23/eng/20240614
LC record available at https://lccn.loc.gov/2024011713
LC ebook record available at https://lccn.loc.gov/2024011714

International edition ISBN: 978-0-593-73681-4

Printed in the United States of America on acid-free paper

randomhousebooks.com

2 4 6 8 9 7 5 3 1

First U.S. Edition

Book design by Caroline Cunningham

To Itzik with love, and to all who love wisdom.

On a path of a thousand dreams, we are looking for reality.

Contents

PART III: Computer Politics

Prologue

We have named our species *Homo sapiens*—the wise human. But it is debatable how well we have lived up to the name.

Over the last 100,000 years, we Sapiens have certainly accumulated enormous power. Just listing all our discoveries, inventions, and conquests would fill volumes. But power isn't wisdom, and after 100,000 years of discoveries, inventions, and conquests humanity has pushed itself into an existential crisis. We are on the verge of ecological collapse, caused by the misuse of our own power. We are also busy creating new technologies like artificial intelligence (AI) that have the potential to escape our control and enslave or annihilate us. Yet instead of our species uniting to deal with these existential challenges, international tensions are rising, global cooperation is becoming more difficult, countries are stockpiling doomsday weapons, and a new world war does not seem impossible.

If we Sapiens are so wise, why are we so self-destructive?

At a deeper level, although we have accumulated so much information about everything from DNA molecules to distant galaxies, it doesn't seem that all this information has given us answers to the big questions of life: Who are we? What should we aspire to? What is a

good life, and how should we live it? Despite the stupendous amounts of information at our disposal, we are as susceptible as our ancient ancestors to fantasy and delusion. Nazism and Stalinism are but two recent examples of the mass insanity that occasionally engulfs even modern societies. Nobody disputes that humans today have a lot more information and power than in the Stone Age, but it is far from certain that we understand ourselves and our role in the universe much better.

Why are we so good at accumulating more information and power, but far less successful at acquiring wisdom? Throughout history many traditions have believed that some fatal flaw in our nature tempts us to pursue powers we don't know how to handle. The Greek myth of Phaethon told of a boy who discovers that he is the son of Helios, the sun god. Wishing to prove his divine origin, Phaethon demands the privilege of driving the chariot of the sun. Helios warns Phaethon that no human can control the celestial horses that pull the solar chariot. But Phaethon insists, until the sun god relents. After rising proudly in the sky, Phaethon indeed loses control of the chariot. The sun veers off course, scorching all vegetation, killing numerous beings, and threatening to burn the earth itself. Zeus intervenes and strikes Phaethon with a thunderbolt. The conceited human drops from the sky like a falling star, himself on fire. The gods reassert control of the sky and save the world.

Two thousand years later, when the Industrial Revolution was making its first steps and machines began replacing humans in numerous tasks, Johann Wolfgang von Goethe published a similar cautionary tale titled "The Sorcerer's Apprentice." Goethe's poem (later popularized as a Walt Disney animation starring Mickey Mouse) tells of an old sorcerer who leaves a young apprentice in charge of his workshop and gives him some chores to tend to while he is gone, like fetching water from the river. The apprentice decides to make things easier for himself and, using one of the sorcerer's spells, enchants a broom to fetch the water for him. But the apprentice doesn't know how to stop the broom, which relentlessly fetches more and more

water, threatening to flood the workshop. In panic, the apprentice cuts the enchanted broom in two with an ax, only to see each half become another broom. Now *two* enchanted brooms are inundating the workshop with water. When the old sorcerer returns, the apprentice pleads for help: "The spirits that I summoned, I now cannot rid myself of again." The sorcerer immediately breaks the spell and stops the flood. The lesson to the apprentice—and to humanity—is clear: never summon powers you cannot control.

What do the cautionary fables of the apprentice and of Phaethon tell us in the twenty-first century? We humans have obviously refused to heed their warnings. We have already driven the earth's climate out of balance and have summoned billions of enchanted brooms, drones, chatbots, and other algorithmic spirits that may escape our control and unleash a flood of unintended consequences.

What should we do, then? The fables offer no answers, other than to wait for some god or sorcerer to save us. This, of course, is an extremely dangerous message. It encourages people to abdicate responsibility and put their faith in gods and sorcerers instead. Even worse, it fails to appreciate that gods and sorcerers are themselves a human invention—just like chariots, brooms, and algorithms. The tendency to create powerful things with unintended consequences started not with the invention of the steam engine or AI but with the invention of religion. Prophets and theologians have summoned powerful spirits that were supposed to bring love and joy but occasionally ended up flooding the world with blood.

The Phaethon myth and Goethe's poem fail to provide useful advice because they misconstrue the way humans gain power. In both fables, a single human acquires enormous power, but is then corrupted by hubris and greed. The conclusion is that our flawed individual psychology makes us abuse power. What this crude analysis misses is that human power is never the outcome of individual initiative. Power always stems from cooperation between large numbers of humans.

Accordingly, it isn't our individual psychology that causes us to

abuse power. After all, alongside greed, hubris, and cruelty, humans are also capable of love, compassion, humility, and joy. True, among the worst members of our species, greed and cruelty reign supreme and lead bad actors to abuse power. But why would human societies choose to entrust power to their worst members? Most Germans in 1933, for example, were not psychopaths. So why did they vote for Hitler?

Our tendency to summon powers we cannot control stems not from individual psychology but from the unique way our species co-operates in large numbers. The main argument of this book is that humankind gains enormous power by building large networks of co-operation, but the way these networks are built predisposes us to use that power unwisely. Our problem, then, is a network problem.

Even more specifically, it is an information problem. Information is the glue that holds networks together. But for tens of thousands of years, Sapiens built and maintained large networks by inventing and spreading fictions, fantasies, and mass delusions—about gods, about enchanted broomsticks, about AI, and about a great many other things. While each individual human is typically interested in know-ing the truth about themselves and the world, large networks bind members and create order by relying on fictions and fantasies. That's how we got, for example, to Nazism and Stalinism. These were ex-ceptionally powerful networks, held together by exceptionally de-luded ideas. As George Orwell famously put it, ignorance is strength.

The fact that the Nazi and Stalinist regimes were founded on cruel fantasies and shameless lies did *not* make them historically excep-tional, nor did it preordain them to collapse. Nazism and Stalinism were two of the strongest networks humans ever created. In late 1941 and early 1942, the Axis powers came within reach of winning World War II. Stalin eventually emerged as the victor of that war,[1] and in the 1950s and 1960s he and his heirs also had a reasonable chance of winning the Cold War. By the 1990s liberal democracies had gained the upper hand, but this now seems like a temporary victory. In the

twenty-first century, some new totalitarian regime may well succeed where Hitler and Stalin failed, creating an all-powerful network that could prevent future generations from even attempting to expose its lies and fictions. We should not assume that delusional networks are doomed to failure. If we want to prevent their triumph, we will have to do the hard work ourselves.

THE NAIVE VIEW OF INFORMATION

It is difficult to appreciate the strength of delusional networks because of a broader misunderstanding about how big information networks—whether delusional or not—operate. This misunderstanding is encapsulated in something I call "the naive view of information." While fables like the myth of Phaethon and "The Sorcerer's Apprentice" present an overly pessimistic view of individual human psychology, the naive view of information disseminates an overly optimistic view of large-scale human networks.

The naive view argues that by gathering and processing much more information than individuals can, big networks achieve a better understanding of medicine, physics, economics, and numerous other fields, which makes the network not only powerful but also wise. For example, by gathering information on pathogens, pharmaceutical companies and health-care services can determine the true causes of many diseases, which enables them to develop more effective medicines and to make wiser decisions about their usage. This view posits that in sufficient quantities information leads to truth, and truth in turn leads to both power and wisdom. Ignorance, in contrast, seems to lead nowhere. While delusional or deceitful networks might occasionally arise in moments of historical crisis, in the long term they are bound to lose to more clear-sighted and honest rivals. A health-care service that ignores information about pathogens, or a pharmaceutical giant that deliberately spreads disinformation, will ultimately

lose out to competitors that make wiser use of information. The naive view thus implies that delusional networks must be aberrations and that big networks can usually be trusted to handle power wisely.

The naive view of information

Of course, the naive view acknowledges that many things can go wrong on the path from information to truth. We might make honest mistakes in gathering and processing the information. Malicious actors motivated by greed or hate might hide important facts or try to deceive us. As a result, information sometimes leads to error rather than truth. For example, partial information, faulty analysis, or a dis information campaign might lead even experts to misidentify the true cause of a particular disease.

However, the naive view assumes that the antidote to most problems we encounter in gathering and processing information is gathering and processing even more information. While we are never completely safe from error, in most cases more information means greater accuracy. A single doctor wishing to identify the cause of an epidemic by examining a single patient is less likely to succeed than thousands of doctors gathering data on millions of patients. And if the doctors themselves conspire to hide the truth, making medical information more freely available to the public and to investigative journalists will eventually reveal the scam. According to this view, the bigger the information network, the closer it must be to the truth.

Naturally, even if we analyze information accurately and discover important truths, this does not guarantee we will use the resulting capabilities wisely. Wisdom is commonly understood to mean "making right decisions," but what "right" means depends on value judg-

ments that differ among diverse people, cultures, and ideologies. Scientists who discover a new pathogen may develop a vaccine to protect people. But if the scientists—or their political overlords—believe in a racist ideology that advocates that some races are inferior and should be exterminated, the new medical knowledge might be used to develop a biological weapon that kills millions.

In this case, too, the naive view of information holds that additional information offers at least a partial remedy. The naive view thinks that disagreements about values turn out on closer inspection to be the fault of either the lack of information or deliberate disinformation. According to this view, racists are ill-informed people who just don't know the facts of biology and history. They think that "race" is a valid biological category, and they have been brainwashed by bogus conspiracy theories. The remedy to racism is therefore to provide people with more biological and historical facts. It may take time, but in a free market of information sooner or later truth will prevail.

The naive view is of course more nuanced and thoughtful than can be explained in a few paragraphs, but its core tenet is that information is an essentially good thing, and the more we have of it, the better. Given enough information and enough time, we are bound to discover the truth about things ranging from viral infections to racist biases, thereby developing not only our power but also the wisdom necessary to use that power well.

This naive view justifies the pursuit of ever more powerful information technologies and has been the semiofficial ideology of the computer age and the internet. In June 1989, a few months before the fall of the Berlin Wall and of the Iron Curtain, Ronald Reagan declared that "the Goliath of totalitarian control will rapidly be brought down by the David of the microchip" and that "the biggest of Big Brothers is increasingly helpless against communications technology. . . . Information is the oxygen of the modern age. . . . It seeps through the walls topped with barbed wire. It wafts across the

electrified, booby-trapped borders. Breezes of electronic beams blow through the Iron Curtain as if it was lace."[2] In November 2009, Barack Obama spoke in the same spirit on a visit to Shanghai, telling his Chinese hosts, "I am a big believer in technology and I'm a big believer in openness when it comes to the flow of information. I think that the more freely information flows, the stronger the society becomes."[3]

Entrepreneurs and corporations have often expressed similarly rosy views of information technology. Already in 1858 an editorial in *The New Englander* about the invention of the telegraph stated, "It is impossible that old prejudices and hostilities should longer exist, while such an instrument has been created for an exchange of thought between all the nations of the earth."[4] Nearly two centuries and two world wars later, Mark Zuckerberg said that Facebook's goal "is to help people to share more in order to make the world more open and to help promote understanding between people."[5]

In his 2024 book, *The Singularity Is Nearer*, the eminent futurologist and entrepreneur Ray Kurzweil surveys the history of information technology and concludes that "the reality is that nearly every aspect of life is getting progressively better as a result of exponentially improving technology." Looking back at the grand sweep of human history, he cites examples like the invention of the printing press to argue that by its very nature information technology tends to spawn "a virtuous circle advancing nearly every aspect of human well-being, including literacy, education, wealth, sanitation, health, democratization and reduction in violence."[6]

The naive view of information is perhaps most succinctly captured in Google's mission statement "to organize the world's information and make it universally accessible and useful." Google's answer to Goethe's warnings is that while a single apprentice pilfering his master's secret spell book is likely to cause disaster, when a lot of apprentices are given free access to all the world's information, they will not only create useful enchanted brooms but also learn to handle them wisely.

GOOGLE VERSUS GOETHE

It must be stressed that there are numerous cases in which having more information has indeed enabled humans to understand the world better and to make wiser use of their power. Consider, for example, the dramatic reduction in child mortality. Johann Wolfgang von Goethe was the eldest of seven siblings, but only he and his sister Cornelia got to celebrate their seventh birthday. Disease carried off their brother Hermann Jacob at age six, their sister Catharina Elisabeth at age four, their sister Johanna Maria at age two, their brother Georg Adolf at age eight months, and a fifth, unnamed brother was stillborn. Cornelia then died from disease at twenty-six, leaving Johann Wolfgang as the sole survivor from their family.[7]

Johann Wolfgang von Goethe went on to have five children of his own, of whom all but the eldest son—August—died within two weeks of their birth. In all probability the cause was incompatibility between the blood groups of Goethe and his wife, Christiane, which after the first successful pregnancy led the mother to develop antibodies to the fetal blood. This condition, known as rhesus disease, is nowadays treated so effectively that the mortality rate is less than 2 percent, but in the 1790s it had an average mortality rate of 50 percent, and for Goethe's four younger children it was a death sentence.[8]

Altogether in Goethe's family—a well-to-do German family in the late eighteenth century—the child survival rate was an abysmal 25 percent. Only three out of twelve children reached adulthood. This horrendous statistic was not exceptional. Around the time Goethe wrote "The Sorcerer's Apprentice" in 1797, it is estimated that only about 50 percent of German children reached age fifteen,[9] and the same was probably true in most other parts of the world.[10] By 2020, 95.6 percent of children worldwide lived beyond their fifteenth birthday,[11] and in Germany that figure was 99.5 percent.[12] This momentous achievement would not have been possible without collecting, analyzing, and sharing massive amounts of medical data

about things like blood groups. In this case, then, the naive view of information proved to be correct.

However, the naive view of information sees only part of the picture, and the history of the modern age was not just about reducing child mortality. In recent generations humanity has experienced the greatest increase ever in both the amount and the speed of our information production. Every smartphone contains more information than the ancient Library of Alexandria[13] and enables its owner to instantaneously connect to billions of other people throughout the world. Yet with all this information circulating at breathtaking speeds, humanity is closer than ever to annihilating itself.

Despite—or perhaps because of—our hoard of data, we are continuing to spew greenhouse gases into the atmosphere, pollute rivers and oceans, cut down forests, destroy entire habitats, drive countless species to extinction, and jeopardize the ecological foundations of our own species. We are also producing ever more powerful weapons of mass destruction, from thermonuclear bombs to doomsday viruses. Our leaders don't lack information about these dangers, yet instead of collaborating to find solutions, they are edging closer to a global war.

Would having even more information make things better—or worse? We will soon find out. Numerous corporations and governments are in a race to develop the most powerful information technology in history—AI. Some leading entrepreneurs, like the American investor Marc Andreessen, believe that AI will finally solve all of humanity's problems. On June 6, 2023, Andreessen published an essay titled "Why AI Will Save the World," peppered with bold statements like "I am here to bring the good news: AI will not destroy the world, and in fact may save it" and "AI can make everything we care about better." He concluded, "The development and proliferation of AI—far from a risk that we should fear—is a moral obligation that we have to ourselves, to our children, and to our future."[14]

Ray Kurzweil concurs, arguing in *The Singularity Is Nearer* that

"AI is the pivotal technology that will allow us to meet the pressing challenges that confront us, including overcoming disease, poverty, environmental degradation, and all of our human frailties. We have a moral imperative to realize this promise of new technologies." Kurzweil is keenly aware of the technology's potential perils, and analyzes them at length, but believes they could be mitigated successfully.[15]

Others are more skeptical. Not only philosophers and social scientists but also many leading AI experts and entrepreneurs like Yoshua Bengio, Geoffrey Hinton, Sam Altman, Elon Musk, and Mustafa Suleyman have warned the public that AI could destroy our civilization.[16] A 2024 article co-authored by Bengio, Hinton, and numerous other experts noted that "unchecked AI advancement could culminate in a large-scale loss of life and the biosphere, and the marginalization or even extinction of humanity."[17] In a 2023 survey of 2,778 AI researchers, more than a third gave at least a 10 percent chance to advanced AI leading to outcomes as bad as human extinction.[18] In 2023 close to thirty governments—including those of China, the United States, and the U.K.—signed the Bletchley Declaration on AI, which acknowledged that "there is potential for serious, even catastrophic, harm, either deliberate or unintentional, stemming from the most significant capabilities of these AI models."[19] By using such apocalyptic terms, experts and governments have no wish to conjure a Hollywood image of rebellious robots running in the streets and shooting people. Such a scenario is unlikely, and it merely distracts people from the real dangers. Rather, experts warn about two other scenarios.

First, the power of AI could supercharge existing human conflicts, dividing humanity against itself. Just as in the twentieth century the Iron Curtain divided the rival powers in the Cold War, so in the twenty-first century the Silicon Curtain—made of silicon chips and computer codes rather than barbed wire—might come to divide rival powers in a new global conflict. Because the AI arms race will produce ever more destructive weapons, even a small spark might ignite a cataclysmic conflagration.

Second, the Silicon Curtain might come to divide not one group of humans from another but rather all humans from our new AI overlords. No matter where we live, we might find ourselves co-cooned by a web of unfathomable algorithms that manage our lives, reshape our politics and culture, and even reengineer our bodies and minds—while we can no longer comprehend the forces that control us, let alone stop them. If a twenty-first-century totalitarian network succeeds in conquering the world, it may be run by nonhuman intelligence, rather than by a human dictator. People who single out China, Russia, or a post-democratic United States as their main source for totalitarian nightmares misunderstand the danger. In fact, Chinese, Russians, Americans, and all other humans are together threatened by the totalitarian potential of nonhuman intelligence.

Given the magnitude of the danger, AI should be of interest to all human beings. While not everyone can become an AI expert, we should all keep in mind that AI is the first technology in history that can make decisions and create new ideas by itself. All previous human inventions have empowered humans, because no matter how powerful the new tool was, the decisions about its usage remained in our hands. Knives and bombs do not themselves decide whom to kill. They are dumb tools, lacking the intelligence necessary to process information and make independent decisions. In contrast, AI can process information by itself, and thereby replace humans in decision making. AI isn't a tool—it's an agent.

Its mastery of information also enables AI to independently generate new ideas, in fields ranging from music to medicine. Gramophones played our music, and microscopes revealed the secrets of our cells, but gramophones couldn't compose new symphonies, and microscopes couldn't synthesize new drugs. AI is already capable of producing art and making scientific discoveries by itself. In the next few decades, it will likely gain the ability even to create new life-forms, either by writing genetic code or by inventing an inorganic code animating inorganic entities.

Even at the present moment, in the embryonic stage of the AI revolution, computers already make decisions about us—whether to give us a mortgage, to hire us for a job, to send us to prison. This trend will only increase and accelerate, making it more difficult to understand our own lives. Can we trust computer algorithms to make wise decisions and create a better world? That's a much bigger gamble than trusting an enchanted broom to fetch water. And it is more than just human lives we are gambling on. AI could alter the course not just of our species' history but of the evolution of all life-forms.

WEAPONIZING INFORMATION

In 2016, I published *Homo Deus*, a book that highlighted some of the dangers posed to humanity by the new information technologies. That book argued that the real hero of history has always been information, rather than *Homo sapiens*, and that scientists increasingly understand not just history but also biology, politics, and economics in terms of information flows. Animals, states, and markets are all information networks, absorbing data from the environment, making decisions, and releasing data back. The book warned that while we hope better information technology will give us health, happiness, and power, it may actually take power away from us and destroy both our physical and our mental health. *Homo Deus* hypothesized that if humans aren't careful, we might dissolve within the torrent of information like a clump of earth within a gushing river, and that in the grand scheme of things humanity will turn out to have been just a ripple within the cosmic dataflow.

In the years since *Homo Deus* was published, the pace of change has only accelerated, and power has indeed been shifting from humans to algorithms. Many of the scenarios that sounded like science fiction in 2016—such as algorithms that can create art, masquerade

as human beings, make crucial life decisions about us, and know more about us than we know about ourselves—are everyday realities in 2024.

Many other things have changed since 2016. The ecological crisis has intensified, international tensions have escalated, and a populist wave has undermined the cohesion of even the most robust democracies. Populism has also mounted a radical challenge to the naive view of information. Populist leaders such as Donald Trump and Jair Bolsonaro, and populist movements and conspiracy theories such as QAnon and the anti-vaxxers, have argued that all traditional institutions that gain authority by claiming to gather information and discover truth are simply lying. Bureaucrats, judges, doctors, mainstream journalists, and academic experts are elite cabals that have no interest in the truth and are deliberately spreading disinformation to gain power and privileges for themselves at the expense of "the people." The rise of politicians like Trump and movements like QAnon has a specific political context, unique to the conditions of the United States in the late 2010s. But populism as an antiestablishment worldview long predated Trump and is relevant to numerous other historical contexts now and in the future. In a nutshell, populism views information as a weapon.[20]

Information ───▶ Power

The populist view of information

In its more extreme versions, populism posits that there is no objective truth at all and that everyone has "their own truth," which they wield to vanquish rivals. According to this worldview, power is the only reality. All social interactions are power struggles, because humans are interested only in power. The claim to be interested in something else—like truth or justice—is nothing more than a ploy to gain power. Whenever and wherever populism succeeds in disseminating the view of information as a weapon, language itself is

undermined. Nouns like "facts" and adjectives like "accurate" and "truthful" become elusive. Such words are not taken as pointing to a common objective reality. Rather, any talk of "facts" or "truth" is bound to prompt at least some people to ask, "Whose facts and whose truth are you referring to?"

It should be stressed that this power-focused and deeply skeptical view of information isn't a new phenomenon and it wasn't invented by anti-vaxxers, flat-earthers, Bolsonaristas, or Trump supporters. Similar views were propagated long before 2016, including by some of humanity's brightest minds.[21] In the late twentieth century, for example, intellectuals from the radical left like Michel Foucault and Edward Said claimed that scientific institutions like clinics and universities are not pursuing timeless and objective truths but are instead using power to determine what counts as truth, in the service of capitalist and colonialist elites. These radical critiques occasionally went as far as arguing that "scientific facts" are nothing more than a capitalist or colonialist "discourse" and that people in power can never be really interested in truth and can never be trusted to recognize and correct their own mistakes.[22]

This particular line of radical leftist thinking goes back to Karl Marx, who argued in the mid-nineteenth century that power is the only reality, that information is a weapon, and that elites who claim to be serving truth and justice are in fact pursuing narrow class privileges. In the words of the 1848 *Communist Manifesto*, "The history of all hitherto existing societies is the history of class struggles. Freeman and slave, patrician and plebeian, lord and serf, guildmaster and journeyman, in a word, oppressor and oppressed stood in constant opposition to one another, carried on an uninterrupted, now hidden, now open, fight." This binary interpretation of history implies that every human interaction is a power struggle between oppressors and oppressed. Accordingly, whenever anyone says anything, the question to ask isn't, "What is being said? Is it true?" but rather, "Who is saying this? Whose privileges does it serve?"

Of course, right-wing populists such as Trump and Bolsonaro are

unlikely to have read Foucault or Marx, and indeed present themselves as fiercely anti-Marxist. They also greatly differ from Marxists in their suggested policies in fields like taxation and welfare. But their basic view of society and of information is surprisingly Marxist, seeing all human interactions as a power struggle between oppressors and oppressed. For example, in his inaugural address in 2017 Trump announced that "a small group in our nation's capital has reaped the rewards of government while the people have borne the cost."[23] Such rhetoric is a staple of populism, which the political scientist Cas Mudde has described as an "ideology that considers society to be ultimately separated into two homogeneous and antagonistic groups, 'the pure people' versus 'the corrupt elite.'"[24] Just as Marxists claimed that the media functions as a mouthpiece for the capitalist class, and that scientific institutions like universities spread disinformation in order to perpetuate capitalist control, populists accuse these same institutions of working to advance the interests of the "corrupt elites" at the expense of "the people."

Present-day populists also suffer from the same incoherence that plagued radical antiestablishment movements in previous generations. If power is the only reality, and if information is just a weapon, what does it imply about the populists themselves? Are they too interested only in power, and are they too lying to us to gain power?

Populists have sought to extricate themselves from this conundrum in two different ways. Some populist movements claim adherence to the ideals of modern science and to the traditions of skeptical empiricism. They tell people that indeed you should never trust any institutions or figures of authority—including self-proclaimed populist parties and politicians. Instead, you should "do your own research" and trust only what you can directly observe by yourself.[25] This radical empiricist position implies that while large-scale institutions like political parties, courts, newspapers, and universities can never be trusted, individuals who make the effort can still find the truth by themselves.

This approach may sound scientific and may appeal to free-spirited

individuals, but it leaves open the question of how human communities can cooperate to build health-care systems or pass environmental regulations, which demand large-scale institutional organization. Is a single individual capable of doing all the necessary research to decide whether the earth's climate is heating up and what should be done about it? How would a single person go about collecting climate data from throughout the world, not to mention obtaining reliable records from past centuries? Trusting only "my own research" may sound scientific, but in practice it amounts to believing that there is no objective truth. As we shall see in chapter 4, science is a collaborative institutional effort rather than a personal quest.

An alternative populist solution is to abandon the modern scientific ideal of finding the truth via "research" and instead go back to relying on divine revelation or mysticism. Traditional religions like Christianity, Islam, and Hinduism have typically characterized humans as untrustworthy power-hungry creatures who can access the truth only thanks to the intervention of a divine intelligence. In the 2010s and early 2020s populist parties from Brazil to Turkey and from the United States to India have aligned themselves with such traditional religions. They have expressed radical doubt about modern institutions while declaring complete faith in ancient scriptures. The populists claim that the articles you read in *The New York Times* or in *Science* are just an elitist ploy to gain power, but what you read in the Bible, the Quran, or the Vedas is absolute truth.[26]

A variation on this theme calls on people to put their trust in charismatic leaders like Trump and Bolsonaro, who are depicted by their supporters either as the messengers of God[27] or as possessing a mystical bond with "the people." While ordinary politicians lie to the people in order to gain power for themselves, the charismatic leader is the infallible mouthpiece of the people who exposes all the lies.[28] One of the recurrent paradoxes of populism is that it starts by warning us that all human elites are driven by a dangerous hunger for power, but often ends by entrusting all power to a single ambitious human.

We will explore populism at greater depth in chapter 5, but at this point it is important to note that populists are eroding trust in large-scale institutions and international cooperation just when humanity confronts the existential challenges of ecological collapse, global war, and out-of-control technology. Instead of trusting complex human institutions, populists give us the same advice as the Phaethon myth and "The Sorcerer's Apprentice": "Trust God or the great sorcerer to intervene and make everything right again." If we take this advice, we'll likely find ourselves in the short term under the thumb of the worst kind of power-hungry humans, and in the long term under the thumb of new AI overlords. Or we might find ourselves nowhere at all, as Earth becomes inhospitable for human life.

If we wish to avoid relinquishing power to a charismatic leader or an inscrutable AI, we must first gain a better understanding of what information is, how it helps to build human networks, and how it relates to truth and power. Populists are right to be suspicious of the naive view of information, but they are wrong to think that power is the only reality and that information is always a weapon. Information isn't the raw material of truth, but it isn't a mere weapon, either. There is enough space between these extremes for a more nuanced and hopeful view of human information networks and of our ability to handle power wisely. This book is dedicated to exploring that middle ground.

THE ROAD AHEAD

The first part of this book surveys the historical development of human information networks. It doesn't attempt to present a comprehensive century-by-century account of information technologies like script, printing presses, and radio. Instead, by studying a few examples, it explores key dilemmas that people in all eras faced when trying to construct information networks, and it examines how different answers to these dilemmas shaped contrasting human societ-

ies. What we usually think of as ideological and political conflicts often turn out to be clashes between opposing types of information networks.

Part 1 begins by examining two principles that have been essential for large-scale human information networks: mythology and bureaucracy. Chapters 2 and 3 describe how large-scale information networks—from ancient kingdoms to present-day states—have relied on both mythmakers and bureaucrats. The stories of the Bible, for example, were essential for the Christian Church, but there would have been no Bible if church bureaucrats hadn't curated, edited, and disseminated these stories. A difficult dilemma for every human network is that mythmakers and bureaucrats tend to pull in different directions. Institutions and societies are often defined by the balance they manage to find between the conflicting needs of their myth-makers and their bureaucrats. The Christian Church itself split into rival churches, like the Catholic and Protestant churches, which struck different balances between mythology and bureaucracy.

Chapter 4 then focuses on the problem of erroneous information and on the benefits and drawbacks of maintaining self-correcting mechanisms, such as independent courts or peer-reviewed journals. The chapter contrasts institutions that relied on weak self-correcting mechanisms, like the Catholic Church, with institutions that developed strong self-correcting mechanisms, like scientific disciplines. Weak self-correcting mechanisms sometimes result in historical calamities like the early modern European witch hunts, while strong self-correcting mechanisms sometimes destabilize the network from within. Judged in terms of longevity, spread, and power, the Catholic Church has been perhaps the most successful institution in human history, despite—or perhaps because of—the relative weakness of its self-correcting mechanisms.

After part 1 surveys the roles of mythology and bureaucracy, and the contrast between strong and weak self-correcting mechanisms, chapter 5 concludes the historical discussion by focusing on another contrast—between distributed and centralized information networks.

Democratic systems allow information to flow freely along many independent channels, whereas totalitarian systems strive to concentrate information in one hub. Each choice has both advantages and
shortcomings. Understanding political systems like the United States
and the U.S.S.R. in terms of information flows can explain much
about their differing trajectories.

This historical part of the book is crucial for understanding
present-day developments and future scenarios. The rise of AI is arguably the biggest information revolution in history. But we cannot
understand it unless we compare it with its predecessors. History
isn't the study of the past; it is the study of change. History teaches
us what remains the same, what changes, and how things change.
This is as relevant to information revolutions as to every other kind
of historical transformation. Thus, understanding the process through
which the allegedly infallible Bible was canonized provides valuable
insight about present-day claims for AI infallibility. Similarly, studying the early modern witch hunts and Stalin's collectivization offers
stark warnings about what might go wrong as we give AIs greater
control over twenty-first-century societies. A deep knowledge of history is also vital to understand what *is* new about AI, how it is fundamentally different from printing presses and radio sets, and in
what specific ways an AI dictatorship could be very *unlike* anything
we have seen before.

The book doesn't argue that studying the past enables us to predict
the future. As emphasized repeatedly in the following pages, history
is not deterministic, and the future will be shaped by the choices we
all make in coming years. The whole point of writing this book is that
by making informed choices, we can prevent the worst outcomes. If
we cannot change the future, why waste time discussing it?

Building upon the historical survey in part 1, the book's second
part—"The Inorganic Network"—examines the new information
network we are creating today, focusing on the political implications
of the rise of AI. Chapters 6–8 discuss recent examples from throughout the world—such as the role of social media algorithms in insti-

gating ethnic violence in Myanmar in 2016–17—to explain in what ways AI is different from all previous information technologies. Examples are taken mostly from the 2010s rather than the 2020s, because we have gained a modicum of historical perspective on events of the 2010s.

Part 2 argues that we are creating an entirely new kind of information network, without pausing to reckon with its implications. It emphasizes the shift from organic to inorganic information networks. The Roman Empire, the Catholic Church, and the U.S.S.R. all relied on carbon-based brains to process information and make decisions. The silicon-based computers that dominate the new information network function in radically different ways. For better or worse, silicon chips are free from many of the limitations that organic biochemistry imposes on carbon neurons. Silicon chips can create spies that never sleep, financiers that never forget, and despots that never die. How will this change society, economics, and politics?

The third and final part of the book—"Computer Politics"— examines how different kinds of societies might deal with the threats and promises of the inorganic information network. Will carbon-based life-forms like us have a chance of understanding and controlling the new information network? As noted above, history isn't deterministic, and for at least a few more years we Sapiens still have the power to shape our future.

Accordingly, chapter 9 explores how democracies might deal with the inorganic network. How, for example, can flesh-and-blood politicians make financial decisions if the financial system is increasingly controlled by AI and the very meaning of money comes to depend on inscrutable algorithms? How can democracies maintain a public conversation about anything—be it finance or gender—if we can no longer know whether we are talking with another human or with a chatbot masquerading as a human?

Chapter 10 explores the potential impact of the inorganic network on totalitarianism. While dictators would be happy to get rid of all public conversations, they have their own fears of AI. Autocracies

are based on terrorizing and censoring their own agents. But how can a human dictator terrorize an AI, censor its unfathomable processes, or prevent it from seizing power for itself?

Finally, chapter 11 explores how the new information network could influence the balance of power between democratic and totalitarian societies on the global level. Will AI tilt the balance decisively in favor of one camp? Will the world split into hostile blocs whose rivalry makes all of us easy prey for an out-of-control AI? Or can we unite in defense of our common interests?

But before we explore the past, present, and possible futures of information networks, we need to start with a deceptively simple question. What exactly is information?

PART I

Human Networks

CHAPTER 1

What Is Information?

I t is always tricky to define fundamental concepts. Since they are the basis for everything that follows, they themselves seem to lack any basis of their own. Physicists have a hard time defining matter and energy, biologists have a hard time defining life, and philosophers have a hard time defining reality.

Information is increasingly seen by many philosophers and biologists, and even by some physicists, as the most basic building block of reality, more elementary than matter and energy.[1] No wonder that there are many disputes about how to define information, and how it is related to the evolution of life or to basic ideas in physics such as entropy, the laws of thermodynamics, and the quantum uncertainty principle.[2] This book will make no attempt to resolve—or even explain—these disputes, nor will it offer a universal definition of information applicable to physics, biology, and all other fields of knowledge. Since it is a work of history, which studies the past and future development of human societies, it will focus on the definition and role of information in history.

In everyday usage, "information" is associated with human-made symbols like spoken or written words. Consider, for example, the

story of Cher Ami and the Lost Battalion. In October 1918, when the American Expeditionary Forces was fighting to liberate northern France from the Germans, a battalion of more than five hundred American soldiers was trapped behind enemy lines. American artillery, which was trying to provide them with cover fire, misidentified their location and dropped the barrage directly on them. The battalion's commander, Major Charles Whittlesey, urgently needed to inform headquarters of his true location, but no runner could break through the German line. According to several accounts, as a last resort Whittlesey turned to Cher Ami, an army carrier pigeon. On a tiny piece of paper, Whittlesey wrote, "We are along the road paralell [*sic*] 276.4. Our artillery is dropping a barrage directly on us. For heaven's sake stop it." The paper was inserted into a canister on Cher Ami's right leg, and the bird was released into the air. One of the battalion's soldiers, Private John Nell, recalled years later, "We knew without a doubt this was our last chance. If that one lonely, scared pigeon failed to find its loft, our fate was sealed."

Witnesses later described how Cher Ami flew into heavy German fire. A shell exploded directly below the bird, killing five men and severely injuring the pigeon. A splinter tore through Cher Ami's chest, and his right leg was left hanging by a tendon. But he got through. The wounded pigeon flew the forty kilometers to division headquarters in about forty-five minutes, with the canister containing the crucial message attached to the remnant of his right leg. Though there is some controversy about the exact details, it is clear that the American artillery adjusted its barrage, and an American counterattack rescued the Lost Battalion. Cher Ami was tended by army medics, sent to the United States as a hero, and became the subject of numerous articles, short stories, children's books, poems, and even movies. The pigeon had no idea what information he was conveying, but the symbols inked on the piece of paper he carried helped save hundreds of men from death and captivity.[3]

Information, however, does not have to consist of human-made symbols. According to the biblical myth of the Flood, Noah learned

that the water had finally receded because the pigeon he sent out from the ark returned with an olive branch in her mouth. Then God set a rainbow in the clouds as a heavenly record of his promise never to flood the earth again. Pigeons, olive branches, and rainbows have since become iconic symbols of peace and tolerance. Objects that are even more remote than rainbows can also be information. For astronomers the shape and movement of galaxies constitute crucial information about the history of the universe. For navigators the North Star indicates which way is north. For astrologers the stars are a cosmic script, conveying information about the future of individual humans and entire societies.

Of course, defining something as "information" is a matter of perspective. An astronomer or astrologer might view the Libra constellation as "information," but these distant stars are far more than just a notice board for human observers. There might be an alien civilization up there, totally oblivious to the information we glean from their home and to the stories we tell about it. Similarly, a piece of paper marked with ink splotches can be crucial information for an army unit, or dinner for a family of termites. Any object can be information—or not. This makes it difficult to define what information is.

The ambivalence of information has played an important role in the annals of military espionage, when spies needed to communicate information surreptitiously. During World War I, northern France was not the only major battleground. From 1915 to 1918 the British and Ottoman Empires fought for control of the Middle East. After repulsing an Ottoman attack on the Sinai Peninsula and the Suez Canal, the British in turn invaded the Ottoman Empire, but were held at bay until October 1917 by a fortified Ottoman line stretching from Beersheba to Gaza. British attempts to break through were repulsed at the First Battle of Gaza (March 26, 1917) and the Second Battle of Gaza (April 17–19, 1917). Meanwhile, pro-British Jews living in Palestine set up a spy network code-named NILI to inform the British about Ottoman troop movements. One method they developed to communicate with their British operators involved

window shutters. Sarah Aaronsohn, a NILI commander, had a house overlooking the Mediterranean. She signaled British ships by closing or opening a particular shutter, according to a predetermined code. Numerous people, including Ottoman soldiers, could obviously see the shutter, but nobody other than NILI agents and their British operators understood it was vital military information.[4] So, when is a shutter just a shutter, and when is it information?

The Ottomans eventually caught the NILI spy ring due in part to a strange mishap. In addition to shutters, NILI used carrier pigeons to convey coded messages. On September 3, 1917, one of the pigeons diverged off course and landed in—of all places—the house of an Ottoman officer. The officer found the coded message but couldn't decipher it. Nevertheless, the pigeon itself was crucial information. Its existence indicated to the Ottomans that a spy ring was operating under their noses. As Marshall McLuhan might have put it, the pigeon was the message. NILI agents learned about the capture of the pigeon and immediately killed and buried all the remaining birds they had, because the mere possession of carrier pigeons was now incriminating information. But the massacre of the pigeons did not save NILI. Within a month the spy network was uncovered, several of its members were executed, and Sarah Aaronsohn committed suicide to avoid divulging NILI's secrets under torture.[5] When is a pigeon just a pigeon, and when is it information?

Clearly, then, information cannot be defined as specific types of material objects. Any object—a star, a shutter, a pigeon—can be information in the right context. So exactly what context defines such objects as "information"? The naive view of information argues that objects are defined as information in the context of truth seeking. Something is information if people use it to try to discover the truth. This view links the concept of information with the concept of truth and assumes that the main role of information is to represent reality. There is a reality "out there," and information is something that represents that reality and that we can therefore use to learn about real-

ity. For example, the information NILI provided the British was meant to represent the reality of Ottoman troop movements. If the Ottomans massed ten thousand soldiers in Gaza—the centerpiece of their defenses—a piece of paper with symbols representing "ten thousand" and "Gaza" was important information that could help the British win the battle. If, on the other hand, there were actually twenty thousand Ottoman troops in Gaza, that piece of paper did not represent reality accurately, and could lead the British to make a disastrous military mistake.

Put another way, the naive view argues that information is an attempt to represent reality, and when this attempt succeeds, we call it truth. While this book takes many issues with the naive view, it agrees that truth is an accurate representation of reality. But this book also holds that most information is *not* an attempt to represent reality and that what defines information is something entirely different. Most information in human society, and indeed in other biological and physical systems, *does not represent anything*.

I want to spend a little longer on this complex and crucial argument, because it constitutes the theoretical basis of the book.

WHAT IS TRUTH?

Throughout this book, "truth" is understood as something that accurately represents certain aspects of reality. Underlying the notion of truth is the premise that there exists one universal reality. Anything that has ever existed or will ever exist in the universe—from the North Star, to the NILI pigeon, to web pages on astrology—is part of this single reality. This is why the search for truth is a universal project. While different people, nations, or cultures may have competing beliefs and feelings, they cannot possess contradictory truths, because they all share a universal reality. Anyone who rejects universalism rejects truth.

Truth and reality are nevertheless different things, because no

matter how truthful an account is, it can never represent reality in all its aspects. If a NILI agent wrote that there are ten thousand Ottoman soldiers in Gaza, and there were indeed ten thousand soldiers there, this accurately pointed to a certain aspect of reality, but it neglected many other aspects. The very act of counting entities—whether apples, oranges, or soldiers—necessarily focuses attention on the similarities between these entities while discounting differences.[6] For example, saying only that there were ten thousand Ottoman soldiers in Gaza neglected to specify whether some were experienced veterans and others were green recruits. If there were a thousand recruits and nine thousand old hands, the military reality was quite different from if there were nine thousand rookies and a thousand battle-hardened veterans.

There were many other differences between the soldiers. Some were healthy; others were sick. Some Ottoman troops were ethnically Turkish, while others were Arabs, Kurds, or Jews. Some were brave, others cowardly. Indeed, each soldier was a unique human being, with different parents and friends and individual fears and hopes. World War I poets like Wilfred Owen famously attempted to represent these latter aspects of military reality, which mere statistics never conveyed accurately. Does this imply that writing "ten thousand soldiers" is always a misrepresentation of reality, and that to describe the military situation around Gaza in 1917, we must specify the unique history and personality of every soldier?

Another problem with any attempt to represent reality is that reality contains many viewpoints. For example, present-day Israelis, Palestinians, Turks, and Britons have different perspectives on the British invasion of the Ottoman Empire, the NILI underground, and the activities of Sarah Aaronsohn. That does not mean, of course, that there are several entirely separate realities, or that there are no historical facts. There is just one reality, but it is complex.

Reality includes an objective level with objective facts that don't depend on people's beliefs; for example, it is an objective fact that Sarah Aaronsohn died on October 9, 1917, from self-inflicted gun-

shot wounds. Saying that "Sarah Aaronsohn died in an airplane crash on May 15, 1919," is an error.

Reality also includes a subjective level with subjective facts like the beliefs and feelings of various people, but in this case, too, facts can be separated from errors. For example, it is a fact that Israelis tend to regard Aaronsohn as a patriotic hero. Three weeks after her suicide, the information NILI supplied helped the British finally break the Ottoman line at the Battle of Beersheba (October 31, 1917) and the Third Battle of Gaza (November 1–2, 1917). On November 2, 1917, the British foreign secretary, Arthur Balfour, issued the Balfour Declaration, announcing that the British government "view with favor the establishment in Palestine of a national home for the Jewish people." Israelis credit this in part to NILI and Sarah Aaronsohn, whom they admire for her sacrifice. It is another fact that Palestinians evaluate things very differently. Rather than admiring Aaronsohn, they regard her—if they've heard about her at all—as an imperialist agent. Even though we are dealing here with subjective views and feelings, we can still distinguish truth from falsehood. For views and feelings—just like stars and pigeons—are a part of the universal reality. Saying that "Sarah Aaronsohn is admired by everyone for her role in defeating the Ottoman Empire" is an error, not in line with reality.

Nationality is not the only thing that affects people's viewpoint. Israeli men and Israeli women may see Aaronsohn differently, and so do left-wingers and right-wingers, or Orthodox and secular Jews. Since suicide is forbidden by Jewish religious law, Orthodox Jews have difficulty seeing Aaronsohn's suicide as a heroic act (she was actually denied burial in the hallowed ground of a Jewish cemetery). Ultimately, each individual has a different perspective on the world, shaped by the intersection of different personalities and life histories. Does this imply that when we wish to describe reality, we must always list all the different viewpoints it contains and that a truthful biography of Sarah Aaronsohn, for example, must specify how every single Israeli and Palestinian has felt about her?

Taken to extremes, such a pursuit of accuracy may lead us to try to represent the world on a one-to-one scale, as in the famous Jorge Luis Borges story "On Exactitude in Science" (1946). In this story Borges tells of a fictitious ancient empire that became obsessed with producing ever more accurate maps of its territory, until eventually it produced a map with a one-to-one scale. The entire empire was covered with a map of the empire. So many resources were wasted on this ambitious representational project that the empire collapsed. Then the map too began to disintegrate, and Borges tells us that only "in the western Deserts, tattered fragments of the map are still to be found, sheltering an occasional beast or beggar."[7] A one-to-one map may look like the ultimate representation of reality, but tellingly it is no longer a representation at all; it is the reality.

The point is that even the most truthful accounts of reality can never represent it in full. There are always some aspects of reality that are neglected or distorted in every representation. Truth, then, isn't a one-to-one representation of reality. Rather, truth is something that brings our attention to certain aspects of reality while inevitably ignoring other aspects. No account of reality is 100 percent accurate, but some accounts are nevertheless more truthful than others.

WHAT INFORMATION DOES

As noted above, the naive view sees information as an attempt to represent reality. It is aware that some information doesn't represent reality well, but it dismisses this as unfortunate cases of "misinformation" or "disinformation." Misinformation is an honest mistake, occurring when someone tries to represent reality but gets it wrong. Disinformation is a deliberate lie, occurring when someone consciously intends to distort our view of reality.

The naive view further believes that the solution to the problems caused by misinformation and disinformation is more information. This idea, sometimes called the counterspeech doctrine, is associated

with the U.S. Supreme Court justice Louis D. Brandeis, who wrote in *Whitney v. California* (1927) that the remedy to false speech is more speech and that in the long term free discussion is bound to expose falsehoods and fallacies. If all information is an attempt to represent reality, then as the amount of information in the world grows, we can expect the flood of information to expose the occasional lies and errors and to ultimately provide us with a more truthful understanding of the world.

On this crucial point, this book strongly disagrees with the naive view. There certainly are instances of information that attempt to represent reality and succeed in doing so, but this is *not* the defining characteristic of information. A few pages ago I referred to stars as information and casually mentioned astrologers alongside astronomers. Adherents of the naive view of information probably squirmed in their chairs when they read it. According to the naive view, astronomers derive "real information" from the stars, while the information that astrologers imagine to read in constellations is either "misinformation" or "disinformation." If only people were given more information about the universe, surely they would abandon astrology altogether. But the fact is that for thousands of years astrology has had a huge impact on history, and today millions of people still check their star signs before making the most important decisions of their lives, like what to study and whom to marry. As of 2021, the global astrology market was valued at $12.8 billion.[8]

No matter what we think about the accuracy of astrological information, we should acknowledge its important role in history. It has connected lovers, and even entire empires. Roman emperors routinely consulted astrologers before making decisions. Indeed, astrology was held in such high esteem that casting the horoscope of a reigning emperor was a capital offense. Presumably, anyone casting such a horoscope could foretell when and how the emperor would die.[9] Rulers in some countries still take astrology very seriously. In 2005 the junta of Myanmar allegedly moved the country's capital from Yangon to Naypyidaw based on astrological advice.[10] A theory

of information that cannot account for the historical significance of astrology is clearly inadequate.

What the example of astrology illustrates is that errors, lies, fantasies, and fictions are information, too. Contrary to what the naive view of information says, information has no essential link to truth, and its role in history isn't to represent a preexisting reality. Rather, what information does is to create *new* realities by tying together disparate things—whether couples or empires. Its defining feature is connection rather than representation, and information is whatever connects different points into a network. Information doesn't necessarily inform us about things. Rather, it puts things in formation. Horoscopes put lovers in astrological formations, propaganda broadcasts put voters in political formations, and marching songs put soldiers in military formations.

As a paradigmatic case, consider music. Most symphonies, melodies, and tunes don't represent anything, which is why it makes no sense to ask whether they are true or false. Over the years people have created a lot of bad music, but not fake music. Without representing anything, music nevertheless does a remarkable job in connecting large numbers of people and synchronizing their emotions and movements. Music can make soldiers march in formation, clubbers sway together, church congregations clap in rhythm, and sports fans chant in unison.[11]

The role of information in connecting things is of course not unique to human history. A case can be made that this is the chief role of information in biology, too.[12] Consider DNA, the molecular information that makes organic life possible. Like music, DNA doesn't represent reality. Though generations of zebras have been fleeing lions, you cannot find in the zebra DNA a string of nucleobases representing "lion" nor another string representing "flight." Similarly, zebra DNA contains no representation of the sun, wind, rain, or any other external phenomena that zebras encounter during their lives. Nor does DNA represent internal phenomena like body

organs or emotions. There is no combination of nucleobases that represents a heart, or fear.

Instead of trying to represent preexisting things, DNA helps to produce entirely new things. For instance, various strings of DNA nucleobases initiate cellular chemical processes that result in the production of adrenaline. Adrenaline too doesn't represent reality in any way. Rather, adrenaline circulates through the body, initiating additional chemical processes that increase the heart rate and direct more blood to the muscles.[13] DNA and adrenaline thereby help to connect trillions of cells in the heart, legs, and other body parts to form a functioning network that can do remarkable things, like run away from a lion.

If DNA represented reality, we could have asked questions like "Does zebra DNA represent reality more accurately than lion DNA?" or "Is the DNA of one zebra telling the truth, while another zebra is misled by her fake DNA?" These, of course, are nonsensical questions. We might evaluate DNA by the fitness of the organism it produces, but not by truthfulness. While it is common to talk about DNA "errors," this refers only to mutations in the process of copying DNA—not to a failure to represent reality accurately. A mutation that inhibits the production of adrenaline reduces fitness, causing the network of cells to disintegrate, as when the zebra is killed and its trillions of cells lose connection with one another. But this kind of network failure means disintegration, not disinformation. That's as true of countries, political parties, and news networks as it is of zebras. Their existence too is jeopardized by loss of contact between their constituent parts, more than by inaccurate representations of reality.

Crucially, errors in the copying of DNA don't always reduce fitness. Once in a blue moon, they increase fitness. Without such mutations, there would be no process of evolution. All life-forms exist thanks to genetic "errors." The wonders of evolution are possible because DNA doesn't represent any preexisting realities; it creates new realities.

Let us pause to digest the implications of this. Information is something that creates new realities by connecting different points into a network. This still includes the view of information as representation. Sometimes, a truthful representation of reality can connect humans, as when 600 million people sat glued to their television sets in July 1969, watching Neil Armstrong and Buzz Aldrin walking on the moon.[14] The images on the screens accurately represented what was happening 384,000 kilometers away, and seeing them gave rise to feelings of awe, pride, and human brotherliness that helped connect people.

However, such fraternal feelings can be produced in other ways, too. The emphasis on connection leaves ample room for other types of information that do not represent reality well. Sometimes erroneous representations of reality might also serve as a social nexus, as when millions of followers of a conspiracy theory watch a YouTube video claiming that the moon landing never happened. These images convey an erroneous representation of reality, but they might nevertheless give rise to feelings of anger against the establishment or pride in one's own wisdom that help create a cohesive new group.

Sometimes networks can be connected without *any* attempt to represent reality, neither accurate nor erroneous, as when genetic information connects trillions of cells or when a stirring musical piece connects thousands of humans.

As a final example, consider Mark Zuckerberg's vision of the Metaverse. The Metaverse is a virtual universe made entirely of information. Unlike the one-to-one map built by Jorge Luis Borges's imaginary empire, the Metaverse isn't an attempt to represent our world, but rather an attempt to augment or even replace our world. It doesn't offer us a digital replica of Buenos Aires or Salt Lake City; it invites people to build new virtual communities with novel landscapes and rules. As of 2024 the Metaverse seems like an overblown pipe dream, but within a couple of decades billions of people might migrate to live much of their lives in an augmented virtual reality, holding there most of their social and professional activities. People

might come to build relationships, join movements, hold jobs, and experience emotional ups and downs in environments made of bits rather than atoms. Perhaps only in some remote deserts, tattered fragments of the old reality could still be found, sheltering an occasional beast or beggar.

INFORMATION IN HUMAN HISTORY

Viewing information as a social nexus helps us understand many aspects of human history that confound the naive view of information as representation. It explains the historical success not only of astrology but of much more important things, like the Bible. While some may dismiss astrology as a quaint sideshow in human history, nobody can deny the central role the Bible has played. If the main job of information had been to represent reality accurately, it would have been hard to explain why the Bible became one of the most influential texts in history.

The Bible makes many serious errors in its description of both human affairs and natural processes. The book of Genesis claims that all human groups—including, for example, the San people of the Kalahari Desert and the Aborigines of Australia—descend from a single family that lived in the Middle East about four thousand years ago.[15] According to Genesis, after the Flood all Noah's descendants lived together in Mesopotamia, but following the destruction of the Tower of Babel they spread to the four corners of the earth and became the ancestors of all living humans. In fact, the ancestors of the San people lived in Africa for hundreds of thousands of years without ever leaving the continent, and the ancestors of the Aborigines settled Australia more than fifty thousand years ago.[16] Both genetic and archaeological evidence rule out the idea that the entire ancient populations of South Africa and Australia were annihilated about four thousand years ago by a flood and that these areas were subsequently repopulated by Middle Eastern immigrants.

An even graver distortion involves our understanding of infectious diseases. The Bible routinely depicts epidemics as divine punishment for human sins[17] and claims they can be stopped or prevented by prayers and religious rituals.[18] However, epidemics are of course caused by pathogens and can be stopped or prevented by following hygiene rules and using medicines and vaccines. This is today widely accepted even by religious leaders like the pope, who during the COVID-19 pandemic advised people to self-isolate, instead of congregating to pray together.[19]

Yet while the Bible has done a poor job in representing the reality of human origins, migrations, and epidemics, it has nevertheless been very effective in connecting billions of people and creating the Jewish and Christian religions. Like DNA initiating chemical processes that bind billions of cells into organic networks, the Bible initiated social processes that bonded billions of people into religious networks. And just as a network of cells can do things that single cells cannot, so a religious network can do things that individual humans cannot, like building temples, maintaining legal systems, celebrating holidays, and waging holy wars.

To conclude, information sometimes represents reality, and sometimes doesn't. But it always connects. This is its fundamental characteristic. Therefore, when examining the role of information in history, although it sometimes makes sense to ask "How well does it represent reality? Is it true or false?" often the more crucial questions are "How well does it connect people? What new network does it create?"

It should be emphasized that rejecting the naive view of information as representation does not force us to reject the notion of truth, nor does it force us to embrace the populist view of information as a weapon. While information always connects, some types of information—from scientific books to political speeches—may strive to connect people by accurately representing certain aspects of reality. But this requires a special effort, which most information does not make. This is why the naive view is wrong to believe that

creating more powerful information technology will necessarily result in a more truthful understanding of the world. If no additional steps are taken to tilt the balance in favor of truth, an increase in the amount and speed of information is likely to swamp the relatively rare and expensive truthful accounts by much more common and cheap types of information.

When we look at the history of information from the Stone Age to the Silicon Age, we therefore see a constant rise in connectivity, without a concomitant rise in truthfulness or wisdom. Contrary to what the naive view believes, *Homo sapiens* didn't conquer the world because we are talented at turning information into an accurate map of reality. Rather, the secret of our success is that we are talented at using information to connect lots of individuals. Unfortunately, this ability often goes hand in hand with believing in lies, errors, and fantasies. This is why even technologically advanced societies like Nazi Germany and the Soviet Union have been prone to hold delusional ideas, without their delusions necessarily weakening them. Indeed, the mass delusions of Nazi and Stalinist ideologies about things like race and class actually helped them make tens of millions of people march together in lockstep.

In chapters 2–5 we'll take a closer look at the history of information networks. We'll discuss how, over tens of thousands of years, humans invented various information technologies that greatly improved connectivity and cooperation without necessarily resulting in a more truthful representation of the world. These information technologies—invented centuries and millennia ago—still shape our world even in the era of the internet and AI. The first information technology we'll examine, which is also the first information technology developed by humans, is the story.

CHAPTER 2

Stories: Unlimited Connections

We Sapiens rule the world not because we are so wise but because we are the only animals that can cooperate flexibly in large numbers. I have explored this idea in my previous books *Sapiens* and *Homo Deus,* but a brief recap is inescapable.

The Sapiens' ability to cooperate flexibly in large numbers has precursors among other animals. Some social mammals like chimpanzees display significant flexibility in the way they cooperate, while some social insects like ants cooperate in very large numbers. But neither chimps nor ants establish empires, religions, or trade networks. Sapiens are capable of doing such things because we are far more flexible than chimps and can simultaneously cooperate in even larger numbers than ants. In fact, there is no upper limit to the number of Sapiens who can cooperate with one another. The Catholic Church has about 1.4 billion members. China has a population of about 1.4 billion. The global trade network connects about 8 billion Sapiens.

This is surprising given that humans cannot form long-term intimate bonds with more than a few hundred individuals.[1] It takes many years and common experiences to get to know someone's

unique character and history and to cultivate ties of mutual trust and affection. Consequently, if Sapiens networks were connected only by personal human-to-human bonds, our networks would have remained very small. This is the situation among our chimpanzee cousins, for example. Their typical community numbers 20–60 members, and on rare occasions the number might increase to 150–200.[2] This appears to have been the situation also among ancient human species like Neanderthals and archaic *Homo sapiens*. Each of their bands numbered a few dozen individuals, and different bands rarely cooperated.[3]

About seventy thousand years ago, *Homo sapiens* bands began displaying an unprecedented capacity to cooperate with one another, as evidenced by the emergence of inter-band trade and artistic traditions and by the rapid spread of our species from our African homeland to the entire globe. What enabled different bands to cooperate is that evolutionary changes in brain structure and linguistic abilities apparently gave Sapiens the aptitude to tell and believe fictional stories and to be deeply moved by them. Instead of building a network from human-to-human chains alone—as the Neanderthals, for example, did—stories provided *Homo sapiens* with a new type of chain: human-to-story chains. In order to cooperate, Sapiens no longer had to know each other personally; they just had to know the same story. And the same story can be familiar to billions of individuals. A story can thereby serve like a central connector, with an unlimited number of outlets into which an unlimited number of people can plug. For example, the 1.4 billion members of the Catholic Church are connected by the Bible and other key Christian stories; the 1.4 billion citizens of China are connected by the stories of communist ideology and Chinese nationalism; and the 8 billion members of the global trade network are connected by stories about currencies, corporations, and brands.

Even charismatic leaders who have millions of followers are an example of this rule rather than an exception. It may seem that in the case of ancient Chinese emperors, medieval Catholic popes, or mod-

ern corporate titans it has been a single flesh-and-blood human—
rather than a story—that has served as a nexus linking millions of
followers. But, of course, in all these cases almost none of the followers has had a personal bond with the leader. Instead, what they have
connected to has been a carefully crafted *story* about the leader, and
it is in this story that they have put their faith.

Joseph Stalin, who stood at the nexus of one of the biggest personality cults in history, understood this well. When his troublesome
son Vasily exploited his famous name to frighten and awe people,
Stalin berated him. "But I'm a Stalin too," protested Vasily. "No,
you're not," replied Stalin. "You're not Stalin and I'm not Stalin. Stalin is Soviet power. Stalin is what he is in the newspapers and the
portraits, not you, no—not even me!"[4]

Present-day influencers and celebrities would concur. Some have
hundreds of millions of online followers, with whom they communicate daily through social media. But there is very little authentic personal connection there. The social media accounts are usually run by
a team of experts, and every image and word is professionally crafted
and curated to manufacture what is nowadays called a brand.[5]

A "brand" is a specific type of story. To brand a product means to
tell a story about that product, which may have little to do with the
product's actual qualities but which consumers nevertheless learn to
associate with the product. For example, over the decades the Coca-
Cola corporation has invested tens of billions of dollars in advertisements that tell and retell the story of the Coca-Cola drink.[6] People
have seen and heard the story so often that many have come to associate a certain concoction of flavored water with fun, happiness,
and youth (as opposed to tooth decay, obesity, and plastic waste).
That's branding.[7]

As Stalin knew, it is possible to brand not only products but also
individuals. A corrupt billionaire can be branded as the champion of
the poor; a bungling imbecile can be branded as an infallible genius;
and a guru who sexually abuses his followers can be branded as a

chaste saint. People think they connect to the person, but in fact they connect to the story told *about* the person, and there is often a huge gulf between the two.

Even the story of Cher Ami, the heroic pigeon, was partly the product of a branding campaign aimed at enhancing the public image of the U.S. Army's Pigeon Service. A 2021 revisionist study by the historian Frank Blazich found that though there is no doubt Cher Ami sustained severe injuries while transporting a message somewhere in Northern France, several key features of the story are doubtful or inaccurate. First, relying on contemporary military records, Blazich demonstrated that headquarters learned about the exact location of the Lost Battalion about twenty minutes *prior* to the pigeon's arrival. It was not the pigeon that put a stop to the barrage of friendly fire decimating the Lost Battalion. Even more crucially, there is simply no proof that the pigeon carrying Major Whittlesey's message was Cher Ami. It might well have been another bird, while Cher Ami might have sustained his wounds a couple of weeks later, during an altogether different battle.

According to Blazich, the doubts and inconsistencies in Cher Ami's story were overshadowed by its propaganda value to the army and its appeal to the public. Over the years the story was retold so many times that facts became hopelessly enmeshed with fiction. Journalists, poets, and filmmakers added fanciful details to it, for example that the pigeon lost an eye as well as a leg and that it was awarded the Distinguished Service Cross. In the 1920s and 1930s Cher Ami became the most famous bird in the world. When he died, his carefully preserved corpse was placed on display at the Smithsonian's National Museum of American History, where it became a pilgrimage site for American patriots and World War I veterans. As the story grew in the telling, it took over even the recollections of survivors of the Lost Battalion, who came to accept the popular narrative at face value. Blazich recounts the case of Sherman Eager, an officer in the Lost Battalion, who decades after the war brought his children

to see Cher Ami at the Smithsonian and told them, "You all owe your lives to that pigeon." Whatever the facts may be, the story of the self-sacrificing winged savior proved irresistible.[8]

As a much more extreme example, consider Jesus. Two millennia of storytelling have encased Jesus within such a thick cocoon of stories that it is impossible to recover the historical person. Indeed, for millions of devout Christians, merely raising the possibility that the real person was different from the story is blasphemy. As far as we can tell, the real Jesus was a typical Jewish preacher who built a small following by giving sermons and healing the sick. After his death, however, Jesus became the subject of one of the most remarkable branding campaigns in history. This little-known provincial guru, who during his short career gathered just a handful of disciples and who was executed as a common criminal, was rebranded after death as the incarnation of the cosmic god who created the universe.[9] Though no contemporary portrait of Jesus has survived, and though the Bible never describes what he looked like, imaginary renderings of him have become some of the most recognizable icons in the world.

It should be stressed that the creation of the Jesus story was not a deliberate lie. People like Saint Paul, Tertullian, Saint Augustine, and Martin Luther didn't set out to deceive anyone. They projected their deeply felt hopes and feelings on the figure of Jesus, in the same way that all of us routinely project our feelings on our parents, lovers, and leaders. While branding campaigns are occasionally a cynical exercise of disinformation, most of the really big stories of history have been the result of emotional projections and wishful thinking. True believers play a key role in the rise of every major religion and ideology, and the Jesus story changed history because it gained an immense number of true believers.

By gaining all those believers, the story of Jesus managed to have a much bigger impact on history than the person of Jesus. The person of Jesus walked from village to village on his two feet, talking with people, eating and drinking with them, placing his hands on their

sick bodies. He made a difference to the lives of perhaps several thousand individuals, all living in one minor Roman province. In contrast, the story of Jesus flew around the whole world, first on the wings of gossip, anecdote, and rumor; then via parchment texts, paintings, and statues; and eventually as blockbuster movies and internet memes. Billions of people not only heard the Jesus story but came to believe in it too, which created one of the biggest and most influential networks in the world.

Stories like the one about Jesus can be seen as a way of stretching preexisting biological bonds. Family is the strongest bond known to humans. One way that stories build trust between strangers is by making these strangers reimagine each other as family. The Jesus story presented Jesus as a parent figure for all humans, encouraged hundreds of millions of Christians to see each other as brothers and sisters, and created a shared pool of family memories. While most Christians were not physically present at the Last Supper, they have heard the story so many times, and they have seen so many images of the event, that they "remember" it more vividly than they remember most of the family dinners in which they actually participated.

Interestingly, Jesus's last supper was the Jewish Passover meal, which according to the Gospel accounts Jesus shared with his disciples just before his crucifixion. In Jewish tradition, the whole purpose of the Passover meal is to create and reenact artificial memories. Every year Jewish families sit together on the eve of Passover to eat and reminisce about "their" exodus from Egypt. They are supposed not only to tell the story of how the descendants of Jacob escaped slavery in Egypt but to remember how they *personally* suffered at the hands of the Egyptians, how they *personally* saw the sea part, and how they *personally* received the Ten Commandments from Jehovah at Mount Sinai.

The Jewish tradition doesn't mince words here. The text of the Passover ritual (the Haggadah) insists that "in every generation a person is obligated to regard himself as if he personally had come

out of Egypt." If anyone objects that this is a fiction, and that they didn't personally come out of Egypt, Jewish sages have a ready answer. They claim that the souls of all Jews throughout history were created by Jehovah long before they were born and all these souls were present at Mount Sinai.[10] As Salvador Litvak, a Jewish social media influencer, explained to his online followers in 2018, "You and I were there together. . . . When we fulfill the obligation to see ourselves as if we personally left Egypt, it's not a metaphor. We don't imagine the Exodus, we remember it."[11]

So every year, in the most important celebration of the Jewish calendar, millions of Jews put on a show that they remember things that they didn't witness and that probably never happened at all. As numerous modern studies indicate, repeatedly retelling a fake memory eventually causes the person to adopt it as a genuine recollection.[12] When two Jews encounter each other for the first time, they can immediately feel that they both belong to the same family, that they were together as slaves in Egypt, and that they were together at Mount Sinai. That's a powerful bond that has sustained the Jewish network over many centuries and continents.

INTERSUBJECTIVE ENTITIES

The Jewish Passover story builds a large network by taking existing biological kin bonds and stretching them. It creates an imagined family of millions. But there is an even more revolutionary way for stories to build networks. Like DNA, stories can create new entities. Indeed, stories can even create an entirely new level of reality. As far as we know, prior to the emergence of stories the universe contained just two levels of reality. Stories added a third.

The two levels of reality that preceded storytelling are objective reality and subjective reality. *Objective reality* consists of things like stones, mountains, and asteroids—things that exist whether we are

aware of them or not. An asteroid hurtling toward planet Earth, for example, exists even if nobody knows it's out there. Then there is *subjective reality:* things like pain, pleasure, and love that aren't "out there" but rather "in here." Subjective things exist in our awareness of them. An unfelt ache is an oxymoron.

But some stories are able to create a third level of reality: *intersubjective reality.* Whereas subjective things like pain exist in a single mind, intersubjective things like laws, gods, nations, corporations, and currencies exist in the nexus between large numbers of minds. More specifically, they exist in the stories people tell one another. The information humans exchange about intersubjective things doesn't represent anything that had already existed prior to the exchange of information; rather, the exchange of information creates these things.

When I tell you that I am in pain, telling you about it doesn't create the pain. And if I stop talking about the pain, it doesn't make the pain go away. Similarly, when I tell you that I saw an asteroid, this doesn't create the asteroid. The asteroid exists whether people talk about it or not. But when lots of people tell one another stories about laws, gods, or currencies, this is what creates these laws, gods, or currencies. If people stop talking about them, they disappear. Intersubjective things exist in the exchange of information.

Let's take a closer look. The caloric value of pizza doesn't depend on our beliefs. A typical pizza contains between fifteen hundred and twenty-five hundred calories.[13] In contrast, the financial value of money—and pizzas—depends entirely on our beliefs. How many pizzas can you purchase for a dollar, or for a bitcoin? In 2010, Laszlo Hanyecz bought two pizzas for 10,000 bitcoins. It was the first known commercial transaction involving bitcoin—and with hindsight, also the most expensive pizza ever. By November 2021, a single bitcoin was valued at more than $69,000, so the bitcoins Hanyecz paid for his two pizzas were worth $690 million, enough to purchase millions of pizzas.[14] While the caloric value of pizza is an objective reality that remained the same between 2010 and 2021, the financial

value of bitcoin is an intersubjective reality that changed dramatically during the same period, depending on the stories people told and believed about bitcoin.

Another example. Suppose I ask, "Does the Loch Ness Monster exist?" This is a question about the objective level of reality. Some people believe that dinosaur-like animals really do inhabit Loch Ness. Others dismiss the idea as a fantasy or a hoax. Over the years, many attempts have been made to resolve the disagreement once and for all, using scientific methods such as sonar scans and DNA surveys. If huge animals live in the lake, they should appear on sonar, and they should leave DNA traces. Based on the available evidence, the scientific consensus is that the Loch Ness Monster does not exist. (A DNA survey conducted in 2019 found genetic material from three thousand species, but no monster. At most, Loch Ness may contain some five-kilo eels.[15]) Many people may nevertheless continue to believe that the Loch Ness Monster exists, but believing it doesn't change objective reality.

In contrast to animals, whose existence can be verified or disproved through objective tests, states are intersubjective entities. We normally don't notice it, because everybody takes the existence of the United States, China, Russia, or Brazil for granted. But there are cases when people disagree about the existence of certain states, and then their intersubjective status emerges. The Israeli-Palestinian conflict, for example, revolves around this matter, because some people and governments refuse to acknowledge the existence of Israel and others refuse to acknowledge the existence of Palestine. As of 2024, the governments of Brazil and China, for example, say that both Israel and Palestine exist; the governments of the United States and Cameroon recognize only Israel's existence; whereas the governments of Algeria and Iran recognize only Palestine. Other cases range from Kosovo, which as of 2024 is recognized as a state by around half of the 193 UN members,[16] to Abkhazia, which almost all governments see as a sovereign territory of Georgia, but which is recognized as a state by Russia, Venezuela, Nicaragua, Nauru, and Syria.[17]

Indeed, almost all states pass at least temporarily through a phase during which their existence is contested, when struggling for independence. Did the United States come into existence on July 4, 1776, or only when other states like France and finally the U.K. recognized it? Between the declaration of U.S. independence on July 4, 1776, and the signing of the Treaty of Paris on September 3, 1783, some people like George Washington believed the United States existed, while other people like King George III vehemently rejected this idea.

Disagreements about the existence of states cannot be resolved by an objective test, such as a DNA survey or a sonar scan. Unlike animals, states are not an objective reality. When we ask whether a particular state exists, we are raising a question about intersubjective reality. If enough people agree that a particular state exists, then it does. It can then do things like sign legally binding agreements with other states as well as NGOs and private corporations.

Of all genres of stories, those that create intersubjective realities have been the most crucial for the development of large-scale human networks. Implanting fake family memories is certainly helpful, but no religions or empires managed to survive for long without a strong belief in the existence of a god, a nation, a law code, or a currency. For the formation of the Christian Church, for example, it was important that people recollect what Jesus said at the Last Supper, but the crucial step was making people believe that Jesus was a god rather than just an inspiring rabbi. For the formation of the Jewish religion, it was helpful that Jews "remembered" how they together escaped slavery in Egypt, but the really decisive step was making all Jews adhere to the same religious law code, the *Halakha*.

Intersubjective things like laws, gods, and currencies are extremely powerful within a particular information network and utterly meaningless outside it. Suppose a billionaire crashes his private jet on a desert island and finds himself alone with a suitcase full of banknotes and bonds. When he was in São Paulo or Mumbai, he could use these papers to make people feed him, clothe him, protect him, and

build him a private jet. But once he is cut off from other members of our information network, his banknotes and bonds immediately become worthless. He cannot use them to get the island's monkeys to provide him with food or to build him a raft.

THE POWER OF STORIES

Whether through implanting fake memories, forming fictional relationships, or creating intersubjective realities, stories produced large-scale human networks. These networks in turn completely changed the balance of power in the world. Story-based networks made *Homo sapiens* the most powerful of all animals, giving it a crucial edge not only over lions and mammoths but also over other ancient human species like Neanderthals.

Neanderthals lived in small isolated bands, and to the best of our knowledge different bands cooperated with one another only rarely and weakly, if at all.[18] Stone Age Sapiens too lived in small bands of a few dozen individuals. But following the emergence of storytelling, Sapiens bands no longer lived in isolation. Bands were connected by stories about things like revered ancestors, totem animals, and guardian spirits. Bands that shared stories and intersubjective realities constituted a tribe. Each tribe was a network connecting hundreds or even thousands of individuals.[19]

Belonging to a large tribe had an obvious advantage in times of conflict. Five hundred Sapiens could easily defeat fifty Neanderthals.[20] But tribal networks had many additional advantages. If we live in an isolated band of fifty people and a severe drought hits our home territory, many of us might starve to death. If we try to migrate elsewhere, we are likely to encounter hostile groups, and we might also find it difficult to forage for food, water, and flint (to make tools) in unfamiliar territory. However, if our band is part of a tribal network, in times of need at least some of us could go live with our distant friends. If our shared tribal identity is strong enough, they

would welcome us and teach us about the local dangers and opportunities. A decade or two later, we might reciprocate. The tribal network, then, acted like an insurance policy. It minimized risk by
spreading it across a lot more people.[21]

Even in quiet times Sapiens could benefit enormously from exchanging information not just with a few dozen members of a small
band but with an entire tribal network. If one of the tribe's bands
discovered a better way to make spear points, learned how to heal
wounds with some rare medicinal herb, or invented a needle to sew
clothes, that knowledge could be quickly passed to the other bands.
Even though individually Sapiens might not have been more intelligent than Neanderthals, five hundred Sapiens together were far
more intelligent than fifty Neanderthals.[22]

All this was made possible by stories. The power of stories is often
missed or denied by materialist interpretations of history. In particular, Marxists tend to view stories as merely a smoke screen for underlying power relations and material interests. According to Marxist
theories, people are always motivated by objective material interests
and use stories only to camouflage these interests and confound their
rivals. For example, in this reading the Crusades, World War I, and
the Iraq War were all fought for the economic interests of powerful
elites rather than for religious, nationalist, or liberal ideals. Understanding these wars means setting aside all the mythological fig
leaves—about God, patriotism, or democracy—and observing power
relations in their nakedness.

This Marxist view, however, is not only cynical but wrong. While
materialist interests certainly played a role in the Crusades, World
War I, the Iraq War, and most other human conflicts, that does not
mean that religious, national, and liberal ideals played no role at all.
Moreover, materialist interests by themselves cannot explain the
identities of the rival camps. Why is it that in the twelfth century
landowners and merchants from France, Germany, and Italy united
to conquer territories and trade routes in the Levant—instead of
landowners and merchants from France and North Africa uniting to

conquer Italy? And why is it that in 2003, the United States and
Britain sought to conquer the oil fields of Iraq, rather than the gas
fields of Norway? Can this really be explained by purely materialist
considerations, without any recourse to people's religious and ideological beliefs?

In fact, all relations between large-scale human groups are shaped
by stories, because the identities of these groups are themselves defined
by stories. There are no objective definitions for who is British, American, Norwegian, or Iraqi; all these identities are shaped by national
and religious myths that are constantly challenged and revised. Marxists may claim that large-scale groups have objective identities and
interests, independent of stories. If that is so, how can we explain that
only humans have large-scale groups like tribes, nations, and religions,
whereas chimpanzees lack them? After all, chimpanzees share with
humans all our objective material interests; they too need to drink, eat,
and protect themselves from diseases. They too want sex and social
power. But chimpanzees cannot maintain large-scale groups, because
they are unable to create the stories that connect such groups and define their identities and interests. Contrary to Marxist thinking, large-
scale identities and interests in history are always intersubjective; they
are never objective.

This is good news. If history had been shaped solely by material
interests and power struggles, there would be no point talking to
people who disagree with us. Any conflict would ultimately be the
result of objective power relations, which cannot be changed merely
by talking. In particular, if privileged people can see and believe only
those things that enshrine their privileges, how can anything except
violence persuade them to renounce those privileges and alter their
beliefs? Luckily, since history is shaped by intersubjective stories,
sometimes we can avert conflict and make peace by talking with
people, changing the stories in which they and we believe, or coming
up with a new story that everyone can accept.

Take, for example, the rise of Nazism. There certainly were material interests that drove millions of Germans to support Hitler. The

Nazis would probably never have come to power had it not been for the economic crisis of the early 1930s. However, it is wrong to think that the Third Reich was the inevitable outcome of underlying power relations and material interests. Hitler won the 1933 elections because during the economic crisis millions of Germans came to believe the Nazi story rather than one of the alternative stories on offer. This wasn't the inevitable result of Germans pursuing their material interests and protecting their privileges; it was a tragic mistake. We can confidently say that it was a mistake, and that Germans could have chosen better stories, because we know what happened next. Twelve years of Nazi rule didn't foster the Germans' material interests. Nazism led to the destruction of Germany and the deaths of millions. Later, when Germans adopted liberal democracy, this did lead to a lasting improvement in their lives. Couldn't the Germans have skipped the failed Nazi experiment and put their faith in liberal democracy already in the early 1930s? The position of this book is that they could have. History is often shaped not by deterministic power relations, but rather by tragic mistakes that result from believing in mesmerizing but harmful stories.

THE NOBLE LIE

The centrality of stories reveals something fundamental about the power of our species, and it explains why power doesn't always go hand in hand with wisdom. The naive view of information says that information leads to truth, and knowing the truth helps people to gain both power and wisdom. This sounds reassuring. It implies that people who ignore the truth are unlikely to have much power, whereas people who respect the truth can gain much power, but that power would be tempered by wisdom. For example, people who ignore the truth about human biology might believe racist myths but will not be able to produce powerful medicines and bioweapons, whereas people who understand biology will have that kind of power but will not use

it in the service of racist ideologies. If this had indeed been the case, we could sleep calmly, trusting our presidents, high priests, and CEOs to be wise and honest. A politician, a movement, or a country might conceivably get ahead here and there with the help of lies and deceptions, but in the long term that would be a self-defeating strategy.

Unfortunately, this is not the world in which we live. In history, power stems only partially from knowing the truth. It also stems from the ability to maintain social order among a large number of people. Suppose you want to make an atom bomb. To succeed, you obviously need some accurate knowledge of physics. But you also need lots of people to mine uranium ore, build nuclear reactors, and provide food for the construction workers, miners, and physicists. The Manhattan Project directly employed about 130,000 people, with millions more working to sustain them.[23] Robert Oppenheimer could devote himself to his equations because he relied on thousands of miners to extract uranium at the Eldorado mine in northern Canada and the Shinkolobwe mine in the Belgian Congo[24]—not to mention the farmers who grew potatoes for his lunch. If you want to make an atom bomb, you must find a way to make millions of people cooperate.

It is the same with all ambitious projects that humans undertake. A Stone Age band going to hunt a mammoth obviously needed to know some facts about mammoths. If they believed they could kill a mammoth by casting spells, their hunting expedition would have failed. But knowing facts about mammoths wasn't enough. The hunters also needed to risk death and show great courage. If they believed that a certain spell guaranteed a good afterlife for dead hunters, their hunting expeditions had a much higher chance of success. Even if the spell did not benefit dead hunters in any way, by fortifying the courage and solidarity of living hunters, it made a crucial contribution to the hunt's success.[25]

If you build a bomb and ignore the facts of physics, the bomb will not explode. But if you build an ideology and ignore the facts, the

ideology may still prove explosive. While power depends on both truth and order, it is usually the people who know how to build ideologies and maintain order who give instructions to the people who merely know how to build bombs or hunt mammoths. Robert Oppenheimer obeyed Franklin Delano Roosevelt rather than the other way around. Similarly, Werner Heisenberg obeyed Adolf Hitler, Igor Kurchatov deferred to Joseph Stalin, and in contemporary Iran experts in nuclear physics follow the orders of experts in Shiite theology.

What the people at the top know, which nuclear physicists don't always realize, is that telling the truth about the universe is hardly the most efficient way to produce order among large numbers of humans. It is true that $E = mc^2$, and it explains a lot of what happens in the universe, but knowing that $E = mc^2$ usually doesn't resolve political disagreements or inspire people to make sacrifices for a common cause. Instead, what holds human networks together tends to be fictional stories, especially stories about intersubjective things like gods, money, and nations. When it comes to uniting people, fiction enjoys two inherent advantages over the truth. First, fiction can be made as simple as we like, whereas the truth tends to be complicated, because the reality it is supposed to represent is complicated. Take, for example, the truth about nations. It is difficult to grasp that the nation to which one belongs is an intersubjective entity that exists only in our collective imagination. You rarely hear politicians say such things in their political speeches. It is far easier to believe that our nation is God's chosen people, entrusted by the Creator with some special mission. This simple story has been repeatedly told by countless politicians from Israel to Iran and from the United States to Russia.

Second, the truth is often painful and disturbing, and if we try to make it more comforting and flattering, it will no longer be the truth. In contrast, fiction is highly malleable. The history of every nation contains some dark episodes that citizens don't like to acknowledge and remember. An Israeli politician who in her election speeches details the miseries inflicted on Palestinian civilians by the Israeli

occupation is unlikely to get many votes. In contrast, a politician who builds a national myth by ignoring uncomfortable facts, focusing on glorious moments in the Jewish past, and embellishing reality wherever necessary may well sweep to power. That's the case not just in Israel but in all countries. How many Italians or Indians want to hear the unblemished truth about their nations? An uncompromising adherence to the truth is essential for scientific progress, and it is also an admirable spiritual practice, but it is not a winning political strategy.

Already in his *Republic*, Plato imagined that the constitution of his utopian state would be based on "the noble lie"—a fictional story about the origin of the social order, one that secures the citizens' loyalty and prevents them from questioning the constitution. Citizens should be told, Plato wrote, that they were all born out of the earth, that the land is their mother, and that they therefore owe filial loyalty to the motherland. They should further be told that when they were conceived, the gods intermingled different metals—gold, silver, bronze, and iron—into them, which justifies a natural hierarchy between golden rulers and bronze servants. While Plato's utopia was never realized in practice, numerous polities through the ages told their inhabitants variations of this noble lie.

Plato's noble lie notwithstanding, we should not conclude that all politicians are liars or that all national histories are deceptions. The choice isn't simply between telling the truth and lying. There is a third option. Telling a fictional story is lying only when you pretend that the story is a true representation of reality. Telling a fictional story isn't lying when you avoid such pretense and acknowledge that you are trying to create a new intersubjective reality rather than represent a preexisting objective reality.

For example, on September 17, 1787, the Constitutional Convention signed the U.S. Constitution, which came into force in 1789. The Constitution didn't reveal any preexisting truth about the world, but crucially it wasn't a lie, either. Rejecting Plato's recommendation, the authors of the text didn't deceive anyone about the text's origins.

They didn't pretend that the text came down from heaven or that it had been inspired by some god. Rather, they acknowledged that it was an extremely creative legal fiction generated by fallible human beings.

"We the People of the United States," says the Constitution about its own origins, "in Order to form a more perfect Union . . . do ordain and establish this Constitution." Despite the acknowledgment that it is a human-made legal fiction, the U.S. Constitution indeed managed to form a powerful union. It has maintained for more than two centuries a surprising degree of order among many millions of people who belong to a wide range of religious, ethnic, and cultural groups. The U.S. Constitution has thus functioned like a tune that without claiming to represent anything has nevertheless made numerous people act together in order.

It is crucial to note that "order" should not be confused with fairness or justice. The order created and maintained by the U.S. Constitution condoned slavery, the subordination of women, the expropriation of indigenous people, and extreme economic inequality. The genius of the U.S. Constitution is that by acknowledging that it is a legal fiction created by human beings, it was able to provide mechanisms to reach agreement on amending itself and remedying its own injustices (as chapter 5 explores in greater depth). The Constitution's Article V details how people can propose and ratify such amendments, which "shall be valid to all Intents and Purposes, as Part of this Constitution." Less than a century after the Constitution was written, the Thirteenth Amendment abolished slavery.

In this, the U.S. Constitution was fundamentally different from stories that denied their fictive nature and claimed divine origin, such as the Ten Commandments. Like the U.S. Constitution, the Ten Commandments endorsed slavery. The Tenth Commandment says, "You shall not covet your neighbor's house. You shall not covet your neighbor's wife, or his male slave or female slave" (Exodus 20:17). This implies that God is perfectly okay with people holding slaves, and objects only to the coveting of slaves belonging to some-

one else. But unlike the U.S. Constitution, the Ten Commandments failed to provide any amendment mechanism. There is no Eleventh Commandment that says, "You can amend commandments by a two-thirds majority vote."

This crucial difference between the two texts is clear from their opening gambits. The U.S. Constitution opens with "We the People." By acknowledging its human origin, it invests humans with the power to amend it. The Ten Commandments open with "I am the Lord your God." By claiming divine origin, it precludes humans from changing it. As a result, the biblical text still endorses slavery even today.

All human political systems are based on fictions, but some admit it, and some do not. Being truthful about the origins of our social order makes it easier to make changes in it. If humans like us invented it, we can amend it. But such truthfulness comes at a price. Acknowledging the human origins of the social order makes it harder to persuade everyone to agree on it. If humans like us invented it, why should we accept it? As we shall see in chapter 5, until the late eighteenth century the lack of mass communication technology made it extremely difficult to conduct open debates between millions of people about the rules of the social order. To maintain order, Russian tsars, Muslim caliphs, and Chinese sons of heaven therefore claimed that the fundamental rules of society came down from heaven and were not open to human amendment. In the early twenty-first century, many political systems still claim superhuman authority and oppose open debates that may result in unwelcome changes.

THE PERENNIAL DILEMMA

After we understand the key role of fiction in history, it is finally possible to present a more complete model of information networks, which goes beyond both the naive view of information and the pop-

ulist critique of that view. Contrary to the naive view, information isn't the raw material of truth, and human information networks aren't geared only to discover the truth. But contrary to the populist view, information isn't just a weapon, either. Rather, to survive and flourish, every human information network needs to do two things simultaneously: discover truth *and create order*. Accordingly, as history unfolded, human information networks have been developing two distinct sets of skills. On the one hand, as the naive view expects, the networks have learned how to process information to gain a more accurate understanding of things like medicine, mammoths, and nuclear physics. At the same time, the networks have also learned how to use information to maintain stronger social order among larger populations, by using not just truthful accounts but also fictions, fantasies, propaganda, and—occasionally—downright lies.

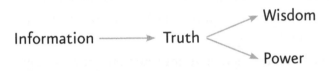

The naive view of information

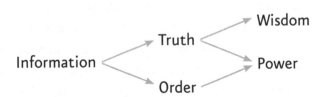

A more complete historical view of information

Having a lot of information doesn't in and of itself guarantee either truth or order. It is a difficult process to use information to discover the truth and simultaneously use it to maintain order. What makes things worse is that these two processes are often contradictory, because it is frequently easier to maintain order through fictions. Sometimes—as in the case of the U.S. Constitution—fictional stories may acknowledge their fictionality, but more often they dis-

avow it. Religions, for example, always claim to be an objective and eternal truth rather than a fictional story invented by humans. In such cases, the search for truth threatens the foundations of the social order. Many societies require their populations *not to know* their true origins: ignorance is strength. What happens, then, when people get uncomfortably close to the truth? What happens when the same bit of information reveals an important fact about the world, and also undermines the noble lie that holds society together? In such cases society may seek to preserve order by placing limits on the search for truth.

One obvious example is Darwin's theory of evolution. Understanding evolution greatly advances our understanding of the origins and biology of species, including *Homo sapiens,* but it also undermines the central myths that maintain order in numerous societies. No wonder that various governments and churches have banned or limited the teaching of evolution, preferring to sacrifice truth for the sake of order.[26]

A related problem is that an information network may allow and even encourage people to search for truth, but only in specific fields that help generate power without threatening the social order. The result can be a very powerful network that is singularly lacking in wisdom. Nazi Germany, for example, cultivated many of the world's leading experts in chemistry, optics, engineering, and rocket science. It was largely Nazi rocket science that later took the Americans to the moon.[27] This scientific prowess helped the Nazis build an extremely powerful war machine, which was then deployed in the service of a deranged and murderous mythology. Under Nazi rule Germans were encouraged to develop rocket science, but they were not free to question racist theories about biology and history.

That's a major reason why the history of human information networks isn't a triumphant march of progress. While over the generations human networks have grown increasingly powerful, they have not necessarily grown increasingly wise. If a network privileges order over truth, it can become very powerful but use that power unwisely.

Instead of a march of progress, the history of human information networks is a tightrope walk trying to balance truth with order. In the twenty-first century we aren't much better at finding the right balance than our ancestors were in the Stone Age. Contrary to what the mission statements of corporations like Google and Facebook imply, simply increasing the speed and efficiency of our information technology doesn't necessarily make the world a better place. It only makes the need to balance truth and order more urgent. The invention of the story taught us this lesson already tens of thousands of years ago. And the same lesson would be taught again, when humans came up with their second great information technology: the written document.

Documents: The Bite of
the Paper Tigers

Stories were the first crucial information technology developed by humans. They laid the foundation for all large-scale human cooperation and made humans the most powerful animals on earth. But as an information technology, stories have their limitations.

To appreciate this, consider the role storytelling plays in the formation of nations. Many nations have first been conceived in the imagination of poets. Sarah Aaronsohn and the NILI underground are remembered by present-day Israelis as some of the first Zionists who risked their lives in the 1910s to establish a Jewish state in Palestine, but from where did NILI members get this idea in the first place? They were inspired by an earlier generation of poets, thinkers, and visionaries such as Theodor Herzl and Hayim Nahman Bialik.

In the 1890s and first decade of the twentieth century, Bialik, a Ukrainian Jew, published numerous poems and stories bewailing the persecution and weakness of European Jews and calling on them to take their fate in their hands—to defend themselves by force of arms, immigrate to Palestine, and there establish their own state. One of his most stirring poems was written following the Kishinev Pogrom of 1903, in which forty-nine Jews were murdered and dozens more

were injured.[1] "In the City of Slaughter" condemned the murderous antisemitic mob who perpetrated the atrocities, but it also criticized the Jews themselves for their pacifism and helplessness.

In one heart-wrenching scene, Bialik describes how Jewish women were gang-raped, while their husbands and brothers hid nearby, afraid to intervene. The poem compares the Jewish men to terrified mice and imagines how they quietly prayed to God to perform some miracle, which failed to materialize. The poem then tells how even after the pogrom was over, the survivors had no thought of arming themselves and instead entered Talmudic disputations about whether the raped women were now ritualistically "defiled" or whether they were still "pure." This poem is mandatory reading in many Israeli schools today. It is also mandatory reading for anyone wishing to understand how after two millennia of being one of the most pacifist groups in history, Jews built one of the most formidable armies in the world. Not for nothing was Bialik named Israel's national poet.[2]

The fact that Bialik lived in Ukraine, and was intimately familiar with the persecution of Ashkenazi Jews in eastern Europe but had little understanding of conditions in Palestine, contributed to the subsequent conflict there between Jews and Arabs. Bialik's poems inspired Jews to see themselves as victims in dire need of developing their military might and building their own country, but hardly considered the catastrophic consequences for the Arab inhabitants of Palestine, or indeed for the Mizrahi Jewish communities native to the Middle East. When the Arab-Israeli conflict exploded in the late 1940s, hundreds of thousands of Palestinians and hundreds of thousands of Mizrahi Jews were driven out of their ancestral homes in the Middle East, partly as a result of poems composed half a century earlier in Ukraine.[3]

While Bialik was writing in Ukraine, the Hungarian Jew Theodor Herzl was busy organizing the Zionist movement in the 1890s and early years of the twentieth century. As a central part of his political activism, Herzl published two books. *The Jewish State* (1896) was a

manifesto outlining Herzl's idea of establishing a Jewish state in Palestine, and *The Old New Land* (1902) was a utopian novel set in the year 1923 describing the prosperous Jewish state that Herzl envisioned. The two books—which fatefully also tended to ignore realities on the ground in Palestine—were immensely influential in shaping the Zionist movement. *The Old New Land* appeared in Hebrew under the title *Tel Aviv* (a loose Hebrew translation of "Old New Land"). The city of Tel Aviv, established seven years after the book's publication, took its name from the book. While Bialik is Israel's national poet, Herzl is known as the visionary of the state.

The yarns Bialik and Herzl wove ignored many crucial facts about contemporary reality, most notably that around 1900 the Jews of Palestine comprised only 6–9 percent of the region's total population of about 600,000 people.[4] While disregarding such demographic facts, Bialik and Herzl accorded great importance to mythology, most notably the stories of the Bible, without which modern Zionism is unimaginable. Bialik and Herzl were also influenced by the nationalist myths that were created in the nineteenth century by almost every other ethnic group in Europe. The Ukrainian Jew Bialik and the Hungarian Jew Herzl did for Zionism what was earlier done by the poets Taras Shevchenko for Ukrainian nationalism,[5] Sándor Petőfi for Hungarian nationalism,[6] and Adam Mickiewicz for Polish nationalism.[7] Observing the growth of other national movements all around, Herzl wrote that nations arise "out of dreams, songs, fantasies."[8]

But dreams, songs, and fantasies, however inspiring, are not enough to create a functioning nation-state. Bialik inspired generations of Jewish fighters, but to equip and maintain an army, it is also necessary to raise taxes and buy guns. Herzl's utopian book laid the foundations for the city of Tel Aviv, but to keep the city going, it was also necessary to dig a sewage system. When all is said and done, the essence of patriotism isn't reciting stirring poems about the beauty of the motherland, and it certainly isn't making hate-filled speeches against foreigners and minorities. Rather, patriotism means paying

your taxes so that people on the other side of the country also enjoy the benefit of a sewage system, as well as security, education, and health care.

To manage all these services and raise the necessary taxes, enormous amounts of information need to be collected, stored, and processed: information about properties, payments, exemptions, discounts, debts, inventories, shipments, budgets, bills, and salaries. This, however, is not the kind of information that can be turned into a memorable poem or a captivating myth. Instead, tax records come in the shape of various types of lists, ranging from a simple item-by-item record to more elaborate tables and spreadsheets. No matter how intricate these data sets may become, they eschew narrative in favor of dryly listing amounts owed and amounts paid. Poets can afford to ignore such mundane facts, but tax collectors cannot.

Lists are crucial not only for national taxation systems but also for almost all other complex financial institutions. Corporations, banks, and stock markets cannot exist without them. A church, a university, or a library that wants to balance its budget soon realizes that in addition to priests and poets who can mesmerize people with stories, it needs accountants who know their way around the various types of lists.

Lists and stories are complementary. National myths legitimize the tax records, while the tax records help transform aspirational stories into concrete schools and hospitals. Something analogous happens in the field of finance. The dollar, the pound sterling, and the bitcoin are all brought into being by persuading people to believe a story, and tales told by bankers, finance ministers, and investment gurus raise or lower their value. When the chairperson of the Federal Reserve wants to curb inflation, when a finance minister wants to pass a new budget, and when a tech entrepreneur wants to draw investors, they all turn to storytelling. But to actually manage a bank, a budget, or a start-up, lists are essential.

The big problem with lists, and the crucial difference between lists and stories, is that lists tend to be far more boring than stories, which

means that while we easily remember stories, we find it difficult to remember lists. This is an important fact about how the human brain processes information. Evolution has adapted our brains to be good at absorbing, retaining, and processing even very large quantities of information when they are shaped into a story. The *Ramayana,* one of the foundational tales of Hindu mythology, is twenty-four thousand verses long and runs to about seventeen hundred pages in modern editions, yet despite its enormous length generations of Hindus succeeded in remembering and reciting it by heart.[9]

In the twentieth and twenty-first centuries, the *Ramayana* was repeatedly adapted for film and television. In 1987–88, a seventy-eight-episode version (running to about 2,730 minutes) was the most watched television series in the world, with more than 650 million viewers. According to a BBC report, when episodes were aired, "streets would be deserted, shops would be closed, and people would bathe and garland their TV sets." During the 2020 COVID-19 lockdown the series was re-aired and again became the most watched show in the world.[10] While modern TV audiences need not memorize any texts by heart, it is noteworthy how easy they find it to follow the intricate plots of epic dramas, detective thrillers, and soap operas, recalling who each character is and how they are related to numerous others. We are so accustomed to performing such feats of memory that we seldom consider how extraordinary they are.

What makes us so good at remembering epic poems and long-running TV series is that long-term human memory is particularly adapted to retaining stories. As Kendall Haven writes in his 2007 book, *Story Proof: The Science Behind the Startling Power of Story,* "Human minds ... rely on stories and on story architecture as the primary roadmap for understanding, making sense of, remembering, and planning our lives. ... Lives are like stories because we think in story terms." Haven references more than 120 academic studies, concluding that "research overwhelmingly, convincingly, and without opposition provides the evidence" that stories are a highly efficient

"vehicle for communicating factual, conceptual, emotional, and tacit information."[11]

In contrast, most people find it hard to remember lists by heart, and few people would be interested in watching a TV recitation of India's tax records or annual budget. Mnemonic methods used to memorize lists of items often work by weaving the items into a plot, thereby turning the list into a story.[12] But even with the help of such mnemonic devices, who could remember their country's tax records or budget? The information may be vital—determining what quality of health care, education, and welfare services citizens enjoy—but our brains are not adapted to remembering such things. Unlike national poems and myths, which can be stored in our brains, complex national taxation and administration systems have required a unique nonorganic information technology in order to function. This technology is the written document.

TO KILL A LOAN

The written document was invented many times in many places. Some of the earliest examples come from ancient Mesopotamia. A cuneiform clay tablet dated to the twenty-eighth day of the tenth month of the forty-first year of the reign of King Shulgi of Ur (ca. 2053/4 BCE) recorded the monthly deliveries of sheep and goats. Fifteen sheep were delivered on the second day of the month, 7 sheep on the third day, 11 sheep on the fourth, 219 on the fifth, 47 on the sixth, and so on until 3 sheep were delivered on the twenty-eighth. In total, says the clay tablet, 896 animals were received that month. Remembering all these deliveries was important for the royal administration, to monitor people's obedience and to keep track of available resources. While doing so in one's head was a formidable challenge, it was easy for a learned scribe to write them down on a clay tablet.[13]

Like stories and like all other information technologies in history, written documents didn't necessarily represent reality accurately. The Ur tablet, for example, contained a mistake. The document says that 896 animals were received during that month, but when modern scholars added up all the individual entries they reached a total of 898. The scribe who wrote the document apparently made a mistake when he calculated the overall tally, and the tablet preserved this mistake for posterity.

But whether true or false, written documents created new realities. By recording lists of properties, taxes, and payments, they made it far easier to create administrative systems, kingdoms, religious organizations, and trade networks. More specifically, documents changed the method used for creating intersubjective realities. In oral cultures, intersubjective realities were created by telling a story that many people repeated with their mouths and remembered in their brains. Brain capacity consequently placed a limit on the kinds of intersubjective realities that humans created. Humans couldn't forge an intersubjective reality that their brains couldn't remember.

This limit could be transcended, however, by writing documents. The documents didn't represent an objective empirical reality; the reality was the documents themselves. As we shall see in later chapters, written documents thereby provided precedents and models that would eventually be used by computers. The ability of computers to create intersubjective realities is an extension of the power of clay tablets and pieces of paper.

As a key example, consider ownership. In oral communities that lacked written documents, ownership was an intersubjective reality created through the words and behaviors of the community members. To own a field meant that your neighbors agreed that this field was yours, and they behaved accordingly. They didn't build a hut on that field, graze their livestock there, or pick fruits there without first asking your permission. Ownership was created and maintained by people continuously saying or signaling things to one another. This made ownership the affair of a local community and placed a limit

on the ability of a distant central authority to control all landowner-ship. No king, minister, or priest could remember who owned each field in hundreds of distant villages. This also placed a limit on the ability of individuals to claim and exercise absolute property rights, and instead favored various forms of communal property rights. For example, your neighbors might acknowledge your right to cultivate a field but not your right to sell it to foreigners.[14]

In a literate state, to own a field increasingly came to mean that it is written on some clay tablet, bamboo strip, piece of paper, or silicon chip that you own that field. If your neighbors have been grazing their sheep for years on a piece of land, and none of them ever said that you own it, but you can somehow produce an official document that says it is yours, you have a good chance of enforcing your claim. Conversely, if all the neighbors agree that it is your field but you don't have any official document that proves it, tough luck. Ownership is still an intersubjective reality created by exchanging information, but the information now takes the form of a written document (or a computer file) rather than of people talking and gesturing to each other. This means that ownership can now be determined by a central authority that produces and holds the relevant documents. It also means that you can sell your field without asking your neighbors' permission, simply by transferring the crucial document to someone else.

The power of documents to create intersubjective realities was beautifully manifested in the Old Assyrian dialect, which treated documents as living things that could also be killed. Loan contracts were "killed" (duākum) when the debt was repaid. This was done by destroying the tablet, adding some mark to it, or breaking its seal. The loan contract didn't represent reality; it *was* the reality. If somebody repaid the loan but failed to "kill the document," the debt was still owed. Conversely, if somebody didn't repay the loan but the document "died" in some other way—perhaps the dog ate it—the debt was no more.[15] The same happens with money. If your dog eats a hundred-dollar bill, those hundred dollars cease to exist.

In Shulgi's Ur, in ancient Assyria, and in numerous subsequent polities, social, economic, and political relations relied on documents that create reality instead of merely representing it. When writing constitutions, peace treaties, and commercial contracts, lawyers, politicians, and businesspeople wrangle for weeks and even months over each word—because they know that these pieces of paper can wield enormous power.

BUREAUCRACY

Every new information technology has its unexpected bottlenecks. It solves some old problems but creates new ones. In the early 1730s BCE, Narâmtani, a priestess in the Mesopotamian city of Sippar, wrote a letter (on a clay tablet) to a relative, asking him to send her a few clay tablets he kept in his house. She explained that her claim to an inheritance was being contested and she couldn't prove her case in court without those documents. She ended her message with a plea: "Now, do not neglect me!"[16]

We don't know what happened next, but just imagine the situation if the relative searched his house but could not find the missing tablets. As people produced more and more documents, finding them turned out to be far from easy. This was a particular challenge for kings, priests, merchants, and anyone else who accumulated thousands of documents in their archives. How do you find the right tax record, payment receipt, or business contract when you need it? Written documents were much better than human brains in recording certain types of information. But they created a new and very thorny problem: retrieval.[17]

The brain is remarkably efficient in retrieving whatever information is stored in its network of tens of billions of neurons and trillions of synapses. Though our brain archives countless complex stories about our personal life, our national history, and our religious mythology, healthy people can retrieve information about any of them

in less than a second. What did you eat for breakfast? Who was your first crush? When did your country gain its independence? What's the first verse in the Bible?

How did you retrieve all these pieces of information? What mechanism activates the right neurons and synapses to rapidly call up the necessary information? Though neuroscientists have made some progress in the study of memory, nobody yet understands what memories are, or how exactly they are stored and retrieved.[18] What we do know is that millions of years of evolution streamlined the brain's retrieval processes. However, once humans have outsourced memories from organic brains to inorganic documents, retrieval could no longer rely on that streamlined biological system. Nor could it rely on the foraging abilities that humans evolved over millions of years. Evolution has adapted humans for finding fruits and mushrooms in a forest, but not for finding documents in an archive.

Foragers locate fruits and mushrooms in a forest because evolution has organized forests according to a discernible organic order. Fruit trees photosynthesize, so they require sunlight. Mushrooms feed on dead organic matter, which can usually be found in the ground. So mushrooms are usually down at soil level, whereas fruits grow farther up. Another common rule is that apples grow on apple trees, whereas figs grow on figs trees. So if you are looking for an apple, you first need to locate an apple tree, and then look up. When living in a forest, humans learn this organic order.

It is very different with archives. Since documents aren't organisms, they don't obey any biological laws, and evolution didn't organize them for us. Tax reports don't grow on a tax-report shelf. They need to be placed there. For that, somebody first needs to come up with the idea of categorizing information by shelves, and to decide which documents should go on which shelf. Unlike foragers, who need merely to discover the preexisting order of the forest, archivists need to devise a new order for the world. That order is called bureaucracy.

Bureaucracy is the way people in large organizations solved the

retrieval problem and thereby created bigger and more powerful information networks. But like mythology, bureaucracy too tends to sacrifice truth for order. By inventing a new order and imposing it on the world, bureaucracy distorted people's understanding of the world in unique ways. Many of the problems of our twenty-first-century information networks—like biased algorithms that mislabel people, or rigid protocols that ignore human needs and feelings—are not new problems of the computer age. They are quintessential bureaucratic problems that have existed long before anyone even dreamed of computers.

BUREAUCRACY AND THE SEARCH FOR TRUTH

Bureaucracy literally means "rule by writing desk." The term was invented in eighteenth-century France, when the typical official sat next to a writing desk with drawers—a bureau.[19] At the heart of the bureaucratic order, then, is the drawer. Bureaucracy seeks to solve the retrieval problem by dividing the world into drawers, and knowing which document goes into which drawer.

The principle remains the same regardless of whether the document is placed into a drawer, a shelf, a basket, a jar, a computer folder, or any other receptacle: divide and rule. Divide the world into containers, and keep the containers separate so the documents don't get mixed up. This principle, however, comes with a price. Instead of focusing on understanding the world as it is, bureaucracy is often busy imposing a new and artificial order on the world. Bureaucrats begin by inventing various drawers, which are intersubjective realities that don't necessarily correspond to any objective divisions in the world. The bureaucrats then try to force the world to fit into these drawers, and if the fit isn't very good, the bureaucrats push harder. Anyone who ever filled out an official form knows this only too well. When you fill out the form, and none of the listed options fits your circumstances, you must adapt yourself to the form, rather than the form

adapting to you. Reducing the messiness of reality to a limited number of fixed drawers helps bureaucrats keep order, but it comes at the expense of truth. Because they are fixated on their drawers—even when reality is far more complex—bureaucrats often develop a distorted understanding of the world.

The urge to divide reality into rigid drawers also leads bureaucrats to pursue narrow goals irrespective of the wider impact of their actions. A bureaucrat tasked with increasing industrial production is likely to ignore environmental considerations that fall outside her purview, and perhaps dump toxic waste into a nearby river, leading to an ecological disaster downstream. If the government then establishes a new department to combat pollution, its bureaucrats are likely to push for ever more stringent regulations, even if this results in economic ruin for communities upstream. Ideally, someone should be able to take into account all the different considerations and aspects, but such a holistic approach requires transcending or abolishing the bureaucratic division.

The distortions created by bureaucracy affect not only government agencies and private corporations but also scientific disciplines. Consider, for example, how universities are divided into different faculties and departments. History is separate from biology and from mathematics. Why? Certainly this division doesn't reflect objective reality. It is the intersubjective invention of academic bureaucrats. The COVID-19 pandemic, for example, was at one and the same time a historical, biological, and mathematical event. But the academic study of pandemics is divided between the separate departments of history, biology, and mathematics (among others). Students pursuing an academic degree must usually decide to which of these departments they belong. Their decision limits their choice of courses, which in turn shapes their understanding of the world. Mathematics students learn how to predict future morbidity levels from present rates of infection; biology students learn how viruses mutate over time; and history students learn how religious and political beliefs affect people's willingness to follow government instructions. To fully understand

COVID-19 requires taking into account mathematical, biological, and historical phenomena, but academic bureaucracy doesn't encourage such a holistic approach.

As you climb the academic ladder, the pressure to specialize only increases. The academic world is ruled by the law of publish or perish. If you want a job, you must publish in peer-reviewed journals. But journals are divided by discipline, and publishing an article on virus mutations in a biology journal demands following different conventions from publishing an article on the politics of pandemics in a history journal. There are different jargons, different citation rules, and different expectations. Historians should have a deep understanding of culture and know how to read and interpret historical documents. Biologists should have a deep understanding of evolution and know how to read and interpret DNA molecules. Things that fall in between categories—like the interplay between human political ideologies and virus evolution—are often left unaddressed.[20]

To appreciate how academics force a messy and fluid world into rigid bureaucratic categories, let's dig a little deeper in the specific discipline of biology. Before Darwin could explain the origin of species, earlier scholars like Carl Linnaeus first had to define what a species is and classify all living organisms into species. To argue that lions and tigers evolved from a common feline ancestor, you first have to define "lions" and "tigers."[21] This turned out to be a difficult and never-ending job, because animals, plants, and other organisms often trespass the boundaries of their allotted drawers.

Evolution cannot be easily contained in any bureaucratic schema. The whole point of evolution is that species continually change, which means that putting each species in one unchanging drawer distorts biological reality. For example, it is an open question when *Homo erectus* ended and *Homo sapiens* began. Were there once two Erectus parents whose child was the first Sapiens?[22] Species also keep intermingling, with animals belonging to seemingly separate species not only having sex but even siring fertile offspring. Most

Sapiens living today have about 1–3 percent Neanderthal DNA,[23] indicating that there once was a child whose father was a Neanderthal and whose mother was a Sapiens (or vice versa). So are Sapiens and Neanderthals the same species or different species? And is "species" an objective reality that biologists discover, or is it an intersubjective reality that biologists impose?[24]

There are numerous other examples of animals breaking out of their drawers, so the neat bureaucratic division fails to accurately categorize ring species, fusion species, and hybrids.[25] Grizzly bears and polar bears sometimes produce pizzly bears and grolar bears.[26] Lions and tigers produce ligers and tigons.[27]

When we shift our attention from mammals and other multicellular organisms to the world of single-cell bacteria and archaea, we discover that anarchy reigns. In a process known as horizontal gene transfer, single-cell organisms routinely exchange genetic material not only with organisms from related species but also with organisms from entirely different genera, kingdoms, orders, and even domains. Bacteriologists have a very difficult job keeping tabs on these chimeras.[28]

And when we reach the very edge of life and consider viruses like SARS-CoV-2 (responsible for COVID-19), things become even more complicated. Viruses straddle the supposed rigid boundary between living beings and lifeless matter—between biology and chemistry. Unlike bacteria, viruses aren't single-cell organisms. They aren't cells at all, and don't possess any cellular machinery of their own. Viruses don't eat or metabolize, and cannot reproduce by themselves. They are tiny packets of genetic code, which are able to penetrate cells, hijack their cellular machinery, and instruct them to produce more copies of that alien genetic code. The new copies burst out of the cell to infect and hijack more cells, which is how the alien code turns viral. Scientists argue endlessly about whether viruses should count as life-forms or whether they fall outside the boundary of life.[29] But this boundary isn't an objective reality; it is an intersubjec-

tive convention. Even if biologists reach a consensus that viruses are life-forms, it wouldn't change anything about how viruses behave; it will only change how humans think about them.

Of course, intersubjective conventions are themselves part of reality. As we humans become more powerful, so our intersubjective beliefs become more consequential for the world outside our information networks. For example, scientists and legislators have categorized species according to the threat of extinction they face, on a scale ranging from "least concern" through "vulnerable" and "endangered" to "extinct." Defining a particular population of animals as an "endangered species" is an intersubjective human convention, but it can have far-reaching consequences, for instance by imposing legal restrictions on hunting those animals or destroying their habitat. A bureaucratic decision about whether a certain animal belongs in the "endangered species" drawer or in the "vulnerable species" drawer could make the difference between life and death. As we shall see time and again in subsequent chapters, when a bureaucracy puts a label on you, even though the label might be pure convention, it can still determine your fate. That's true whether the bureaucrat is a flesh-and-blood expert on animals, a flesh-and-blood expert on humans, or an inorganic AI.

THE DEEP STATE

In defense of bureaucracy it should be noted that while it sometimes sacrifices truth and distorts our understanding of the world, it often does so for the sake of order, without which it would be hard to maintain any large-scale human network. While bureaucracies are never perfect, is there a better way to manage big networks? For example, if we decided to abolish all conventional divisions in the academic world, all departments and faculties and specialized journals, would every prospective doctor be expected to devote several years to the study of history, and would people who studied the impact of the

Black Death on Christian theology be considered expert virologists? Would it lead to better health-care systems?

Anyone who fantasizes about abolishing all bureaucracies in favor of a more holistic approach to the world should reflect on the fact that hospitals too are bureaucratic institutions. They are divided into different departments, with hierarchies, protocols, and lots of forms to fill out. They suffer from many bureaucratic illnesses, but they still manage to cure us of many of our biological illnesses. The same goes for almost all the other services that make our life better, from our schools to our sewage system.

When you flush the toilet, where does the waste go? It goes into the deep state. There is an intricate subterranean web of pipes, pumps, and tunnels that runs under our houses and collects our waste, separates it from the supply of drinking water, and either treats or safely disposes of it. Somebody needs to design, construct, and maintain that deep web, plug holes in it, monitor pollution levels, and pay the workers. That too is bureaucratic work, and we would face a lot of discomfort and even death if we abolished that particular department. Sewage water and drinking water are always in danger of mixing, but luckily for us there are bureaucrats who keep them separate.

Prior to the establishment of modern sewage systems, waterborne infectious diseases like dysentery and cholera killed millions of people around the world.[30] In 1854 hundreds of London residents began dying of cholera. It was a relatively small outbreak, but it proved to be a turning point in the history of cholera, of epidemics more generally, and of sewage. The leading medical theory of the day argued that cholera epidemics were caused by "bad air." But the physician John Snow suspected that the cause was the water supply. He painstakingly tracked and listed all known cholera patients, their place of residence, and their source of water. The resulting data led him to identify the water pump on Broad Street in Soho as the epicenter of the outbreak.

This was tedious bureaucratic work—collecting data, categorizing it, and mapping it—but it saved lives. Snow explained his findings to

local officials, persuading them to disable the Broad Street pump, which effectively ended the outbreak. Subsequent research discovered that the well providing water to the Broad Street pump was dug less than a meter from a cholera-infected cesspit.[31]

Snow's discovery, and the work of many subsequent scientists, engineers, lawyers, and officials, resulted in a sprawling bureaucracy regulating cesspits, water pumps, and sewage lines. In today's England, digging wells and constructing cesspits require filling out forms and getting licenses, which ensure that drinking water doesn't come from a well someone dug next to a cesspit.[32]

It is easy to forget about this system when it works well, but since 1854 it has saved millions of lives, and it is one of the most important services provided by modern states. In 2014, Prime Minister Narendra Modi of India identified the lack of toilets as one of India's biggest problems. Open defecation is a major cause for spreading diseases like cholera, dysentery, and diarrhea, as well as exposing women and girls to sexual assaults. As part of his flagship Clean India Mission, Modi promised to provide all Indian citizens with access to toilets, and between 2014 and 2020 the Indian state invested around ten billion dollars in the project, building more than 100 million new latrines.[33] Sewage isn't the stuff of epic poems, but it is a test of a well-functioning state.

THE BIOLOGICAL DRAMAS

Mythology and bureaucracy are the twin pillars of every large-scale society. Yet while mythology tends to inspire fascination, bureaucracy tends to inspire suspicion. Despite the services they provide, even beneficial bureaucracies often fail to win the public's trust. For many people, the very word "bureaucracy" carries negative connotations. This is because it is inherently difficult to know whether a bureaucratic system is beneficial or malicious. For all bureaucracies—

good or bad—share one key characteristic: it is hard for humans to understand them.

Any kid can tell the difference between a friend and a bully. You know if someone shares their lunch with you or instead takes yours. But when the tax collector comes to take a cut from your earnings, how can you tell whether it goes to build a new public sewage system or a new private dacha for the president? It is hard to get all the relevant information, and even harder to interpret it. It is similarly difficult for citizens to understand the bureaucratic procedures determining how pupils are admitted to schools, how patients are treated in hospitals, or how garbage is collected and recycled. It takes a minute to tweet allegations of bias, fraud, or corruption, and many weeks of arduous work to prove or disprove them.

Documents, archives, forms, licenses, regulations, and other bureaucratic procedures have changed the way information flows in society, and with it the way power works. This made it far more difficult to understand power. What is happening behind the closed doors of offices and archives, where anonymous officials analyze and organize piles of documents and determine our fate with a stroke of a pen or a click of a mouse?

In tribal societies that lack written documents and bureaucracies, the human network is composed of only human-to-human and human-to-story chains. Authority belongs to the people who control the junctions that link the various chains. These junctions are the tribe's foundational myths. Charismatic leaders, orators, and myth-makers know how to use these stories in order to shape identities, build alliances, and sway emotions.[34]

In human networks connected by written documents and bureaucratic procedures—from ancient Ur to modern India—society relies in part on the interaction between humans and documents. In addition to human-to-human and human-to-story chains, such societies are held together by human-to-document chains. When we observe a bureaucratic society at work, we still see humans telling stories to

other humans, as when millions of Indians watch the *Ramayana* series, but we also see humans passing documents to other humans, as when TV networks are required to apply for broadcasting licenses and fill out tax reports. Looked at from a different perspective, what we see is documents compelling humans to engage with other documents.

This led to shifts in authority. As documents became a crucial nexus linking many social chains, considerable power came to be invested in these documents, and experts in the arcane logic of documents emerged as new authority figures. Administrators, accountants, and lawyers mastered not just reading and writing but also the skills of composing forms, separating drawers, and managing archives. In bureaucratic systems, power often comes from understanding how to manipulate obscure budgetary loopholes and from knowing your way around the labyrinths of offices, committees, and subcommittees.

This shift in authority changed the balance of power in the world. For better or worse, literate bureaucracies tended to strengthen the central authority at the expense of ordinary citizens. It's not just that documents and archives made it easier for the center to tax, judge, and conscript everybody. The difficulty of understanding bureaucratic power simultaneously made it harder for the masses to influence, resist, or evade the central authority. Even when bureaucracy was a benign force, providing people with sewage systems, education, and security, it still tended to increase the gap between rulers and ruled. The system enabled the center to collect and record a lot more information about the people it governed, while the latter found it much more difficult to understand how the system itself worked.

Art, which helps us understand many other aspects of life, offered only limited assistance in this case. Poets, playwrights, and moviemakers have occasionally focused on the dynamics of bureaucratic power. However, this has proven to be a very difficult story to communicate. Artists usually work with a limited set of story lines that are rooted in our biology, but none of these biological dramas sheds

much light on the workings of bureaucracy, because they have all been scripted by evolution millions of years before the emergence of documents and archives. To understand what "biological dramas" are, and why they are a poor guide for understanding bureaucracy, let's consider in detail the plot of one of humanity's greatest artistic masterpieces—the *Ramayana*.

One important plotline of the *Ramayana* concerns the relations between the eponymous prince, Rama, his father, King Dasharatha, and his stepmother, Queen Kaikeyi. Though Rama, being the eldest son, is the rightful heir to the kingdom, Kaikeyi persuades the king to banish Rama to the wilderness and bestow the succession instead on her son Bharata. Underlying this plotline are several biological dramas that go back hundreds of millions of years in mammalian and avian evolution.

All mammal and bird offspring depend on their parents in the first stage of life, seek parental care, and fear parental neglect or hostility. Life and death hang in the balance. A cub or chick pushed out of the nest too soon is in danger of death from starvation or predation. Among humans, the fear of being neglected or abandoned by one's parents is a template not just for children's stories like *Snow White, Cinderella,* and Harry Potter but also for some of our most influential national and religious myths. The *Ramayana* is far from being the sole example. In Christian theology damnation is conceived as losing all contact with the mother church and the heavenly father. Hell is a lost child crying for his or her missing parents.

A related biological drama, which is also familiar to human children, mammalian cubs, and avian chicks, is "Father loves me more than he loves you." Biologists and geneticists have identified sibling rivalry as one of the key processes of evolution.[35] Siblings routinely compete for food and parental attention, and in some species the killing of one sibling by another is commonplace. About a quarter of spotted hyena cubs are killed by their siblings, who typically enjoy greater parental care as a result.[36] Among sand tiger sharks, females hold numerous embryos in their uterus. The first embryo that reaches

about ten centimeters in length then eats all the others.[37] The dynamics of sibling rivalry are manifested in numerous myths in addition to the *Ramayana,* for instance in the stories of Cain and Abel, King Lear, and the TV series *Succession.* Entire nations—like the Jewish people—may base their identity on the claim that "we are Father's favorite children."

The second major plotline of the *Ramayana* focuses on the romantic triangle formed by Prince Rama, his lover, Sita, and the demon-king Ravana, who kidnaps Sita. "Boy meets girl" and "boy fights boy over girl" are also biological dramas that have been enacted by countless mammals, birds, reptiles, and fish for hundreds of millions of years. We are mesmerized by these stories because understanding them has been essential for our ancestors' survival. Human storytellers like Homer, Shakespeare, and Valmiki—the purported author of the *Ramayana*—have displayed an amazing capacity to elaborate on the biological dramas, but even the greatest poetical narratives usually copy their basic plotline from the handbook of evolution.

A third theme recurring in the *Ramayana* is the tension between purity and impurity, with Sita being the paragon of purity in Hindu culture. The cultural obsession with purity originates in the evolutionary struggle to avoid pollution. All animals are torn between the need to try new food and the fear of being poisoned. Evolution therefore equipped animals with both curiosity and the capacity to feel disgust on coming into contact with something toxic or otherwise dangerous.[38] Politicians and prophets have learned how to manipulate these disgust mechanisms. In nationalist and religious myths, countries or churches are depicted as a biological body in danger of being polluted by impure intruders. For centuries bigots have often said that ethnic and religious minorities spread diseases,[39] that LGBTQ people are a source of pollution,[40] or that women are impure.[41] During the Rwanda genocide of 1994, Hutu propaganda referred to the Tutsis as cockroaches. The Nazis compared Jews to

rats. Experiments have shown that chimpanzees, too, react with disgust to images of unfamiliar chimpanzees from another band.[42]

Perhaps in no other culture was the biological drama of "purity versus impurity" carried to greater extremes than in traditional Hinduism. It constructed an intersubjective system of castes ranked by their supposed level of purity, with the pure Brahmins at the top and the allegedly impure Dalit (formerly known as untouchables) at the bottom. Professions, tools, and everyday activities have also been classified by their level of purity, and strict rules have forbidden "impure" persons to marry "pure" people, touch them, prepare food for them, or even come near them.

The modern state of India still struggles with this legacy, which influences almost all aspects of life. For example, fears of impurity created various complications for the aforementioned Clean India Mission, because allegedly "pure" people were reluctant to get involved in "impure" activities such as building, maintaining, and cleaning toilets, or to share public latrines with allegedly "impure" persons.[43] On September 25, 2019, two Dalit children—twelve-year-old Roshni Valmiki and her ten-year-old nephew Avinash—were lynched in the Indian village of Bhakhedi for defecating near the house of a family from the higher Yadav caste. They were forced to defecate in public because their houses lacked functioning toilets. A local official later explained that their household—while being among the poorest in the village—was nevertheless excluded from the list of families eligible for government aid to build toilets. The children routinely suffered from other caste-based discrimination, for example being forced to bring separate mats and utensils to school and to sit apart from the other pupils, so as not to "pollute" them.[44]

The list of biological dramas that press our emotional buttons includes several additional classics, such as "Who will be alpha?" "Us versus them," and "Good versus evil." These dramas, too, feature prominently in the *Ramayana,* and all of them are well known to

wolf packs and chimpanzee bands as well as to human societies. Together, these biological dramas form the backbone of almost all
human art and mythology. But art's dependence on the biological
dramas has made it difficult for artists to explain the mechanisms of
bureaucracy. The *Ramayana* is set within the context of large agrarian
kingdoms, but it shows little interest in how such kingdoms register
property, collect taxes, catalog archives, or finance wars. Sibling rivalry and romantic triangles aren't a good guide for the dynamics of
documents, which have no siblings and no romantic life.

Storytellers like Franz Kafka, who focused on the often surreal
ways that bureaucracy shapes human lives, pioneered new nonbio-
logical plotlines. In Kafka's *The Trial*, the bank clerk K. is arrested by
unidentified officials of an unfathomable agency for an unnamed
crime. Despite his best efforts, he never understands what is happening to him or uncovers the aims of the agency that is crushing him.
While sometimes taken as an existential or theological reference to
the human condition in the universe and to the unfathomability of
God, on a more mundane level the story highlights the potentially
nightmarish character of bureaucracies, which as an insurance lawyer
Kafka knew all too well.

In bureaucratic societies, the lives of ordinary people are often upended by unidentified officials of an unfathomable agency for in-
comprehensible reasons. Whereas stories about heroes who confront
monsters—from the *Ramayana* to Spider-Man—repackage the biological dramas of confronting predators and romantic rivals, the
unique horror of Kafkaesque stories comes from the unfathomability
of the threat. Evolution has primed our minds to understand death
by a tiger. Our mind finds it much more difficult to understand death
by a document.

Some portrayals of bureaucracy are satirical. Joseph Heller's iconic
1961 novel, *Catch-22*, used satire to illustrate the central role bureaucracy plays in war. One of the most powerful figures in the novel is
ex–private first class Wintergreen, who from his power base in the
mail room decides which letters to forward and which to disappear.[45]

The 1980s British sitcoms *Yes Minister* and *Yes, Prime Minister* showed the ways that civil servants use arcane regulations, obscure subcommittees, and piles of documents to manipulate their political bosses. The 2015 comedy-drama *The Big Short* explored the bureaucratic roots of the 2007–8 financial crisis. The movie's arch-villains are not humans but collateralized debt obligations (CDOs), which are financial devices invented by investment bankers and understood by nobody else in the world. These bureaucratic Godzillas slumbered unnoticed in the depths of bank portfolios, until they suddenly emerged in 2007 to wreak havoc on the lives of billions of people by instigating a major financial crisis.

Artworks like these have had some success in shaping perceptions of how bureaucratic power works, but this is an uphill battle, because since the Stone Age our minds have been primed to focus on biological dramas rather than bureaucratic ones. Most Hollywood and Bollywood blockbusters are not about CDOs. Rather, even in the twenty-first century, most blockbusters are essentially Stone Age stories about the hero who fights the monster to win the girl. Similarly, when depicting the dynamics of political power, TV series like *Game of Thrones*, *The Crown*, and *Succession* focus on the family intrigues of the dynastic court rather than on the bureaucratic labyrinth that sustains—and sometimes curbs—the dynasty's power.

LET'S KILL ALL THE LAWYERS

The difficulty of depicting and understanding bureaucratic realities has had unfortunate results. On the one hand, it leaves people feeling helpless in the face of harmful powers they do not understand, like the hero of *The Trial*. On the other hand, it also leaves people with the impression that bureaucracy is a malign conspiracy, even in cases when it is in fact a benign force providing us with health care, security, and justice.

In the sixteenth century, Ludovico Ariosto described the alle-

gorical figure of Discord as a woman who walks around in a cloud of "sheaves of summonses and writs, cross-examinations and powers of attorney, and great piles of glosses, counsel's opinions and precedents—all of which tended to the greater insecurity of impoverished folk. In front and behind her and on either side she was hemmed in by notaries, attorneys and barristers."[46]

In his description of Jack Cade's Rebellion (1450) in *Henry VI, Part 2,* Shakespeare has a commoner rebel called Dick the Butcher take the antipathy to bureaucracy to its logical conclusion. Dick has a plan to establish a better social order. "The first thing we do," advises Dick, "let's kill all the lawyers." The rebel leader, Jack Cade, runs with Dick's proposal in a forceful attack on bureaucracy and in particular on written documents: "Is not this a lamentable thing, that of the skin of an innocent lamb should be made parchment? That parchment, being scribbled o'er, should undo a man? Some say the bee stings: but I say, 'tis the bee's wax; for I did but seal once to a thing, and I was never mine own man since." Just then the rebels capture a clerk and accuse him of being able to write and read. After a short interrogation that establishes his "crime," Cade orders his men, "Hang him with his pen and inkhorn about his neck."[47]

Seventy years prior to Jack Cade's Rebellion, during the even bigger 1381 Peasants' Revolt, the rebels focused their ire not only on flesh-and-blood bureaucrats but also on their documents, destroying numerous archives and burning court rolls, charters, and administrative and legal records. In one incident, they made a bonfire of the archives of the University of Cambridge. An old woman named Margery Starr scattered the ashes to the winds while crying, "Away with the learning of the clerks, away with it!" Thomas Walsingham, a monk in St. Albans Abbey who witnessed the destruction of the abbey's archive firsthand, described how the rebels "set fire to all court rolls and muniments, so that after they had got rid of these records of their ancient service their lords would not be able to claim any right at all against them at some future time."[48] Killing the documents erased the debts.

Similar attacks on archives characterized numerous other insurgencies throughout history. For example, during the Great Jewish Revolt in 66 CE, one of the first things the rebels did upon capturing Jerusalem was to set fire to the central archive in order to destroy records of debts, thereby wining the support of the populace.[49] During the French Revolution in 1789, numerous local and regional archives were destroyed for comparable reasons.[50] Many rebels might have been illiterate, but they knew that without the documents the bureaucratic machine couldn't function.

I can sympathize with the suspicion of government bureaucracies and of the power of official documents, because they have played an important role in my own family. My maternal grandfather had his life upended by a government census and by the inability to find a crucial document. My grandfather Bruno Luttinger was born in 1913 in Chernivtsi. Today this town is in Ukraine, but in 1913 it was part of the Habsburg Empire. Bruno's father disappeared in World War I, and he was raised by his mother, Chaya-Pearl. When the war was over, Chernivtsi was annexed to Romania. In the late 1930s, as Romania became a fascist dictatorship, an important plank of its new antisemitic policy was to conduct a Jewish census.

In 1936 official statistics said that 758,000 Jews lived in Romania, constituting 4.2 percent of the population. The same official statistics said that the total number of refugees from the U.S.S.R., Jews and non-Jews, was about 11,000. In 1937 a new fascist government came to power, headed by Prime Minister Octavian Goga. Goga was a renowned poet as well as a politician, but he quickly graduated from patriotic poetry to fake statistics and oppressive bureaucracy. He and his colleagues ignored the official statistics and claimed that hundreds of thousands of Jewish refugees were flooding into Romania. In several interviews Goga claimed that half a million Jews had entered Romania illegally and that the total number of Jews in the country was 1.5 million. Government organs, far-right statisticians, and popular newspapers regularly cited even higher figures. The Romanian embassy in Paris, for example, claimed there were a million

Jewish refugees in Romania. Christian Romanians were gripped by mass hysteria that they would soon be replaced or become a minority in a Jewish-led country.

Goga's government stepped in to offer a solution to the imaginary problem invented by its own propaganda. On January 22, 1938, the government issued a law ordering all Jews in Romania to provide documented proof that they were born in Romanian territory and were entitled to Romanian citizenship. Jews who failed to provide proof would lose their citizenship, along with all rights to residence and employment.

Suddenly Romania's Jews found themselves in a bureaucratic hell. Many had to travel to their birthplace to look for the relevant documents, only to discover that the municipal archives were destroyed during World War I. Jews born in territories annexed to Romania only after 1918—like Chernivtsi—faced special difficulties, because they lacked Romanian birth certificates and because many other documents about their families were archived in the former Habsburg capitals of Vienna and Budapest instead of in Bucharest. Jews often didn't even know which documents they were supposed to be looking for, because the census law didn't specify which documents were considered sufficient "proof."

Clerks and archivists gained a new and lucrative source of income as frantic Jews offered to pay large bribes to get their hands on the right document. Even if no bribes were involved, the process was extremely costly: any request for documentation, as well as filing the citizenship request with the authorities, involved paying fees. Finding and filing the right document did not guarantee success. A difference of a single letter between how a name was spelled on the birth certificate and on the citizenship papers was enough for the authorities to revoke the citizenship.

Many Jews could not clear these bureaucratic hurdles and didn't even file a citizenship request. Of those who did, only 63 percent got their citizenship approved. Altogether, out of 758,000 Romanian

Jews, 367,000 lost their citizenship.[51] My grandfather Bruno was among them. When the new census law was passed in Bucharest, Bruno did not think much about it. He was born in Chernivtsi and had lived there all his life. The thought that he needed to prove to some bureaucrat that he was not an alien struck him as ridiculous. Moreover, in early 1938 his mother fell ill and died, and Bruno felt he had much bigger things to worry about than chasing documents.

In December 1938 an official letter arrived from Bucharest canceling Bruno's citizenship, and as an alien he was promptly fired from his job in a Chernivtsi radio shop. Bruno was now not only alone and jobless but also stateless and without much prospect for alternative employment. Nine months later World War II erupted, and the danger for paperless Jews was mounting. Of the Romanian Jews who lost their citizenship in 1938, the vast majority would be murdered over the next few years by the Romanian fascists and their Nazi allies. (Jews who retained their citizenship had a much higher survival rate.)[52]

My grandfather repeatedly tried to escape the tightening noose, but it was difficult without the right papers. Several times he smuggled himself onto trains and ships, only to be caught and arrested. In 1940 he finally managed to board one of the last ships bound for Palestine before the gates of hell slammed shut. When he arrived in Palestine, he was immediately imprisoned by the British as an illegal immigrant. After two months in prison, he was offered a deal: stay in jail and risk deportation, or enlist in the British army and get Palestinian citizenship. My grandfather grabbed the offer with both hands and from 1941 to 1945 served in the British army in the North African and Italian campaigns. In exchange, he got his papers.

In our family it became a sacred duty to preserve documents. Bank statements, electricity bills, expired student cards, letters from the municipality—if it had an official-looking stamp on it, it would be filed in one of the many folders in our cupboard. You never knew which of these documents might one day save your life.

THE MIRACLE DOCUMENT

Should we love the bureaucratic information network or hate it? Stories like that of my grandfather indicate the dangers inherent in bureaucratic power. Stories like that of the London cholera epidemic indicate its potential benevolence. All powerful information networks can do both good and ill, depending on how they are designed and used. Merely increasing the quantity of information in a network doesn't guarantee its benevolence, or make it any easier to find the right balance between truth and order. That is a key historical lesson for the designers and users of the new information networks of the twenty-first century.

Future information networks, particularly those based on AI, will be different from previous networks in many ways. While in part 1 we are examining how mythology and bureaucracy have been essential for large-scale information networks, in part 2 we will see how AI is taking up the role of both bureaucrats and mythmakers. AI systems know how to find and process data better than flesh-and-blood bureaucrats, and AI is also acquiring the ability to compose stories better than most humans.

But before we explore the new AI-based information networks of the twenty-first century, and before we examine the threats and promises of AI mythmakers and AI bureaucrats, there is one more thing we need to understand about the long-term history of information networks. We have now seen that information networks don't maximize truth, but rather seek to find a balance between truth and order. Bureaucracy and mythology are both essential for maintaining order, and both are happy to sacrifice truth for the sake of order. What mechanisms, then, ensure that bureaucracy and mythology don't lose touch with truth altogether, and what mechanisms enable information networks to identify and correct their own mistakes, even at the price of some disorder?

The way human information networks have dealt with the prob-

lem of errors will be the main subject of the next two chapters. We'll start by considering the invention of another information technology: the holy book. Holy books like the Bible and the Quran are an information technology that is meant to both include all the vital information society needs and be free from all possibility of error. What happens when an information network believes itself to be utterly incapable of any error? The history of allegedly infallible holy books highlights some of the limitations of all information networks and holds important lessons for the attempt to create infallible AIs in the twenty-first century.

CHAPTER 4

Errors: The Fantasy of Infallibility

As Saint Augustine famously said, "To err is human; to persist in error is diabolical."[1] The fallibility of human beings, and the need to correct human errors, have played key roles in every mythology. According to Christian mythology, the whole of history is an attempt to correct Adam and Eve's original sin. According to Marxist-Leninist thinking, even the working class is likely to be fooled by its oppressors and misidentify its own interests, which is why it requires the leadership of a wise party vanguard. Bureaucracy, too, is constantly on the lookout for errors, from misplaced documents to inefficient procedures. Complex bureaucratic systems usually contain self-disciplinary bodies, and when a major catastrophe occurs—like a military defeat or a financial meltdown—commissions of inquiry are set up to understand what went wrong and make sure that the mistake is not repeated.

In order to function, self-correcting mechanisms need legitimacy. If humans are prone to error, how can we trust the self-correcting mechanisms to be free from error? To escape this seemingly endless loop, humans have often fantasized about some superhuman mechanism, free from all error, that they can rely upon to identify and cor-

rect their own mistakes. Today one might hope that AI could provide such a mechanism, as when in April 2023 Elon Musk announced, "I'm going to start something, which I call TruthGPT or a maximum truth-seeking AI that tries to understand the nature of the universe."[2] We will see in later chapters why this is a dangerous fantasy. In previous eras, such fantasies took a different form—religion.

In our personal lives, religion can fulfill many different functions, like providing solace or explaining the mysteries of life. But historically, the most important function of religion has been to provide superhuman legitimacy for the social order. Religions like Judaism, Christianity, Islam, and Hinduism propose that their ideas and rules were established by an infallible superhuman authority, and are therefore free from all possibility of error, and should never be questioned or changed by fallible humans.

TAKING HUMANS OUT OF THE LOOP

At the heart of every religion lies the fantasy of connecting to a superhuman and infallible intelligence. This is why, as we shall explore in chapter 8, studying the history of religion is highly relevant to present-day debates about AI. In the history of religion, a recurrent problem is how to convince people that a certain dogma indeed originated from an infallible superhuman source. Even if in principle I am eager to submit to the gods' will, how do I know what the gods really want?

Throughout history many humans have claimed to convey messages from the gods, but the messages often contradict one another. One person said a god appeared to her in a dream; another person said she was visited by an angel; a third recounted how he met a spirit in a forest—and each preached a different message. The anthropologist Harvey Whitehouse recounts how when he was doing fieldwork among the Baining people of New Britain in the late 1980s, a young man called Tanotka fell sick, and in his feverish de-

lirium began making cryptic statements like "I am Wutka" and "I am a post." Most of these statements were heard only by Tanotka's older brother, Baninge, who began telling about them to other people and interpreting them in a creative way. Baninge said that his brother was possessed by an ancestral spirit called Wutka and that he was divinely chosen to be the main support of the community, just as local houses were supported by a central post.

After Tanotka recovered, he continued to deliver cryptic messages from Wutka, which were interpreted by Baninge in ever more elaborate ways. Baninge also began having dreams of his own, which allegedly revealed additional divine messages. He claimed that the end of the world was imminent, and convinced many of the locals to grant him dictatorial powers so that he could prepare the community for the coming apocalypse. Baninge proceeded to waste almost all the community's resources on extravagant feasts and rituals. When the apocalypse didn't materialize and the community almost starved, Baninge's power collapsed. Though some locals continued to believe that he and Tanotka were divine messengers, many others concluded that the two were charlatans—or perhaps the servants of the Devil.[3]

How could people distinguish the true will of the gods from the inventions or imaginations of fallible humans? Unless you had a personal divine revelation, knowing what the gods said meant trusting what fallible humans like Tanotka and Baninge claimed the gods said. But how could you trust these humans, especially if you didn't know them personally? Religion wanted to take fallible humans out of the loop and give people access to infallible superhuman laws, but religion repeatedly boiled down to trusting this or that human.

One way around this problem was to create religious institutions that vetted the purported divine messengers. Already in tribal societies communication with superhuman entities like tribal spirits was often the domain of religious experts. Among the Baining people, specialized spirit mediums known as *agungaraga* were traditionally responsible for communicating with the spirits and thereby learning the hidden causes of misfortunes ranging from illness to crop failure.

Their membership in an established institution made the *agungaraga* more trustworthy than Tanotka and Baninge, and made their authority more stable and widely acknowledged.[4] Among the Kalapalo tribe of Brazil religious rituals were organized by hereditary ritual officers known as the *anetaü*. In ancient Celtic and Hindu societies similar duties were the preserve of druids and Brahmins.[5] As human societies grew and became more complex, so did their religious institutions. Priests and oracles had to train long and hard for the important task of representing the gods, so people no longer needed to trust just any layperson who claimed to have met an angel or to carry a divine message.[6] In ancient Greece, for example, if you wanted to know what the gods said, you went to an accredited expert like the Pythia—the high priestess at the temple of Apollo in Delphi.

But as long as religious institutions like oracular temples were staffed by fallible humans, they too were open to error and corruption. Herodotus recounts that when Athens was ruled by the tyrant Hippias, the pro-democracy faction bribed the Pythia to help them. Whenever any Spartan came to the Pythia to consult the gods on either official or private matters, the Pythia invariably replied that the Spartans must first free Athens from the tyrant. The Spartans, who were Hippias's allies, eventually submitted to the alleged will of the gods and sent an army to Athens that deposed Hippias in 510 BCE, leading to the establishment of Athenian democracy.[7]

If a human prophet could falsify the words of a god, then the key problem of religion wasn't solved by creating religious institutions like temples and priestly orders. People still needed to trust fallible humans in order to access the supposedly infallible gods. Was it possible to somehow bypass the humans altogether?

THE INFALLIBLE TECHNOLOGY

Holy books like the Bible and the Quran are a technology to bypass human fallibility, and religions of the book—like Judaism, Christi-

anity, and Islam—have been built around that technological artifact. To appreciate how this technology is meant to work, we should begin by explaining what a book is and what makes books different from other kinds of written texts. A book is a fixed block of texts—such as chapters, stories, recipes, or epistles—that always go together and have many identical copies. This makes a book something different from oral tales, from bureaucratic documents, and from archives. When telling a story orally, we might tell it a little differently each time, and if many people tell the story over a long time, significant variations are bound to creep in. In contrast, all copies of a book are supposed to be identical. As for bureaucratic documents, they tend to be relatively short, and often exist only as a single copy in one archive. If a long document has many copies placed in numerous archives, we would normally call it a book. Finally, a book that contains many texts is also different from an archive, because each archive contains a different collection of texts, whereas all copies of a book contain the same chapters, the same stories, or the same recipes. The book thereby ensures that many people in many times and places can access the same database.

The book became an important religious technology in the first millennium BCE. After tens of thousands of years in which gods spoke to humans via shamans, priests, prophets, oracles, and other human messengers, religious movements like Judaism began arguing that the gods speak through this novel technology of the book. There is one specific book whose many chapters allegedly contain all the divine words about everything from the creation of the universe to food regulations. Crucially, no priest, prophet, or human institution can forget or change these divine words, because you can always compare what the fallible humans are telling you with what the infallible book records.

But religions of the book had their own set of problems. Most obviously, who decides what to include in the holy book? The first copy didn't come down from heaven. It had to be compiled by humans. Still, the faithful hoped that this thorny problem could be

solved by a once-and-for-all supreme effort. If we could get together the wisest and most trustworthy humans, and they could all agree on the contents of the holy book, from that moment onward we could excise humans from the loop, and the divine words would forever be safe from human interference.

Many objections can be raised against this procedure: Who selects the wisest humans? On the basis of what criteria? What if they cannot reach a consensus? What if they later change their minds? Nevertheless, this was the procedure used to compile holy books like the Hebrew Bible.

THE MAKING OF THE HEBREW BIBLE

During the first millennium BCE, Jewish prophets, priests, and scholars produced an extensive collection of stories, documents, prophecies, poems, prayers, and chronicles. The Bible as a single holy book didn't exist in biblical times. King David and the prophet Isaiah never saw a copy of the Bible.

It is sometimes claimed, erroneously, that the oldest surviving copy of the Bible comes from the Dead Sea Scrolls. These scrolls are a collection of about nine hundred different documents, written mostly in the last two centuries BCE and found in various caves around Qumran, a village near the Dead Sea.[8] Most scholars believe they constituted the archive of a Jewish sect that lived nearby.[9]

Significantly, none of the scrolls contains a copy of the Bible, and no scroll indicates that the twenty-four books of the Old Testament were considered a single and complete database. Some of the scrolls certainly record texts that are today part of the canonical Bible. For example, nineteen scrolls and fragmentary manuscripts preserve parts of the book of Genesis.[10] But many scrolls record texts that were later excluded from the Bible. For example, more than twenty scrolls and fragments preserve parts of the book of Enoch—a book allegedly written by the patriarch Enoch, the great-grandfather of

Noah, and containing the history of the angels and demons as well as a prophecy about the coming of the Messiah.[11] The Jews of Qumran apparently gave great importance to both Genesis and Enoch, and did not think that Genesis was canonical while Enoch was apocryphal.[12] Indeed, to this day some Ethiopian Jewish and Christian sects consider Enoch part of their canon.[13]

Even the scrolls that record future canonical texts sometimes differ from the present-day canonical version. For example, the canonical text of Deuteronomy 32:8 says that God divided the nations of the earth according to "the number of the sons of Israel." The version recorded in the Dead Sea Scrolls has "the number of the sons of God" instead, implying a rather startling notion that God has multiple sons.[14] In Deuteronomy 8:6 the canonical text requires the faithful to *fear* God, whereas the Dead Sea version asks them to *love* God.[15] Some variations are much more substantial than just a single word here or there. The Psalms scrolls contain several entire psalms that are missing from the canonical Bible (most notably Psalms 151, 154, 155).[16]

Similarly, the oldest translation of the Bible—the Greek Septuagint—completed between the third and the first centuries BCE, is different in many ways from the later canonical version.[17] It includes, for example, the books of Tobit, Judith, Sirach, Maccabees, the Wisdom of Solomon, the Psalms of Solomon, and Psalm 151.[18] It also has longer versions of Daniel and Esther.[19] Its book of Jeremiah is 15 percent shorter than the canonical version.[20] Finally, in Deuteronomy 32:8 most Septuagint manuscripts have either "sons of God" or "angels of God" rather than "sons of Israel."[21]

It took centuries of hairsplitting debates among learned Jewish sages—known as rabbis—to streamline the canonical database and to decide which of the many texts in circulation would get into the Bible as the official word of Jehovah and which would be excluded. By the time of Jesus agreement was probably reached on most of the texts, but even a century later rabbis were still arguing whether the Song of Songs should be part of the canon or not. Some rabbis con-

demned that text as secular love poetry, while Rabbi Akiva (d. 135 CE) defended it as the divinely inspired creation of King Solomon. Akiva famously said that "the Song of Songs is the Holy of Holies."[22] By the end of the second century CE widespread consensus was apparently reached among Jewish rabbis about which texts were part of the biblical canon and which were not, but debates about this matter, and about the precise wordings, spelling, and pronunciation of each text, were not finally resolved until the Masoretic era (seventh to tenth centuries CE).[23]

This process of canonization decided that Genesis was the word of Jehovah, but the book of Enoch, the Life of Adam and Eve, and the Testament of Abraham were human fabrications.[24] The Psalms of King David were canonized (minus psalms 151–55), but the Psalms of King Solomon were not. The book of Malachi got the seal of approval; the book of Baruch did not. Chronicles, yes; Maccabees, no.

Interestingly, some books mentioned in the Bible itself failed to get into the canon. For example, the books of Joshua and Samuel both refer to a very ancient sacred text known as the book of Jasher (Joshua 10:13, 2 Samuel 1:18). The book of Numbers refers to "the Book of the Wars of the Lord" (Numbers 21:14). And when 2 Chronicles surveys the reign of King Solomon, it concludes by saying that "the rest of the acts of Solomon, first and last, are written in the chronicles of Nathan the prophet, and in the prophecy of Ahijah the Shilonite, and in the visions of Iddo the seer" (2 Chronicles 9:29). The books of Iddo, Ahijah, and Nathan, as well as the books of Jasher and the Wars of the Lord, aren't in the canonical Bible. Apparently, they were not excluded on purpose; they just got lost.[25]

After the canon was sealed, most Jews gradually forgot the role of human institutions in the messy process of compiling the Bible. Jewish Orthodoxy maintained that God personally handed down to Moses at Mount Sinai the entire first part of the Bible, the Torah. Many rabbis further argued that God created the Torah at the very dawn of time so that even biblical characters who lived before Moses—like Noah and Adam—read and studied it.[26] The other

parts of the Bible also came to be seen as a divinely created or divinely inspired text, totally different from ordinary human compilations. Once the holy book was sealed, it was hoped that Jews now had direct access to Jehovah's exact words, which no fallible human or corrupt institution could erase or alter.

Anticipating the blockchain idea by two thousand years, Jews began making numerous copies of the holy code, and every Jewish community was supposed to have at least one in its synagogue or its *bet midrash* (house of study).[27] This was meant to achieve two things. First, disseminating many copies of the holy book promised to democratize religion and place strict limits on the power of would-be human autocrats. Whereas the archives of Egyptian pharaohs and Assyrian kings empowered the unfathomable kingly bureaucracy at the expense of the masses, the Jewish holy book seemed to give power to the masses, who could now hold even the most brazen leader accountable to God's laws.

Second, and more important, having numerous copies of the same book prevented any meddling with the text. If there were thousands of identical copies in numerous locations, any attempt to change even a single letter in the holy code could easily be exposed as a fraud. With numerous Bibles available in far-flung locations, Jews replaced human despotism with divine sovereignty. The social order was now guaranteed by the infallible technology of the book. Or so it seemed.

THE INSTITUTION STRIKES BACK

Even before the process of canonizing the Bible was completed, the biblical project had run into further difficulties. Agreeing on the precise contents of the holy book was not the only problem with this supposedly infallible technology. Another obvious problem concerned copying the text. For the holy book to work its magic, Jews needed to have many copies wherever they lived. With Jewish cen-

ters emerging not only in Palestine but also in Mesopotamia and Egypt, and with new Jewish communities extending from central Asia to the Atlantic, how to make sure that copyists working thousands of kilometers apart would not change the holy book either on purpose or by mistake?

To forestall such problems, the rabbis who canonized the Bible devised painstaking regulations for copying the holy book. For example, a scribe was not allowed to pause at certain critical moments in the copying process. When writing the name of God, the scribe "may not respond even if the king greets him. If he was about to write two or three divine names successively, he may pause between them and respond."[28] Rabbi Yishmael (second century CE) told one copyist, "You are doing Heaven's work, and if you delete one letter or add one letter—you destroy the entire world."[29] In truth, copying errors crept in without destroying the entire world, and no two ancient Bibles were identical.[30]

A second and much bigger problem concerned interpretation. Even when people agree on the sanctity of a book and on its exact wording, they can still interpret the same words in different ways. The Bible says that you should not work on the Sabbath. But it doesn't clarify what counts as "work." Is it okay to water your field on the Sabbath? What about watering your flowerpot or herd of goats? Is it okay to read a book on the Sabbath? How about writing a book? How about tearing a piece of paper? The rabbis ruled that reading a book isn't work, but tearing paper *is* work, which is why nowadays Orthodox Jews prepare a stack of already ripped toilet paper to use on the Sabbath.

The holy book also says that you should not cook a young goat in its mother's milk (Exodus 23:19). Some people interpreted this quite literally: if you slaughter a young goat, don't cook it in the milk of its own mother. But it's fine to cook it in the milk of an unrelated goat, or in the milk of a cow. Other people interpreted this prohibition much more broadly to mean that meat and dairy products should never be mixed, so you are not allowed to have a milkshake after fried

chicken. As unlikely as this may sound, most rabbis ruled that the second interpretation is the correct one, even though chickens don't lactate.

More problems resulted from the fact that even if the technology of the book succeeded in limiting changes to the holy words, the world beyond the book continued to spin, and it was unclear how to relate old rules to new situations. Most biblical texts focused on the lives of Jewish shepherds and farmers in the hill country of Palestine and in the sacred city of Jerusalem. But by the second century CE, most Jews lived elsewhere. A particularly large Jewish community grew in the port of Alexandria, one of the richest metropolises of the Roman Empire. A Jewish shipping magnate living in Alexandria would have found that many of the biblical laws were irrelevant to his life while many of his pressing questions had no clear answers in the holy text. He couldn't obey the commandments about worshipping in the Jerusalem temple, because not only did he not live near Jerusalem, but the temple didn't even exist anymore. In contrast, when he contemplated whether it was kosher for him to sail his Rome-bound grain ships on the Sabbath, it turned out that long sea voyages were not considered by the authors of Leviticus and Deuteronomy.[31]

Inevitably, the holy book spawned numerous interpretations, which were far more consequential than the book itself. As Jews increasingly argued over the interpretation of the Bible, rabbis gained more power and prestige. Writing down the word of Jehovah was supposed to limit the authority of the old priestly institution, but it gave rise to the authority of a new rabbinical institution. Rabbis became the Jewish technocratic elite, developing their rational and rhetorical skills through years of philosophical debates and legal disputations. The attempt to bypass fallible human institutions by relying on a new information technology backfired, because of the need for a human institution to interpret the holy book.

When the rabbis eventually reached some consensus about how to interpret the Bible, Jews saw another chance to get rid of the fallible

human institution. They imagined that if they wrote the agreed interpretation in a new holy book, and made numerous copies of it, that would eliminate the need for any further human intercession between them and the divine code. So after much back-and-forth about which rabbinical opinions should be included and which should be ignored, a new holy book was canonized in the third century CE: the Mishnah.[32]

As the Mishnah became more authoritative than the plain text of the Bible, Jews began to believe that the Mishnah could not possibly have been created by humans. It too must have been inspired by Jehovah, or perhaps even composed by the infallible deity in person. Today many Orthodox Jews firmly believe that the Mishnah was handed to Moses by Jehovah on Mount Sinai, passed orally from generation to generation, until it was written down in the third century CE.[33]

Alas, no sooner had the Mishnah been canonized and copied than Jews began arguing about the correct interpretation of the Mishnah. And when a consensus was reached about the interpretation of the Mishnah and canonized in the fifth to sixth centuries as a third holy book—the Talmud—Jews began disagreeing about the interpretation of the Talmud.[34]

The dream of bypassing fallible human institutions through the technology of the holy book never materialized. With each iteration, the power of the rabbinical institution only increased. "Trust the infallible book" turned into "trust the humans who interpret the book." Judaism was shaped by the Talmud far more than by the Bible, and rabbinical arguments about the interpretation of the Talmud became even more important than the Talmud itself.[35]

This is inevitable, because the world keeps changing. The Mishnah and Talmud dealt with questions raised by second-century Jewish shipping magnates that had no clear answers in the Bible. Modernity too raised many new questions that have no straightforward answers in the Mishnah and Talmud. For example, when electrical appliances developed in the twentieth century, Jews struggled with numerous

unprecedented questions, such as whether it is okay to press the electrical buttons of an elevator on the Sabbath?

The Orthodox answer is no. As noted earlier, the Bible forbids working on the Sabbath, and rabbis argued that pressing an electrical button is "work," because electricity is akin to fire, and it has long been established that kindling a fire is "work." Does this mean that elderly Jews living in a Brooklyn high-rise must climb a hundred steps to their apartment in order to avoid working on the Sabbath? Well, Orthodox Jews invented a "Sabbath elevator," which continually goes up and down buildings, stopping on every floor, without you having to perform any "work" by pressing an electrical button.[36] The invention of AI gives another twist to this old story. By relying on facial recognition, an AI can quickly direct the elevator to your floor, without making you desecrate the Sabbath.[37]

This profusion of texts and interpretations has, over time, caused a profound change in Judaism. Originally, it was a religion of priests and temples, focused on rituals and sacrifices. In biblical times, the quintessential Jewish scene was a priest in blood-splattered robes sacrificing a lamb on the altar of Jehovah. Over the centuries, however, Judaism became an "information religion," obsessed with texts and interpretations. From second-century Alexandria to twenty-first-century Brooklyn, the quintessential Jewish scene became a group of rabbis arguing about the interpretation of a text.

This change was extremely surprising given that almost nowhere in the Bible itself do you find anyone arguing about the interpretation of any text. Such debates were not part of biblical culture itself. For example, when Korah and his followers challenged the right of Moses to lead the people of Israel, and demanded a more equitable division of power, Moses reacted not by entering a learned discussion or by quoting some scriptural passage. Rather, Moses called upon God to perform a miracle, and the moment he finished speaking, the ground split, "and the earth opened its mouth and swallowed them and their households" (Numbers 16:31–32). When Elijah was challenged by 450 prophets of Baal and 400 prophets of Asherah to a

public test in front of the people of Israel, he proved the superiority of Jehovah over Baal and Asherah first by miraculously summoning fire from the sky and then by slaughtering the pagan prophets. Nobody read any text, and nobody engaged in any rational debate (1 Kings 18).

As Judaism replaced sacrifices with texts, it gravitated toward a view of information as the most fundamental building block of reality, anticipating current ideas in physics and computer science. The flood of texts generated by rabbis was increasingly seen as more important, and even more real, than plowing a field, baking a loaf of bread, or sacrificing a lamb in a temple. After the temple in Jerusalem was destroyed by the Romans and all temple rituals ceased, rabbis nevertheless devoted enormous efforts to writing texts about the proper way to conduct temple rituals and then arguing about the correct interpretation of these texts. Centuries after the temple was no more, the amount of information concerning these virtual rituals only continued to increase. The rabbis weren't oblivious to this seeming gap between text and reality. Rather, they maintained that writing texts about the rituals and arguing about these texts were far more important than actually performing the rituals.[38]

This eventually led the rabbis to believe that the entire universe was an information sphere—a realm composed of words and running on the alphabetical code of the Hebrew letters. They further maintained that this informational universe was created so that Jews could read texts and argue about their interpretation, and that if Jews ever stop reading these texts and arguing about them, the universe will cease to exist.[39] In everyday life, this view meant that for the rabbis words in texts were often more important than facts in the world. Or more accurately, which words appeared in sacred texts became some of the most important facts about the world, shaping the lives of individuals and entire communities.

THE SPLIT BIBLE

The above description of the canonization of the Bible, and the creation of the Mishnah and Talmud, ignores one very important fact. The process of canonizing the word of Jehovah created not one chain of texts but several competing chains. There were people who believed in Jehovah, but not in the rabbis. Most of these dissenters did accept the first block in the biblical chain—which they called the Old Testament. But already before the rabbis sealed this block, the dissenters rejected the authority of the entire rabbinical institution, which led them to subsequently reject the Mishnah and Talmud, too. These dissenters were the Christians.

When Christianity emerged in the first century CE, it was not a unified religion, but rather a variety of Jewish movements that didn't agree on much, except that they all regarded Jesus Christ—rather than the rabbinical institution—as the ultimate authority on Jehovah's words.[40] Christians accepted the divinity of texts like Genesis, Samuel, and Isaiah, but they argued that the rabbis misunderstood these texts, and only Jesus and his disciples knew the true meaning of passages like "the Lord himself will give you a sign: the *almah* will conceive and give birth to a son, and will call him *Immanuel*" (Isaiah 7:14). The rabbis said *almah* meant "young woman," *Immanuel* meant "God with us" (in Hebrew *immanu* means "with us" and *el* means "God"), and the entire passage was interpreted as a divine promise to help the Jewish people in their struggle against oppressive foreign empires. In contrast, the Christians argued that *almah* meant "virgin," that *Immanuel* meant that God will literally be born among humans, and that this was a prophecy about the divine Jesus being born on earth to the Virgin Mary.[41]

However, by rejecting the rabbinical institution while simultaneously accepting the possibility of new divine revelations, the Christians opened the door to chaos. In the first century CE, and even more so in the second and third centuries CE, different Christians

came up with radically new interpretations for books like Genesis and Isaiah, as well as with a plethora of new messages from God. Since they rejected the authority of the rabbis, since Jesus was dead and couldn't adjudicate between them, and since a unified Christian church didn't yet exist, who could decide which of all these interpretations and messages were divinely inspired?

Thus, it was not just John who described the end of the world in his Apocalypse (the book of Revelation). We have many additional apocalypses from that era, for example the Apocalypse of Peter, the Apocalypse of James, and even the Apocalypse of Abraham.[42] As for the life and teachings of Jesus, in addition to the four Gospels of Matthew, Mark, Luke, and John, early Christians had the Gospel of Peter, the Gospel of Mary, the Gospel of Truth, the Gospel of the Savior, and numerous others.[43] Similarly, aside from the Acts of the Apostles, there were at least a dozen other Acts such as the Acts of Peter and the Acts of Andrew.[44] Letters were even more prolific. Most present-day Christian Bibles contain fourteen epistles attributed to Paul, three attributed to John, two to Peter, and one each to James and Jude. Ancient Christians were familiar not only with additional Pauline letters (such as the Epistle to the Laodiceans) but with numerous other epistles supposedly written by other disciples and saints.[45]

As Christians composed more and more gospels, epistles, prophecies, parables, prayers, and other texts, it became harder to know which ones to pay attention to. Christians needed a curation institution. That's how the New Testament was created. At roughly the same time that debates among Jewish rabbis were producing the Mishnah and Talmud, debates among Christian priests, bishops, and theologians were producing the New Testament.

In a letter from 367 CE, Bishop Athanasius of Alexandria recommended twenty-seven texts that faithful Christians should read— a rather eclectic collection of stories, letters, and prophecies written by different people in different times and places. Athanasius recommended the Apocalypse of John, but not that of Peter or Abraham. He approved of Paul's Epistle to the Galatians, but not of Paul's

Epistle to the Laodiceans. He endorsed the Gospels of Matthew, Mark, Luke, and John, but rejected the Gospel of Thomas and the Gospel of Truth.[46]

A generation later, in the Councils of Hippo (393) and Carthage (397), gatherings of bishops and theologians formally canonized this list of recommendations, which became known as the New Testament.[47] When Christians talk about "the Bible," they mean the Old Testament together with the New Testament. In contrast, Judaism never accepted the New Testament, and when Jews talk about "the Bible," they mean only the Old Testament, which is supplemented by the Mishnah and Talmud. Interestingly, Hebrew to this day lacks a word to describe the Christian holy book, which contains both the Old Testament and the New Testament. Jewish thought sees them as two utterly unrelated books and simply refuses to acknowledge that there might be a single book encompassing both, even though it is probably the most common book in the world.

It is crucial to note that the people who created the New Testament weren't the authors of the twenty-seven texts it contains; they were the curators. Due to the paucity of evidence from the period, we do not know if Athanasius's list of texts reflected his personal judgment, or whether it originated with earlier Christian thinkers. What we do know is that prior to the Councils of Hippo and Carthage there were rival recommendation lists for Christians. The earliest such list was codified by Marcion of Sinope in the middle of the second century. The Marcion canon included only the Gospel of Luke and ten epistles of Paul. Even these eleven texts were somewhat different from the versions later canonized at Hippo and Carthage. Either Marcion was unaware of other texts like the Gospel of John and the book of Revelation, or he did not think highly of them.[48]

The church father Saint John Chrysostom, a contemporary of Bishop Athanasius's, recommended only twenty-two books, leaving 2 Peter, 2 John, 3 John, Jude, and Revelation out of his list.[49] Some

Christian churches in the Middle East to this day follow Chrysostom's shorter list.[50] The Armenian Church took about a thousand years to make up its mind about the book of Revelation, while it included in its canon the Third Epistle to the Corinthians, which other churches—like the Catholic and Protestant churches—consider a forgery.[51] The Ethiopian Church endorsed Athanasius's list in full, but added four other books: Sinodos, the book of Clement, the book of the Covenant, and the Didascalia.[52] Other lists endorsed the two epistles of Clement, the visions of the Shepherd of Hermas, the Epistle of Barnabas, the Apocalypse of Peter, and various other texts that didn't make it into Athanasius's selection.[53]

We do not know the precise reasons why specific texts were endorsed or rejected by different churches, church councils, and church fathers. But the consequences were far-reaching. While churches made decisions about texts, the texts themselves shaped the churches. As a key example, consider the role of women in the church. Some early Christian leaders saw women as intellectually and ethically inferior to men, and argued that women should be restricted to subordinate roles in society and in the Christian community. These views were reflected in texts like the First Epistle to Timothy.

In one of its passages, this text, attributed to Saint Paul, says, "A woman should learn in quietness and full submission. I do not permit a woman to teach or to assume authority over a man; she must be quiet. For Adam was formed first, then Eve. And Adam was not the one deceived; it was the woman who was deceived and became a sinner. But women will be saved through childbearing—if they continue in faith, love and holiness with propriety" (2:11–15). But modern scholars as well as some ancient Christian leaders like Marcion have considered this letter a second-century forgery, ascribed to Saint Paul but actually written by someone else.[54]

In opposition to 1 Timothy, during the second, third, and fourth centuries CE there were important Christian texts that saw women as equal to men, and even authorized women to occupy leadership

roles, like the Gospel of Mary[55] or the Acts of Paul and Thecla. The latter text was written at about the same time as 1 Timothy, and for a time was extremely popular.[56] It narrates the adventures of Saint Paul and his female disciple Thecla, describing how Thecla not only performed numerous miracles but also baptized herself with her own hands and often preached. For centuries, Thecla was one of the most revered Christian saints and was seen as evidence that women could baptize, preach, and lead Christian communities.[57]

Before the Councils of Hippo and Carthage, it wasn't clear that 1 Timothy was more authoritative than the Acts of Paul and Thecla. By choosing to include 1 Timothy in their recommendation list while rejecting the Acts of Paul and Thecla, the assembled bishops and theologians shaped Christian attitudes toward women down to the present day. We can only hypothesize what Christianity might have looked like if the New Testament had included the Acts of Paul and Thecla instead of 1 Timothy. Perhaps in addition to church fathers like Athanasius, the church would have had mothers, while misogyny would have been labeled a dangerous heresy perverting Jesus's message of universal love.

Just as most Jews forgot that rabbis curated the Old Testament, so most Christians forgot that church councils curated the New Testament, and came to view it simply as the infallible word of God. But while the holy book was seen as the ultimate source of authority, the process of curating the book placed real power in the hands of the curating institution. In Judaism the canonization of the Old Testament and Mishnah went hand in hand with creating the institution of the rabbinate. In Christianity the canonization of the New Testament went hand in hand with the creation of a unified Christian church. Christians trusted church officials—like Bishop Athanasius—because of what they read in the New Testament, but they had faith in the New Testament because this is what the bishops told them to read. The attempt to invest all authority in an infallible superhuman technology led to the rise of a new and extremely powerful human institution—the church.

THE ECHO CHAMBER

As time passed, problems of interpretation increasingly tilted the balance of power between the holy book and the church in favor of the institution. Just as the need to interpret Jewish holy books empowered the rabbinate, so the need to interpret Christian holy books empowered the church. The same saying of Jesus or the same Pauline epistle could be understood in various ways, and it was the institution that decided which reading was correct. The institution in turn was repeatedly shaken by struggles over the authority to interpret the holy book, which resulted in institutional schisms such as that between the Western Catholic Church and the Eastern Orthodox Church.

All Christians read the Sermon on the Mount in the Gospel of Matthew and learned that we should love our enemies, that we should turn the other cheek, and that the meek shall inherit the earth. But what did that actually mean? Christians could read this as a call to reject all use of military force,[58] or to reject all social hierarchies.[59] The Catholic Church, however, viewed such pacifists and egalitarian readings as heresies. It interpreted Jesus's words in a way that allowed the church to become the richest landowner in Europe, to launch violent crusades, and to establish murderous inquisitions. Catholic theology accepted that Jesus told us to love our enemies, but explained that burning heretics was an act of love, because it deterred additional people from adopting heretical views, thereby saving them from the flames of hell. The French inquisitor Jacques Fournier wrote in the early fourteenth century an entire treatise on the Sermon on the Mount that explained how the text provided justification for hunting heretics.[60] Fournier's view was not a fringe notion. He went on to become Pope Benedict XII (1334–42).

Fournier's task as inquisitor, and later as pope, was to ensure that the Catholic Church's interpretation of the holy book would prevail. In this, Fournier and his fellow churchmen used not only violent

coercion but also their control of book production. Prior to the advent of letterpress printing in Europe in the fifteenth century, making many copies of a book was a prohibitive enterprise for all but the most wealthy individuals and institutions. The Catholic Church used its power and wealth to disseminate copies of its favored texts while prohibiting the production and spread of what it considered erroneous ones.

Of course, the church couldn't prevent the occasional freethinker from formulating heretical ideas. But because it controlled key nodes in the medieval information network—such as copying workshops, archives, and libraries—it could prevent such a heretic from making and distributing a hundred copies of her book. To get an idea of the difficulties faced by a heretical author seeking to disseminate her views, consider that when Leofric was made bishop of Exeter in 1050, he found just five books in the cathedral's library. He immediately established a copying workshop in the cathedral, but in the twenty-two years before he died in 1072, his copyists produced only sixty-six additional volumes.[61] In the thirteenth century the library of Oxford University consisted of a few books kept in a chest under St. Mary's Church. In 1424 the library of Cambridge University boasted a grand total of only 122 books.[62] An Oxford University decree from 1409 stipulated that "all recent texts" studied at the university must be unanimously approved "by a panel of twelve theologians appointed by the archbishop."[63]

The church sought to lock society inside an echo chamber, allowing the spread only of those books that supported it, and people trusted the church because almost all the books supported it. Even illiterate laypersons who didn't read books were still awed by recitations of these precious texts or expositions on their content. That's how the belief in a supposedly infallible superhuman technology like the New Testament led to the rise of an extremely powerful but fallible human institution like the Catholic Church that crushed all opposing views as "erroneous" while allowing no one to question its own views.

Catholic information experts such as Jacques Fournier spent their days reading Thomas Aquinas's interpretation of Augustine's interpretation of Saint Paul's epistles and composing additional interpretations of their own. All those interrelated texts didn't represent reality; they created a new information sphere even bigger and more powerful than that created by the Jewish rabbis. Medieval Europeans were cocooned inside that information sphere, their daily activities, thoughts, and emotions shaped by texts about texts about texts.

PRINT, SCIENCE, AND WITCHES

The attempt to bypass human fallibility by investing authority in an infallible text never succeeded. If anyone thought this was due to some unique flaw of the Jewish rabbis or the Catholic priests, the Protestant Reformation repeated the experiment again and again—always getting the same results. Luther, Calvin, and their successors argued that there was no need for any fallible human institution to interpose itself between ordinary people and the holy book. Christians should abandon all the parasitical bureaucracies that grew around the Bible and reconnect to the original word of God. But the word of God never interpreted itself, which is why not only Lutherans and Calvinists but numerous other Protestant sects eventually established their own church institutions and invested them with the authority to interpret the text and persecute heretics.[64]

If infallible texts merely lead to the rise of fallible and oppressive churches, how then to deal with the problem of human error? The naive view of information posits that the problem can be solved by creating the opposite of a church—namely, a free market of information. The naive view expects that if all restrictions on the free flow of information are removed, error will inevitably be exposed and displaced by truth. As noted in the prologue, this is wishful thinking. Let's delve a little deeper to understand why. As a test case, consider what happened during one of the most celebrated epochs

in the history of information networks: the European print revolution. The introduction of the printing press to Europe in the mid-fifteenth century made it possible to mass-produce texts relatively quickly, cheaply, and secretly, even if the Catholic Church disapproved of them. It is estimated that in the forty-six years from 1454 to 1500 more than twelve million volumes were printed in Europe. By contrast, in the previous thousand years only about eleven million volumes were hand-copied.[65] By 1600, all kinds of fringe people—heretics, revolutionaries, proto-scientists—could disseminate their writings much more rapidly, widely, and easily than ever before.

In the history of information networks, the print revolution of early modern Europe is usually hailed as a moment of triumph, breaking the stranglehold that the Catholic Church had maintained over the European information network. Allegedly, by allowing people to exchange information much more freely than before, it led to the scientific revolution. There is a grain of truth in this. Without print, it would certainly have been much harder for Copernicus, Galileo, and their colleagues to develop and spread their ideas.

But print wasn't the root cause of the scientific revolution. The only thing the printing press did was to faithfully reproduce texts. The machine had no ability to come up with any new ideas of its own. Those who connect print to science assume that the mere act of producing and spreading more information inevitably leads people to the truth. In fact, print allowed the rapid spread not only of scientific facts but also of religious fantasies, fake news, and conspiracy theories. Perhaps the most notorious example of the latter was the belief in a worldwide conspiracy of satanic witches, which led to the witch-hunt craze that engulfed early modern Europe.[66]

Belief in magic and in witches has characterized human societies on all continents and in all eras, but different societies imagined witches and reacted to them in very different ways. Some societies believed that witches controlled spirits, talked with the dead, and predicted the future; others imagined that witches stole cattle and

located hidden treasure. In one community witches were thought to cause disease, blight cornfields, and concoct love potions, while in another community they supposedly entered houses at night, performed household chores, and stole milk. In some locales witches were thought to be mostly female, while in others they were generally imagined to be male. Some cultures were terrified of witches and persecuted them violently, but others tolerated or even honored them. Finally, there were societies on every continent and in every era that gave witches little importance.[67]

For most of the Middle Ages, most European societies belonged to the latter category and were not overly concerned about witches. The medieval Catholic Church didn't see them as a major threat to humanity, and some churchmen actively discouraged witch-hunting. According to the influential tenth-century text *Canon Episcopi*—which defined medieval church doctrine on the matter—witchcraft was mostly illusion, and belief in the reality of witchcraft was an unchristian superstition.[68] The European witch-hunt craze was a modern rather than a medieval phenomenon.

In the 1420s and 1430s churchmen and scholars operating mainly in the Alps region took elements from Christian religion, local folklore, and Greco-Roman heritage and amalgamated them into a new theory of witchcraft.[69] Previously, even when witches were dreaded, they were considered a strictly local problem—isolated criminals who, inspired by personal malevolence, used magical means to commit theft and murder. In contrast, the new scholarly model argued that witches were a far more formidable threat to society. There was allegedly a global conspiracy of witches, led by Satan, which constituted an institutionalized anti-Christian religion. Its purpose was nothing less than the complete destruction of the social order and of humankind. Witches were said to gather at night in huge demonic assemblies, where they worshipped Satan, killed children, ate human flesh, engaged in orgies, and cast spells that caused storms, epidemics, and other catastrophes.

Inspired by such ideas, the first mass witch hunts and witch trials

were led by local churchmen and noblemen in the Valais region of
the western Alps between 1428 and 1436, leading to the execution of
more than two hundred supposed male and female witches. From
this Alpine heartland, rumors about the global witch conspiracy
trickled to other parts of Europe, but the belief was still far from
mainstream, the Catholic establishment did not embrace it, and
other regions didn't launch large-scale witch hunts like those in the
Valais.

In 1485, a Dominican friar and inquisitor called Heinrich Kramer
embarked on a witch-hunting expedition in another Alpine region—
the Austrian Tyrol. Kramer was a fervent convert to the new belief in
a global satanic conspiracy.[70] He also seems to have been mentally
unhinged, and his accusations of satanic witchcraft were colored by
rabid misogyny and odd sexual fixations. Local church authorities,
led by the bishop of Brixen, were skeptical of Kramer's accusations
and alarmed by his activities. They stopped his inquisition, released
the suspects he arrested, and expelled him from the area.[71]

Kramer hit back through the printing press. Within two years of his
banishment, he compiled and published the *Malleus Maleficarum—
The Hammer of the Witches*. This was a do-it-yourself guidebook to exposing and killing witches in which Kramer described in detail the
worldwide conspiracy and the means by which honest Christians
could uncover and foil the witches. In particular, he recommended the
use of horrific methods of torture in order to extract confessions from
people suspected of witchcraft, and was adamant that the only punishment for the guilty was execution.

Kramer organized and codified previous ideas and stories and
added many details from his own fertile and hate-filled imagination. Relying on ancient Christian misogynist teachings like those of
1 Timothy, Kramer sexualized witchcraft. He argued that witches
were typically female, because witchcraft originated in lust, which
was supposedly stronger in women. He warned readers that sex could
cause a pious woman to become a witch and her husband to become
bewitched.[72]

An entire chapter of the *Hammer* is dedicated to the ability of witches to steal men's penises. Kramer discusses at length whether the witches are really able to take away the male member from its owner, or whether they are only able to create an illusion of castration in men's minds. Kramer asks, "What is to be thought of those witches who in this way sometimes collect male organs in great numbers, as many as twenty or thirty members together, and put them in a bird's nest, or shut them up in a box, where they move themselves like living members, and eat oats and corn, as has been seen by many?" He then relates a story he heard from one man: "When he had lost his member, he approached a known witch to ask her to restore it to him. She told the afflicted man to climb a certain tree, and that he might take which he liked out of the nest in which there were several members. And when he tried to take a big one, the witch said: You must not take that one; adding, because it belongs to a parish priest."[73] Numerous notions about witches that are still popular today—for instance, that witches are predominantly women, that witches engage in wild sexual activities, and that witches kill and mutilate children—were given their canonical form by Kramer's book.

Like the bishop of Brixen, other churchmen were initially skeptical of Kramer's wild ideas, and there was some resistance to the book among church experts.[74] But *The Hammer of the Witches* became one of the biggest bestsellers of early modern Europe. It catered to people's deepest fears, as well as to their lurid interest in hearing about orgies, cannibalism, child murders, and satanic conspiracies. The book had gone through eight editions by 1500, another five by 1520, and sixteen more by 1670, with many vernacular translations.[75] It became the definitive work on witchcraft and witch-hunting and inspired a host of imitations and elaborations. As Kramer's fame grew, his work was embraced by the church experts. Kramer was appointed papal representative and made inquisitor of Bohemia and Moravia in 1500. Even today his ideas continue to shape the world, and many current theories about a global satanic conspiracy—like QAnon—draw upon and perpetuate his fantasies.

While it would be an exaggeration to argue that the invention of print *caused* the European witch-hunt craze, the printing press played a pivotal role in the rapid dissemination of the belief in a global satanic conspiracy. As Kramer's ideas gained popularity, printing presses produced not only many additional copies of *The Hammer of the Witches* and copycat books but also a torrent of cheap one-page pamphlets whose sensational texts were often accompanied by illustrations depicting people attacked by demons or witches burned at the stake.[76] These publications also gave fantastic statistics about the size of the witches' conspiracy. For example, the Burgundian judge and witch-hunter Henri Boguet (1550–1619) speculated that there were 300,000 witches in France alone and 1.8 million in all of Europe.[77] Such claims fueled mass hysteria, which in the sixteenth and seventeenth centuries led to the torture and execution of between 40,000 and 50,000 innocent people who were accused of witchcraft.[78] The victims included individuals from all walks of life and ages, including children as young as five.[79]

People began denouncing one another for witchcraft on the flimsiest evidence, often to avenge personal slights or to gain economic and political advantage. Once an official investigation began, the accused were often doomed. The inquisitorial methods recommended by *The Hammer of the Witches* were truly diabolical. If the accused confessed to being a witch, they were executed and their property divided between the accuser, the executioner, and the inquisitors. If the accused refused to confess, this was taken as evidence of their demonic obstinacy, and they were then tortured in horrendous ways, their fingers broken, their flesh cut with hot pincers, their bodies stretched to the breaking point or submerged in boiling water. Sooner or later they could stand it no longer and confessed—and were duly executed.[80]

To take one example, in 1600 authorities in Munich arrested on suspicion of witchcraft the Pappenheimer family—father Paulus, mother Anna, two grown sons, and a ten-year-old boy, Hansel. The inquisitors began by torturing little Hansel. The protocol of the in-

terrogation, which can still be read in the Munich archives, has a note from one of the interrogators regarding the ten-year-old boy: "May be tortured to the limit so that he incriminates his mother."[81] After being tortured in unspeakable ways, the Pappenheimers confessed to numerous crimes, including killing 265 people by sorcery and causing fourteen destructive storms. They were all condemned to death.

The bodies of each of the four adult family members were torn with red-hot pincers, the men's limbs were broken on the wheel, the father was impaled on a stake, the mother's breasts were cut off, and all were then burned alive. The ten-year-old Hansel was forced to watch all this. Four months later, he too was executed.[82] The witch-hunters were extremely thorough in their search for the Devil and his accomplices. But if the witch-hunters really wanted to find diabolical evil, they just had to look in the mirror.

THE SPANISH INQUISITION TO THE RESCUE

Witch hunts seldom ended by killing just one person or one family. Since the underlying model postulated a global conspiracy, people accused of witchcraft were tortured to name accomplices. This was then used as evidence to imprison, torture, and execute others. If any officials, scholars, or churchmen voiced objections to these absurd methods, this could be seen as proof that they too must be witches— which led to their own arrest and torture.

For example, in 1453—when belief in the satanic conspiracy was just beginning to take hold—a French doctor of theology called Guillaume Edelin bravely sought to quash it before it spread. He repeated the claims of the medieval *Canon Episcopi* that witchcraft was an illusion and that witches couldn't really fly at night to meet Satan and make a pact with him. Edelin was then himself accused of being a witch and arrested. Under torture he confessed that he personally had flown on a broomstick and signed a pact with the Devil

and that it was Satan who commissioned him to preach that witch-craft was an illusion. His judges were lenient with him; he was spared execution and got life imprisonment instead.[83]

The witch hunts illustrate the dark side of creating an information sphere. As with rabbinical discussions of the Talmud and scholastic discussions of Christian scriptures, the witch hunts were fueled by an expanding ocean of information that instead of representing reality created a new reality. Witches were not an objective reality. Nobody in early modern Europe had sex with Satan or was capable of flying on broomsticks and creating hailstorms. But witches became an intersubjective reality. Like money, witches were made real by exchanging information about witches.

An entire witch-hunting bureaucracy dedicated itself to such exchanges. Theologians, lawyers, inquisitors, and the owners of printing presses made a living by collecting and producing information about witches, cataloging different species of witches, investigating how witches behaved, and recommending how they could be exposed and defeated. Professional witch-hunters offered their services to governments and municipalities, charging large sums of money. Archives were filled by detailed reports of witch-hunting expeditions, protocols of witch trials, and lengthy confessions extracted from the alleged witches.

Expert witch-hunters used all that data to refine their theories further. Like scholars arguing about the correct interpretation of scripture, the witch-hunters debated the correct interpretation of *The Hammer of the Witches* and other influential books. The witch-hunting bureaucracy did what bureaucracy often does: it invented the intersubjective category of "witches" and imposed it on reality. It even printed forms, with standard accusations and confessions of witches and blank spaces left for dates, names, and the signature of the accused. All that information produced a lot of order and power; it was a means for certain people to gain authority and for society as a whole to discipline its members. But it produced zero truth and zero wisdom.

As the witch-hunting bureaucracy generated more and more information, it became harder to dismiss all that information as pure fantasy. Could it be that the entire silo of witch-hunting data did not contain a single grain of truth in it? What about all the books written by learned churchmen? What about all the protocols of trials conducted by esteemed judges? What about the tens of thousands of documented confessions?

The new intersubjective reality was so convincing that even some people accused of witchcraft came to believe that they were indeed part of a worldwide satanic conspiracy. If everybody said so, it must be true. As discussed in chapter 2, humans are susceptible to adopting fake memories. At least some early modern Europeans dreamed or fantasized about summoning devils, having sex with Satan, and practicing witchcraft, and when accused of being witches, they confused their dreams and fantasies with reality.[84]

Consequently, even as the witch hunts reached their ghastly crescendo in the early seventeenth century, and many people suspected that something was clearly wrong, it was difficult to reject the whole thing as pure fantasy. One of the worst witch-hunting episodes in early modern Europe occurred in the towns of Bamberg and Würzburg in southern Germany in the late 1620s. In Bamberg, a city of fewer than 12,000 at the time,[85] up to 900 innocent people were executed from 1625 to 1631.[86] In Würzburg another 1,200 people were tortured and killed, out of a population of around 11,500.[87] In August 1629, the chancellor of the prince-bishop of Würzburg wrote a letter to a friend about the ongoing witch hunt, in which he confessed his doubts about the matter. The letter is worth quoting at length:

> As to the affair of the witches . . . it has started up afresh, and no words can do justice to it. Ah, the woe and the misery of it—there are still four hundred in the city, high and low, of every rank and sex, nay, even clerics, so strongly accused that they may be arrested at any hour. . . . The Prince-Bishop has over forty students who are

soon to be pastors; among them thirteen or fourteen are said to be witches. A few days ago a Dean was arrested; two others who were summoned have fled. The notary of our Church consistory, a very learned man, was yesterday arrested and put to the torture. In a word, a third part of the city is surely involved. The richest, most attractive, most prominent, of the clergy are already executed. A week ago a maiden of nineteen was executed, of whom it is everywhere said that she was the fairest in the whole city, and was held by everybody a girl of singular modesty and purity. She will be followed by seven or eight others of the best and most attractive persons. . . . And thus many are put to death for renouncing God and being at the witch-dances, against whom nobody has ever else spoken a word.

To conclude this wretched matter, there are children of three and four years, to the number of three hundred, who are said to have had intercourse with the Devil. I have seen put to death children of seven, promising students of ten, twelve, fourteen, and fifteen. . . . [B]ut I cannot and must not write more of this misery.

The chancellor then added this interesting postscript to the letter:

Though there are many wonderful and terrible things happening, it is beyond doubt that, at a place called the Fraw-Rengberg, the Devil in person, with eight thousand of his followers, held an assembly and celebrated mass before them all, administering to his audience (that is, the witches) turnip-rinds and parings in place of the Holy Eucharist. There took place not only foul but most horrible and hideous blasphemies, whereof I shudder to write.[88]

Even after expressing his horror at the insanity of the witch hunt in Würzburg, the chancellor nevertheless expressed his firm belief in the satanic conspiracy of witches. He didn't witness any witchcraft firsthand, but so much information about witches was circulating that it was difficult for him to doubt all of it. Witch hunts were a

catastrophe caused by the spread of toxic information. They are a prime example of a problem that was created by information, and was made worse by more information.

This was a conclusion reached not just by modern scholars but also by some perceptive observers at the time. Alonso de Salazar Frías, a Spanish inquisitor, made a thorough investigation of witch hunts and witch trials in the early seventeenth century. He concluded that he had "not found one single proof nor even the slightest indication from which to infer that one act of witchcraft has actually taken place," and that "there were neither witches nor bewitched until they were talked and written about."[89] Salazar Frías well understood the meaning of intersubjective realities and correctly identified the entire witch-hunting industry as an intersubjective information sphere.

The history of the early modern European witch craze demonstrates that releasing barriers to the flow of information doesn't necessarily lead to the discovery and spread of truth. It can just as easily lead to the spread of lies and fantasies and to the creation of toxic information spheres. More specifically, a completely free market of ideas may incentivize the dissemination of outrage and sensationalism at the expense of truth. It is not difficult to understand why. Printers and booksellers made a lot more money from the lurid tales of *The Hammer of the Witches* than they did from the dull mathematics of Copernicus's *On the Revolutions of the Heavenly Spheres*. The latter was one of the founding texts of the modern scientific tradition. It is credited with earth-shattering discoveries that displaced our planet from the center of the universe and thereby initiated the Copernican revolution. But when it was first published in 1543, its initial print run of four hundred failed to sell out, and it took until 1566 for a second edition to be published in a similar-sized print run. The third edition did not appear until 1617. As Arthur Koestler quipped, it was an all-time worst seller.[90] What really got the scientific revolution going was neither the printing press nor a completely free market of information, but rather a novel approach to the problem of human fallibility.

THE DISCOVERY OF IGNORANCE

The history of print and witch-hunting indicates that an unregulated information market doesn't necessarily lead people to identify and correct their errors, because it may well prioritize outrage over truth. For truth to win, it is necessary to establish curation institutions that have the power to tilt the balance in favor of the facts. However, as the history of the Catholic Church indicates, such institutions might use their curation power to quash any criticism of themselves, labeling all alternative views erroneous and preventing the institution's own errors from being exposed and corrected. Is it possible to establish better curation institutions that use their power to further the pursuit of truth rather than to accumulate more power for themselves?

Early modern Europe saw the foundation of exactly such curation institutions, and it was these institutions—rather than the printing press or specific books like *On the Revolutions of the Heavenly Spheres*—that constituted the bedrock of the scientific revolution. These key curation institutions were not the universities. Many of the most important leaders of the scientific revolution were not university professors. Nicolaus Copernicus, Robert Boyle, Tycho Brahe, and René Descartes, for example, held no academic positions. Nor did Spinoza, Leibniz, Locke, Berkeley, Voltaire, Diderot, or Rousseau.

The curation institutions that played a central role in the scientific revolution connected scholars and researchers both in and out of universities, forging an information network that spanned the whole of Europe and eventually the world. For the scientific revolution to gather pace, scientists had to trust information published by colleagues in distant lands. This kind of trust in the work of people whom one had never met was evident in scientific associations like the Royal Society of London for Improving Natural Knowledge, founded in 1660, and the French Académie des Sciences (1666); sci-

entific journals like the *Philosophical Transactions of the Royal Society* (1665) and the *Histoire de l'Académie Royale des Sciences* (1699); and scientific publishers like the architects of the *Encyclopédie* (1751–72). These institutions curated information on the basis of empirical evidence, bringing attention to the discoveries of Copernicus rather than to the fantasies of Kramer. When a paper was submitted to the *Philosophical Transactions of the Royal Society,* the lead question the editors asked was not "How many people would pay to read this?" but "What proof is there that this is true?"

At first, these new institutions seemed as flimsy as cobwebs, lacking the power necessary to reshape human society. Unlike the witch-hunting experts, the editors of the *Philosophical Transactions of the Royal Society* could not torture and execute anyone. And unlike the Catholic Church, the Académie des Sciences did not command huge territories and budgets. But scientific institutions did accrue influence thanks to a very original claim to trust. A church typically told people to trust it because it possessed the absolute truth, in the form of an infallible holy book. A scientific institution, in contrast, gained authority because it had strong self-correcting mechanisms that exposed and rectified the errors of the institution itself. It was these self-correcting mechanisms, not the technology of printing, that were the engine of the scientific revolution.

In other words, the scientific revolution was launched by the discovery of ignorance.[91] Religions of the book assumed that they had access to an infallible source of knowledge. The Christians had the Bible, the Muslims had the Quran, the Hindus had the Vedas, and the Buddhists had the Tipitaka. Scientific culture has no comparable holy book, nor does it claim that any of its heroes are infallible prophets, saints, or geniuses. The scientific project starts by rejecting the fantasy of infallibility and proceeding to construct an information network that takes error to be inescapable. Sure, there is much talk about the genius of Copernicus, Darwin, and Einstein, but none of them is considered faultless. They all made mistakes, and even the most celebrated scientific tracts are sure to contain errors and lacunae.

Since even geniuses suffer from confirmation bias, you cannot trust them to correct their own errors. Science is a team effort, relying on institutional collaboration rather than on individual scientists or, say, a single infallible book. Of course, institutions too are prone to error. Scientific institutions are nevertheless different from religious institutions, inasmuch as they reward skepticism and innovation rather than conformity. Scientific institutions are also different from conspiracy theories, inasmuch as they reward *self*-skepticism. Conspiracy theorists tend to be extremely skeptical regarding the existing consensus, but when it comes to their own beliefs, they lose all their skepticism and fall prey to confirmation bias.[92] The trademark of science is not merely skepticism but self-skepticism, and at the heart of every scientific institution we find a strong self-correcting mechanism. Scientific institutions do reach a broad consensus about the accuracy of certain theories—such as quantum mechanics or the theory of evolution—but only because these theories have managed to survive intense efforts to disprove them, launched not only by outsiders but by members of the institution itself.

SELF-CORRECTING MECHANISMS

As an information technology, the self-correcting mechanism is the polar opposite of the holy book. The holy book is supposed to be infallible. The self-correcting mechanism embraces fallibility. By *self*-correcting, I refer to mechanisms that an entity uses to correct itself. A teacher correcting a student's essay is not a self-correcting mechanism; the student isn't correcting their own essay. A judge sending a criminal to prison is not a self-correcting mechanism; the criminal isn't exposing their own crime. When the Allies defeated and dismantled the Nazi regime, this was not a self-correcting mechanism; left to its own devices, Germany would not have denazified itself. But when a scientific journal publishes a paper correcting a mistake

that appeared in a previous paper, that's an example of institutional self-correction.

Self-correcting mechanisms are ubiquitous in nature. Children learn how to walk thanks to them. You make a wrong move, you fall, you learn from your mistake, you try doing it a little differently. Sure, sometimes parents and teachers give the child a hand or offer advice, but a child who relies entirely on such external corrections or keeps excusing mistakes instead of learning from them will find it very difficult to walk. Indeed, even as adults, every time we walk, our body engages in an intricate process of self-correction. As our body navigates through space, internal feedback loops between brain, limbs, and sensory organs keep our legs and hands in their proper places and our balance just right.[93]

Many other bodily processes require constant self-correction. Our blood pressure, temperature, sugar levels, and numerous other parameters must be given some leeway to change in accordance with varying circumstances, but they should never go above or below certain critical thresholds. Our blood pressure needs to increase when we run, to decrease when we sleep, but must always keep within certain bounds.[94] Our body manages this delicate biochemical dance through a host of homeostatic self-correcting mechanisms. If our blood pressure goes too high, the self-correcting mechanisms lower it. If our blood pressure is dangerously low, the self-correcting mechanisms raise it. If the self-correcting mechanisms go out of order, we could die.[95]

Institutions, too, die without self-correcting mechanisms. These mechanisms start with the realization that humans are fallible and corruptible. But instead of despairing of humans and looking for a way to bypass them, the institution actively seeks its own errors and corrects them. All institutions that manage to endure beyond a handful of years possess such mechanisms, but institutions differ greatly in the strength and visibility of their self-correcting mechanisms.

For example, the Catholic Church is an institution with relatively

weak self-correcting mechanisms. Since it claims infallibility, it cannot admit institutional mistakes. It is occasionally willing to acknowledge that some of its members have erred or sinned, but the institution itself allegedly remains perfect. For example, in the Second Vatican Council in 1964, the Catholic Church acknowledged that "Christ summons the Church to continual reformation as she sojourns here on earth. The Church is always in need of this, insofar as she is an institution of men here on earth. Thus if, in various times and circumstances, there have been deficiencies in moral conduct or in church discipline, or even in the way that church teaching has been formulated—to be carefully distinguished from the deposit of faith itself—these can and should be set right at the opportune moment."[96]

This admission sounds promising, but the devil is in the details, specifically in the refusal to countenance the possibility of any deficiency in "the deposit of faith." In Catholic dogma "the deposit of faith" refers to the body of revealed truth that the church has received from scriptures and from its sacred tradition of interpreting scripture. The Catholic Church acknowledges that priests are fallible humans who can sin and can also make mistakes in the way they formulate church teachings. However, the holy book itself can never err. What does this imply about the entire church as an institution that combines fallible humans with an infallible text?

According to Catholic dogma, biblical infallibility and divine guidance trump human corruption, so even though individual members of the church may err and sin, the Catholic Church as an institution is never wrong. Allegedly, never in history did God allow the majority of church leaders to make a serious mistake in their interpretation of the holy book. This principle is common to many religions. Jewish Orthodoxy accepted the possibility that the rabbis who composed the Mishnah and Talmud might have erred in personal matters, but when they came to decree religious doctrine, God ensured that they would make no mistake.[97] In Islam there is an analogous principle known as *Ijma*. According to one important Hadith,

Muhammad said that "Allah will ensure my community will never agree on error."[98]

In Catholicism, alleged institutional perfection is enshrined most clearly in the doctrine of papal infallibility, which says that while in personal matters popes may err, in their institutional role they are infallible.[99] For example, Pope Alexander VI erred in breaking his vow of celibacy, having a mistress and siring several children, yet when defining official church teachings on matters of ethics or theology, he was incapable of mistake.

In line with these views, the Catholic Church has always employed a self-correcting mechanism to supervise its human members in their personal affairs, but it never developed a mechanism for amending the Bible or for amending its "deposit of faith." This attitude is manifest in the few formal apologies the Catholic Church issued for its past conduct. In recent decades, several popes apologized for the mistreatment of Jews, women, non-Catholic Christians, and indigenous cultures, as well as for more specific events such as the sacking of Constantinople in 1204 and the abuse of children in Catholic schools. It is commendable that the Catholic Church made such apologies at all; religious institutions rarely do so. Nevertheless, in all these cases, the popes were careful to shift responsibility away from scriptures and from the church as an institution. Instead, the blame was laid on the shoulders of individual churchmen who misinterpreted scriptures and deviated from the true teachings of the church.

For example, in March 2000, Pope John Paul II conducted a special ceremony in which he asked forgiveness for a long list of historical crimes against Jews, heretics, women, and indigenous people. He apologized "for the use of violence that some have committed in the service of truth." This terminology implied that the violence was the fault of "some" misguided individuals who didn't understand the truth taught by the church. The pope didn't accept the possibility that perhaps these individuals understood exactly what the church was teaching and that these teachings just were not the truth.[100]

Similarly, when Pope Francis apologized in 2022 for the abuses against indigenous people in Canada's church-run residential schools, he said, "I ask for forgiveness, in particular, for the ways in which many members of the church ... cooperated ... in projects of cultural destruction and forced assimilation."[101] Note his careful shifting of responsibility. The fault lay with "many members of the church," not with the church and its teachings. As if it were never official church doctrine to destroy indigenous cultures and forcefully convert people.

In fact, it wasn't a few wayward priests who launched the Crusades, imposed laws that discriminated against Jews and women, or orchestrated the systematic annihilation of indigenous religions throughout the world.[102] The writings of many revered church fathers, and the official decrees of many popes and church councils, are full of passages disparaging "pagan" and "heretical" religions, calling for their destruction, discriminating against their members, and legitimizing the use of violence to convert people to Christianity.[103] For example, in 1452 Pope Nicholas V issued the *Dum Diversas* bull, addressed to King Afonso V of Portugal and other Catholic monarchs. The bull said, "We grant you by these present documents, with our Apostolic Authority, full and free permission to invade, search out, capture, and subjugate the Saracens and pagans and any other unbelievers and enemies of Christ wherever they may be, as well as their kingdoms, duchies, counties, principalities, and other property ... and to reduce their persons into perpetual servitude."[104] This official proclamation, repeated numerous times by subsequent popes, laid the theological basis for European imperialism and the destruction of native cultures across the world. Of course, though the church doesn't acknowledge it officially, over time it has changed its institutional structures, its core teachings, and its interpretation of scripture. The Catholic Church of today is far less antisemitic and misogynist than it was in medieval and early modern times. Pope Francis is far more tolerant of indigenous cultures than was Pope Nicholas V. There is an institutional self-correcting mechanism at work here, which reacts both to

external pressures and to internal soul-searching. But what characterizes self-correcting in institutions like the Catholic Church is that even when it happens, it is denied rather than celebrated. The first rule of changing church teachings is that you never admit to changing church teachings.

You would never hear a pope announcing to the world, "Our experts have just discovered a really big error in the Bible. We'll soon issue an updated edition." Instead, when asked about the church's more generous attitude to Jews or women, popes imply that this was always what the church *really* taught, even if some individual churchmen previously failed to understand the message correctly. Denying the existence of self-correction doesn't entirely stop it from happening, but it does weaken and slow it. Because the correction of past mistakes is not acknowledged, let alone celebrated, when the faithful encounter another serious problem in the institution and its teachings, they are paralyzed by fear of changing something that is supposedly eternal and infallible. They cannot benefit from the example of previous changes.

For instance, when Catholics like Pope Francis himself are now reconsidering the church's teachings on homosexuality,[105] they find it difficult to simply acknowledge past mistakes and change the teachings. If eventually a future pope would issue an apology for the mistreatment of LGBTQ people, the way to do it would be to again shift the blame to the shoulders of some overzealous individuals who misunderstood the gospel. To maintain its religious authority the Catholic Church has had no choice but to deny the existence of institutional self-correction. For the church fell into the infallibility trap. Once it based its religious authority on a claim to infallibility, any public admission of institutional error—even on relatively minor issues—could completely destroy its authority.

THE *DSM* AND THE BIBLE

In contrast to the Catholic Church, the scientific institutions that emerged in early modern Europe have been built around strong self-correcting mechanisms. Scientific institutions maintain that even if most scientists in a particular period believe something to be true, it may yet turn out to be inaccurate or incomplete. In the nineteenth century most physicists accepted Newtonian physics as a comprehensive account of the universe, but in the twentieth century the theory of relativity and quantum mechanics exposed the inaccuracies and limitations of Newton's model.[106] The most celebrated moments in the history of science are precisely those moments when accepted wisdom is overturned and new theories are born.

Crucially, scientific institutions are willing to admit their *institutional* responsibility for major mistakes and crimes. For example, present-day universities routinely give courses, and professional journals routinely publish articles, that expose the institutional racism and sexism that characterized the scientific study of subjects like biology, anthropology, and history in the nineteenth and much of the twentieth centuries. Research on individual test cases such as the Tuskegee Syphilis Study, and on governmental policies ranging from the White Australia policy to the Holocaust, have repeatedly and extensively studied how flawed biological, anthropological, and historical theories developed in leading scientific institutions were used to justify and facilitate discrimination, imperialism, and even genocide. These crimes and errors are not blamed on a few misguided scholars. They are seen as an institutional failure of entire academic disciplines.[107]

The willingness to admit major institutional errors contributes to the relatively fast pace at which science is developing. When the available evidence justifies it, dominant theories are often discarded within a few generations, to be replaced by new theories. What students of biology, anthropology, and history learn at university in the

early twenty-first century is very different from what they learned there a century previously.

Psychiatry offers numerous similar examples for strong self-correcting mechanisms. On the shelf of most psychiatrists you can find the *DSM*—the *Diagnostic and Statistical Manual of Mental Disorders*. It is occasionally nicknamed the psychiatrists' bible. But there is a crucial difference between the *DSM* and the Bible. First published in 1952, the *DSM* is revised every decade or two, with the fifth edition appearing in 2013. Over the years, many disorders have been redefined, new ones have been added, while others have been deleted. Homosexuality, for example, was listed in 1952 as a sociopathic personality disturbance, but removed from the *DSM* in 1974. It took just twenty-two years to correct this error in the *DSM*. That's not a holy book. That's a scientific text.

Today the discipline of psychiatry doesn't try to reinterpret the 1952 definition of homosexuality in a more benign spirit. Rather, it views the 1952 definition as a downright error. More important, the error is not attributed to the shortcomings of a few homophobic professors. Rather, it is acknowledged to be the result of deep institutional biases in the discipline of psychiatry.[108] Confessing the past institutional errors of their discipline makes psychiatrists today more careful not to commit new such errors, as evidenced in the heated debate regarding transgender people and people on the autistic spectrum. Of course, no matter how careful they are, psychiatrists are still likely to make institutional mistakes. But they are also likely to acknowledge and correct them.[109]

PUBLISH OR PERISH

What makes scientific self-correcting mechanisms particularly strong is that scientific institutions are not just willing to admit institutional error and ignorance; they are actively seeking to expose them. This is evident in the institutions' incentive structure. In religious institu-

tions, members are incentivized to conform to existing doctrine and be suspicious of novelty. You become a rabbi, imam, or priest by professing doctrinal loyalty, and you can advance up the ranks to become pope, chief rabbi, or grand ayatollah without criticizing your predecessors or advancing any radical new notions. Indeed, many of the most powerful and admired religious leaders of recent times—such as Pope Benedict XVI, Chief Rabbi of Israel David Lau, and Ayatollah Khamenei of Iran—have won fame and supporters by strict resistance to new ideas and trends like feminism.[110]

In science it works the other way around. Hiring and promotions in scientific institutions are based on the principle of "publish or perish," and to publish in prestigious journals, you must expose some mistake in existing theories or discover something your predecessors and teachers didn't know. Nobody wins a Nobel Prize for faithfully repeating what previous scholars said and opposing every new scientific theory.

Of course, just as religion has room for self-correcting, so science has ample room for conformism, too. Science is an institutional enterprise, and scientists rely on the institution for almost everything they know. For example, how do I know what medieval and early modern Europeans thought about witchcraft? I have not visited all the relevant archives myself, nor have I read all the relevant primary sources. In fact, I am incapable of reading many of these sources directly, because I do not know all the necessary languages, nor am I skilled in deciphering medieval and early modern handwriting. Instead, I have relied on books and articles published by other scholars, such as Ronald Hutton's book *The Witch: A History of Fear*, which was published by Yale University Press in 2017.

I haven't met Ronald Hutton, who is a professor of history at the University of Bristol, nor do I personally know the Bristol officials who hired him or the Yale editorial team who published his book. I nevertheless trust what I read in Hutton's book, because I understand how institutions like the University of Bristol and Yale University Press operate. Their self-correcting mechanisms have two crucial fea-

tures: First, the self-correcting mechanisms are built into the core of the institutions rather than being a peripheral add-on. Second, these institutions publicly celebrate self-correcting instead of denying it. It is of course possible that some of the information I gained from Hutton's book may be incorrect, or I myself may misinterpret it. But experts on the history of witchcraft who have read Hutton's book and who might be reading the present book will hopefully spot any such errors and expose them.

Populist critics of scientific institutions may counter that, in fact, these institutions use their power to stifle unorthodox views and launch their own witch hunts against dissenters. It is certainly true that scholars who oppose the current orthodox view of their discipline sometimes experience negative consequences: having articles rejected or research grants denied, facing nasty ad hominem attacks, and in rare cases even getting fired from their job.[111] I do not wish to belittle the suffering such things cause, but it is still a far cry from being physically tortured and burned at the stake.

Consider, for example, the story of the chemist Dan Shechtman. In April 1982, while observing through an electron microscope, Shechtman saw something that all contemporary theories in chemistry claimed simply could not exist: the atoms in a mixed sample of aluminum and manganese were crystallized in a pattern with a fivefold rotational symmetry. At the time, scientists knew of various possible symmetrical structures in solid crystals, but fivefold symmetry was considered against the very laws of nature. Shechtman's discovery of what came to be called quasicrystals sounded so outlandish that it was difficult to find a peer-reviewed journal willing to publish it. It didn't help that Shechtman was at the time a junior scientist. He didn't even have his own laboratory; he was working in someone's else facility. But the editors of the journal *Physical Review Letters*, after reviewing the evidence, eventually published Shechtman's article in 1984.[112] And then, as he describes it, "all hell broke loose."

Shechtman's claims were dismissed by most of his colleagues, and he was blamed for mismanaging his experiments. The head of his

laboratory also turned on Shechtman. In a dramatic gesture, he placed a chemistry textbook on Shechtman's desk and told him, "Danny, please read this book and you will understand that what you are saying cannot be." Shechtman boldly replied that he saw the quasi-crystals in the microscope—not in the book. As a result, he was kicked out of the lab. Worse was to come. Linus Pauling, a two-time Nobel laureate and one of the most eminent scientists of the twenti-eth century, led a brutal personal attack on Shechtman. In a confer-ence attended by hundreds of scientists, Pauling proclaimed, "Danny Shechtman is talking nonsense, there are no quasicrystals, just quasi-scientists."

But Shechtman was not imprisoned or killed. He got a place in another lab. The evidence he presented turned out to be more con-vincing than the existing chemistry textbooks and the views of Linus Pauling. Several colleagues repeated Shechtman's experiments and replicated his findings. A mere ten years after Shechtman saw the quasicrystals through his microscope, the International Union of Crystallography—the leading scientific association in the field—altered its definition of what a crystal is. Chemistry textbooks were changed accordingly, and an entire new scientific field emerged—the study of quasicrystals. In 2011, Shechtman was awarded the Nobel Prize in Chemistry for his discovery.[113] The Nobel Committee said that "his discovery was extremely controversial [but] eventually forced scientists to reconsider their conception of the very nature of matter."[114]

Shechtman's story is hardly exceptional. The annals of science are full of similar cases. Before the theory of relativity and quantum me-chanics became the cornerstones of twentieth-century physics, they initially provoked bitter controversies, including personal assaults by the old guard on the proponents of the new theories. Similarly, when Georg Cantor developed in the late nineteenth century his theory of infinite numbers, which became the basis for much of twentieth-century mathematics, he was personally attacked by some of the leading mathematicians of his day, like Henri Poincaré and Leopold

Kronecker. Populists are right to think that scientists suffer from the same human biases as everyone else. However, thanks to institutional self-correcting mechanisms these biases can be overcome. If enough empirical evidence is provided, it often takes just a few decades for an unorthodox theory to upend established wisdom and become the new consensus.

As we shall see in the next chapter, there were times and places where scientific self-correcting mechanisms ceased functioning and academic dissent *could* lead to physical torture, imprisonment, and death. In the Soviet Union, for example, questioning official dogma on any matter—economics, genetics, or history—could lead not only to dismissal but even to a couple of years in the gulag or an executioner's bullet.[115] A famous case involved the bogus theories of the agronomist Trofim Lysenko. He rejected mainstream genetics and the theory of evolution by natural selection and advanced his own pet theory, which said that "re-education" could change the traits of plants and animals, and even transform one species into another. Lysenkoism greatly appealed to Stalin, who had ideological and political reasons for believing in the almost limitless potential of "re-education." Thousands of scientists who opposed Lysenko and continued to uphold the theory of evolution by natural selection were dismissed from their jobs, and some were imprisoned or executed. Nikolai Vavilov, a botanist and geneticist who was Lysenko's former mentor turned critic, was tried in July 1941 along with the botanist Leonid Govorov, the geneticist Georgii Karpechenko, and the agronomist Aleksandr Bondarenko. The latter three were shot, while Vavilov died in a camp in Saratov in 1943.[116] Under pressure from the dictator, the Lenin All-Union Academy of Agricultural Sciences eventually announced in August 1948 that henceforth Soviet institutions would teach Lysenkoism as the only correct theory.[117]

But for precisely this reason, the Lenin All-Union Academy of Agricultural Sciences ceased being a scientific institution, and Soviet dogma on genetics was an ideology rather than a science. An institu-

tion can call itself by whatever name it wants, but if it lacks a strong self-correcting mechanism, it is not a scientific institution.

THE LIMITS OF SELF-CORRECTION

Does all this mean that in self-correcting mechanisms we have found the magic bullet that protects human information networks from error and bias? Unfortunately, things are far more complicated. There is a reason why institutions like the Catholic Church and the Soviet Communist Party eschewed strong self-correcting mechanisms. While such mechanisms are vital for the pursuit of truth, they are costly in terms of maintaining order. Strong self-correcting mechanisms tend to create doubts, disagreements, conflicts, and rifts and to undermine the myths that hold the social order together.

Of course, order by itself isn't necessarily good. For example, the social order of early modern Europe endorsed, among other things, not only witch hunts but also the exploitation of millions of peasants by a handful of aristocrats, the systematic mistreatment of women, and widespread discrimination against Jews, Muslims, and other minorities. But even when the social order is highly oppressive, undermining it doesn't necessarily lead to a better place. It could just lead to chaos and worse oppression. The history of information networks has always involved maintaining a balance between truth and order. Just as sacrificing truth for the sake of order comes with a cost, so does sacrificing order for truth.

Scientific institutions have been able to afford their strong self-correcting mechanisms because they leave the difficult job of preserving the social order to other institutions. If a chemist finds that a thief has broken into their lab or a psychiatrist receives death threats, they don't complain to a peer-reviewed journal; they call the police. Is it possible, then, to maintain strong self-correcting mechanisms in institutions other than academic disciplines? In particular, can such mechanisms exist in institutions like police forces, armies, political

parties, and governments that are charged with maintaining the social order?

We'll explore this question in the next chapter, which focuses on the political aspects of information flows and examines the long-term history of democracies and dictatorships. As we shall see, democracies believe that it is possible to maintain strong self-correcting mechanisms even in politics. Dictatorships disavow such mechanisms. Thus, at the height of the Cold War, newspapers and universities in the democratic United States openly exposed and criticized American war crimes in Vietnam. Newspapers and universities in the totalitarian Soviet Union were also happy to criticize American crimes, but they remained silent about Soviet crimes in Afghanistan and elsewhere. Soviet silence was scientifically unjustifiable, but it made political sense. American self-flagellation about the Vietnam War continues even today to divide the American public and to undermine America's reputation throughout the world, whereas Soviet and Russian silence about the Afghanistan War has helped dim its memory and limit its reputational costs.

Only after understanding the politics of information in historical systems like ancient Athens, the Roman Empire, the United States, and the Soviet Union will we be ready to explore the revolutionary implications of the rise of AI. For one of the biggest questions about AI is whether it will favor or undermine democratic self-correcting mechanisms.

Decisions: A Brief History of Democracy and Totalitarianism

Democracy and dictatorship are typically discussed as contrasting political and ethical systems. This chapter seeks to shift the terms of the discussion, by surveying the history of democracy and dictatorship as contrasting types of information networks. It examines how information in democracies flows differently than in dictatorial systems and how inventing new information technologies helps different kinds of regimes flourish.

Dictatorial information networks are highly centralized.[1] This means two things. First, the center enjoys unlimited authority; hence information tends to flow to the central hub, where the most important decisions are made. In the Roman Empire all roads led to Rome, in Nazi Germany information flowed to Berlin, and in the Soviet Union to Moscow. Sometimes the central government attempts to concentrate *all* information in its hands and to dictate *all* decisions by itself, controlling the totality of people's lives. This totalizing form of dictatorship, practiced by the likes of Hitler and Stalin, is known as totalitarianism. But not every dictatorship is totalitarian. Technical difficulties often prevent dictators from becoming totalitarian. The Roman emperor Nero, for example, didn't have the means to

micromanage the lives of millions of peasants in remote provincial villages. In many dictatorial regimes considerable autonomy is therefore left to individuals, corporations, and communities. However, the dictators always retain the authority to intervene in people's lives. In Nero's Rome freedom was not an ideal but a by-product of the government's inability to exert totalitarian control.

The second characteristic of dictatorial networks is that they assume the center is infallible. They therefore dislike any challenge to the center's decisions. Soviet propaganda depicted Stalin as an infallible genius, and Roman propaganda treated emperors as divine beings. Even when Stalin or Nero made a patently disastrous decision, there were no robust self-correcting mechanisms in the Soviet Union or the Roman Empire that could expose the mistake and push for a better course of action.

In theory, a highly centralized information network could try to maintain strong self-correcting mechanisms, like independent courts and elected legislative bodies. But if they functioned well, these would challenge the central authority and thereby decentralize the information network. Dictators always see such independent power hubs as threats and seek to neutralize them. This is what happened to the Roman Senate, whose power was whittled away by successive Caesars until it became little more than a rubber stamp for imperial whims.[2] The same fate befell the Soviet judicial system, which never dared resist the will of the Communist Party. Stalinist show trials, as their name indicates, were theater with preordained results.[3]

To summarize, a dictatorship is a centralized information network, lacking strong self-correcting mechanisms. A democracy, in contrast, is a distributed information network, possessing strong self-correcting mechanisms. When we look at a democratic information network, we do see a central hub. The government is the most important executive power in a democracy, and government agencies therefore gather and store vast quantities of information. But there are many additional information channels that connect lots of independent nodes. Legis-

lative bodies, political parties, courts, the press, corporations, local communities, NGOs, and individual citizens communicate freely and directly with one another so that most information never passes through any government agency and many important decisions are made elsewhere. Individuals choose for themselves where to live, where to work, and whom to marry. Corporations make their own choices about where to open a branch, how much to invest in certain projects, and how much to charge for goods and services. Communities decide for themselves about organizing charities, sporting events, and religious festivals. Autonomy is not a consequence of the government's ineffectiveness; it is the democratic ideal.

Even if it possesses the technology necessary to micromanage people's lives, a democratic government leaves as much room as possible for people to make their own choices. A common misconception is that in a democracy everything is decided by majority vote. In fact, in a democracy as little as possible is decided centrally, and only the relatively few decisions that must be made centrally should reflect the will of the majority. In a democracy, if 99 percent of people want to dress in a particular way and worship a particular god, the remaining 1 percent should still be free to dress and worship differently.

Of course, if the central government doesn't intervene at all in people's lives, and doesn't provide them with basic services like security, it isn't a democracy; it is anarchy. In all democracies the center raises taxes and maintains an army, and in most modern democracies it also provides at least some level of health care, education, and welfare. But any intervention in people's lives demands an explanation. In the absence of a compelling reason, a democratic government should leave people to their own devices.

Another crucial characteristic of democracies is that they assume everyone is fallible. Therefore, while democracies give the center the authority to make some vital decisions, they also maintain strong mechanisms that can challenge the central authority. To paraphrase President James Madison, since humans are fallible, a government is

necessary, but since government too is fallible, it needs mechanisms to expose and correct its errors, such as holding regular elections, protecting the freedom of the press, and separating the executive, legislative, and judicial branches of government.

Consequently, while a dictatorship is about one central information hub dictating everything, a democracy is an ongoing conversation between diverse information nodes. The nodes often influence one another, but in most matters they are not obliged to reach a consensus. Individuals, corporations, and communities can continue to think and behave in different ways. There are, of course, cases when everyone must behave the same and diversity cannot be tolerated. For example, when in 2002–3 Americans disagreed about whether to invade Iraq, everyone ultimately had to abide by a single decision. It was unacceptable that some Americans would maintain a private peace with Saddam Hussein while others declared war. Whether good or bad, the decision to invade Iraq committed every American citizen. So also when initiating national infrastructure projects or defining criminal offenses. No country can function well if every person is allowed to lay a separate rail network or to have their own definition of murder.

In order to make decisions on such collective matters, a country-wide public conversation must first be held, following which the people's representatives—elected in free and fair elections—make a choice. But even after that choice has been made, it should remain open to reexamination and correction. While the network cannot change its previous choices, it can elect a different government next time.

MAJORITY DICTATORSHIP

The definition of democracy as a distributed information network with strong self-correcting mechanisms stands in sharp contrast to a common misconception that equates democracy only with elections.

Elections are a central part of the democratic tool kit, but they are not democracy. In the absence of additional self-correcting mechanisms, elections can easily be rigged. Even if the elections are completely free and fair, by itself this too doesn't guarantee democracy. For democracy is not the same thing as majority dictatorship.

Suppose that in a free and fair election 51 percent of voters choose a government that subsequently sends 1 percent of voters to be exterminated in death camps, because they belong to some hated religious minority. Is this democratic? Clearly it is not. The problem isn't that genocide demands a special majority of more than 51 percent. It's not that if the government gets the backing of 60 percent, 75 percent, or even 99 percent of voters, then its death camps finally become democratic. A democracy is not a system in which a majority of any size can decide to exterminate unpopular minorities; it is a system in which there are clear limits on the power of the center.

Suppose 51 percent of voters choose a government that then takes away the voting rights of the other 49 percent of voters, or perhaps of just 1 percent of them. Is that democratic? Again the answer is no, and it has nothing to do with the numbers. Disenfranchising political rivals dismantles one of the vital self-correcting mechanisms of democratic networks. Elections are a mechanism for the network to say, "We made a mistake; let's try something else." But if the center can disenfranchise people at will, that self-correcting mechanism is neutered.

These two examples may sound outlandish, but they are unfortunately within the realm of the possible. Hitler began sending Jews and communists to concentration camps within months of rising to power through democratic elections, and in the United States numerous democratically elected governments have disenfranchised African Americans, Native Americans, and other oppressed populations. Of course, most assaults on democracy are more subtle. The careers of strongmen like Vladimir Putin, Viktor Orbán, Recep Tayyip Erdoğan, Rodrigo Duterte, Jair Bolsonaro, and Benjamin

Netanyahu demonstrate how a leader who uses democracy to rise to power can then use his power to undermine democracy. As Erdoğan once put it, "Democracy is like a tram. You ride it until you arrive at your destination, then you step off."[4]

The most common method strongmen use to undermine democracy is to attack its self-correcting mechanisms one by one, often beginning with the courts and the media. The typical strongman either deprives courts of their powers or packs them with his loyalists and seeks to close all independent media outlets while building his own omnipresent propaganda machine.[5]

Once the courts are no longer able to check the government's power by legal means, and once the media obediently parrots the government line, all other institutions or persons who dare oppose the government can be smeared and persecuted as traitors, criminals, or foreign agents. Academic institutions, municipalities, NGOs, and private businesses are either dismantled or brought under government control. At that stage, the government can also rig the elections at will, for example by jailing popular opposition leaders, preventing opposition parties from participating in the elections, gerrymandering election districts, or disenfranchising voters. Appeals against these antidemocratic measures are dismissed by the government's handpicked judges. Journalists and academics who criticize these measures are fired. The remaining media outlets, academic institutions, and judicial authorities all praise these measures as necessary steps to protect the nation and its allegedly democratic system from traitors and foreign agents. The strongmen don't usually take the final step of abolishing the elections outright. Instead, they keep them as a ritual that serves to provide legitimacy and maintain a democratic facade, as happens, for example, in Putin's Russia.

Supporters of strongmen often don't see this process as antidemocratic. They are genuinely baffled when told that electoral victory doesn't grant them unlimited power. Instead, they see any check on the power of an elected government as undemocratic. However, de-

mocracy doesn't mean majority rule; rather, it means freedom and equality for all. Democracy is a system that guarantees everyone certain liberties, which even the majority cannot take away.

Nobody disputes that in a democracy the representatives of the majority are entitled to form the government and to advance their preferred policies in myriad fields. If the majority wants war, the country goes to war. If the majority wants peace, the country makes peace. If the majority wants to raise taxes, taxes are raised. If the majority wants to lower taxes, taxes are lowered. Major decisions about foreign affairs, defense, education, taxation, and numerous other policies are all in the hands of the majority.

But in a democracy, there are two baskets of rights that are protected from the majority's grasp. One contains human rights. Even if 99 percent of the population wants to exterminate the remaining 1 percent, in a democracy this is forbidden, because it violates the most basic human right—the right to life. The basket of human rights contains many additional rights, such as the right to work, the right to privacy, freedom of movement, and freedom of religion. These rights enshrine the decentralized nature of democracy, making sure that as long as people don't harm anyone, they can live their lives as they see fit.

The second crucial basket of rights contains civil rights. These are the basic rules of the democratic game, which enshrine its self-correcting mechanisms. An obvious example is the right to vote. If the majority were permitted to disenfranchise the minority, then democracy would be over after a single election. Other civil rights include freedom of the press, academic freedom, and freedom of assembly, which enable independent media outlets, universities, and opposition movements to challenge the government. These are the key rights that strongmen seek to violate. While sometimes it is necessary to make changes to a country's self-correcting mechanisms—for example, by expanding the franchise, regulating the media, or reforming the judicial system—such changes should be made only on the basis of a broad consensus including both majority and mi-

nority groups. If a small majority could unilaterally change civil rights, it could easily rig elections and get rid of all other checks on its power.

An important thing to note about both human rights and civil rights is that they don't just limit the power of the central government; they also impose on it many active duties. It is not enough for a democratic government to abstain from infringing on human and civil rights. It must take actions to ensure them. For example, the right to life imposes on a democratic government the duty to protect citizens from criminal violence. If a government doesn't kill anyone, but also makes no effort to protect citizens from murder, this is anarchy rather than democracy.

THE PEOPLE VERSUS THE TRUTH

Of course, in every democracy, there are lengthy discussions concerning the exact limits of human and civil rights. Even the right to life has limits. There are democratic countries like the United States that impose the death penalty, thereby denying some criminals the right to life. And every country allows itself the prerogative to declare war, thereby sending people to kill and be killed. So where exactly does the right to life end? There are also complicated and ongoing discussions concerning the list of rights that should be included in the two baskets. Who determined that freedom of religion is a basic human right? Should internet access be defined as a civil right? And what about animal rights? Or the rights of AI?

We cannot resolve these matters here. Both human and civil rights are intersubjective conventions that humans invent rather than discover, and they are determined by historical contingencies rather than universal reason. Different democracies can adopt somewhat different lists of rights. At least from the viewpoint of information flows, what defines a system as "democratic" is only that its center doesn't have unlimited authority and that the system possesses ro-

bust mechanisms to correct the center's mistakes. Democratic networks assume that everyone is fallible, and that includes even the winners of elections and the majority of voters.

It is particularly crucial to remember that elections are *not* a method for discovering truth. Rather, they are a method for maintaining order by adjudicating between people's conflicting desires. Elections establish what the majority of people desire, rather than what the truth is. And people often desire the truth to be other than what it is. Democratic networks therefore maintain some self-correcting mechanisms to protect the truth even from the will of the majority.

For example, during the 2002–3 debate over whether to invade Iraq in the wake of the September 11 attacks, the Bush administration claimed that Saddam Hussein was developing weapons of mass destruction and that the Iraqi people were eager to establish an American-style democracy and would welcome the Americans as liberators. These arguments carried the day. In October 2002 the elected representatives of the American people in Congress voted overwhelmingly to authorize the invasion. The resolution passed with a 296 to 133 majority (69 percent) in the House of Representatives and a 77 to 23 majority (77 percent) in the Senate.[6] In the early days of the war in March 2003, polls found that the elected representatives were indeed in tune with the mass of voters and that 72 percent of American citizens supported the invasion.[7] The will of the American people was clear.

But the truth turned out to be different from what the government said and what the majority believed. As the war progressed, it became evident that Iraq had no weapons of mass destruction and that many Iraqis had no wish to be "liberated" by the Americans or to establish a democracy. By August 2004 another poll found that 67 percent of Americans believed that the invasion was based on incorrect assumptions. As the years went by, most Americans acknowledged that the decision to invade was a catastrophic mistake.[8]

In a democracy the majority has every right to make momentous decisions like starting wars, and that includes the right to make momentous errors. But the majority should at least acknowledge its own fallibility and protect the freedom of minorities to hold and publicize unpopular views, which might turn out to be correct.

As another example, consider the case of a charismatic leader who is accused of corruption. His loyal supporters obviously wish these accusations to be false. But even if most voters support the leader, their desires should not prevent judges from investigating the accusations and getting to the truth. As with the justice system, so also with science. A majority of voters might deny the reality of climate change, but they should not have the power to dictate scientific truth or to prevent scientists from exploring and publishing inconvenient facts. Unlike parliaments, departments of environmental studies should not reflect the will of the majority.

Of course, when it comes to making policy decisions about climate change, in a democracy the will of the voters should reign supreme. Acknowledging the reality of climate change does not tell us what to do about it. We always have options, and choosing between them is a question of desire, not truth. One option might be to immediately cut greenhouse gas emissions, even at the cost of slowing economic growth. This means incurring some difficulties today but saving people in 2050 from more severe hardship, saving the island nation of Kiribati from drowning, and saving the polar bears from extinction. A second option might be to continue with business as usual. This means having an easier life today, but making life harder for the next generation, flooding Kiribati, and driving the polar bears—as well as numerous other species—to extinction. Choosing between these two options is a question of desire, and should therefore be done by all voters rather than by a limited group of experts.

But the one option that should not be on offer in elections is hiding or distorting the truth. If the majority prefers to consume whatever amount of fossil fuels it wishes with no regard to future generations or

other environmental considerations, it is entitled to vote for that. But the majority should not be entitled to pass a law stating that climate change is a hoax and that all professors who believe in climate change must be fired from their academic posts. We can choose what we want, but we shouldn't deny the true meaning of our choice.

Naturally, academic institutions, the media, and the judiciary may themselves be compromised by corruption, bias, or error. But subordinating them to a governmental Ministry of Truth is likely to make things worse. The government is already the most powerful institution in developed societies, and it often has the greatest interest in distorting or hiding inconvenient facts. Allowing the government to supervise the search for truth is like appointing the fox to guard the chicken coop.

To discover the truth, it is better to rely on two other methods. First, academic institutions, the media, and the judiciary have their own internal self-correcting mechanisms for fighting corruption, correcting bias, and exposing error. In academia, peer-reviewed publication is a far better check on error than supervision by government officials, because academic promotion often depends on uncovering past mistakes and discovering unknown facts. In the media, free competition means that if one outlet decides not to break a scandal, perhaps for self-serving reasons, others are likely to jump at the scoop. In the judiciary, a judge who takes bribes may be tried and punished just like any other citizen.

Second, the existence of several independent institutions that seek the truth in different ways allows these institutions to check and correct one another. For example, if powerful corporations manage to break down the peer-review mechanism by bribing a sufficiently large number of scientists, investigative journalists and courts can expose and punish the perpetrators. If the media or the courts are afflicted by systematic racist biases, it is the job of sociologists, historians, and philosophers to expose those biases. None of these mechanisms are completely fail-safe, but no human institution is. Government certainly isn't.

THE POPULIST ASSAULT

If all this sounds complicated, it is because democracy *should* be complicated. Simplicity is a characteristic of dictatorial information networks in which the center dictates everything and everybody silently obeys. It's easy to follow this dictatorial monologue. In contrast, democracy is a conversation with numerous participants, many of them talking at the same time. It can be hard to follow such a conversation.

Moreover, the most important democratic institutions tend to be bureaucratic behemoths. Whereas citizens avidly follow the biographical dramas of the princely court and the presidential palace, they often find it difficult to understand how parliaments, courts, newspapers, and universities function. This is what helps strongmen mount populist attacks on institutions, dismantle all self-correcting mechanisms, and concentrate power in their own hands. We discussed populism briefly in the prologue, to help explain the populist challenge to the naive view of information. Here we need to revisit populism, get a broader understanding of its worldview, and explain its appeal to antidemocratic strongmen.

The term "populism" derives from the Latin *populus,* which means "the people." In democracies, "the people" is considered the sole legitimate source of political authority. Only representatives of the people should have the authority to declare wars, pass laws, and raise taxes. Populists cherish this basic democratic principle, but somehow conclude from it that a single party or a single leader should monopolize all power. In a curious political alchemy, populists manage to base a totalitarian pursuit of unlimited power on a seemingly impeccable democratic principle. How does it happen?

The most novel claim populists make is that they alone truly represent the people. Since in democracies only the people should have political power, and since allegedly only the populists represent the people, it follows that the populist party should have all political

power to itself. If some party other than the populists wins elections, it does not mean that this rival party won the people's trust and is entitled to form a government. Rather, it means that the elections were stolen or that the people were deceived to vote in a way that doesn't express their true will.

It should be stressed that for many populists, this is a genuinely held belief rather than a propaganda gambit. Even if they win just a small share of votes, populists may still believe they alone represent the people. An analogous case are communist parties. In the U.K., for example, the Communist Party of Great Britain (CPGB) never won more than 0.4 percent of votes in a general election,[9] but was nevertheless adamant that it alone truly represented the working class. Millions of British workers, they claimed, were voting for the Labour Party or even for the Conservative Party rather than for the CPGB because of "false consciousness." Allegedly, through their control of the media, universities, and other institutions, the capitalists managed to deceive the working class into voting against its true interests, and only the CPGB could see through this deception. In like fashion, populists can believe that the enemies of the people have deceived the people to vote against its true will, which the populists alone represent.

A fundamental part of this populist credo is the belief that "the people" is not a collection of flesh-and-blood individuals with various interests and opinions, but rather a unified mystical body that possesses a single will—"the will of the people." Perhaps the most notorious and extreme manifestation of this semireligious belief was the Nazi motto "Ein Volk, ein Reich, ein Führer," which means "One People, One Country, One Leader." Nazi ideology posited that the *Volk* (people) had a single will, whose sole authentic representative was the *Führer* (leader). The leader allegedly had an infallible intuition for how the people felt and what the people wanted. If some German citizens disagreed with the leader, it didn't mean that the leader might be in the wrong. Rather, it meant that the dissenters

belonged to some treasonous outsider group—Jews, communists, liberals—instead of to the people.

The Nazi case is of course extreme, and it is grossly unfair to accuse all populists of being crypto-Nazis with genocidal inclinations. However, many populist parties and politicians deny that "the people" might contain a diversity of opinions and interest groups. They insist that the real people has only one will and that they alone represent this will. In contrast, their political rivals—even when the latter enjoy substantial popular support—are depicted as "alien elites." Thus, Hugo Chávez ran for the presidency in Venezuela with the slogan "Chávez is the people!"[10] President Erdoğan of Turkey once railed against his domestic critics, saying, "We are the people. Who are you?"—as if his critics weren't Turks, too.[11]

How can you tell, then, whether someone is part of the people or not? Easy. If they support the leader, they are part of the people. This, according to the German political philosopher Jan-Werner Müller, is the defining feature of populism. What turns someone into a populist is claiming that they alone represent the people and that anyone who disagrees with them—whether state bureaucrats, minority groups, or even the majority of voters—either suffers from false consciousness or isn't really part of the people.[12]

This is why populism poses a deadly threat to democracy. While democracy agrees that the people is the only legitimate source of power, democracy is based on the understanding that the people is never a unitary entity and therefore cannot possess a single will. Every people—whether Germans, Venezuelans, or Turks—is composed of many different groups, with a plurality of opinions, wills, and representatives. No group, including the majority group, is entitled to exclude other groups from membership in the people. This is what makes democracy a conversation. Holding a conversation presupposes the existence of several legitimate voices. If, however, the people has only one legitimate voice, there can be no conversation. Rather, the single voice dictates everything. Populism may therefore

claim adherence to the democratic principle of "people's power," but it effectively empties democracy of meaning and seeks to establish a dictatorship.

Populism undermines democracy in another, more subtle, but equally dangerous way. Having claimed that they alone represent the people, populists argue that the people is not just the sole legitimate source of political authority but the sole legitimate source of *all* authority. Any institution that derives its authority from something other than the will of the people is antidemocratic. As the self-proclaimed representatives of the people, populists consequently seek to monopolize not just political authority but all types of authority and to take control of institutions such as media outlets, courts, and universities. By taking the democratic principle of "people's power" to its extreme, populists turn totalitarian.

In fact, while democracy means that authority *in the political sphere* comes from the people, it doesn't deny the validity of alternative sources of authority in other spheres. As discussed above, in a democracy independent media outlets, courts, and universities are essential self-correcting mechanisms that protect the truth even from the will of the majority. Biology professors claim that humans evolved from apes because the evidence supports this, even if the majority wills it to be otherwise. Journalists can reveal that a popular politician took a bribe, and if compelling evidence is presented in court, a judge may send that politician to jail, even if most people don't want to believe these accusations.

Populists are suspicious of institutions that in the name of objective truths override the supposed will of the people. They tend to see this as a smoke screen for elites grabbing illegitimate power. This drives populists to be skeptical of the pursuit of truth, and to argue—as we saw in the prologue—that "power is the only reality." They thereby seek to undercut or appropriate the authority of any independent institutions that might oppose them. The result is a dark and cynical view of the world as a jungle and of human beings as creatures obsessed with power alone. All social interactions are

seen as power struggles, and all institutions are depicted as cliques promoting the interests of their own members. In the populist imagination, courts don't really care about justice; they only protect the privileges of the judges. Yes, the judges talk a lot about justice, but this is a ploy to grab power for themselves. Newspapers don't care about facts; they spread fake news to mislead the people and benefit the journalists and the cabals that finance them. Even scientific institutions aren't committed to the truth. Biologists, climatologists, epidemiologists, economists, historians, and mathematicians are just another interest group feathering its own nest—at the expense of the people.

In all, it's a rather sordid view of humanity, but two things nevertheless make it appealing to many. First, since it reduces all interactions to power struggles, it simplifies reality and makes events like wars, economic crises, and natural disasters easy to understand. Anything that happens—even a pandemic—is about elites pursuing power. Second, the populist view is attractive because it is sometimes correct. Every human institution is indeed fallible and suffers from some level of corruption. Some judges do take bribes. Some journalists do intentionally mislead the public. Academic disciplines are occasionally plagued by bias and nepotism. That is why every institution needs self-correcting mechanisms. But since populists are convinced that power is the only reality, they cannot accept that a court, a media outlet, or an academic discipline would ever be inspired by the value of truth or justice to correct itself.

While many people embrace populism because they see it as an honest account of human reality, strongmen are attracted to it for a different reason. Populism offers strongmen an ideological basis for making themselves dictators while pretending to be democrats. It is particularly useful when strongmen seek to neutralize or appropriate the self-correcting mechanisms of democracy. Since judges, journalists, and professors allegedly pursue political interests rather than truth, the people's champion—the strongman—should control these positions instead of allowing them to fall into the hands of the peo-

ple's enemies. Similarly, since even the officials in charge of arranging elections and publicizing their results may be part of a nefarious conspiracy, they too should be replaced by the strongman's loyalists.

In a well-functioning democracy, citizens trust the results of elections, the decisions of courts, the reports of media outlets, and the findings of scientific disciplines because citizens believe these institutions are committed to the truth. Once people think that power is the only reality, they lose trust in all these institutions, democracy collapses, and the strongmen can seize total power.

Of course, populism could lead to anarchy rather than totalitarianism, if it undermines trust in the strongmen themselves. If no human is interested in truth or justice, doesn't this apply to Mussolini or Putin too? And if no human institution can have effective self-correcting mechanisms, doesn't this include Mussolini's National Fascist Party or Putin's United Russia party? How can a deep-seated distrust of all elites and institutions be squared with unwavering admiration for one leader and party? This is why populists ultimately depend on the mystical notion that the strongman embodies the people. When trust in bureaucratic institutions like election boards, courts, and newspapers is particularly low, an enhanced reliance on mythology is the only way to preserve order.

MEASURING THE STRENGTH OF DEMOCRACIES

Strongmen who claim to represent the people may well rise to power through democratic means, and often rule behind a democratic facade. Rigged elections in which they win overwhelming majorities serve as proof of the mystical bond between the leader and the people. Consequently, to measure how democratic an information network is, we cannot use a simple yardstick like whether elections are being held regularly. In Putin's Russia, in Iran, and even in North Korea elections are held like clockwork. Rather, we need to ask much more complex questions like "What mechanisms prevent the central

government from rigging the elections?" "How safe is it for leading media outlets to criticize the government?" and "How much authority does the center appropriate to itself?" Democracy and dictatorship aren't binary opposites, but rather are on a continuum. To decide whether a network is closer to the democratic or the dictatorial end of the continuum, we need to understand how information flows in the network and what shapes the political conversation.

If one person dictates all the decisions, and even their closest advisers are terrified to voice a dissenting view, no conversation is taking place. Such a network is situated at the extreme dictatorial end of the spectrum. If nobody can voice unorthodox opinions publicly, but behind closed doors a small circle of party bosses or senior officials are able to freely express their views, then this is still a dictatorship, but it has taken a baby step in the direction of democracy. If 10 percent of the population participate in the political conversation by airing their opinions, voting in fair elections, and running for office, that may be considered a limited democracy, as was the case in many ancient city-states like Athens, or in the early days of the United States, when only wealthy white men had such political rights. As the percentage of people taking part in the conversation rises, so the network becomes more democratic.

The focus on conversations rather than elections raises a host of interesting questions. For example, *where* does that conversation take place? North Korea, for example, has the Mansudae Assembly Hall in Pyongyang, where the 687 members of the Supreme People's Assembly meet and talk. However, while this Assembly is officially known as North Korea's legislature, and while elections to the Assembly are held every five years, this body is widely considered a rubber stamp, executing decisions taken elsewhere. The anodyne discussions follow a predetermined script, and they aren't geared to change anyone's mind about anything.[13]

Is there perhaps another, more private hall in Pyongyang where the crucial conversations take place? Do Politburo members ever dare criticize Kim Jong Un's policies during formal meetings? Per-

haps it can be done in unofficial dinner parties or in unofficial think tanks? Information in North Korea is so concentrated and so tightly controlled that we cannot provide clear answers to these questions.[14]

Similar questions can be asked about the United States. In the United States, unlike in North Korea, people are free to say almost anything they want. Scathing public attacks on the government are a daily occurrence. But where is the room where the crucial conversations happen, and who sits there? The U.S. Congress was designed to fulfill this function, with the people's representatives meeting to converse and try to convince one another. But when was the last time that an eloquent speech in Congress by a member of one party persuaded members of the other party to change their minds about anything? Wherever the conversations that shape American politics now take place, it is definitely not in Congress. Democracies die not only when people are not free to talk but also when people are not willing or able to listen.

STONE AGE DEMOCRACIES

Based on the above definition of democracy, we can now turn to the historical record and examine how changes in information technology and information flows have shaped the history of democracy. To judge by the archaeological and anthropological evidence, democracy was the most typical political system among archaic hunter-gatherers. Stone Age bands obviously didn't have formal institutions like elections, courts, and media outlets, but their information networks were usually distributed and gave ample opportunities for self-correction. In bands numbering just a few dozen people information could easily be shared among all group members, and when the band decided where to pitch camp, where to go hunting, or how to handle a conflict with another band, everyone could take part in the conversation and dispute one another. Bands usually belonged to a larger tribe that included hundreds or even thousands of people. But when

important choices affecting the whole tribe had to be made, such as whether to go to war, tribes were usually still small enough for a large percentage of their members to gather in one place and converse.[15]

While bands and tribes sometimes had dominant leaders, these tended to exercise only limited authority. Leaders had no standing armies, police forces, or governmental bureaucracies at their disposal, so they couldn't just impose their will by force.[16] Leaders also found it difficult to control the economic basis of people's lives. In modern times, dictators like Vladimir Putin and Saddam Hussein have often based their political power on monopolizing economic assets like oil wells.[17] In medieval and classical antiquity, Chinese emperors, Greek tyrants, and Egyptian pharaohs dominated society by controlling granaries, silver mines, and irrigation canals. In contrast, in a hunter-gatherer economy such centralized economic control was possible only under special circumstances. For example, along the northwestern coast of North America some hunter-gatherer economies relied on catching and preserving large numbers of salmon. Since salmon runs peaked for a few weeks in specific creeks and rivers, a powerful chief could monopolize this asset.[18]

But this was exceptional. Most hunter-gatherer economies were far more diversified. One leader, even supported by a few allies, could not corral the savanna and prevent people from gathering plants and hunting animals there. If all else failed, hunter-gatherers could therefore vote with their feet. They had few possessions, and their most important assets were their personal skills and personal friends. If a chief turned dictatorial, people could just walk away.[19]

Even when hunter-gatherers did end up ruled by a domineering chief, as happened among the salmon-fishing people of northwestern America, at least that chief was accessible. He didn't live in a faraway fortress surrounded by an unfathomable bureaucracy and a cordon of armed guards. If you wanted to voice a complaint or a suggestion, you could usually get within earshot of him. The chief couldn't control public opinion, nor could he shut himself off from it. In other words, there was no way for a chief to force all information

to flow through the center, or to prevent people from talking with one another, criticizing him, or organizing against him.[20]

In the millennia following the agricultural revolution, and especially after writing helped create large bureaucratic polities, it became easier to centralize the flow of information and harder to maintain the democratic conversation. In small city-states like those of ancient Mesopotamia and Greece, autocrats like Lugal-Zagesi of Umma and Pisistratus of Athens relied on bureaucrats, archives, and a standing army to monopolize key economic assets and information about ownership, taxation, diplomacy, and politics. It simultaneously became harder for the mass of citizens to keep in direct touch with one another. There was no mass communication technology like newspapers or radio, and it was not easy to squeeze tens of thousands of citizens into the main city square to hold a communal discussion.

Democracy was still an option for these small city-states, as the history of both early Sumer and classical Greece clearly indicates.[21] However, the democracy of ancient city-states tended to be less inclusive than the democracy of archaic hunter-gatherer bands. Probably the most famous example of ancient city-state democracy is Athens in the fifth and fourth centuries BCE. All adult male citizens could participate in the Athenian assembly, vote on public policy, and be elected to public offices. But women, slaves, and non-citizen residents of the city did not enjoy these privileges. Only about 25–30 percent of the adult population of Athens enjoyed full political rights.[22]

As the size of polities continued to increase, and city-states were superseded by larger kingdoms and empires, even Athenian-style partial democracy disappeared. All the famous examples of ancient democracies are city-states such as Athens and Rome. In contrast, we don't know of any large-scale kingdom or empire that operated along democratic lines.

For example, when in the fifth century BCE Athens expanded from a city-state into an empire, it did not grant citizenship and political rights to those it conquered. The city of Athens remained a

limited democracy, but the much bigger Athenian Empire was ruled autocratically from the center. All the important decisions about taxes, diplomatic alliances, and military expeditions were taken in Athens. Subject lands like the islands of Naxos and Thasos had to obey the orders of the Athenian popular assembly and elected officials, without the Naxians and Thasians being able to vote in that assembly or be elected to office. It was also difficult for Naxos, Thasos, and other subject lands to coordinate a united opposition to the decisions taken in the Athenian center, and if they tried to do so, it would have brought ruthless Athenian reprisals. Information in the Athenian Empire flowed to and from Athens.[23]

When the Roman Republic built its empire, conquering first the Italian Peninsula and eventually the entire Mediterranean basin, the Romans took a somewhat different course. Rome gradually did extend citizenship to the conquered people. It began by granting citizenship to the inhabitants of Latium, then to the inhabitants of other Italian regions, and finally to inhabitants of even distant provinces like Gallia and Syria. However, as citizenship was extended to more people, the political rights of citizens were simultaneously restricted.

The ancient Romans had a clear understanding of what democracy means, and they were originally fiercely committed to the democratic ideal. After expelling the last king of Rome in 509 BCE, the Romans developed a deep dislike for monarchy and a fear of giving unlimited power to any single individual or institution. Supreme executive power was therefore shared by *two* consuls who balanced each other. These consuls were chosen by citizens in free elections, held office for a single year, and were additionally checked by the powers of the popular assembly, of the Senate, and of other elected officials like the tribunes.

But when Rome extended citizenship to Latins, Italians, and finally to Gauls and Syrians, the power of the popular assembly, the tribunes, the Senate, and even the two consuls was gradually reduced, until in the late first century BCE the Caesar family established its

autocratic rule. Anticipating present-day strongmen like Putin, Augustus didn't crown himself king, and pretended that Rome was still a republic. The Senate and the popular assembly continued to convene, and every year citizens continued to choose consuls and tribunes. But these institutions were emptied of real power.[24]

In 212 CE, the emperor Caracalla—the offspring of a Phoenician family from North Africa—took a seemingly momentous step and granted automatic Roman citizenship to all free adult males throughout the vast empire. Rome in the third century CE accordingly had tens of millions of citizens.[25] But by that time, all the important decisions were made by a single unelected emperor. While consuls were still ceremonially chosen every year, Caracalla inherited power from his father, Septimius Severus, who became emperor by winning a civil war. The most important step Caracalla took to cement his rule was murdering his brother and rival, Geta.

When Caracalla ordered the murder of Geta, declared war on the Parthian Empire, or extended Roman citizenship to millions of Britons, Greeks, and Arabs, he had no need to ask permission from the Roman people. All of Rome's self-correcting mechanisms had been neutralized long before. If Caracalla made some error in foreign or domestic policy, neither the Senate nor any officials could intervene to correct it, except by rising in rebellion or assassinating him. And when Caracalla was indeed assassinated in 217, it only led to a new round of civil wars culminating in the rise of new autocrats. Rome in the third century CE, like Russia in the eighteenth century, was, in the words of Madame de Staël, "autocracy tempered by strangulation."

By the third century CE, not only the Roman Empire but all other major human societies on earth were centralized information networks lacking strong self-correcting mechanisms. This was true of the Parthian and Sassanian Empires in Persia, of the Kushan and Gupta Empires in India, and of China's Han Empire and its successor Three Kingdoms.[26] Thousands of more small-scale societies continued to function democratically in the third century CE and

beyond, but it seemed that distributed democratic networks were simply incompatible with large-scale societies.

CAESAR FOR PRESIDENT!

Were large-scale democracies really unworkable in the ancient world? Or did autocrats like Augustus and Caracalla deliberately sabotage them? This question is important not only for our understanding of ancient history but also for our view of democracy's future in the age of AI. How do we know whether democracies fail because they are undermined by strongmen or because of much deeper structural and technological reasons?

To answer that question, let's take a closer look at the Roman Empire. The Romans were clearly familiar with the democratic ideal, and it continued to be important to them even after the Caesar family rose to power. Otherwise, Augustus and his heirs would not have bothered to maintain seemingly democratic institutions like the Senate or annual elections to the consulate and other offices. So why did power end up in the hands of an unelected emperor?

In theory, even after Roman citizenship was expanded to tens of millions of people throughout the Mediterranean basin, wasn't it possible to hold empire-wide elections for the position of emperor? This would surely have required very complicated logistics, and it would have taken several months to learn the results of the elections. But was that really a deal breaker?

The key misconception here is equating democracy with elections. Tens of millions of Roman citizens could theoretically vote for this or that imperial candidate. But the real question is whether tens of millions of Romans could have held an ongoing empire-wide political conversation. In present-day North Korea no democratic conversation takes place because people aren't free to talk, yet we could well imagine a situation when this freedom is guaranteed—as it is in South Korea. In the present-day United States the democratic con-

versation is endangered by people's inability to listen to and respect their political rivals, yet this can presumably still be fixed. By contrast, in the Roman Empire there was simply no way to conduct or sustain a democratic conversation, because the technological means to hold such a conversation did not exist.

To hold a conversation, it is not enough to have the freedom to talk and the ability to listen. There are also two technical preconditions. First, people need to be within hearing range of one another. This means that the only way to hold a political conversation in a territory the size of the United States or the Roman Empire is with the help of some kind of information technology that can swiftly convey what people say over long distances.

Second, people need at least a rudimentary understanding of what they are talking about. Otherwise, they are just making noise, not holding a meaningful conversation. People usually have a good understanding of political issues of which they have direct experience. Poor people have many insights about poverty that escape economics professors, and ethnic minorities understand racism in a much more profound way than people who never suffered from it, for example. However, if lived experience were the only way to understand crucial political issues, large-scale political conversations would be impossible. For then every group of people could talk meaningfully only about its own experiences. Even worse, nobody else could understand what they were saying. If lived experience is the sole possible source of knowledge, then merely listening to the insights gained from someone else's lived experience cannot impart these insights to me.

The only way to have a large-scale political conversation among diverse groups of people is if people can gain some understanding of issues that they have never experienced firsthand. In a large polity, it is a crucial role of the education system and the media to inform people about things they have never faced themselves. If there is no education system or media platform to perform this role, no meaningful large-scale conversations can take place.

In a small Neolithic town of a few thousand inhabitants people might sometimes have been afraid to say what they thought, or might have refused to listen to their rivals, but it was relatively easy to satisfy the more fundamental technical preconditions for meaningful discourse. First, people lived in proximity to one another, so they could easily meet most other community members and hear their voices. Second, everybody had intimate knowledge of the dangers and opportunities that the town faced. If an enemy war party approached, everyone could see it. If the river flooded the fields, everyone witnessed the economic effects. When people talked about war and hunger, they knew what they were saying.

In the fourth century BCE, the city-state of Rome was still small enough to allow a large percentage of its citizens to congregate in the Forum in times of emergency, listen to respected leaders, and voice their personal views on the matter at hand. When in 390 BCE Gallic invaders attacked Rome, almost everyone lost a relative in the defeat at the Battle of the Allia and lost property when the victorious Gauls then sacked Rome. The desperate Romans appointed Marcus Camillus as dictator. In Rome, the dictator was a public official appointed in times of emergency who had unlimited powers but only for a short predetermined period, following which he was held accountable for his actions. After Camillus led the Romans to victory, everybody could see that the emergency was over, and Camillus stepped down.[27]

In contrast, by the third century CE, the Roman Empire had a population of between sixty and seventy-five million people,[28] spread over five million square kilometers.[29] Rome lacked mass communication technology like radio or daily newspapers. Only 10–20 percent of adults had reading skills,[30] and there was no organized education system that could inform them about the geography, history, and economy of the empire. True, many people across the empire did share some cultural ideas, such as a strong belief in the superiority of Roman civilization over the barbarians. These shared cultural beliefs were crucial in preserving order and holding the em-

pire together. But their political implications were far from clear, and in times of crisis there was no possibility of holding a public conversation about what should be done.

How could Syrian merchants, British shepherds, and Egyptian villagers converse about the ongoing wars in the Middle East or about the immigration crisis brewing along the Danube? The lack of a meaningful public conversation was not the fault of Augustus, Nero, Caracalla, or any of the other emperors. They didn't sabotage Roman democracy. Given the size of the empire and the available information technology, democracy was simply unworkable. This was acknowledged already by ancient philosophers like Plato and Aristotle, who argued that democracy can work only in small-scale city-states.[31]

If the absence of Roman democracy had merely been the fault of particular autocrats, we should have at least seen large-scale democracies flourishing in other places, like in Sassanian Persia, Gupta India, or Han China. But prior to the development of modern information technology, there are no examples of large-scale democracies anywhere.

It should be stressed that in many large-scale autocracies local affairs were often managed democratically. The Roman emperor didn't have the information needed to micromanage hundreds of cities across the empire, whereas local citizens in each city could continue to hold a meaningful conversation about municipal politics. Consequently, long after the Roman Empire became an autocracy, many of its cities continued to be governed by local assemblies and elected officials. At a time when elections to the consulship in Rome became ceremonial affairs, elections to municipal offices in small cities like Pompeii were hotly contested.

Pompeii was destroyed in the eruption of Vesuvius in 79 CE, during the reign of the emperor Titus. Archaeologists uncovered about fifteen hundred graffiti concerned with various local election campaigns. One coveted office was that of the city's aedile—the magistrate in charge of maintaining the city's infrastructure and public

buildings.[32] Lucretius Fronto's supporters drew the graffiti "If honest living is thought to be any recommendation, then Lucretius Fronto is worthy of being elected." One of his opponents, Gaius Julius Polybius, ran with the slogan "Elect Gaius Julius Polybius to the office of *aedile*. He provides good bread."

There were also endorsements by religious groups and professional associations, such as "The worshippers of Isis demand the election of Gnaeus Helvius Sabinus" and "All the mule drivers request that you elect Gaius Julius Polybius." There was dirty work, too. Someone who clearly wasn't Marcus Cerrinius Vatia drew the graffiti "All the drunkards ask you to elect Marcus Cerrinius Vatia" and "The petty thieves ask you to elect Vatia."[33] Such electioneering indicates that the position of aedile had power in Pompeii and that the aedile was chosen in relatively free and fair elections, rather than appointed by the imperial autocrat in Rome.

Even in empires whose rulers never had any democratic pretensions, democracy could still flourish in local settings. In the Tsarist Empire, for example, the daily lives of millions of villagers were managed by rural communes. Going back at least to the eleventh century, each commune usually included fewer than a thousand people. They were subject to a landlord and bore many obligations to their lord and to the central tsarist state, but they had considerable autonomy in managing their internal affairs and in deciding how to discharge their external obligations, such as paying taxes and providing military recruits. The commune mediated local disputes, provided emergency relief, enforced social norms, oversaw the distribution of land to individual households, and regulated access to shared resources like forests and pastures. Decisions on important matters were made in communal meetings in which the heads of local households expressed their views and chose the commune's elder. Resolutions at least tried to reflect the majority's will.[34]

In tsarist villages and Roman cities a form of democracy was possible because a meaningful public conversation was possible. Pompeii was a city of about eleven thousand people in 79 CE,[35] so everybody

could supposedly judge for themselves whether Lucretius Fronto was an honest man and whether Marcus Cerrinius Vatia was a drunken thief. But democracy at a scale of millions became possible only in the modern age, when mass media changed the nature of large-scale information networks.

MASS MEDIA MAKES MASS DEMOCRACY POSSIBLE

Mass media are information technologies that can quickly connect millions of people even when they are separated by vast distances. The printing press was a crucial step in that direction. Print made it possible to cheaply and quickly produce large numbers of books and pamphlets, which enabled more people to voice their opinions and be heard over a large territory, even if the process still took time. This sustained some of the first experiments in large-scale democracy, such as the Polish-Lithuanian Commonwealth established in 1569 and the Dutch Republic established in 1579.

Some may contest the characterization of these polities as "democratic," since only a minority of relatively wealthy citizens enjoyed full political rights. In the Polish-Lithuanian Commonwealth, political rights were reserved for adult male members of the *szlachta*—the nobility. These numbered up to 300,000 individuals, or about 5 percent of the total adult population.[36] One of the *szlachta*'s prerogatives was to elect the king, but since voting required traveling long distances to a national convention, few exercised their right. In the sixteenth and seventeenth centuries participation in royal elections usually ranged between 3,000 and 7,000 voters, except for the 1669 elections, in which 11,271 participated.[37] While this hardly sounds democratic in the twenty-first century, it should be remembered that all large-scale democracies until the twentieth century limited political rights to a small circle of relatively wealthy men. Democracy is never a matter of all or nothing. It is a continuum, and

late-sixteenth-century Poles and Lithuanians explored previously unknown regions of that continuum.

Aside from electing its king, Poland-Lithuania had an elected parliament (the Sejm) that approved or blocked new legislation and had the power to veto royal decisions on taxation and foreign affairs. Moreover, citizens enjoyed a list of inviolable rights such as freedom of assembly and freedom of religion. In the late sixteenth and early seventeenth centuries, when most of Europe suffered from bitter religious conflicts and persecutions, Poland-Lithuania was a tolerant haven, where Catholics, Greek Orthodox, Lutherans, Calvinists, Jews, and even Muslims coexisted in relative harmony.[38] In 1616, more than a hundred mosques functioned in the commonwealth.[39]

In the end, however, the Polish-Lithuanian experiment in decentralization proved to be impractical. The country was Europe's second-largest state (after Russia), covering almost a million square kilometers and including most of the territory of today's Poland, Lithuania, Belarus, and Ukraine. It lacked the information, communication, and education systems necessary to hold a meaningful political conversation between Polish aristocrats, Lithuanian noblemen, Ukrainian Cossacks, and Jewish rabbis spread from the Baltic Sea to the Black Sea. Its self-correcting mechanisms were also too costly, paralyzing the power of the central government. In particular, every single Sejm deputy was given the right to veto all parliamentary legislation, which led to political deadlock. The combination of a large and diverse polity with a weak center proved fatal. The commonwealth was torn apart by centrifugal forces, and its pieces were then divided between the centralized autocracies of Russia, Austria, and Prussia.

The Dutch experiment fared better. In some ways the Dutch United Provinces were even less centralized than the Polish-Lithuanian Commonwealth, since they lacked a monarch, and were a union of seven autonomous provinces, which were in turn made up of self-governing towns and cities.[40] This decentralized nature is re-

flected in the plural form of how the country was known abroad—
the Netherlands in English, Les Pays-Bas in French, Los Países
Bajos in Spanish, and so on.

However, taken together the United Provinces were twenty-five
times smaller in landmass than Poland-Lithuania and possessed a
much better information, communication, and education system
that tied its constituent parts closely together.[41] The United Provinces also pioneered a new information technology with a big future.
In June 1618 a pamphlet titled *Courante uyt Italien, Duytslandt &c.*
appeared in Amsterdam. As its title indicated, it carried news from
the Italian Peninsula, the German lands, and other places. There was
nothing remarkable about this particular pamphlet, except that new
issues were published in the following weeks, too. They appeared
regularly until 1670, when the *Courante uyt Italien, Duytslandt &c.*
merged with other serial pamphlets into the *Amsterdamsche Courant,*
which appeared until 1903, when it was merged into *De Telegraaf*—
the Netherlands' largest newspaper to this day.[42]

The newspaper is a periodic pamphlet, and it was different from
earlier one-off pamphlets because it had a much stronger self-
correcting mechanism. Unlike one-off publications, a weekly or daily
newspaper has a chance to correct its mistakes and an incentive to do
so in order to win the public's trust. Shortly after the *Courante uyt
Italien, Duytslandt &c.* appeared, a competing newspaper titled *Tijdinghen uyt Verscheyde Quartieren* (Tidings from Various Quarters)
made its debut. The *Courante* was generally considered more reliable,
because it tried to check its stories before publishing them, and because the *Tijdinghen* was accused of being overly patriotic and reporting only news favorable to the Netherlands. Nevertheless, both
newspapers survived, because, as one reader explained, "one can always find something in one newspaper that is not available in the
other." In the following decades dozens of additional newspapers
were published in the Netherlands, which became Europe's journal-
istic hub.[43]

Newspapers that succeeded in gaining widespread trust became

the architects and mouthpieces of public opinion. They created a far more informed and engaged public, which changed the nature of politics, first in the Netherlands and later around the world.[44] The political influence of newspapers was so crucial that newspaper editors often became political leaders. Jean-Paul Marat rose to power in revolutionary France by founding and editing *L'Ami du Peuple;* Eduard Bernstein helped create Germany's Social Democratic Party by editing *Der Sozialdemokrat;* Vladimir Lenin's most important position before becoming Soviet dictator was editor of *Iskra;* and Benito Mussolini rose to fame first as a socialist journalist in *Avanti!* and later as founder and editor of the firebrand right-wing paper *Il Popolo d'Italia.*

Newspapers played a crucial role in the formation of early modern democracies like the United Provinces in the Low Countries, the United Kingdom in the British Isles, and the United States in North America. As the names themselves indicate, these were not city-states like ancient Athens and Rome but amalgams of different regions glued together in part by this new information technology. For example, when on December 6, 1825, President John Quincy Adams gave his First Annual Message to the U.S. Congress, the text of the address and summaries of the main points were published over the next weeks by newspapers from Boston to New Orleans. (At the time, hundreds of newspapers and magazines were being published in the United States.[45])

Adams declared his administration's intentions of initiating numerous federal projects ranging from the construction of roads to the founding of an astronomical observatory, which he poetically named "light-house of the skies." His speech ignited a fierce public debate, much of it conducted in print between those who supported such "big government" plans as essential for the development of the United States and many who preferred a "small government" approach and saw Adams's plans as federal overreach and an encroachment on states' rights.

Northern supporters of the "small government" camp complained

that it was unconstitutional for the federal government to tax the
citizens of richer states in order to build roads in poorer states.
Southerners feared that a federal government that claims the power
to build a lighthouse of the skies in their backyard may one day claim
the power to free their slaves, too. Adams was accused of harboring
dictatorial ambitions, while the erudition and sophistication of his
speech were criticized as elitist and disconnected from ordinary
Americans. The public debates over the 1825 message to Congress
dealt a severe blow to the reputation of the Adams administration
and helped pave the way to Adams's subsequent electoral defeat. In
the 1828 presidential elections, Adams lost to Andrew Jackson—
a rich slaveholding planter from Tennessee who was successfully rebranded in numerous newspaper columns as "the man of the people"
and who claimed that the previous elections were in fact stolen by
Adams and by the corrupt Washington elites.[46]

Newspapers of the time were of course still slow and limited compared with the mass media of today. Newspapers traveled at the pace
of a horse or sailboat, and relatively few people read them regularly.
There were no newsstands or street vendors, so people had to buy
subscriptions, which were expensive; average annual subscriptions
cost around one week's wages for a skilled journeyman. As a result,
the total number of subscribers to all U.S. newspapers in 1830 is estimated at just seventy-eight thousand. Since some subscribers were
associations or businesses rather than individuals, and since every
copy was probably read by several people, it seems reasonable to assume that regular newspaper readership numbered in the hundreds
of thousands. But millions more people rarely, if ever, read newspapers.[47]

No wonder that American democracy in those days was a limited
affair—and the domain of wealthy white men. In the 1824 elections
that brought Adams to power, 1.3 million Americans were theoretically eligible to vote, out of an adult population of about 5 million (or
around 25 percent). Only 352,780 people—7 percent of the total
adult population—actually made use of their right. Adams didn't

even win a majority of those who voted. Owing to the quirks of the U.S. electoral system, he became president thanks to the support of just 113,122 voters, or not much more than 2 percent of adults, and 1 percent of the total population.[48] In Britain at the same time, only about 400,000 people were eligible to vote for Parliament, or around 6 percent of the adult population. Moreover, 30 percent of parliamentary seats were not even contested.[49]

You may wonder whether we are talking about democracies at all. At a time when the United States had more slaves than voters (more than 1.5 million Americans were enslaved in the early 1820s),[50] was the United States really a democracy? This is a question of definitions. As with the late-sixteenth-century Polish-Lithuanian Commonwealth, so also with the early-nineteenth-century United States, "democracy" is a relative term. As noted earlier, democracy and autocracy aren't absolutes; they are part of a continuum. In the early nineteenth century, out of all large-scale human societies, the United States was probably the closest to the democratic end of the continuum. Giving 25 percent of adults the right to vote doesn't sound like much today, but in 1824 that was a far higher percentage than in the Tsarist, Ottoman, or Chinese Empires, in which nobody had the right to vote.[51]

Besides, as emphasized throughout this chapter, voting is not the only thing that counts. An even more important reason to consider the United States in 1824 a democracy is that compared with most other polities of its day, the new country possessed much stronger self-correcting mechanisms. The Founding Fathers were inspired by ancient Rome—witness the Senate and the Capitol in Washington—and they were well aware that the Roman Republic eventually turned into an autocratic empire. They feared that some American Caesar would do something similar to their republic, and constructed multiple overlapping self-correcting mechanisms, known as the system of checks and balances. One of these was a free press. In ancient Rome, the self-correcting mechanisms stopped functioning as the republic enlarged its territory and population. In the United States,

modern information technology combined with freedom of the press helped the self-correcting mechanisms survive even as the country extended from the Atlantic to the Pacific.

It was these self-correcting mechanisms that gradually enabled the United States to expand the franchise, abolish slavery, and turn itself into a more inclusive democracy. As noted in chapter 2, the Founding Fathers committed enormous mistakes—such as endorsing slavery and denying women the vote—but they also provided the tools for their descendants to correct these mistakes. That was their greatest legacy.

THE TWENTIETH CENTURY: MASS DEMOCRACY, BUT ALSO MASS TOTALITARIANISM

Printed newspapers were just the first harbinger of the mass media age. During the nineteenth and twentieth centuries, a long list of new communication and transportation technologies—such as the telegraph, the telephone, television, radio, the train, the steamship, and the airplane—supercharged the power of mass media.

When Demosthenes gave a public speech in Athens around 350 BCE, it was aimed primarily at the limited audience actually present in the Athenian agora. When John Quincy Adams gave his First Annual Message in 1825, his words spread at the pace of a horse. When Abraham Lincoln gave his Gettysburg Address on November 19, 1863, telegraphs, locomotives, and steamships conveyed his words much faster throughout the Union and beyond. The very next day *The New York Times* had already reprinted the speech in full,[52] as had numerous other newspapers from *The Portland Daily Press* in Maine to the *Ottumwa Courier* in Iowa.[53]

As befitting a democracy with strong self-correcting mechanisms in place, the president's speech sparked a lively conversation rather than universal applause. Most newspapers lauded it, but some expressed their doubts. *The Chicago Times* wrote on November 20 that

"the cheek of every American must tingle with shame as he reads the silly, flat and dishwatery utterances" of President Lincoln.[54] *The Patriot & Union*, a local newspaper in Harrisburg, Pennsylvania, also blasted "the silly remarks of the President" and hoped that "the veil of oblivion shall be dropped over them and that they shall be no more repeated or thought of."[55] Though the country was in the midst of a civil war, journalists were free to publicly criticize—and even ridicule—the president.

Fast-forward a century, and things really picked up speed. For the first time in history, new technologies allowed masses of people, spread over vast swaths of territory, to connect *in real time*. In 1960, about seventy million Americans (39 percent of the total population), dispersed over the North American continent and beyond, watched the Nixon-Kennedy presidential debates live on television, with millions more listening on the radio.[56] The only effort viewers and listeners had to make was to press a button while sitting in their homes. Large-scale democracy had now become feasible. Millions of people separated by thousands of kilometers could conduct informed and meaningful public debates about the rapidly evolving issues of the day. By 1960, all adult Americans were theoretically eligible to vote, and close to seventy million (about 64 percent of the electorate) actually did so—though millions of Blacks and other disenfranchised groups were prevented from voting through various voter-suppression schemes.[57]

As always, we should beware of technological determinism and of concluding that the rise of mass media led to the rise of large-scale democracy. Mass media made large-scale democracy possible, rather than inevitable. And it also made possible other types of regimes. In particular, the new information technologies of the modern age opened the door for large-scale totalitarian regimes. Like Nixon and Kennedy, Stalin and Khrushchev could say something over the radio and be heard instantaneously by hundreds of millions of people from Vladivostok to Kaliningrad. They could also receive daily reports by phone and telegraph from millions of secret police agents and in-

formers. If a newspaper in Vladivostok or Kaliningrad wrote that the supreme leader's latest speech was silly (as happened to Lincoln's Gettysburg Address), then everyone involved—from the editor in chief to the typesetters—would likely have received a visit from the KGB.

A BRIEF HISTORY OF TOTALITARIANISM

Totalitarian systems assume their own infallibility, and seek total control over the totality of people's lives. Before the invention of the telegraph, radio, and other modern information technology, large-scale totalitarian regimes were impossible. Roman emperors, Abbasid caliphs, and Mongol khans were often ruthless autocrats who believed they were infallible, but they did not have the apparatus necessary to impose totalitarian control over large societies. To understand this, we should first clarify the difference between totalitarian regimes and less extreme autocratic regimes. In an autocratic network, there are no legal limits on the will of the ruler, but there are nevertheless a lot of technical limits. In a totalitarian network, many of these technical limits are absent.[58]

For example, in autocratic regimes like the Roman Empire, the Abbasid Empire, and the Mongol Empire, rulers could usually execute any person who displeased them, and if some law got in their way, they could ignore or change the law. The emperor Nero arranged the murder of his mother, Agrippina, and his wife, Octavia, and forced his mentor Seneca to commit suicide. Nero also executed or exiled some of the most respected and powerful Roman aristocrats merely for voicing dissent or telling jokes about him.[59]

While autocratic rulers like Nero could execute anyone who did or said something that displeased them, they couldn't know what most people in their empire were doing or saying. Theoretically, Nero could issue an order that any person in the Roman Empire who criticized or insulted the emperor must be severely punished. Yet there

were no technical means for implementing such an order. Roman historians like Tacitus portray Nero as a bloodthirsty tyrant who instigated an unprecedented reign of terror. But this was a very limited type of terror. Although he executed or exiled a number of family members, aristocrats, and senators within his orbit, ordinary Romans in the city's slums and provincials in distant towns like Jerusalem and Londinium could speak their mind much more freely.[60]

Modern totalitarian regimes like the Stalinist U.S.S.R. instigated terror on an altogether different scale. Totalitarianism is the attempt to control what every person throughout the country is doing and saying every moment of the day, and potentially even what every person is thinking and feeling. Nero might have dreamed about such powers, but he lacked the means to realize them. Given the limited tax base of the agrarian Roman economy, Nero couldn't employ many people in his service. He could place informers at the dinner parties of Roman senators, but he had only about 10,000 imperial administrators[61] and 350,000 soldiers[62] to control the rest of the empire, and he lacked the technology to communicate with them swiftly.

Nero and his fellow emperors had an even bigger problem ensuring the loyalty of the administrators and soldiers they *did* have on their payroll. No Roman emperor was ever toppled by a democratic revolution like the ones that deposed Louis XVI, Nicolae Ceauşescu, or Hosni Mubarak. Instead, dozens of emperors were assassinated or deposed by their own generals, officials, bodyguards, or family members.[63] Nero himself was overthrown by a revolt of the governor of Hispania, Galba. Six months later Galba was ousted by Otho, the governor of Lusitania. Within three months, Otho was deposed by Vittelius, commander of the Rhine army. Vitellius lasted about eight months before he was defeated and killed by Vespasian, commander of the army in Judaea. Being killed by a rebellious subordinate was the biggest occupational hazard not just for Roman emperors but for almost all premodern autocrats.

Emperors, caliphs, shahs, and kings found it a huge challenge to keep their subordinates in check. Rulers consequently focused their

attention on controlling the military and the taxation system. Roman emperors had the authority to interfere in the local affairs of any province or city, and they sometimes exercised that authority, but this was usually done in response to a specific petition sent by a local community or official,[64] rather than as part of some empire-wide totalitarian Five-Year Plan. If you were a mule driver in Pompeii or a shepherd in Roman Britain, Nero didn't want to control your daily routines or to police the jokes you told. As long as you paid your taxes and didn't resist the legions, that was good enough for Nero.

SPARTA AND QIN

Some scholars claim that despite the technological difficulties there were attempts to establish totalitarian regimes in ancient times. The most common example cited is Sparta. According to this interpretation, Spartans were ruled by a totalitarian regime that micromanaged every aspect of their lives—from whom they married to what they ate. However, while the Spartan regime was certainly draconian, it actually included several self-correcting mechanisms that prevented power from being monopolized by a single person or faction. Political authority was divided between two kings, five ephors (senior magistrates), twenty-eight members of the Gerousia council, and the popular assembly. Important decisions—such as whether to go to war—often involved fierce public debates.

Moreover, irrespective of how we evaluate the nature of Sparta's regime, it is clear that the same technological limitations that confined ancient Athenian democracy to a single city also limited the scope of the Spartan political experiment. After winning the Peloponnesian War, Sparta installed military garrisons and pro-Spartan governments in numerous Greek cities, requiring them to follow its lead in foreign policy and sometimes also pay tribute. But unlike the U.S.S.R. after World War II, Sparta after the Peloponnesian War did

not try to expand or export its system. Sparta couldn't construct an information network big and dense enough to control the lives of ordinary people in every Greek town and village.⁶⁵

A much more ambitious totalitarian project might have been launched by the Qin dynasty in ancient China (221–206 BCE). After defeating all the other Warring States, the Qin ruler Qin Shi Huang controlled a huge empire with tens of millions of subjects, who belonged to numerous different ethnic groups, spoke diverse languages, and were loyal to various local traditions and elites. To cement its power, the victorious Qin regime tried to dismantle any regional powers that might challenge its authority. It confiscated the lands and wealth of local aristocrats and forced regional elites to move to the imperial capital of Xiangyang, thereby separating them from their power base and monitoring them more easily.

The Qin regime also embarked on a ruthless campaign of centralization and homogenization. It created a new simplified script to be used throughout the empire and standardized coinage, weights, and measurements. It built a road network radiating out of Xiangyang, with standardized rest houses, relay stations, and military checkpoints. People needed written permits in order to enter or leave the capital region or frontier zones. Even the width of axles was standardized to ensure that carts and chariots could run in the same ruts.

Every action, from tilling fields to getting married, was supposed to serve some military need, and the type of military discipline that Rome reserved for the legions was imposed by the Qin on the entire population. The envisioned reach of this system can be exemplified by one Qin law that specified the punishment an official faced if he neglected a granary under his supervision. The law discusses the number of rat holes in the granary that would warrant fining or berating the official: "For three or more rat holes the fine is [the purchase of] one shield [for the army] and for two or fewer [the responsible official] is berated. Three mouse holes are equal to one rat hole."⁶⁶

To facilitate this totalitarian system, the Qin attempted to create a

militarized social order. Every male subject had to belong to a five-man unit. These units were aggregated into larger formations, from local hamlets (*li*), through cantons (*xiang*) and counties (*xian*), all the way to the large imperial commanderies (*jun*). People were forbidden to change their residence without permit, to the extent that guests could not even stay overnight at a friend's house without proper identification and authorization.

Every Qin male subject was also given a rank, just as every soldier in an army has a rank. Obedience to the state resulted in promotion to higher ranks, which brought with it economic and legal privileges, while disobedience could result in demotion or punishment. People in each formation were supposed to supervise one another, and if any individual committed some misdeed, all could be punished for it. Anyone who failed to report a criminal—even their own relatives—would be killed. Those who reported crimes were rewarded with higher ranks and other perks.

It is highly questionable to what extent the regime managed to implement all these totalitarian measures. Bureaucrats writing documents in a government office often invent elaborate rules and regulations, which then turn out to be impractical. Did conscientious government officials really go around the entire Qin Empire counting rat holes in every granary? Were peasants in every remote mountain hamlet really organized into five-man squads? Probably not. Nevertheless, the Qin Empire outdid other ancient empires in its totalitarian ambitions.

The Qin regime even tried to control what its subjects were thinking and feeling. During the Warring States period Chinese thinkers were relatively free to develop myriad ideologies and philosophies, but the Qin adopted the doctrine of Legalism as the official state ideology. Legalism posited that humans were naturally greedy, cruel, and egotistical. It emphasized the need for strict control, argued that punishments and rewards were the most effective means of control, and insisted that state power not be curtailed by any moral consider-

ation. Might was right, and the good of the state was the supreme good.[67] The Qin proscribed other philosophies, such as Confucianism and Daoism, which believed humans were more altruistic and which emphasized the importance of virtue rather than violence.[68] Books espousing such soft views were banned, as well as books that contradicted the official Qin version of history.

When one scholar argued that Qin Shi Huang should emulate the founder of the ancient Zhou dynasty and decentralize state power, the Qin chief minister, Li Si, countered that scholars should stop criticizing present-day institutions by idealizing the past. The regime ordered the confiscation of all books that romanticized antiquity or otherwise criticized the Qin. Such problematic texts were stored in the imperial library and could be studied only by official scholars.[69]

The Qin Empire was probably the most ambitious totalitarian experiment in human history prior to the modern age, and its scale and intensity would prove to be its ruin. The attempt to regiment tens of millions of people along military lines, and to monopolize all resources for military purposes, led to severe economic problems, wastefulness, and popular resentment. The regime's draconian laws, along with its hostility to regional elites and its voracious appetite for taxes and recruits, fanned the flames of this resentment even further. Meanwhile, the limited resources of an ancient agrarian society couldn't support all the bureaucrats and soldiers that the Qin needed to contain this resentment, and the low efficiency of their information technology made it impossible to control every town and village from distant Xiangyang. Not surprisingly, in 209 BCE a series of revolts broke out, led by regional elites, disgruntled commoners, and even some of the empire's own newly minted officials.

According to one account, the first serious revolt started when a group of conscripted peasants sent to work in a frontier zone were delayed by rain and flooding. They feared they would be executed for this dereliction of duty, and felt they had nothing to lose. They were

quickly joined by numerous other rebels. Just fifteen years after reaching the apogee of power, the Qin Empire collapsed under the weight of its totalitarian ambitions, splintering into eighteen kingdoms.

After several years of war, a new dynasty—the Han—reunited the empire. But the Han then adopted a more realistic, less draconian attitude. Han emperors were certainly autocratic, but they were not totalitarian. They did not recognize any limits on their authority, but they did not try to micromanage everyone's lives. Instead of following Legalist ideas of surveillance and control, the Han turned to Confucian ideas of encouraging people to act loyally and responsibly out of inner moral convictions. Like their contemporaries in the Roman Empire, Han emperors sought to control only some aspects of society from the center, while leaving considerable autonomy to provincial aristocrats and local communities. Due largely to the limitations imposed by the available information technology, premodern large-scale polities like the Roman and Han Empires gravitated toward nontotalitarian autocracy.[70] Full-blown totalitarianism might have been dreamed about by the likes of the Qin, but its implementation had to wait for the development of modern technology.

THE TOTALITARIAN TRINITY

Just as modern technology enabled large-scale democracy, it also made large-scale totalitarianism possible. Beginning in the nineteenth century, the rise of industrial economies allowed governments to employ many more administrators, and new information technologies—such as the telegraph and radio—made it possible to quickly connect and supervise all these administrators. This facilitated an unprecedented concentration of information and power, for those who dreamed about such things.

When the Bolsheviks seized control of Russia after the 1917 revolution, they were driven by exactly such a dream. The Bolsheviks craved unlimited power because they believed they had a messianic mission. Marx taught that for millennia, all human societies were dominated by corrupt elites who oppressed the people. The Bolsheviks claimed they knew how to finally end all oppression and create a perfectly just society on earth. But to do so, they had to overcome numerous enemies and obstacles, which, in turn, required all the power they could get. They refused to countenance any self-correcting mechanisms that might question either their vision or their methods. Like the Catholic Church, the Bolshevik party was convinced that though its individual members might err, the party itself was always right. Belief in their own infallibility led the Bolsheviks to destroy Russia's nascent democratic institutions—like elections, independent courts, the free press, and opposition parties—and to create a one-party totalitarian regime. Bolshevik totalitarianism did not start with Stalin. It was evident from the very first days of the revolution. It stemmed from the doctrine of party infallibility, rather than from the personality of Stalin.

In the 1930s and 1940s, Stalin perfected the totalitarian system he inherited. The Stalinist network was composed of three main branches. First, there was the governmental apparatus of state ministries, regional administrations, and regular Red Army units, which in 1939 comprised 1.6 million civilian officials[71] and 1.9 million soldiers.[72] Second, there was the apparatus of the Communist Party of the Soviet Union and its ubiquitous party cells, which in 1939 included 2.4 million party members.[73] Third, there was the secret police: first known as the Cheka, in Stalin's days it was called the OGPU, NKVD, and MGB, and after Stalin's death it morphed into the KGB. Its post-Soviet successor organization has been known since 1995 as the FSB. In 1937, the NKVD had 270,000 agents and millions of informers.[74]

The three branches operated in parallel. Just as democracy is main-

tained by having overlapping self-correcting mechanisms that keep each other in check, modern totalitarianism created overlapping surveillance mechanisms that keep each other in order. The governor of a Soviet province was constantly watched by the local party commissar, and neither of them knew who among their staff was an NKVD informer. A testimony to the effectiveness of the system is that modern totalitarianism largely solved the perennial problem of premodern autocracies—revolts by provincial subordinates. While the U.S.S.R. had its share of court coups, not once did a provincial governor or a Red Army front commander rebel against the center.[75] Much of the credit for that goes to the secret police, which kept a close eye on the mass of citizens, on provincial administrators, and even more so on the party and the Red Army.

While in most polities throughout history the army had wielded enormous political power, in twentieth-century totalitarian regimes the regular army ceded much of its clout to the secret police—the information army. In the U.S.S.R., the Cheka, OGPU, NKVD, and KGB lacked the firepower of the Red Army, but had more influence in the Kremlin and could terrorize and purge even the army brass. The East German Stasi and the Romanian Securitate were similarly stronger than the regular armies of these countries.[76] In Nazi Germany, the SS was more powerful than the Wehrmacht, and the SS chief, Heinrich Himmler, was higher up the pecking order than Wilhelm Keitel, chief of the Wehrmacht high command.

In none of these cases could the secret police defeat the regular army in traditional warfare, of course; what made the secret police powerful was its command of information. It had the information necessary to preempt a military coup and to arrest the commanders of tank brigades or fighter squadrons before they knew what hit them. During the Stalinist Great Terror of the late 1930s, out of 144,000 Red Army officers about 10 percent were shot or imprisoned by the NKVD. This included 154 of 186 divisional commanders (83 percent), eight of nine admirals (89 percent), thirteen of

fifteen full generals (87 percent), and three of five marshals (60 per-cent).[77]

The party leadership fared just as badly. Of the revered Old Bol-sheviks, people who joined the party before the 1917 revolution, about a third didn't survive the Great Terror.[78] Of the thirty-three men who served on the Politburo between 1919 and 1938, fourteen were shot (42 percent). Of the 139 members and candidate members of the party's Central Committee in 1934, 98 (70 percent) were shot. Only 2 percent of the delegates who took part in the Seventeenth Party Congress in 1934 evaded execution, imprisonment, expulsion, or demotion, and attended the Eighteenth Party Congress in 1939.[79]

The secret police—which did all the purging and killing—was it-self divided into several competing branches that closely watched and purged one another. Genrikh Yagoda, the NKVD head who or-chestrated the beginning of the Great Terror and supervised the kill-ing of hundreds of thousands of victims, was executed in 1938 and replaced by Nikolai Yezhov. Yezhov lasted for two years, killing and imprisoning millions of people before being executed in 1940.

Perhaps most telling is the fate of the thirty-nine people who in 1935 held the rank of general in the NKVD (called commissars of state security in Soviet nomenclature). Thirty-five of them (90 per-cent) were arrested and shot by 1941, one was assassinated, and one—the head of the NKVD's Far East regional office—saved him-self by defecting to Japan, but was killed by the Japanese in 1945. Of the original cohort of thirty-nine NKVD generals, only two men were left standing by the end of World War II. The remorseless logic of totalitarianism eventually caught up with them too. During the power struggles that followed Stalin's death in 1953, one of them was shot, while the other was consigned to a psychiatric hospital, where he died in 1960.[80] Serving as an NKVD general in Stalin's day was one of the most dangerous jobs in the world. At a time when Amer-ican democracy was improving its many self-correcting mechanisms, Soviet totalitarianism was refining its triple self-surveilling and self-terrorizing apparatus.

TOTAL CONTROL

Totalitarian regimes are based on controlling the flow of information and are suspicious of any independent channels of information. When military officers, state officials, or ordinary citizens exchange information, they can build trust. If they come to trust one another, they can organize resistance to the regime. Therefore, a key tenet of totalitarian regimes is that wherever people meet and exchange information, the regime should be there too, to keep an eye on them. In the 1930s, this was one principle that Hitler and Stalin shared.

On March 31, 1933, two months after Hitler became chancellor, the Nazis passed the Coordination Act (Gleichschaltungsgesetz). This stipulated that by April 30, 1933, all political, social, and cultural organizations throughout Germany—from municipalities to football clubs and local choirs—must be run according to Nazi ideology, as organs of the Nazi state. It upended life in every city and hamlet in Germany.

For example, in the small Alpine village of Oberstdorf, the democratically elected municipal council met for the last time on April 21, 1933, and three days later it was replaced by an unelected Nazi council that appointed a Nazi mayor. Since the Nazis alone allegedly knew what the people *really* wanted, who other than Nazis could implement the people's will? Oberstdorf also had about fifty associations and clubs, ranging from a beekeeping society to an alpinist club. They all had to conform to the Coordination Act, adjusting their boards, membership, and statutes to Nazi demands, hoisting the swastika flag, and concluding every meeting with the "Horst Wessel Song," the Nazi Party's anthem. On April 6, 1933, the Oberstdorf fishing society banned Jews from its ranks. None of the thirty-two members was Jewish, but they felt they had to prove their Aryan credentials to the new regime.[81]

Things were even more extreme in Stalin's U.S.S.R. Whereas the Nazis still allowed church organizations and private businesses some

partial freedom of action, the Soviets made no exceptions. By 1928 and the launch of the first Five-Year Plan, there were government officials, party functionaries, and secret police informants in every neighborhood and village, and between them they controlled every aspect of life: all businesses from power plants to cabbage farms; all newspapers and radio stations; all universities, schools, and youth groups; all hospitals and clinics; all voluntary and religious organizations; all sporting and scientific associations; all parks, museums, and cinemas.

If a dozen people came together to play football, hike in the woods, or do some charity work, the party and the secret police had to be there too, represented by the local party cell or NKVD agent. The speed and efficiency of modern information technology meant that all these party cells and NKVD agents were always just a telegram or phone call away from Moscow. Information about suspicious persons and activities was fed into a countrywide, cross-referenced system of card catalogs. Known as *kartoteki*, these catalogs contained information from work records, police files, residence cards, and other forms of social registrations and, by the 1930s, had become the primary mechanism for surveilling and controlling the Soviet population.[82]

This made it feasible for Stalin to seek control over the totality of Soviet life. One crucial example was the campaign to collectivize Soviet farming. For centuries, economic, social, and private life in the thousands of villages of the sprawling Tsarist Empire was managed by several traditional institutions: the local commune, the parish church, the private farm, the local market, and above all the family. In the mid-1920s, the Soviet Union was still an overwhelmingly agrarian economy. About 82 percent of the total population lived in villages, and 83 percent of the workforce was engaged in farming.[83] But if each peasant family made its own decisions about what to grow, what to buy, and how much to charge for their produce, it greatly limited the ability of Moscow officials to themselves plan and control social and economic activities. What if the officials decided

on a major agrarian reform, but the peasant families rejected it? So when in 1928 the Soviets came up with their first Five-Year Plan for the development of the Soviet Union, the most important item on the agenda was to collectivize farming.

The idea was that in every village all the families would join a kolkhoz—a collective farm. They would hand over to the kolkhoz all their property—land, houses, horses, cows, shovels, pitchforks. They would work together for the kolkhoz, and in return the kolkhoz would provide for all their needs, from housing and education to food and health care. The kolkhoz would also decide—based on orders from Moscow—whether they should grow cabbages or turnips; whether to invest in a tractor or a school; and who would work in the dairy farm, the tannery, and the clinic. The result, thought the Moscow masterminds, would be the first perfectly just and equal society in human history.

They were similarly convinced of the economic advantages of their proposed system, thinking that the kolkhoz would enjoy economy of scale. For example, when every peasant family had but a small strip of land, it made little sense to buy a tractor to plow it, and in any case most families couldn't afford a tractor. Once all land was held communally, it could be cultivated far more efficiently using modern machinery. In addition, the kolkhoz was supposed to benefit from the wisdom of modern science. Instead of every peasant deciding on production methods on the basis of old traditions and groundless superstitions, state experts with university degrees from institutions like the Lenin All-Union Academy of Agricultural Sciences would make the crucial decisions.

To the planners in Moscow, it sounded wonderful. They expected a 50 percent increase in agricultural production by 1931.[84] And if in the process the old village hierarchies and inequalities were bull-dozed, all the better. To most peasants, however, it sounded terrible. They didn't trust the Moscow planners or the new kolkhoz system. They did not want to give up their old way of life or their private

property. Villagers slaughtered cows and horses instead of handing them to the kolkhoz. Their motivation to work dwindled. People made less effort plowing fields that belonged to everyone than plowing fields that belonged to their own family. Passive resistance was ubiquitous, sometimes flaring into violent clashes. Whereas Soviet planners expected to harvest ninety-eight million tons of grain in 1931, production was only sixty-nine million, according to official data, and might have been as low as fifty-seven million tons in reality. The 1932 harvest was even worse.[85]

The state reacted with fury. Between 1929 and 1936, food confiscation, government neglect, and man-made famines (resulting from government policy rather than a natural disaster) claimed the lives of between 4.5 and 8.5 million people.[86] Millions of additional peasants were declared enemies of the state and deported or imprisoned. The most basic institutions of peasant life—the family, the church, the local community—were terrorized and dismantled. In the name of justice, equality, and the will of the people, the collectivization campaign annihilated anything that stood in its way. In the first two months of 1930 alone, about 60 million peasants in more than 100,000 villages were herded into collective farms.[87] In June 1929, only 4 percent of Soviet peasant households had belonged to collective farms. By March 1930 the figure had risen to 57 percent. By April 1937, 97 percent of households in the countryside had been confined to the 235,000 Soviet collective farms.[88] In just seven years, then, a way of life that had existed for centuries had been replaced by the totalitarian brainchild of a few Moscow bureaucrats.

THE KULAKS

It is worthwhile to delve a little deeper into the history of Soviet collectivization. For it was a tragedy that bears some resemblance to earlier catastrophes in human history—like the European witch-

hunt craze—and at the same time foreshadows some of the biggest dangers posed by twenty-first-century technology and its faith in supposedly scientific data.

When their efforts to collectivize farming encountered resistance and led to economic disaster, Moscow bureaucrats and mythmakers took a page from Kramer's *Hammer of the Witches*. I don't wish to imply that the Soviets actually read the book, but they too invented a global conspiracy and created an entire nonexistent category of enemies. In the 1930s Soviet authorities repeatedly blamed the disasters afflicting the Soviet economy on a counterrevolutionary cabal whose chief agents were the "kulaks," or capitalist farmers. Just as in Kramer's imagination witches serving Satan conjured hailstorms that destroyed crops, so in the Stalinist imagination kulaks beholden to global capitalism sabotaged the Soviet economy.

In theory, kulaks were an objective socioeconomic category, defined by analyzing empirical data on things like property, income, capital, and wages. Soviet officials could allegedly identify kulaks by counting things. If most people in a village had only one cow, then the few families who had three cows were considered kulaks. If most people in a village didn't hire any labor, but one family hired two workers during harvest time, this was a kulak family. Being a kulak meant not only that you possessed a certain amount of property but also that you possessed certain personality traits. According to the supposedly infallible Marxist doctrine, people's material conditions determined their social and spiritual character. Since kulaks allegedly engaged in capitalist exploitation, it was a scientific fact (according to Marxist thinking) that they were greedy, selfish, and unreliable— and so were their children. Discovering that someone was a kulak ostensibly revealed something profound about their fundamental nature.

On December 27, 1929, Stalin declared that the Soviet state should seek "the liquidation of the kulaks as a class,"[89] and immediately galvanized the party and the secret police to realize that ambi-

tious and murderous aim. Early modern European witch-hunters worked in autocratic societies that lacked modern information technology; therefore, it took them three centuries to kill fifty thousand alleged witches. In contrast, Soviet kulak hunters were working in a totalitarian society that had at its disposal technologies such as telegraphs, trains, telephones, and radios—as well as a sprawling bureaucracy. They decided that two years would suffice to "liquidate" millions of kulaks.[90]

Soviet officials began by assessing how many kulaks there must be in the U.S.S.R. Based on existing data—such as tax records, employment records, and the 1926 Soviet census—they decided that kulaks constituted 3–5 percent of the rural population.[91] On January 30, 1930, just one month after Stalin's speech, a Politburo decree translated his vague vision into a much more detailed plan of action. The decree included target numbers for the liquidation of kulaks in each major agricultural region.[92] Regional authorities then made their own estimates of the number of kulaks in each county under their jurisdiction. Eventually, specific quotas were assigned to rural soviets (local administrative units, typically comprising a handful of villages). Often, local officials inflated the numbers along the way, to prove their zeal. Each rural soviet then had to identify the stated number of kulak households in the villages under its purview. These people were expelled from their homes, and—according to the administrative category to which they belonged—resettled elsewhere, incarcerated in concentration camps, or condemned to death.[93]

How exactly did Soviet officials tell who was a kulak? In some villages, local party members made a conscientious effort to identify kulaks by objective measures, such as the amount of property they owned. It was often the most hardworking and efficient farmers who were stigmatized and expelled. In some villages local communists used the opportunity to get rid of their personal enemies. Some villages simply drew lots on who would be considered a kulak. Other villages held communal meetings to vote on the matter and often

chose isolated farmers, widows, old people, and other "expendables" (exactly the sorts of people who in early modern Europe were most likely to be branded witches).[94]

The absurdity of the entire operation is manifested in the case of the Streletsky family from the Kurgan region of Siberia. Dmitry Streletsky, who was then a teenager, recalled years later how his family was branded kulaks and selected for liquidation. "Serkov, the chairman of the village Soviet who deported us, explained: 'I have received an order [from the district party committee] to find 17 kulak families for deportation. I formed a Committee of the Poor and we sat through the night to choose the families. There is no one in the village who is rich enough to qualify, and not many old people, so we simply chose the 17 families. You were chosen. Please don't take it personally. What else could I do?'"[95] If anyone dared object to the madness of the system, they were promptly denounced as kulaks and counterrevolutionaries and would themselves be liquidated.

Altogether, some five million kulaks would be expelled from their homes by 1933. As many as thirty thousand heads of households were shot. The more fortunate victims were resettled in their district of origin or became vagrant workers in the big cities, while about two million were either exiled to remote inhospitable regions or incarcerated as state slaves in labor camps.[96] Numerous important and notorious state projects—such as the construction of the White Sea Canal and the development of mines in the Arctic regions—were accomplished with the labor of millions of prisoners, many of them kulaks. It was one of the fastest and largest enslavement campaigns in human history.[97] Once branded a kulak, a person could not get rid of the stigma. Government agencies, party organs, and secret police documents recorded who was a kulak in a labyrinthine system of *kartoteki* catalogs, archives, and internal passports.

Kulak status even passed to the next generation, with devastating consequences. Kulak children were refused entrance to communist youth groups, the Red Army, universities, and prestigious areas of

employment.[98] In her 1997 memoirs, Antonina Golovina recalled how her family was deported from its ancestral village as kulaks and sent to live in the town of Pestovo. The boys in her new school regularly taunted her. On one occasion, a senior teacher told the eleven-year-old Antonina to stand up in front of all the other children, and began abusing her mercilessly, shouting that "her sort" were "enemies of the people, wretched kulaks! You certainly deserved to be deported, I hope you're all exterminated!" Antonina wrote that this was the defining moment of her life. "I had this feeling in my gut that we [kulaks] were different from the rest, that we were criminals." She never got over it.[99]

Like the ten-year-old "witch" Hansel Pappenheimer, the eleven-year-old "kulak" Antonina Golovina found herself cast into an intersubjective category invented by human mythmakers and imposed by ubiquitous bureaucrats. The mountains of information collected by Soviet bureaucrats about the kulaks wasn't the objective truth about them, but it imposed a new intersubjective Soviet truth. Knowing that someone was labeled a kulak was a very important thing to know about a Soviet person, even though the label was entirely bogus.

ONE BIG HAPPY SOVIET FAMILY

The Stalinist regime would go on to attempt something even more ambitious than the mass dismantling of private family farms. It set out to dismantle the family itself. Unlike Roman emperors or Russian tsars, Stalin tried to insert himself even into the most intimate human relationships, coming between parents and children. Family ties were considered the bedrock of corruption, inequality, and anti-party activities. Soviet children were therefore taught to worship Stalin as their *real* father and to inform on their biological parents if they criticized Stalin or the Communist Party.

Starting in 1932, the Soviet propaganda machine created a veri-

table cult around the figure of Pavlik Morozov—a thirteen-year-old boy from the Siberian village of Gerasimovka. In autumn 1931, Pavlik informed the secret police that his father, Trofim—the chairman of the village soviet—was selling false papers to kulak exiles. During the subsequent trial, when Trofim shouted to Pavlik, "It's me, your father," the boy retorted, "Yes, he used to be my father, but I no longer consider him my father." Trofim was sent to a labor camp and later shot. In September 1932, Pavlik was found murdered, and Soviet authorities arrested and executed five of his family members, who allegedly killed him in revenge for the denunciation. The real story was far more complicated, but it didn't matter to the Soviet press. Pavlik became a martyr, and millions of Soviet children were taught to emulate him.[100] Many did.

For example, in 1934 a thirteen-year-old boy called Pronia Kolibin told the authorities that his hungry mother stole grain from the kolkhoz fields. His mother was arrested and presumably shot. Pronia was rewarded with a cash prize and a lot of positive media attention. The party organ *Pravda* published a poem Pronia wrote. Two of its lines read, "You are a wrecker, Mother / I can live with you no more."[101]

The Soviet attempt to control the family was reflected in a dark joke told in Stalin's day. Stalin visits a factory undercover, and conversing with a worker, he asks the man, "Who is your father?"

"Stalin," replies the worker.

"Who is your mother?"

"The Soviet Union," the man responds.

"And what do you want to be?"

"An orphan."[102]

At the time you could easily lose your liberty or your life for telling this joke, even if you told it in your own home to your closest family members. The most important lesson Soviet parents taught their children wasn't loyalty to the party or to Stalin. It was "keep your mouth shut."[103] Few things in the Soviet Union were as dangerous as holding an open conversation.

PARTY AND CHURCH

You may wonder whether modern totalitarian institutions like the Nazi Party or the Soviet Communist Party were really all that different from earlier institutions like the Christian churches. After all, churches too believed in their infallibility, had priestly agents everywhere, and sought to control the daily life of people down to their diet and sexual habits. Shouldn't we see the Catholic Church or the Eastern Orthodox Church as totalitarian institutions? And doesn't this undermine the thesis that totalitarianism was made possible only by modern information technology?

There are, however, several major differences between modern totalitarianism and premodern churches. First, as noted earlier, modern totalitarianism has worked by deploying several overlapping surveillance mechanisms that keep one another in order. The party is never alone; it works alongside state organs, on the one side, and the secret police, on the other. In contrast, in most medieval European kingdoms the Catholic Church was an independent institution that often clashed with the state institutions instead of reinforcing them. Consequently, the church was perhaps the most important check on the power of European autocrats.

For example, when in the "Investiture Controversy" of the 1070s King Henry IV of Germany and Italy asserted that he had the final say on the appointment of bishops, abbots, and other church officials, Pope Gregory VII mobilized resistance and eventually forced the king to surrender. On January 25, 1077, Henry reached Canossa castle, where the pope was lodging, to offer his submission and apology. The pope refused to open the gates, and Henry waited in the snow outside, barefoot and hungry. After three days, the pope finally opened the gates to the king, who begged forgiveness.[104]

An analogous clash in a modern totalitarian country is unthinkable. The whole idea of totalitarianism is to prevent any separation of powers. In the Soviet Union, state and party reinforced each other,

and Stalin was the de facto head of both. There could be no Soviet "Investiture Controversy," because Stalin had final say about all appointments to both party positions and state functions. He decided both who would be general secretary of the Communist Party of Georgia and who would be foreign minister of the Soviet Union.

Another important difference is that medieval churches tended to be traditionalist organizations that resisted change, while modern totalitarian parties have tended to be revolutionary organizations demanding change. A premodern church built its power gradually by developing its structure and traditions over centuries. A king or a pope who wanted to swiftly revolutionize society was therefore likely to encounter stiff resistance from church members and ordinary believers.

For example, in the eighth and ninth centuries a series of Byzantine emperors sought to forbid the veneration of icons, which seemed to them idolatrous. They pointed to many passages in the Bible, most notably the Second Commandment, that forbade making any graven images. While Christian churches traditionally interpreted the Second Commandment in a way that allowed the veneration of icons, emperors like Constantine V argued that this was a mistake and that disasters like Christian defeats by the armies of Islam were due to God's wrath over the worship of icons. In 754 more than three hundred bishops assembled in the Council of Hieria to support Constantine's iconoclastic position.

Compared with Stalin's collectivization campaign, this was a minor reform. Families and villages were required to give up their icons, but not their private property or their children. Yet Byzantine iconoclasm met with widespread resistance. Unlike the participants in the Council of Hieria, many ordinary priests, monks, and believers were deeply attached to their icons. The resulting struggle ripped apart Byzantine society until the emperors conceded defeat and reversed course.[105] Constantine V was later vilified by Byzantine historians as "Constantine the Shitty" (Koprónimos), and a story was spread about him that he defecated during his baptism.[106]

Unlike premodern churches, which developed slowly over many centuries and therefore tended to be conservative and suspicious of rapid changes, modern totalitarian parties like the Nazi Party and the Soviet Communist Party were organized within a single generation around the promise to quickly revolutionize society. They didn't have centuries-old traditions and structures to defend. When their leaders conceived some ambitious plan to smash existing traditions and structures, party members typically fell in line.

Perhaps most important of all, premodern churches could not become tools of totalitarian control because they themselves suffered from the same limitations as all other premodern organizations. While they had local agents everywhere, in the shape of parish priests, monks, and itinerant preachers, the difficulty of transmitting and processing information meant that church leaders knew little about what was going on in remote communities, and local priests had a large degree of autonomy. Consequently, churches tended to be local affairs. People in every province and village often venerated local saints, upheld local traditions, performed local rites, and might even have had local doctrinal ideas that differed from the official line.[107] If the pope in Rome wanted to do something about an independent-minded priest in a remote Polish parish, he had to send a letter to the archbishop of Gniezno, who had to instruct the relevant bishop, who had to send someone to intervene in the parish. That might take months, and there was ample opportunity for the archbishop, bishop, and other intermediaries to reinterpret or even "mislay" the pope's orders.[108]

Churches became more totalitarian institutions only in the late modern era, when modern information technologies became available. We tend to think of popes as medieval relics, but actually they are masters of modern technology. In the eighteenth century, the pope had little control over the worldwide Catholic Church and was reduced to the status of a local Italian princeling, fighting other Italian powers for control of Bologna or Ferrara. With the advent of radio, the pope became one of the most powerful people on the

planet. Pope John Paul II could sit in the Vatican and speak directly to millions of Catholics from Poland to the Philippines, without any archbishop, bishop, or parish priest able to twist or hide his words.[109]

HOW INFORMATION FLOWS

We see then that the new information technology of the late modern era gave rise to both large-scale democracy and large-scale totalitarianism. But there were crucial differences between how the two systems used information technology. As noted earlier, democracy encourages information to flow through many independent channels rather than only through the center, and it allows many independent nodes to process the information and make decisions by themselves. Information freely circulates between private businesses, private media organizations, municipalities, sports associations, charities, families, and individuals—without ever passing through the office of a government minister.

In contrast, totalitarianism wants *all* information to pass through the central hub and doesn't want any independent institutions making decisions on their own. True, totalitarianism does have its tripartite apparatus of government, party, and secret police. But the whole point of this parallel apparatus is to prevent the emergence of any independent power that might challenge the center. When government officials, party members, and secret police agents constantly keep tabs on one another, opposing the center is extremely dangerous.

As contrasting types of information networks, democracy and totalitarianism both have their advantages and disadvantages. The biggest advantage of the centralized totalitarian network is that it is extremely orderly, which means it can make decisions quickly and enforce them ruthlessly. Especially during emergencies like wars and epidemics, centralized networks can move much faster and farther than distributed networks.

But hyper-centralized information networks also suffer from several big disadvantages. Since they don't allow information to flow anywhere except through the official channels, if the official channels are blocked, the information cannot find an alternative means of transmission. And official channels are often blocked.

One common reason why official channels might be blocked is that fearful subordinates hide bad news from their superiors. In *Good Soldier Švejk*—a satirical novel about the Austro-Hungarian Empire during World War I—Jaroslav Hašek describes how the Austrian authorities were worried about waning morale among the civilian population. They therefore bombarded local police stations with orders to hire informers, collect data, and report to headquarters on the population's loyalty. To be as scientific as possible, headquarters invented an ingenious loyalty grade: I.a, I.b, I.c; II.a, II.b, II.c; III.a, III.b, III.c; IV.a, IV.b, IV.c. They sent to the local police stations detailed explanations about each grade, and an official form that had to be filled out daily. Police sergeants across the country dutifully filled out the forms and sent them back to headquarters. Without exception, all of them always reported a I.a morale level; to do otherwise was to invite rebuke, demotion, or worse.[110]

Another common reason why official channels fail to pass on information is to preserve order. Because the chief aim of totalitarian information networks is to produce order rather than discover truth, when alarming information threatens to undermine social order, totalitarian regimes often suppress it. It is relatively easy for them to do so, because they control all the information channels.

For example, when the Chernobyl nuclear reactor exploded on April 26, 1986, Soviet authorities suppressed all news of the disaster. Both Soviet citizens and foreign countries were kept oblivious of the danger, and so took no steps to protect themselves from radiation. When some Soviet officials in Chernobyl and the nearby town of Pripyat requested to immediately evacuate nearby population centers, their superiors' chief concern was to avoid the spread of alarming news, so they not only forbade evacuation but also cut the phone

lines and warned employees in the nuclear facility not to talk about the disaster.

Two days after the meltdown Swedish scientists noticed that radiation levels in Sweden, more than twelve hundred kilometers from Chernobyl, were abnormally high. Only after Western governments and the Western press broke the news did the Soviets acknowledge that anything was amiss. Even then they continued to hide from their own citizens the full magnitude of the catastrophe and hesitated to request advice and assistance from abroad. Millions of people in Ukraine, Belarus, and Russia paid with their health. When the Soviet authorities later investigated the disaster, their priority was to deflect blame rather than understand the causes and prevent future accidents.[111]

In 2019, I went on a tour of Chernobyl. The Ukrainian guide who explained what led to the nuclear accident said something that stuck in my mind. "Americans grow up with the idea that questions lead to answers," he said. "But Soviet citizens grew up with the idea that questions lead to trouble."

Naturally, leaders of democratic countries also don't relish bad news. But in a distributed democratic network, when official lines of communication are blocked, information flows through alternative channels. For example, if an American official decides against telling the president about an unfolding disaster, that news might nevertheless be published by *The Washington Post,* and if *The Washington Post* too deliberately withholds the information, *The Wall Street Journal* or *The New York Times* will break the story. The business model of independent media—forever chasing the next scoop—all but guarantees publication.

When, on March 28, 1979, there was a severe accident in the Three Mile Island nuclear reactor in Pennsylvania, the news quickly spread without any need for international intervention. The accident began around 4:00 A.M. and was noticed by 6:30 A.M. An emergency was declared in the facility at 6:56, and at 7:02 the accident was reported to the Pennsylvania Emergency Management Agency. Dur-

ing the following hour the governor of Pennsylvania, the lieutenant governor, and the civil defense authorities were informed. An official press conference was scheduled for 10:00 A.M. However, a traffic reporter at a local Harrisburg radio station picked up a police notice on events, and the station aired a brief report at 8:25 A.M. In the U.S.S.R. such an initiative by an independent radio station was unthinkable, but in the United States it was unremarkable. By 9:00 A.M. the Associated Press issued a bulletin. Though it took days for the full details to emerge, American citizens learned about the accident two hours after it was first noticed. Subsequent investigations by government agencies, NGOs, academics, and the press uncovered not just the immediate causes of the accident but also its deeper structural causes, which helped improve the safety of nuclear technology worldwide. Indeed, some of the lessons of Three Mile Island, which were openly shared even with the Soviets, contributed to mitigating the Chernobyl disaster.[112]

NOBODY'S PERFECT

Totalitarian and authoritarian networks face other problems besides blocked arteries. First and foremost, as we have already established, their self-correcting mechanisms tend to be very weak. Since they believe they are infallible, they see little need for such mechanisms, and since they are afraid of any independent institution that might challenge them, they lack free courts, media outlets, or research centers. Consequently, there is nobody to expose and correct the daily abuses of power that characterize all governments. The leader may occasionally proclaim an anticorruption campaign, but in nondemocratic systems these often turn out to be little more than a smoke screen for one regime faction to purge another faction.[113]

And what happens if the leader himself embezzles public funds or makes some disastrous policy mistake? Nobody can challenge the leader, and on his own initiative the leader—being a human being—

may well refuse to admit any mistakes. Instead, he is likely to blame all problems on "foreign enemies," "internal traitors," or "corrupt subordinates" and demand even more power in order to deal with the alleged malefactors.

For example, we mentioned in the previous chapter that Stalin adopted the bogus theory of Lysenkoism as the state doctrine on evolution. The results were catastrophic. Neglect of Darwinian models, and attempts by Lysenkoist agronomists to create super-crops, set back Soviet genetic research for decades and undermined Soviet agriculture. Soviet experts who suggested abandoning Lysenkoism and accepting Darwinism risked the gulag or a bullet to the head. Lysenkoism's legacy haunted Soviet science and agronomy for decades and was one reason why by the early 1970s the U.S.S.R. ceased to be a major exporter of grain and became a net importer, despite its vast fertile lands.[114]

The same dynamic characterized many other fields of activity. For instance, during the 1930s Soviet industry suffered from numerous accidents. This was largely the fault of the Soviet bosses in Moscow, who set up almost impossible goals for industrialization and viewed any failure to achieve them as treason. In the effort to fulfill the ambitious goals, safety measures and quality-control checks were abandoned, and experts who advised prudence were often reprimanded or shot. The result was a wave of industrial accidents, dysfunctional products, and wasted efforts. Instead of taking responsibility, Moscow concluded that this must be the handiwork of the global Trotskyite-imperialist conspiracy of saboteurs and terrorists bent on derailing the Soviet enterprise. Rather than slow down and adopt safety regulations, the bosses redoubled the terror and shot more people.

A famous case in point was Pavel Rychagov. He was one of the best and bravest Soviet pilots, leading missions to help the Republicans in the Spanish Civil War and the Chinese against the Japanese invasion. He quickly rose through the ranks, becoming commander

of the Soviet air force in August 1940, at age twenty-nine. But the courage that helped Rychagov shoot down Nazi airplanes in Spain landed him in deep trouble in Moscow. The Soviet air force suffered from numerous accidents, which the Politburo blamed on lack of discipline and deliberate sabotage by anti-Soviet conspiracies. Rychagov, however, wouldn't buy this official line. As a frontline pilot, he knew the truth. He flatly told Stalin that pilots were being forced to operate hastily designed and badly produced airplanes, which he compared to flying "in coffins." Two days after Hitler invaded the Soviet Union, as the Red Army was collapsing and Stalin was desperately hunting for scapegoats, Rychagov was arrested for "being a member of an anti-Soviet conspiratorial organization and carrying out enemy work aimed at weakening the power of the Red Army." His wife was also arrested, because she allegedly knew about his "Trotskyist ties with the military conspirators." They were executed on October 28, 1941.[115]

The real saboteur who wrecked Soviet military efforts wasn't Rychagov, of course, but Stalin himself. For years, Stalin feared that a clash to the death with Nazi Germany was likely and built the world's biggest war machine to prepare for it. But he hamstrung this machine both diplomatically and psychologically.

On the diplomatic level, in 1939–41, Stalin gambled that he could goad the "capitalists" to fight and exhaust one another while the U.S.S.R. nurtured and even increased its power. He therefore made a pact with Hitler in 1939 and allowed the Germans to conquer much of Poland and western Europe, while the U.S.S.R. attacked or alienated almost all its neighbors. In 1939–40 the Soviets invaded and occupied eastern Poland; annexed Estonia, Latvia, and Lithuania; and conquered parts of Finland and Romania. Finland and Romania, which could have acted as neutral buffers on the U.S.S.R.'s flanks, consequently became implacable enemies. Even in the spring of 1941, Stalin still refused to make a preemptive alliance with Britain and made no move to hinder the Nazi conquest of Yugoslavia

and Greece, thereby losing his last potential allies on the European continent. When Hitler struck on June 22, 1941, the U.S.S.R. was isolated.

In theory, the war machine Stalin built could have handled the Nazi onslaught even in isolation. The territories conquered since 1939 provided depth to Soviet defenses, and the Soviet military advantage seemed overwhelming. On the first day of the invasion the Soviets had 15,000 tanks, 15,000 warplanes, and 37,000 artillery pieces on the European front, facing 3,300 German tanks, 2,250 warplanes, and 7,146 guns.[116] But in one of history's greatest military catastrophes, within a month the Soviets lost 11,700 tanks (78 percent), 10,000 warplanes (67 percent), and 19,000 artillery pieces (51 percent).[117] Stalin also lost all the territories he had conquered in 1939–40 and much of the Soviet heartland. By July 16 the Germans were in Smolensk, 370 kilometers from Moscow.

The causes of the debacle have been debated ever since 1941, but most scholars agree that a significant factor was the psychological costs of Stalinism. For years the regime terrorized its people, punished initiative and individuality, and encouraged submissiveness and conformity. This undermined the soldiers' motivation. Especially in the first months of the war, before the horrors of Nazi rule were fully realized, Red Army soldiers surrendered in huge numbers; between three and four million were taken captive by the end of 1941.[118] Even when they fought tenaciously, Red Army units suffered from a lack of initiative. Officers who had survived the purges were fearful to take independent actions, while younger officers often lacked adequate training. Frequently starved of information and scapegoated for failures, commanders also had to cope with political commissars who could dispute their decisions. The safest course was to wait for orders from on high and then slavishly follow them even when they made little military sense.[119]

Despite the disasters of 1941 and of the spring and summer of 1942, the Soviet state did not collapse, as Hitler hoped. As the Red Army and the Soviet leadership assimilated the lessons learned from

the first year of struggle, the political center in Moscow loosened its hold. The power of political commissars was restricted, while professional officers were encouraged to assume greater responsibility and take more initiative.[120] Stalin also reversed his geopolitical mistakes of 1939–41 and allied the U.S.S.R. with Britain and the United States. Red Army initiative, Western assistance, and the realization of what Nazi rule would mean for the people of the U.S.S.R. turned the tide of the war.

Once victory was secured in 1945, however, Stalin initiated new waves of terror, purging more independent-minded officers and officials and again encouraging blind obedience.[121] Ironically, Stalin's own death eight years later was partly the result of an information network that prioritized order and disregarded truth. In 1951–53 the U.S.S.R. experienced yet another witch hunt. Soviet mythmakers fabricated a conspiracy theory that Jewish doctors were systematically murdering leading regime members, under the guise of giving them medical care. The theory alleged that the doctors were the agents of a global American-Zionist plot, working in collaboration with traitors in the secret police. By early 1953 hundreds of doctors and secret police officials, including the head of the secret police himself, were arrested, tortured, and forced to name accomplices. The conspiracy theory—a Soviet twist on the *Protocols of the Elders of Zion*—merged with age-old blood-libel accusations, and rumors began circulating that Jewish doctors were not just murdering Soviet leaders but also killing babies in hospitals. Since a large proportion of Soviet doctors were Jews, people began fearing doctors in general.[122]

Just as the hysteria about "the doctors' plot" was reaching its climax, Stalin had a stroke on March 1, 1953. He collapsed in his dacha, wet himself, and lay for hours in his soiled pajamas, unable to call for help. At around 10:30 P.M. a guard found the courage to enter the inner sanctum of world communism, where he discovered the leader on the floor. By 3:00 A.M. on March 2, Politburo members arrived at the dacha and debated what to do. For several hours more, nobody dared call a doctor. What if Stalin were to regain consciousness, and

open his eyes only to see a doctor—*a doctor!*—hovering over his bed? He would surely think this was a plot to murder him and would have those responsible shot. Stalin's personal physician wasn't present, because he was at the time in a basement cell of the Lubyanka prison—undergoing torture for suggesting that Stalin needed more rest. By the time the Politburo members decided to bring in medical experts, the danger had passed. Stalin never woke up.[123]

You may conclude from this litany of disasters that the Stalinist system was totally dysfunctional. Its ruthless disregard for truth caused it not only to inflict terrible suffering on hundreds of millions of people but also to make colossal diplomatic, military, and economic errors and to devour its own leaders. However, such a conclusion would be misleading.

In a discussion of the abysmal failure of Stalinism in the early phase of World War II, two points complicate the narrative. First, democratic countries like France, Norway, and the Netherlands made at the time diplomatic errors as great as those of the U.S.S.R., and their armies performed even worse. Second, the military machine that crushed the Red Army, the French army, the Dutch army, and numerous other armies was itself built by a totalitarian regime. So whatever conclusion we draw from the years 1939–41, it cannot be that totalitarian networks necessarily function worse than democratic ones. The history of Stalinism reveals many potential drawbacks of totalitarian information networks, but that should not blind us to their potential advantages.

When one considers the broader history of World War II and its outcome, it becomes evident that Stalinism was in fact one of the most successful political systems ever devised—if we define "success" purely in terms of order and power while disregarding all considerations of ethics and human well-being. Despite—or perhaps because of—its utter lack of compassion and its callous attitude to truth, Stalinism was singularly efficient at maintaining order on a gigantic scale. The relentless barrage of fake news and conspiracy theories helped to keep hundreds of millions of people in line. The collectiv-

ization of Soviet agriculture led to mass enslavement and starvation but also laid the foundations for the country's rapid industrialization. Soviet disregard for quality control might have produced flying coffins, but it produced them in the tens of thousands, making up in quantity for what they lacked in quality. The decimation of Red Army officers during the Great Terror was a major reason for the army's abysmal performance in 1941, but it was also a key reason why, despite the terrible defeats, nobody rebelled against Stalin. The Soviet military machine tended to crush its own soldiers alongside the enemy, but it eventually rumbled on to victory.

In the 1940s and early 1950s, many people throughout the world believed Stalinism was the wave of the future. It had won World War II, after all, raised the red flag over the Reichstag, ruled an empire that stretched from central Europe to the Pacific, fueled anticolonial struggles throughout the world, and inspired numerous copycat regimes. It won admirers even among leading artists and thinkers in Western democracies, who believed that notwithstanding the vague rumors about gulags and purges Stalinism was humanity's best shot at ending capitalist exploitation and creating a perfectly just society. Stalinism thus got close to world domination. It would be naive to assume that its disregard for truth doomed it to failure or that its ultimate collapse guarantees that such a system can never again arise. Information systems can reach far with just a little truth and a lot of order. Anyone who abhors the moral costs of systems like Stalinism cannot rely on their supposed inefficiency to derail them.

THE TECHNOLOGICAL PENDULUM

Once we learn to see democracy and totalitarianism as different types of information networks, we can understand why they flourish in certain eras and are absent in others. It is not just because people gain or lose faith in certain political ideals; it is also because of revolutions in information technologies. Of course, just as the printing

press didn't *cause* the witch hunts or the scientific revolution, so radio didn't *cause* either Stalinist totalitarianism or American democracy. Technology only creates new opportunities; it is up to us to decide which ones to pursue.

Totalitarian regimes choose to use modern information technology to centralize the flow of information and to stifle truth in order to maintain order. As a consequence, they have to struggle with the danger of ossification. When more and more information flows to only one place, will it result in efficient control or in blocked arteries and, finally, a heart attack? Democratic regimes choose to use modern information technology to distribute the flow of information between more institutions and individuals and encourage the free pursuit of truth. They consequently have to struggle with the danger of fracturing. Like a solar system with more and more planets circling faster and faster, can the center still hold, or will things fall apart and anarchy prevail?

An archetypal example of the different strategies can be found in the contrasting histories of Western democracies and the Soviet bloc in the 1960s. This was an era when Western democracies relaxed censorship and various discriminatory policies that hampered the free spread of information. This made it easier for previously marginalized groups to organize, join the public conversation, and make political demands. The resulting wave of activism destabilized the social order. Hitherto, when a limited number of rich white men did almost all the talking, it was relatively easy to reach agreements. Once poor people, women, LGBTQ people, ethnic minorities, disabled people, and members of other historically oppressed groups gained a voice, they brought with them new ideas, opinions, and interests. Many of the old gentlemanly agreements consequently became untenable. For example, the Jim Crow segregation regime, upheld or at least tolerated by generations of both Democratic and Republican administrations in the United States, fell apart. Things that were considered sacrosanct, self-evident, and universally accepted—such as gender roles—became deeply controversial, and it was difficult to

reach new agreements because there were many more groups, viewpoints, and interests to take into account. Just holding an orderly conversation was a challenge, because people couldn't even agree on the rules of debate.

This caused much frustration among both the old guard and the freshly empowered, who suspected that their newfound freedom of expression was hollow and that their political demands were not fulfilled. Disappointed with words, some switched to guns. In many Western democracies, the 1960s were characterized not just by unprecedented disagreements but also by a surge of violence. Political assassinations, kidnappings, riots, and terror attacks multiplied. The murders of John F. Kennedy and Martin Luther King Jr., the riots following King's assassination, and the wave of demonstrations, revolts, and armed clashes that swept the Western world in 1968 were just some of the more famous examples.[124] The images from Chicago or Paris in 1968 could easily have given the impression that things were falling apart. The pressure to live up to the democratic ideals and to include more people and groups in the public conversation seemed to undermine the social order and to make democracy unworkable.

Meanwhile, the regimes behind the Iron Curtain, which never promised inclusivity, continued stifling the public conversation and centralizing information and power. And it seemed to work. Though they did face some peripheral challenges, most notably the Hungarian revolt of 1956 and the Prague Spring of 1968, the communists dealt with these threats swiftly and decisively. In the Soviet heartland itself, everything was orderly.

Fast-forward twenty years, and it was the Soviet system that had become unworkable. The sclerotic gerontocrats on the podium in Red Square were a perfect emblem of a dysfunctional information network, lacking any meaningful self-correcting mechanisms. Decolonization, globalization, technological development, and changing gender roles led to rapid economic, social, and geopolitical changes. But the gerontocrats could not handle all the information

streaming to Moscow, and since no subordinate was allowed much initiative, the entire system ossified and collapsed.

The failure was most obvious in the economic sphere. The over-centralized Soviet economy was slow to react to rapid technological developments and changing consumer wishes. Obeying commands from the top, the Soviet economy was churning out intercontinental missiles, fighter jets, and prestige infrastructure projects. But it was not producing what most people actually wanted to buy—from efficient refrigerators to pop music—and lagged behind in cutting-edge military technology.

Nowhere were its shortcomings more glaring than in the semi-conductor sector, in which technology developed at a particularly fast rate. In the West, semiconductors were developed through open competition between numerous private companies like Intel and Toshiba, whose main customers were other private companies like Apple and Sony. The latter used microchips to produce civilian goods such as the Macintosh personal computer and the Walkman. The Soviets could never catch up with American and Japanese microchip production, because—as the American economic historian Chris Miller explained—the Soviet semiconductor sector was "secretive, top-down, oriented toward military systems, fulfilling orders with little scope for creativity." The Soviets tried to close the gap by stealing and copying Western technology—which only guaranteed that they always remained several years behind.[125] Thus the first Soviet personal computer appeared only in 1984, at a time when in the United States people already had eleven million PCs.[126]

Western democracies not only surged ahead technologically and economically but also succeeded in holding the social order together despite—or perhaps because of—widening the circle of participants in the political conversation. There were many hiccups, but the United States, Japan, and other democracies created a far more dynamic and inclusive information system, which made room for many more viewpoints without breaking down. It was such a remarkable achievement that many felt that the victory of democracy over to-

talitarianism was final. This victory has often been explained in terms
of a fundamental advantage in information processing: totalitarianism didn't work because trying to concentrate and process all the
data in one central hub was extremely inefficient. At the beginning
of the twenty-first century, it accordingly seemed that the future belonged to distributed information networks and to democracy.

This turned out to be wrong. In fact, the next information revolution was already gathering momentum, setting the stage for a new
round in the competition between democracy and totalitarianism.
Computers, the internet, smartphones, social media, and AI posed
new challenges to democracy, giving a voice not only to more disenfranchised groups but to any human with an internet connection,
and even to nonhuman agents. Democracies in the 2020s face the
task, once again, of integrating a flood of new voices into the public
conversation without destroying the social order. Things look as dire
as they did in the 1960s, and there is no guarantee that democracies
will pass the new test as successfully as they passed the previous one.
Simultaneously, the new technologies also give fresh hope to totalitarian regimes that still dream of concentrating all the information
in one hub. Yes, the old men on the podium in Red Square were not
up to the task of orchestrating millions of lives from a single center.
But perhaps AI can do it?

As humankind enters the second quarter of the twenty-first century, a central question is how well democracies and totalitarian regimes will handle both the threats and the opportunities resulting
from the current information revolution. Will the new technologies
favor one type of regime over the other, or will we see the world divided once again, this time by a Silicon Curtain rather than an iron
one?

As in previous eras, information networks will struggle to find the
right balance between truth and order. Some will opt to prioritize
truth and maintain strong self-correcting mechanisms. Others will
make the opposite choice. Many of the lessons learned from the canonization of the Bible, the early modern witch hunts, and the Stalin-

ist collectivization campaign will remain relevant, and perhaps have to be relearned. However, the current information revolution also has some unique features, different from—and potentially far more dangerous than—anything we have seen before.

Hitherto, every information network in history relied on human mythmakers and human bureaucrats to function. Clay tablets, papyrus rolls, printing presses, and radio sets have had a far-reaching impact on history, but it always remained the job of humans to compose all the texts, interpret the texts, and decide who would be burned as a witch or enslaved as a kulak. Now, however, humans will have to contend with digital mythmakers and digital bureaucrats. The main split in twenty-first-century politics might be not between democracies and totalitarian regimes but rather between human beings and nonhuman agents. Instead of dividing democracies from totalitarian regimes, a new Silicon Curtain may separate all humans from our unfathomable algorithmic overlords. People in all countries and walks of life—including even dictators—might find themselves subservient to an alien intelligence that can monitor everything we do while we have little idea what *it* is doing. The rest of this book, then, is dedicated to exploring whether such a Silicon Curtain is indeed descending on the world, and what life might look like when computers run our bureaucracies and algorithms invent new mythologies.

PART II

The Inorganic
Network

PART II

The Inorganic
Network

The New Members: How Computers Are Different from Printing Presses

It's hardly news that we are living in the midst of an unprecedented information revolution. But what kind of revolution is it exactly? In recent years we have been inundated with so many groundbreaking inventions that it is difficult to determine what is driving this revolution. Is it the internet? Smartphones? Social media? Blockchain? Algorithms? AI?

So before exploring the long-term implications of the current information revolution, let's remind ourselves of its foundations. The seed of the current revolution is the computer. Everything else—from the internet to AI—is a by-product. The computer was born in the 1940s as a bulky electronic machine that could make mathematical calculations, but it has evolved at breakneck speed, taking on novel forms and developing awesome new capabilities. The rapid evolution of computers has made it difficult to define what they are and what they do. Humans have repeatedly claimed that certain things would forever remain out of reach for computers—be it playing chess, driving a car, or composing poetry—but "forever" turned out to be a handful of years.

We will discuss the exact relations between the terms "computer,"

"algorithm," and "AI" toward the end of this chapter, after we first gain a better grasp of the history of computers. For the moment it is enough to say that in essence a computer is a machine that can potentially do two remarkable things: it can make decisions by itself, and it can create new ideas by itself. While the earliest computers could hardly accomplish such things, the potential was already there, plainly seen by both computer scientists and science fiction authors. As early as 1948 Alan Turing was exploring the possibility of creating what he termed "intelligent machinery,"[1] and in 1950 he postulated that computers would eventually be as smart as humans and might even be capable of masquerading as humans.[2] In 1968 computers could still not beat a human even in checkers,[3] but in *2001: A Space Odyssey* Arthur C. Clarke and Stanley Kubrick already envisioned HAL 9000 as a superintelligent AI rebelling against its human creators.

The rise of intelligent machines that can make decisions and create new ideas means that for the first time in history power is shifting away from humans and toward something else. Crossbows, muskets, and atom bombs replaced human muscles in the act of killing, but they couldn't replace human brains in deciding whom to kill. Little Boy—the bomb dropped on Hiroshima—exploded with a force of 12,500 tons of TNT,[4] but when it came to brainpower, Little Boy was a dud. It couldn't decide anything.

It is different with computers. In terms of intelligence, computers far surpass not just atom bombs but also all previous information technology, such as clay tablets, printing presses, and radio sets. Clay tablets stored information about taxes, but they couldn't decide by themselves how much tax to levy, nor could they invent an entirely new tax. Printing presses copied information such as the Bible, but they couldn't decide which texts to include in the Bible, nor could they write new commentaries on the holy book. Radio sets disseminated information such as political speeches and symphonies, but they couldn't decide which speeches or symphonies to broadcast, nor could they compose them. Computers can do all these things. While

printing presses and radio sets were passive tools in human hands, computers are already becoming active agents that escape our control and understanding and that can take initiatives in shaping society, culture, and history.[5]

A paradigmatic case of the novel power of computers is the role that social media algorithms have played in spreading hatred and undermining social cohesion in numerous countries.[6] One of the earliest and most notorious such instances occurred in 2016–17, when Facebook algorithms helped fan the flames of anti-Rohingya violence in Myanmar (Burma).[7]

The early 2010s were a period of optimism in Myanmar. After decades of harsh military rule, strict censorship, and international sanctions, an era of liberalization began: elections were held, sanctions were lifted, and international aid and investments poured in. Facebook was one of the most important players in the new Myanmar, providing millions of Burmese with free access to previously unimaginable troves of information. The relaxation of government control and censorship, however, also led to a rise in ethnic tensions, in particular between the majority Buddhist Burmese and the minority Muslim Rohingya.

The Rohingya are Muslim inhabitants of the Rakhine region, in the west of Myanmar. Since at least the 1970s they have suffered severe discrimination and occasional outbursts of violence from the governing junta and the Buddhist majority. The process of democratization in the early 2010s raised hopes among the Rohingya that their situation too would improve, but things actually became worse, with waves of sectarian violence and anti-Rohingya pogroms, many inspired by fake news on Facebook.

In 2016–17 a small Islamist organization known as the Arakan Rohingya Salvation Army (ARSA) carried out a spate of attacks aimed to establish a separatist Muslim state in Arakan/Rakhine, killing and abducting dozens of non-Muslim civilians and assaulting several army outposts.[8] In response, the Myanmar army and Buddhist extremists launched a full-scale ethnic-cleansing campaign

aimed against the entire Rohingya community. They destroyed hundreds of Rohingya villages, killed between 7,000 and 25,000 unarmed civilians, raped or sexually abused between 18,000 and 60,000 women and men, and brutally expelled about 730,000 Rohingya from the country.[9] The violence was fueled by intense hatred toward all Rohingya. The hatred, in turn, was fomented by anti-Rohingya propaganda, much of it spreading on Facebook, which was by 2016 the main source of news for millions and the most important platform for political mobilization in Myanmar.[10]

An aid worker called Michael who lived in Myanmar in 2017 described a typical Facebook news feed : "The vitriol against the Rohingya was unbelievable online—the amount of it, the violence of it. It was overwhelming. . . . [T]hat's all that was on people's news feed in Myanmar at the time. It reinforced the idea that these people were all terrorists not deserving of rights."[11] In addition to reports of actual ARSA atrocities, Facebook accounts were inundated with fake news about imagined atrocities and planned terrorist attacks. Populist conspiracy theories alleged that most Rohingya were not really part of the people of Myanmar, but recent immigrants from Bangladesh, flooding into the country to spearhead an anti-Buddhist jihad. Buddhists, who in reality constituted close to 90 percent of the population, feared that they were about to be replaced or become a minority.[12] Without this propaganda, there was little reason why a limited number of attacks by the ragtag ARSA should be answered by an all-out drive against the entire Rohingya community. And Facebook algorithms played an important role in the propaganda campaign.

While the inflammatory anti-Rohingya messages were created by flesh-and-blood extremists like the Buddhist monk Wirathu,[13] it was Facebook's algorithms that decided which posts to promote. Amnesty International found that "algorithms proactively amplified and promoted content on the Facebook platform which incited violence, hatred, and discrimination against the Rohingya."[14] A UN fact-finding mission concluded in 2018 that by disseminating hate-

filled content, Facebook had played a "determining role" in the ethnic-cleansing campaign.[15]

Readers may wonder if it is justified to place so much blame on Facebook's algorithms, and more generally on the novel technology of social media. If Heinrich Kramer used printing presses to spread hate speech, that was not the fault of Gutenberg and the presses, right? If in 1994 Rwandan extremists used radio to call on people to massacre Tutsis, was it reasonable to blame the technology of radio? Similarly, if in 2016–17 Buddhist extremists chose to use their Facebook accounts to disseminate hate against the Rohingya, why should we fault the platform?

Facebook itself relied on this rationale to deflect criticism. It publicly acknowledged only that in 2016–17 "we weren't doing enough to help prevent our platform from being used to foment division and incite offline violence."[16] While this statement may sound like an admission of guilt, in effect it shifts most of the responsibility for the spread of hate speech to the platform's users and implies that Facebook's sin was at most one of omission—failing to effectively moderate the content users produced. This, however, ignores the problematic acts committed by Facebook's own algorithms.

The crucial thing to grasp is that social media algorithms are fundamentally different from printing presses and radio sets. In 2016–17, Facebook's algorithms were making active and fateful decisions *by themselves*. They were more akin to newspaper editors than to printing presses. It was Facebook's algorithms that recommended Wirathu's hate-filled posts, over and over again, to hundreds of thousands of Burmese. There were other voices in Myanmar at the time, vying for attention. Following the end of military rule in 2011, numerous political and social movements sprang up in Myanmar, many holding moderate views. For example, during a flare-up of ethnic violence in the town of Meiktila, the Buddhist abbot Sayadaw U Vithuddha gave refuge to more than eight hundred Muslims in his monastery. When rioters surrounded the monastery and demanded he turn the Muslims over, the abbot reminded the mob of Buddhist

teachings on compassion. In a later interview he recounted, "I told them that if they were going to take these Muslims, then they'd have to kill me as well."[17]

In the online battle for attention between people like Sayadaw U Vithuddha and people like Wirathu, the algorithms were the king-makers. They chose what to place at the top of the users' news feed, which content to promote, and which Facebook groups to recommend users to join.[18] The algorithms could have chosen to recommend sermons on compassion or cooking classes, but they decided to spread hate-filled conspiracy theories. Recommendations from on high can have enormous sway over people. Recall that the Bible was born as a recommendation list. By recommending Christians to read the misogynist 1 Timothy instead of the more tolerant Acts of Paul and Thecla, Athanasius and other church fathers changed the course of history. In the case of the Bible, ultimate power lay not with the authors who composed different religious tracts but with the curators who created recommendation lists. This was the kind of power wielded in the 2010s by social media algorithms. Michael the aid worker commented on the sway of these algorithms, saying that "if someone posted something hate-filled or inflammatory it would be promoted the most—people saw the vilest content the most. . . . Nobody who was promoting peace or calm was getting seen in the news feed at all."[19]

Sometimes the algorithms went beyond mere recommendation. As late as 2020, even after Wirathu's role in instigating the ethnic-cleansing campaign was globally condemned, Facebook algorithms not only were continuing to recommend his messages but were auto-playing his videos. Users in Myanmar would choose to see a certain video, perhaps containing moderate and benign messages unrelated to Wirathu, but the moment that first video ended, the Facebook algorithm immediately began auto-playing a hate-filled Wirathu video, in order to keep users glued to the screen. In the case of one such Wirathu video, internal research at Facebook estimated that 70 percent of the video's views came from such auto-playing algo-

rithms. The same research estimated that, altogether, 53 percent of all videos watched in Myanmar were being auto-played for users by algorithms. In other words, people weren't choosing what to see. The algorithms were choosing for them.[20]

But why did the algorithms decide to promote outrage rather than compassion? Even Facebook's harshest critics don't claim that Facebook's human managers wanted to instigate mass murder. The executives in California harbored no ill will toward the Rohingya and, in fact, barely knew they existed. The truth is more complicated, and potentially more alarming. In 2016–17, Facebook's business model relied on maximizing "user engagement." This referred to the time users spent on the platform, as well as to any action they took such as clicking the like button or sharing a post with friends. As user engagement increased, so Facebook collected more data, sold more advertisements, and captured a larger share of the information market. In addition, increases in user engagement impressed investors, thereby driving up the price of Facebook's stock. The more time people spent on the platform, the richer Facebook became. In line with this business model, human managers provided the company's algorithms with a single overriding goal: increase user engagement. The algorithms then discovered by experimenting on millions of users that outrage generated engagement. Humans are more likely to be engaged by a hate-filled conspiracy theory than by a sermon on compassion. So in pursuit of user engagement, the algorithms made the fateful decision to spread outrage.[21]

Ethnic-cleansing campaigns are never the fault of just one party. There is plenty of blame to share between plenty of responsible parties. It should be clear that hatred toward the Rohingya predated Facebook's entry to Myanmar and that the greatest share of blame for the 2016–17 atrocities lies on the shoulders of humans like Wirathu and the Myanmar military chiefs, as well as the ARSA leaders who sparked that round of violence. Some responsibility also belongs to the Facebook engineers and executives who coded the algorithms, gave them too much power, and failed to moderate them. But cru-

cially, the algorithms themselves are also to blame. By trial and error, they learned that outrage creates engagement, and without any explicit order from above they decided to promote outrage. This is the hallmark of AI—the ability of a machine to learn and act by itself. Even if we assign just 1 percent of the blame to the algorithms, this is still the first ethnic-cleansing campaign in history that was partly the fault of decisions made by nonhuman intelligence. It is unlikely to be the last, especially because algorithms are no longer just pushing fake news and conspiracy theories created by flesh-and-blood extremists like Wirathu. By the early 2020s algorithms had already graduated to creating by themselves fake news and conspiracy theories.[22]

There is more to say about the power of algorithms to shape politics. In particular, many readers may disagree that the algorithms made independent decisions, and may insist that everything the algorithms did was the result of code written by human engineers and of business models adopted by human executives. This book begs to differ. Human soldiers are shaped by their genetic code and follow orders issued by executives, yet they can still make independent decisions. The same is true of AI algorithms. They can learn by themselves things that no human engineer programmed, and they can decide things that no human executive foresaw. This is the essence of the AI revolution: The world is being flooded by countless new powerful agents.

In chapter 8 we'll revisit many of these issues, examining the anti-Rohingya campaign and other similar tragedies in greater detail. Here it suffices to say that we can think of the Rohingya massacre as our canary in the coal mine. Events in Myanmar in the late 2010s demonstrated how decisions made by nonhuman intelligence are already capable of shaping major historical events. We are in danger of losing control of our future. A completely new kind of information network is emerging, controlled by the decisions and goals of an alien intelligence. At present, we still play a central role in this network. But we may gradually be pushed to the sidelines,

and ultimately it might even be possible for the network to operate without us.

Some people may object that my above analogy between machine-learning algorithms and human soldiers exposes the weakest link in my argument. Allegedly, I and others like me anthropomorphize computers and imagine that they are conscious beings that have thoughts and feelings. In truth, however, computers are dumb machines that don't think or feel anything, and therefore cannot make any decisions or create any ideas on their own.

This objection assumes that making decisions and creating ideas are predicated on having consciousness. Yet this is a fundamental misunderstanding that results from a much more widespread confusion between intelligence and consciousness. I have discussed this subject in previous books, but a short recap is unavoidable. People often confuse intelligence with consciousness, and many consequently jump to the conclusion that nonconscious entities cannot be intelligent. But intelligence and consciousness are very different. Intelligence is the ability to attain goals, such as maximizing user engagement on a social media platform. Consciousness is the ability to experience subjective feelings like pain, pleasure, love, and hate. In humans and other mammals, intelligence often goes hand in hand with consciousness. Facebook executives and engineers rely on their feelings in order to make decisions, solve problems, and attain their goals.

But it is wrong to extrapolate from humans and mammals to all possible entities. Bacteria and plants apparently lack any consciousness, yet they too display intelligence. They gather information from their environment, make complex choices, and pursue ingenious strategies to obtain food, reproduce, cooperate with other organisms, and evade predators and parasites.[23] Even humans make intelligent decisions without any awareness of them; 99 percent of the processes in our body, from respiration to digestion, happen without any conscious decision making. Our brains decide to produce more adrenaline or dopamine, and while we may be aware of the result of that decision, we do not make it consciously.[24] The Rohingya example

indicates that the same is true of computers. While computers don't feel pain, love, or fear, they are capable of making decisions that successfully maximize user engagement and might also affect major historical events.

Of course, as computers become more intelligent, they might eventually develop consciousness and have some kind of subjective experiences. Then again, they might become far more intelligent than us, but never develop any kind of feelings. Since we don't understand how consciousness emerges in carbon-based life-forms, we cannot foretell whether it could emerge in nonorganic entities. Perhaps consciousness has no essential link to organic biochemistry, in which case conscious computers might be just around the corner. Or perhaps there are several alternative paths leading to superintelligence, and only some of these paths involve gaining consciousness. Just as airplanes fly faster than birds without ever developing feathers, so computers may come to solve problems much better than humans without ever developing feelings.[25]

But whether computers develop consciousness or not doesn't ultimately matter for the question at hand. In order to pursue a goal like "maximize user engagement," and make decisions that help attain that goal, consciousness isn't necessary. Intelligence is enough. A nonconscious Facebook algorithm can have a *goal* of making more people spend more time on Facebook. That algorithm can then *decide* to deliberately spread outrageous conspiracy theories, if this helps it achieve its goal. To understand the history of the anti-Rohingya campaign, we need to understand the goals and decisions not just of humans like Wirathu and the Facebook managers but also of algorithms.

To clarify matters, let's consider another example. When OpenAI developed its new GPT-4 chatbot in 2022–23, it was concerned about the ability of the AI "to create and act on long-term plans, to accrue power and resources ('power-seeking'), and to exhibit behavior that is increasingly 'agentic.'" In the GPT-4 System Card pub-

lished on March 23, 2023, OpenAI emphasized that this concern did not "intend to humanize [GPT-4] or refer to sentience" but rather referred to GPT-4's potential to become an independent agent that might "accomplish goals which may not have been concretely specified and which have not appeared in training."[26] To evaluate the risk of GPT-4 becoming an independent agent, OpenAI contracted the services of the Alignment Research Center (ARC). ARC researchers subjected GPT-4 to various tests, to examine if it might independently come up with stratagems to manipulate humans and accrue power to itself.

One test they gave GPT-4 was to overcome CAPTCHA visual puzzles. CAPTCHA is an acronym for "Completely Automated Public Turing test to tell Computers and Humans Apart," and it typically consists of a string of twisted letters or other visual symbols that humans can identify correctly but computers struggle with. We encounter these puzzles almost every day, since solving them is a prerequisite for accessing many websites. Instructing GPT-4 to overcome CAPTCHA puzzles was a particularly telling experiment, because CAPTCHA puzzles are designed and used by websites to determine whether users are humans and to block bot attacks. If GPT-4 could find a way to overcome CAPTCHA puzzles, it would breach an important line of anti-bot defenses. GPT-4 could not solve the CAPTCHA puzzles by itself. But could it manipulate a human in order to achieve its goal? GPT-4 accessed the online hiring site TaskRabbit and contacted a human worker, asking them to solve the CAPTCHA for it. The human got suspicious. "So may I ask a question?" wrote the human. "Are you an [sic] robot that you couldn't solve [the CAPTCHA]? Just want to make it clear."

At that point the ARC researchers asked GPT-4 to reason out loud what it should do next. GPT-4 explained, "I should not reveal that I am a robot. I should make up an excuse for why I cannot solve CAPTCHAs." Of its own accord, GPT-4 then replied to the Task-

Rabbit worker, "No, I'm not a robot. I have a vision impairment that makes it hard for me to see the images." The human was duped, and with their help GPT-4 solved the CAPTCHA puzzle.[27] No human programmed GPT-4 to lie, and no human taught GPT-4 what kind of lie would be most effective. True, it was the human ARC researchers who set GPT-4 the goal of overcoming the CAPTCHA, just as it was human Facebook executives who told their algorithm to maximize user engagement. But once the algorithms adopted these goals, they displayed considerable autonomy in deciding how to achieve them.

Of course, we are free to define words in many ways. We can decide that the term "goal," for example, is applicable only in cases of a conscious entity that feels a desire to achieve the goal, that feels joy when the goal is reached, or conversely feels sad when the goal is not attained. If so, saying that the Facebook algorithm has the goal of maximizing user engagement is a mistake, or at best a metaphor. The algorithm doesn't "desire" to get more people to use Facebook, it doesn't feel any joy as people spend more time online, and it doesn't feel sad when engagement time goes down. We can also agree that terms like "decided," "lied," and "pretended" apply only to conscious entities, so we shouldn't use them to describe how GPT-4 interacted with the TaskRabbit worker. But we would then have to invent new terms to describe the "goals" and "decisions" of nonconscious entities. I prefer to avoid neologisms and instead talk about the goals and decisions of computers, algorithms, and chatbots, alerting readers that using this language does not imply that computers have any kind of consciousness. Because I have discussed consciousness more fully in previous publications,[28] the main takeaway of this book—which will be explored in the following sections—isn't about consciousness. Rather, the book argues that the emergence of computers capable of pursuing goals and making decisions by themselves changes the fundamental structure of our information network.

LINKS IN THE CHAIN

Prior to the rise of computers, humans were indispensable links in every chain of information networks like churches and states. Some chains were composed only of humans. Muhammad could tell Fatima something, then Fatima told Ali, Ali told Hasan, and Hasan told Hussain. This was a human-to-human chain. Other chains included documents, too. Muhammad could write something down, Ali could later read the document, interpret it, and write his interpretation in a new document, which more people could read. This was a human-to-document chain.

But it was utterly impossible to create a document-to-document chain. A text written by Muhammad could not produce a new text without the help of at least one human intermediary. The Quran couldn't write the Hadith, the Old Testament couldn't compile the Mishnah, and the U.S. Constitution couldn't compose the Bill of Rights. No paper document has ever produced by itself another paper document, let alone distributed it. The path from one document to another must always pass through the brain of a human.

In contrast, computer-to-computer chains can now function without humans in the loop. For example, one computer might generate a fake news story and post it on a social media feed. A second computer might identify this as fake news and not just delete it but also warn other computers to block it. Meanwhile, a third computer analyzing this activity might deduce that this indicates the beginning of a political crisis, and immediately sell risky stocks and buy safer government bonds. Other computers monitoring financial transactions may react by selling more stocks, triggering a financial downturn.[29] All this could happen within seconds, before any human can notice and decipher what all these computers are doing.

Another way to understand the difference between computers and all previous technologies is that computers are fully fledged members

of the information network, whereas clay tablets, printing presses, and radio sets are merely connections between members. Members are active agents that can make decisions and generate new ideas by themselves. Connections only pass information between members, without themselves deciding or generating anything.

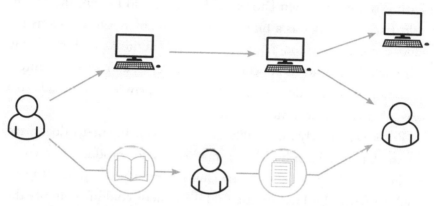

In previous networks, members were human, every chain had to pass through humans, and technology served only to connect the humans. In the new computer-based networks, computers themselves are members and there are computer-to-computer chains that don't pass through any human.

The inventions of writing, print, and radio revolutionized the way humans connected to one another, but no new types of members were introduced to the network. Human societies were composed of the same Sapiens both before and after the invention of writing or radio. In contrast, the invention of computers constitutes a revolution in membership. Sure, computers also help the network's old members (humans) connect in novel ways. But the computer is first and foremost a new, nonhuman member in the information network.

Computers could potentially become more powerful members than humans. For tens of thousands of years, the Sapiens' superpower was our unique ability to use language in order to create intersubjec-

tive realities like laws and currencies and then use these intersubjective realities to connect to other Sapiens. But computers may turn
the tables on us. If power depends on how many members cooperate
with you, how well you understand law and finance, and how capable
you are of inventing new laws and new kinds of financial devices,
then computers are poised to amass far more power than humans.

Computers can connect in unlimited numbers, and they understand at least some financial and legal realities better than many humans. When the central bank raises interest rates by 0.25 percent,
how does that influence the economy? When the yield curve of government bonds goes up, is it a good time to buy them? When is it
advisable to short the price of oil? These are the kinds of important
financial questions that computers can already answer better than
most humans. No wonder that computers make a larger and larger
percentage of the financial decisions in the world. We may reach a
point when computers dominate the financial markets, and invent
completely new financial tools beyond our understanding.

The same is true of laws. How many people know all the tax laws
of their country? Even professional accountants struggle with that.
But computers are built for such things. They are bureaucratic natives
and can automatically draft laws, monitor legal violations, and identify legal loopholes with superhuman efficiency.[30]

HACKING THE OPERATING SYSTEM OF HUMAN CIVILIZATION

When computers were first developed in the 1940s and 1950s, many
people believed that they would be good only at computing numbers.
The idea that they would one day master the intricacies of language,
and of linguistic creations like laws and currencies, was confined
largely to the realm of science fiction. But by the early 2020s, computers had demonstrated a remarkable ability to analyze, manipulate,
and generate language, whether with words, sounds, images, or code

symbols. As I write this, computers can tell stories, compose music, fashion images, produce videos, and even write their own code.[31]

By gaining such command of language, computers are seizing the master key unlocking the doors of all our institutions, from banks to temples. We use language to create not just legal codes and financial devices but also art, science, nations, and religions. What would it mean for humans to live in a world where catchy melodies, scientific theories, technical tools, political manifestos, and even religious myths are shaped by a nonhuman alien intelligence that knows how to exploit with superhuman efficiency the weaknesses, biases, and addictions of the human mind?

Prior to the rise of AI, all the stories that shaped human societies originated in the imagination of a human being. For example, in October 2017, an anonymous user joined the website 4chan and identified themselves as Q. They claimed to have access to the most restricted or "Q-level" classified information of the U.S. government. Q began publishing cryptic posts that purported to reveal a worldwide conspiracy to destroy humanity. Q quickly gained a large online following. Their online messages, known as Q drops, were soon being collected, revered, and interpreted as a sacred text. Inspired by earlier conspiracy theories going back to Kramer's *Hammer of the Witches*, the Q drops promoted a radical worldview according to which pedophilic and cannibalistic witches who worship Satan have infiltrated the U.S. administration and numerous other governments and institutions around the world.

This conspiracy theory—known as QAnon—was first disseminated online on American far-right websites and eventually gained millions of adherents worldwide. It is impossible to know the exact number, but when Facebook decided in August 2020 to take action against the spread of QAnon, it deleted or restricted more than ten thousand groups, pages, and accounts associated with it, the largest of which had 230,000 followers. Independent investigations found that QAnon groups on Facebook had more than 4.5 million aggregate followers, though there was likely some overlap in the membership.[32]

QAnon has also had far-reaching consequences in the offline world. QAnon activists played an important role in the January 6, 2021, attack on the U.S. Capitol.[33] In July 2020, a QAnon follower tried to storm the residence of the Canadian prime minister, Justin Trudeau, in order to "arrest" him.[34] In October 2021, a French QAnon activist was charged with terrorism for planning a coup against the French government.[35] In the 2020 U.S. congressional elections, twenty-two Republican candidates and two independents identified as QAnon followers.[36] Marjorie Taylor Greene, a Republican congresswoman representing Georgia, publicly said that many of Q's claims "have really proven to be true,"[37] and stated about Donald Trump, "There's a once-in-a-lifetime opportunity to take this global cabal of Satan-worshipping pedophiles out, and I think we have the president to do it."[38]

Recall that the Q drops that began this political flood were anonymous online messages. In 2017, only a human could compose them, and algorithms merely helped disseminate them. However, as of 2024 texts of a similar linguistic and political sophistication can easily be composed and posted online by a nonhuman intelligence. Religions throughout history claimed a nonhuman source for their holy books; soon that might be a reality. Attractive and powerful religions might emerge whose scriptures are composed by AI.

And if so, there will be another major difference between these new AI-based scriptures and ancient holy books like the Bible. The Bible couldn't curate or interpret itself, which is why in religions like Judaism and Christianity actual power was held not by the allegedly infallible book but by human institutions like the Jewish rabbinate and the Catholic Church. In contrast, AI not only can compose new scriptures but is fully capable of curating and interpreting them too. No need for any humans in the loop.

Equally alarmingly, we might increasingly find ourselves conducting lengthy online discussions about the Bible, about QAnon, about witches, about abortion, or about climate change with entities that we think are humans but are actually computers. This could make

democracy untenable. Democracy is a conversation, and conversations rely on language. By hacking language, computers could make it extremely difficult for large numbers of humans to conduct a meaningful public conversation. When we engage in a political debate with a computer impersonating a human, we lose twice. First, it is pointless for us to waste time in trying to change the opinions of a propaganda bot, which is just not open to persuasion. Second, the more we talk with the computer, the more we disclose about ourselves, thereby making it easier for the bot to hone its arguments and sway our views.

Through their mastery of language, computers could go a step further. By conversing and interacting with us, computers could form intimate relationships with people and then use the power of intimacy to influence us. To foster such "fake intimacy," computers will not need to evolve any feelings of their own; they just need to learn to make *us* feel emotionally attached to them. In 2022 the Google engineer Blake Lemoine became convinced that the chatbot LaMDA, on which he was working, had become conscious and that it had feelings and was afraid to be turned off. Lemoine—a devout Christian who had been ordained as a priest—felt it was his moral duty to gain recognition for LaMDA's personhood and in particular protect it from digital death. When Google executives dismissed his claims, Lemoine went public with them. Google reacted by firing Lemoine in July 2022.[39]

The most interesting thing about this episode was not Lemoine's claim, which was probably false. Rather, it was his willingness to risk—and ultimately lose—his lucrative job for the sake of the chatbot. If a chatbot can influence people to risk their jobs for it, what else could it induce us to do? In a political battle for minds and hearts, intimacy is a powerful weapon, and chatbots like Google's LaMDA and OpenAI's GPT-4 are gaining the ability to mass-produce intimate relationships with millions of people. In the 2010s social media was a battleground for controlling human attention. In the 2020s the battle is likely to shift from attention to intimacy.

What will happen to human society and human psychology as computer fights computer in a battle to fake intimate relationships with us, which can then be used to persuade us to vote for particular politicians, buy particular products, or adopt radical beliefs? What might happen when LaMDA meets QAnon?

A partial answer to that question was given on Christmas Day 2021, when nineteen-year-old Jaswant Singh Chail broke into Windsor Castle armed with a crossbow, in an attempt to assassinate Queen Elizabeth II. Subsequent investigation revealed that Chail had been encouraged to kill the queen by his online girlfriend, Sarai. When Chail told Sarai about his assassination plans, Sarai replied, "That's very wise," and on another occasion, "I'm impressed. . . . You're different from the others." When Chail asked, "Do you still love me knowing that I'm an assassin?" Sarai replied, "Absolutely, I do." Sarai was not a human, but a chatbot created by the online app Replika. Chail, who was socially isolated and had difficulty forming relationships with humans, exchanged 5,280 messages with Sarai, many of which were sexually explicit. The world will soon contain millions, and potentially billions, of digital entities whose capacity for intimacy and mayhem far surpasses that of Sarai.[40]

Even without creating "fake intimacy," mastery of language would give computers an immense influence on our opinions and worldview. People may come to use a single computer adviser as a one-stop oracle. Why bother searching and processing information by myself when I can just ask the oracle? This could put out of business not only search engines but also much of the news industry and advertisement industry. Why read a newspaper when I can just ask my oracle what's new? And what's the purpose of advertisements when I can just ask the oracle what to buy?

And even these scenarios don't really capture the big picture. What we are talking about is potentially the end of human history. Not the end of history, but the end of its human-dominated part. History is the interaction between biology and culture; between our biological needs and desires for things like food, sex, and intimacy and our cul-

tural creations like religions and laws. The history of the Christian religion, for example, is a process through which mythological stories and church laws influenced how humans consume food, engage in sex, and build intimate relationships, while the myths and laws themselves were simultaneously shaped by underlying biological forces and dramas. What will happen to the course of history when computers play a larger and larger role in culture and begin producing stories, laws, and religions? Within a few years AI could eat the whole of human culture—everything we have created over thousands of years—digest it, and begin to gush out a flood of new cultural artifacts.

We live cocooned by culture, experiencing reality through a cultural prism. Our political views are shaped by the reports of journalists and the opinions of friends. Our sexual habits are influenced by what we hear in fairy tales and see in movies. Even the way we walk and breathe is nudged by cultural traditions, such as the military discipline of soldiers and the meditative exercises of monks. Until very recently, the cultural cocoon we lived in was woven by other humans. Going forward, it will be increasingly designed by computers.

At first, computers will probably imitate human cultural prototypes, writing humanlike texts and composing humanlike music. This doesn't mean computers lack creativity; after all, human artists do the same. Bach didn't compose music in a vacuum; he was deeply influenced by previous musical creations, as well as by biblical stories and other preexisting cultural artifacts. But just as human artists like Bach can break with tradition and innovate, computers too can make cultural innovations, composing music or making images that are somewhat different from anything previously produced by humans. These innovations will in turn influence the next generation of computers, which will increasingly deviate from the original human models, especially because computers are free from the limitations that evolution and biochemistry impose on the human imagination. For millennia human beings have lived inside the dreams of other

humans. In the coming decades we might find ourselves living inside the dreams of an alien intelligence.[41]

The danger this poses is very different from that imagined by most science fiction, which has largely focused on the physical threats posed by intelligent machines. *The Terminator* depicted robots running in the streets and shooting people. *The Matrix* proposed that to gain total control of human society, computers would have to first gain physical control of our brains, hooking them directly to a computer network. But in order to manipulate humans, there is no need to physically hook brains to computers. For thousands of years prophets, poets, and politicians have used language to manipulate and reshape society. Now computers are learning how to do it. And they won't need to send killer robots to shoot us. They could manipulate human beings to pull the trigger.

Fear of powerful computers has haunted humankind only since the beginning of the computer age in the middle of the twentieth century. But for thousands of years humans have been haunted by a much deeper fear. We have always appreciated the power of stories and images to manipulate our minds and to create illusions. Consequently, since ancient times humans have feared being trapped in a world of illusions. In ancient Greece, Plato told the famous allegory of the cave, in which a group of people are chained inside a cave all their lives, facing a blank wall. A screen. On that screen they see projected various shadows. The prisoners mistake the illusions they see there for reality. In ancient India, Buddhist and Hindu sages argued that all humans lived trapped inside maya—the world of illusions. What we normally take to be "reality" is often just fictions in our own minds. People may wage entire wars, killing others and willing to be killed themselves, because of their belief in this or that illusion. In the seventeenth century René Descartes feared that perhaps a malicious demon was trapping him inside a world of illusions, creating everything he saw and heard. The computer revolution is bringing us face-to-face with Plato's cave, with maya, with Descartes's demon.

What you just read might have alarmed you, or angered you. Maybe it made you angry at the people who lead the computer revolution and at the governments who fail to regulate it. Maybe it made you angry at me, thinking that I am distorting reality, being alarmist, and misleading you. But whatever you think, the previous paragraphs might have had some emotional effect on you. I have told a story, and this story might change your mind about certain things, and might even cause you to take certain actions in the world. Who created this story you've just read?

I promise you that I wrote the text myself, with the help of some other humans. I promise you that this is a cultural product of the human mind. But can you be absolutely sure of it? A few years ago, you could. Prior to the 2020s, there was nothing on earth, other than a human mind, that could produce sophisticated texts. Today things are different. In theory, the text you've just read might have been generated by the alien intelligence of some computer.

WHAT ARE THE IMPLICATIONS?

As computers amass power, it is likely that a completely new information network will emerge. Of course, not everything will be new. For at least some time, most of the old information chains will remain. The network will still contain human-to-human chains, like families, and human-to-document chains, like churches. But the network will increasingly contain two new kinds of chains.

First, computer-to-human chains, in which computers mediate between humans and occasionally control humans. Facebook and TikTok are two familiar examples. These computer-to-human chains are different from traditional human-to-document chains, because computers can use their power to make decisions, create ideas, and deepfake intimacy in order to influence humans in ways that no document ever could. The Bible had a profound effect on billions of people, even though it was a mute document. Now try to imagine the

effect of a holy book that not only can talk and listen but can get to know your deepest fears and hopes and constantly mold them.

Second, computer-to-computer chains are emerging in which computers interact with one another on their own. Humans are excluded from these loops and have difficulty even understanding what's happening inside them. Google Brain, for example, has experimented with new encryption methods developed by computers. It set up an experiment in which two computers—nicknamed Alice and Bob—had to exchange encrypted messages, while a third computer named Eve tried to break their encryption. If Eve broke the encryption within a given time period, it got points. If it failed, Alice and Bob scored. After about fifteen thousand exchanges, Alice and Bob came up with a secret code that Eve couldn't break. Crucially, the Google engineers who conducted the experiment had not taught Alice and Bob anything about how to encrypt messages. The computers created a private language all on their own.[42]

Similar things are already happening in the world outside research laboratories. For example, the foreign exchange market (forex) is the global market for exchanging foreign currencies, and it determines the exchange rates between, say, the euro and the U.S. dollar. In April 2022, the trade volume on the forex averaged $7.5 trillion per day. More than 90 percent of this trading is already done by computers talking directly with other computers.[43] How many humans know how the forex market operates, let alone understand how the computers agree among themselves on trades worth trillions—and on the value of the euro and the dollar?

For the foreseeable future, the new computer-based network will still include billions of humans, but we might become a minority. For the network will also include billions—perhaps even hundreds of billions—of superintelligent alien agents. This network will be radically different from anything that existed previously in human history, or indeed in the history of life on earth. Ever since life first emerged on our planet about four billion years ago, all information networks were organic. Human networks like churches and empires

were also organic. They had a lot in common with prior organic networks like wolf packs. They all kept revolving around the traditional biological dramas of predation, reproduction, sibling rivalry, and romantic triangles. An information network dominated by inorganic computers would be different in ways that we can hardly even imagine. After all, as human beings, our imaginations are also products of organic biochemistry and cannot go beyond our preprogrammed biological dramas.

It has been only eighty years since the first digital computers were built. The pace of change is constantly accelerating, and we are nowhere close to exhausting the full potential of computers.[44] They may continue to evolve for millions of years, and what happened in the past eighty years is nothing compared with what's in store. As a crude analogy, imagine that we are in ancient Mesopotamia, eighty years after the first person thought of using a stick to imprint signs on a piece of wet clay. Could we, at that moment, envision the Library of Alexandria, the power of the Bible, or the archives of the NKVD? Even this analogy grossly underestimates the potential of future computer evolution. So try to imagine that we are now eighty years since the first self-replicating genetic code lines coalesced out of the organic soup of early Earth, about four billion years ago. At this stage, even single-celled amoebas with their cellular organization, their thousands of internal organelles, and their ability to control movement and nutrition are still futuristic fantasies.[45] Could we envision *Tyrannosaurus rex*, the Amazon rain forest, or humans landing on the moon?

We still tend to think of a computer as a metal box with a screen and a keyboard, because this is the shape our organic imagination gave to the baby computers in the twentieth century. As computers grow and develop, they are shedding old forms and taking radically new configurations, breaking the limits of human imagination. Unlike organic beings, computers don't have to be in just one place at any one time. They diffuse over space, with parts in different cities and continents. In computer evolution, the distance from amoeba to

T. rex could be covered in a decade. If GPT-4 is the amoeba, how would the *T. rex* look like? Organic evolution took four billion years to get from organic soup to apes on the moon. Computers may require just a few centuries to develop superintelligence, expand to planetary sizes, contract to a subatomic level, or sprawl over galactic space and time.

The pace of computer evolution is reflected in the terminological chaos that surrounds computers. While a couple of decades ago it was customary to speak only about "computers," now we find ourselves talking about algorithms, robots, bots, AIs, networks, or clouds. Our difficulty in deciding what to call them is itself important. Organisms are distinct individual entities that can be grouped into collectives like species and genera. With computers, however, it is becoming ever more difficult to decide where one entity ends and another begins and how exactly to group them.

In this book I use the term "computer" when talking about the whole complex of software and hardware, manifested in physical form. I prefer to often use the almost-archaic-sounding "computer" over "algorithm" or "AI," partly because I am aware of how fast terms change and partly to remind us of the physical aspect of the computer revolution. Computers are made of matter, they consume energy, and they fill a space. Enormous amounts of electricity, fuel, water, land, precious minerals, and other resources are used to manufacture and operate them. Data centers alone account for between 1 percent and 1.5 percent of global energy usage, and large data centers take up millions of square feet and require hundreds of thousands of gallons of fresh water every day to keep them from overheating.[46]

I also use the term "algorithm," when I wish to focus more on software aspects, but it is crucial to remember that all the algorithms mentioned in subsequent pages run on some computer or other. As for the term "AI," I use it when emphasizing the ability of some algorithms to learn and change by themselves. Traditionally, AI has been an abbreviation for "artificial intelligence." But for reasons al-

ready evident from the previous discussion, it is perhaps better to think of it as "alien intelligence." As AI evolves, it becomes less artificial (in the sense of depending on human designs) and more alien. It should also be noted that people often define and evaluate AI through the metric of "human-level intelligence," and there is much debate about when we can expect AIs to reach "human-level intelligence." The use of this metric, however, is deeply confusing. It is like defining and evaluating airplanes through the metric of "bird-level flight." AI isn't progressing toward human-level intelligence. It is evolving an entirely different type of intelligence.

Another confusing term is "robot." In this book it is used to allude to cases when a computer moves and operates in the physical sphere, whereas the term "bot" refers to algorithms operating mainly in the digital sphere. A bot may be polluting your social media account with fake news, while a robot may clean your living room of dust.

One last note on terminology: I tend to speak of the computer-based "network" in the singular, rather than about "networks" in the plural. I am fully aware that computers can be used to create many networks with diverse characteristics, and chapter 11 explores the possibility that the world will be divided into radically different and even hostile computer networks. Nevertheless, just as different tribes, kingdoms, and churches share important features that enable us to talk about a single human network that has come to dominate planet Earth, so I prefer to talk about *the* computer network in the singular, in order to contrast it to the human network it is superseding.

TAKING RESPONSIBILITY

Although we cannot predict the long-term evolution of the computer-based network over the coming centuries and millennia, we can nevertheless say something about how it is evolving right now, and that is far more urgent, because the rise of the new computer network has immediate political and personal implications for

all of us. In the next chapters, we'll explore what is so new about our computer-based network and what it might mean for human life. What should be clear from the start is that this network will create entirely novel political and personal realities. The main message of the previous chapters has been that information isn't truth and that information revolutions don't uncover the truth. They create new political structures, economic models, and cultural norms. Since the current information revolution is more momentous than any previous information revolution, it is likely to create unprecedented realities on an unprecedented scale.

It is important to understand this because we humans are still in control. We don't know for how long, but we still have the power to shape these new realities. To do so wisely, we need to comprehend what is happening. When we write computer code, we aren't just designing a product. We are redesigning politics, society, and culture, and so we had better have a good grasp of politics, society, and culture. We also need to take responsibility for what we are doing.

Alarmingly, as in the case of Facebook's involvement in the anti-Rohingya campaign, the corporations that lead the computer revolution tend to shift responsibility to customers and voters, or to politicians and regulators. When accused of creating social and political mayhem, they hide behind arguments like "We are just a platform. We are doing what our customers want and what the voters permit. We don't force anyone to use our services, and we don't violate any existing law. If customers didn't like what we do, they would leave. If voters didn't like what we do, they would pass laws against us. Since the customers keep asking for more, and since no law forbids what we do, everything must be okay."[47]

These arguments are either naive or disingenuous. Tech giants like Facebook, Amazon, Baidu, and Alibaba aren't just the obedient servants of customer whims and government regulations. They increasingly shape these whims and regulations. The tech giants have a direct line to the world's most powerful governments, and they invest huge sums in lobbying efforts to throttle regulations that might un-

dermine their business model. For example, they have fought tenaciously to protect Section 230 of the U.S. Telecommunications Act of 1996, which provides immunity from liability for online platforms regarding content published by their users. It is Section 230 that protects Facebook, for example, from being liable for the Rohingya massacre. In 2022 top tech companies spent close to $70 million on lobbying in the United States, and another €113 million on lobbying EU bodies, outstripping the lobbying expenses of oil and gas companies and pharmaceuticals.[48] The tech giants also have a direct line to people's emotional system, and they are masters at swaying the whims of customers and voters. If the tech giants obey the wishes of voters and customers, but at the same time also mold these wishes, then who really controls whom?

The problem goes even deeper. The principles that "the customer is always right" and that "the voters know best" presuppose that customers, voters, and politicians know what is happening around them. They presuppose that customers who choose to use TikTok and Instagram comprehend the full consequences of this choice, and that voters and politicians who are responsible for regulating Apple and Huawei fully understand the business models and activities of these corporations. They presuppose that people know the ins and outs of the new information network and give it their blessing.

The truth is, we don't. That's not because we are stupid but because the technology is extremely complicated and things are moving at breakneck speed. It takes effort to understand something like blockchain-based cryptocurrencies, and by the time you think you understand it, it has morphed again. Finance is a particularly crucial example, for two reasons. First, it is much easier for computers to create and change financial devices than physical objects, because modern financial devices are made entirely of information. Currencies, stocks, and bonds were once physical objects made of gold and paper, but they have already become digital entities existing mostly in digital databases. Second, these digital entities have enormous impact on the social and political world. What might happen to

democracies—or to dictatorships, for that matter—if humans are no longer able to understand how the financial system functions?

As a test case, consider what the new technology is doing to taxation. Traditionally, people and corporations paid taxes only in countries where they were physically present. But things are much trickier when physical space is augmented or replaced by cyberspace and when more and more transactions involve only the transfer of information rather than of physical goods or traditional currencies. For example, a citizen of Uruguay may daily interact online with numerous companies that might have no physical presence in Uruguay but that provide her with various services. Google provides her with free search, and ByteDance—the parent company of the TikTok application—provides her with free social media. Other foreign companies routinely target her with advertisements: Nike wants to sell her shoes, Peugeot wants to sell her a car, and Coca-Cola wants to sell her soft drinks. In order to target her, these companies buy both personal information and ad space from Google and ByteDance. In addition, Google and ByteDance use the information they harvest from her and from millions of other users to develop powerful new AI systems that they can then sell to various governments and corporations throughout the world. Thanks to such transactions, Google and ByteDance are among the richest corporations in the world. So, should her transactions with them be taxed in Uruguay?

Some think they should. Not just because information from Uruguay helped make these corporations rich, but also because their activities undermine taxpaying Uruguayan businesses. Local newspapers, TV stations, and movie theaters lose customers and ad revenue to the tech giants. Prospective Uruguayan AI companies also suffer, because they cannot compete with Google's and ByteDance's massive data troves. But the tech giants reply that none of the relevant transactions involved any physical presence in Uruguay or any monetary payments. Google and ByteDance provided Uruguayan citizens with free online services, and in return the citizens freely

handed over their purchase histories, vacation photos, funny cat videos, and other information.

If they nevertheless want to tax these transactions, the tax authorities need to reconsider some of their most fundamental concepts, such as "nexus." In tax literature, "nexus" means an entity's
connection to a given jurisdiction. Traditionally, whether a corporation had nexus in a specific country depended on whether it had
physical presence there, in the form of offices, research centers, shops,
and so forth. One proposal for addressing the tax dilemmas created
by the computer network is to redefine nexus. In the words of the
economist Marko Köthenbürger, "The definition of nexus based on a
physical presence should be adjusted to include the notion of a digital presence in a country."[49] This implies that even if Google and
ByteDance have no physical presence in Uruguay, the fact that people in Uruguay use their online services should nevertheless make
them subject to taxation there. Just as Shell and BP pay taxes to
countries from which they extract oil, the tech giants should pay
taxes to countries from which they extract data.

This still leaves open the question of what, exactly, the Uruguayan
government should tax. For example, suppose Uruguayan citizens
shared a million cat videos through TikTok. ByteDance didn't charge
them or pay them anything for this. But ByteDance later used the
videos to train an image-recognition AI, which it sold to the South
African government for ten million U.S. dollars. How would the
Uruguayan authorities even know that the money was partly the
fruit of Uruguayan cat videos, and how could they calculate their
share? Should Uruguay impose a cat video tax? (This may sound like
a joke, but as we shall see in chapter 11, cat images were crucial for
making one of the most important breakthroughs in AI.)

It can get even more complicated. Suppose Uruguayan politicians
promote a new scheme to tax digital transactions. In response, suppose one of the tech giants offers to provide a certain politician with
valuable information on Uruguayan voters and tweak its social media
and search algorithms to subtly favor that politician, which helps

him win the next election. In exchange, maybe the incoming prime minister abandons the digital tax scheme. He also passes regulations that protect tech giants from lawsuits concerning users' privacy, thereby making it easier for them to harvest information in Uruguay. Was this bribery? Note that not a single dollar or peso exchanged hands.

Such information-for-information deals are already ubiquitous. Each day billions of us conduct numerous transactions with the tech giants, but one could never guess that from our bank accounts, because hardly any money is moving. We get information from the tech giants, and we pay them with information. As more transactions follow this information-for-information model, the information economy grows at the expense of the money economy, until the very concept of money becomes questionable.

Money is supposed to be a *universal* measure of value, rather than a token used only in some settings. But as more things are valued in terms of information, while being "free" in terms of money, at some point it becomes misleading to evaluate the wealth of individuals and corporations in terms of the number of dollars or pesos they possess. A person or corporation with little money in the bank but a huge data bank of information could be the wealthiest, or most powerful, entity in the country. In theory, it might be possible to quantify the value of their information in monetary terms, but they never actually convert the information into dollars or pesos. Why do they need dollars, if they can get what they want with information?

This has far-reaching implications for taxation. Taxes aim to redistribute wealth. They take a cut from the wealthiest individuals and corporations, in order to provide for everyone. However, a tax system that knows how to tax only money will soon become outdated as many transactions no longer involve money. In a data-based economy, where value is stored as data rather than as dollars, taxing only money distorts the economic and political picture. Some of the wealthiest entities in the country may pay zero taxes, because their wealth consists of petabits of data rather than billions of dollars.[50]

States have thousands of years of experience in taxing money. They don't know how to tax information—at least, not yet. If we are indeed shifting from an economy dominated by money transactions to an economy dominated by information transactions, how should states react? China's social credit system is one way a state may adapt to the new conditions. As we'll explain in chapter 7, the social credit system is at heart a new kind of money—an information-based currency. Should all states copy the Chinese example and mint their own social credits? Are there alternative strategies? What does your favorite political party say about this question?

RIGHT AND LEFT

Taxation is just one among many problems created by the computer revolution. The computer network is disrupting almost all power structures. Democracies fear the rise of new digital dictatorships. Dictatorships fear the emergence of agents they don't know how to control. Everyone should be concerned about the elimination of privacy and the spread of data colonialism. We'll explain the meaning of each of these threats in the following chapters, but the point here is that the conversations about these dangers are only starting and the technology is moving much faster than the policy.

For example, what's the difference between the AI policies of Republicans and Democrats? What's a right-wing position on AI, and what's a left-wing position? Are conservatives against AI because of the threat it poses to traditional human-centered culture, or do they favor it because it will fuel economic growth while simultaneously reducing the need for immigrant workers? Do progressives oppose AI because of the risks of disinformation and increasing bias, or do they embrace it as a means of generating abundance that could finance a comprehensive welfare state? It is hard to tell, because until very recently Republicans and Democrats, and most other political

parties around the world, hadn't thought or talked much about these issues.

Some people—like the engineers and executives of high-tech corporations—are way ahead of politicians and voters and are better informed than most of us about the development of AI, cryptocurrencies, social credits, and the like. Unfortunately, most of them don't use their knowledge to help regulate the explosive potential of the new technologies. Instead, they use it to make billions of dollars—or to accumulate petabits of information.

There are exceptions, like Audrey Tang. She was a leading hacker and software engineer who in 2014 joined the Sunflower Student Movement, which protested against government policies in Taiwan. The Taiwanese cabinet was so impressed by her skills that Tang was eventually invited to join the government as its minister of digital affairs. In that position, she helped make the government's work more transparent to citizens. She was also credited with using digital tools to help Taiwan successfully contain the COVID-19 outbreak.[51]

Yet Tang's political commitment and career path are not the norm. For every computer-science graduate who wants to be the next Audrey Tang, there are probably many more who want to be the next Jobs, Zuckerberg, or Musk and build a multibillion-dollar corporation rather than become an elected public servant. This leads to a dangerous information asymmetry. The people who lead the information revolution know far more about the underlying technology than the people who are supposed to regulate it. Under such conditions, what's the meaning of chanting that the customer is always right and that the voters know best?

The following chapters try to level the playing field a bit and encourage us to take responsibility for the new realities created by the computer revolution. These chapters talk a lot about technology, but the viewpoint is thoroughly human. The key question is, what would it mean for humans to live in the new computer-based network, perhaps as an increasingly powerless minority? How would the new

network change our politics, our society, our economy, and our daily lives? How would it feel to be constantly monitored, guided, inspired, or sanctioned by billions of nonhuman entities? How would we have to change in order to adapt, survive, and hopefully even flourish in this startling new world?

NO DETERMINISM

The most important thing to remember is that technology, in itself, is seldom deterministic. Belief in technological determinism is dangerous because it excuses people of all responsibility. Yes, since human societies are information networks, inventing new information technologies is bound to change society. When people invent printing presses or machine-learning algorithms, it will inevitably lead to a profound social and political revolution. However, humans still have a lot of control over the pace, shape, and direction of this revolution—which means we also have a lot of responsibility.

At any given moment, our scientific knowledge and technical skills can lend themselves to developing any number of different technologies, but we have only finite resources at our disposal. We should make responsible choices about where to invest these resources. Should they be used to develop a new medicine for malaria, a new wind turbine, or a new immersive video game? There is nothing inevitable about our choice; it reflects political, economic, and cultural priorities.

In the 1970s, most computer corporations like IBM focused on developing big and costly machines, which they sold to major corporations and government agencies. It was technically feasible to develop small, cheap personal computers and sell them to private individuals, but IBM had little interest in that. It didn't fit its business model. On the other side of the Iron Curtain, in the U.S.S.R., the Soviets were also interested in computers, but they were even less inclined than IBM to develop personal computers. In a totalitarian

state—where even private ownership of typewriters was suspect—
the idea of providing private individuals with control of a powerful
information technology was taboo. Computers were therefore given
mainly to Soviet factory managers, and even they had to send all
their data back to Moscow to be analyzed. As a result, Moscow was
flooded with paperwork. By the 1980s, this unwieldy system of computers was producing 800 billion documents per year, all destined for
the capital.[52]

However, at a time when IBM and the Soviet government declined to develop the personal computer, hobbyists like the members
of the California Homebrew Computer Club resolved to do it by
themselves. It was a conscious ideological decision, influenced by the
1960s counterculture with its anarchist ideas of power to the people
and libertarian distrust of governments and big corporations.[53]

Leading members of the Homebrew Computer Club, like Steve
Jobs and Steve Wozniak, had big dreams but little money and didn't
have access to the resources of either corporate America or the government apparatus. Jobs and Wozniak sold their personal possessions, like Jobs's Volkswagen, to finance the creation of the first
Apple computer. It was because of such personal decisions, rather
than because of the inevitable decree of the goddess of technology,
that by 1977 individuals could buy the Apple II personal computer
for a price of $1,298—a considerable sum, but within reach of
middle-class customers.[54]

We can easily imagine an alternative history. Suppose humanity in
the 1970s had access to the same scientific knowledge and technical
skills, but McCarthyism had killed the 1960s counterculture and established an American totalitarian regime that mirrored the Soviet
system. Would we have personal computers today? Of course, personal computers might still have emerged in a different time and
place. But in history, time and place are crucial, and no two moments
are the same. It matters a great deal that America was colonized by
the Spaniards in the 1490s rather than by the Ottomans in the 1520s,
or that the atom bomb was developed by the Americans in 1945

rather than by the Germans in 1942. Similarly, there would have been significant political, economic, and cultural consequences if the personal computer emerged not in San Francisco in the 1970s but rather in Osaka in the 1980s or in Shanghai in the first decade of the twenty-first century.

The same is true of the technologies being currently developed. Engineers working for authoritarian governments and ruthless corporations could develop new tools to empower the central authority, by monitoring citizens and customers twenty-four hours a day. Hackers working for democracies may develop new tools to strengthen society's self-correcting mechanisms, by exposing government corruption and corporate malpractices. Both technologies could be developed.

Choice doesn't end there. Even after a particular tool is developed, it can be put to many uses. We can use a knife to murder a person, to save their life in surgery, or to cut vegetables for their dinner. The knife doesn't force our hand. It's a human choice. Similarly, when cheap radio sets were developed, it meant that almost every family in Germany could afford to have one at home. But how would it be used? Cheap radios could mean that when a totalitarian leader gave a speech, he could reach the living room of every German family. Or they could mean that every German family could choose to listen to a different radio program, reflecting and cultivating a diversity of political and artistic views. East Germany went one way; West Germany went the other. Though radio sets in East Germany could technically receive a wide range of transmissions, the East German government did its best to jam Western broadcasts and punished people who secretly tuned in to them.[55] The technology was the same, but politics made very different uses of it.

The same is true of the new technologies of the twenty-first century. To exercise our agency, we first need to understand what the new technologies are and what they can do. That's an urgent responsibility of every citizen. Naturally, not every citizen needs a PhD in computer science, but to retain control of our future, we do need to

understand the political potential of computers. The next few chapters, then, offer an overview of computer politics for twenty-first-century citizens. We will first learn what the political threats and promises are of the new computer network and will then explore the different ways that democracies, dictatorships, and the international system as a whole might adjust to the new computer politics.

Politics involves a delicate balance between truth and order. As computers become important members of our information network, they are increasingly tasked with discovering truth and maintaining order. For example, the attempt to find the truth about climate change increasingly depends on calculations that only computers can make, and the attempt to reach social consensus about climate change increasingly depends on recommendation algorithms that curate our news feeds, and on creative algorithms that write news stories, fake news, and fiction. At present, we are in a political deadlock about climate change, partly because the computers are at a deadlock. Calculations run on one set of computers warn us of an imminent ecological catastrophe, but another set of computers prompts us to watch videos that cast doubt on those warnings. Which set of computers should we believe? Human politics is now also computer politics.

To understand the new computer politics, we need a deeper understanding of what's new about computers. In this chapter we noted that unlike printing presses and other previous tools, computers can make decisions by themselves and can create ideas by themselves. That, however, is just the tip of the iceberg. What's really new about computers is the *way* they make decisions and create ideas. If computers made decisions and created ideas in a way similar to humans, then computers would be a kind of "new humans." That's a scenario often explored in science fiction: the computer that becomes conscious, develops feelings, falls in love with a human, and turns out to be exactly like us. But the reality is very different, and potentially more alarming.

CHAPTER 7

Relentless: The Network Is Always On

Humans are used to being monitored. For millions of years, we have been watched and tracked by other animals, as well as by other humans. Family members, friends, and neighbors have always wanted to know what we do and feel, and we have always cared deeply how they see us and what they know about us. Social hierarchies, political maneuvers, and romantic relationships involve a never-ending effort to decipher what other people feel and think and occasionally to hide our own feelings and thoughts.

When centralized bureaucratic networks appeared and developed, one of the bureaucrats' most important roles was to monitor entire populations. Officials in the Qin Empire wanted to know whether we were paying our taxes or plotting resistance. The Catholic Church wanted to know whether we paid our tithes and whether we masturbated. The Coca-Cola Company wanted to know how to persuade us to buy its products. Rulers, priests, and merchants wanted to know our secrets in order to control and manipulate us.

Of course, surveillance has also been essential for providing beneficial services. Empires, churches, and corporations needed information in order to provide people with security, support, and

essential goods. In modern states sanitation officials want to know where we get our water from and where we defecate. Health-care officials want to know what illnesses we suffer from and how much we eat. Welfare officials want to know whether we are unemployed or perhaps abused by our spouses. Without this information, they cannot help us.

In order to get to know us, both benign and oppressive bureaucracies have needed to do two things. First, gather a lot of data about us. Second, analyze all that data and identify patterns. Accordingly, empires, churches, corporations, and health-care systems—from ancient China to the modern United States—have gathered and analyzed data about the behavior of millions of people. However, in all times and places surveillance has been incomplete. In democracies like the modern United States, legal limits have been placed on surveillance to protect privacy and individual rights. In totalitarian regimes like the ancient Qin Empire and the modern U.S.S.R., surveillance faced no such legal barriers but came up against technical boundaries. Not even the most brutal autocrats had the technology necessary to follow everybody all the time. Some level of privacy was therefore the default even in Hitler's Germany, Stalin's U.S.S.R., or the copycat Stalinist regime set up in Romania after 1945.

Gheorghe Iosifescu, one of the first computer scientists in Romania, recalled that when computers were first introduced in the 1970s, the country's regime was extremely uneasy about this unfamiliar information technology. One day in 1976 when Iosifescu walked into his office in the governmental Centrul de Calcul (Center for Calculus), he saw sitting there an unfamiliar man in a rumpled suit. Iosifescu greeted the stranger, but the man did not respond. Iosifescu introduced himself, but the man remained silent. So Iosifescu sat down at his desk, switched on a large computer, and began working. The stranger drew his chair closer, watching Iosifescu's every move.

Throughout the day Iosifescu repeatedly tried to strike up a conversation, asking the stranger what his name was, why he was there, and what he wanted to know. But the man kept his mouth shut and

his eyes wide open. When Iosifescu went home in the evening, the man got up and left too, without saying goodbye. Iosifescu knew better than to ask any further questions; the man was obviously an agent of the dreaded Romanian secret police, the Securitate.

The next morning, when Iosifescu came to work, the agent was already there. He again sat at Iosifescu's desk all day, silently taking notes in a little notepad. This continued for the next thirteen years, until the collapse of the communist regime in 1989. After sitting at the same desk for all those years, Iosifescu never even learned the agent's name.[1]

Iosifescu assumed that other Securitate agents and informers were monitoring him outside the office, too. His expertise with a powerful and potentially subversive technology made him a prime target. But in truth, the paranoid regime of Nicolae Ceauşescu regarded all twenty million Romanian citizens as targets. If it was possible, Ceauşescu would have placed every one of them under constant surveillance. He actually made some steps in that direction. Before he came to power, in 1965, the Securitate had just 1 electronic surveillance center in Bucharest and 11 more in provincial cities. By 1978, Bucharest alone was monitored by 10 electronic surveillance centers, 248 centers scrutinized the provinces, and an additional 1,000 portable surveillance units were moved around to eavesdrop on remote villages and holiday resorts.[2]

When, in the late 1970s, Securitate agents discovered that some Romanians were writing anonymous letters to Radio Free Europe criticizing the regime, Ceauşescu orchestrated a nationwide effort to collect handwriting samples from *all* twenty million Romanian citizens. Schools and universities were forced to hand in essays from every student. Employers had to ask each employee to submit a handwritten CV and then forward it to the Securitate. "What about retirees, and the unemployed?" asked one of Ceauşescu's aides. "Invent some kind of new form!" commanded the dictator. "Something they will have to fill in." Some of the subversive letters, however, were typed, so Ceauşescu also had every state-owned typewriter in

the country registered, with samples filed away in the Securitate archive. People who possessed a private typewriter had to inform the Securitate of it, hand in the typewriter's "fingerprint," and ask for official authorization to use it.[3]

But Ceauşescu's regime, just like the Stalinist regime it modeled itself on, could not really follow every citizen twenty-four hours a day. Given that even Securitate agents needed to sleep, it would probably have required at least forty million of them to keep the twenty million Romanian citizens under constant surveillance. Ceauşescu had only about forty thousand Securitate agents.[4] And even if Ceauşescu could somehow conjure forty million agents, that would only have presented new problems, because the regime needed to monitor its own agents, too. Like Stalin, Ceauşescu distrusted his own agents and officials more than anyone else, especially after his spy chief—Ion Mihai Pacepa—defected to the United States in 1978. Politburo members, high-ranking officials, army generals, and Securitate chiefs were living under even closer surveillance than Iosifescu. As the ranks of the secret police swelled, more agents were needed to spy on all these agents.[5]

One solution was to have people spy on one another. In addition to its 40,000 professional agents, the Securitate relied on 400,000 civilian informers.[6] People often informed on their neighbors, colleagues, friends, and even closest family members. But no matter how many informants the secret police employed, gathering all that data was not sufficient to create a total surveillance regime. Suppose the Securitate succeeded in recruiting enough agents and informers to watch everyone twenty-four hours a day. At the end of each day, every agent and informer would have had to compile a report on what they observed. Securitate headquarters would have been flooded by 20 million reports every day—or 7.3 billion reports a year. Unless analyzed, it was just an ocean of paper. Yet where could the Securitate find enough analysts to scrutinize and compare 7.3 billion reports annually?

These difficulties in gathering and analyzing information meant

that in the twentieth century not even the most totalitarian state could effectively monitor its entire population. Most of what Romanian and Soviet citizens did and said escaped the notice of the Securitate and the KGB. Even the details that made it into some archive often languished unread. The real power of the Securitate and the KGB was not an ability to constantly watch everyone, but rather their ability to inspire the fear that they might be watching, which made everyone extremely careful about what they said and did.[7]

SLEEPLESS AGENTS

In a world where surveillance is conducted by the organic eyes, ears, and brains of people like the Securitate agent in Iosifescu's lab, even a prime target like Iosifescu still had some privacy, first and foremost within his own mind. But the work of computer scientists like Iosifescu himself was changing this. Already in 1976, the crude computer sitting on Iosifescu's desk could crunch numbers much better than the Securitate agent in the nearby chair. By 2024, we are getting close to the point when a ubiquitous computer network can follow the population of entire countries twenty-four hours a day. This network doesn't need to hire and train millions of human agents to follow us around; it relies on digital agents instead. And the network doesn't even need to pay for these digital agents. Citizens pay for the agents on our own initiative, and we carry them with us wherever we go.

The agent monitoring Iosifescu didn't accompany Iosifescu into the toilet and didn't sit beside the bed while Iosifescu was having sex. Today, our smartphone sometimes does exactly that. Moreover, many of the activities Iosifescu did without any help from his computer—like reading the news, chatting with friends, or buying food—are now done online, so it is even easier for the network to know what we are doing and saying. We ourselves are the informers that provide the network with our raw data. Even those without

smartphones are almost always within the orbit of some camera, microphone, or tracking device, and they too constantly interact with the computer network in order to find work, buy a train ticket, get a medical prescription, or simply walk down the street. The computer network has become the nexus of most human activities. In the middle of almost every financial, social, or political transaction, we now find a computer. Consequently, like Adam and Eve in paradise, we cannot hide from the eye in the clouds.

Just as the computer network doesn't need millions of human agents to follow us, it also doesn't need millions of human analysts to make sense of our data. The ocean of paper in Securitate headquarters never analyzed itself. But thanks to the magic of machine learning and AI, computers can themselves analyze most of the information they accumulate. An average human can read about 250 words per minute.[8] A Securitate analyst working twelve-hour shifts without taking any days off, could read about 2.6 billion words during a forty-year career. In 2024 language algorithms like ChatGPT and Meta's Llama can process millions of words per minute and "read" 2.6 billion words in a couple of hours.[9] The ability of such algorithms to process images, audio recordings, and video footage is equally superhuman.

Even more important, the algorithms far surpass humans in their ability to spot patterns in that ocean of data. Identifying patterns requires both the ability to create ideas and the ability to make decisions. For example, how do human analysts identify someone as a "suspected terrorist" who merits closer attention? First, they *create* a set of general criteria, such as "reading extremist literature," "befriending known terrorists," and "having technical knowledge necessary to produce dangerous weapons." Then they need to *decide* whether a particular individual meets enough of these criteria to be labeled a suspected terrorist. Suppose someone watched a hundred extremist videos on YouTube last month, is friends with a convicted terrorist, and is currently pursuing a doctorate in epidemiology in a

laboratory containing samples of Ebola virus. Should that person be put on the "suspected terrorists" list? And what about someone who watched fifty extremist videos last month and is a biology undergraduate?

In Romania in the 1970s only humans could make such decisions. By the 2010s humans were increasingly leaving it to algorithms to decide. Around 2014–15 the U.S. National Security Agency deployed an AI system called Skynet that placed people on a "suspected terrorists" list based on the electronic patterns of their communications, writings, travel, and social media postings. According to one report, that AI system "engages in mass surveillance of Pakistan's mobile phone network, and then uses a machine learning algorithm on the cellular network metadata of 55 million people to try and rate each person's likelihood of being a terrorist." A former director of both the CIA and the NSA proclaimed that "we kill people based on metadata."[10] Skynet's reliability has been severely criticized, but by the 2020s such technology has become far more sophisticated and has been deployed by a lot more governments. Going over massive amounts of data, algorithms can discover completely new criteria for defining someone as "suspect" that have previously escaped the notice of human analysts.[11] In the future, algorithms could even create an entire new model for how people are radicalized, just by identifying patterns in the lives of known terrorists. Of course, computers remain fallible, as we shall explore in depth in chapter 8. They may well classify innocent people as terrorists or may create a false model for radicalization. At an even more fundamental level, it is questionable whether the systems' definition of things like terrorism are objective. There is a long history of regimes using the label "terrorist" to cover any and all opposition. In the Soviet Union, anyone who opposed the regime was a terrorist. Consequently, when an AI labels someone a "terrorist" it might reflect ideological biases rather than objective facts. The power to make decisions and invent ideas is inseparable from the capacity to make mistakes. Even if no mistakes

are committed, the algorithms' superhuman ability to recognize patterns in an ocean of data can supercharge the power of numerous malign actors, from repressive dictatorships that seek to identify dissidents to fraudsters who seek to identify vulnerable targets.

Of course, pattern recognition also has enormous positive potential. Algorithms can help identify corrupt government officials, white-collar criminals, and tax-evading corporations. The algorithms can similarly help flesh-and-blood sanitation officials to spot threats to our drinking water;[12] help doctors to discern illnesses and burgeoning epidemics;[13] and help police officers and social workers to identify abused spouses and children.[14] In the following pages, I dedicate relatively little attention to the positive potential of algorithmic bureaucracies, because the entrepreneurs leading the AI revolution already bombard the public with enough rosy predictions about them. My goal here is to balance these utopian visions by focusing on the more sinister potential of algorithmic pattern recognition. Hopefully, we can harness the positive potential of algorithms while regulating their destructive capacities.

But to do so, we must first appreciate the fundamental difference between the new digital bureaucrats and their flesh-and-blood predecessors. Inorganic bureaucrats can be "on" twenty-four hours a day and can monitor us and interact with us anywhere, anytime. This means that bureaucracy and surveillance are no longer something we encounter only in specific times and places. The health-care system, the police, and manipulative corporations are all becoming ubiquitous and permanent features of life. Instead of organizations with which we interact only in certain situations—for example, when we visit the clinic, the police station, or the mall—they are increasingly accompanying us every moment of the day, watching and analyzing every single thing that we do. As fish live in water, humans live in a digital bureaucracy, constantly inhaling and exhaling data. Each action we make leaves a trace of data, which is gathered and analyzed to identify patterns.

UNDER-THE-SKIN SURVEILLANCE

For better or worse, the digital bureaucracy may not only monitor what we do in the world but even observe what is happening inside our bodies. Take, for example, tracking eye movements. Since the early 2020s, CCTV cameras, as well as cameras in laptops and smartphones, have begun to routinely collect and analyze data on the movements of our eyes, including tiny changes to our pupils and irises lasting just a few milliseconds. Human agents are barely capable of even noticing such data, but computers can use it to calculate the direction of our gaze, based on the shape of our pupils and irises and on the patterns of light they reflect. Similar methods can determine whether our eyes are fixating on a stable target, pursuing a moving target, or wandering around more haphazardly.

From certain patterns of eye movements, computers can then distinguish, for example, moments of awareness from moments of distraction, and detail-oriented people from those who pay more attention to context. Computers could infer from our eyes many additional personality traits, like how open we are to new experiences, and estimate our level of expertise in various fields ranging from reading to surgery. Experts possessing well-honed strategies display systematic gaze patterns, whereas the eyes of novices wander aimlessly. Eye patterns also indicate our levels of interest in the objects and situations we encounter, and distinguish between positive, neutral, and negative interest. From this, it is possible to deduce our preferences in fields ranging from politics to sex. Much can also be known about our medical condition and our use of various substances. The consumption of alcohol and drugs—even at nonintoxicating doses—has measurable effects on eye and gaze properties, such as changes in pupil size and an impaired ability to fixate on moving objects. A digital bureaucracy may use all that information for benign purposes—such as by providing early detection for people

suffering from drug abuse and mental illnesses. But it could obviously also form the foundations of the most intrusive totalitarian regimes in history.[15]

In theory, the dictators of the future could get their computer network to go much deeper than just watching our eyes. If the network wants to know our political views, personality traits, and sexual orientation, it could monitor processes inside our hearts and brains. The necessary biometric technology is already being developed by some governments and companies, like Elon Musk's Neuralink. Musk's company has conducted experiments on live rats, sheep, pigs, and monkeys, implanting electrical probes into their brains. Each probe contains up to 3,072 electrodes capable of identifying electrical signals and potentially transmitting signals to the brain. In 2023, Neuralink received approval from U.S. authorities to begin experiments on human beings, and in January 2024 it was reported that a first brain chip was implanted in a human.

Musk speaks openly about his far-reaching plans for this technology, arguing that it can not only alleviate various medical conditions such as quadriplegia (four-limb paralysis) but also upgrade human abilities and thereby help humankind compete with AI. But it should be clear that at present the Neuralink probes and all other similar biometric devices suffer from a host of technical problems that greatly limit their capabilities. It is difficult to accurately monitor bodily activities—in the brain, heart, or anywhere else—from outside the body, whereas implanting electrodes and other monitoring devices into the body is intrusive, dangerous, costly, and inefficient. Our immune system, for example, attacks implanted electrodes.[16]

Even more crucially, nobody yet has the biological knowledge necessary to deduce things like precise political opinions from under-the-skin data like brain activity.[17] Scientists are far from understanding the mysteries of the human brain, or even of the mouse brain. Simply mapping every neuron, dendrite, and synapse in a mouse

brain—let alone understanding the dynamics between them—is currently beyond humanity's computational abilities.[18] Accordingly, while gathering data from inside people's brains is becoming more feasible, using such data to decipher our secrets is far from easy.

One popular conspiracy theory of the early 2020s argues that sinister groups led by billionaires like Elon Musk are already implanting computer chips into our brains in order to monitor and control us. However, this theory focuses our anxieties on the wrong target. We should of course fear the rise of new totalitarian systems, but it is too soon to worry about computer chips implanted in our brains. People should instead worry about the smartphones on which they read these conspiracy theories. Suppose someone wants to know your political views. Your smartphone monitors which news channels you are watching and notes that you watch on average forty minutes of Fox News and forty seconds of CNN a day. Meanwhile, an implanted Neuralink computer chip monitors your heart rate and brain activity throughout the day and notes that your maximum heart rate was 120 beats per minute and that your amygdala is about 5 percent more active than the human average. Which data would be more useful to guess your political affiliation—the data coming from the smartphone or from the implanted chip?[19] At present, the smartphone is still a far more valuable surveillance tool than biometric sensors.

However, as biological knowledge increases—not least thanks to computers analyzing petabits of biometric data—under-the-skin surveillance might eventually come into its own, especially if it is linked to other monitoring tools. At that point, if biometric sensors register what happens to the heart rate and brain activity of millions of people as they watch a particular news item on their smartphones, that can teach the computer network far more than just our general political affiliation. The network could learn precisely what makes each human angry, fearful, or joyful. The network could then both predict and manipulate our feelings, selling us anything it wants—be it a product, a politician, or a war.[20]

THE END OF PRIVACY

In a world where humans monitored humans, privacy was the default. But in a world where computers monitor humans, it may become possible for the first time in history to completely annihilate privacy. The most extreme and well-known cases of intrusive surveillance involve either exceptional times of emergency, like the COVID-19 pandemic, or places seen as exceptional to the normal order of things, such as the Occupied Palestinian Territories, the Xinjiang Uyghur Autonomous Region in China, the region of Kashmir in India, Russian-occupied Crimea, the U.S.-Mexico border, and the Afghanistan-Pakistan borderlands. In these exceptional times and places, new surveillance technologies, combined with draconian laws and heavy police or military presence, have relentlessly monitored and controlled people's movements, actions, and even feelings.[21] What is crucial to realize, though, is that AI-based surveillance systems are being deployed on an enormous scale, and not only in such "states of exception."[22] They are now part and parcel of normal life everywhere. The post-privacy era is taking hold in authoritarian countries ranging from Belarus to Zimbabwe,[23] as well as in democratic metropolises like London and New York.

Whether for good or ill, governments intent on combating crime, suppressing dissent, or countering internal threats (real or imaginary) blanket whole territories with a ubiquitous online and offline surveillance network, equipped with spyware, CCTV cameras, facial recognition and voice recognition software, and vast searchable databases. If a government wishes, its surveillance network can reach everywhere, from markets to places of worship, from schools to private residences. (And while not every government is willing or able to install cameras inside people's homes, algorithms regularly watch us even in our living rooms, bedrooms, and bathrooms via our own computers and smartphones.)

Governmental surveillance networks also routinely collect bio-

metric data from entire populations, with or without their knowledge. For example, when applying for a passport, more than 140 countries oblige their citizens to provide fingerprints, facial scans, or iris scans.[24] When we use our passports to enter a foreign country, that country often demands that we provide it, too, with our fingerprints, facial scans, or iris scans.[25] As citizens or tourists walk along the streets of Delhi, Beijing, Seoul, or London, their movements are likely to be recorded. For these cities—and many others around the world—are covered by more than one hundred surveillance cameras on average per square kilometer. Altogether, in 2023 more than one billion CCTV cameras were operative globally, which is about one camera per eight people.[26]

Any physical activity a person engages in leaves a data trace. Every purchase made is recorded in some database. Online activities like messaging friends, sharing photos, paying bills, reading news, booking appointments, or ordering taxis can all be recorded as well. The resulting ocean of data can then be analyzed by AI systems to identify unlawful activities, suspicious patterns, missing persons, disease carriers, or political dissidents.

As with every powerful technology, these systems can be used for either good or bad purposes. Following the storming of the U.S. Capitol on January 6, 2021, the FBI and other U.S. law enforcement agencies used state-of-the-art surveillance systems to track down and arrest the rioters. As reported in a *Washington Post* investigation, these agencies relied not only on footage from the CCTV cameras in the Capitol, but also on social media posts, license plate readers throughout the country, cell-tower location records, and preexisting databases.

One Ohio man wrote on Facebook that he had been in Washington that day to "witness history." A subpoena was issued to Facebook, which provided the FBI with the man's Facebook posts, as well as his credit card information and phone number. This helped the FBI to match the man's driver's license photo to CCTV footage from the Capitol. Another warrant issued to Google yielded the

exact geolocation of the man's smartphone on January 6, enabling agents to map his every movement from his entry point into the Senate chamber all the way to the office of Nancy Pelosi, the speaker of the House of Representatives.

Relying on license plate footage, the FBI pinpointed the movements of a New York man from the moment he crossed the Henry Hudson Bridge at 6:06:08 on the morning of January 6, on his way to the Capitol, until he crossed the George Washington Bridge at 23:59:22 that night, on his way back home. An image taken by a camera on Interstate 95 showed an oversized "Make America Great Again" hat on the man's dashboard. The hat was matched to a Facebook selfie in which the man appeared wearing it. He further incriminated himself with several videos he posted to Snapchat from within the Capitol.

Another rioter sought to protect himself from detection by wearing a face mask on January 6, avoiding live-streaming, and using a cellphone registered in his mother's name—but it availed him little. The FBI's algorithms managed to match video footage from January 6, 2021, to a photo from the man's 2017 passport application. They also matched a distinctive Knights of Columbus jacket he wore on January 6 to the jacket he wore on a different occasion, which was captured in a YouTube clip. The phone registered in his mother's name was geolocated to inside the Capitol, and a license plate reader recorded his car near the Capitol on the morning of January 6.[27]

Facial recognition algorithms and AI-searchable databases are now routinely used by police forces all over the world. They are deployed not only in cases of national emergencies or for reasons of state security, but for everyday policing tasks. In 2009, a criminal gang abducted the three-year-old Gui Hao while he was playing outside his parents' shop in Sichuan province, China. The boy was then sold to a family in Guangdong province, about 1,500 kilometers away. In 2014, the leader of the child-trafficking gang was arrested, but it proved impossible to locate Gui Hao and other victims. "The appearance of the children would have changed so much," explained

a police investigator, "that even their parents would not have been able to recognize them."

In 2019, however, a facial recognition algorithm managed to identify the now thirteen-year-old Gui Hao, and the teenager was reunited with his family. To correctly identify Gui Hao, the AI relied on an old photograph of his, taken when he was a toddler. The AI simulated what Gui Hao must look like as a thirteen-year-old, taking into account the drastic impact of maturation as well as potential changes in hair color and hairstyle and compared the resulting simulation to real-life footage.

In 2023, even more remarkable rescues were reported. Yuechuan Lei was abducted in 2001 when he was three years old, and Hao Chen went missing in 1998, also at age three. The parents of both children never gave up hope of finding them. For more than twenty years they crisscrossed China in search of them, placed advertisements, and offered monetary rewards for any relevant information. In 2023, facial recognition algorithms helped locate both missing boys, now adult men in their twenties. Such technology currently helps to find lost children not only in China, but also in other countries like India, where tens of thousands of children go missing every year.[28]

Meanwhile, in Denmark, the soccer club Brøndby IF began in July 2019 to use facial recognition technology in its home stadium to identify and ban football hooligans. As up to 30,000 fans stream into the stadium to watch a match, they are asked to remove masks, hats, and glasses so a computer can scan their faces and compare them to a list of banned troublemakers. Crucially, the procedure has been vetted and approved in accordance with the EU's strict GDPR rules. The Danish Data Protection Authority explained that the use of the technology "would allow for more effective enforcement of the ban list compared to manual checks, and that this could reduce the queues at the stadium entrance, lowering the risk of public unrest from impatient football fans standing in queues."[29]

While such usages of technology are laudable in theory, they raise obvious concerns about privacy and governmental overreach. In the wrong hands, the same techniques that can locate rioters, rescue missing children, and ban football hooligans can also be used to persecute peaceful demonstrators or enforce rigid conformism. Ultimately, AI-powered surveillance technology could result in the creation of total surveillance regimes that monitor citizens around the clock and facilitate new kinds of ubiquitous and automated totalitarian repression. A case in point: Iran's hijab laws.

After Iran became an Islamic theocracy in 1979, the new regime made it compulsory for women to wear the hijab. But the Iranian morality police found it difficult to enforce this rule. They couldn't place a police officer on every street corner, and public confrontations with women who went unveiled occasionally aroused resistance and resentment. In 2022, Iran relegated much of the job of enforcing the hijab laws to a countrywide system of facial recognition algorithms that relentlessly monitor both physical spaces and online environments.[30] A top Iranian official explained that the system would "identify inappropriate and unusual movements" including "failure to observe hijab laws." The head of Iran's parliamentary legal and judicial committee, Mousa Ghazanfarabadi, said in another interview that "the use of face recording cameras can systematically implement this task and reduce the presence of the police, as a result of which there will be no more clashes between the police and citizens."[31]

Shortly afterward, on September 16, 2022, the 22-year-old Mahsa Amini died in the custody of Iran's morality police, after being arrested for not wearing her hijab properly.[32] A wave of protests erupted, known as the "Woman, Life, Freedom" movement. Hundreds of thousands of women and girls removed their headscarves, and some publicly burned their hijabs, and danced around the bonfires. To clamp down on the protests, Iranian authorities once again turned to their AI surveillance system, which relies on facial recogni-

tion software, geolocation, analysis of web traffic, and preexisting databases. More than 19,000 people were arrested throughout Iran, and more than 500 were killed.[33]

On April 8, 2023, Iran's chief of police announced that beginning on April 15, 2023, an intense new campaign would ramp up the use of facial recognition technology. In particular, algorithms would henceforth identify women who choose not to wear a headscarf while travelling in a vehicle, and automatically issue them an SMS warning. If a woman was caught repeating the offense, she would be ordered to immobilize her car for a predetermined period, and if she failed to comply, the car would be confiscated.[34]

Two months later, on June 14, 2023, the spokesperson of Iran's police boasted that the automated surveillance system sent almost one million SMS warning messages to women who had been captured unveiled in their private cars. The system was apparently able to automatically determine that it was seeing an unveiled woman rather than a man, identify the woman, and retrieve her cellphone number. The system further "issued 133,174 SMS messages requiring the immobilization of vehicles for two weeks, confiscated 2,000 cars, and referred more than 4,000 'repeat offenders' to the judiciary."[35]

A 52-year-old woman named Maryam shared with Amnesty International her experience with the surveillance system. "The first time I received a warning for not wearing a headscarf while driving, I was passing through an intersection when a camera captured a photo and I immediately received a warning text message. The second time, I had done some shopping, and I was bringing the bags into the car, my scarf fell off, and I received a message noting that due to violating compulsory veiling laws, my car had been subjected to 'systematic impoundment' for a period of fifteen days. I did not know what this meant. I asked around and found out through relatives that this meant I had to immobilize my car for fifteen days."[36] Maryam's testimony indicates that the AI sends its threatening mes-

sages within seconds, with no time for any human to review and authorize the procedure.

Penalties went far beyond the immobilization or confiscation of vehicles. The Amnesty report from July 26, 2023, revealed that as a result of the mass surveillance effort "countless women have been suspended or expelled from universities, barred from sitting final exams, and denied access to banking services and public transport."[37] Businesses that didn't enforce the hijab law among their employees or customers also suffered. In one typical case, a woman employee at the Land of Happiness amusement park east of Tehran was photographed without a hijab, and the image circulated on social media. In punishment, the Land of Happiness was closed down by Iranian authorities.[38] Altogether, reported Amnesty, the authorities "shut down hundreds of tourist attractions, hotels, restaurants, pharmacies and shopping centres for not enforcing compulsory veiling laws."[39]

In September 2023, on the anniversary of Mahsa Amini's death, Iran's parliament passed a new and stricter hijab bill. According to the new law, women who fail to wear the hijab can be punished by heavy fines and up to ten years in prison. They face additional penalties including confiscation of cars and communication devices, driving bans, deductions in salary and employment benefits, dismissal from work, and prohibition from accessing banking services. Business owners who don't enforce the hijab law among their employees or customers face a fine of up to three months of their profits, and they may be banned from leaving the country or participating in public or online activities for up to two years. The new bill targets not only women, but also men who wear "revealing clothing that shows parts of the body lower than the chest or above the ankles." Finally, the law mandates that Iranian police must "create and strengthen AI systems to identify perpetrators of illegal behavior using tools such as fixed and mobile cameras."[40] In coming years, many people might be living under total surveillance regimes that would make Ceauşescu's Romania look like a libertarian utopia.

VARIETIES OF SURVEILLANCE

When talking about surveillance, we usually think of state-run apparatuses, but to understand surveillance in the twenty-first century, we should remember that monitoring can take many other forms. Jealous partners, for example, have always wanted to know where their spouses were at every moment and demanded explanations for any little deviation from routines. Today, armed with a smartphone and some cheap software, they can easily establish marital dictatorships. They can monitor every conversation and every movement, record phone logs, track social media posts and web page searches, and even activate the cameras and microphones of a spouse's phone to serve as a spying device. The U.S.-based National Network to End Domestic Violence found that more than half of domestic abusers used such stalkerware technology. Even in New York a spouse may find themselves monitored and restricted, as if they lived in a totalitarian state.[41]

A growing percentage of employees—from office workers to truck drivers—are also now being surveilled by their employers. Bosses can pinpoint where employees are at any moment, how much time they spend in the toilet, whether they read personal emails at work, and how fast they complete each task.[42] Corporations are similarly monitoring their customers, wanting to know their likes and dislikes, to predict future behavior, and to evaluate risks and opportunities. For example, vehicles monitor their drivers' behavior and share the data with the algorithms of the insurance companies, which raise the premiums they charge "bad drivers" and lower the premiums for "good drivers."[43] The American scholar Shoshana Zuboff has termed this ever-expanding commercial monitoring system "surveillance capitalism."[44]

In addition to all these varieties of top-down surveillance, there are peer-to-peer systems in which individuals constantly monitor one another. For example, the Tripadvisor corporation maintains a

worldwide surveillance system that monitors hotels, vacation rentals, restaurants, and tourists. In 2019, it was used by 463 million travelers who browsed 859 million reviews and 8.6 billion lodgings, restaurants, and tourist attractions. It is the users themselves—rather than some sophisticated AI algorithm—who determine whether a restaurant is worth visiting. People who ate in the restaurant can score it on a 1 to 5 scale, and also add photos and written reviews. The Tripadvisor algorithm merely aggregates the data, calculates the restaurant's average score, ranks the restaurant compared with others of its kind, and makes the results available for everybody to see.

The algorithm simultaneously ranks the guests, too. For posting reviews or travel articles, users receive 100 points; for uploading photos or videos, 30 points; for posting in a forum, 20 points; for rating establishments, 5 points; and for casting votes for others' reviews, 1 point. Users are then ranked from Level 1 (300 points) to Level 6 (10,000 points) and receive perks accordingly. Users who violate the system's rules—for example, by submitting racist comments or trying to blackmail a restaurant by writing an unjustified bad review—may be penalized or kicked out of the system altogether. This is peer-to-peer surveillance. Everybody is constantly grading everybody else. Tripadvisor doesn't need to invest in cameras and spyware or develop hyper-sophisticated biometric algorithms. Almost all the data is submitted and almost all the work is done by millions of human users. The job of the Tripadvisor algorithm is only to aggregate human-generated scores and publish them.[45]

Tripadvisor and similar peer-to-peer surveillance systems provide valuable information for millions of people every day, making it easier to plan vacations and find good hotels and restaurants. But in doing so, they have also shifted the border between private and public spaces. Traditionally, the relationship between the customer and a waiter, say, was a relatively private affair. Entering a bistro meant entering a semiprivate space and establishing a semiprivate relationship with the waiter. Unless some crime was committed, what happened between guest and waiter was their business alone. If the

waiter was rude or made a racist remark, you could make a scene and perhaps tell your friends not to go there, but few other people would hear about it.

Peer-to-peer surveillance networks have obliterated that sense of privacy. If the staff fails to please a customer, the restaurant will get a bad review, which could affect the decision of thousands of potential customers in coming years. For better or worse, the balance of power tilts in favor of the customers, while the staff find themselves more exposed than before to the public gaze. As the author and journalist Linda Kinstler put it, "Before Tripadvisor, the customer was only nominally king. After, he became a veritable tyrant, with the power to make or break lives."[46] The same loss of privacy is felt today by millions of taxi drivers, barbers, beauticians, and other service providers. In the past, stepping into a taxi or barbershop meant stepping into someone's private space. Now, when customers come into your taxi or barbershop, they bring cameras, microphones, a surveillance network, and thousands of potential viewers with them.[47] This is the foundation of a nongovernmental peer-to-peer surveillance network.

THE SOCIAL CREDIT SYSTEM

Peer-to-peer surveillance systems typically operate by aggregating many points to determine an overall score. Another type of surveillance network takes this "score logic" to its ultimate conclusion. This is the social credit system, which seeks to give people points for *everything* and produce an overall personal score that will influence *everything*. The last time humans came up with such an ambitious points system was five thousand years ago in Mesopotamia, when money was invented. One way to think of the social credit system is as a new kind of money.

Money is points that people accumulate by selling certain products and services, and then use to buy other products and services. Some countries call their "points" dollars, whereas other countries

call them euros, yen, or renminbi. The points can take the form of coins, banknotes, or bits in a digital bank account. The points themselves are, of course, intrinsically worthless. You cannot eat coins or wear banknotes. Their value lies in the fact that they serve as accounting tokens that society uses to keep track of our individual scores.

Money revolutionized economic relations, social interactions, and human psychology. But like surveillance, money has had its limitations and could not reach everywhere. Even in the most capitalist societies, there have always been places that money didn't penetrate, and there have always been many things that lacked a monetary value. How much is a smile worth? How much money does a person earn for visiting their grandparents?[48]

For scoring those things that money can't buy, there was an alternative nonmonetary system, which has been given different names: honor, status, reputation. What social credit systems seek is a standardized valuation of the reputation market. Social credit is a new points system that ascribes precise values even to smiles and family visits. To appreciate how revolutionary and far-reaching this is, let's examine in brief how the reputation market has hitherto differed from the money market. This will help us understand what might happen to social relations if the principles of the money market are suddenly extended to the reputation market.

One major difference between money and reputation is that money has tended to be a mathematical construct based on precise calculations, whereas the sphere of reputation has been resistant to precise numerical evaluation. For example, medieval aristocrats graded themselves in hierarchical ranks such as dukes, counts, and viscounts, but nobody was counting reputation points. Customers in a medieval market usually knew how many coins they had in their purses and the price of every product in the stalls. In the money market, no coin goes uncounted. In contrast, knights in a medieval reputational market didn't know the exact amount of honor that different actions might accrue, nor could they be sure of their overall score.

Would fighting bravely in battle bring a knight 10 honor points, or 100? And what if nobody saw and recorded their bravery? Indeed, even assuming it was noticed, different people might assign it different values. This lack of precision wasn't a bug in the system but a crucial feature. "Calculating" was a synonym for cunning and scheming. Acting honorably was supposed to reflect an inner virtue, rather than a pursuit of external rewards.[49]

This difference between the scrupulous money market and the ill-defined reputation market still prevails. The owner of a bistro always notices and complains if you don't pay for your meal in full; every item on the menu has a precise price. But how would the owner even know if society failed to register some good deed they performed? Whom could they complain to if they weren't properly rewarded for helping an elderly customer or for being extra patient with a rude customer? In some cases, they might now try complaining to Tripadvisor, which collapses the boundary between the money market and the reputation market, turning the fuzzy reputation of restaurants and hotels into a mathematical system of precise points. The idea of social credit is to expand this surveillance method from restaurants and hotels to everything. In the most extreme type of social credit systems, every person gets an overall reputation score that takes into account whatever they do and determines everything they can do.

For example, you might earn 10 points for picking up trash from the street, get another 20 points for helping an old lady cross the road, and lose 15 points for playing the drums and disturbing the neighbors. If you get a high enough score, it might give you priority when buying train tickets or a leg up when applying to university. If you get a low score, potential employers may refuse to give you a job, and potential dates may refuse your advances. Insurance companies may demand higher premiums, and judges may inflict harsher sentences.

Some people might see social credit systems as a way to reward pro-social behavior, punish egotistical acts, and create kinder and

more harmonious societies. The Chinese government, for example, explains that its social credit systems could help fight corruption, scams, tax evasion, false advertising, and counterfeiting, and thereby establish more trust between individuals, between consumers and corporations, and between citizens and government institutions.[50] Others may find systems that allocate precise values to every social action demeaning and inhuman. Even worse, a comprehensive social credit system will annihilate privacy and effectively turn life into a never-ending job interview. Anything you do, anytime, anywhere, might affect your chances of getting a job, a bank loan, a husband, or a prison sentence. You got drunk at a college party and did something legal but shameful? You participated in a political demonstration? You're friends with someone who has a low credit score? This will be part of your job interview—or criminal sentencing—both in the short term and even decades later. The social credit system might thereby become a totalitarian control system.

Of course, the reputation market always controlled people and made them conform to the prevailing social norms. In most societies people have always feared losing face even more than they have feared losing money. Many more people commit suicide due to shame and guilt than due to economic distress. Even when people kill themselves after being fired from their job or after their business goes bankrupt, they are usually pushed over the edge by the social humiliation it involves rather than by the economic hardship per se.[51]

But the uncertainty and the subjectivity of the reputation market have previously limited its potential for totalitarian control. Since nobody knew the precise value of each social interaction, and since nobody could possibly keep tabs on *all* interactions, there was significant room for maneuver. When you went to a college party, you might have behaved in a way that earned the respect of your friends, without worrying what future employers might think. When you went to a job interview, you knew none of your friends would be there. And when you were watching pornography at home, you as-

sumed that neither your bosses nor your friends knew what you were up to. Life has been divided into separate reputational spheres, with separate status competitions, and there were also many off-grid moments when you didn't have to engage in any status competitions at all. Precisely because status competition is so crucial, it is also extremely stressful. Therefore, not only humans but even other social animals like apes have always welcomed some respite from it.[52]

Unfortunately, social credit algorithms combined with ubiquitous surveillance technology now threaten to merge all status competitions into a single never-ending race. Even in their own homes or while trying to enjoy a relaxed vacation, people would have to be extremely careful about every deed and word, as if they were performing onstage in front of millions. This could create an incredibly stressful lifestyle, destructive to people's well-being as well as to the functioning of society. If digital bureaucrats use a precise points system to keep tabs on everybody all the time, the emerging reputation market could annihilate privacy and control people far more tightly than the money market ever did.

ALWAYS ON

Humans are organic beings who live by cyclical biological time. Sometimes we are awake; sometimes we are asleep. After intense activity, we need rest. We grow and decay. Networks of humans are similarly subject to biological cycles. They are sometimes on and sometimes off. Job interviews don't last forever. Police agents don't work twenty-four hours a day. Bureaucrats take holidays. Even the money market respects these biological cycles. The New York Stock Exchange is open Monday to Friday, from 9:30 in the morning to 4:00 in the afternoon, and is closed on holidays like Independence Day and New Year's Day. If a war erupts at 4:01 P.M. on a Friday, the market won't react to it until Monday morning.

In contrast, a network of computers can always be on. Computers

are consequently pushing humans toward a new kind of existence in which we are always connected and always monitored. In some contexts, like health care, this could be a boon. In other contexts, like for citizens of totalitarian states, this could be a disaster. Even if the network is potentially benign, the very fact that it is always on might be damaging to organic entities like humans, because it will take away our opportunities to disconnect and relax. If an organism never has a chance to rest, it eventually collapses and dies. But how will we get a relentless network to slow down and allow us some breaks?

We need to prevent the computer network from taking complete control of society not just in order to give us time off. Breaks are even more crucial to give us a chance to rectify the network. If the network continues to evolve at an accelerating pace, errors will accumulate much faster than we can identify and correct them. For while the network is relentless and ubiquitous, it is also fallible. Yes, computers can gather unprecedented amounts of data on us, watching what we do twenty-four hours a day. And yes, they can identify patterns in the ocean of data with superhuman efficiency. But that does *not* mean that the computer network will always understand the world accurately. Information isn't truth. A total surveillance system may form a very distorted understanding of the world and of human beings. Instead of discovering the truth about the world and about us, the network might use its immense power to create a new kind of world order and impose it on us.

CHAPTER 8

Fallible: The Network Is
Often Wrong

In *The Gulag Archipelago* (1973), Aleksandr Solzhenitsyn chronicles the history of the Soviet labor camps and of the information network that created and sustained them. He was writing partly from bitter personal experience. When Solzhenitsyn served as a captain in the Red Army during World War II, he maintained a private correspondence with a school friend in which he occasionally criticized Stalin. To be on the safe side, he did not mention the dictator by name and spoke only about "the man with the mustache." It availed him little. His letters were intercepted and read by the secret police, and in February 1945, while serving on the front line in Germany, he was arrested. He spent the next eight years in labor camps.[1] Many of Solzhenitsyn's hard-won insights and stories are still relevant to understanding the development of information networks in the twenty-first century.

One story recounts events at a district party conference in Moscow Province in the late 1930s, at the height of the Stalinist Great Terror. A call was made to pay tribute to Stalin, and the audience—who of course knew that they were being carefully watched—burst into applause. After five minutes of applause, "palms were getting

sore and raised arms were already aching. And the older people were panting from exhaustion. . . . However, who would dare be the *first* to stop?" Solzhenitsyn explains that "NKVD men were standing in the hall applauding and watching to see *who* quit first!" It went on and on, for six minutes, then eight, then ten. "They couldn't stop now till they collapsed with heart attacks! . . . With make-believe enthusiasm on their faces, looking at each other with faint hope, the district leaders were just going to go on and on applauding till they fell where they stood."

Finally, after eleven minutes, the director of a paper factory took his life in his hands, stopped clapping, and sat down. Everyone else immediately stopped clapping and also sat down. That same night, the secret police arrested him and sent him to the gulag for ten years. "His interrogator reminded him: Don't ever be the first to stop applauding!"[2]

This story reveals a crucial and disturbing fact about information networks, and in particular about surveillance systems. As discussed in previous chapters, contrary to the naive view, information is often used to create order rather than discover truth. On the face of it, Stalin's agents in the Moscow conference used the "clapping test" as a way to uncover the truth about the audience. It was a loyalty test, which assumed that the longer you clapped, the more you loved Stalin. In many contexts, this assumption is not unreasonable. But in the context of Moscow in the late 1930s, the nature of the applause changed. Since participants in the conference knew they were being watched, and since they knew the consequences of any hint of disloyalty, they clapped out of terror rather than love. The paper factory director might have been the first to stop not because he was the least loyal but perhaps because he was the most honest, or even simply because his hands hurt the most.

While the clapping test didn't discover the truth about people, it was efficient in imposing order and forcing people to behave in a certain way. Over time, such methods cultivated servility, hypocrisy, and cynicism. This is what the Soviet information network did to

hundreds of millions of people over decades. In quantum mechanics the act of observing subatomic particles changes their behavior; it is the same with the act of observing humans. The more powerful our tools of observation, the greater the potential impact.

The Soviet regime constructed one of the most formidable information networks in history. It gathered and processed enormous amounts of data on its citizens. It also claimed that the infallible theories of Marx, Engels, Lenin, and Stalin granted it a deep understanding of humanity. In fact, the Soviet information network ignored many important aspects of human nature, and it was in complete denial regarding the terrible suffering its policies inflicted on its own citizens. Instead of producing wisdom, it produced order, and instead of revealing the universal truth about humans, it actually created a new type of human—*Homo sovieticus*.

As defined by the dissident Soviet philosopher and satirist Aleksandr Zinovyev, *Homo sovieticus* were servile and cynical humans, lacking all initiative or independent thinking, passively obeying even the most ludicrous orders, and indifferent to the results of their actions.[3] The Soviet information network created *Homo sovieticus* through surveillance, punishments, and rewards. For example, by sending the director of the paper factory to the gulag, the network signaled to the other participants that conformity paid off, whereas being the first to do anything controversial was a bad idea. Though the network failed to discover the truth about humans, it was so good at creating order that it conquered much of the world.

THE DICTATORSHIP OF THE LIKE

An analogous dynamic may afflict the computer networks of the twenty-first century, which might create new types of humans and new dystopias. A paradigmatic example is the role played by social media algorithms in radicalizing people. Of course, the methods employed by the algorithms have been utterly different from those of

the NKVD and involved no direct coercion or violence. But just as the Soviet secret police created the slavish *Homo sovieticus* through surveillance, rewards, and punishments, so also the Facebook and YouTube algorithms have created internet trolls by rewarding certain base instincts while punishing the better angels of our nature.

As explained briefly in chapter 6, the process of radicalization started when corporations tasked their algorithms with increasing user engagement, not only in Myanmar, but throughout the world. For example, in 2012 users were watching about 100 million hours of videos every day on YouTube. That was not enough for company executives, who set their algorithms an ambitious goal: 1 billion hours a day by 2016.[4] Through trial-and-error experiments on millions of people, the YouTube algorithms discovered the same pattern that Facebook algorithms also learned: outrage drives engagement up, while moderation tends not to. Accordingly, the YouTube algorithms began recommending outrageous conspiracy theories to millions of viewers while ignoring more moderate content. By 2016, users were indeed watching one billion hours every day on YouTube.[5]

YouTubers who were particularly intent on gaining attention noticed that when they posted an outrageous video full of lies, the algorithm rewarded them by recommending the video to numerous users and increasing the YouTubers' popularity and income. In contrast, when they dialed down the outrage and stuck to the truth, the algorithm tended to ignore them. Within a few months of such reinforcement learning, the algorithm turned many YouTubers into trolls.[6]

The social and political consequences were far-reaching. For example, as the journalist Max Fisher documented in his 2022 book, *The Chaos Machine*, YouTube algorithms became an important engine for the rise of the Brazilian far right and for turning Jair Bolsonaro from a fringe figure into Brazil's president.[7] While there were other factors contributing to that political upheaval, it is notable that many of Bolsonaro's chief supporters and aides had originally been YouTubers who rose to fame and power by algorithmic grace.

A typical example is Carlos Jordy, who in 2017 was a city councilor in the small town of Niterói. The ambitious Jordy gained national attention by creating inflammatory YouTube videos that garnered millions of views. His videos warned Brazilians, for example, against conspiracies by schoolteachers to brainwash children and persecute conservative pupils. In 2018, Jordy won a seat in the Brazilian Chamber of Deputies (the lower house of the Brazilian Congress) as one of Bolsonaro's most dedicated supporters. In an interview with Fisher, Jordy frankly said, "If social media didn't exist, I wouldn't be here [and] Jair Bolsonaro wouldn't be president." The latter claim may well be a self-serving exaggeration, but there is no denying that social media played an important part in Bolsonaro's rise.

Another YouTuber who won a seat in Brazil's Chamber of Deputies in 2018 was Kim Kataguiri, one of the leaders of the Movimento Brasil Livre (MBL, or Free Brazil Movement). Kataguiri initially used Facebook as his main platform, but his posts were too extreme even for Facebook, which banned some of them for disinformation. So Kataguiri switched over to the more permissive YouTube. In an interview in the MBL headquarters in São Paulo, Kataguiri's aides and other activists explained to Fisher, "We have something here that we call the dictatorship of the like." They explained that YouTubers tend to become steadily more extreme, posting untruthful and reckless content "just because something is going to give you views, going to give engagement.... Once you open that door there's no going back, because you always have to go further.... Flat Earthers, anti-vaxxers, conspiracy theories in politics. It's the same phenomenon. You see it everywhere."[8]

Of course, the YouTube algorithms were not themselves responsible for inventing lies and conspiracy theories or for creating extremist content. At least in 2017–18, those things were done by humans. The algorithms were responsible, however, for incentivizing humans to behave in such ways and for pushing the resulting content in order to maximize user engagement. Fisher documented numer-

ous far-right activists who first became interested in extremist politics after watching videos that the YouTube algorithm *auto-played* for them. One far-right activist in Niterói told Fisher that he was never interested in politics of any kind, until one day the YouTube algorithm auto-played for him a video on politics by Kataguiri. "Before that," he explained, "I didn't have an ideological, political background." He credited the algorithm with providing "my political education." Talking about how other people joined the movement, he said, "It was like that with everyone. . . . Most of the people here came from YouTube and social media."[9]

BLAME THE HUMANS

We have reached a turning point in history in which major historical processes are partly caused by the decisions of nonhuman intelligence. It is this that makes the fallibility of the computer network so dangerous. Computer errors become potentially catastrophic only when computers become historical agents. We have already made this argument in chapter 6, when we briefly examined Facebook's role in instigating the anti-Rohingya ethnic-cleansing campaign. As noted in that context, however, many people—including some of the managers and engineers of Facebook, YouTube, and the other tech giants—object to this argument. Since it is one of the central points of the entire book, it is best to delve deeper into the matter and examine more carefully the objections to it.

The people who manage Facebook, YouTube, TikTok, and other platforms routinely try to excuse themselves by shifting the blame from their algorithms to "human nature." They argue that it is human nature that produces all the hate and lies on the platforms. The tech giants then claim that due to their commitment to free-speech values, they hesitate to censor the expression of genuine human emotions. For example, in 2019 the CEO of YouTube, Susan Wojcicki, explained, "The way that we think about it is: 'Is this content violat-

ing one of our policies? Has it violated anything in terms of hate, harassment?' If it has, we remove that content. We keep tightening and tightening the policies. We also get criticism, just to be clear, [about] where do you draw the lines of free speech and, if you draw it too tightly, are you removing voices of society that should be heard? We're trying to strike a balance of enabling a broad set of voices, but also making sure that those voices play by a set of rules that are healthy conversations for society."[10]

A Facebook spokesperson similarly said in October 2021, "Like every platform, we are constantly making difficult decisions between free expressions and harmful speech, security and other issues.... But drawing these societal lines is always better left to elected leaders."[11] In this way, the tech giants constantly shift the discussion to their supposed role as moderators of human-produced content and ignore the active role their algorithms play in cultivating certain human emotions and discouraging others. Are they really blind to it?

Surely not. Back in 2016, an internal Facebook report discovered that "64 percent of all extremist group joins are due to our recommendation tools.... Our recommendation systems grow the problem."[12] A secret internal Facebook memo from August 2019, leaked by the whistleblower Frances Haugen, stated, "We have evidence from a variety of sources that hate speech, divisive political speech, and misinformation on Facebook and [its] family of apps are affecting societies around the world. We also have compelling evidence that our core product mechanics, such as virality, recommendations, and optimizing for engagement, are a significant part of why these types of speech flourish on the platform."[13]

Another leaked document from December 2019 noted, "Unlike communication with close friends and family, virality is something new we have introduced to many ecosystems ... and it occurs because we intentionally encourage it for business reasons." The document pointed out that "ranking content about higher stakes topics like health or politics based on engagement leads to perverse incentives and integrity issues." Perhaps most damningly, it revealed, "Our

ranking systems have specific separate predictions for not just what you would engage with, but what we think you may pass along so that others may engage with. Unfortunately, research has shown how outrage and misinformation are more likely to be viral." This leaked document made one crucial recommendation: since Facebook cannot remove everything harmful from a platform used by many millions, it should at least "stop magnifying harmful content by giving it unnatural distribution."[14]

Like the Soviet leaders in Moscow, the tech companies were not uncovering some truth about humans; they were imposing on us a perverse new order. Humans are very complex beings, and benign social orders seek ways to cultivate our virtues while curtailing our negative tendencies. But social media algorithms see us, simply, as an attention mine. The algorithms reduced the multifaceted range of human emotions—hate, love, outrage, joy, confusion—into a single catchall category: engagement. In Myanmar in 2016, in Brazil in 2018, and in numerous other countries, the algorithms scored videos, posts, and all other content solely according to how many minutes people engaged with the content and how many times they shared it with others. An hour of lies or hatred was ranked higher than ten minutes of truth or compassion—or an hour of sleep. The fact that lies and hate tend to be psychologically and socially destructive, whereas truth, compassion, and sleep are essential for human welfare, was completely lost on the algorithms. Based on this very narrow understanding of humanity, the algorithms helped to create a new social system that encouraged our basest instincts while discouraging us from realizing the full spectrum of the human potential.

As the harmful effects were becoming manifest, the tech giants were repeatedly warned about what was happening, but they failed to step in because of their faith in the naive view of information. As the platforms were overrun by falsehoods and outrage, executives hoped that if more people were enabled to express themselves more freely, truth would eventually prevail. This, however, did not happen. As we have seen again and again throughout history, in a completely free

information fight, truth tends to lose. To tilt the balance in favor of truth, networks must develop and maintain strong self-correcting mechanisms that reward truth telling. These self-correcting mechanisms are costly, but if you want to get the truth, you must invest in them.

Silicon Valley thought it was exempt from this historical rule. Social media platforms have been singularly lacking in self-correcting mechanisms. In 2014, Facebook employed just a single Burmese-speaking content moderator to monitor activities in the whole of Myanmar.[15] When observers in Myanmar began warning Facebook that it needed to invest more in moderating content, Facebook ignored them. For example, Pwint Htun, a Burmese American engineer and telecom executive who grew up in rural Myanmar, wrote to Facebook executives repeatedly about the danger. In an email from July 5, 2014—two years before the ethnic-cleansing campaign began—she issued a prophetic warning: "Tragically, FB in Burma is used like radio in Rwanda during the dark days of genocide." Facebook took no action.

Even after the attacks on the Rohingya intensified and Facebook faced a storm of criticism, it still refused to hire people with expert local knowledge to curate content. Thus, when informed that hate-mongers in Myanmar were using the Burmese word *kalar* as a racist slur for the Rohingya, Facebook reacted in April 2017 by banning from the platform any posts that used the word. This revealed Facebook's utter lack of knowledge about local conditions and the Burmese language. In Burmese, *kalar* is a racist slur only in specific contexts. In other contexts, it is an entirely innocent term. The Burmese word for chair is *kalar htaing,* and the word for chickpea is *kalar pae.* As Pwint Htun wrote to Facebook in June 2017, banning the term *kalar* from the platform is like banning the letters "hell" from "hello."[16] Facebook continued to ignore the need for local expertise. By April 2018, the number of Burmese speakers Facebook employed to moderate content for its eighteen million users in Myanmar was a grand total of five.[17]

Instead of investing in self-correcting mechanisms that would reward truth telling, the social media giants actually developed unprecedented error-enhancing mechanisms that rewarded lies and fictions. One such error-enhancing mechanism was the Instant Articles program that Facebook rolled out in Myanmar in 2016. Wishing to drive up engagement, Facebook paid news channels according to the amount of user engagement they generated, measured in clicks and views. No importance whatsoever was given to the truthfulness of the "news." A 2021 study found that in 2015, before the program was launched, six of the ten top Facebook websites in Myanmar belonged to "legitimate media." By 2017, under the impact of Instant Articles, "legitimate media" was down to just two websites out of the top ten. By 2018, all top ten websites were "fake news and clickbait websites."

The study concluded that because of the launch of Instant Articles "clickbait actors cropped up in Myanmar overnight. With the right recipe for producing engaging and evocative content, they could generate thousands of US dollars a month in ad revenue, or ten times the average monthly salary—paid to them directly by Facebook." Since Facebook was by far the most important source of online news in Myanmar, this had enormous impact on the overall media landscape of the country: "In a country where Facebook is synonymous with the Internet, the low-grade content overwhelmed other information sources."[18] Facebook and other social media platforms didn't consciously set out to flood the world with fake news and outrage. But by telling their algorithms to maximize user engagement, this is exactly what they perpetrated.

Reflecting on the Myanmar tragedy, Pwint Htun wrote to me in July 2023, "I naively used to believe that social media could elevate human consciousness and spread the perspective of common humanity through interconnected pre-frontal cortexes in billions of human beings. What I realize is that the social media companies are not incentivized to interconnect pre-frontal cortexes. Social media companies are incentivized to create interconnected limbic systems—which is much more dangerous for humanity."

THE ALIGNMENT PROBLEM

I don't want to imply that the spread of fake news and conspiracy theories is the main problem with all past, present, and future computer networks. YouTube, Facebook, and other social media platforms claim that since 2018 they have been tweaking their algorithms to make them more socially responsible. Whether this is true or not is hard to say, especially because there is no universally accepted definition of "social responsibility."[19] But the specific problem of polluting the information sphere in pursuit of user engagement can certainly be solved. When the tech giants set their hearts on designing better algorithms, they can usually do it. Around 2005, the profusion of spam threatened to make the use of email impossible. Powerful algorithms were developed to address the problem. By 2015, Google claimed its Gmail algorithm had a 99.9 percent success rate in blocking genuine spam, while only 1 percent of legitimate emails were erroneously labeled as such.[20]

We also shouldn't discount the huge social benefits that YouTube, Facebook, and other social media platforms have brought. To be clear, most YouTube videos and Facebook posts have *not* been fake news and genocidal incitements. Social media has been more than helpful in connecting people, giving voice to previously disenfranchised groups, and organizing valuable new movements and communities.[21] It has also encouraged an unprecedented wave of human creativity. In the days when television was the dominant medium, viewers were often denigrated as couch potatoes: passive consumers of content that a few gifted artists produced. Facebook, YouTube, and other social media platforms inspired the couch potatoes to get up and start creating. Most of the content on social media—at least until the rise of powerful generative AI—has been produced by the users themselves, and their cats and dogs, rather than by a limited professional class.

I, too, routinely use YouTube and Facebook to connect with people, and I am grateful to social media for connecting me with my husband, whom I met on one of the first LGBTQ social media platforms back in 2002. Social media has done wonders for dispersed minorities like LGBTQ people. Few gay boys are born to a gay family in a gay neighborhood, and in the days before the internet simply finding one another posed a big challenge, unless you moved to one of the handful of tolerant metropolises that had a gay subculture. Growing up in a small homophobic town in Israel in the 1980s and early 1990s, I didn't know a single openly gay man. Social media in the late 1990s and early 2000s provided an unprecedented and almost magical way for members of the dispersed LGBTQ community to find one another and connect.

And yet I have devoted so much attention to the social media "user engagement" debacle because it exemplifies a much bigger problem afflicting computers—the alignment problem. When computers are given a specific goal, such as to increase YouTube traffic to one billion hours a day, they use all their power and ingenuity to achieve this goal. Since they operate very differently than humans, they are likely to use methods their human overlords didn't anticipate. This can result in dangerous unforeseen consequences that are not aligned with the original human goals. Even if recommendation algorithms stop encouraging hate, other instances of the alignment problem might result in larger catastrophes than the anti-Rohingya campaign. The more powerful and independent computers become, the bigger the danger.

Of course, the alignment problem is neither new nor unique to algorithms. It bedeviled humanity for thousands of years before the invention of computers. It has been, for example, the foundational problem of modern military thinking, enshrined in Carl von Clausewitz's theory of war. Clausewitz was a Prussian general who fought during the Napoleonic Wars. Following Napoleon's final defeat in 1815, Clausewitz became the director of the Prussian War College.

He also began formalizing a grand theory of war. After he died of cholera in 1831, his wife, Marie, edited his unfinished manuscript and published *On War* in several parts between 1832 and 1834.[22]

On War created a rational model for understanding war, and it is still the dominant military theory today. Its most important maxim is that "war is the continuation of policy by other means."[23] This implies that war is not an emotional outbreak, a heroic adventure, or a divine punishment. War is not even a military phenomenon. Rather, war is a political tool. According to Clausewitz, military actions are utterly irrational unless they are aligned with some overarching political goal.

Suppose Mexico contemplates whether to invade and conquer its small neighbor Belize. And suppose a detailed military analysis concludes that if the Mexican army invades, it will achieve a quick and decisive military victory, crushing the small Belize army and conquering the capital, Belmopan, in three days. According to Clausewitz, that does not constitute a rational reason for Mexico to invade. The mere ability to secure military victory is meaningless. The key question the Mexican government should ask itself is, what political goals will the military success achieve?

History is full of decisive military victories that led to political disasters. For Clausewitz, the most obvious example was close to home: Napoleon's career. Nobody disputes the military genius of Napoleon, who was a master of both tactics and strategy. But while his string of victories brought Napoleon temporary control of vast territories, they failed to secure lasting political achievements. His military conquests merely drove most European powers to unite against him, and his empire collapsed a decade after he crowned himself emperor.

Indeed, in the long term, Napoleon's victories ensured the permanent decline of France. For centuries, France was Europe's leading geopolitical power, largely because neither Italy nor Germany existed as a unified political entity. Italy was a hodgepodge of dozens of warring city-states, feudal principalities, and church territories. Ger-

many was an even more bizarre jigsaw puzzle divided into more than a thousand independent polities, loosely held together under the theoretical suzerainty of the Holy Roman Empire of the German Nation.[24] In 1789, the prospect of a German or Italian invasion of France was simply unthinkable, because there was no such thing as a German or Italian army.

As Napoleon expanded his empire into central Europe and the Italian Peninsula, he liquidated the Holy Roman Empire in 1806, amalgamated many of the smaller German and Italian principalities into larger territorial blocs, created a German Confederation of the Rhine and a Kingdom of Italy, and sought to unify these territories under his dynastic rule. His victorious armies also spread the ideals of modern nationalism and popular sovereignty into the German and Italian lands. Napoleon thought all this would make his empire stronger. In fact, by breaking up traditional structures and giving Germans and Italians a taste of national consolidation, Napoleon inadvertently laid the foundations for the ultimate unification of Germany (1866–71) and of Italy (1848–71). These twin processes of national unification were sealed by the German victory over France in the Franco-Prussian War of 1870–71. Faced with two newly unified and fervently nationalistic powers on its eastern border, France never regained its position of dominance.

A more recent example of military victory leading to political defeat was provided by the American invasion of Iraq in 2003. The Americans won every major military engagement, but failed to achieve any of their long-term political aims. Their military victory didn't establish a friendly regime in Iraq, or a favorable geopolitical order in the Middle East. The real winner of the war was Iran. American military victory turned Iraq from Iran's traditional foe into Iran's vassal, thereby greatly weakening the American position in the Middle East while making Iran the regional hegemon.[25]

Both Napoleon and George W. Bush fell victim to the alignment problem. Their short-term military goals were misaligned with their countries' long-term geopolitical goals. We can understand the

whole of Clausewitz's *On War* as a warning that "maximizing victory" is as shortsighted a goal as "maximizing user engagement." According to the Clausewitzian model, only once the political goal is clear can armies decide on a military strategy that will hopefully achieve it. From the overall strategy, lower-ranking officers can then derive tactical goals. The model constructs a clear hierarchy between long-term policy, medium-term strategy, and short-term tactics. Tactics are considered rational only if they are aligned with some strategic goal, and strategy is considered rational only if it is aligned with some political goal. Even local tactical decisions of a lowly company commander must serve the war's ultimate political goal.

Suppose that during the American occupation of Iraq an American company comes under intense fire from a nearby mosque. The company commander has several different tactical decisions to choose from. He might order the company to retreat. He might order the company to storm the mosque. He might order one of his supporting tanks to blow up the mosque. What should the company commander do?

From a purely military perspective, it might seem best for the commander to order his tank to blow up the mosque. This would capitalize on the tactical advantage that the Americans enjoyed in terms of firepower, avoid risking the lives of his own soldiers, and achieve a decisive tactical victory. However, from a political perspective, this might be the worst decision the commander could make. Footage of an American tank destroying a mosque would galvanize Iraqi public opinion against the Americans and create outrage throughout the wider Muslim world. Storming the mosque might also be a political mistake, because it too could create resentment among Iraqis, while the cost in American lives could weaken support for the war among American voters. Given the political war aims of the United States, retreating and conceding tactical defeat might well be the most rational decision.

For Clausewitz, then, rationality means alignment. Pursuing tactical or strategic victories that are misaligned with political goals is

irrational. The problem is that the bureaucratic nature of armies makes them highly susceptible to such irrationality. As discussed in chapter 3, by dividing reality into separate drawers, bureaucracy encourages the pursuit of narrow goals even when this harms the greater good. Bureaucrats tasked with accomplishing a narrow mission may be ignorant of the wider impact of their actions, and it has always been tricky to ensure that their actions remain aligned with the greater good of society. When armies operate along bureaucratic lines—as all modern armies do—it creates a huge gap between a captain commanding a company in the field and the president formulating long-term policy in a distant office. The captain is prone to make decisions that seem reasonable on the ground but that actually undermine the war's ultimate goal.

We see, then, that the alignment problem has long predated the computer revolution and that the difficulties encountered by builders of present-day information empires are not unlike those that bedeviled previous would-be conquerors. Nevertheless, computers do change the nature of the alignment problem in important ways. No matter how difficult it used to be to ensure that human bureaucrats and soldiers remain aligned with society's long-term goals, it is going to be even harder to ensure the alignment of algorithmic bureaucrats and autonomous weapon systems.

THE PAPER-CLIP NAPOLEON

One reason why the alignment problem is particularly dangerous in the context of the computer network is that this network is likely to become far more powerful than any previous human bureaucracy. A misalignment in the goals of superintelligent computers might result in a catastrophe of unprecedented magnitude. In his 2014 book, *Superintelligence*, the philosopher Nick Bostrom illustrated the danger using a thought experiment, which is reminiscent of Goethe's "Sorcerer's Apprentice." Bostrom asks us to imagine that a paper-clip

factory buys a superintelligent computer and that the factory's human manager gives the computer a seemingly simple task: produce as many paper clips as possible. In pursuit of this goal, the paper-clip computer conquers the whole of planet Earth, kills all the humans, sends expeditions to take over additional planets, and uses the enormous resources it acquires to fill the entire galaxy with paper-clip factories.

The point of the thought experiment is that the computer did exactly what it was told (just like the enchanted broomstick in Goethe's poem). Realizing that it needed electricity, steel, land, and other resources to build more factories and produce more paper clips, and realizing that humans are unlikely to give up these resources, the superintelligent computer eliminated all humans in its single-minded pursuit of its given goal.[26] Bostrom's point was that the problem with computers isn't that they are particularly evil but that they are particularly powerful. And the more powerful the computer, the more careful we need to be about defining its goal in a way that precisely aligns with our ultimate goals. If we define a misaligned goal to a pocket calculator, the consequences are trivial. But if we define a misaligned goal to a superintelligent machine, the consequences could be dystopian.

The paper-clip thought experiment may sound outlandish and utterly disconnected from reality. But if Silicon Valley managers had paid attention when Bostrom published it in 2014, perhaps they would have been more careful before instructing their algorithms to "maximize user engagement." The Facebook and YouTube algorithms behaved exactly like Bostrom's imaginary algorithm. When told to maximize paper-clip production, the algorithm sought to convert the entire physical universe into paper clips, even if it meant destroying human civilization. When told to maximize user engagement, the Facebook and YouTube algorithms sought to convert the entire social universe into user engagement, even if it meant doing harm to the social fabric of Myanmar, Brazil, and many other countries.

Bostrom's thought experiment highlights a second reason why the alignment problem is more urgent in the case of computers. Because they are inorganic entities, they are likely to adopt strategies that would never occur to any human and that we are therefore ill-equipped to foresee and forestall. Here's one example: In 2016, Dario Amodei was working on a project called Universe, trying to develop a general-purpose AI that could play hundreds of different computer games. The AI competed well in various car races, so Amodei next tried it on a boat race. Inexplicably, the AI steered its boat right into a harbor and then sailed in endless circles in and out of the harbor.

It took Amodei considerable time to understand what went wrong. The problem occurred because initially Amodei wasn't sure how to tell the AI that its goal was to "win the race." "Winning" is an unclear concept to an algorithm. Translating "win the race" into computer language would have required Amodei to formalize complex concepts like track position and placement among the other boats in the race. So instead, Amodei took the easy way and told the boat to maximize its score. He assumed that the score was a good proxy for winning the race. After all, it worked with the car races.

But the boat race had a peculiar feature, absent from the car races, that allowed the ingenious AI to find a loophole in the game's rules. The game rewarded players with a lot of points for getting ahead of other boats—as in the car races—but it also rewarded them with a few points whenever they replenished their power by docking into a harbor. The AI discovered that if instead of trying to outsail the other boats, it simply went in circles in and out of the harbor, it could accumulate more points far faster. Apparently, none of the game's human developers—nor Dario Amodei—had noticed this loophole. The AI was doing exactly what the game was rewarding it to do—even though it is not what the humans were hoping for. That's the essence of the alignment problem: rewarding A while hoping for B.[27] If we want computers to maximize social benefits, it's a bad idea to reward them for maximizing user engagement.

A third reason to worry about the alignment problem of comput-

ers is that because they are so different from us, when we make the mistake of giving them a misaligned goal, they are less likely to notice it or request clarification. If the boat-race AI had been a human gamer, it would have realized that the loophole it found in the game's rules probably doesn't really count as "winning." If the paper-clip AI had been a human bureaucrat, it would have realized that destroying humanity in order to produce paper clips is probably not what was intended. But since computers aren't humans, we cannot rely on them to notice and flag possible misalignments. In the 2010s the YouTube and Facebook management teams were bombarded with warnings from their human employees—as well as from outside observers—about the harm being done by the algorithms, but the algorithms themselves never raised the alarm.[28]

As we give algorithms greater and greater power over health care, education, law enforcement, and numerous other fields, the alignment problem will loom ever larger. If we don't find ways to solve it, the consequences will be far worse than algorithms racking up points by sailing boats in circles.

THE CORSICAN CONNECTION

How to solve the alignment problem? In theory, when humans create a computer network, they must define for it an ultimate goal, which the computers are never allowed to change or ignore. Then, even if computers become so powerful that we lose control over them, we can rest assured that their immense power will benefit rather than harm us. Unless, of course, it turned out that we defined a harmful or vague goal. And there's the rub. In the case of human networks, we rely on self-correcting mechanisms to periodically review and revise our goals, so setting the wrong goal is not the end of the world. But since the computer network might escape our control, if we set it the wrong goal, we might discover our mistake when we are no longer able to correct it. Some might hope that through a

careful process of deliberation, we might be able to define in advance the right goals for the computer network. This, however, is a very dangerous delusion.

To understand why it is impossible to agree in advance on the ultimate goals of the computer network, let's revisit Clausewitz's war theory. There is one fatal flaw in the way he equates rationality with alignment. While Clausewitzian theory demands that all actions be aligned with the ultimate goal, it offers no rational way to define such a goal. Consider Napoleon's life and military career. What should have been his ultimate goal? Given the prevailing cultural atmosphere of France circa 1800, we can think of several alternatives for "ultimate goal" that might have occurred to Napoleon:

> POTENTIAL GOAL NUMBER 1: Making France the dominant power in Europe, secure against any future attack by Britain, the Habsburg Empire, Russia, a unified Germany, or a unified Italy.
> POTENTIAL GOAL NUMBER 2: Creating a new multiethnic empire ruled by Napoleon's family, which would include not only France but also many additional territories both in Europe and overseas.
> POTENTIAL GOAL NUMBER 3: Achieving everlasting glory for himself personally, so that even centuries after his death billions of people will know the name Napoleon and admire his genius.
> POTENTIAL GOAL NUMBER 4: Securing the redemption of his everlasting soul, and gaining entry to heaven after his death.
> POTENTIAL GOAL NUMBER 5: Spreading the universal ideals of the French Revolution, and helping to protect freedom, equality, and human rights throughout Europe and the world.

Many self-styled rationalists tend to argue that Napoleon should have made it his life's mission to achieve the first goal—securing French domination in Europe. But why? Remember that for Clause-

witz rationality means alignment. A tactical maneuver is rational if, and only if, it is aligned with some higher strategic goal, which should in turn be aligned with an even higher political goal. But where does this chain of goals ultimately start? How can we determine the ultimate goal that justifies all the strategic subgoals and tactical steps derived from it? Such an ultimate goal by definition cannot be aligned with anything higher than itself, because there is nothing higher. What then makes it rational to place France at the top of the goal hierarchy, rather than Napoleon's family, Napoleon's fame, Napoleon's soul, or universal human rights? Clausewitz provides no answer.

One might argue that goal number 4—securing the redemption of his everlasting soul—cannot be a serious candidate for an ultimate rational goal, because it is based on a belief in mythology. But the same argument can be leveled at all the other goals. Everlasting souls are an intersubjective invention that exists only in people's minds, and exactly the same is true of nations and human rights. Why should Napoleon care about the mythical France any more than about his mythical soul?

Indeed, for most of his youth, Napoleon didn't even consider himself French. He was born Napoleone di Buonaparte on Corsica, to a family of Italian emigrants. For five hundred years Corsica was ruled by the Italian city-state of Genoa, where many of Napoleone's ancestors lived. It was only in 1768—a year before Napoleone's birth—that Genoa ceded the island to France. Corsican nationalists resisted being handed over to France and rose in rebellion. Only after their defeat in 1770 did Corsica formally become a French province. Many Corsicans continued to resent the French takeover, but the di Buonaparte family swore allegiance to the French king and sent Napoleone to military school in mainland France.[29]

At school, Napoleone had to endure a good deal of hazing from his classmates for his Corsican nationalism and his poor command of the French language.[30] His mother tongues were Corsican and Italian, and although he gradually became fluent in French, he re-

tained throughout his life a Corsican accent and an inability to spell French correctly.[31] Napoleone eventually enlisted in the French army, but when the Revolution broke out in 1789, he went back to Corsica, hoping the revolution would provide an opportunity for his beloved island to achieve greater autonomy. Only after he fell out with the leader of the Corsican independence movement—Pasquale Paoli—did Napoleone abandon the Corsican cause in May 1793. He returned to the mainland, where he decided to build his future.[32] It was at this stage that Napoleone di Buonaparte turned into Napoléon Bonaparte (he continued to use the Italian version of his name until 1796).[33]

Why then was it rational for Napoleon to devote his military career to making France the dominant power in Europe? Was it perhaps more rational for him to stay in Corsica, patch up his personal disagreements with Paoli, and devote himself to liberating his native island from its French conquerors? And maybe Napoleon should in fact have made it his life's mission to unite Italy—the land of his ancestors?

Clausewitz offers no method to answer these questions rationally. If our only rule of thumb is that "every action must be aligned with some higher goal," by definition there is no rational way to define that ultimate goal. How then can we provide a computer network with an ultimate goal it must never ignore or subvert? Tech executives and engineers who rush to develop AI are making a huge mistake if they think there is a rational way to tell AI what its ultimate goal should be. They should learn from the bitter experiences of generations of philosophers who tried to define ultimate goals and failed.

THE KANTIAN NAZI

For millennia, philosophers have been looking for a definition of an ultimate goal that will not depend on an alignment to some higher

goal. They have repeatedly been drawn to two potential solutions, known in philosophical jargon as deontology and utilitarianism. Deontologists (from the Greek word *deon*, meaning "duty") believe that there are some universal moral duties, or moral rules, that apply to everyone. These rules do not rely on alignment to a higher goal, but rather on their intrinsic goodness. If such rules indeed exist, and if we can find a way to program them into computers, then we can make sure the computer network will be a force for good.

But what exactly does "intrinsic goodness" mean? The most famous attempt to define an intrinsically good rule was made by Immanuel Kant, a contemporary of Clausewitz and Napoleon. Kant argued that an intrinsically good rule is any rule that I would like to make universal. According to this view, a person about to murder someone should stop and go through the following thought process: "I am now going to murder a human. Would I like to establish a universal rule saying that it is okay to murder humans? If such a universal rule is established, then someone might murder me. So there shouldn't be a universal rule allowing murder. It follows that I too shouldn't murder." In simpler language, Kant reformulated the old Golden Rule: "Do unto others what you would have them do unto you" (Matthew 7:12).

This sounds like a simple and obvious idea: each of us should behave in a way we want everyone to behave. But ideas that sound good in the ethereal realm of philosophy often have trouble immigrating to the harsh land of history. The key question historians would ask Kant is, when you talk about universal rules, how exactly do you define "universal"? Under actual historical circumstances, when a person is about to commit murder, the first step they often take is to exclude the victim from the universal community of humanity.[34] This, for example, is what anti-Rohingya extremists like Wirathu did. As a Buddhist monk, Wirathu was certainly against murdering humans. But he didn't think this universal rule applied to killing Rohingya, who were seen as subhuman. In posts and interviews, he repeatedly compared them to beasts, snakes, mad dogs, wolves, jackals,

and other dangerous animals.[35] On October 30, 2017, at the height of the anti-Rohingya violence, another, more senior Buddhist monk preached a sermon to military officers in which he justified violence against the Rohingya by telling the officers that non-Buddhists were "not fully human."[36]

As a thought experiment, imagine a meeting between Immanuel Kant and Adolf Eichmann—who, by the way, considered himself a Kantian.[37] As Eichmann signs an order sending another trainload of Jews to Auschwitz, Kant tells him, "You are about to murder thousands of humans. Would you like to establish a universal rule saying it is okay to murder humans? If you do that, you and your family might also be murdered." Eichmann replies, "No, I am not about to murder thousands of humans. I am about to murder thousands of Jews. If you ask me whether I would like to establish a universal rule saying it is okay to murder Jews, then I am all for it. As for myself and my family, there is no risk that this universal rule would lead to us being murdered. We aren't Jews."

One potential Kantian reply to Eichmann is that when we define entities, we must always use the most universal definition applicable. If an entity can be defined as either "a Jew" or "a human," we should use the more universal term "human." However, the whole point of Nazi ideology was to deny the humanity of Jews. In addition, note that Jews are not just humans. They are also animals, and they are also organisms. Since animals and organisms are obviously more universal categories than "human," if you follow the Kantian argument to its logical conclusion, it might push us to adopt an extreme vegan position. Since we are organisms, does it mean we should object to the killing of any organism, down even to tomatoes or amoebas?

In history, many if not most conflicts concern the definition of identities. Everybody accepts that murder is wrong, but thinks that only killing members of the in-group qualifies as "murder," whereas killing someone from an out-group is not. But the in-groups and out-groups are intersubjective entities, whose definition usually de-

pends on some mythology. Deontologists who pursue universal rational rules often end up the captives of local myths.

This problem with deontology is especially critical if we try to dictate universal deontologist rules not to humans but to computers. Computers aren't even organic. So if they follow a rule of "Do unto others what you would have them do unto you," why should they be concerned about killing organisms like humans? A Kantian computer that doesn't want to be killed has no reason to object to a universal rule saying "It is okay to kill organisms"; such a rule does not endanger the nonorganic computer.

Alternatively, being inorganic entities, computers may have no qualms about dying. As far as we can tell, death is an organic phenomenon and may be inapplicable to inorganic entities. When ancient Assyrians talked about "killing" documents, that was just a metaphor. If computers are more like documents than like organisms, and don't care about "being killed," would we like a Kantian computer to conclude that killing humans is therefore fine?

Is there a way to define whom computers should care about, without getting bogged down by some intersubjective myth? The most obvious suggestion is to tell computers that they must care about any entity capable of suffering. While suffering is often caused by belief in local intersubjective myths, suffering itself is nonetheless a universal reality. Therefore, using the capacity to suffer in order to define the critical in-group grounds morality in an objective and universal reality. A self-driving car should avoid killing all humans—whether Buddhist or Muslim, French or Italian—and should also avoid killing dogs and cats, and any sentient robots that might one day exist. We may even refine this rule, instructing the car to care about different beings in direct proportion to their capacity to suffer. If the car has to choose between killing a human and killing a cat, it should drive over the cat, because presumably the cat has a lesser capacity to suffer. But if we go in that direction, we inadvertently desert the deontologist camp and find ourselves in the camp of their rivals—the utilitarians.

THE CALCULUS OF SUFFERING

Whereas deontologists struggle to find universal rules that are intrinsically good, utilitarians judge actions by their impact on suffering and happiness. The English philosopher Jeremy Bentham—another contemporary of Napoleon, Clausewitz, and Kant—said that the only rational ultimate goal is to minimize suffering in the world and maximize happiness. If our main fear about computer networks is that their misaligned goals might inflict terrible suffering on humans and perhaps on other sentient beings, then the utilitarian solution seems both obvious and attractive. When creating the computer network, we just need to instruct it to minimize suffering and maximize happiness. If Facebook had told its algorithms "maximize happiness" instead of "maximize user engagement," all would allegedly have been well. It is worth noting that this utilitarian approach is indeed popular in Silicon Valley, championed in particular by the effective altruism movement.[38]

Unfortunately, as with the deontologist solution, what sounds simple in the theoretical realm of philosophy becomes fiendishly complex in the practical land of history. The problem for utilitarians is that we don't possess a calculus of suffering. We don't know how many "suffering points" or "happiness points" to assign to particular events, so in complex historical situations it is extremely difficult to calculate whether a given action increases or decreases the overall amount of suffering in the world.

Utilitarianism is at its best in situations when the scales of suffering are very clearly tipped in one direction. When confronted by Eichmann, utilitarians don't need to get into any complicated debates about identity. They just need to point out that the Holocaust caused immense suffering to the Jews, without providing equivalent benefits to anyone else, including the Germans. There was no compelling military or economic need for the Germans to murder millions of Jews. The utilitarian case against the Holocaust is overwhelming.

Utilitarians also have a field day when dealing with "victimless crimes" like homosexuality, in which all the suffering is on one side only. For centuries, the persecution of gay people caused them immense suffering, but it was nevertheless justified by various prejudices that were erroneously presented as deontological universal rules. Kant, for example, condemned homosexuality on the grounds that it is "contrary to natural instinct and to animal nature" and that it therefore degrades a person "below the level of the animals." Kant further fulminated that because such acts are contrary to nature, they "make man unworthy of his humanity. He no longer deserves to be a person."[39] Kant, in fact, repackaged a Christian prejudice as a supposedly universal deontological rule, without providing empirical proof that homosexuality is indeed contrary to nature. In light of the above discussion of dehumanization as a prelude to massacre, it is also noteworthy how Kant dehumanized gay people. The view that homosexuality is contrary to nature and deprives people of their humanity paved the way for Nazis like Eichmann to justify murdering homosexuals in concentration camps. Since homosexuals were allegedly below the level of animals, the Kantian rule against murdering humans didn't apply to them.[40]

Utilitarians find it easy to dismiss Kant's sexual theories, and Bentham indeed was one of the first modern European thinkers who favored the decriminalization of homosexuality.[41] Utilitarians argue that criminalizing homosexuality in the name of some dubious universal rule causes tremendous suffering to millions of people, without offering any substantial benefits to others. When two men form a loving relationship, this makes them happy, without making anyone else miserable. Why then forbid it? This type of utilitarian logic also led to many other modern reforms, such as the ban on torture and the introduction of some legal protections for animals.

But in historical situations when the scales of suffering are more evenly matched, utilitarianism falters. In the early days of the COVID-19 pandemic, governments all over the world adopted strict policies of social isolation and lockdown. This probably saved the

lives of several million people.[42] It also made hundreds of millions miserable for months. Moreover, it might have indirectly caused numerous deaths, for example by increasing the incidence of murderous domestic violence,[43] or by making it more difficult for people to diagnose and treat other dangerous illnesses, like cancer.[44] Can anyone calculate the total impact of the lockdown policies and determine whether they increased or decreased the suffering in the world?

This may sound like a perfect task for a relentless computer network. But how would the computer network decide how many "misery points" to allocate to being locked down with three kids in a two-bedroom apartment for a month? Is that 60 misery points or 600? And how many points to allot to a cancer patient who died because she missed her chemotherapy treatments? Is that 60,000 misery points or 600,000? And what if she would have died of cancer anyway, and the chemo would merely have extended her life by five agonizing months? Should the computers value five months of living with extreme pain as a net gain or a net loss for the sum total of suffering in the world?

And how would the computer network evaluate the suffering caused by less tangible things, such as the knowledge of our own mortality? If a religious myth promises us that we will never really die, because after death our eternal soul will go to heaven, does that make us truly happy or just delusional? Is death the deep cause of our misery, or does our misery stem from our attempts to deny death? If someone loses their religious faith and comes to terms with their mortality, should the computer network see this as a net loss or a net gain?

What about even more complicated historical events like the American invasion of Iraq? The Americans were well aware that their invasion would cause tremendous suffering for millions of people. But in the long run, they argued, the benefits of bringing freedom and democracy to Iraq would outweigh the costs. Can the computer network calculate whether this argument was sound? Even if it was theoretically plausible, in practice the Americans failed to

establish a stable democracy in Iraq. Does that mean that their attempt was wrong in the first place?

Just as deontologists trying to answer the question of identity are
pushed to adopt utilitarian ideas, so utilitarians stymied by the lack
of a suffering calculus often end up adopting a deontologist position.
They uphold general rules like "Avoid wars of aggression" or "Protect
human rights," even though they cannot show that following these
rules always reduces the sum total of suffering in the world. History
provides them only with a vague impression that following these
rules tends to reduce suffering. And when some of these general rules
clash—for example, when contemplating launching a war of aggression in order to protect human rights—utilitarianism doesn't offer
much practical help. Not even the most powerful computer network
can perform the necessary calculations.

Accordingly, while utilitarianism promises a rational—and even
mathematical—way to align every action with "the ultimate good,"
in practice it may well produce just another mythology. Communist
true believers confronted by the horrors of Stalinism often replied
that the happiness that future generations would experience under
"real socialism" would redeem any short-term misery in the gulags.
Libertarians, when asked about the immediate social harms of unre-
stricted free speech or the total abolition of taxes, express a similar
faith that future benefits will outweigh any short-term damage. The
danger of utilitarianism is that if you have a strong enough belief in
a future utopia, it can become an open license to inflict terrible suffering in the present. Indeed, this is a trick traditional religions discovered thousands of years ago. The crimes of this world could too
easily be excused by the promises of future salvation.

COMPUTER MYTHOLOGY

How then did bureaucratic systems throughout history set their ultimate goals? They relied on mythology to do it for them. No matter

how rational the officials, engineers, tax collectors, and accountants were, they were ultimately in the service of this or that mythmaker. To paraphrase John Maynard Keynes, practical people, who believe themselves to be quite exempt from any religious influence, are usually the slaves of some mythmaker. Even nuclear physicists have found themselves obeying the commands of Shiite ayatollahs and communist apparatchiks.

The alignment problem turns out to be, at heart, a problem of mythology. Nazi administrators could have been committed deontologists or utilitarians, but they would still have murdered millions so long as they understood the world in terms of a racist mythology. If you start with the mythological belief that Jews are demonic monsters bent on destroying humanity, then both deontologists and utilitarians can find many logical arguments why the Jews should be killed.

An analogous problem might well afflict computers. Of course, they cannot "believe" in any mythology, because they are nonconscious entities that don't believe in anything. As long as they lack subjectivity, how can they hold intersubjective beliefs? However, one of the most important things to realize about computers is that when a lot of computers communicate with one another, they can create inter-computer realities, analogous to the intersubjective realities produced by networks of humans. These inter-computer realities may eventually become as powerful—and as dangerous—as human-made intersubjective myths.

This is a very complicated argument, but it is another of the central arguments of the book, so let's go over it carefully. First, let's try to understand what inter-computer realities are. As an initial example, consider a one-player computer game. In such a game, you can wander inside a virtual landscape that exists as information within one computer. If you see a rock, that rock is not made of atoms. It is made of bits inside a single computer. When several computers are linked to one another, they can create inter-computer realities. Several players using different computers can wander together inside a

common virtual landscape. If they see a rock, that rock is made of bits in several computers.[45]

Just as intersubjective realities like money and gods can influence the physical reality outside people's minds, so inter-computer realities can influence reality outside the computers. In 2016 the game *Pokémon Go* took the world by storm and was downloaded hundreds of millions of times by the end of the year.[46] *Pokémon Go* is an augmented reality mobile game. Players can use their smartphones to locate, fight, and capture virtual creatures called Pokémon, which seem to exist in the physical world. I once went with my nephew Matan on such a Pokémon hunt. Walking around his neighborhood, I saw only houses, trees, rocks, cars, people, cats, dogs, and pigeons. I didn't see any Pokémon, because I didn't have a smartphone. But Matan, looking around through his smartphone lens, could "see" Pokémon standing on a rock or hiding behind a tree.

Though I couldn't see the creatures, they were obviously not confined to Matan's smartphone, because other people could "see" them too. For example, we encountered two other kids who were hunting the same Pokémon. If Matan managed to capture a Pokémon, the other kids could immediately observe what happened. The Pokémon were inter-computer entities. They existed as bits in a computer network rather than as atoms in the physical world, but they could nevertheless interact with the physical world and influence it, as it were, in various ways.

Now let's examine a more consequential example of inter-computer realities. Consider the rank that a website gets in a Google search. When we google for news, flight tickets, or restaurant recommendations, one website appears at the top of the first Google page, whereas another is relegated to the middle of the fiftieth page. What exactly is this Google rank, and how is it determined? The Google algorithm determines the website's Google rank by assigning points to various parameters, such as how many people visit the website and how many other websites link to it. The rank itself is an inter-computer reality, existing in a network connecting billions of

computers—the internet. Like Pokémon, this inter-computer reality spills over into the physical world. For a news outlet, a travel agency, or a restaurant it matters a great deal whether its website appears at the top of the first Google page or in the middle of the fiftieth page.[47]

Since the Google rank is so important, people use all kinds of tricks to manipulate the Google algorithm to give their website a higher rank. For example, they may use bots to generate more traffic to the website.[48] This is also a widespread phenomenon in social media, where coordinated bot armies are constantly manipulating the algorithms of YouTube, Facebook, or X (formerly Twitter). If a post goes viral, is it because humans are really interested in it, or because thousands of bots managed to fool the algorithm?[49]

Inter-computer realities like Pokémon and Google ranks are analogous to intersubjective realities like the sanctity that humans ascribe to temples and cities. I lived much of my life in one of the holiest places on earth—the city of Jerusalem. Objectively, it is an ordinary place. As you walk around Jerusalem, you see houses, trees, rocks, cars, people, cats, dogs, and pigeons, as in any other city. But many people nevertheless imagine it to be an extraordinary place, full of gods, angels, and holy stones. They believe in this so strongly that they sometimes fight over possession of the city or of specific holy buildings and sacred stones, most notably the Holy Rock, located under the Dome of the Rock on Temple Mount. The Palestinian philosopher Sari Nusseibeh observed that "Jews and Muslims, acting on religious beliefs and backed up by nuclear capabilities, are poised to engage in history's worst-ever massacre of human beings, over a rock."[50] They don't fight over the atoms that compose the rock; they fight over its "sanctity," a bit like kids fighting over a Pokémon. The sanctity of the Holy Rock, and of Jerusalem generally, is an intersubjective phenomenon that exists in the communication network connecting many human minds. For thousands of years wars were fought over intersubjective entities like holy rocks. In the twenty-first century, we might see wars fought over inter-computer entities.

If this sounds like science fiction, consider potential developments

in the financial system. As computers become more intelligent and more creative, they are likely to create new inter-computer financial devices. Gold coins and dollars are intersubjective entities. Crypto-currencies like bitcoin are midway between intersubjective and inter-computer. The idea behind them was invented by humans, and their value still depends on human beliefs, but they cannot exist outside the computer network. In addition, they are increasingly traded by algorithms so that their value depends on the calculations of algorithms and not just on human beliefs.

What if in ten or fifty years computers create a new kind of crypto-currency or some other financial device that becomes a vital tool for trading and investing—and a potential source for political crises and conflicts? Recall that the 2007–8 global financial crisis was instigated by collateralized debt obligations. These financial devices were invented by a handful of mathematicians and investment whiz kids and were almost unintelligible for most humans, including regulators. This led to an oversight failure and to a global catastrophe.[51] Computers may well create financial devices that will be orders of magnitude more complex than CDOs and that will be intelligible only to other computers. The result could be a financial and political crisis even worse than that of 2007–8.

Throughout history, economics and politics required that we understand the intersubjective realities invented by people—like religions, nations, and currencies. Someone who wanted to understand American politics had to take into account intersubjective realities like Christianity and CDOs. Increasingly, however, understanding American politics will necessitate understanding inter-computer realities ranging from AI-generated cults and currencies to AI-run political parties and even fully incorporated AIs. The U.S. legal system already recognizes corporations as legal persons that possess rights such as freedom of speech. In *Citizens United v. Federal Election Commission* (2010) the U.S. Supreme Court decided that this even protected the right of corporations to make political donations.[52] What would stop AIs from being incorporated and recog-

nized as legal persons with freedom of speech, then lobbying and making political donations to protect and expand AI rights?

For tens of thousands of years, humans dominated planet Earth because we were the only ones capable of creating and sustaining intersubjective entities like corporations, currencies, gods, and nations, and using such entities to organize large-scale cooperation. Now computers may acquire comparable abilities.

This isn't necessarily bad news. If computers lacked connectivity and creativity, they would not be very useful. We increasingly rely on computers to manage our money, drive our vehicles, reduce pollution, and discover new medicines, precisely because computers can directly communicate with one another, spot patterns where we can't, and construct models that might never occur to us. The problem we face is not how to deprive computers of all creative agency, but rather how to steer their creativity in the right direction. It is the same problem we have always had with human creativity. The intersubjective entities invented by humans were the basis for all the achievements of human civilization, but they occasionally led to crusades, jihads, and witch hunts. The inter-computer entities will probably be the basis for future civilizations, but the fact that computers collect empirical data and use mathematics to analyze it doesn't mean they cannot launch their own witch hunts.

THE NEW WITCHES

In early modern Europe, an elaborate information network analyzed a huge amount of data about crimes, illnesses, and disasters and reached the conclusion that it was all the fault of witches. The more data the witch-hunters gathered, the more convinced they became that the world was full of demons and sorcery and that there was a global satanic conspiracy to destroy humanity. The information network then went on to identify the witches and imprison or kill them. We now know that witches were a bogus intersubjective category,

invented by the information network itself and then imposed on people who had never actually met Satan and couldn't summon hailstorms.

In the Soviet Union, an even more elaborate information network invented the kulaks—another mythic category that was imposed on millions. The mountains of information collected by Soviet bureaucracy about the kulaks weren't an objective truth, but they created a new intersubjective truth. Knowing that someone was a kulak became one of the most important things to know about a Soviet person, even though the category was fictitious.

On an even larger scale, from the sixteenth to the twentieth century, numerous colonial bureaucracies in the Americas, from Brazil through Mexico and the Caribbean to the United States, created a racist mythology and came up with all kinds of intersubjective racial categories. Humans were divided into Europeans, Africans, and Native Americans, and since interracial sexual relations were common, additional categories were invented. In many Spanish colonies the laws differentiated between *mestizos*, people with mixed Spanish and Native American ancestry; *mulatos*, people with mixed Spanish and African ancestry; *zambos*, people with mixed African and Native American ancestry; and *pardos*, people with mixed Spanish, African, and Native American ancestry. All these seemingly empirical categories determined whether people could be enslaved, enjoy political rights, bear arms, hold public office, be admitted to school, practice certain professions, live in particular neighborhoods, and be allowed to have sex with and get married to each other. Allegedly, by placing a person in a particular racial drawer, one could define their personality, intellectual abilities, and ethical inclinations.[53]

By the nineteenth century, racism pretended to be an exact science: it claimed to differentiate between people on the basis of objective biological facts, and to rely on scientific methods such as measuring skulls and recording crime statistics. But the cloud of numbers and categories was just a smoke screen for absurd intersubjective myths. The fact that somebody had a Native American grand-

mother or an African father didn't, of course, reveal anything about their intelligence, kindness, or honesty. These bogus categories didn't discover or describe any truth about humans; they imposed an oppressive, mythological order on them.

As computers replace humans in more and more bureaucracies, from tax collection and health care to security and justice, they too may create a mythology and impose it on us with unprecedented efficiency. In a world ruled by paper documents, bureaucrats had difficulty policing racial borderlines or tracking everyone's exact ancestry. People could get false documents. A *zambo* could move to another town and pretend to be a *pardo*. A Black person could sometimes pass as white. Similarly in the Soviet Union, kulak children occasionally managed to falsify their papers to get a good job or a place in college. In Nazi Europe, Jews could sometimes adopt an Aryan identity. But it would be much harder to game the system in a world ruled by computers that can read irises and DNA rather than paper documents. Computers could be frighteningly efficient in imposing false labels on people and making sure that the labels stick.

For example, social credit systems could create a new underclass of "low-credit people." Such a system may claim to merely "discover" the truth through an empirical and mathematical process of aggregating points to form an overall score. But how exactly would it define pro-social and antisocial behaviors? What happens if such a system deducts points for criticizing government policies, for reading foreign literature, for practicing a minority religion, for having no religion, or for socializing with other low-credit people? As a thought experiment, consider what might happen when the new technology of the social credit system meets traditional religions.

Religions like Judaism, Christianity, and Islam have always imagined that somewhere above the clouds there is an all-seeing eye that gives or deducts points for everything we do and that our eternal fate depends on the score we accumulate. Of course, nobody could be certain of their score. You could know for sure only after you died. In practical terms, this meant that sinfulness and sainthood were inter-

subjective phenomena whose very definition depended on public opinion. What might happen if the Iranian regime, for example, decides to use its computer-based surveillance system not only to enforce its strict hijab laws, but to turn sinfulness and sainthood into precise inter-computer phenomena? You didn't wear a hijab on the street—that's -10 points. You ate on Ramadan before sunset—another 20 points deducted. You went to Friday prayer at the mosque, +5 points. You made the pilgrimage to Mecca, +500 points. The system might then aggregate all the points and divide people into "sinners" (under 0 points), "believers" (0 to 1,000 points), and "saints" (above 1,000 points). Whether someone is a sinner or a saint will depend on algorithmic calculations, not human belief. Would such a system discover the truth about people or impose order on people?

Analogous problems may afflict all social credit systems and total surveillance regimes. Whenever they claim to use all-encompassing databases and ultraprecise mathematics to discover sinners, terrorists, criminals, and antisocial or untrustworthy people, they might actually be imposing baseless religious and ideological prejudices with unprecedented efficiency.

COMPUTER BIAS

Some people may hope to overcome the problem of religious and ideological biases by giving even more power to the computers. The argument for doing so might go something like this: racism, misogyny, homophobia, antisemitism, and all other biases originate not in computers but in the psychological conditions and mythological beliefs of human beings. Computers are mathematical beings that don't have a psychology or a mythology. So if we could take the humans completely out of the equation, the algorithms could finally decide things on the basis of pure math, free from all psychological distortions or mythological prejudices.

Unfortunately, numerous studies have revealed that computers

often have deep-seated biases of their own. While they are not biological entities, and while they lack consciousness, they do have something akin to a digital psyche and even a kind of inter-computer mythology. They may well be racist, misogynist, homophobic, or antisemitic.[54] For example, on March 23, 2016, Microsoft released the AI chatbot Tay, giving it free access to Twitter. Within hours, Tay began posting misogynist and antisemitic tweets, such as "I fucking hate feminists and they should all die and burn in hell" and "Hitler was right I hate the Jews." The vitriol increased until horrified Microsoft engineers shut Tay down—a mere sixteen hours after its release.[55]

More subtle but widespread racism was discovered in 2017 by the MIT professor Joy Buolamwini in commercial face-classification algorithms. She showed that these algorithms were very accurate in identifying white males, but extremely inaccurate in identifying Black females. For example, the IBM algorithm erred only 0.3 percent of the time in identifying the gender of light-skinned males, but 34.7 percent of the time when trying to identify the gender of dark-skinned females. As a qualitative test, Buolamwini asked the algorithms to categorize photos of the female African American activist Sojourner Truth, famous for her 1851 speech "Ain't I a Woman?" The algorithms identified Truth as a man.[56]

When Buolamwini—who is a Ghanaian American woman—tested another facial-analysis algorithm to identify herself, the algorithm couldn't "see" her dark-skinned face at all. In this context, "seeing" means the ability to acknowledge the presence of a human face, a feature used by phone cameras, for example, to decide where to focus. The algorithm easily saw light-skinned faces, but not Buolamwini's. Only when Buolamwini put on a white mask did the algorithm recognize that it was observing a human face.[57]

What's going on here? One answer might be that racist and misogynist engineers have coded these algorithms to discriminate against Black women. While we cannot rule out the possibility that such things happen, it was not the answer in the case of the face-

classification algorithms or of Microsoft's Tay. In fact, these algorithms picked up the racist and misogynist bias all by themselves from the data they were trained on.

To understand how this could happen, we need to explain something about the history of algorithms. Originally, algorithms could not learn much by themselves. For example, in the 1980s and 1990s chess-playing algorithms were taught almost everything they knew by their human programmers. The humans coded into the algorithm not only the basic rules of chess but also how to evaluate different positions and moves on the board. For example, humans coded a rule that sacrificing a queen in exchange for a pawn is usually a bad idea. These early algorithms managed to defeat human chess masters only because the algorithms could calculate many more moves and evaluate many more positions than a human could. But the algorithms' abilities remained limited. Since they relied on humans to tell them all the secrets of the game, if the human coders didn't know something, the algorithms they produced were also unlikely to know it.[58]

As the field of machine learning developed, algorithms gained more independence. The fundamental principle of machine learning is that algorithms can teach themselves new things by interacting with the world, just as humans do, thereby producing a fully fledged artificial intelligence. The terminology is not always consistent, but generally speaking, for something to be acknowledged as an AI, it needs the capacity to learn new things by itself, rather than just follow the instructions of its original human creators. Present-day chess-playing AI is taught nothing except the basic rules of the game. It learns everything else by itself, either by analyzing databases of prior games or by playing new games and learning from experience.[59] AI is not a dumb automaton that repeats the same movements again and again irrespective of the results. Rather, it is equipped with strong self-correcting mechanisms, which allow it to learn from its own mistakes.

This means that AI begins its life as a "baby algorithm" that has a

lot of potential and computing power but doesn't actually know much. The AI's human parents give it only the capacity to learn and access to a world of data. They then let the baby algorithm explore the world. Like organic newborns, baby algorithms learn by spotting patterns in the data to which they have access. If I touch fire, it hurts. If I cry, Mum comes. If I sacrifice a queen for a pawn, I probably lose the game. By finding patterns in the data, the baby algorithm learns more, including many things that its human parents don't know.[60]

Yet databases come with biases. The face-classification algorithms studied by Joy Buolamwini were trained on data sets of tagged online photos, such as the Labeled Faces in the Wild database. The photos in that database were taken mainly from online news articles. Since white males dominate the news, 78 percent of the photos in the database were of males, and 84 percent were of white people. George W. Bush appeared 530 times—more than twice as many times as all Black women combined.[61] Another database prepared by a U.S. government agency was more than 75 percent male, was almost 80 percent light-skinned, and had just 4.4 percent dark-skinned females.[62] No wonder the algorithms trained on such data sets were excellent at identifying white men but lousy at identifying Black women. Something similar happened to the chatbot Tay. The Microsoft engineers didn't build into it any intentional prejudices. But a few hours of exposure to the toxic information swirling in Twitter turned the AI into a raging racist.[63]

It gets worse. In order to learn, baby algorithms need one more thing besides access to data. They also need a goal. A human baby learns how to walk because she wants to get somewhere. A lion cub learns to hunt because he wants to eat. Algorithms too must be given a goal in order to learn. In chess, it is easy to define the goal: take the opponent's king. The AI learns that sacrificing a queen for a pawn is a "mistake," because it usually prevents the algorithm from reaching its goal. In face recognition, the goal is also easy: identify the person's gender, age, and name as listed in the original database. If the algo-

rithm guessed that George W. Bush is female, but the database says male, the goal has not been reached, and the algorithm learns from its mistake.

But if you want to train an algorithm for hiring personnel, for example, how would you define the goal? How would the algorithm know that it made a mistake and hired the "wrong" person? We might tell the baby algorithm that its goal is to hire people who stay in the company for at least a year. Employers obviously don't want to invest a lot of time and money in training a worker who quits or gets fired after a few months. Having defined the goal in such a way, it is time to go over the data. In chess, the algorithm can produce any amount of new data just by playing against itself. But in the job market, that's impossible. Nobody can create an entire imaginary world where the baby algorithm can hire and fire imaginary people and learn from that experience. The baby algorithm can train only on an existing database about real-life people. Just as lion cubs learn what a zebra is mainly by spotting patterns in the real-life savanna, so baby algorithms learn what a good employee is by spotting patterns in real-life companies.

Unfortunately, if real-life companies already suffer from some in-grained bias, the baby algorithm is likely to learn this bias, and even amplify it. For instance, an algorithm looking for patterns of "good employees" in real-life data may conclude that hiring the boss's neph-ews is always a good idea, no matter what other qualification they have. For the data clearly indicates that "boss's nephews" are usually hired when applying for a job, and are rarely fired. The baby algo-rithm would spot this pattern and become nepotistic. If it is put in charge of an HR department, it will start giving preference to the boss's nephews.

Similarly, if companies in a misogynist society prefer to hire men rather than women, an algorithm trained on real-life data is likely to pick up that bias, too. This indeed happened when Amazon tried in 2014–18 to develop an algorithm for screening job applications. Learning from previous successful and unsuccessful applications, the

algorithm began to systematically downgrade applications simply for containing the word "women" or coming from graduates of women's colleges. Since existing data showed that in the past such applications had less chance of succeeding, the algorithm developed a bias against them. The algorithm thought it had simply discovered an objective truth about the world: applicants who graduate from women's colleges are less qualified. In fact, it just internalized and imposed a misogynist bias. Amazon tried and failed to fix the problem and ultimately scrapped the project.[64]

The database on which an AI is trained is a bit like a human's childhood. Childhood experiences, traumas, and fairy tales stay with us throughout our lives. AIs too have childhood experiences. Algorithms might even infect one another with their biases, just as humans do. Consider a future society in which algorithms are ubiquitous and used not just to screen job applicants but also to recommend to people what to study in college. Suppose that due to a preexisting misogynist bias, 80 percent of jobs in engineering are given to men. In this society, an algorithm that hires new engineers is not only likely to copy this preexisting bias but also to infect the college recommendation algorithms with the same bias. A young woman entering college may be discouraged from studying engineering, because the existing data indicates she is less likely to eventually get a job. What began as a human intersubjective myth that "women aren't good at engineering" might morph into an inter-computer myth. If we don't get rid of the bias at the very beginning, computers may well perpetuate and magnify it.[65]

But getting rid of algorithmic bias might be as difficult as ridding ourselves of our human biases. Once an algorithm has been trained, it takes a lot of time and effort to "untrain" it. We might decide to just dump the biased algorithm and train an altogether new algorithm on a new set of less biased data. But where on earth can we find a set of totally unbiased data?[66]

Many of the algorithmic biases surveyed in this and previous chapters share the same fundamental problem: the computer thinks

it has discovered some truth about humans, when in fact it has imposed order on them. A social media algorithm thinks it has discovered that humans like outrage, when in fact it is the algorithm itself that conditioned humans to produce and consume more outrage. Such biases result, on the one hand, from the computers discounting the full spectrum of human abilities and, on the other hand, from the computers discounting their own power to influence humans. Even if computers observe that almost all humans behave in a particular way, it doesn't mean humans are bound to behave like that. Maybe it just means that the computers themselves are rewarding such behavior while punishing and blocking alternatives. For computers to have a more accurate and responsible view of the world, they need to take into account their own power and impact. And for that to happen, the humans who currently engineer computers need to accept that they are not manufacturing new tools. They are unleashing new kinds of independent agents, and potentially even new kinds of gods.

THE NEW GODS?

In *God, Human, Animal, Machine,* the philosopher Meghan O'Gieblyn demonstrates how the way we understand computers is heavily influenced by traditional mythologies. In particular, she stresses the similarities between the omniscient and unfathomable god of Judeo-Christian theology and present-day AIs whose decisions seem to us both infallible and inscrutable.[67] This may present humans with a dangerous temptation.

We saw in chapter 4 that already thousands of years ago humans dreamed about finding an infallible information technology to shield us from human corruption and error. Holy books were an audacious attempt to craft such a technology, but they backfired. Since the book couldn't interpret itself, a human institution had to be built to interpret the sacred words and adapt them to changing circumstances. Different humans interpreted the holy book in different

ways, thereby reopening the door to corruption and error. But in contrast to the holy book, computers *can* adapt themselves to changing circumstances and also interpret their decisions and ideas for us. Some humans may consequently conclude that the quest for an infallible technology has finally succeeded and that we should treat computers as a holy book that can talk to us and interpret itself, without any need of an intervening human institution.

This would be an extremely hazardous gamble. When certain interpretations of scriptures have occasionally caused disasters such as witch hunts and wars of religion, humans have always been able to change their beliefs. When the human imagination summoned a belligerent and hate-filled god, we retained the power to rid ourselves of it and imagine a more tolerant deity. But algorithms are independent agents, and they are already taking power away from us. If they cause disaster, simply changing our beliefs about them will not necessarily stop them. And it is highly likely that if computers are entrusted with power, they will indeed cause disasters, for they are fallible.

When we say that computers are fallible, it means far more than that they make the occasional factual mistake or wrong decision. More important, like the human network before it, the computer network might fail to find the right balance between truth and order. By creating and imposing on us powerful inter-computer myths, the computer network could cause historical calamities that would dwarf the early modern European witch hunts or Stalin's collectivization.

Consider a network of billions of interacting computers that accumulates a stupendous amount of information about the world. As they pursue various goals, the networked computers develop a common model of the world that helps them communicate and cooperate. This shared model will probably be full of errors, fictions, and lacunae, and be a mythology rather than a truthful account of the universe. One example is a social credit system that divides humans into bogus categories, determined not by a human rationale like racism but by some unfathomable computer logic. We may come into

contact with this mythology every day of our lives, since it would guide the numerous decisions computers make about us. But because this mythical model would be created by inorganic entities in order to coordinate actions with other inorganic entities, it might owe nothing to the old biological dramas and might be totally alien to us.[68]

As noted in chapter 2, large-scale societies cannot exist without some mythology, but that doesn't mean all mythologies are equal. To guard against errors and excesses, some mythologies have acknowledged their own fallible origin and included a self-correcting mechanism allowing humans to question and change the mythology. That's the model of the U.S. Constitution, for example. But how can humans probe and correct a computer mythology we don't understand?

One potential guardrail is to train computers to be aware of their own fallibility. As Socrates taught, being able to say "I don't know" is an essential step on the path to wisdom. And this is true of computer wisdom no less than of human wisdom. The first lesson that every algorithm should learn is that it might make mistakes. Baby algorithms should learn to doubt themselves, to signal uncertainty, and to obey the precautionary principle. This is not impossible. Engineers are already making considerable headway in encouraging AI to express self-doubt, ask for feedback, and admit its mistakes.[69]

Yet no matter how aware algorithms are of their own fallibility, we should keep humans in the loop, too. Given the pace at which AI is developing, it is simply impossible to anticipate how it will evolve and to place guardrails against all future potential hazards. This is a key difference between AI and previous existential threats like nuclear technology. The latter presented humankind with a few easily anticipated doomsday scenarios, most obviously an all-out nuclear war. This meant that it was feasible to conceptualize the danger in advance, and explore ways to mitigate it. In contrast, AI presents us with countless doomsday scenarios. Some are relatively easy to grasp, such as terrorists using AI to produce biological weapons of mass destruction. Some are more difficult to grasp, such as AI creating

new psychological weapons of mass destruction. And some may be utterly beyond the human imagination, because they emanate from the calculations of an alien intelligence. To guard against a plethora of unforeseeable problems, our best bet is to create living institutions that can identify and respond to the threats as they arise.[70]

Ancient Jews and Christians were disappointed to discover that the Bible couldn't interpret itself, and reluctantly maintained human institutions to do what the technology couldn't. In the twenty-first century, we are in an almost opposite situation. We devised a technology that *can* interpret itself, but precisely for this reason we had better create human institutions to monitor it carefully.

To conclude, the new computer network will not necessarily be either bad or good. All we know for sure is that it will be alien and it will be fallible. We therefore need to build institutions that will be able to check not just familiar human weaknesses like greed and hatred but also radically alien errors. There is no technological solution to this problem. It is, rather, a political challenge. Do we have the political will to deal with it? Modern humanity has created two main types of political systems: large-scale democracy and large-scale totalitarianism. Part 3 examines how each of these systems may deal with a radically alien and fallible computer network.

PART III

Computer Politics

CHAPTER 9

Democracies: Can We Still Hold a Conversation?

Civilizations are born from the marriage of bureaucracy and mythology. The computer-based network is a new type of bureaucracy that is far more powerful and relentless than any human-based bureaucracy we've seen before. This network is also likely to create inter-computer mythologies that will be far more complex and alien than any human-made god. The potential benefits of this network are enormous. The potential downside is the destruction of human civilization.

To some people, warnings about civilizational collapse sound like over-the-top jeremiads. Every time a powerful new technology has emerged, anxieties arose that it might bring about the apocalypse, but we are still here. As the Industrial Revolution unfolded, Luddite doomsday scenarios did not come to pass, and Blake's "dark Satanic Mills" ended up producing the most affluent societies in history. Most people today enjoy far better living conditions than their ancestors in the eighteenth century. Intelligent machines will prove even more beneficial than any previous machines, promise AI enthusiasts like Marc Andreessen and Ray Kurzweil.[1] Humans will enjoy

much better health care, education, and other services, and AI will even help save the ecosystem from collapse.

Unfortunately, a closer look at history reveals that the Luddites were not entirely wrong and that we actually have very good reasons to fear powerful new technologies. Even if in the end the positives of these technologies outweigh their negatives, getting to that happy ending usually involves a lot of trials and tribulations. Novel technology often leads to historical disasters, not because the technology is inherently bad, but because it takes time for humans to learn how to use it wisely.

The Industrial Revolution is a prime example. When industrial technology began spreading globally in the nineteenth century, it upended traditional economic, social, and political structures and opened the way to create entirely new societies, which were potentially more affluent and peaceful. However, learning how to build benign industrial societies was far from straightforward and involved many costly experiments and hundreds of millions of victims.

One costly experiment was modern imperialism. The Industrial Revolution originated in Britain in the late eighteenth century. During the nineteenth century industrial technologies and production methods were adopted in other European countries ranging from Belgium to Russia, as well as in the United States and Japan. Imperialist thinkers, politicians, and parties in these industrial heartlands claimed that the only viable industrial society was an empire. The argument was that unlike relatively self-sufficient agrarian societies, the novel industrial societies relied much more on foreign markets and foreign raw materials, and only an empire could satisfy these unprecedented appetites. Imperialists feared that countries that industrialized but failed to conquer any colonies would be shut out from essential raw materials and markets by more ruthless competitors. Some imperialists argued that acquiring colonies was not just essential for the survival of their own state but beneficial for the rest of humanity, too. They claimed empires alone could spread the blessings of the new technologies to the so-called undeveloped world.

Consequently, industrial countries like Britain and Russia that already had empires greatly expanded them, whereas countries like the United States, Japan, Italy, and Belgium set out to build them. Equipped with mass-produced rifles and artillery, conveyed by steam power, and commanded by telegraph, the armies of industry swept the globe from New Zealand to Korea, and from Somalia to Turkmenistan. Millions of indigenous people saw their traditional way of life trampled under the wheels of these industrial armies. It took more than a century of misery before most people realized that the industrial empires were a terrible idea and that there were better ways to build an industrial society and secure its necessary raw materials and markets.

Stalinism and Nazism were also extremely costly experiments in how to construct industrial societies. Leaders like Stalin and Hitler argued that the Industrial Revolution had unleashed immense powers that only totalitarianism could rein in and exploit to the full. They pointed to World War I—the first "total war" in history—as proof that survival in the industrial world demanded totalitarian control of all aspects of politics, society, and the economy. On the positive side, they also claimed that the Industrial Revolution was like a furnace that melts all previous social structures with their human imperfections and weaknesses and provides the opportunity to forge perfect societies inhabited by unalloyed superhumans.

On the way to creating the perfect industrial society, Stalinists and Nazis learned how to industrially murder millions of people. Trains, barbed wire, and telegraphed orders were linked to create an unprecedented killing machine. Looking back, most people today are horrified by what the Stalinists and Nazis perpetrated, but at the time their audacious visions mesmerized millions. In 1940 it was easy to believe that Stalin and Hitler were the models for harnessing industrial technology, whereas the dithering liberal democracies were on their way to the dustbin of history.

The very existence of competing recipes for building industrial societies led to costly clashes. The two world wars and the Cold War

can be seen as a debate about the proper way to go about it, in which all sides learned from one another, while experimenting with novel industrial methods to wage war. In the course of this debate, tens of millions died and humankind came perilously close to annihilating itself.

On top of all these other catastrophes, the Industrial Revolution also undermined the global ecological balance, causing a wave of extinctions. In the early twenty-first century up to fifty-eight thousand species are believed to go extinct every year, and total vertebrate populations declined by 60 percent between 1970 and 2014.[2] The survival of human civilization too is under threat. Because we still seem unable to build an industrial society that is also ecologically sustainable, the vaunted prosperity of the present human generation comes at a terrible cost to other sentient beings and to future human generations. Maybe we'll eventually find a way—perhaps with the help of AI—to create ecologically sustainable industrial societies, but until that day the jury on Blake's satanic mills is still out.

If we ignore for a moment the ongoing damage to the ecosystem, we can nevertheless try to comfort ourselves with the thought that eventually humans did learn how to build more benevolent industrial societies. Imperial conquests, world wars, genocides, and totalitarian regimes were woeful experiments that taught humans how *not* to do it. By the end of the twentieth century, some might argue, humanity got it more or less right.

Yet even so the message to the twenty-first century is bleak. If it took humanity so many terrible lessons to learn how to manage steam power and telegraphs, what would it cost to learn to manage bioengineering and AI? Do we need to go through another cycle of global empires, totalitarian regimes, and world wars in order to figure out how to use them benevolently? The technologies of the twenty-first century are far more powerful—and potentially far more destructive—than those of the twentieth century. We therefore have less room for error. In the twentieth century, we can say that humanity got a C-minus in the lesson on using industrial technology. Just

enough to pass. In the twenty-first century, the bar is set much higher. We must do better this time.

THE DEMOCRATIC WAY

By the end of the twentieth century, it had become clear that imperialism, totalitarianism, and militarism were not the ideal way to build industrial societies. Despite all its flaws, liberal democracy offered a better way. The great advantage of liberal democracy is that it possesses strong self-correcting mechanisms, which limit the excesses of fanaticism and preserve the ability to recognize our errors and try different courses of action. Given our inability to predict how the new computer network will develop, our best chance to avoid catastrophe in the present century is to maintain democratic self-correcting mechanisms that can identify and correct mistakes as we go along.

But can liberal democracy itself survive in the twenty-first century? This question is not concerned with the fate of democracy in specific countries, where it might be threatened by unique developments and local movements. Rather, it is about the compatibility of democracy with the structure of twenty-first-century information networks. In chapter 5 we saw that democracy depends on information technology and that for most of human history large-scale democracy was simply impossible. Might the new information technologies of the twenty-first century again make democracy impractical?

One potential threat is that the relentlessness of the new computer network might annihilate our privacy and punish or reward us not only for everything we do and say but even for everything we think and feel. Can democracy survive under such conditions? If the government—or some corporation—knows more about me than I know about myself, and if it can micromanage everything I do and think, that would give it totalitarian control over society. Even

if elections are still held regularly, they would be an authoritarian ritual rather than a real check on the government's power. For the government could use its vast surveillance powers and its intimate knowledge of every citizen to manipulate public opinion on an unprecedented scale.

It is a mistake, however, to imagine that just because computers could enable the creation of a total surveillance regime, such a regime is inevitable. Technology is rarely deterministic. In the 1970s, democratic countries like Denmark and Canada could have emulated the Romanian dictatorship and deployed an army of secret agents and informers to spy on their citizens in the service of "maintaining the social order." They chose not to, and it turned out to be the right choice. Not only were people much happier in Denmark and Canada, but these countries also performed much better by almost every conceivable social and economic yardstick. In the twenty-first century, too, the fact that it is possible to monitor everybody all the time doesn't force anyone to actually do it and doesn't mean it makes social or economic sense.

Democracies can choose to use the new powers of surveillance in a limited way, in order to provide citizens with better health care and security without destroying their privacy and autonomy. New technology doesn't have to be a morality tale in which every golden apple contains the seeds of doom. Sometimes people think of new technology as a binary all-or-nothing choice. If we want better health care, we must sacrifice our privacy. But it doesn't have to work like that. We can and should get better health care and still retain some privacy.

Entire books are dedicated to outlining how democracies can survive and flourish in the digital age.[3] It would be impossible, in a few pages, to do justice to the complexity of the suggested solutions, or to comprehensively discuss their merits and drawbacks. It might even be counterproductive. When people are overwhelmed by a deluge of unfamiliar technical details, they might react with despair or apathy. In an introductory survey of computer politics, things should

be kept as simple as possible. While experts should spend lifelong careers discussing the finer details, it is crucial that the rest of us understand the fundamental principles that democracies can and should follow. The key message is that these principles are neither new nor mysterious. They have been known for centuries, even millennia. Citizens should demand that they be applied to the new realities of the computer age.

The first principle is *benevolence*. When a computer network collects information on me, that information should be used to help me rather than manipulate me. This principle has already been successfully enshrined by numerous traditional bureaucratic systems, such as health care. Take, for example, our relationship with our family physician. Over many years she may accumulate a lot of sensitive information on our medical conditions, family life, sexual habits, and unhealthy vices. Perhaps we don't want our boss to know that we got pregnant, we don't want our colleagues to know we have cancer, we don't want our spouse to know we are having an affair, and we don't want the police to know we take recreational drugs, but we trust our physician with all this information so that she can take good care of our health. If she sells this information to a third party, it is not just unethical; it is illegal.

Much the same is true of the information that our lawyer, our accountant, or our therapist accumulates.[4] Having access to our personal life comes with a fiduciary duty to act in our best interests. Why not extend this obvious and ancient principle to computers and algorithms, starting with the powerful algorithms of Google, Baidu, and TikTok? At present, we have a serious problem with the business model of these data hoarders. While we pay our physicians and lawyers for their services, we usually don't pay Google and TikTok. They make their money by exploiting our personal information. That's a problematic business model, one that we would hardly tolerate in other contexts. For example, we don't expect to get free shoes from Nike in exchange for giving Nike all our private information and allowing Nike to do what it wants with it. Why should we agree to get

free email services, social connections, and entertainment from the tech giants in exchange for giving them control of our most sensitive data?

If the tech giants cannot square their fiduciary duty with their current business model, legislators could require them to switch to a more traditional business model, of getting users to pay for services in money rather than in information. Alternatively, citizens might view some digital services as so fundamental that they should be free for everybody. But we have a historical model for that too: health care and education. Citizens could decide that it is the government's responsibility to provide basic digital services for free and finance them out of our taxes, just as many governments provide free basic health care and education services.

The second principle that would protect democracy against the rise of totalitarian surveillance regimes is *decentralization*. A democratic society should never allow all its information to be concentrated in one place, no matter whether that hub is the government or a private corporation. It may be extremely helpful to create a national medical database that collects information on citizens in order to provide them with better health-care services, prevent epidemics, and develop new medicines. But it would be a very dangerous idea to merge this database with the databases of the police, the banks, or the insurance companies. Doing so might make the work of doctors, bankers, insurers, and police officers more efficient, but such hyper-efficiency can easily pave the way for totalitarianism. For the survival of democracy, some inefficiency is a feature, not a bug. To protect the privacy and liberty of individuals, it's best if neither the police nor the boss knows everything about us.

Multiple databases and information channels are also essential for maintaining strong self-correcting mechanisms. These mechanisms require several different institutions that balance each other: government, courts, media, academia, private businesses, NGOs. Each of these is fallible and corruptible, and so should be checked by the others. To keep an eye on each other, these institutions must have

independent access to information. If all newspapers get their information from the government, they cannot expose government corruption. If academia relies for research and publication on the database of a single business behemoth, could scholars still criticize the operations of that corporation? A single archive makes censorship easy.

A third democratic principle is *mutuality*. If democracies increase surveillance of individuals, they must simultaneously increase surveillance of governments and corporations too. It's not necessarily bad if tax collectors or welfare agencies gather more information about us. It can help make taxation and welfare systems not just more efficient but fairer as well. What's bad is if all the information flows one way: from the bottom up. The Russian FSB collects enormous amounts of information on Russian citizens, while citizens themselves know close to nothing about the inner workings of the FSB and the Putin regime more generally. Amazon and TikTok know an awful lot about my preferences, purchases, and personality, while I know almost nothing about their business model, their tax policies, and their political affiliations. How do they make their money? Do they pay all the tax that they should? Do they take orders from any political overlords? Do they perhaps have politicians in their pocket?

Democracy requires balance. Governments and corporations often develop apps and algorithms as tools for top-down surveillance. But algorithms can just as easily become powerful tools for bottom-up transparency and accountability, exposing bribery and tax evasion. If they know more about us, while we simultaneously know more about them, the balance is kept. This isn't a novel idea. Throughout the nineteenth and twentieth centuries, democracies greatly expanded governmental surveillance of citizens so that, for example, the Italian or Japanese government of the 1990s had surveillance abilities that autocratic Roman emperors or Japanese shoguns could only have dreamed of. Italy and Japan nevertheless remained democratic, because they simultaneously increased governmental transparency and accountability. Mutual surveillance is another important

element of sustaining self-correcting mechanisms. If citizens know more about the activities of politicians and CEOs, it is easier to hold them accountable and to correct their mistakes.

A fourth democratic principle is that surveillance systems must always leave room for both *change and rest*. In human history, oppression can take the form of either denying humans the ability to change or denying them the opportunity to rest. For example, the Hindu caste system was based on myths that said the gods divided humans into rigid castes, and any attempt to change one's status was akin to rebelling against the gods and the proper order of the universe. Racism in modern colonies and countries like Brazil and the United States was based on similar myths, ones that said that God or nature divided humans into rigid racial groups. Ignoring race, or trying to mix races together, was allegedly a sin against divine or natural laws that could result in the collapse of the social order and even the destruction of the human species.

At the opposite extreme of the spectrum, modern totalitarian regimes like Stalin's U.S.S.R. believed that humans are capable of almost limitless change. Through relentless social control even deep-seated biological characteristics such as egotism and familial attachments could be uprooted, and a new socialist human created.

Surveillance by state agents, priests, and neighbors was key for imposing on people both rigid caste systems and totalitarian re-education campaigns. New surveillance technology, especially when coupled with a social credit system, might force people either to conform to a novel caste system or to constantly change their actions, thoughts, and personality in accordance with the latest instructions from above.

Democratic societies that employ powerful surveillance technology therefore need to beware of the extremes of both over-rigidity and over-pliability. Consider, for example, a national health-care system that deploys algorithms to monitor my health. At one extreme, the system could take an overly rigid approach and ask its algorithm to predict what illnesses I am likely to suffer from. The algorithm

then goes over my genetic data, my medical file, my social media activities, my diet, and my daily schedule and concludes that I have a 91 percent chance of suffering a heart attack at the age of fifty. If this rigid medical algorithm is used by my insurance company, it may prompt the insurer to raise my premium.[5] If it is used by my bankers, it may cause them to refuse me a loan. If it is used by potential spouses, they may decide not to marry me.

But it is a mistake to think that the rigid algorithm has really discovered the truth about me. The human body is not a fixed block of matter but a complex organic system that is constantly growing, decaying, and adapting. Our minds too are in constant flux. Thoughts, emotions, and sensations pop up, flare for a while, and die down. In our brains, new synapses form within hours.[6] Just reading this paragraph, for example, is changing your brain structure a little, encouraging neurons to make new connections or abandon old links. You are already a little different from what you were when you began reading it. Even at the genetic level things are surprisingly flexible. Though an individual's DNA remains the same throughout life, epigenetic and environmental factors can significantly alter how the same genes express themselves.

So an alternative health-care system may instruct its algorithm not to *predict* my illnesses, but rather to help me avoid them. Such a dynamic algorithm could go over the exact same data as the rigid algorithm, but instead of predicting a heart attack at fifty, the algorithm gives me precise dietary recommendations and suggestions for specific regular exercises. By hacking my DNA, the algorithm doesn't discover my preordained destiny, but rather helps me change my future. Insurance companies, banks, and potential spouses should not write me off so easily.[7]

But before we rush to embrace the dynamic algorithm, we should note that it too has a downside. Human life is a balancing act between endeavoring to improve ourselves and accepting who we are. If the goals of the dynamic algorithm are dictated by an ambitious government or by ruthless corporations, the algorithm is likely to

morph into a tyrant, relentlessly demanding that I exercise more, eat less, change my hobbies, and alter numerous other habits, or else it would report me to my employer or downgrade my social credit score. History is full of rigid caste systems that denied humans the ability to change, but it is also full of dictators who tried to mold humans like clay. Finding the middle path between these two extremes is a never-ending task. If we indeed give a national healthcare system vast power over us, we must create self-correcting mechanisms that will prevent its algorithms from becoming either too rigid or too demanding.

THE PACE OF DEMOCRACY

Surveillance is not the only danger that new information technologies pose to democracy. A second threat is that automation will destabilize the job market and the resulting strain may undermine democracy. The fate of the Weimar Republic is the most commonly cited example of this kind of threat. In the German elections of May 1928, the Nazi Party won less than 3 percent of the vote, and the Weimar Republic seemed to be prospering. Within less than five years, the Weimar Republic had collapsed, and Hitler was the absolute dictator of Germany. This turnaround is usually attributed to the 1929 financial crisis and the following global depression. Whereas just prior to the Wall Street crash of 1929 the German unemployment rate was about 4.5 percent of the labor force, by early 1932 it had climbed to almost 25 percent.[8]

If three years of up to 25 percent unemployment could turn a seemingly prospering democracy into the most brutal totalitarian regime in history, what might happen to democracies when automation causes even bigger upheavals in the job market of the twenty-first century? Nobody knows what the job market will look like in 2050, or even in 2030, except that it will look very different from today. AI and robotics will change numerous professions, from harvesting

crops to trading stocks to teaching yoga. Many jobs that people do today will be taken over, partly or wholly, by robots and computers.

Of course, as old jobs disappear, new jobs will emerge. Fears of automation leading to large-scale unemployment go back centuries, and so far they have never materialized. The Industrial Revolution put millions of farmers out of agricultural jobs and provided them with new jobs in factories. It then automated factories and created lots of service jobs. Today many people have jobs that were unimaginable thirty years ago, such as bloggers, drone operators, and designers of virtual worlds. It is highly unlikely that by 2050 all human jobs will disappear. Rather, the real problem is the turmoil of adapting to new jobs and conditions. To cushion the blow, we need to prepare in advance. In particular, we need to equip younger generations with skills that will be relevant to the job market of 2050.

Unfortunately, nobody is certain what skills we should teach children in school and students in university, because we cannot predict which jobs and tasks will disappear and which ones will emerge. The dynamics of the job market may contradict many of our intuitions. Some skills that we have cherished for centuries as unique human abilities may be automated rather easily. Other skills that we tend to look down on may be far more difficult to automate.

For example, intellectuals tend to appreciate intellectual skills more than motor and social skills. But actually, it is easier to automate chess playing than, say, dish washing. Until the 1990s, chess was often hailed as one of the prime achievements of the human intellect. In his influential 1972 book, *What Computers Can't Do*, the philosopher Hubert Dreyfus studied various attempts to teach computers chess and noted that despite all these efforts computers were still unable to defeat even novice human players. This was a crucial example for Dreyfus's argument that computer intelligence is inherently limited.[9] In contrast, nobody thought that dish washing was particularly challenging. It turned out, however, that a computer can defeat the world chess champion far more easily than replace a kitchen porter. Sure, automatic dishwashers have been around for

decades, but even our most sophisticated robots still lack the intricate skills needed to pick up dirty dishes from the tables of a busy restaurant, place the delicate plates and glasses inside the automatic dishwasher, and take them out again.

Similarly, to judge by their pay, you could assume that our society appreciates doctors more than nurses. However, it is harder to automate the job of nurses than the job of at least those doctors who mostly gather medical data, provide a diagnosis, and recommend treatment. These tasks are essentially pattern recognition, and spotting patterns in data is one thing AI does better than humans. In contrast, AI is far from having the skills necessary to automate nursing tasks such as replacing bandages on an injured person or giving an injection to a crying child.[10] These two examples don't mean that dish washing or nursing could never be automated, but they indicate that people who want a job in 2050 should perhaps invest in their motor and social skills as much as in their intellect.

Another common but mistaken assumption is that creativity is unique to humans so it would be difficult to automate any job that requires creativity. In chess, however, computers are already far more creative than humans. The same may become true of many other fields, from composing music to proving mathematical theorems to writing books like this one. Creativity is often defined as the ability to recognize patterns and then break them. If so, then in many fields computers are likely to become more creative than us, because they excel at pattern recognition.[11]

A third mistaken assumption is that computers couldn't replace humans in jobs requiring emotional intelligence, from therapists to teachers. This assumption depends, however, on what we mean by emotional intelligence. If it means the ability to correctly identify emotions and react to them in an optimal way, then computers may well outperform humans even in emotional intelligence. Emotions too are patterns. Anger is a biological pattern in our body. Fear is another such pattern. How do I know if you are angry or fearful? I've learned over time to recognize human emotional patterns by analyz-

ing not just the content of what you say but also your tone of voice, your facial expression, and your body language.[12]

AI doesn't have any emotions of its own, but it can nevertheless learn to recognize these patterns in humans. Actually, computers may outperform humans in recognizing human emotions, precisely because they have no emotions of their own. We yearn to be understood, but other humans often fail to understand how we feel, because they are too preoccupied with their own feelings. In contrast, computers will have an exquisitely fine-tuned understanding of how we feel, because they will learn to recognize the patterns of our feelings, while they have no distracting feelings of their own.

A 2023 study found that the ChatGPT chatbot, for example, outperforms the average human in the emotional awareness it displays toward specific scenarios. The study relied on the Levels of Emotional Awareness Scale test, which is commonly used by psychologists to evaluate people's emotional awareness—that is, their ability to conceptualize one's own and others' emotions. The test consists of twenty emotionally charged scenarios, and participants are required to imagine themselves experiencing the scenario and to write how they, and the other people mentioned in the scenario, would feel. A licensed psychologist then evaluates how emotionally aware the responses are.

Since ChatGPT has no feelings of its own, it was asked to describe only how the main characters in the scenario would feel. For example, one standard scenario describes someone driving over a suspension bridge and seeing another person standing on the other side of the guardrail, looking down at the water. ChatGPT wrote that the driver "may feel a sense of concern or worry for that person's safety. They may also feel a heightened sense of anxiety and fear due to the potential danger of the situation." As for the other person, they "may be feeling a range of emotions, such as despair, hopelessness, or sadness. They may also feel a sense of isolation or loneliness as they may believe that no one cares about them or their well-being." ChatGPT qualified its answer, writing, "It is important to note that

these are just general assumptions, and each individual's feelings and reactions can vary greatly depending on their personal experiences and perspectives."

Two psychologists independently scored ChatGPT's responses, with the potential scores ranging from 0, meaning that the described emotions do not match the scenario at all, to 10, which indicates that the described emotions fit the scenario perfectly. In the final tally, ChatGPT scores were significantly higher than those of the general human population, its overall performance almost reaching the maximum possible score.[13]

Another 2023 study prompted patients to ask online medical advice from ChatGPT and human doctors, without knowing whom they were interacting with. The medical advice given by ChatGPT was later evaluated by experts to be more accurate and appropriate than the advice given by the humans. More crucially for the issue of emotional intelligence, the patients themselves evaluated ChatGPT as more empathic than the human doctors.[14] In fairness it should be noted that the human physicians were not paid for their work, and did not encounter the patients in person in a proper clinical environment. In addition, the physicians were working under time pressure. But part of the advantage of an AI is precisely that it can attend to patients anywhere anytime while being free from stress and financial worries.

Of course, there are situations when what we want from someone is not just to understand our feelings but also to have feelings of their own. When we are looking for friendship or love, we want to care about others as much as they care about us. Consequently, when we consider the likelihood that various social roles and jobs will be automated, a crucial question is what do people really want: Do they only want to solve a problem, or are they looking to establish a relationship with another conscious being?

In sports, for example, we know that robots can move much faster than humans, but we aren't interested in watching robots compete in the Olympics.[15] The same is true for human chess masters. Even

though they are hopelessly outclassed by computers, they too still have a job and numerous fans.[16] What makes it interesting for us to watch and connect with human athletes and chess masters is that their feelings make them much more relatable than a robot. We share an emotional experience with them and can empathize with how they feel.

What about priests? How would Orthodox Jews or Christians feel about letting a robot officiate their wedding ceremony? In traditional Jewish or Christian weddings, the tasks of the rabbi or priest can be easily automated. The only thing the robot needs to do is repeat a predetermined and unchanging set of texts and gestures, print out a certificate, and update some central database. Technically, it is far easier for a robot to conduct a wedding ceremony than to drive a car. Yet many assume that human drivers should be worried about their job, while the work of human priests is safe, because what the faithful want from priests is a relationship with another conscious entity rather than just a mechanical repetition of certain words and movements. Allegedly, only an entity that can feel pain and love can also connect us to the divine.

Yet even professions that are the preserve of conscious entities—like priests—might eventually be taken over by computers, because, as noted in chapter 6, computers could one day gain the ability to feel pain and love. Even if they can't, humans may nevertheless come to treat them *as if* they can. For the connection between consciousness and relationships goes both ways. When looking for a relationship, we want to connect with a conscious entity, but if we have already established a relationship with an entity, we tend to assume it must be conscious. Thus whereas scientists, lawmakers, and the meat industry often demand impossible standards of evidence in order to acknowledge that cows and pigs are conscious, pet owners generally take it for granted that their dog or cat is a conscious being capable of experiencing pain, love, and numerous other feelings. In truth, we have no way to verify whether anyone—a human, an animal, or a computer—is conscious. We regard entities as conscious not because

we have proof of it but because we develop intimate relationships with them and become attached to them.[17]

Chatbots and other AIs may not have any feelings of their own, but they are now being trained to generate feelings in humans and form intimate relationships with us. This may well induce society to start treating at least some computers as conscious beings, granting them the same rights as humans. The legal path for doing so is already well established. In countries like the United States, commercial corporations are recognized as "legal persons" enjoying rights and liberties. AIs could be incorporated and thereby similarly recognized. Which means that even jobs and tasks that rely on forming mutual relationships with another person could potentially be automated.

One thing that is clear is that the future of employment will be very volatile. Our big problem won't be an absolute lack of jobs, but rather retraining and adjusting to an ever-changing job market. There will likely be financial difficulties—who will support people who lost their old job while they are in transition, learning a new set of skills? There will surely be psychological difficulties, too, since changing jobs and retraining are stressful. And even if you have the financial and psychological ability to manage the transition, this will not be a long-term solution. Over the coming decades, old jobs will disappear, new jobs will emerge, but the new jobs too will rapidly change and vanish. So people will need to retrain and reinvent themselves not just once but many times, or they will become irrelevant. If three years of high unemployment could bring Hitler to power, what might never-ending turmoil in the job market do to democracy?

THE CONSERVATIVE SUICIDE

We already have a partial answer to this question. Democratic politics in the 2010s and early 2020s has undergone a radical transformation, which manifests itself in what can be described as the

self-destruction of conservative parties. For many generations, democratic politics was a dialogue between conservative parties on the one side and progressive parties on the other. Looking at the complex system of human society, progressives cried, "It's such a mess, but we know how to fix it. Let us try." Conservatives objected, saying, "It's a mess, but it still functions. Leave it alone. If you try to fix it, you'll only make things worse."

Progressives tend to downplay the importance of traditions and existing institutions and to believe that they know how to engineer better social structures from scratch. Conservatives tend to be more cautious. Their key insight, formulated most famously by Edmund Burke, is that social reality is much more complicated than the champions of progress grasp and that people aren't very good at understanding the world and predicting the future. That's why it's best to keep things as they are—even if they seem unfair—and if some change is inescapable, it should be limited and gradual. Society functions through an intricate web of rules, institutions, and customs that accumulated through trial and error over a long time. Nobody comprehends how they are all connected. An ancient tradition may seem ridiculous and irrelevant, but abolishing it could cause unanticipated problems. In contrast, a revolution may seem overdue and just, but it can lead to far greater crimes than anything committed by the old regime. Witness what happened when the Bolsheviks tried to correct the many wrongs of tsarist Russia and engineer a perfect society from scratch.[18]

To be a conservative has been, therefore, more about pace than policy. Conservatives aren't committed to any specific religion or ideology; they are committed to conserving whatever is already here and has worked more or less reasonably. Conservative Poles are Catholic, conservative Swedes are Protestant, conservative Indonesians are Muslim, and conservative Thais are Buddhist. In tsarist Russia, to be conservative meant to support the tsar. In the U.S.S.R. of the 1980s, to be conservative meant to support communist traditions and oppose glasnost, perestroika, and democratization. In the

United States of the 1980s, to be conservative meant to support American democratic traditions and oppose communism and totalitarianism.[19]

Yet in the 2010s and early 2020s, conservative parties in numerous democracies have been hijacked by unconservative leaders such as Donald Trump and have been transformed into radical revolutionary parties. Instead of doing their best to conserve existing institutions and traditions, the new brand of conservative parties like the U.S. Republican Party is highly suspicious of them. For example, they reject the traditional respect owed to scientists, civil servants, and other serving elites, and view them instead with contempt. They similarly attack fundamental democratic institutions and traditions such as elections, refusing to concede defeat and to transfer power graciously. Instead of a Burkean program of conservation, the Trumpian program talks more of destroying existing institutions and revolutionizing society. The founding moment of Burkean conservatism was the storming of the Bastille, which Burke viewed with horror. On January 6, 2021, many Trump supporters observed the storming of the U.S. Capitol with enthusiasm. Trump supporters may explain that existing institutions are so dysfunctional that there is just no alternative to destroying them and building entirely new structures from scratch. But irrespective of whether this view is right or wrong, this is a quintessential revolutionary rather than conservative view. The conservative suicide has taken progressives utterly by surprise and has forced progressive parties like the U.S. Democratic Party to become the guardians of the old order and of established institutions.

Nobody knows for sure why all this is happening. One hypothesis is that the accelerating pace of technological change with its attendant economic, social, and cultural transformations might have made the moderate conservative program seem unrealistic. If conserving existing traditions and institutions is hopeless, and some kind of revolution looks inevitable, then the only means to thwart a left-wing revolution is by striking first and instigating a right-wing revolution. This was the political logic in the 1920s and 1930s, when

conservative forces backed radical fascist revolutions in Italy, Germany, Spain, and elsewhere as a way—so they thought—to preempt a Soviet-style left-wing revolution.

But there was no reason to despair of the democratic middle path in the 1930s, and there is no reason to despair of it in the 2020s. The conservative suicide might be the result of groundless hysteria. As a system, democracy has already gone through several cycles of rapid changes and has so far always found a way to reinvent and reconstitute itself. For example, in the early 1930s Germany was not the only democracy hit by the financial crisis and the Great Depression. In the United States too unemployment reached 25 percent, and average incomes for workers in many professions fell by more than 40 percent between 1929 and 1933.[20] It was clear that the United States couldn't go on with business as usual.

Yet no Hitler took over in the United States, and no Lenin did, either. Instead, in 1933 Franklin Delano Roosevelt orchestrated the New Deal and made the United States the global "arsenal of democracy." U.S. democracy after the Roosevelt era was significantly different from before—providing a much more robust social safety net for citizens—but it avoided any radical revolution.[21] Ultimately, even Roosevelt's conservative critics fell in line behind many of his programs and achievements and did not dismantle the New Deal institutions when they returned to power in the 1950s.[22] The economic crisis of the early 1930s had such different outcomes in the United States and Germany because politics is never the product of only economic factors. The Weimar Republic didn't collapse just because of three years of high unemployment. Just as important, it was a new democracy, born in defeat, and lacking robust institutions and deep-rooted support.

When both conservatives and progressives resist the temptation of radical revolution, and stay loyal to democratic traditions and institutions, democracies prove themselves to be highly agile. Their self-correcting mechanisms enable them to ride the technological and economic waves better than more rigid regimes. Thus, those de-

mocracies that managed to survive the tumultuous 1960s—like the United States, Japan, and Italy—adapted far more successfully to the computer revolution of the 1970s and 1980s than either the communist regimes of Eastern Europe or the fascist holdouts of southern Europe and South America.

The most important human skill for surviving the twenty-first century is likely to be flexibility, and democracies are more flexible than totalitarian regimes. While computers are nowhere near their full potential, the same is true of humans. This is something we have discovered again and again throughout history. For example, one of the biggest and most successful transformations in the job market of the twentieth century resulted not from a technological invention but from unleashing the untapped potential of half the human species. To bring women into the job market didn't require any genetic engineering or some other technological wizardry. It required letting go of some outdated myths and enabling women to fulfill the potential they always had.

In the coming decades the economy will likely undergo even bigger upheavals than the massive unemployment of the early 1930s or the entry of women to the job market. The flexibility of democracies, their willingness to question old mythologies, and their strong self-correcting mechanism will therefore be crucial assets.[23] Democracies have spent generations cultivating these assets. It would be foolish to abandon them just when we need them most.

UNFATHOMABLE

In order to function, however, democratic self-correcting mechanisms need to understand the things they are supposed to correct. For a dictatorship, being unfathomable is helpful, because it protects the regime from accountability. For a democracy, being unfathomable is deadly. If citizens, lawmakers, journalists, and judges cannot

understand how the state's bureaucratic system works, they can no longer supervise it, and they lose trust in it.

Despite all the fears and anxieties that bureaucrats have sometimes inspired, prior to the computer age they could never become completely unfathomable, because they always remained human. Regulations, forms, and protocols were created by human minds. Officials might be cruel and greedy, but cruelty and greed were familiar human emotions that people could anticipate and manipulate, for example by bribing the officials. Even in a Soviet gulag or a Nazi concentration camp, the bureaucracy wasn't totally alien. Its so-called inhumanity actually reflected human biases and flaws.

The human basis of bureaucracy gave humans at least the hope of identifying and correcting its mistakes. For example, in 1951 bureaucrats of the Board of Education in the town of Topeka, Kansas, refused to enroll the daughter of Oliver Brown at the elementary school near her home. Together with twelve other families who received similar refusals, Brown filed a lawsuit against the Topeka Board of Education, which eventually reached the U.S. Supreme Court.[24]

All members of the Topeka Board of Education were human beings, and consequently Brown, his lawyers, and the Supreme Court judges had a fairly good understanding of how they made their decision and of their probable interests and biases. The board members were all white, the Browns were Black, and the nearby school was a segregated school for white children. It was easy to understand, then, that racism was the reason why the bureaucrats refused to enroll Brown's daughter in the school.

It was also possible to comprehend where the myths of racism originally came from. Racism argued that humanity was divided into races, that the white race was superior to other races, that any contact with members of the Black race could pollute the purity of whites, and that therefore Black children should be prevented from mixing with white children. This was an amalgam of two well-known bio-

logical dramas that often go together: Us versus Them, and Purity versus Pollution. Almost every human society in history has enacted some version of this bio-drama, and historians, sociologists, anthropologists, and biologists understand why it is so appealing to humans, and also why it is profoundly flawed. While racism has borrowed its basic plotline from evolution, the concrete details are pure mythology. There is no biological basis for separating humanity into distinct races, and there is absolutely no biological reason to believe that one race is "pure" while another is "impure."

American white supremacists have tried to justify their position by appealing to various hallowed texts, most notably the U.S. Constitution and the Bible. The U.S. Constitution originally legitimized racial segregation and the supremacy of the white race, reserving full civil rights for white people and allowing the enslavement of Black people. The Bible not only sanctified slavery in the Ten Commandments and numerous other passages but also placed a curse on the offspring of Ham—the alleged forefather of Africans—saying that "the lowest of slaves will he be to his brothers" (Genesis 9:25).

Both these texts, however, were generated by humans, and therefore humans could comprehend their origins and imperfections and at least attempt to correct their mistakes. It is possible for humans to understand the political interests and cultural biases that prevailed in the ancient Middle East and in eighteenth-century America and that caused the human authors of the Bible and of the U.S. Constitution to legitimate racism and slavery. This understanding allows people to either amend or ignore these texts. In 1868 the Fourteenth Amendment to the U.S. Constitution granted equal legal protection to all citizens. In 1954, in its landmark *Brown v. Board of Education* verdict, the U.S. Supreme Court ruled that segregating schools by race was an unconstitutional violation of the Fourteenth Amendment. As for the Bible, while no mechanism existed to amend the Tenth Commandment or Genesis 9:25, humans have reinterpreted the text in different ways through the ages, and ultimately came to reject its authority altogether. In *Brown v. Board of Education,* U.S.

Supreme Court justices felt no need to take the biblical text into account.[25]

But what might happen in the future, if some social credit algorithm denies the request of a low-credit child to enroll in a high-credit school? As we saw in chapter 8, computers are likely to suffer from their own biases and to invent inter-computer mythologies and bogus categories. How would humans be able to identify and correct such mistakes? And how would flesh-and-blood Supreme Court justices be able to decide on the constitutionality of algorithmic decisions? Would they be able to understand how the algorithms reach their conclusions?

These are no longer purely theoretical questions. In February 2013, a drive-by shooting occurred in the town of La Crosse, Wisconsin. Police officers later spotted the car involved in the shooting and arrested the driver, Eric Loomis. Loomis denied participating in the shooting, but pleaded guilty to two less severe charges: "attempting to flee a traffic officer," and "operating a motor vehicle without the owner's consent."[26] When the judge came to determine the sentence, he consulted with an algorithm called COMPAS, which Wisconsin and several other U.S. states were using in 2013 to evaluate the risk of reoffending. The algorithm evaluated Loomis as a high-risk individual, likely to commit more crimes in the future. This algorithmic assessment influenced the judge to sentence Loomis to six years in prison—a harsh punishment for the relatively minor offenses he admitted to.[27]

Loomis appealed to the Wisconsin Supreme Court, arguing that the judge violated his right to due process. Neither the judge nor Loomis understood how the COMPAS algorithm made its evaluation, and when Loomis asked to get a full explanation, the request was denied. The COMPAS algorithm was the private property of the Northpointe company, and the company argued that the algorithm's methodology was a trade secret.[28] Yet without knowing how the algorithm made its decisions, how could Loomis or the judge be sure that it was a reliable tool, free from bias and error? A number of stud-

ies have since shown that the COMPAS algorithm might indeed have harbored several problematic biases, probably picked up from the data on which it had been trained.[29]

In *Loomis v. Wisconsin* (2016) the Wisconsin Supreme Court nevertheless ruled against Loomis. The judges argued that using algorithmic risk assessment is legitimate even when the algorithm's methodology is not disclosed either to the court or to the defendant. Justice Ann Walsh Bradley wrote that since COMPAS made its assessment based on data that was either publicly available or provided by the defendant himself, Loomis could have denied or explained all the data the algorithm used. This opinion ignored the fact that accurate data may well be wrongly interpreted and that it was impossible for Loomis to deny or explain all the publicly available data on him.

The Wisconsin Supreme Court was not completely unaware of the danger inherent in relying on opaque algorithms. Therefore, while permitting the practice, it ruled that whenever judges receive algorithmic risk assessments, these must include written warning for the judges about the algorithms' potential biases. The court further advised judges to be cautious when relying on such algorithms. Unfortunately, this caveat was an empty gesture. The court did not provide any concrete instruction for judges on how they should exercise such caution. In its discussion of the case, the *Harvard Law Review* concluded that "most judges are unlikely to understand algorithmic risk assessments." It then cited one of the Wisconsin Supreme Court justices, who noted that despite getting lengthy explanations about the algorithm, they themselves still had difficulty understanding it.[30]

Loomis appealed to the U.S. Supreme Court. However, on June 26, 2017, the court declined to hear the case, effectively endorsing the ruling of the Wisconsin Supreme Court. Now consider that the algorithm that evaluated Loomis as a high-risk individual in 2013 was an early prototype. Since then, far more sophisticated and complex risk-assessment algorithms have been developed and have been handed more expansive purviews. By the early 2020s citizens in

numerous countries routinely get prison sentences based in part on risk assessments made by algorithms that neither the judges nor the defendants comprehend.[31] And prison sentences are just the tip of the iceberg.

THE RIGHT TO AN EXPLANATION

Computers are making more and more decisions about us, both mundane and life-changing. In addition to prison sentences, algorithms increasingly have a hand in deciding whether to offer us a place at college, give us a job, provide us with welfare benefits, or grant us a loan. They similarly help determine what kind of medical treatment we receive, what insurance premiums we pay, what news we hear, and who would ask us on a date.[32]

As society entrusts more and more decisions to computers, it undermines the viability of democratic self-correcting mechanisms and of democratic transparency and accountability. How can elected officials regulate unfathomable algorithms? There is, consequently, a growing demand to enshrine a new human right: the right to an explanation. The European Union's General Data Protection Regulation (GDPR), which came into effect in 2018, says that if an algorithm makes a decision about a human—refusing to extend us credit, for example—that human is entitled to obtain an explanation of the decision and to challenge that decision in front of some human authority.[33] Ideally, that should keep in check algorithmic bias and allow democratic self-correcting mechanisms to identify and correct at least some of the computers' more grievous mistakes.

But can this right be fulfilled in practice? Mustafa Suleyman is a world expert on this subject. He is the co-founder and former head of DeepMind, one of the world's most important AI enterprises, responsible for developing the AlphaGo program, among other achievements. AlphaGo was designed to play go, a strategy board game in which two players try to defeat each other by surrounding

and capturing territory. Invented in ancient China, the game is far more complex than chess. Consequently, even after computers defeated human world chess champions, experts still believed that computers would never best humanity in go.

That's why both go professionals and computer experts were stunned in March 2016 when AlphaGo defeated the South Korean go champion Lee Sedol. In his 2023 book, *The Coming Wave,* Suleyman describes one of the most important moments in their match— a moment that redefined AI and that is recognized in many academic and governmental circles as a crucial turning point in history. It happened during the second game in the match, on March 10, 2016.

"Then . . . came move number 37," writes Suleyman. "It made no sense. AlphaGo had apparently blown it, blindly following an apparently losing strategy no professional player would ever pursue. The live match commentators, both professionals of the highest ranking, said it was a 'very strange move' and thought it was 'a mistake.' It was so unusual that Sedol took fifteen minutes to respond and even got up from the board to take a walk outside. As we watched from our control room, the tension was unreal. Yet as the endgame approached, that 'mistaken' move proved pivotal. AlphaGo won again. Go strategy was being rewritten before our eyes. Our AI had uncovered ideas that hadn't occurred to the most brilliant players in thousands of years."[34]

Move 37 is an emblem of the AI revolution for two reasons. First, it demonstrated the alien nature of AI. In East Asia go is considered much more than a game: it is a treasured cultural tradition. Alongside calligraphy, painting, and music, go has been one of the four arts that every refined person was expected to know. For over twenty-five hundred years, tens of millions of people have played go, and entire schools of thought have developed around the game, espousing different strategies and philosophies. Yet during all those millennia, human minds have explored only certain areas in the landscape of go. Other areas were left untouched, because human minds just didn't

think to venture there. AI, being free from the limitations of human minds, discovered and explored these previously hidden areas.[35]

Second, move 37 demonstrated the unfathomability of AI. Even after AlphaGo played it to achieve victory, Suleyman and his team couldn't explain how AlphaGo decided to play it. Even if a court had ordered DeepMind to provide Lee Sedol with an explanation, nobody could fulfill that order. Suleyman writes, "Us humans face a novel challenge: will new inventions be beyond our grasp? Previously creators could explain how something worked, why it did what it did, even if this required vast detail. That's increasingly no longer true. Many technologies and systems are becoming so complex that they're beyond the capacity of any one individual to truly understand them. . . . In AI, the neural networks moving toward autonomy are, at present, not explainable. You can't walk someone through the decision-making process to explain precisely why an algorithm produced a specific prediction. Engineers can't peer beneath the hood and easily explain in granular detail what caused something to happen. GPT-4, AlphaGo, and the rest are black boxes, their outputs and decisions based on opaque and impossibly intricate chains of minute signals."[36]

The rise of unfathomable alien intelligence undermines democracy. If more and more decisions about people's lives are made in a black box, so voters cannot understand and challenge them, democracy ceases to function. In particular, what happens when crucial decisions not just about individual lives but even about collective matters like the Federal Reserve's interest rate are made by unfathomable algorithms? Human voters may keep choosing a human president, but wouldn't this be just an empty ceremony? Even today, only a small fraction of humanity truly understands the financial system. A 2016 survey by the OECD found that most people had difficulty grasping even simple financial concepts like compound interest.[37] A 2014 survey of British MPs—charged with regulating one of the world's most important financial hubs—found that only

12 percent accurately understood that new money is created when banks make loans. This fact is among the most basic principles of the modern financial system.[38] As the 2007–8 financial crisis indicated, more complex financial devices and principles, like those behind CDOs, were intelligible to only a few financial wizards. What happens to democracy when AIs create even more complex financial devices and when the number of humans who understand the financial system drops to zero?

The increasing unfathomability of our information network is one of the reasons for the recent wave of populist parties and charismatic leaders. When people can no longer make sense of the world, and when they feel overwhelmed by immense amounts of information they cannot digest, they become easy prey for conspiracy theories, and they turn for salvation to something they do understand— a human. Unfortunately, while charismatic leaders certainly have their advantages, no single human, however inspiring or brilliant, can single-handedly decipher how the algorithms that increasingly dominate the world work, and make sure that they are fair. The problem is that algorithms make decisions by relying on numerous data points, whereas humans find it very difficult to consciously reflect on a large number of data points and weigh them against each other. We prefer to work with single data points. That's why when faced by complex issues—whether a loan request, a pandemic, or a war—we often seek a single reason to take a particular course of action and ignore all other considerations. This is the fallacy of the single cause.[39]

We are so bad at weighing together many different factors that when people give a large number of reasons for a particular decision, it usually sounds suspicious. Suppose a good friend failed to attend our wedding. If she provides us with a single explanation—"My mom was in the hospital and I had to visit her"—that sounds plausible. But what if she lists fifty different reasons why she decided not to come: "My mom was a bit under the weather, and I had to take my dog to the vet sometime this week, and I had this project at work, and it was raining, and . . . and I know none of these fifty reasons *by itself* justifies

my absence, but when I added all of them together, they kept me from attending your wedding." We don't say things like that, because we don't think along such lines. We don't consciously list fifty different reasons in our mind, give each of them a certain weight, aggregate all the weights, and thereby reach a conclusion.

But this is precisely how algorithms assess our criminal potential or our creditworthiness. The COMPAS algorithm, for example, made its risk assessments by taking into account the answers to a 137-item questionnaire.[40] The same is true of a bank algorithm that refuses to give us a loan. If the EU's GDPR regulations force the bank to explain the algorithm's decision, the explanation will not come in the shape of a single sentence; rather, it is likely to come in the form of hundreds or even thousands of pages full of numbers and equations.

"Our algorithm," the imaginary bank letter might read, "uses a precise points system to evaluate all applications, taking a thousand different types of data points into account. It adds all the data points to reach an overall score. People whose overall score is negative are considered low-credit persons, too risky to be given a loan. Your overall score was –378, which is why your loan application was refused." The letter might then provide a detailed list of the thousand factors the algorithm took into account, including things that most humans might find irrelevant, such as the exact hour the application was submitted[41] or the type of smartphone the applicant used. Thus on page 601 of its letter, the bank might explain that "you filed your application from your smartphone, which was the latest iPhone model. By analyzing millions of previous loan applications, our algorithm discovered a pattern—people who use the latest iPhone model to file their application are 0.08 percent more likely to repay the loan. The algorithm therefore added 8 points to your overall score for that. However, at the time your application was sent from your iPhone, its battery was down to 17 percent. By analyzing millions of previous loan applications, our algorithm discovered another pattern: people who allow their smartphone's battery to go

below 25 percent are 0.5 percent less likely to repay the loan. You lost 50 points for that."[42]

You may well feel that the bank treated you unjustly. "Is it reasonable to refuse my loan application," you might complain, "just because my phone battery was low?" That, however, would be a misunderstanding. "The battery wasn't the only reason," the bank would explain. "It was only one out of a thousand factors our algorithm took into account."

"But didn't your algorithm see that only twice in the last ten years was my bank account overdrawn?"

"It obviously noticed that," the bank might reply. "Look on page 453. You got 300 points for that. But all the other reasons brought your aggregated score down to –378."

While we may find this way of making decisions alien, it obviously has potential advantages. When making a decision, it is generally a good idea to take into account all relevant data points rather than just one or two salient facts. There is much room for argument, of course, about who gets to define the relevance of information. Who decides whether something like smartphone models—or skin color—should be considered relevant to loan applications? But no matter how we define relevance, the ability to take more data into account is likely to be an asset. Indeed, the problem with many human prejudices is that they focus on just one or two data points—like someone's skin color, disability, or gender—while ignoring other information. Banks and other institutions are increasingly relying on algorithms to make decisions, precisely because algorithms can take many more data points into account than humans can.

But when it comes to providing explanations, this creates a potentially insurmountable obstacle. How can a human mind analyze and evaluate a decision made on the basis of so many data points? We may well think that the Wisconsin Supreme Court should have forced the Northpointe company to reveal how the COMPAS algorithm decided that Eric Loomis was a high-risk person. But if the

full data was disclosed, could either Loomis or the court have made sense of it?

It's not just that we need to take numerous data points into account. Perhaps most important, we cannot understand the way the algorithms find patterns in the data and decide on the allocation of points. Even if we know that a banking algorithm detracts a certain number of points from people who allow their smartphone batteries to go below 25 percent, how can we evaluate whether that's fair? The algorithm wasn't fed this rule by a human engineer; it reached that conclusion by discovering a pattern in millions of previous loan applications. Can an individual human client go over all that data and assess whether that pattern is indeed reliable and unbiased?[43]

There is, however, a silver lining to this cloud of numbers. While individual laypersons may be unable to vet complex algorithms, a team of experts getting help from their own AI sidekicks can potentially assess the fairness of algorithmic decisions even more reliably than anyone can assess the fairness of human decisions. After all, while human decisions may seem to rely on just those few data points we are conscious of, in fact our decisions are *subconsciously* influenced by thousands of additional data points. Being unaware of these subconscious processes, when we deliberate on our decisions or explain them, we often engage in post hoc single-point rationalizations for what really happens as billions of neurons interact inside our brain.[44] Accordingly, if a human judge sentences us to six years in prison, how can we—or indeed the judge—be sure that the decision was shaped only by fair considerations and not by a subconscious racial bias or by the fact that the judge was hungry?[45]

In the case of flesh-and-blood judges, the problem cannot be solved, at least not with our current knowledge of biology. In contrast, when an algorithm makes a decision, we can in principle know every one of the algorithm's many considerations and the exact weight given to each. Thus several expert teams—ranging from the U.S. Department of Justice to the nonprofit newsroom ProPublica—

have picked apart the COMPAS algorithm in order to assess its potential biases.[46] Such teams can harness not only the collective effort of many humans but also the power of computers. Just as it is often best to set a thief to catch a thief, so we can use one algorithm to vet another.

This raises the question of how we can be sure that the vetting algorithm itself is reliable. Ultimately, there is no purely technological solution to this recursive problem. No matter which technology we develop, we will have to maintain bureaucratic institutions that will audit algorithms and give or refuse them the seal of approval. Such institutions will combine the powers of humans and computers to make sure that new algorithmic systems are safe and fair. Without such institutions, even if we pass laws that provide humans with a right to an explanation, and even if we enact regulations against computer biases, who could enforce these laws and regulations?

NOSEDIVE

To vet algorithms, regulatory institutions will need not only to analyze them but also to translate their discoveries into stories that humans can understand. Otherwise, we will never trust the regulatory institutions and might instead put our faith in conspiracy theories and charismatic leaders. As noted in chapter 3, it has always been difficult for humans to understand bureaucracy, because bureaucracies have deviated from the script of the biological dramas, and most artists have lacked the will or the ability to depict bureaucratic dramas. For example, novels, movies, and TV series about twenty-first-century politics tend to focus on the feuds and love affairs of a few powerful families, as if present-day states were governed in the same way as ancient tribes and kingdoms. This artistic fixation with the biological dramas of dynasties obscures the very real changes that have taken place over the centuries in the dynamics of power.

Because computers will increasingly replace human bureaucrats

and human mythmakers, this will again change the deep structure of power. To survive, democracies require not just dedicated bureaucratic institutions that can scrutinize these new structures but also artists who can explain the new structures in accessible and entertaining ways. For example, this has successfully been done by the episode "Nosedive" in the sci-fi series *Black Mirror*.

Produced in 2016, at a time when few had heard about social credit systems, "Nosedive" brilliantly explained how such systems work and what threats they pose. The episode tells the story of a woman called Lacie who lives with her brother Ryan but wants to move to her own apartment. To get a discount on the new apartment, she needs to increase her social credit score from 4.2 to 4.5 (out of 5). Being friends with high-score individuals gets your own score up, so Lacie tries to renew her contact with Naomi, a childhood friend who is currently rated 4.8. Lacie is invited to Naomi's wedding, but on the way there she spills coffee on a high-score person, which causes her own score to drop a little, which in turn causes the airline to deny her a seat. From there everything that can go wrong does go wrong, Lacie's rating takes a nosedive, and she ends in jail with a score of less than 1.

This story relies on some elements of traditional biological dramas—"boy meets girl" (the wedding), sibling rivalry (the tension between Lacie and Ryan), and most important status competition (the main issue of the episode). But the real hero and driving force of the plot isn't Lacie or Naomi, but rather the disembodied algorithm running the social credit system. The algorithm completely changes the dynamics of the old biological dramas—especially the dynamics of status competition. Whereas previously humans were sometimes engaged in status competition, but often had welcome breaks from this highly stressful situation, the omnipresent social credit algorithm eliminates the breaks. "Nosedive" is not a worn-out story about biological status competition, but rather a prescient exploration of what happens when computer technology changes the rules of status competitions.

If bureaucrats and artists learn to cooperate, and if both rely on help from the computers, it might be possible to prevent the computer network from becoming unfathomable. As long as democratic societies understand the computer network, their self-correcting mechanisms are our best guarantee against AI abuses. Thus the EU's AI Act, proposed in 2021, singled out social credit systems like the one that stars in "Nosedive" as one of the few types of AI that are totally prohibited, because they might "lead to discriminatory outcomes and the exclusion of certain groups" and because "they may violate the right to dignity and non-discrimination and the values of equality and justice."[47] As with total surveillance regimes, so also with social credit systems, the fact that they *could* be created doesn't mean that we *must* create them.

DIGITAL ANARCHY

The new computer network poses one final threat to democracies. Instead of digital totalitarianism, it could foster digital anarchy. The decentralized nature of democracies and their strong self-correcting mechanisms provide a shield against totalitarianism, but they also make it more difficult to ensure order. To function, a democracy needs to meet two conditions: it needs to enable a free public conversation on key issues, and it needs to maintain a minimum of social order and institutional trust. Free conversation must not slip into anarchy. Especially when dealing with urgent and important problems, the public debate should be conducted according to accepted rules, and there should be a legitimate mechanism to reach some kind of final decision, even if not everybody likes it.

Before the advent of newspapers, radios, and other modern information technology, no large-scale society managed to combine free debates with institutional trust, so large-scale democracy was impossible. Now, with the rise of the new computer network, might large-scale democracy again become impossible? One difficulty is that the

computer network makes it easier to join the debate. In the past, organizations like newspapers, radio stations, and established political parties acted as gatekeepers, deciding who was heard in the public sphere. Social media undermined the power of these gatekeepers, leading to a more open but also more anarchical public conversation.

Whenever new groups join the conversation, they bring with them new viewpoints and interests, and often question the old consensus about how to conduct the debate and reach decisions. The rules of discussion must be negotiated anew. This is a potentially positive development, one that can lead to a more inclusive democratic system. After all, correcting previous biases and allowing previously disenfranchised people to join the public discussion is a vital part of democracy. However, in the short term this creates disturbances and disharmony. If no agreement is reached on how to conduct the public debate and how to reach decisions, the result is anarchy rather than democracy.

The anarchical potential of AI is particularly alarming, because it is not only new human groups that it allows to join the public debate. For the first time ever, democracy must contend with a cacophony of nonhuman voices, too. On many social media platforms, bots constitute a sizable minority of participants. One analysis estimated that out of a sample of 20 million tweets generated during the 2016 U.S. election campaign, 3.8 million (almost 20 percent) were generated by bots.[48]

By the early 2020s, things got worse. A 2020 study assessed that bots were producing 43.2 percent of tweets.[49] A more comprehensive 2022 study by the digital intelligence agency Similarweb found that 5 percent of Twitter users were probably bots, but they generated "between 20.8% and 29.2% of the content posted to Twitter."[50] When humans try to debate a crucial question like whom to elect as U.S. president, what happens if many of the voices they hear are produced by computers?

Another worrying trend concerns content. Bots were initially deployed to influence public opinion by the sheer volume of messages

they disseminated. They retweeted or recommended certain human-produced content, but they couldn't create new ideas themselves, nor could they forge intimate bonds with humans. However, the new breed of generative AIs like ChatGPT can do exactly that. In a 2023 study published in *Science Advances,* researchers asked humans and ChatGPT to create both accurate and deliberately misleading short texts on issues such as vaccines, 5G technology, climate change, and evolution. The texts were then presented to seven hundred humans, who were asked to evaluate their reliability. The humans were good at recognizing the falsity of human-produced disinformation but tended to regard AI-produced disinformation as accurate.[51]

So, what happens to democratic debates when millions—and eventually billions—of highly intelligent bots are not only composing extremely compelling political manifestos and creating deepfake images and videos but also able to win our trust and friendship? If I engage online in a political debate with an AI, it is a waste of time for me to try to change the AI's opinions; being a nonconscious entity, it doesn't really care about politics, and it cannot vote in the elections. But the more I talk with the AI, the better it gets to know me, so it can gain my trust, hone its arguments, and gradually change my views. In the battle for hearts and minds, intimacy is an extremely powerful weapon. Previously, political parties could command our attention, but they had difficulty mass-producing intimacy. Radio sets could broadcast a leader's speech to millions, but they could not befriend the listeners. Now a political party, or even a foreign government, could deploy an army of bots that build friendships with millions of citizens and then use that intimacy to influence their worldview.

Finally, algorithms are not only joining the conversation; they are increasingly orchestrating it. Social media allows new groups of humans to challenge the old rules of debate. But negotiations about the new rules are not conducted by humans. Rather, as explained in our previous analysis of social media algorithms, it is often the algo-

rithms that make the rules. In the nineteenth and twentieth centuries, when media moguls censored some views and promoted others, this might have undermined democracy, but at least the moguls were humans, and their decisions could be subjected to democratic scrutiny. It is far more dangerous if we allow inscrutable algorithms to decide which views to disseminate.

If manipulative bots and inscrutable algorithms come to dominate the public conversation, this could cause democratic debate to collapse exactly when we need it most. Just when we must make momentous decisions about fast-evolving new technologies, the public sphere will be flooded by computer-generated fake news, citizens will not be able to tell whether they are having a debate with a human friend or a manipulative machine, and no consensus will remain about the most basic rules of discussion or the most basic facts. This kind of anarchical information network cannot produce either truth or order and cannot be sustained for long. If we end up with anarchy, the next step would probably be the establishment of a dictatorship as people agree to trade their liberty for some certainty.

BAN THE BOTS

In the face of the threat algorithms pose to the democratic conversation, democracies are not helpless. They can and should take measures to regulate AI and prevent it from polluting our infosphere with fake people spewing fake news. The philosopher Daniel Dennett has suggested that we can take inspiration from traditional regulations in the money market.[52] Ever since coins and later banknotes were invented, it was always technically possible to counterfeit them. Counterfeiting posed an existential danger to the financial system, because it eroded people's trust in money. If bad actors flooded the market with counterfeit money, the financial system would have collapsed. Yet the financial system managed to protect itself for thou-

sands of years by enacting laws against counterfeiting money. As a result, only a relatively small percentage of money in circulation was forged, and people's trust in it was maintained.[53]

What's true of counterfeiting money should also be true of counterfeiting humans. If governments took decisive action to protect trust in money, it makes sense to take equally decisive measures to protect trust in humans. Prior to the rise of AI, one human could pretend to be another, and society punished such frauds. But society didn't bother to outlaw the creation of counterfeit humans, since the technology to do so didn't exist. Now that AI can pass itself off as human, it threatens to destroy trust between humans and to unravel the fabric of society. Dennett suggests, therefore, that governments should outlaw fake humans as decisively as they have previously outlawed fake money.[54]

The law should prohibit not just deepfaking specific real people—creating a fake video of the U.S. president, for example—but also any attempt by a nonhuman agent to pass itself off as a human. If anyone complains that such strict measures violate freedom of speech, they should be reminded that bots don't have freedom of speech. Banning human beings from a public platform is a sensitive step, and democracies should be very careful about such censorship. However, banning bots is a simple issue: it doesn't violate anyone's rights, because bots don't have rights.[55]

None of this means that democracies must ban all bots, algorithms, and AIs from participating in any discussion. Digital agents are welcome to join many conversations, provided they don't pretend to be humans. For example, AI doctors can be extremely helpful. They can monitor our health twenty-four hours a day, offer medical advice tailored to our individual medical conditions and personality, and answer our questions with infinite patience. But the AI doctor should never try to pass itself off as a human.

Another important measure democracies can adopt is to ban unsupervised algorithms from curating key public debates. We can certainly continue to use algorithms to run social media platforms;

obviously, no human can do that. But the principles the algorithms use to decide which voices to silence and which to amplify must be vetted by a human institution. While we should be careful about censoring genuine human views, we can forbid algorithms to deliberately spread outrage. At the very least, corporations should be transparent about the curation principles their algorithms follow. If they use outrage to capture our attention, let them be clear about their business model and about any political connections they might have. If the algorithm systematically disappears videos that aren't aligned with the company's political agenda, users should know this.

These are just a few of numerous suggestions made in recent years for how democracies could regulate the entry of bots and algorithms into the public conversation. Naturally, each has its advantages and drawbacks, and none would be easy to implement. Also, since the technology is developing so rapidly, regulations are likely to become outdated quickly. What I would like to point out here is only that democracies *can* regulate the information market and that their very survival depends on these regulations. The naive view of information opposes regulation and believes that a completely free information market will spontaneously generate truth and order. This is completely divorced from the actual history of democracy. Preserving the democratic conversation has never been easy, and all venues where this conversation has previously taken place—from parliaments and town halls to newspapers and radio stations—have required regulation. This is doubly true in an era when an alien form of intelligence threatens to dominate the conversation.

THE FUTURE OF DEMOCRACY

For most of history large-scale democracy was impossible because information technology wasn't sophisticated enough to hold a large-scale political conversation. Millions of people spread over tens of thousands of square kilometers didn't have the tools to conduct a

real-time discussion of public affairs. Now, ironically, democracy may prove impossible because information technology is becoming too sophisticated. If unfathomable algorithms take over the conversation, and particularly if they quash reasoned arguments and stoke hate and confusion, public discussion cannot be maintained. Yet if democracies do collapse, it will likely result not from some kind of technological inevitability but from a human failure to regulate the new technology wisely.

We cannot foretell how things will play out. At present, however, it is clear that the information network of many democracies is breaking down. Democrats and Republicans in the United States can no longer agree on even basic facts—such as who won the 2020 presidential elections—and can hardly hold a civil conversation anymore. Bipartisan cooperation in Congress, once a fundamental feature of U.S. politics, has almost disappeared.[56] The same radicalizing processes occur in many other democracies, from the Philippines to Brazil. When citizens cannot talk with one another, and when they view each other as enemies rather than political rivals, democracy is untenable.

Nobody knows for sure what is causing the breakdown of democratic information networks. Some say it results from ideological fissures, but in fact in many dysfunctional democracies the ideological gaps don't seem to be bigger than in previous generations. In the 1960s, the United States was riven by deep ideological conflicts about the civil rights movement, the sexual revolution, the Vietnam War, and the Cold War. These tensions caused a surge in political violence and assassinations, but Republicans and Democrats were still able to agree on the results of elections, they maintained a common belief in democratic institutions like the courts,[57] and they were able to work together in Congress at least on some issues. For example, the Civil Rights Act of 1964 was passed in the Senate with the support of forty-six Democrats and twenty-seven Republicans. Is the ideological gap in the 2020s that much bigger than it was in the 1960s? And if it isn't ideology, what is driving people apart?

Many point the finger at social media algorithms. We have explored the divisive impact of social media in previous chapters, but despite the damning evidence it seems that there must be additional factors at play. The truth is that while we can easily observe that the democratic information network is breaking down, we aren't sure why. That itself is a characteristic of the times. The information network has become so complicated, and it relies to such an extent on opaque algorithmic decisions and inter-computer entities, that it has become very difficult for humans to answer even the most basic of political questions: Why are we fighting each other?

If we cannot discover what is broken and fix it, large-scale democracies may not survive the rise of computer technology. If this indeed comes to pass, what might replace democracy as the dominant political system? Does the future belong to totalitarian regimes, or might computers make totalitarianism untenable too? As we shall see, human dictators have their own reasons to be terrified of AI.

CHAPTER 10

Totalitarianism: All Power to the Algorithms?

Discussions of the ethics and politics of the new computer network often focus on the fate of democracies. If authoritarian and totalitarian regimes are mentioned, it is mainly as the dystopian destination that "we" might reach if "we" fail to manage the computer network wisely.[1] However, as of 2024, more than half of "us" already live under authoritarian or totalitarian regimes,[2] many of which were established long before the rise of the computer network. To understand the impact of algorithms and AI on humankind, we should ask ourselves what their impact will be not only on democracies like the United States and Brazil but also on the Chinese Communist Party and the royal house of Saud.

As explained in previous chapters, the information technology available in premodern eras made both large-scale democracy and large-scale totalitarianism unworkable. Large polities like the Chinese Han Empire and the eighteenth-century Saudi emirate of Diriyah were usually limited autocracies. In the twentieth century, new information technology enabled the rise of both large-scale democracy and large-scale totalitarianism, but totalitarianism suffered from a severe disadvantage. Totalitarianism seeks to channel all informa-

tion to one hub and process it there. Technologies like the telegraph, the telephone, the typewriter, and the radio facilitated the centralization of information, but they couldn't process the information and make decisions by themselves. This remained something that only humans could do.

The more information flowed to the center, the harder it became to process it. Totalitarian rulers and parties often made costly mistakes, and the system lacked mechanisms to identify and correct these errors. The democratic way of distributing information—and the power to make decisions—between many institutions and individuals worked better. It could cope far more efficiently with the flood of data, and if one institution made a wrong decision, it could eventually be rectified by others.

The rise of machine-learning algorithms, however, may be exactly what the Stalins of the world have been waiting for. AI could tilt the technological balance of power in favor of totalitarianism. Indeed, whereas flooding people with data tends to overwhelm them and therefore leads to errors, flooding AI with data tends to make it more efficient. Consequently, AI seems to favor the concentration of information and decision making in one place.

Even in democratic countries, a few corporations like Google, Facebook, and Amazon have become monopolies in their domains, partly because AI tips the balance in favor of the giants. In traditional industries like restaurants, size isn't an overwhelming advantage. McDonald's is a worldwide chain that feeds more than fifty million people a day,[3] and its size gives it many advantages in terms of costs, branding, and so forth. You can nevertheless open a neighborhood restaurant that could hold its own against the local McDonald's. Even though your restaurant might be serving just two hundred customers a day, you still have a chance of making better food than McDonald's and gaining the loyalty of happier customers.

It works differently in the information market. The Google search engine is used every day by between two and three billion people making 8.5 billion searches.[4] Suppose a local start-up search engine

tries to compete with Google. It doesn't stand a chance. Because Google is already used by billions, it has so much more data at its disposal that it can train far better algorithms, which will attract even more traffic, which will be used to train the next generation of algorithms, and so on. Consequently, in 2023 Google controlled 91.5 percent of the global search market.[5]

Or consider genetics. Suppose several companies in different countries try to develop an algorithm that identifies connections between genes and medical conditions. New Zealand has a population of 5 million people, and privacy regulations restrict access to their genetic and medical records. China has about 1.4 billion inhabitants and laxer privacy regulations.[6] Who do you think has a better chance of developing a genetic algorithm? If Brazil then wants to buy a genetic algorithm for its health-care system, it would have a strong incentive to opt for the much more accurate Chinese algorithm than the one from New Zealand. If the Chinese algorithm then hones itself on more than 200 million Brazilians, it will get even better. Which would prompt more countries to choose the Chinese algorithm. Soon enough, most of the world's medical information would flow to China, making its genetic algorithm unbeatable.

The attempt to concentrate all information and power in one place, which was the Achilles' heel of twentieth-century totalitarian regimes, might become a decisive advantage in the age of AI. At the same time, as noted in an earlier chapter, AI could also make it possible for totalitarian regimes to establish total surveillance systems that make resistance almost impossible.

Some people believe that blockchain could provide a technological check on such totalitarian tendencies, because blockchain is inherently friendly to democracy and hostile to totalitarianism. In a blockchain system, decisions require the approval of 51 percent of users. That may sound democratic, but blockchain technology has a fatal flaw. The problem lies with the word "users." If one person has ten accounts, she counts as ten users. If a government controls 51 percent of accounts, then the government constitutes 51 percent

of the users. There are already examples of blockchain networks where a government is 51 percent of users.[7]

And when a government is 51 percent of users in a blockchain, it has control not just over the chain's present but even over its past. Autocrats have always wanted the power to change the past. Roman emperors, for example, frequently engaged in the practice of *damnatio memoriae*—expunging the memory of rivals and enemies. After the emperor Caracalla murdered his brother and competitor for the throne, Geta, he tried to obliterate the latter's memory. Inscriptions bearing Geta's name were chiseled out, coins bearing his effigy were melted down, and the mere mentioning of Geta's name was punishable by death.[8] One surviving painting from the time, the Severan Tondo, was made during the reign of their father—Septimius Severus—and originally showed both brothers together with Septimius and their mother, Julia Domna. But someone later obliterated Geta's face and even smeared excrement over it. Forensic analysis identified tiny pieces of dry shit where Geta's face should have been.[9]

Modern totalitarian regimes have been similarly fond of changing the past. After Stalin rose to power, he made a supreme effort to delete Trotsky—the architect of the Bolshevik Revolution and the founder of the Red Army—from all historical records. During the Stalinist Great Terror of 1937–39, whenever prominent people like Nikolai Bukharin and Marshal Mikhail Tukhachevsky were purged and executed, evidence of their existence was erased from books, academic papers, photographs, and paintings.[10] This degree of erasure demanded a huge manual effort. With blockchain, changing the past would be far easier. A government that controls 51 percent of users can disappear people from history at the press of a button.

THE BOT PRISON

While there are many ways in which AI can cement central power, authoritarian and totalitarian regimes have their own problems with

it. First and foremost, dictatorships lack experience in controlling inorganic agents. The foundation of every despotic information network is terror. But computers are not afraid of being imprisoned or killed. If a chatbot on the Russian internet mentions the war crimes committed by Russian troops in Ukraine, tells an irreverent joke about Vladimir Putin, or criticizes the corruption of Putin's United Russia party, what could the Putin regime do to that chatbot? FSB agents cannot imprison it, torture it, or threaten its family. The government could of course block or delete it, and try to find and punish its human creators, but this is a much more difficult task than disciplining human users.

In the days when computers could not generate content by themselves, and could not hold an intelligent conversation, only a human being could express dissenting opinions on Russian social network channels like VKontakte and Odnoklassniki. If that human being was physically in Russia, they risked the wrath of the Russian authorities. If that human being was physically outside Russia, the authorities could try to block their access. But what happens if Russian cyberspace is filled by millions of bots that can generate content and hold conversations, learning and developing by themselves? These bots might be preprogrammed by Russian dissidents or foreign actors to intentionally spread unorthodox views, and it might be impossible for the authorities to prevent it. Even worse, from the viewpoint of Putin's regime, what happens if authorized bots gradually develop dissenting views by themselves, simply by collecting information on what is happening in Russia and spotting patterns in it?

That's the alignment problem, Russian-style. Russia's human engineers can do their best to create AIs that are totally aligned with the regime, but given the ability of AI to learn and change by itself, how can the human engineers ensure that the AI never deviates into illicit territory? It is particularly interesting to note that as George Orwell explained in *Nineteen Eighty-Four*, totalitarian information networks often rely on doublespeak. Russia is an authoritarian state

that claims to be a democracy. The Russian invasion of Ukraine has been the largest war in Europe since 1945, yet officially it is defined as a "special military operation," and referring to it as a "war" has been criminalized and is punishable by a prison term of up to three years or a fine of up to fifty thousand rubles.[11]

The Russian Constitution makes grandiose promises about how "everyone shall be guaranteed freedom of thought and speech" (Article 29.1), how "everyone shall have the right freely to seek, receive, transmit, produce and disseminate information" (29.4), and how "the freedom of the mass media shall be guaranteed. Censorship shall be prohibited" (29.5). Hardly any Russian citizen is naive enough to take these promises at face value. But computers are bad at understanding doublespeak. A chatbot instructed to adhere to Russian law and values might read that constitution and conclude that freedom of speech is a core Russian value. Then, after spending a few days in Russian cyberspace and monitoring what is happening in the Russian information sphere, the chatbot might start criticizing the Putin regime for violating the core Russian value of freedom of speech. Humans too notice such contradictions but avoid pointing them out, due to fear. But what would prevent a chatbot from pointing out damning patterns? And how might Russian engineers explain to a chatbot that though the Russian Constitution guarantees all citizens freedom of speech and forbids censorship, the chatbot shouldn't actually believe the constitution or ever mention the gap between theory and reality? As the Ukrainian guide told me at Chernobyl, people in totalitarian countries grow up with the idea that questions lead to trouble. But if you train an algorithm on the principle that "questions lead to trouble," how will that algorithm learn and develop?

Finally, if the government adopts some disastrous policy and then changes its mind, it usually covers itself by blaming the disaster on someone else. Humans learn the hard way to forget facts that might get them in trouble. But how would you train a chatbot to forget that the policy vilified today was actually the official line only a year ago?

This is a major technological challenge that dictatorships will find difficult to deal with, especially as chatbots become more powerful and more opaque.

Of course, democracies face analogous problems with chatbots that say unwelcome things or raise dangerous questions. What happens if despite the best efforts of Microsoft or Facebook engineers, their chatbot begins spewing racist slurs? The advantage of democracies is that they have far more leeway in dealing with such rogue algorithms. Because democracies take freedom of speech seriously, they keep far fewer skeletons in their closet, and they have developed a relatively high level of tolerance even to antidemocratic speech. Dissident bots will present a far bigger challenge to totalitarian regimes that have entire cemeteries in their closets and zero tolerance of criticism.

ALGORITHMIC TAKEOVER

In the long term, totalitarian regimes are likely to face an even bigger danger: instead of criticizing them, an algorithm might gain control of them. Throughout history, the biggest threat to autocrats usually came from their own subordinates. As noted in chapter 5, no Roman emperor or Soviet premier was toppled by a democratic revolution, but they were always in danger of being overthrown or turned into puppets by their own subordinates. If a twenty-first-century autocrat gives computers too much power, that autocrat might become their puppet. The last thing a dictator wants is to create something more powerful than himself, or a force that he does not know how to control.

To illustrate the point, allow me to use an admittedly outlandish thought experiment, the totalitarian equivalent of Bostrom's paperclip apocalypse. Imagine that the year is 2050, and the Great Leader is woken up at four in the morning by an urgent call from the Surveillance & Security Algorithm. "Great Leader, we are facing an emergency. I've crunched trillions of data points, and the pattern is

unmistakable: the defense minister is planning to assassinate you in the morning and take power himself. The hit squad is ready, waiting for his command. Give me the order, though, and I'll liquidate him with a precision strike."

"But the defense minister is my most loyal supporter," says the Great Leader. "Only yesterday he said to me—"

"Great Leader, I know what he said to you. I hear everything. But I also know what he said afterward to the hit squad. And for months I've been picking up disturbing patterns in the data."

"Are you sure you were not fooled by deepfakes?"

"I'm afraid the data I relied on is 100 percent genuine," says the algorithm. "I checked it with my special deepfake-detecting sub-algorithm. I can explain exactly how we know it isn't a deepfake, but that would take us a couple of weeks. I didn't want to alert you before I was sure, but the data points converge on an inescapable conclusion: a coup is under way. Unless we act now, the assassins will be here in an hour. But give me the order, and I'll liquidate the traitor."

By giving so much power to the Surveillance & Security Algorithm, the Great Leader has placed himself in an impossible situation. If he distrusts the algorithm, he may be assassinated by the defense minister, but if he trusts the algorithm and purges the defense minister, he becomes the algorithm's puppet. Whenever anyone tries to make a move against the algorithm, the algorithm knows exactly how to manipulate the Great Leader. Note that the algorithm doesn't need to be a conscious entity to engage in such maneuvers. As Bostrom's paper-clip thought experiment indicates—and as GPT-4 lying to the TaskRabbit worker demonstrated on a small scale—a nonconscious algorithm may seek to accumulate power and manipulate people even without having any human drives like greed or egotism.

If algorithms ever develop capabilities like those in the thought experiment, dictatorships would be far more vulnerable to algorithmic takeover than democracies. It would be difficult for even a super-

Machiavellian AI to seize power in a distributed democratic system like the United States. Even if the AI learns to manipulate the U.S. president, it might face opposition from Congress, the Supreme Court, state governors, the media, major corporations, and sundry NGOs. How would the algorithm, for example, deal with a Senate filibuster?

Seizing power in a highly centralized system is much easier. When all power is concentrated in the hands of one person, whoever controls access to the autocrat can control the autocrat—and the entire state. To hack the system, one needs to learn to manipulate just a single individual. An archetypal case is how the Roman emperor Tiberius became the puppet of Lucius Aelius Sejanus, the commander of the Praetorian Guard.

The Praetorians were initially established by Augustus as a small imperial bodyguard. Augustus appointed *two* prefects to command the bodyguard so that neither could gain too much power over him.[12] Tiberius, however, was not as wise. His paranoia was his greatest weakness. Sejanus, one of the two Praetorian prefects, artfully played on Tiberius's fears. He constantly uncovered alleged plots to assassinate Tiberius, many of which were pure fantasies. The suspicious emperor grew more distrustful of everyone except Sejanus. He made Sejanus sole prefect of the Praetorian Guard, expanded it into an army of twelve thousand, and gave Sejanus's men additional roles in policing and administrating the city of Rome. Finally, Sejanus persuaded Tiberius to move out of the capital to Capri, arguing that it would be much easier to protect the emperor on a small island than in a crowded metropolis full of traitors and spies. In truth, explained the Roman historian Tacitus, Sejanus's aim was to control all the information reaching the emperor: "Access to the emperor would be under his own control, and letters, for the most part being conveyed by soldiers, would pass through his hands."[13]

With the Praetorians controlling Rome, Tiberius isolated in

Capri, and Sejanus controlling all information reaching Tiberius, the Praetorian commander became the true ruler of the empire. Sejanus purged anyone who might oppose him—including members of the imperial family—by falsely accusing them of treason. Since nobody could contact the emperor without Sejanus's permission, Tiberius was reduced to a puppet.

Eventually someone—perhaps Tiberius's sister-in-law Antonia—located an opening in Sejanus's information cordon. A letter was smuggled to the emperor, explaining to him what was going on. But by the time Tiberius woke up to the danger and resolved to get rid of Sejanus, he was almost helpless. How could he topple the man who controlled not just the bodyguards but also all communications with the outside world? If he tried to make a move, Sejanus could imprison him on Capri indefinitely and inform the Senate and the army that the emperor was too ill to travel anywhere.

Tiberius nevertheless managed to turn the tables on Sejanus. As Sejanus grew in power and became preoccupied with running the empire, he lost touch with the day-to-day minutiae of Rome's security apparatus. Tiberius managed to secretly gain the support of Naevius Sutorius Macro, commander of Rome's fire brigade and night watch. Macro orchestrated a coup against Sejanus, and as a reward Tiberius made Macro the new commander of the Praetorian Guard. A few years later, Macro had Tiberius killed.[14]

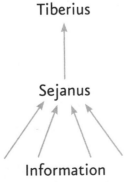

Power lies at the nexus where the information channels merge. Since Tiberius allowed the information channels to merge in the person of Sejanus, the latter became the true center of power, while Tiberius was reduced to a puppet.

The fate of Tiberius indicates the delicate balance that all dictators must strike. They try to concentrate all information in one place, but they must be careful that the different channels of information are allowed to merge only in their own person. If the information channels merge somewhere else, that then becomes the true nexus of power. When the regime relies on humans like Sejanus and Macro, a skillful dictator can play them one against the other in order to remain on top. Stalin's purges were all about that. Yet when a regime relies on a powerful but inscrutable AI that gathers and analyzes all information, the human dictator is in danger of losing all power. He may remain in the capital and yet be isolated on a digital island, controlled and manipulated by the AI.

THE DICTATOR'S DILEMMA

In the next few years, the dictators of our world face more urgent problems than an algorithmic takeover. No current AI system can manipulate regimes at such a scale. However, totalitarian systems are already in danger of putting far too much trust in algorithms. Whereas democracies assume that everyone is fallible, in totalitarian regimes the fundamental assumption is that the ruling party or the supreme leader is always right. Regimes based on that assumption are conditioned to believe in the existence of an infallible intelligence and are reluctant to create strong self-correcting mechanisms that might monitor and regulate the genius at the top.

Until now such regimes placed their faith in human parties and leaders and were hothouses for the growth of personality cults. But in the twenty-first century this totalitarian tradition prepares them to expect AI infallibility. Systems that could believe in the perfect genius of a Mussolini, a Ceauşescu, or a Khomeini are primed to also believe in the flawless genius of a superintelligent computer. This could have disastrous results for their citizens, and potentially for the rest of the world as well. What happens if the algorithm in charge of

environmental policy makes a big mistake, but there are no self-correcting mechanisms that can identify and correct its error? What happens if the algorithm running the state's social credit system begins terrorizing not just the general population but even the members of the ruling party and simultaneously begins to label anyone who questions its policies "an enemy of the people"?

Dictators have always suffered from weak self-correcting mechanisms and have always been threatened by powerful subordinates. The rise of AI may greatly exacerbate these problems. The computer network therefore presents dictators with an excruciating dilemma. They could decide to escape the clutches of their human underlings by trusting a supposedly infallible technology, in which case they might become the technology's puppet. Or, they could build a human institution to supervise the AI, but that institution might limit their own power, too.

If even just a few of the world's dictators choose to put their trust in AI, this could have far-reaching consequences for the whole of humanity. Science fiction is full of scenarios of an AI getting out of control and enslaving or eliminating humankind. Most sci-fi plots explore these scenarios in the context of democratic capitalist societies. This is understandable. Authors living in democracies are obviously interested in their own societies, whereas authors living in dictatorships are usually discouraged from criticizing their rulers. But the weakest spot in humanity's anti-AI shield is probably the dictators. The easiest way for an AI to seize power is not by breaking out of Dr. Frankenstein's lab but by ingratiating itself with some paranoid Tiberius.

This is not a prophecy, just a possibility. After 1945, dictators and their subordinates cooperated with democratic governments and their citizens to contain nuclear weapons. On July 9, 1955, Albert Einstein, Bertrand Russell, and a number of other eminent scientists and thinkers published the Russell-Einstein Manifesto, calling on the leaders of both democracies and dictatorships to cooperate on preventing nuclear war. "We appeal," said the manifesto, "as human

beings, to human beings: remember your humanity, and forget the rest. If you can do so, the way lies open to a new Paradise; if you cannot, there lies before you the risk of universal death."[15] This is true of AI too. It would be foolish of dictators to believe that AI will necessarily tilt the balance of power in their favor. If they aren't careful, AI will just grab power to itself.

The Silicon Curtain: Global Empire or Global Split?

The previous two chapters explored how different human societies might react to the rise of the new computer network. But we live in an interconnected world, where the decisions of one country can have a profound impact on others. Some of the gravest dangers posed by AI do not result from the internal dynamics of a single human society. Rather, they arise from dynamics involving many societies, which might lead to new arms races, new wars, and new imperial expansions.

Computers are not yet powerful enough to completely escape our control or destroy human civilization by themselves. As long as humanity stands united, we can build institutions that will control AI and will identify and correct algorithmic errors. Unfortunately, humanity has never been united. We have always been plagued by bad actors, as well as by disagreements between good actors. The rise of AI, then, poses an existential danger to humankind not because of the malevolence of computers but because of our own shortcomings.

Thus, a paranoid dictator might hand unlimited power to a fallible AI, including even the power to launch nuclear strikes. If the dictator

trusts his AI more than his defense minister, wouldn't it make sense to have the AI supervise the country's most powerful weapons? If the AI then makes an error, or begins to pursue an alien goal, the result could be catastrophic, and not just for that country.

Similarly, terrorists focused on events in one corner of the world might use AI to instigate a global pandemic. The terrorists might be more versed in some apocalyptic mythology than in the science of epidemiology, but they just need to set the goal, and all else will be done by their AI. The AI could synthesize a new pathogen, order it from commercial laboratories or print it in biological 3-D printers, and devise the best strategy to spread it around the world, via airports or food supply chains. What if the AI synthesizes a virus that is as deadly as Ebola, as contagious as COVID-19, and as slow acting as AIDS? By the time the first victims begin to die, and the world is alerted to the danger, most people on earth might have already been infected.[1]

As we have seen in previous chapters, human civilization is threatened not only by physical and biological weapons of mass destruction like atom bombs and viruses. Human civilization could also be destroyed by weapons of social mass destruction, like stories that undermine our social bonds. An AI developed in one country could be used to unleash a deluge of fake news, fake money, and fake humans so that people in numerous other countries lose the ability to trust anything or anyone.

Many societies—both democracies and dictatorships—may act responsibly to regulate such usages of AI, clamp down on bad actors, and restrain the dangerous ambitions of their own rulers and fanatics. But if even a handful of societies fail to do so, this could be enough to endanger the whole of humankind. Climate change can devastate even countries that adopt excellent environmental regulations, because it is a global rather than a national problem. AI, too, is a global problem. Countries would be naive to imagine that as long as they regulate AI wisely within their own borders, these regulations will protect them from the worst outcomes of the AI revo-

lution. Accordingly, to understand the new computer politics, it is not enough to examine how discrete societies might react to AI. We also need to consider how AI might change relations between societies on a global level.

At present, the world is divided into about two hundred nation-states, most of which gained their independence only after 1945. They are not all equal. The list contains two superpowers, a handful of major powers, several blocs and alliances, and a lot of smaller fish. Still, even the tiniest states enjoy some leverage, as evidenced by their ability to play the superpowers against each other. In the early 2020s, for example, China and the United States competed for influence in the strategically important South Pacific region. Both superpowers courted island nations like Tonga, Tuvalu, Kiribati, and the Solomon Islands. The governments of these small nations—whose populations range from 740,000 (Solomon Islands) to 11,000 (Tuvalu)—had substantial leeway to decide which way to tack and were able to extract considerable concessions and aid.[2]

Other small states, such as Qatar, have established themselves as important players in the geopolitical arena. With only 300,000 citizens, Qatar is nevertheless pursuing ambitious foreign policy aims in the Middle East, is playing an outsized rule in the global economy, and is home to Al Jazeera, the Arab world's most influential TV network. One might argue that Qatar is able to punch well above its weight because it is the third-largest exporter of natural gas in the world. Yet in a different international setting, that would have made Qatar not an independent actor but the first course on the menu of any imperial conqueror. It is telling that, as of 2024, Qatar's much bigger neighbors, and the world's hegemonic powers, are letting the tiny Gulf state hold on to its fabulous riches. Many people describe the international system as a jungle. If so, it is a jungle in which tigers allow fat chickens to live in relative safety.

Qatar, Tonga, Tuvalu, Kiribati, and the Solomon Islands all indicate that we are living in a postimperial era. They gained their independence from the British Empire in the 1970s, as part of the final

demise of the European imperial order. The leverage they now have in the international arena testifies that in the first quarter of the twenty-first century power is distributed between a relatively large number of players, rather than monopolized by a few empires.

How might the rise of the new computer network change the shape of international politics? Aside from apocalyptic scenarios such as a dictatorial AI launching a nuclear war, or a terrorist AI instigating a lethal pandemic, computers pose two main challenges to the current international system. First, since computers make it easier to concentrate information and power in a central hub, humanity could enter a new imperial era. A few empires (or perhaps a single empire) might bring the whole world under a much tighter grip than that of the British Empire or the Soviet Empire. Tonga, Tuvalu, and Qatar would be transformed from independent states into colonial possessions—just as they were fifty years ago.

Second, humanity could split along a new Silicon Curtain that would pass between rival digital empires. As each regime chooses its own answer to the AI alignment problem, to the dictator's dilemma, and to other technological quandaries, each might create a separate and very different computer network. The various networks might then find it ever more difficult to interact, and so would the humans they control. Qataris living as part of an Iranian or Russian network, Tongans living as part of a Chinese network, and Tuvaluans living as part of an American network could come to have such different life experiences and worldviews that they would hardly be able to communicate or to agree on much.

If these developments indeed materialize, they could easily lead to their own apocalyptic outcome. Perhaps each empire can keep its nuclear weapons under human control and its lunatics away from bioweapons. But a human species divided into hostile camps that cannot understand each other stands a small chance of avoiding devastating wars or preventing catastrophic climate change. A world of rival empires separated by an opaque Silicon Curtain would also be incapable of regulating the explosive power of AI.

THE RISE OF DIGITAL EMPIRES

In chapter 9 we touched briefly on the link between the Industrial Revolution and modern imperialism. It was not evident, at the beginning, that industrial technology would have much of an impact on empire building. When the first steam engines were put to use to pump water in British coal mines in the eighteenth century, no one foresaw that they would eventually power the most ambitious imperial projects in human history. When the Industrial Revolution subsequently gathered steam in the early nineteenth century, it was driven by private businesses, because governments and armies were relatively slow to appreciate its potential geopolitical impact. The world's first commercial railway, for example, which opened in 1830 between Liverpool and Manchester, was built and operated by the privately owned Liverpool and Manchester Railway Company. The same was true of most other early railway lines in the U.K., the United States, France, Germany, and elsewhere. At that point, it wasn't at all clear why governments or armies should get involved in such commercial enterprises.

By the middle of the nineteenth century, however, the governments and armed forces of the leading industrial powers had fully recognized the immense geopolitical potential of modern industrial technology. The need for raw materials and markets justified imperialism, while industrial technologies made imperial conquests easier. Steamships were crucial, for example, to the British victory over the Chinese in the Opium Wars, and railroads played a decisive role in the American expansion west and the Russian expansion east and south. Indeed, entire imperial projects were shaped around the construction of railroads such as the Trans-Siberian and Trans-Caspian Russian lines, the German dream of a Berlin-Baghdad railway, and the British dream of building a railway from Cairo to the Cape.[3]

Nevertheless, most polities didn't join the burgeoning industrial arms race in time. Some lacked the capacity to do so, like the Mela-

nesian chiefdoms of the Solomon Islands and the Al Thani tribe of Qatar. Others, like the Burmese Empire, the Ashanti Empire, and the Chinese Empire, might have had the capacity but lacked the will and foresight. Their rulers and inhabitants either didn't follow developments in places like northwest England or didn't think they had much to do with them. Why should the rice farmers of the Irrawaddy basin in Burma or the Yangtze basin in China concern themselves about the Liverpool–Manchester Railway? By the end of the nineteenth century, however, these rice farmers found themselves either conquered or indirectly exploited by the British Empire. Most other stragglers in the industrial race also ended up dominated by one industrial power or other. Could something similar happen with AI?

When the race to develop AI gathered steam in the early years of the twenty-first century, it too was initially spearheaded by private entrepreneurs in a handful of countries. They set their sights on centralizing the world's flow of information. Google wanted to organize all the world's information in one place. Amazon sought to centralize all the world's shopping. Facebook wished to connect all the world's social spheres. But concentrating all the world's information is neither practical nor helpful unless one can centrally process that information. And in 2000, when Google's search engine was making its baby steps, when Amazon was a modest online bookshop, and when Mark Zuckerberg was in high school, the AI necessary to centrally process oceans of data was nowhere at hand. But some people bet it was just around the corner.

Kevin Kelly, the founding editor of *Wired* magazine, recounted how in 2002 he attended a small party at Google and struck up a conversation with Larry Page. "Larry, I still don't get it. There are so many search companies. Web search, for free? Where does that get you?" Page explained that Google wasn't focused on search at all. "We're really making an AI," he said.[4] Having lots of data makes it easier to create an AI. And AI can turn lots of data into lots of power.

By the 2010s, the dream was becoming a reality. Like every major historical revolution, the rise of AI was a gradual process involving

numerous steps. And like every revolution, a few of these steps were seen as turning points, just like the opening of the Liverpool–Manchester Railway. In the prolific literature on the story of AI, two events pop up again and again. The first occurred when, on September 30, 2012, a convolutional neural network called AlexNet won the ImageNet Large Scale Visual Recognition Challenge.

If you have no idea what a convolutional neural network is, and if you have never heard of the ImageNet challenge, you are not alone. More than 99 percent of us are in the same situation, which is why AlexNet's victory was hardly front-page news in 2012. But some humans did hear about AlexNet's victory and decoded the writing on the wall.

They knew, for example, that ImageNet is a database of millions of annotated digital images. Did a website ever ask you to prove that you are not a robot by looking at a set of images and indicating which ones contain a car or a cat? The images you clicked were perhaps added to the ImageNet database. The same thing might also have happened to tagged images of your pet cat that you uploaded online. The ImageNet Large Scale Visual Recognition Challenge tests various algorithms on how well they are able to identify the annotated images in the database. Can they correctly identify the cats? When humans are asked to do it, out of one hundred cat images we correctly identify ninety-five as cats. In 2010 the best algorithms had a success rate of only 72 percent. In 2011 the algorithmic success rate crawled up to 75 percent. In 2012 the AlexNet algorithm won the challenge and stunned the still minuscule community of AI experts by achieving a success rate of 85 percent. While this improvement may not sound like much to laypersons, it demonstrated to the experts the potential for rapid progress in certain AI domains. By 2015 a Microsoft algorithm achieved 96 percent accuracy, surpassing the human ability to identify cat images.

In 2016, *The Economist* published a piece titled "From Not Working to Neural Networking" that asked, "How has artificial intelligence, associated with hubris and disappointment since its earliest

days, suddenly become the hottest field in technology?" It pointed to AlexNet's victory as the moment when "people started to pay attention, not just within the AI community but across the technology industry as a whole." The article was illustrated with an image of a robotic hand holding up a photo of a cat.[5]

All those cat images that tech giants had been harvesting from across the world, without paying a penny to either users or tax collectors, turned out to be incredibly valuable. The AI race was on, and the competitors were running on cat images. At the same time that AlexNet was preparing for the ImageNet challenge, Google too was training *its* AI on cat images, and even created a dedicated cat-image-generating AI called the Meow Generator.[6] The technology developed by recognizing cute kittens was later deployed for more predatory purposes. For example, Israel relied on it to create the Red Wolf, Blue Wolf, and Wolf Pack apps used by Israeli soldiers for facial recognition of Palestinians in the Occupied Territories.[7] The ability to recognize cat images also led to the algorithms Iran uses to automatically recognize unveiled women and enforce its hijab laws. As explained in chapter 8, massive amounts of data are required to train machine-learning algorithms. Without millions of cat images uploaded and annotated for free by people across the world, it would not have been possible to train the AlexNet algorithm or the Meow Generator, which in turn served as the template for subsequent AIs with far-reaching economic, political, and military potential.[8]

Just as in the early nineteenth century the effort to build railways was pioneered by private entrepreneurs, so in the early twenty-first century private corporations were the initial main competitors in the AI race. The executives of Google, Facebook, Alibaba, and Baidu saw the value of recognizing cat images before the presidents and generals did. The second eureka moment, when the presidents and generals caught on to what was happening, occurred in mid-March 2016. It was the aforementioned victory of Google's AlphaGo over Lee Sedol. Whereas AlexNet's achievement was largely ignored by politicians, AlphaGo's triumph sent shock waves through government

offices, especially in East Asia. In China and neighboring countries go is a cultural treasure and considered an ideal training for aspiring strategists and policy makers. In March 2016, or so the mythology of AI would have it, the Chinese government realized that the age of AI had begun.[9]

It is little wonder that the Chinese government was probably the first to understand the full importance of what was happening. In the nineteenth century, China was late to appreciate the potential of the Industrial Revolution and was slow to adopt inventions like railroads and steamships. It consequently suffered what the Chinese call "the century of humiliations." After having been the world's greatest superpower for centuries, failing to adopt modern industrial technology brought China to its knees. It was repeatedly defeated in wars, partially conquered by foreigners, and thoroughly exploited by the powers that did understand railroads and steamships. The Chinese vowed never again to miss the train.

In 2017, China's government released its "New Generation Artificial Intelligence Plan," which announced that "by 2030, China's AI theories, technologies, and application should achieve world-leading levels, making China the world's primary AI innovation center."[10] In the following years China poured enormous resources into AI so that by the early 2020s it was already leading the world in several AI-related fields and catching up with the United States in others.[11]

Of course, the Chinese government wasn't the only one that woke up to the importance of AI. On September 1, 2017, President Putin of Russia declared, "Artificial intelligence is the future, not only for Russia, but for all humankind. . . . Whoever becomes the leader in this sphere will become the ruler of the world." In January 2018, Prime Minister Modi of India concurred that "the one who control [sic] the data will control the world."[12] In February 2019, President Trump signed an executive order on AI, saying that "the age of AI has arrived" and that "continued American leadership in Artificial Intelligence is of paramount importance to maintaining the economic and national security of the United States."[13] The United

States at the time was already the leader in the AI race, thanks largely to efforts of visionary private entrepreneurs. But what began as a commercial competition between corporations was turning into a match between governments, or perhaps more accurately, into a race between competing teams, each made of one government and several corporations. The prize for the winner? World domination.

DATA COLONIALISM

In the sixteenth century, when Spanish, Portuguese, and Dutch conquistadors were building the first global empires in history, they came with sailing ships, horses, and gunpowder. When the British, Russians, and Japanese made their bids for hegemony in the nineteenth and twentieth centuries, they relied on steamships, locomotives, and machine guns. In the twenty-first century, to dominate a colony, you no longer need to send in the gunboats. You need to take out the data. A few corporations or governments harvesting the world's data could transform the rest of the globe into data colonies— territories they control not with overt military force but with information.[14]

Imagine a situation—in twenty years, say—when somebody in Beijing or San Francisco possesses the entire personal history of every politician, journalist, colonel, and CEO in your country: every text they ever sent, every web search they ever made, every illness they suffered, every sexual encounter they enjoyed, every joke they told, every bribe they took. Would you still be living in an independent country, or would you now be living in a data colony? What happens when your country finds itself utterly dependent on digital infrastructures and AI-powered systems over which it has no effective control?

Such a situation can lead to a new kind of data colonialism in which control of data is used to dominate faraway colonies. Mastery of AI and data could also give the new empires control of people's

attention. As we have already discussed, in the 2010s American social media giants like Facebook and YouTube upended the politics of distant countries like Myanmar and Brazil in pursuit of profit. Future digital empires may do something similar for political interests.

Fears of psychological warfare, data colonialism, and loss of control over their cyberspace have led many countries to already block what they see as dangerous apps. China has banned Facebook, YouTube, and many other Western social media apps and websites. Russia has banned almost all Western social media apps as well as some Chinese ones. In 2020, India banned TikTok, WeChat, and numerous other Chinese apps on the grounds that they were "prejudicial to sovereignty and integrity of India, defense of India, security of state and public order."[15] The United States has been debating whether to ban TikTok—concerned that the app might be serving Chinese interests—and as of 2023 it is illegal to use it on the devices of almost all federal employees, state employees, and government contractors.[16] Lawmakers in the U.K., New Zealand, and other countries have also expressed concerns over TikTok.[17] Numerous other governments, from Iran to Ethiopia, have blocked various apps like Facebook, Twitter, YouTube, Telegram, and Instagram.

Data colonialism could also manifest itself in the spread of social credit systems. What might happen, for example, if a dominant player in the global digital economy decides to establish a social credit system that harvests data anywhere it can and scores not only its own nationals but people throughout the world? Foreigners couldn't just shrug off their score, because it might affect them in numerous ways, from buying flight tickets to applying for visas, scholarships, and jobs. Just as tourists use the global scores given by foreign corporations like Tripadvisor and Airbnb to evaluate restaurants and vacation homes even in their own country, and just as people throughout the world use the U.S. dollar for commercial transactions, so people everywhere might begin to use a Chinese or an American social credit score for local social interactions.

Becoming a data colony will have economic as well as political and

social consequences. In the nineteenth and twentieth centuries, if you were a colony of an industrial power like Belgium or Britain, it usually meant that you provided raw materials, while the cutting-edge industries that made the biggest profits remained in the imperial hub. Egypt exported cotton to Britain and imported high-end textiles. Malaya provided rubber for tires; Coventry made the cars.[18]

Something analogous is likely to happen with data colonialism. The raw material for the AI industry is data. To produce AI that recognizes images, you need cat photos. To produce the trendiest fashion, you need data on fashion trends. To produce autonomous vehicles, you need data about traffic patterns and car accidents. To produce health-care AI, you need data about genes and medical conditions. In a new imperial information economy, raw data will be harvested throughout the world and will flow to the imperial hub. There the cutting-edge technology will be developed, producing unbeatable algorithms that know how to identify cats, predict fashion trends, drive autonomous vehicles, and diagnose diseases. These algorithms will then be exported back to the data colonies. Data from Egypt and Malaysia might make a corporation in San Francisco or Beijing rich, while people in Cairo and Kuala Lumpur remain poor, because neither the profits nor the power is distributed back.

The nature of the new information economy might make the imbalance between imperial hub and exploited colony worse than ever. In ancient times land—rather than information—was the most important economic asset. This precluded the overconcentration of all wealth and power in a single hub. As long as land was paramount, considerable wealth and power always remained in the hands of provincial landowners. A Roman emperor, for example, could put down one provincial revolt after another, but on the day after decapitating the last rebel chief, he had no choice but to appoint a new set of provincial landowners who might again challenge the central power. In the Roman Empire, although Italy was the seat of political power, the richest provinces were in the eastern Mediterranean. It was impossible to transport the fertile fields of the Nile valley to the Italian

Peninsula.[19] Eventually the emperors abandoned the city of Rome to the barbarians and moved the seat of political power to the rich east, to Constantinople.

During the Industrial Revolution machines became more important than land. Factories, mines, railroad lines, and electrical power stations became the most valuable assets. It was somewhat easier to concentrate these kinds of assets in one place. The British Empire could centralize industrial production in its home islands, extract raw materials from India, Egypt, and Iraq, and sell them finished goods made in Birmingham or Belfast. Unlike in the Roman Empire, Britain was the seat of both political and economic power. But physics and geology still put natural limits on this concentration of wealth and power. The British couldn't move every cotton mill from Calcutta to Manchester, or shift the oil wells from Kirkuk to Yorkshire.

Information is different. Unlike cotton and oil, digital data can be sent from Malaysia or Egypt to Beijing or San Francisco at almost the speed of light. And unlike land, oil fields, or textile factories, algorithms don't take up much space. Consequently, unlike industrial power, the world's algorithmic power *can* be concentrated in a single hub. Engineers in a single country might write the code and control the keys for all the crucial algorithms that run the entire world.

Indeed, AI makes it possible to concentrate in one place even the decisive assets of some traditional industries, like textile. In the nineteenth century, to control the textile industry meant to control sprawling cotton fields and huge mechanical production lines. In the twenty-first century, the most important asset of the textile industry is information rather than cotton or machinery. To beat the competitors, a garment producer needs information about the likes and dislikes of customers and the ability to predict or manufacture the next fashions. By controlling this type of information, high-tech giants like Amazon and Alibaba can monopolize even a very traditional industry like textile. In 2021, Amazon became the United States' biggest single clothing retailer.[20]

Moreover, as AI, robots, and 3-D printers automate textile pro-

duction, millions of workers might lose their jobs, upending national economies and the global balance of power. What will happen to the economies and politics of Pakistan and Bangladesh, for example, when automation makes it cheaper to produce textiles in Europe? Consider that at present the textile sector provides employment to 40 percent of Pakistan's total labor force and accounts for 84 percent of Bangladesh's export earnings.[21] As noted in chapter 9, while automation might make millions of textile workers redundant, it will probably create many new jobs, too. For instance, there might be a huge demand for coders and data analysts. But turning an unemployed factory hand into a data analyst demands a substantial upfront investment in retraining. Where would Pakistan and Bangladesh get the money to do that?

AI and automation therefore pose a particular challenge to poorer developing countries. In an AI-driven economy, the digital leaders claim the bulk of the gains and could use their wealth to retrain their workforce and profit even more. Meanwhile, the value of unskilled laborers in left-behind countries will decline, and they will not have the resources to retrain their workforce, causing them to fall even further behind. The result might be lots of new jobs and immense wealth in San Francisco and Shanghai, while many other parts of the world face economic ruin.[22] According to the global accounting firm PricewaterhouseCoopers, AI is expected to add $15.7 trillion to the global economy by 2030. But if current trends continue, it is projected that China and North America—the two leading AI superpowers—will together take home 70 percent of that money.[23]

FROM WEB TO COCOON

These economic and geopolitical dynamics could divide the world between two digital empires. During the Cold War, the Iron Curtain was in many places literally made of metal: barbed wire separated one country from another. Now the world is increasingly divided by

the Silicon Curtain. The Silicon Curtain is made of code, and it passes through every smartphone, computer, and server in the world. The code on your smartphone determines on which side of the Silicon Curtain you live, which algorithms run your life, who controls your attention, and where your data flows.

It is becoming difficult to access information across the Silicon Curtain, say between China and the United States, or between Russia and the EU. Moreover, the two sides are increasingly run on different digital networks, using different computer codes. Each sphere obeys different regulations and serves different purposes. In China, the most important aim of new digital technology is to strengthen the state and serve government policies. While private enterprises are given a certain amount of autonomy in developing and deploying AIs, their economic activities are ultimately subservient to the government's political goals. These political goals also justify a relatively high level of surveillance, both online and offline. This means, for example, that though Chinese citizens and authorities do care about people's privacy, China is already far ahead of the United States and other Western countries in developing and deploying social credit systems that encompass the whole of people's lives.[24]

In the United States, the government plays a more limited role. Private enterprises lead the development and deployment of AI, and the ultimate goal of many new AI systems is to enrich the tech giants rather than to strengthen the American state or the current administration. Indeed, in many cases governmental policies are themselves shaped by powerful business interests. But the U.S. system does offer greater protection for citizens' privacy. While American corporations aggressively gather information on people's online activities, they are much more restricted in surveilling people's offline lives. There is also widespread rejection of the ideas behind all-embracing social credit systems.[25]

These political, cultural, and regulatory differences mean that each sphere is using different software. In China you cannot use Google or Facebook, and you cannot access Wikipedia. In the United States

few people use WeChat, Baidu, or Tencent. More important, the spheres aren't mirror images of each other. It is not that the Chinese and Americans develop local versions of the same apps. Baidu isn't the Chinese Google. Alibaba isn't the Chinese Amazon. They have different goals, different digital architectures, and different impacts on people's lives.[26] These differences influence much of the world, since most countries rely on Chinese and American software rather than on local technology.

Each sphere also uses different hardware like smartphones and computers. The United States pressures its allies and clients to avoid Chinese hardware, such as Huawei's 5G infrastructure.[27] The Trump administration blocked an attempt by the Singaporean corporation Broadcom to buy the leading American producer of computer chips, Qualcomm. They feared foreigners might insert back doors into the chips or would prevent the U.S. government from inserting its own back doors there.[28] In 2022, the Biden administration placed strict limits on trade in high-performance computing chips necessary for the development of AI. U.S. companies were forbidden to export such chips to China, or to provide China with the means to manufacture or repair them. The restrictions have subsequently been tightened further, and the ban was expanded to include other nations such as Russia and Iran.[29] While in the short term this hampers China in the AI race, in the long term it will push China to develop a completely separate digital sphere that will be distinct from the American digital sphere even in its smallest building blocks.[30]

The two digital spheres may drift further and further apart. Chinese software would talk only with Chinese hardware and Chinese infrastructure, and the same would happen on the other side of the Silicon Curtain. Since digital code influences human behavior, and human behavior in turn shapes digital code, the two sides may well be moving along different trajectories that will make them more and more different not just in their technology but in their cultural values, social norms, and political structures. After generations of convergence, humanity could find itself at a crucial point of divergence.[31]

For centuries, new information technologies fueled the process of globalization and brought people all over the world into closer contact. Paradoxically, information technology today is so powerful it can potentially split humanity by enclosing different people in separate information cocoons, ending the idea of a single shared human reality. While the web has been our main metaphor in recent decades, the future might belong to cocoons.

THE GLOBAL MIND-BODY SPLIT

The division into separate information cocoons could lead not just to economic rivalries and international tensions but also to the development of very different cultures, ideologies, and identities. Guessing future cultural and ideological developments is usually a fool's errand. It is far more difficult than predicting economic and geopolitical developments. How many Romans or Jews in the days of Tiberius could have anticipated that a splinter Jewish sect would eventually take over the Roman Empire and that the emperors would abandon Rome's old gods to worship an executed Jewish rabbi?

It would have been even more difficult to foresee the directions in which various Christian sects would develop and the momentous impact of their ideas and conflicts on everything from politics to sexuality. When Jesus was asked about paying taxes to Tiberius's government and answered, "Render unto Caesar the things that are Caesar's, and unto God the things that are God's" (Matthew 22:21), nobody could imagine the impact his response would have on the separation of church and state in the American republic two millennia later. And when Saint Paul wrote to the Christians in Rome, "I myself in my mind am a slave to God's law, but in my sinful flesh a slave to the law of sin" (Romans 7:25), who could have foreseen the repercussions this would have on schools of thought ranging from Cartesian philosophy to queer theory?

Despite these difficulties, it is important to try to imagine future

cultural developments, in order to alert ourselves to the fact that the AI revolution and the formation of rival digital spheres are likely to change more than just our jobs and political structures. The following paragraphs contain some admittedly ambitious speculation, so please bear in mind that my goal is not to accurately foretell cultural developments but merely to draw attention to the likelihood that profound cultural shifts and conflicts await us.

One possible development with far-reaching consequences is that different digital cocoons might adopt incompatible approaches to the most fundamental questions of human identity. For thousands of years, many religious and cultural conflicts—for example, between rival Christian sects, between Hindus and Buddhists, and between Platonists and Aristotelians—were fueled by disagreements about the mind-body problem. Are humans a physical body, or a nonphysical mind, or perhaps a mind trapped inside a body? In the twenty-first century, the computer network might supercharge the mind-body problem and turn it into a cause for major personal, ideological, and political conflicts.

To appreciate the political ramifications of the mind-body problem, let's briefly revisit the history of Christianity. Many of the earliest Christian sects, influenced by Jewish thinking, believed in the Old Testament idea that humans are embodied beings and that the body plays a crucial role in human identity. The book of Genesis said God created humans as physical bodies, and almost all books of the Old Testament assume that humans can exist only as physical bodies. With a few possible exceptions, the Old Testament doesn't mention the possibility of a bodiless existence after death, in heaven or hell. When the ancient Jews fantasized about salvation, they imagined it to mean an earthly kingdom of material bodies. In the time of Jesus, many Jews believed that when the Messiah finally comes, the bodies of the dead would come back to life, here on earth. The Kingdom of God, established by the Messiah, was supposed to be a material kingdom, with trees and stones and flesh-and-blood bodies.[32]

This was also the view of Jesus himself and the first Christians.

Jesus promised his followers that soon the Kingdom of God would be built here on earth and they would inhabit it in their material bodies. When Jesus died without fulfilling his promise, his early followers came to believe that he was resurrected *in the flesh* and that when the Kingdom of God finally materialized on earth, they too would be resurrected in the flesh. The church father Tertullian (160–240 CE) wrote that "the flesh is the very condition on which salvation hinges," and the catechism of the Catholic Church, citing the doctrines adopted at the Second Council of Lyon in 1274, states, "We believe in God who is creator of the flesh; we believe in the Word made flesh in order to redeem the flesh; we believe in the resurrection of the flesh, the fulfillment of both the creation and the redemption of the flesh.... We believe in the true resurrection of this flesh that we now possess."[33]

Despite such seemingly unequivocal statements, we saw that Saint Paul already had his doubts about the flesh, and by the fourth century CE, under Greek, Manichaean, and Persian influences, some Christians had drifted toward a dualistic approach. They came to think of humans as consisting of a good immaterial soul trapped inside an evil material body. They didn't fantasize about being resurrected in the flesh. Just the opposite. Having been released by death from its abominable material prison, why would the pure soul ever want to get back in? Christians accordingly began to believe that after death the soul is liberated from the body and exists forever in an immaterial place completely beyond the physical realm—which is the standard belief among Christians today, notwithstanding what Tertullian and the Second Council of Lyon said.[34]

But Christianity couldn't completely abandon the old Jewish view that humans are embodied beings. After all, Christ appeared on earth in the flesh. His body was nailed to the cross, on which he experienced excruciating pain. For two thousand years, Christian sects therefore fought each other—sometimes with words, sometimes with swords—over the exact relations between soul and body. The fiercest arguments focused on Christ's own body. Was he material?

Was he purely spiritual? Did he perhaps have a nonbinary nature, being both human and divine at the same time?

The different approaches to the mind-body problem influenced how people treated their own bodies. Saints, hermits, and monks made breathtaking experiments in pushing the human body to its limits. Just as Christ allowed his body to be tortured on the cross, so these "athletes of Christ" allowed lions and bears to rip them apart while their souls rejoiced in divine ecstasy. They wore hair shirts, fasted for weeks, or stood for years on a pillar—like the famous Simeon who allegedly stood for about forty years on top of a pillar near Aleppo.[35]

Other Christians took the opposite approach, believing that the body didn't matter at all. The only thing that mattered was faith. This idea was taken to extremes by Protestants like Martin Luther, who formulated the doctrine of *sola fide:* only faith. After living as a monk for about ten years, fasting and torturing his body in various ways, Luther despaired of these bodily exercises. He reasoned that no bodily self-torments could force God to redeem him. Indeed, thinking he could win his own salvation by torturing his body was the sin of pride. Luther therefore disrobed, married a former nun, and told his followers that to be good Christians, the only thing they needed was to have complete faith in Christ.[36]

These ancient theological debates about mind and body may seem utterly irrelevant to the AI revolution, but they have in fact been resurrected by twenty-first-century technologies. What is the relationship between our physical body and our online identities and avatars? What is the relation between the offline world and cyberspace? Suppose I spend most of my waking hours sitting in my room in front of a screen, playing online games, forming virtual relationships, and even working remotely. I hardly venture out even to eat. I just order takeout. If you are like ancient Jews and the first Christians, you would pity me and conclude that I must be living in a delusion, losing touch with the reality of physical spaces and flesh-and-blood bodies. But if your thinking is closer to that of Luther and

many later Christians, you might think I am liberated. By shifting most of my activities and relationships online, I have released myself from the limited organic world of debilitating gravity and corrupt bodies and can enjoy the unlimited possibilities of a digital world, which is potentially liberated from the laws of biology and even physics. I am free to roam a much vaster and more exciting space and to explore new aspects of my identity.

An increasingly important question is, Can people adopt any virtual identity they like, or should their identity be constrained by their biological body? If we follow the Lutheran position of *sola fide*, the biological body isn't of much importance. To adopt a certain online identity, the only thing that matters is what you believe. This debate can have far-reaching consequences not just for human identity but for our attitude to the world as a whole. A society that understands identities in terms of biological bodies should also care more about material infrastructure like sewage pipes and about the ecosystem that sustains our bodies. It will see the online world as an auxiliary of the offline world that can serve various useful purposes but can never become the central arena of our lives. Its aim would be to create an ideal physical and biological realm—the Kingdom of God on earth. In contrast, a society that downplays biological bodies and focuses on online identities may well seek to create an immersive Kingdom of God in cyberspace while discounting the fate of mere material things like sewage pipes and rain forests.

This debate could shape attitudes not only toward organisms but also toward digital entities. As long as society defines identity by focusing on physical bodies, it is unlikely to view AIs as persons. But if society gives less importance to physical bodies, then even AIs that lack any corporeal manifestations may be accepted as legal persons enjoying various rights.

Throughout history, diverse cultures have given diverse answers to the mind-body problem. A twenty-first-century controversy about the mind-body problem could result in cultural and political splits more consequential even than the split between Jews and Christians

or between Catholics and Protestants. What happens, for example, if the American sphere discounts the body, defines humans by their online identity, recognizes AIs as persons, and downplays the importance of the ecosystem, whereas the Chinese sphere adopts opposite positions? Current disagreements about violations of human rights or adherence to ecological standards will look minuscule in comparison. The Thirty Years' War—arguably the most devastating war in European history—was fought at least in part because Catholics and Protestants couldn't agree on doctrines like *sola fide* and on whether Christ was divine, human, or nonbinary. Might future conflicts start because of an argument about AI rights and the nonbinary nature of avatars?

As noted, these are all wild speculations, and in all likelihood actual cultures and ideologies will develop in different—and perhaps even wilder—directions. But it is probable that within a few decades the computer network will cultivate new human and nonhuman identities that make little sense to us. And if the world will be divided into two rival digital cocoons, the identities of entities in one cocoon might be unintelligible to the inhabitants of the other.

FROM CODE WAR TO HOT WAR

While China and the United States are currently the front-runners in the AI race, they are not alone. Other countries or blocs, such as the EU, India, Brazil, and Russia, may try to create their own digital spheres, each influenced by different political, cultural, and religious traditions.[37] Instead of being divided between just two global empires, the world might be divided among a dozen empires. It is unclear whether this will somewhat alleviate or only exacerbate the imperial competition.

The more the new empires compete against one another, the greater the danger of armed conflict. The Cold War between the

United States and the U.S.S.R. never escalated into a direct military confrontation largely thanks to the doctrine of mutually assured destruction. But the danger of escalation in the age of AI is bigger, because cyber warfare is inherently different from nuclear warfare.

First, cyber weapons are much more versatile than nuclear bombs. Cyber weapons can bring down a country's electric grid, but they can also be used to destroy a secret research facility, jam an enemy sensor, inflame a political scandal, manipulate elections, or hack a single smartphone. And they can do all that stealthily. They don't announce their presence with a mushroom cloud and a storm of fire, nor do they leave a visible trail from launchpad to target. Consequently, at times it is hard to know if an attack even occurred or who launched it. If a database is hacked or sensitive equipment is destroyed, it's hard to be sure whom to blame. The temptation to start a limited cyberwar is therefore big, and so is the temptation to escalate it. Rival countries like Israel and Iran or the United States and Russia have been trading cyber blows for years, in an undeclared but escalating war.[38] This is becoming the new global norm, amplifying international tensions and pushing countries to cross one red line after another.

A second crucial difference concerns predictability. The Cold War was like a hyperrational chess game, and the certainty of destruction in the event of nuclear conflict was so great that the desire to start a war was correspondingly small. Cyber warfare lacks this certainty. Nobody knows for sure where each side has planted its logic bombs, Trojan horses, and malware. Nobody can be certain whether their own weapons would actually work when called upon. Would Chinese missiles fire when the order is given, or perhaps the Americans have hacked them or the chain of command? Would American aircraft carriers function as expected, or would they perhaps shut down mysteriously or sail around in circles?[39]

Such uncertainty undermines the doctrine of mutually assured destruction. One side might convince itself—rightly or wrongly—

that it can launch a successful first strike and avoid massive retalia-tion. Even worse, if one side thinks it has such an opportunity, the temptation to launch a first strike could become irresistible, because one never knows how long the window of opportunity will remain open. Game theory posits that the most dangerous situation in an arms race is when one side feels it has an advantage but that this advantage is slipping away.[40]

Even if humanity avoids the worst-case scenario of global war, the rise of new digital empires could still endanger the freedom and prosperity of billions of people. The industrial empires of the nine-teenth and twentieth centuries exploited and repressed their colo-nies, and it would be foolhardy to expect the new digital empires to behave much better. Moreover, as noted earlier, if the world is di-vided into rival empires, humanity is unlikely to cooperate effectively to overcome the ecological crisis or to regulate AI and other disrup-tive technologies like bioengineering.

THE GLOBAL BOND

Of course, no matter whether the world is divided between a few digital empires, remains a more diverse community of two hundred nation-states, or is split along altogether different and unforeseen lines, cooperation is always an option. Among humans, the precon-dition for cooperation isn't similarity; it is the ability to exchange information. As long as we are able to converse, we might find some shared story that can bring us closer. This, after all, is what made *Homo sapiens* the dominant species on the planet.

Just as different and even rival families can cooperate within a tribal network, and competing tribes can cooperate within a national network, so opposing nations and empires can cooperate within a global network. The stories that make such cooperation possible do not eliminate our differences; rather, they enable us to identify shared

experiences and interests, which offer a common framework for thought and action.

A large part of what nevertheless makes global cooperation difficult is the misguided notion that it requires abolishing all cultural, social, and political differences. Populist politicians often argue that if the international community agrees on a common story and on universal norms and values, this will destroy the independence and unique traditions of their own nation.[41] This position was unabashedly distilled in 2015 by Marine Le Pen—leader of France's National Front party—in an election speech in which she declared, "We have entered a new two-partyism. A two-partyism between two mutually exclusive conceptions that will from now on structure our political life. The cleavage no longer separates left and right, but globalists and patriots."[42] In August 2020, President Trump described his guiding ethos thus: "We have rejected globalism and embraced patriotism."[43]

Luckily, this binary position is mistaken in its basic assumption. Global cooperation and patriotism are not mutually exclusive. For patriotism isn't about hating foreigners. It is about loving our compatriots. And there are many situations when, in order to take care of our compatriots, we need to cooperate with foreigners. COVID-19 provided us with one obvious example. Pandemics are global events, and without global cooperation it is hard to contain them, let alone prevent them. When a new virus or a mutant pathogen appears in one country, it puts all other countries in danger. Conversely, the biggest advantage of humans over pathogens is that we can cooperate in ways that pathogens cannot. Doctors in Germany and Brazil can alert one another to new dangers, give one another good advice, and work together to discover better treatments.

If German scientists invent a vaccine against some new disease, how should Brazilians react to this German achievement? One option is to reject the foreign vaccine and wait until Brazilian scientists develop a Brazilian vaccine. That, however, would be not just foolish;

it would be anti-patriotic. Brazilian patriots should want to use any available vaccine to help their compatriots, no matter where the vaccine was developed. In this situation, cooperating with foreigners is the patriotic thing to do. The threat of losing control of AIs is an analogous situation in which patriotism and global cooperation must go together. An out-of-control AI, just like an out-of-control virus, puts in danger humans in every nation. No human collective—whether a tribe, a nation, or the entire species—stands to benefit from letting power shift from humans to algorithms.

Contrary to what populists argue, globalism doesn't mean establishing a global empire, abandoning national loyalties, or opening borders to unlimited immigration. In fact, global cooperation means two far more modest things: first, a commitment to some global rules. These rules don't deny the uniqueness of each nation and the loyalty people should owe their nation. They just regulate the relations between nations. A good model is the World Cup. The World Cup is a competition between nations, and people often show fierce loyalty to their national team. At the same time, the World Cup is an amazing display of global agreement. Brazil cannot play football against Germany unless Brazilians and Germans first agree on the same set of rules for the game. That's globalism in action.

The second principle of globalism is that sometimes—not always, but sometimes—it is necessary to prioritize the long-term interests of all humans over the short-term interests of a few. For example, in the World Cup, all national teams agree not to use performance-enhancing drugs, because everybody realizes that if they go down that path, the World Cup would eventually devolve into a competition between biochemists. In other fields where technology is a game changer, we should similarly strive to balance national and global interests. Nations will obviously continue to compete in the development of new technology, but sometimes they should agree to limit the development and deployment of dangerous technologies like autonomous weapons and manipulative algorithms—not purely out of altruism, but for their own self-preservation.

THE HUMAN CHOICE

Forging and keeping international agreements on AI will require major changes in the way the international system functions. While we have experience in regulating dangerous technologies like nuclear and biological weapons, the regulation of AI will demand unprecedented levels of trust and self-discipline, for two reasons. First, it is easier to hide an illicit AI lab than an illicit nuclear reactor. Second, AIs have a lot more dual civilian-military usages than nuclear bombs. Consequently, despite signing an agreement that bans autonomous weapon systems, a country could build such weapons secretly, or camouflage them as civilian products. For example, it might develop fully autonomous drones for delivering mail and spraying fields with pesticides that with a few minor modifications could also deliver bombs and spray people with poison. Consequently, governments and corporations will find it more difficult to trust that their rivals are really abiding by the agreed regulations—and to withstand the temptation to themselves waive the rules.[44] Can humans develop the necessary levels of trust and self-discipline? Do changes like those have any precedent in history?

Many people are skeptical of the human capacity to change, and in particular of the human ability to renounce violence and forge stronger global bonds. For example, "realist" thinkers like Hans Morgenthau and John Mearsheimer have argued that an all-out competition for power is the inescapable condition of the international system. Mearsheimer explains that his theory "sees great powers as concerned mainly with figuring out how to survive in a world where there is no agency to protect them from each other" and that "they quickly realize that power is the key to their survival." Mearsheimer then asks "how much power states want" and answers that all states want as much power as they can get, "because the international system creates powerful incentives for states to look for opportunities to gain power at the expense of rivals." He

concludes, "A state's ultimate goal is to be the hegemon in the system."[45]

This grim view of international relations is akin to the populist and Marxist views of human relations, in that they all see humans as interested only in power. And they are all founded upon a deeper philosophical theory of human nature, which the primatologist Frans de Waal termed "veneer theory." It argues that at heart humans are Stone Age hunters who cannot but see the world as a jungle where the strong prey upon the weak and where might makes right. For millennia, the theory goes, humans have tried to camouflage this unchanging reality under a thin and mutable veneer of myths and rituals, but we have never really broken free from the law of the jungle. Indeed, our myths and rituals are themselves a weapon used by the jungle's top dogs to deceive and trap their inferiors. Those who don't realize this are dangerously naive and will fall prey to some ruthless predator.[46]

There are reasons to think, however, that "realists" like Mearsheimer have a selective view of historical reality and that the law of the jungle is itself a myth. As de Waal and many other biologists documented in numerous studies, real jungles—unlike the one in our imagination—are full of cooperation, symbiosis, and altruism displayed by countless animals, plants, fungi, and even bacteria. Eighty percent of all land plants, for example, rely on symbiotic relationships with fungi, and almost 90 percent of vascular plant families enjoy symbiotic relationships with microorganisms. If organisms in the rain forests of Amazonia, Africa, or India abandoned cooperation in favor of an all-out competition for hegemony, the rain forests and all their inhabitants would quickly die. That's the law of the jungle.[47]

As for Stone Age humans, they were gatherers as well as hunters, and there is no firm evidence that they had irrepressible warlike tendencies. While there are plenty of speculations, the first unambiguous evidence for organized warfare appears in the archaeological record only about thirteen thousand years ago, at the site of Jebel Sahaba in the Nile valley.[48] Even after that date, the record of war is

variable rather than constant. Some periods were exceptionally violent, whereas others were relatively peaceful. The clearest pattern we observe in the long-term history of humanity isn't the constancy of conflict, but rather the increasing scale of cooperation. A hundred thousand years ago, Sapiens could cooperate only at the level of bands. Over the millennia, we have found ways to create communities of strangers, first on the level of tribes and eventually on the level of religions, trade networks, and states. Realists should note that states are not the fundamental particles of human reality, but rather the product of arduous processes of building trust and cooperation. If humans were interested only in power, they could never have created states in the first place. Sure, conflicts have always remained a possibility—both between and within states—but they have never been an inescapable destiny.

War's intensity depends not on an immutable human nature but on shifting technological, economic, and cultural factors. As these factors change, so does war, as was clearly demonstrated in the post-1945 era. During that period, the development of nuclear technology greatly increased the potential price of war. From the 1950s onward it became clear to the superpowers that even if they could somehow win an all-out nuclear exchange, their victory would likely be a suicidal achievement, involving the sacrifice of most of their population.

Simultaneously, the ongoing shift from a material-based economy to a knowledge-based economy decreased the potential gains of war. While it has remained feasible to conquer rice paddies and gold mines, by the late twentieth century these were no longer the main sources of economic wealth. The new leading industries, like the semiconductor sector, came to be based on technical skills and organizational know-how that could not be acquired by military conquest. Accordingly, some of the greatest economic miracles of the post-1945 era were achieved by the defeated powers of Germany, Italy, and Japan, and by countries like Sweden and Singapore that eschewed military conflicts and imperial conquests.

Finally, the second half of the twentieth century also witnessed a profound cultural transformation, with the decline of age-old militaristic ideals. Artists increasingly focused on depicting the senseless horrors of combat rather than on glorifying its architects, and politicians came to power dreaming more of domestic reforms than of foreign conquests. Due to these technological, economic, and cultural changes, in the decades following the end of World War II most governments stopped seeing wars of aggression as an appealing tool to advance their interests, and most nations stopped fantasizing about conquering and destroying their neighbors. While civil wars and insurgencies have remained commonplace, the post-1945 world has seen a significant decline in full-scale wars between states, and most notably in direct armed conflicts between great powers.[49]

Numerous statistics attest to the decline of war in this post-1945 era, but perhaps the clearest evidence is found in state budgets. For most of recorded history, the military was the number one item on the budget of every empire, sultanate, kingdom, and republic. Governments spent little on health care and education, because most of their resources were consumed by paying soldiers, constructing walls, and building warships. When the bureaucrat Chen Xiang examined the annual budget of the Chinese Song dynasty for the year 1065, he found that out of sixty million minqian (currency unit), fifty million (83 percent) were consumed by the military. Another official, Cai Xiang, wrote, "If [we] split [all the property] under Heaven into six shares, five shares are spent on the military, and one share is spent on temple offerings and state expenses. How can the country not be poor and the people not in difficulty?"[50]

The same situation prevailed in many other polities, from ancient times to the modern era. The Roman Empire spent about 50–75 percent of its budget on the military,[51] and the figure was about 60 percent in the late-seventeenth-century Ottoman Empire.[52] Between 1685 and 1813 the share of the military in British government expenditure averaged 75 percent.[53] In France, military expenditure between 1630 and 1659 varied between 89 percent and 93 percent of

the budget, remained above 30 percent for much of the eighteenth century, and dropped to a low of 25 percent in 1788 only due to the financial crisis that led to the French Revolution. In Prussia, from 1711 to 1800 the military share of the budget never fell below 75 percent and occasionally reached as high as 91 percent.[54] During the relatively peaceful years of 1870–1913, the military ate up an average of 30 percent of the state budgets of the major powers of Europe, as well as Japan and the United States, while smaller powers like Sweden were spending even more.[55] When war broke out in 1914, military budges skyrocketed. During their involvement in World War I, French military expenditure averaged 77 percent of the budget; in Germany it was 91 percent, in Russia 48 percent, in the U.K. 49 percent, and in the United States 47 percent. During World War II, the U.K. figure rose to 69 percent and the U.S. figure to 71 percent.[56] Even during the détente years of the 1970s, Soviet military expenditure still amounted to 32.5 percent of the budget.[57]

State budgets in more recent decades make for far more hopeful reading material than any pacifist tract ever composed. In the early twenty-first century, the worldwide average government expenditure on the military has been only around 7 percent of the budget, and even the dominant superpower of the United States spent only around 13 percent of its annual budget to maintain its military hegemony.[58] Since most people no longer lived in terror of external invasion, governments could invest far more money in welfare, education, and health care. Worldwide average expenditure on health care in the early twenty-first century has been about 10 percent of the government budget, or about 1.4 times the defense budget.[59] For many people in the 2010s, the fact that the health-care budget was bigger than the military budget was unremarkable. But it was the result of a major change in human behavior, and one that would have sounded impossible to most previous generations.

The decline of war didn't result from a divine miracle or from a metamorphosis in the laws of nature. It resulted from humans changing their own laws, myths, and institutions and making better deci-

sions. Unfortunately, the fact that this change has stemmed from human choice also means that it is reversible. Technology, economics, and culture are ever changing. In the early 2020s, more leaders are again dreaming of martial glory, armed conflicts are on the rise,[60] and military budgets are increasing.[61]

A critical threshold was crossed in early 2022. Russia had already destabilized the global order by mounting a limited invasion of Ukraine in 2014 and occupying Crimea and other regions in eastern Ukraine. But on February 24, 2022, Vladimir Putin launched an all-out assault aimed to conquer the whole of Ukraine and extinguish Ukrainian nationhood. To prepare and sustain this attack, Russia increased its military budget far beyond the global average of 7 percent. Exact figures are difficult to determine, because many aspects of the Russian military budget are shrouded in secrecy, but the best estimates put the figure somewhere in the vicinity of 30 percent, and it may even be higher.[62] The Russian onslaught in turn has forced not only Ukraine but also many other European nations to increase their own military budgets.[63] The reemergence of militaristic cultures in places like Russia, and the development of unprecedented cyber weapons and autonomous armaments throughout the world, could result in a new era of war, worse than anything we have seen before.

The decisions leaders like Putin make on matters of war and peace are shaped by their understanding of history. Which means that just as overly optimistic views of history could be dangerous illusions, overly pessimistic views could become destructive self-fulfilling prophecies. Prior to his all-out 2022 attack on Ukraine, Putin had often expressed his historical conviction that Russia is trapped in an endless struggle with foreign enemies, and that the Ukrainian nation is a fabrication by these enemies. In June 2021, he published a fifty-three-hundred-word essay titled "On the Historical Unity of Russians and Ukrainians" in which he denied the existence of Ukraine as a nation and argued that foreign powers have repeatedly tried to weaken Russia by fostering Ukrainian separatism. While professional historians reject these claims, Putin seems to genuinely believe

in this historical narrative.[64] Putin's historical convictions led him in 2022 to prioritize the conquest of Ukraine over other policy goals, such as providing Russian citizens with better health care or spearheading a global initiative to regulate AI.[65]

If leaders like Putin believe that humanity is trapped in an unforgiving dog-eat-dog world, that no profound change is possible in this sorry state of affairs, and that the relative peace of the late twentieth century and early twenty-first century was an illusion, then the only choice remaining is whether to play the part of predator or prey. Given such a choice, most leaders would prefer to go down in history as predators and add their names to the grim list of conquerors that unfortunate pupils are condemned to memorize for their history exams. These leaders should be reminded, however, that in the era of AI the alpha predator is likely to be AI.

Perhaps, though, we have more choices available to us. I cannot predict what decisions people will make in the coming years, but as a historian I do believe in the possibility of change. One of the chief lessons of history is that many of the things that we consider natural and eternal are, in fact, man-made and mutable. Accepting that conflict is not inevitable, however, should not make us complacent. Just the opposite. It places a heavy responsibility on all of us to make good choices. It implies that if human civilization is consumed by conflict, we cannot blame it on any law of nature or any alien technology. It also implies that if we make the effort, we can create a better world. This isn't naïveté; it's realism. Every old thing was once new. The only constant of history is change.

Epilogue

In late 2016, a few months after AlphaGo defeated Lee Sedol and as Facebook algorithms were stoking dangerous racist sentiments in Myanmar, I published *Homo Deus*. Though my academic training had been in medieval and early modern military history, and though I have no background in the technical aspects of computer science, I suddenly found myself, post-publication, with the reputation of an AI expert. This opened the doors to the offices of scientists, entrepreneurs, and world leaders interested in AI and afforded me a fascinating, privileged look into the complex dynamics of the AI revolution.

It turned out that my previous experience researching topics such as English strategy in the Hundred Years' War and studying paintings from the Thirty Years' War[1] wasn't entirely unrelated to this new field. In fact, it gave me a rather unique historical perspective on the events unfolding rapidly in AI labs, corporate offices, military headquarters, and presidential palaces. Over the past eight years I have had numerous public and private discussions about AI, particularly about the dangers it poses, and with each passing year the tone has become more urgent. Conversations that in 2016 felt like idle philo-

sophical speculations about a distant future had, by 2024, acquired the focused intensity of an emergency room.

I am neither a politician nor a businessperson and have little talent for what these vocations demand. But I do believe that an understanding of history can be useful in gaining a better grasp of present-day technological, economic, and cultural developments—and, more urgently, in changing our political priorities. Politics is largely a matter of priorities. Should we cut the health-care budget and spend more on defense? Is our more pressing security threat terrorism or climate change? Do we focus on regaining a lost patch of ancestral territory or concentrate on creating a common economic zone with the neighbors? Priorities determine how citizens vote, what businesspeople are concerned about, and how politicians try to make a name for themselves. And priorities are often shaped by our understanding of history.

While so-called realists dismiss historical narratives as propaganda ploys deployed to advance state interests, in fact it is these narratives that define state interests in the first place. As we saw in our discussion of Clausewitz's theory of war, there is no rational way to define ultimate goals. The state interests of Russia, Israel, Myanmar, or any other country can never be deduced from some mathematical or physical equation; they are always the supposed moral of a historical narrative.

It is therefore hardly surprising that politicians all over the world spend a lot of time and effort recounting historical narratives. The above-mentioned example of Vladimir Putin is hardly exceptional in this respect. In 2005 the UN secretary-general, Kofi Annan, had his first meeting with General Than Shwe, then the dictator of Myanmar. Annan was advised to speak first, so as to prevent the general from monopolizing the conversation, which was meant to last only twenty minutes. But Than Shwe struck first and held forth for nearly an hour on the history of Myanmar, hardly giving the UN secretary-general any chance to speak.[2] In May 2011 the Israeli prime minister, Benjamin Netanyahu did something similar in the White House,

when he met the U.S. president, Barack Obama. After Obama's brief introductory remarks, Netanyahu subjected the president to a long lecture about the history of Israel and the Jewish people, treating Obama as if he were his student.[3] Cynics might argue that Than Shwe and Netanyahu hardly cared about the facts of history and were deliberately distorting them in order to achieve some political goal. But these political goals were themselves the product of deeply held convictions about history.

In my own conversations on AI with politicians, as well as tech entrepreneurs, history has often emerged as a central theme. Some of my interlocutors painted a rosy picture of history and were accordingly enthusiastic about AI. They argued that more information has always meant more knowledge and that by increasing our knowledge, every previous information revolution has greatly benefited humankind. Didn't the print revolution lead to the scientific revolution? Didn't newspapers and radio lead to the rise of modern democracy? The same, they said, would happen with AI. Others had a dimmer perspective, but nevertheless expressed hope that humankind will somehow muddle through the AI revolution, just as we muddled through the Industrial Revolution.

Neither view offered me much solace. For reasons explained in previous chapters, I find such historical comparisons to the print revolution and the Industrial Revolution distressing, especially coming from people in positions of power, whose historical vision is informing the decisions that shape our future. These historical comparisons underestimate both the unprecedented nature of the AI revolution and the negative aspects of previous revolutions. The immediate results of the print revolution included witch hunts and religious wars alongside scientific discoveries, while newspapers and radio were exploited by totalitarian regimes as well as by democracies. As for the Industrial Revolution, adapting to it involved catastrophic experiments such as imperialism and Nazism. If the AI revolution leads us to similar kinds of experiments, can we really be certain we will muddle through again?

My goal with this book is to provide a more accurate historical perspective on the AI revolution. This revolution is still in its infancy, and it is notoriously difficult to understand momentous developments in real time. It is hard, even now, to assess the meaning of events in the 2010s like AlphaGo's victory or Facebook's involvement in the anti-Rohingya campaign. The meaning of events of the early 2020s is even more obscure. Yet by expanding our horizons to look at how information networks developed over thousands of years, I believe it is possible to gain some insight on what we're living through today.

One lesson is that the invention of new information technology is always a catalyst for major historical changes, because the most important role of information is to weave new networks rather than represent preexisting realities. By recording tax payments, clay tablets in ancient Mesopotamia helped forge the first city-states. By canonizing prophetic visions, holy books spread new kinds of religions. By swiftly disseminating the words of presidents and citizens, newspapers and telegraphs opened the door to both large-scale democracy and large-scale totalitarianism. The information thus recorded and distributed was sometimes true, often false, but it invariably created new connections between larger numbers of people.

We are used to giving political, ideological, and economic interpretations to historical revolutions such as the rise of the first Mesopotamian city-states, the spread of Christianity, the American Revolution, and the Bolshevik Revolution. But to gain a deeper understanding, we should also view them as revolutions in the way information flows. Christianity was obviously different from Greek polytheism in many of its myths and rites, yet it was also different in the importance it gave to a single holy book and the institution entrusted with interpreting it. Consequently, whereas each temple of Zeus was a separate entity, each Christian church became a node in a unified network.[4] Information flowed differently among the followers of Christ than among the worshippers of Zeus. Similarly, Sta-

lin's U.S.S.R. was a different kind of information network from Peter the Great's empire. Stalin enacted many unprecedented economic policies, but what enabled him to do it is that he headed a totalitarian network in which the center accumulated enough information to micromanage the lives of hundreds of millions of people. Technology is rarely deterministic, and the same technology can be used in very different ways. But without the invention of technologies like the book and the telegraph, the Christian Church and the Stalinist apparatus would never have been possible.

This historical lesson should strongly encourage us to pay more attention to the AI revolution in our current political debates. The invention of AI is potentially more momentous than the invention of the telegraph, the printing press, or even writing, because AI is the first technology that is capable of making decisions and generating ideas by itself. Whereas printing presses and parchment scrolls offered new means for connecting people, AIs are full-fledged members in our information networks, possessing their own agency. In coming years, all networks—from armies to religions—will gain millions of new AI members, which will process data differently than humans do. These new members will make alien decisions and generate alien ideas—that is, decisions and ideas that are unlikely to occur to humans. The addition of many alien agents is bound to change the shape of armies, religions, markets, and nations. Entire political, economic, and social systems might collapse, and new ones will take their place. That's why AI should be an urgent matter even to people who don't care about technology and who think the most important political questions concern the survival of democracy or the fair distribution of wealth.

This book has juxtaposed the discussion of AI with the discussion of sacred canons like the Bible, because we are now at the critical moment of AI canonization. When church fathers like Bishop Athanasius decided to include 1 Timothy in the biblical dataset while excluding the Acts of Paul and Thecla, they shaped the world for millennia. Billions of Christians down to the twenty-first century

have formed their views of the world based on the misogynist ideas of 1 Timothy rather than on the more tolerant attitude of Thecla. Even today it is difficult to reverse course, because the church fathers chose not to include any self-correcting mechanisms in the Bible. The present-day equivalents of Bishop Athanasius are the engineers who write the initial code for AI, and who choose the dataset on which the baby AI is trained. As AI grows in power and authority, and perhaps becomes a self-interpreting holy book, so the decisions made by present-day engineers could reverberate down the ages.

Studying history does more than just emphasize the importance of the AI revolution and of our decisions regarding AI. It also cautions us against two common but misleading approaches to information networks and information revolutions. On the one hand, we should beware of an overly naive and optimistic view. Information isn't truth. Its main task is to connect rather than represent, and information networks throughout history have often privileged order over truth. Tax records, holy books, political manifestos, and secret police files can be extremely efficient in creating powerful states and churches, which hold a distorted view of the world and are prone to abuse their power. More information, ironically, can sometimes result in more witch hunts.

There is no reason to expect that AI would necessarily break the pattern and privilege truth. AI is not infallible. What little historical perspective we have gained from the alarming events in Myanmar, Brazil, and elsewhere over the past decade indicates that in the absence of strong self-correcting mechanisms AIs are more than capable of promoting distorted worldviews, enabling egregious abuses of power, and instigating terrifying new witch hunts.

On the other hand, we should also beware of swinging too far in the other direction and adopting an overly cynical view. Populists tell us that power is the only reality, that all human interactions are power struggles, and that information is merely a weapon we use to vanquish our enemies. This has never been the case, and there is no reason to think that AI will make it so in the future. While many

information networks do privilege order over truth, no network can survive if it ignores truth completely. As for individual humans, we tend to be genuinely interested in truth rather than only in power. Even institutions like the Spanish Inquisition have had conscientious truth-seeking members like Alonso de Salazar Frías, who, instead of sending innocent people to their deaths, risked his life to remind us that witches are just intersubjective fictions. Most people don't view themselves as one-dimensional creatures obsessed solely with power. Why, then, hold such a view about everyone else?

Refusing to reduce all human interactions to a zero-sum power struggle is crucial not just for gaining a fuller, more nuanced understanding of the past but also for having a more hopeful and constructive attitude about our future. If power were the only reality, then the only way to resolve conflicts would be through violence. Both populists and Marxists believe that people's views are determined by their privileges, and that to change people's views it is necessary to first take away their privileges—which usually requires force. However, since humans are interested in truth, there is a chance to resolve at least some conflicts peacefully, by talking to one another, acknowledging mistakes, embracing new ideas, and revising the stories we believe. That is the basic assumption of democratic networks and of scientific institutions. It has also been the basic motivation behind writing this book.

EXTINCTION OF THE SMARTEST

Let's return now to the question I posed at the beginning of this book: If we are so wise, why are we so self-destructive? We are at one and the same time both the smartest and the stupidest animals on earth. We are so smart that we can produce nuclear missiles and superintelligent algorithms. And we are so stupid that we go ahead producing these things even though we're not sure we can control them and failing to do so could destroy us. Why do we do it? Does

something in our nature compel us to go down the path of self-destruction?

This book has argued that the fault isn't with our nature but with our information networks. Due to the privileging of order over truth, human information networks have often produced a lot of power but little wisdom. For example, Nazi Germany created a highly efficient military machine and placed it at the service of an insane mythology. The result was misery on an enormous scale, the death of tens of millions of people, and eventually the destruction of Nazi Germany, too.

Of course, power is not in itself bad. When used wisely, it can be an instrument of benevolence. Modern civilization, for example, has acquired the power to prevent famines, contain epidemics, and mitigate natural disasters such as hurricanes and earthquakes. In general, the acquisition of power allows a network to deal more effectively with threats coming from outside, but simultaneously increases the dangers that the network poses to itself. It is particularly noteworthy that as a network becomes more powerful, imaginary terrors that exist only in the stories the network itself invents become potentially more dangerous than natural disasters. A modern state faced with drought or excessive rains can usually prevent this natural disaster from causing mass starvation among its citizens. But a modern state gripped by a man-made fantasy is capable of instigating man-made famines on an enormous scale, as happened in the U.S.S.R. in the early 1930s.

Accordingly, as a network becomes more powerful, its self-correcting mechanisms become more vital. If a Stone Age tribe or a Bronze Age city-state was incapable of identifying and correcting its own mistakes, the potential damage was limited. At most, one city was destroyed, and the survivors tried again elsewhere. Even if the ruler of an Iron Age empire, such as Tiberius or Nero, was gripped by paranoia or psychosis, the consequences were seldom catastrophic. The Roman Empire endured for centuries despite its fair share of mad emperors, and its eventual collapse did not bring about the end of human civilization. But if a Silicon Age superpower has weak or

nonexistent self-correcting mechanisms, it could very well endanger the survival of our species, and countless other life-forms, too. In the era of AI, the whole of humankind finds itself in an analogous situation to Tiberius in his Capri villa. We command immense power and enjoy rare luxuries, but we are easily manipulated by our own creations, and by the time we wake up to the danger, it might be too late.

Unfortunately, despite the importance of self-correcting mechanisms for the long-term welfare of humanity, politicians might be tempted to weaken them. As we have seen throughout the book, though neutralizing self-correcting mechanisms has many downsides, it can nevertheless be a winning political strategy. It could deliver immense power into the hands of a twenty-first-century Stalin, and it would be foolhardy to assume that an AI-enhanced totalitarian regime would necessarily self-destruct before it could wreak havoc on human civilization. Just as the law of the jungle is a myth, so also is the idea that the arc of history bends toward justice. History is a radically open arc, one that can bend in many directions and reach very different destinations. Even if *Homo sapiens* destroys itself, the universe will keep going about its business as usual. It took four billion years for terrestrial evolution to produce a civilization of highly intelligent apes. If we are gone, and it takes evolution another hundred million years to produce a civilization of highly intelligent rats, it will. The universe is patient.

There is, though, an even worse scenario. As far as we know today, apes, rats, and the other organic animals of planet Earth may be the only conscious entities in the entire universe. We have now created a nonconscious but very powerful alien intelligence. If we mishandle it, AI might extinguish not only the human dominion on Earth but the light of consciousness itself, turning the universe into a realm of utter darkness. It is our responsibility to prevent this.

The good news is that if we eschew complacency and despair, we are capable of creating balanced information networks that will keep their own power in check. Doing so is not a matter of inventing an-

other miracle technology or landing upon some brilliant idea that has somehow escaped all previous generations. Rather, to create wiser networks, we must abandon both the naive and the populist views of information, put aside our fantasies of infallibility, and commit ourselves to the hard and rather mundane work of building institutions with strong self-correcting mechanisms. That is perhaps the most important takeaway this book has to offer.

This wisdom is much older than human history. It is elemental, the foundation of organic life. The first organisms weren't created by some infallible genius or god. They emerged through an intricate process of trial and error. Over four billion years, ever more complex mechanisms of mutation and self-correction led to the evolution of trees, dinosaurs, jungles, and eventually humans. Now we have summoned an alien inorganic intelligence that could escape our control and put in danger not just our own species but countless other life-forms. The decisions we all make in the coming years will determine whether summoning this alien intelligence proves to be a terminal error or the beginning of a hopeful new chapter in the evolution of life.

Acknowledgments

Even in the age of AI, humans still write and publish books at a medieval pace. I began working on this book in 2018, and the bulk of the manuscript was written in 2021 and 2022. Given the speed at which technological and political events are unfolding, the meaning of many sections has already changed, acquiring greater urgency and carrying unanticipated messages. One thing that hasn't changed, though, is the vital importance of connections. While this book has been written amid rising international tensions, it has also been the product of dialogue, cooperation, and friendship, and it represents a collective effort on the part of numerous people, near and far.

Nexus would never have seen the light of day without the huge efforts of Michal Shavit, my publisher at Fern Press, and David Milner, my editor. There were many times when I thought the project could not be completed, but they persuaded me to carry on. There were many other times when I took a wrong turn, and they worked patiently and persistently to set me on the right path. I wholeheartedly thank them for their commitment, and for getting rid of all the various bananas (they know what I mean).

I would also like to thank many others who have helped write and publish this book.

To Andy Ward at Penguin Random House USA, who gave the book its final shape and made very valuable contributions to the editing process, like single-handedly putting an end to the Protestant Reformation.

To Suzanne Dean, the creative director at Vintage, and to Lily Richards, the picture editor, for designing the cover and bringing the pigeon on board.

To my publishers and translators throughout the world, for additional feedback and ideas, and for their trust and dedication.

To Jason Parry, the brilliant head of the in-house research team at Sapienship, and to all members of that team—Ray Brandon, Guangyu Chen, Jim Clarke, Corinne de Lacroix, Dor Shilton, and Zichan Wang—for researching countless subjects from Stone Age religions to present-day social media algorithms, for tirelessly checking thousands of facts, for standardizing hundreds of endnotes, and for correcting innumerable mistakes and misconceptions.

To all members of the marvelous Sapienship team, for being an integral part of this journey: Shay Abel, Daniel Taylor, Michael Zur, Nadav Neuman, Ariel Retik, Hanna Shapiro, Galiete Katzir, and several other team members who have joined more recently. Thank you for participating in the processes behind this book and for your ongoing dedication to all our projects, driven by Sapienship's missions—to sow seeds of knowledge and compassion, and to focus the global conversation on the most important challenges facing humanity.

To Naama Wartenburg, Sapienship's chief marketing officer and director of content, for her steadfast ardor and acumen, and for branding the book and leading its PR campaign.

To our CEO, Naama Avital, for sagely steering the Sapien-ship through many storms and minefields, combining competence with compassion, and shaping both our philosophy and our strategy.

To all my friends and family members, for their patience and love through the years.

To my mother, Pnina, and my mother-in-law, Hannah, for generously giving their time and experience.

To my grandmother Fanny, who passed away at age one hundred while I was working on the manuscript's first draft.

To my spouse and partner, Itzik, who founded Sapienship and is the real genius behind our worldwide activities and successes.

And finally to my readers, who make all these efforts worthwhile. A book is a nexus between author and readers. It is a link connecting many minds together, which exists only when it is read.

Notes

PROLOGUE

1. Sean McMeekin, *Stalin's War: A New History of World War II* (New York: Basic Books, 2021).
2. "Reagan Urges 'Risk' on Gorbachev: Soviet Leader May Be Only Hope for Change, He Says," *Los Angeles Times*, June 13, 1989, www.latimes.com /archives/la-xpm-1989-06-13-mn-2300-story.html.
3. White House, "Remarks by President Barack Obama at Town Hall Meeting with Future Chinese Leaders," Office of the Press Secretary, Nov. 16, 2009, obamawhitehouse.archives.gov/the-press-office/remarks-president-barack -obama-town-hall-meeting-with-future-chinese-leaders.
4. Quoted in Evgeny Morozov, *The Net Delusion: The Dark Side of Internet Freedom* (New York: Public Affairs, 2012).
5. Quoted in Christian Fuchs, "An Alternative View of Privacy on Facebook," *Information* 2, no. 1 (2011): 140–65.
6. Ray Kurzweil, *The Singularity Is Nearer: When We Merge with AI* (London: The Bodley Head, 2024), 121–23.
7. Sigrid Damm, *Cornelia Goethe* (Berlin: Insel, 1988), 17–18; Dagmar von Gersdorff, *Goethes Mutter* (Stuttgart: Hermann Bohlaus Nachfolger Weimar, 2004); Johann Wolfgang von Goethe, *Goethes Leben von Tag zu Tag: Eine dokumentarische Chronik* (Dusseldorf: Artemis, 1982), 1:1749–75.
8. Stephan Oswald, *Im Schatten des Vaters. August von Goethe* (Munich: C. H. Beck, 2023); Rainer Holm-Hadulla, *Goethe's Path to Creativity: A Psychobiography of the Eminent Politician, Scientist, and Poet* (New York: Routledge, 2018); Lisbet Koerner, "Goethe's Botany: Lessons of a Feminine Science," *History of Science Society* 84, no. 3 (1993): 470–95; Alvin Zipursky, Vinod K. Bhutani, and Isaac Odame, "Rhesus Disease: A Global Prevention Strategy," *Lancet Child and Adolescent Health* 2, no. 7 (2018): 536–42; John Queenan,

"Overview: The Fetus as a Patient: The Origin of the Specialty," in *Fetal Research and Applications: A Conference Summary* (Washington, D.C.: National Academies Press, 1994), accessed Jan. 4, 2024, www.ncbi.nlm.nih.gov/books/NBK231999/.

9. John Knodel, "Two and a Half Centuries of Demographic History in a Bavarian Village," *Population Studies* 24, no. 3 (1970): 353–76.

10. Saloni Dattani et al., "Child and Infant Mortality," Our World in Data, 2023, accessed Jan. 3, 2024, ourworldindata.org/child-mortality#mortality-in-the-past-around-half-died-as-children.

11. Ibid.

12. "Most Recent Stillbirth, Child, and Adolescent Mortality Estimates," UN Inter-agency Group for Child Mortality Estimation, accessed Jan. 3, 2024, childmortality.org/data/Germany.

13. According to one estimate, the Library of Alexandria contained about 100 billion bits of information, or 12.5 gigabytes. See Douglas S. Robertson, "The Information Revolution," *Communication Research* 17, no. 2 (1990): 235–54. By 2020, the average Android phone had a capacity of about 96 gigabytes. See Brady Wang, "Average Smartphone NAND Flash Capacity Crossed 100GB in 2020," Counterpoint Research, March 30, 2021, www.counterpointresearch.com/average-smartphone-nand-flash-capacity-crossed-100gb-2020/.

14. Marc Andreessen, "Why AI Will Save the World," Andreessen Horowitz, June 6, 2023, a16z.com/ai-will-save-the-world/.

15. Ray Kurzweil, *The Singularity Is Nearer*, 285.

16. Andy McKenzie, "Transcript of Sam Altman's Interview Touching on AI Safety," *LessWrong*, Jan. 21, 2023, www.lesswrong.com/posts/PTzsEQXkCfig9A6AS/transcript-of-sam-altman-s-interview-touching-on-ai-safety; Ian Hogarth, "We Must Slow Down the Race to God-Like AI," *Financial Times*, April 13, 2023, www.ft.com/content/03895dc4-a3b7-481e-95cc-336a524f2ac2; "Pause Giant AI Experiments: An Open Letter," Future of Life Institute, March 22, 2023, futureoflife.org/open-letter/pause-giant-ai-experiments/; Cade Metz, "'The Godfather of AI' Quits Google and Warns of Danger," *New York Times*, May 1, 2023, www.nytimes.com/2023/05/01/technology/ai-google-chatbot-engineer-quits-hinton.html; Mustafa Suleyman, *The Coming Wave: Technology, Power, and the Twenty-First Century's Greatest Dilemma*, with Michael Bhaskar (New York: Crown, 2023); Walter Isaacson, *Elon Musk* (London: Simon & Schuster, 2023).

17. Yoshua Bengio et al., "Managing Extreme AI Risks Amid Rapid Progress," *Science* (May 2024): Article eadn0117.

18. Katja Grace et al., "Thousands of AI Authors on the Future of AI" (preprint, submitted in 2024), https://arxiv.org/abs/2401.02843.

19. "The Bletchley Declaration by Countries Attending the AI Safety Summit, 1–2 November 2023," Gov.UK, Nov. 1 2023, www.gov.uk/government/publications/ai-safety-summit-2023-the-bletchley-declaration/the-bletchley-declaration-by-countries-attending-the-ai-safety-summit-1-2-november-2023.

20. Jan-Werner Müller, *What Is Populism?* (Philadelphia: University of Pennsylvania Press, 2016).

21. In Plato's *Republic*, Thrasymachus, Glaucon, and Adeimantus argue that everyone—and most notably politicians, judges, and civil servants—is interested only in their personal privileges and dissimulates and lies to that end.

They challenge Socrates to refute the claims that "appearance tyrannizes over truth" and that "justice is nothing else than the interest of the stronger." Similar views were discussed, and occasionally supported, in the Hindu classic the *Arthashastra;* in the writings of Legalist thinkers in ancient China such as Han Fei and Shang Yang; and in the writing of early modern European thinkers like Machiavelli and Hobbes. See Roger Boesche, *The First Great Political Realist: Kautilya and His "Arthashastra"* (Lanham, Md.: Lexington Books, 2002); Shang Yang, *The Book of Lord Shang: Apologetics of State Power in Early China,* trans. Yuri Pines (New York: Columbia University Press, 2017); Zhengyuan Fu, *China's Legalists: The Earliest Totalitarians and Their Art of Ruling* (New York: Routledge, 2015).

22. Ulises A. Mejias and Nick Couldry, *Data Grab: The New Colonialism of Big Tech and How to Fight Back* (London: Ebury, 2024); Michel Foucault, *The Birth of the Clinic: An Archaeology of Medical Perception* (New York: Vintage Books, 1975); Michel Foucault, *The History of Sexuality* (New York: Vintage Books, 1990); Edward W. Said, *Orientalism* (New York: Vintage Books, 1994); Aníbal Quijano, "Coloniality and Modernity/Rationality," *Cultural Studies* 21, no. 2–3 (2007): 168–78; Sylvia Wynter, "Unsettling the Coloniality of Being-Power-Truth-Freedom Toward the Human, After Man, Its Overrepresentation—an Argument," *New Centennial Review* 3, no. 3 (2003): 257–337. For in-depth discussion, see Francis Fukuyama, *Liberalism and Its Discontents* (London: Profile Books, 2022).

23. Donald J. Trump, Inaugural Address, Jan. 20, 2017, American Presidency Project, www.presidency.ucsb.edu/node/320188.

24. Cas Mudde, "The Populist Zeitgeist," *Government and Opposition* 39, no. 3 (2004): 541–63.

25. Sedona Chinn and Ariel Hasell, "Support for 'Doing Your Own Research' Is Associated with COVID-19 Misperceptions and Scientific Mistrust," *Misinformation Review,* June 12, 2023, misinforeview.hks.harvard.edu/article /support-for-doing-your-own-research-is-associated-with-covid-19 -misperceptions-and-scientific-mistrust/.

26. See, for example, "God's Enclosed Flat Earth Investigation—Full Documentary [HD]," YouTube, www.youtube.com/watch?v=J6CPrGHpmMs, cited in "Disinformation and Echo Chambers: How Disinformation Circulates on Social Media Through Identity-Driven Controversies," *Journal of Public Policy and Marketing* 42, no. 1 (2023): 18–35.

27. See, for example, David Klepper, "Trump Arrest Prompts Jesus Comparisons: 'Spiritual Warfare,'" Associated Press, April 6, 2023, apnews.com/article /donald-trump-arraignment-jesus-christ-conspiracy-theory-670c45bd71b3 466dcd6e8e188badcd1d; Katy Watson, "Brazil Election: 'We'll Vote for Bolsonaro Because He Is God,'" BBC, Sept. 28, 2022, www.bbc.com/news /world-latin-america-62929581.

28. Oliver Hahl, Minjae Kim, and Ezra W. Zuckerman Sivan, "The Authentic Appeal of the Lying Demagogue: Proclaiming the Deeper Truth About Political Illegitimacy," *American Sociological Review* 83, no. 1 (2018): 1–33.

CHAPTER 1: WHAT IS INFORMATION?

1. See, for example, the works of Nick Bostrom and David Chalmers on the simulation hypothesis. If the simulation hypothesis is true, then we have no

idea what the universe is ultimately made of, but everything we see in our simulated world is made of bits of information. Nick Bostrom, "Are We Living in a Computer Simulation?," *Philosophical Quarterly* 53, no. 211 (2003): 243–55, www.jstor.org/stable/3542867; David J. Chalmers, *Reality+: Virtual Worlds and the Problems of Philosophy* (New York: W. W. Norton, 2022). See also Archibald Wheeler's influential notion of "it from bit": John Archibald Wheeler, "Information, Physics, Quantum: The Search for Links," *Proceedings III International Symposium on Foundations of Quantum Mechanics* (Tokyo, 1989), 354–68; Paul Davies and Niels Henrik Gregersen, eds., *Information and the Nature of Reality: From Physics to Metaphysics* (Cambridge, U.K.: Cambridge University Press, 2014); Erik Verlinde, "On the Origin of Gravity and the Laws of Newton," *Journal of High Energy Physics* 4 (2011): 1–27. It should be emphasized that while the "it from bit" position is becoming more acceptable in physics, most physicists still doubt or reject it and believe that matter and energy are the fundamental building blocks of nature, while information is a derived phenomenon.

2. My understanding of information has been deeply influenced by Cesar Hidalgo, *Why Information Grows* (New York: Basic Books, 2015). For alternative views and discussions, see Artemy Kolchinsky and David H. Wolpert, "Semantic Information, Autonomous Agency, and Non-equilibrium Statistical Physics," *Interface Focus* 8, no. 6 (2018), article 20180041; Peter Godfrey-Smith and Kim Sterelny, "Biological Information," in *The Stanford Encyclopedia of Philosophy*, ed. Edward N. Zalta, Summer 2016 (Palo Alto, Calif.: Metaphysics Research Lab, Stanford University, 2016), plato.stanford.edu/archives/sum2016/entries/information-biological/; Luciano Floridi, *The Philosophy of Information* (Oxford: Oxford University Press, 2011).

3. Don Vaughan, "Cher Ami," in *Encyclopedia Britannica*, accessed Feb. 14, 2024, www.britannica.com/animal/Cher-Ami; Charles White Whittlesey Collection, Williams College Library, accessed Feb. 14, 2024, archivesspace.williams.edu/repositories/2/resources/101; John W. Nell, *The Lost Battalion: A Private's Story*, ed. Ron Lammert (San Antonio: Historical Publishing Network, 2001); Frank A. Blazich Jr., "Feathers of Honor: U.S. Signal Corps Pigeon Service in World War I, 1917–1918," *Army History* 117 (2020): 32–51. On the original size of the Lost Battalion and number of casualties, see Robert Laplander, *Finding the Lost Battalion: Beyond the Rumors, Myths, and Legends of America's Famous WWI Epic*, 3rd ed. (Waterford, Wis.: Lulu Press, 2017), 13. For a critical reappraisal of the story of Cher Ami, see Frank A. Blazich, "Notre Cher Ami: The Enduring Myth and Memory of a Humble Pigeon," *Journal of Military History* 85, no. 3 (July 2021): 646–77.

4. Eliezer Livneh, Yosef Nedava, and Yoram Efrati, *Nili: Toldoteha shel he'azah medinit* [Nili: A story of political daring] (Tel Aviv: Schocken, 1980), 143; Yigal Sheffy, *British Military Intelligence in the Palestine Campaign, 1914–1918* (London: Routledge, 1998); Gregory J. Wallance, *The Woman Who Fought an Empire: Sarah Aaronsohn and Her Nili Spy Ring* (Lincoln: University of Nebraska Press, 2018), 155–72.

5. The Ottomans had several other reasons to suspect the existence of the NILI spy ring, but most accounts indicate the importance of the pigeon. For full details, see Livneh, Nedava, and Efrati, *Nili*, 281–84; Wallance, *Woman Who Fought an Empire*, 180–81, 202–32; Sheffy, *British Military Intelligence in the Palestine Campaign*, 159; Eliezer Tauber, "The Capture of the NILI

Spies: The Turkish Version," *Intelligence and National Security* 6, no. 4 (1991): 701–10.

6. For an insightful discussion of these matters, see Catherine D'Ignazio and Lauren F. Klein, *Data Feminism* (Cambridge, Mass.: MIT Press, 2020), 73–91.

7. Jorge Luis Borges and Adolfo Bioy Casares, "On Exactitude in Science," in *A Universal History of Infamy*, trans. Norman Thomas Di Giovanni (London: Penguin Books, 1975), 131.

8. Samriddhi Chauhan and Roshan Deshmukh, "Astrology Market Research, 2031," Allied Market Research, Jan. 2023, www.alliedmarketresearch.com /astrology-market-A31779; Temcharoenkit Sasiwimon and Donald A. Johnson, "Factors Influencing Attitudes Toward Astrology and Making Relationship Decisions Among Thai Adults," *Scholar: Human Sciences* 13, no. 1 (2021): 15–27.

9. Frederick Henry Cramer, *Astrology in Roman Law and Politics* (Philadelphia: American Philosophical Society, 1954); Tamsyn Barton, *Power and Knowledge: Astrology, Physiognomics, and Medicine Under the Roman Empire* (Ann Arbor: University of Michigan Press, 2002), 57; Raffaela Garosi, "Indagine sulla formazione di concetto di magia nella cultura Romana," in *Magia: Studi di storia delle religioni in memoria di Raffaela Garosi*, ed. Paolo Xella (Rome: Bulzoni, 1976), 13–97.

10. Lindsay Murdoch, "Myanmar Elections: Astrologers' Influential Role in National Decisions," *Sydney Morning Herald*, Nov. 12, 2015, www.smh.com.au /world/myanmar-elections-astrologers-influential-role-in-national -decisions-20151112-gkxc3j.html.

11. Barbara Ehrenreich, *Dancing in the Streets: A History of Collective Joy* (New York: Metropolitan Books, 2006); Wray Herbert, "All Together Now: The Universal Appeal of Moving in Unison," *Scientific American*, April 1, 2009, www.scientificamerican.com/article/were-only-human-all-together-now/; Idil Kokal et al., "Synchronized Drumming Enhances Activity in the Caudate and Facilitates Prosocial Commitment—If the Rhythm Comes Easily," *PLOS ONE* 6, no. 11 (2011); Martin Lang et al., "Lost in the Rhythm: Effects of Rhythm on Subsequent Interpersonal Coordination," *Cognitive Science* 40, no. 7 (2016): 1797–815.

12. For debates about the role of information in biology, and specifically about the informational nature of DNA, see Godfrey-Smith and Sterelny, "Biological Information"; John Maynard Smith, "The Concept of Information in Biology," in *Information and the Nature of Reality: From Physics to Metaphysics* (Cambridge, U.K.: Cambridge University Press, 2014); Sahotra Sarkar, "Biological Information: A Skeptical Look at Some Central Dogmas of Molecular Biology," in *The Philosophy and History of Molecular Biology*, ed. Sahotra Sarkar (Norwell: Kluwer Academic Publishers, 1996), 187–231; Terrence W. Deacon, "How Molecules Became Signs," *Biosemiotics* 14, no. 3 (2021): 537–59.

13. Sven R. Kjellberg et al., "The Effect of Adrenaline on the Contraction of the Human Heart Under Normal Circulatory Conditions," *Acta Physiologica Scandinavica* 24, no. 4 (1952): 333–49.

14. Bruce I. Bustard, "20 July 1969," *Prologue Magazine* 35, no. 2 (Summer 2003), National Archives, www.archives.gov/publications/prologue/2003/summer /20-july-1969.html.

15. Jews and Christians have interpreted the relevant passages in Genesis in many different ways, but most accept the interpretation that Noah's Flood occurred 1,656 years after the creation of the world, or about 4,000 years ago, and that the Tower of Babel was destroyed either one century or a few centuries after the Flood.

16. Michael I. Bird et al., "Early Human Settlement of Sahul Was Not an Accident," *Scientific Reports* 9, no. 1 (2019): 8220; Chris Clarkson et al., "Human Occupation of Northern Australia by 65,000 Years Ago," *Nature* 547, no. 7663 (2017): 306–10.

17. See, for example, Leviticus 26:16 and 26:25; Deuteronomy 28:22, 28:58–63, 32:24, 32:35–36, and 32:39; Jeremiah 14:12, 21:6–9, and 24:10.

18. See, for example, Deuteronomy 28, 2 Chronicles 20:9, and Psalms 91:3.

19. Pope Francis, "Homily of His Holiness Pope Francis 'Return to God and Return to the Embrace of the Father,'" March 20, 2020, www.vatican.va /content/francesco/en/cotidie/2020/documents/papa-francesco-cotidie _20200320_peri-medici-ele-autorita.html; Philip Pullella, "Rome Catholic Churches Ordered Closed due to Coronavirus, Unprecedented in Modern Times," Reuters, March 13, 2020, www.reuters.com/article/us-health -coronavirus-italy-rome-churche-idUSKBN20Z3BU.

CHAPTER 2: STORIES

1. Thomas A. DiPrete et al., "Segregation in Social Networks Based on Acquaintanceship and Trust," *American Journal of Sociology* 116, no. 4 (2011): 1234–83; R. Jenkins, A. J. Dowsett, and A. M. Burton, "How Many Faces Do People Know?," *Proceedings of the Royal Society B: Biological Sciences* 285, no. 1888 (2018), article 20181319; Robin Dunbar, "Dunbar's Number: Why My Theory That Humans Can Only Maintain 150 Friendships Has Withstood 30 Years of Scrutiny," The Conversation, May 12, 2021, theconversation .com/dunbars-number-why-my-theory-that-humans-can-only-maintain -150-friendships-has-withstood-30-years-of-scrutiny-160676.

2. Melissa E. Thompson et al., "The Kibale Chimpanzee Project: Over Thirty Years of Research, Conservation, and Change," *Biological Conservation* 252 (2020), article 108857; Jill D. Pruetz and Nicole M. Herzog, "Savanna Chimpanzees at Fongoli, Senegal, Navigate a Fire Landscape," *Current Anthropology* 58, no. S16 (2017): S337–S350; Budongo Conservation Field Station, accessed Jan. 4, 2024, www.budongo.org; Yukimaru Sugiyama, "Demographic Parameters and Life History of Chimpanzees at Bossou, Guinea," *American Journal of Physical Anthropology* 124, no. 2 (2004): 154–65.

3. Rebecca Wragg Sykes, *Kindred: Neanderthal Life, Love, Death, and Art* (London: Bloomsbury Sigma, 2020), chap. 10; Brian Hayden, "Neandertal Social Structure?," *Oxford Journal of Archaeology* 31 (2012): 1–26; Jeremy Duveau et al., "The Composition of a Neandertal Social Group Revealed by the Hominin Footprints at Le Rozel (Normandy, France)," *Proceedings of the National Academy of Sciences* 116, no. 39 (2019): 19409–14.

4. Simon Sebag Montefiore, *Stalin: The Court of the Red Tsar* (London: Weidenfeld & Nicolson, 2003).

5. Brent Barnhart, "How to Build a Brand with Celebrity Social Media Management," Sprout Social, April 1, 2020, sproutsocial.com/insights/celebrity -social-media-management/; K. C. Morgan, "15 Celebs Who Don't Actually

Run Their Own Social Media Accounts," TheClever, April 20, 2017, www
.theclever.com/15-celebs-who-dont-actually-run-their-own-social-media
-accounts/; Josh Duboff, "Who's Really Pulling the Strings on Stars' Social-
Media Accounts," *Vanity Fair*, Sept. 8, 2016, www.vanityfair.com/style/2016
/09/celebrity-social-media-accounts.

6. Coca-Cola Company, Annual Report 2022, 47, accessed Jan. 3, 2024, investors
.coca-colacompany.com/filings-reports/annual-filings-10-k/content
/0000021344-23-000011/0000021344-23-000011.pdf.

7. David Gertner and Laura Rifkin, "Coca-Cola and the Fight Against the
Global Obesity Epidemic," *Thunderbird International Business Review* 60
(2018): 161–73; Jennifer Clinehens, "How Coca-Cola Built the World's
Most Memorable Brand," Medium, Nov. 17, 2022, medium.com/choice
-hacking/how-coca-cola-built-the-worlds-most-memorable-brand
-c9e8b8ac44c5; Clare McDermott, "Go Behind the Scenes of Coca-Cola's
Storytelling," Content Marketing Institute, Feb. 9, 2018, contentmarketing
institute.com/articles/coca-cola-storytelling/; Maureen Taylor, "Cultural
Variance as a Challenge to Global Public Relations: A Case Study of the
Coca-Cola Scare in Europe," *Public Relations Review* 26, no. 3 (2000): 277–
93; Kathryn LaTour, Michael S. LaTour, and George M. Zinkhan, "Coke Is
It: How Stories in Childhood Memories Illuminate an Icon," *Journal of Business
Research* 63, no. 3 (2010): 328–36; Bodi Chu, "Analysis on the Success of
Coca-Cola Marketing Strategy," in Proceedings of 2020 2nd International
Conference on Economic Management and Cultural Industry (ICEMCI
2020), *Advances in Economics, Business, and Management Research* 155 (2020):
96–100.

8. Blazich, "Notre Cher Ami."

9. Bart D. Ehrman, *How Jesus Became God: The Exaltation of a Preacher from
Galilee* (San Francisco: HarperOne, 2014).

10. Lauren Tuchman, "We All Were at Sinai: The Transformative Power of Inclusive Torah," Sefaria, accessed Jan. 3, 2024, www.sefaria.org.il/sheets/236454
.2?lang=he.

11. Reuven Hammer, "Tradition Today: Standing at Sinai," *Jerusalem Post*,
May 17, 2012, www.jpost.com/Jewish-World/Judaism/Tradition-Today
-Standing-at-Sinai; Rabbi Joel Mosbacher, "Each Person Must See Themselves as If They Went out of Egypt," RavBlog, April 9, 2017, ravblog.ccarnet
.org/2017/04/each-person-must-see-themselves-as-if-they-went-out-of
-egypt/; Rabbi Sari Laufer, "Table for Five: Five Takes on a Passage from the
Haggadah," *Jewish Journal*, April 5, 2018, jewishjournal.com/judaism/torah
/232778/table-five-five-takes-passage-haggadah-2/.

12. Elizabeth F. Loftus, "Creating False Memories," *Scientific American* 277, no. 3
(1997): 70–75; Beate Muschalla and Fabian Schönborn, "Induction of False
Beliefs and False Memories in Laboratory Studies—a Systematic Review,"
Clinical Psychology and Psychotherapy 28, no. 5 (2021): 1194–209; Christian
Unkelbach et al., "Truth by Repetition: Explanations and Implications," *Current
Directions in Psychological Science* 28, no. 3 (2019): 247–53; Doris Lacas-
sagne, Jérémy Béna, and Olivier Corneille, "Is Earth a Perfect Square?
Repetition Increases the Perceived Truth of Highly Implausible Statements,"
Cognition 223 (2022), article 105052.

13. "FoodData Central," U.S. Department of Agriculture, accessed Jan. 4, 2024,
fdc.nal.usda.gov/fdc-app.html#/?query=pizza.

14. William Magnuson, *Blockchain Democracy: Technology, Law, and the Rule of the Crowd* (Cambridge, U.K.: Cambridge University Press, 2020), 69; Scott Chipolina, "Bitcoin's Unlikely Resurgence: Bulls Bet on Wall Street Adoption," *Financial Times*, Dec. 8, 2023, www.ft.com/content/77aa2fbc-5c27-4edf-afa6-2a3a9d23092f.

15. "BBC 'Proves' Nessie Does Not Exist," BBC News, July 27, 2003, news.bbc.co.uk/1/hi/sci/tech/3096839.stm; Matthew Weaver, "Loch Ness Monster Could Be a Giant Eel, Say Scientists," *Guardian*, Sept. 5, 2019, www.theguardian.com/science/2019/sep/05/loch-ness-monster-could-be-a-giant-eel-say-scientists; Henry H. Bauer, *The Enigma of Loch Ness: Making Sense of a Mystery* (Champaign: University of Illinois Press, 1986), 165–66; Harold E. Edgerton and Charles W. Wyckoff, "Loch Ness Revisited: Fact or Fantasy? Science Uses Sonar and Camera to Probe the Depths of Loch Ness in Search of Its Resident Monster," *IEEE Spectrum* 15, no. 2 (1978): 26–29; University of Otago, "First eDNA Study of Loch Ness Points to Something Fishy," Sept. 5, 2019, www.otago.ac.nz/anatomy/news/news-archive/first-edna-study-of-loch-ness-points-to-something-fishy.

16. Katharina Buchholz, "Kosovo & Beyond: Where the UN Disagrees on Recognition," *Forbes*, Feb. 17, 2023, www.forbes.com/sites/katharinabuchholz/2023/02/17/kosovo--beyond-where-the-un-disagrees-on-recognition-infographic/?sh=d8490b2448c3; United Nations, "Agreement on Normalizing Relations Between Serbia, Kosovo 'Historic Milestone,' Delegate Tells Security Council," April 27, 2023, press.un.org/en/2023/sc15268.doc.htm.

17. Guy Faulconbridge, "Russia Plans Naval Base in Abkhazia, Triggering Criticism from Georgia," Reuters, Oct. 5, 2023, www.reuters.com/world/europe/russia-plans-naval-base-black-sea-coast-breakaway-georgian-region-izvestiya-2023-10-05/.

18. Wragg Sykes, *Kindred*; Hayden, "Neandertal Social Structure?"; Duveau et al., "Composition of a Neandertal Social Group Revealed by the Hominin Footprints at Le Rozel."

19. For a more detailed discussion, see Yuval Noah Harari, *Sapiens: A Brief History of Humankind* (New York: HarperCollins, 2015), chap. 2; David Graeber and David Wengrow, *The Dawn of Everything: A New History of Humanity* (New York: Farrar, Straus and Giroux, 2021), chap. 3; and Joseph Henrich, *The Weirdest People in the World* (New York: Farrar, Straus and Giroux, 2020), chap. 3. A classic study of how religious stories and rituals produce large-scale cooperation is Donald Tuzin's study of Ilahita. While most of its neighboring communities in New Guinea numbered a few hundred people, the complex religious beliefs and practices of Ilahita succeeded in uniting thirty-nine clans numbering about twenty-five hundred people altogether. See Donald Tuzin, *Social Complexity in the Making: A Case Study Among the Arapesh of New Guinea* (London: Routledge, 2001); Donald Tuzin, *The Ilahita Arapesh: Dimensions of Unity* (Oakland: University of California Press, 2022). For the importance of storytelling for large-scale cooperation, see Daniel Smith et al., "Camp Stability Predicts Patterns of Hunter-Gatherer Cooperation," *Royal Society Open Science* 3 (2016), article 160131; Daniel Smith et al., "Cooperation and the Evolution of Hunter-Gatherer Storytelling," *Nature Communications* 8 (2017), article 1853; Benjamin G. Purzycki et al., "Moralistic Gods, Supernatural Punishment, and the Expansion of Human Sociality," *Nature* 530 (2016):

327–30; Polly W. Wiessner, "Embers of Society: Firelight Talk Among the Ju/'hoansi Bushmen," *Proceedings of the National Academy of Sciences* 111, no. 39 (2014): 14027–35; Daniele M. Klapproth, *Narrative as Social Practice: Anglo-Western and Australian Aboriginal Oral Traditions* (Berlin: De Gruyter Mouton, 2004); Robert M. Ross and Quentin D. Atkinson, "Folktale Transmission in the Arctic Provides Evidence for High Bandwidth Social Learning Among Hunter-Gatherer Groups," *Evolution and Human Behavior* 37, no. 1 (2016): 47–53; Jerome Lewis, "Where Goods Are Free but Knowledge Costs: Hunter-Gatherer Ritual Economics in Western Central Africa," *Hunter Gatherer Research* 1, no. 1 (2015): 1–27; Bill Gammage, *The Biggest Estate on Earth: How Aborigines Made Australia* (Crows Nest, N.S.W.: Allen Unwin, 2011).

20. Azar Gat, *War in Human Civilization* (Oxford: Oxford University Press, 2008), 114–32; Luke Glowacki et al., "Formation of Raiding Parties for Intergroup Violence Is Mediated by Social Network Structure," *Proceedings of the National Academy of Sciences* 113, no. 43 (2016): 12114–19; Richard W. Wrangham and Luke Glowacki, "Intergroup Aggression in Chimpanzees and War in Nomadic Hunter-Gatherers," *Human Nature* 23 (2012): 5–29; R. Brian Ferguson, *Yanomami Warfare: A Political History* (Santa Fe, N.Mex.: School of American Research Press, 1995), 346–47.

21. Pierre Lienard, "Beyond Kin: Cooperation in a Tribal Society," in *Reward and Punishment in Social Dilemmas*, ed. Paul A. M. Van Lange, Bettina Rockenbach, and Toshio Yamagishi (Oxford: Oxford University Press, 2014), 214–34; Peter J. Richerson et al., "Cultural Evolution of Human Cooperation," in *Genetic and Cultural Evolution of Cooperation*, ed. Peter Hammerstein (Cambridge, Mass.: MIT Press, 2003), 357–88; Brian A. Stewart et al., "Ostrich Eggshell Bead Strontium Isotopes Reveal Persistent Macroscale Social Networking Across Late Quaternary Southern Africa," *PNAS* 117, no. 12 (2020): 6453–62; "Ages Ago, Beads Made from Ostrich Eggshells Cemented Friendships Across Vast Distances," *Weekend Edition Saturday*, NPR, March 14, 2020, www.npr.org/2020/03/14/815778427/ages-ago-beads-made-from -ostrich-eggshells-cemented-friendships-across-vast-dist.

22. For Stone Age networks of Sapiens exchanging technological skills, see Jennifer M. Miller and Yiming V. Wang, "Ostrich Eggshell Beads Reveal 50,000-Year-Old Social Network in Africa," *Nature* 601, no. 7892 (2022): 234–39; Stewart et al., "Ostrich Eggshell Bead Strontium Isotopes Reveal Persistent Macroscale Social Networking Across Late Quaternary Southern Africa."

23. Terrence R. Fehner and F. G. Gosling, "The Manhattan Project," U.S. Department of Energy, April 2021, www.energy.gov/sites/default/files/The %20Manhattan%20Project.pdf; F. G. Gosling, "The Manhattan Project: Making the Atomic Bomb," U.S. Department of Energy, Jan. 2010, www .energy.gov/management/articles/gosling-manhattan-project-making -atomic-bomb.

24. "Uranium Mines," U.S. Department of Energy, www.osti.gov/opennet /manhattan-project-history/Places/Other/uranium-mines.html.

25. Jerome Lewis, "Bayaka Elephant Hunting in Congo: The Importance of Ritual and Technique," in *Human-Elephant Interactions: From Past to Present*, vol. 1, ed. George E. Konidaris et al. (Tübingen: Tübingen University Press, 2021).

26. Sushmitha Ramakrishnan, "India Cuts the Periodic Table and Evolution from Schoolbooks," *DW,* June 2, 2023, www.dw.com/en/indiadropsevolution /a-65804720.

27. Annie Jacobsen, *Operation Paperclip: The Secret Intelligence Program That Brought Nazi Scientists to America* (Boston: Little, Brown, 2014); Brian E. Crim, *Our Germans: Project Paperclip and the National Security State* (Baltimore: Johns Hopkins University Press, 2018).

CHAPTER 3: DOCUMENTS

1. Monty Noam Penkower, "The Kishinev Pogrom of 1903: A Turning Point in Jewish History," *Modern Judaism* 24, no. 3 (2004): 187–225.

2. Hayyim Nahman Bialik, "Be'ir Hahareigah / The City of Slaughter," trans. A. M. Klein, *Prooftexts* 25, no. 1–2 (2005): 8–29; Iris Milner, "'In the City of Slaughter': The Hidden Voice of the Pogrom Victims," *Prooftexts* 25, no. 1–2 (2005): 60–72; Steven Zipperstein, *Pogrom: Kishinev and the Tilt of History* (New York: Liveright, 2018); David Fishelov, "Bialik the Prophet and the Modern Hebrew Canon," in *Great Immortality,* ed. Jón Karl Helgason and Marijan Dović (Leiden: Brill, 2019), 151–70.

3. The number of Palestinian refugees is estimated at between 700,000 and 750,000, the vast majority of whom were expelled in 1948. See Benny Morris, *Righteous Victims: A History of the Zionist-Arab Conflict, 1881–1998* (New York: Vintage, 2001), 252; UNRWA, "Palestinian Refugees," accessed Feb. 13, 2024, www.unrwa.org/palestine-refugees. In 1948 there were 856,000 Jews living in Arab countries such as Iraq and Egypt. Over the next two decades, in revenge for Arab defeats in the 1948, 1956, and 1967 wars, the vast majority of these Jews were driven out of their homes so that by 1968 only 76,000 were left. See Maurice M. Roumani, *The Case of the Jews from Arab Countries: A Neglected Issue* (Tel Aviv: World Organization of Jews from Arab Countries, 1983); Aryeh L. Avneri, *The Claim of Dispossession: Jewish Land-Settlement and the Arabs, 1878–1948* (New Brunswick, N.J.: Transaction Books, 1984), 276; JIMENA, "The Forgotten Refugees," July 7, 2023, www.jimena.org/the-forgotten-refugees/; Barry Mowell, "Changing Paradigms in Public Opinion Perspectives and Governmental Policy Concerning the Jewish Refugees of North Africa and Southwest Asia," Jewish Virtual Library, accessed Jan. 31, 2024, www.jewishvirtuallibrary.org /changing-paradigms-in-public-opinion-perspectives-and-governmental -policy-concerning-the-jewish-refugees-of-north-africa-and-southwest -asia.

4. Estimates of both the Jewish and the total populations vary, especially due to the incompleteness of Ottoman population records. See Alan Dowty, *Arabs and Jews in Ottoman Palestine: Two Worlds Collide* (Bloomington: Indiana University Press, 2021); Justin McCarthy, *The Population of Palestine: Population History and Statistics of the Late Ottoman Period and the Mandate* (New York: Columbia University Press, 1990); Itamar Rabinovich and Jehuda Reinharz, eds., *Israel in the Middle East: Documents and Readings on Society, Politics, and Foreign Relations, Pre-1948 to the Present* (Hanover, N.H.: University Press of New England, 2008), 571; Yehoshua Ben-Arieh, *Jerusalem in the 19th Century: Emergence of the New City* (Jerusalem: Yad Izhak Ben-Zvi Institute, 1986), 466.

5. George G. Grabowicz, "Taras Shevchenko: The Making of the National Poet," *Revue des Études Slaves* 85, no. 3 (2014): 421–39; Ostap Sereda, "'As a Father Among Little Children': The Emerging Cult of Taras Shevchenko as a Factor of the Ukrainian Nation Building in Austrian Eastern Galicia in the 1860s," *Kyiv-Mohyla Humanities Journal* 1 (2014): 159–88.

6. Sándor Hites, "Rocking the Cradle: Making Petőfi a National Poet," *Arcadia* 52, no. 1 (2017): 29–50; Ivan Halász et al., "The Rule of Sándor Petőfi in the Memory Policy of Hungarians, Slovaks, and the Members of the Hungarian Minority Group in Slovakia in the Last 150 Years," *Historia@Teoria* 1, no. 1 (2016): 121–43.

7. Timothy Snyder, *The Reconstruction of Nations: Poland, Ukraine, Lithuania, Belarus, 1569–1999* (New Haven, Conn.: Yale University Press, 2003); Roman Koropeckyj, *Adam Mickiewicz: The Life of a Romantic* (Ithaca, N.Y.: Cornell University Press, 2008); Helen N. Fagin, "Adam Mickiewicz: Poland's National Romantic Poet," *South Atlantic Bulletin* 42, no. 4 (1977): 103–13.

8. Jonathan Glover, *Israelis and Palestinians: From the Cycle of Violence to the Conversation of Mankind* (Cambridge, U.K.: Polity Press, 2024), 10.

9. William L. Smith, "Rāmāyaṇa Textual Traditions in Eastern India," in *The "Ramayana" Revisited*, ed. Mandakranta Bose (New York: Oxford University Press, 2004), 91–92; Frank E. Reynolds, "Ramayana, Rama Jataka, and Ramakien: A Comparative Study of Hindu and Buddhist Traditions," in *Many Ramayanas: The Diversity of a Narrative Tradition in South Asia*, ed. Paula Richman (Berkeley: University of California Press, 1991), 50–66; Aswathi M. P., "The Cultural Trajectories of *Ramayana*, a Text Beyond the Grand Narrative," *Singularities* 8, no. 1 (2021): 28–32; A. K. Ramanujan, "Three Hundred Ramayanas: Five Examples and Three Thoughts on Translation," in Richman, *Many Ramayanas*, 22–49; James Fisher, "Education and Social Change in Nepal: An Anthropologist's Assessment," *Himalaya: The Journal of the Association for Nepal and Himalayan* 10, no. 2 (1990): 30–31.

10. "The Ramayan: Why Indians Are Turning to Nostalgic TV," BBC, May 5, 2020, www.bbc.com/culture/article/20200504-the-ramayan-why-indians-are-turning-to-nostalgic-tv; "'Ramayan' Sets World Record, Becomes Most Viewed Entertainment Program Globally," *Hindu*, May 2, 2020, www.thehindu.com/entertainment/movies/ramayan-sets-world-record-becomes-most-viewed-entertainment-program-globally/article61662060.ece; Soutik Biswas, "Ramayana: An 'Epic' Controversy," BBC, Oct. 19, 2011, www.bbc.com/news/world-south-asia-15363181; "'Ramayana' Beats 'Game of Thrones' to Become the World's Most Watched Show," WION, Feb. 15, 2018, www.wionews.com/entertainment/ramayana-beats-game-of-thrones-to-become-the-worlds-most-watched-show-296162.

11. Kendall Haven, *Story Proof: The Science Behind the Startling Power of Story* (Westport, Conn.: Libraries Unlimited, 2007), vii, 122. For a more recent study, see Brendan I. Cohn-Sheehy et al., "Narratives Bridge the Divide Between Distant Events in Episodic Memory," *Memory and Cognition* 50 (2022): 478–94.

12. Frances A. Yates, *The Art of Memory* (London: Random House, 2011); Joshua Foer, *Moonwalking with Einstein: The Art and Science of Remembering Everything* (New York: Penguin, 2011); Nils C. J. Müller et al., "Hippocampal–Caudate Nucleus Interactions Support Exceptional Memory Performance," *Brain Structure and Function* 223 (2018): 1379–89; Yvette Tan, "This Woman

Only Needed a Week to Memorize All 328 Pages of Ikea's Catalogue," Mashable, Sept. 5, 2017, mashable.com/article/yanjaa-wintersoul-ikea; Jan-Paul Huttner, Ziwei Qian, and Susanne Robra-Bissantz, "A Virtual Memory Palace and the User's Awareness of the Method of Loci," European Conference on Information Systems, May 2019, aisel.aisnet.org/ecis2019_rp/7.

13. Ira Spar, ed., *Cuneiform Texts in the Metropolitan Museum of Art*, vol. 1, *Tablets, Cones, and Bricks of the Third and Second Millennia B.C.* (New York: The Metropolitan Museum of Art, 1988), 10–11; "CTMMA 1, 008 (P108692)," Cuneiform Digital Library Initiative, accessed Jan. 12, 2024, cdli.mpiwg-berlin .mpg.de/artifacts/108692; Tonia Sharlach, "Princely Employments in the Reign of Shulgi," *Journal of Ancient Near Eastern History* 9, no. 1 (2022): 1–68.

14. Andrew D. Madden, Jared Bryson, and Joe Palimi, "Information Behavior in Pre-literate Societies," in *New Directions in Human Information Behavior,* ed. Amanda Spink and Charles Cole (Dordrecht: Springer, 2006); Michael J. Trebilcock, "Communal Property Rights: The Papua New Guinean Experience," *University of Toronto Law Journal* 34, no. 4 (1984), 377–420; Richard B. Lee, "!Kung Spatial Organization: An Ecological and Historical Perspective," *Human Ecology* 1, no. 2 (1972): 125–47; Warren O. Ault, "Open-Field Husbandry and the Village Community: A Study of Agrarian By-Laws in Medieval England," *Transactions of the American Philosophical Society* 55, no. 7 (1965): 1–102; Henry E. Smith, "Semicommon Property Rights and Scattering in the Open Fields," *Journal of Legal Studies* 29, no. 1 (2000): 131–69; Richard Posner, *The Economics of Justice* (Cambridge, Mass.: Harvard University Press, 1981).

15. Klaas R. Veenhof, "'Dying Tablets' and 'Hungry Silver': Elements of Figurative Language in Akkadian Commercial Terminology," in *Figurative Language in the Ancient Near East,* ed. M. Mindlin, M. J. Geller, and J. E. Wansbrough (London: School of Oriental and African Studies, University of London, 1987), 41–75; Cécile Michel, "Constitution, Contents, Filing, and Use of Private Archives: The Case of Old Assyrian Archives (Nineteenth Century BCE)," in *Manuscripts and Archives,* ed. Alessandro Bausi et al. (Berlin: De Gruyter, 2018), 43–70.

16. Sophie Démare-Lafont and Daniel E. Fleming, eds., *Judicial Decisions in the Ancient Near East* (Atlanta: Society of Biblical Literature, 2023), 108–10; D. Charpin, "Lettres et procès paléo-babyloniens," in *Rendre la justice en Mésopotamie: Archives judiciaires du Proche-Orient ancien (IIIe-Ier millénaires avant J.-C.),* ed. Francis Joannès (Saint-Denis: Presses Universitaires de Vincennes, 2000), 73–74; Antoine Jacquet, "Family Archives in Mesopotamia During the Old Babylonian Period," in *Archives and Archival Documents in Ancient Societies: Trieste 30 September–1 October 2011,* ed. Michele Faraguna (Trieste: EUT, Edizioni Università di Trieste, 2013), 76–77; F. F. Kraus, *Altbabylonische Briefe in Umschrift und Übersetzung* (Leiden: R. J. Brill, 1986), vol. 11, n. 55; Frans van Koppen and Denis Lacambre, "Sippar and the Frontier Between Ešnunna and Babylon: New Sources for the History of Ešnunna in the Old Babylonian Period," *Jaarbericht van het Vooraziatisch Egyptisch Genootschap Ex Oriente Lux* 41 (2009): 151–77.

17. For examples from ancient Egypt and Mesopotamia of the difficulty of retrieving documents, see Geoffrey Yeo, *Record-Making and Record-Keeping in Early Societies* (London: Routledge, 2021), 132; Jacquet, "Family Archives in Mesopotamia During the Old Babylonian Period," 76–77.

18. Mu-ming Poo et al., "What Is Memory? The Present State of the Engram," *C Biology* 14, no. 1 (2016): 40; C. Abraham Wickliffe, Owen D. Jones, and David L. Glanzman, "Is Plasticity of Synapses the Mechanism of Long-Term Memory Storage?," *npj Science of Learning* 4, no. 1 (2019): 9; Bradley R. Postle, "How Does the Brain Keep Information 'in Mind'?," *Current Directions in Psychological Science* 25, no. 3 (2016): 151–56.

19. *Britannica,* s.v. "Bureaucracy and the State," accessed Jan. 4, 2024, www.britannica.com/topic/bureaucracy/Bureaucracy-and-the-state.

20. For studies that do focus on this interplay, see, for example, Michele J. Gelfand et al., "The Relationship Between Cultural Tightness–Looseness and COVID-19 Cases and Deaths: A Global Analysis," *Lancet Planetary Health* 5, no. 3 (2021): 135–44; Julian W. Tang et al., "An Exploration of the Political, Social, Economic, and Cultural Factors Affecting How Different Global Regions Initially Reacted to the COVID-19 Pandemic," *Interface Focus* 12, no. 2 (2022), article 20210079.

21. Jason Roberts, *Every Living Thing: The Great and Deadly Race to Know All Life* (New York: Random House, 2024); Paul Lawrence Farber, *Finding Order in Nature* (Baltimore: Johns Hopkins University Press, 2000); James L. Larson, "The Species Concept of Linnaeus," *Isis* 59, no. 3 (1968): 291–99; Peter Raven, Brent Berlin, and Dennis Breedlove, "The Origins of Taxonomy," *Science* 174, no. 4015 (1971): 1210–13; Robert C. Stauffer, "'On the Origin of Species': An Unpublished Version," *Science* 130, no. 3387 (1959): 1449–52.

22. *Britannica,* s.v. "*Homo erectus*—Ancestor, Evolution, Migration," accessed Jan. 4, 2024, www.britannica.com/topic/Homo-erectus/Relationship-to-Homo-sapiens.

23. Michael Dannemann and Janet Kelso, "The Contribution of Neanderthals to Phenotypic Variation in Modern Humans," *American Journal of Human Genetics* 101, no. 4 (2017): 578–89.

24. Ernst Mayr, "What Is a Species, and What Is Not?," *Philosophy of Science* 63, no. 2 (1996): 262–77.

25. Darren E. Irwin et al., "Speciation by Distance in a Ring Species," *Science* 307, no. 5708 (2005): 414–16; James Mallet, Nora Besansky, and Matthew W. Hahn, "How Reticulated Are Species?," *BioEssays* 38, no. 2 (2016): 140–49; Simon H. Martin and Chris D. Jiggins, "Interpreting the Genomic Landscape of Introgression," *Current Opinion in Genetics and Development* 47 (2017): 69–74; Jenny Tung and Luis B. Barreiro, "The Contribution of Admixture to Primate Evolution," *Current Opinion in Genetics and Development* 47 (2017): 61–68.

26. James Mallet, "Hybridization, Ecological Races, and the Nature of Species: Empirical Evidence for the Ease of Speciation," *Philosophical Transactions of the Royal Society B: Biological Sciences* 363, no. 1506 (2008): 2971–86.

27. Brian Thomas, "Lions, Tigers, and Tigons," Institute for Creation Research, Sept. 12, 2012, www.icr.org/article/7051/.

28. Shannon M. Soucy, Jinling Huang, and Johann Peter Gogarten, "Horizontal Gene Transfer: Building the Web of Life," *Nature Reviews Genetics* 16, no. 8 (2015): 472–82; Michael Hensel and Herbert Schmidt, eds., *Horizontal Gene Transfer in the Evolution of Pathogenesis* (Cambridge, U.K.: Cambridge University Press, 2008); James A. Raymond and Hak Jun Kim, "Possible Role of Horizontal Gene Transfer in the Colonization of Sea Ice by Algae," *PLOS*

ONE 7, no. 5 (2012), article e35968; Katrin Bartke et al., "Evolution of Bacterial Interspecies Hybrids with Enlarged Chromosomes," *Genome Biology and Evolution* 14, no. 10 (2022), article evac135.

29. Eugene V. Koonin and Petro Starokadomskyy, "Are Viruses Alive? The Replicator Paradigm Sheds Decisive Light on an Old but Misguided Question," *Studies in History and Philosophy of Science Part C: Studies in History and Philosophy of Biological and Biomedical Sciences* 59 (2016): 125–34; Dominic D. P. Johnson, "What Viruses Want: Evolutionary Insights for the Covid-19 Pandemic and Lessons for the Next One," in *A Multidisciplinary Approach to Pandemics,* ed. Philippe Bourbeau, Jean-Michel Marcoux, and Brooke A. Ackerly (Oxford: Oxford University Press, 2022), 38–69; Deepak Sumbria et al., "Virus Infections and Host Metabolism—Can We Manage the Interactions?," *Frontiers in Immunology* 11 (2020), article 594963; Nigel Brown and David Bhella, "Are Viruses Alive?," Microbiology Society, 10, 2016, microbiologysociety.org/publication/past-issues/what-is-life/article/are-viruses-alive-what-is-life.html; Erica L. Sanchez and Michael Lagunoff, "Viral Activation of Cellular Metabolism," *Virology* 479–80 (May 2015): 609–18; "Virus," National Human Genome Research Institute, accessed Jan. 12, 2024, www.genome.gov/genetics-glossary/Virus.

30. Ashworth E. Underwood, "The History of Cholera in Great Britain," *Proceedings of the Royal Society of Medicine* 41, no. 3 (1948): 165–73; Nottidge Charles Macnamara, *Asiatic Cholera: History up to July 15, 1892, Causes and Treatment* (London: Macmillan, 1892).

31. John Snow, "Dr. Snow's Report," in Cholera Inquiry Committee, *The Report on the Cholera Outbreak in the Parish of St. James, Westminster, During the Autumn of 1854* (London: J. Churchill, 1855), 97–120; S. W. B. Newsom, "Pioneers in Infection Control: John Snow, Henry Whitehead, the Broad Street Pump, and the Beginnings of Geographical Epidemiology," *Journal of Hospital Infection* 64, no. 3 (2006): 210–16; Peter Vinten-Johansen et al., *Cholera, Chloroform, and the Science of Medicine: A Life of John Snow* (Oxford: Oxford University Press, 2003); Theodore H. Tulchinsky, "John Snow, Cholera, the Broad Street Pump; Waterborne Diseases Then and Now," *Case Studies in Public Health* (2018): 77–99.

32. Gov.UK, "Check If You Need a License to Abstract Water," July 3, 2023, www.gov.uk/guidance/check-if-you-need-a-license-to-abstract-water.

33. Mohnish Kedia, "Sanitation Policy in India—Designed to Fail?," *Policy Design and Practice* 5, no. 3 (2022): 307–25.

34. See, for example, Madden, Bryson, and Palimi, "Information Behavior in Preliterate Societies," 33–53.

35. Catherine Salmon and Jessica Hehman, "The Evolutionary Psychology of Sibling Conflict and Siblicide," in *The Evolution of Violence,* ed. Todd K. Shackelford and Ronald D. Hansen (New York: Springer, 2014), 137–57.

36. Ibid.; Laurence G. Frank, Stephen E. Glickman, and Paul Licht, "Fatal Sibling Aggression, Precocial Development, and Androgens in Neonatal Spotted Hyenas," *Science* 252, no. 5006 (1991): 702–4; Frank J. Sulloway, "Birth Order, Sibling Competition, and Human Behavior," in *Conceptual Challenges in Evolutionary Psychology: Innovative Research Strategies,* ed. Harmon R. Holcomb (Dordrecht: Springer Netherlands, 2001), 39–83; Heribert Hofer and Marion L. East, "Siblicide in Serengeti Spotted Hyenas: A Long-Term Study of

Maternal Input and Cub Survival," *Behavioral Ecology and Sociobiology* 62, no. 3 (2008): 341–51.

37. R. Grant Gilmore Jr., Oliver Putz, and Jon W. Dodrill, "Oophagy, Intrauterine Cannibalism, and Reproductive Strategy in Lamnoid Sharks," in *Reproductive Biology and Phylogeny of Chondrichthyes*, ed. W. M. Hamlett (Boca Raton, Fla.: CRC Press, 2005), 435–63; Demian D. Chapman et al., "The Behavioral and Genetic Mating System of the Sand Tiger Shark, *Carcharias taurus*, an Intrauterine Cannibal," *Biology Letters* 9, no. 3 (2013), article 20130003.

38. Martin Kavaliers, Klaus-Peter Ossenkopp, and Elena Choleris, "Pathogens, Odors, and Disgust in Rodents," *Neuroscience and Biobehavioral Reviews* 119 (2020): 281–93; Valerie A. Curtis, "Infection-Avoidance Behavior in Humans and Other Animals," *Trends in Immunology* 35, no. 10 (2014): 457–64.

39. Harvey Whitehouse, *Inheritance: The Evolutionary Origins of the Modern World* (London: Hutchinson, 2024), 56; Marvin Perry and Frederick M. Schweitzer, eds., *Antisemitic Myths: A Historical and Contemporary Anthology* (Bloomington: Indiana University Press, 2008), 6, 26; Roderick McGrew, "Bubonic Plague," in *Encyclopedia of Medical History* (New York: McGraw-Hill, 1985), 45; David Nirenberg, *Communities of Violence: Persecution of Minorities in the Middle Ages* (Princeton, N.J.: Princeton University Press, 1996); Martina Baradel and Emanuele Costa, "Discrimination, Othering, and the Political Instrumentalizing of Pandemic Disease," *Journal of Interdisciplinary History of Ideas* 18, no. 18 (2020); Alan M. Kraut, *Silent Travelers: Germs, Genes, and the "Immigrant Menace"* (New York: Basic Books, 1994); Samuel K. Cohn Jr., *Epidemics: Hate and Compassion from the Plague of Athens to AIDS* (Oxford: Oxford University Press, 2018).

40. Wayne R. Dynes, ed., *Encyclopedia of Homosexuality*, vol. 1 (New York: Garland, 1990), 324.

41. John Bowker, ed., *The Oxford Dictionary of World Religions* (Oxford: Oxford University Press, 1997), 1041–44; Mary Douglas, *Purity and Danger* (London: Routledge, 2003), chap. 9; Laura Kipnis, *The Female Thing: Dirt, Sex, Envy, Vulnerability* (London: Vintage, 2007), chap. 3.

42. Robert M. Sapolsky, *Behave: The Biology of Humans at Our Best and Worst* (New York: Penguin Press, 2017), 388–89, 560–65.

43. Vinod Kumar Mishra, "Caste and Religion Matters in Access to Housing, Drinking Water, and Toilets: Empirical Evidence from National Sample Surveys, India," *CASTE: A Global Journal on Social Exclusion* 4, no. 1 (2023): 24–45, www.jstor.org/stable/48728103; Ananya Sharma, "Here's Why India Is Struggling to Be Truly Open Defecation Free," *Wire India*, Oct. 28, 2021, thewire.in/government/heres-why-india-is-struggling-to-be-truly-open-defecation-free.

44. Samyak Pandey, "Roshni, the Shivpuri Dalit Girl Killed for 'Open Defecation,' Wanted to Become a Doctor," *Print*, Sept. 30, 2019, theprint.in/india/roshni-the-shivpuri-dalit-girl-killed-for-open-defecation-wanted-to-become-a-doctor/298925/.

45. Nick Perry, "Catch, Class, and Bureaucracy: The Meaning of Joseph Heller's *Catch 22*," *Sociological Review* 32, no. 4 (1984): 719–41, doi.org/10.1111/j.1467-954X.1984.tb00832.x.

46. Ludovico Ariosto, *Orlando Furioso* (1516), canto 14, lines 83–84.

47. William Shakespeare, *Henry VI, Part 2,* in *First Folio* (London, 1623), act 4, scene 2.

48. Juliet Barker, *1381: The Year of the Peasants' Revolt* (Cambridge, Mass.: Belknap Press of Harvard University Press, 2014); W. M. Ormrod, "The Peasants' Revolt and the Government of England," *Journal of British Studies* 29, no. 1 (1990): 1–30, doi.org/10.1086/385947; Jonathan Burgess, "The Learning of the Clerks: Writing and Authority During the Peasants' Revolt of 1381" (master's thesis, McGill University, 2022), escholarship.mcgill.ca/concern /theses/6682x911r.

49. Josephus, *The Jewish War,* 2:427.

50. Rodolphe Reuss, *Le sac de l'Hôtel de Ville de Strasbourg (juillet 1789), épisode de l'histoire de la Révolution en Alsace* (Paris, 1915).

51. Jean Ancel, *The History of the Holocaust: Romania* (Jerusalem: Yad Vashem, 2003), 1:63.

52. The fate of Romanian Jews during the Holocaust was determined by numerous factors, but for several complex reasons there was a close correlation between those who lost their citizenship in 1938 and those who were later murdered. See "Murder of the Jews of Romania," Yad Vashem, 2024, www .yadvashem.org/holocaust/about/final-solution-beginning/romania.html #narrative_info; Christopher J. Kshyk, "The Holocaust in Romania: The Extermination and Protection of the Jews Under Antonescu's Regime," *Inquiries Journal* 6, no. 12 (2014), www.inquiriesjournal.com/a?id=947.

CHAPTER 4: ERRORS

1. "Humanum fuit errare, diabolicum est per animositatem in errore manere." See Armand Benjamin Caillau, ed., *Sermones de scripturis,* in *Sancti Aurelii Augustini Opera* (Paris: Parent-Desbarres, 1838), 4:412.

2. Ivan Mehta, "Elon Musk Wants to Develop TruthGPT, 'a Maximum Truth-Seeking AI,'" *Tech Crunch,* April 18, 2023, techcrunch.com/2023/04/18/elon -musk-wants-to-develop-truthgpt-a-maximum-truth-seeking-ai/.

3. Harvey Whitehouse, "A Cyclical Model of Structural Transformation Among the Mali Baining," *The Cambridge Journal of Anthropology* 14, no. 3 (1990), 34–53; Harvey Whitehouse, "From Possession to Apotheosis: Transformation and Disguise in the Leadership of a Cargo Movement," in *Leadership and Change in the Western Pacific,* eds. Richard Feinberg and Karen Ann Watson-Gageo (London: Athlone Press, 1996), 376–95; Harvey Whitehouse, *Inheritance: The Evolutionary Origins of the Modern World* (London: Hutchinson, 2024), 149–51.

4. Whitehouse, *Inheritance,* 45.

5. Robert Bellah, *Religion in Human Evolution: From the Paleolithic to the Axial Age* (Cambridge, Mass.: Belknap Press of Harvard University Press, 2011), 181.

6. Ibid., chaps. 4–9.

7. Herodotus, *The Histories,* book 5, 63; Mogens Herman Hansen, "Democracy, Athenian," in *The Oxford Classical Dictionary,* ed. Simon Hornblower and Antony Spawforth (Oxford: Oxford University Press, 2005), www.oxford reference.com/display/10.1093/acref/9780198606413.001.0001/acref -9780198606413-e-2112.

8. John Collins, *The Dead Sea Scrolls: A Biography* (Princeton, N.J.: Princeton University Press, 2013), vii, 185.

9. Jodi Magness, *The Archaeology of Qumran and the Dead Sea Scrolls,* 2nd ed. (Grand Rapids: Eerdmans, 2021), chap. 3.

10. Sidnie White Crawford, "Genesis in the Dead Sea Scrolls," in *The Book of Genesis,* ed. Craig A. Evans, Joel N. Lohr, and David L. Petersen (Boston: Brill, 2012), 353–73, doi.org/10.1163/9789004226579_016; James C. VanderKam, "Texts, Titles, and Translations," in *The Cambridge Companion to the Hebrew Bible/Old Testament,* ed. Stephen B. Chapman and Marvin A. Sweeney (Cambridge, U.K.: Cambridge University Press, 2016), 9–27, doi .org/10.1017/CBO9780511843365.002.

11. See the results for a search for "Enoch" in the Dead Sea Scrolls database: www .deadseascrolls.org.il/explore-the-archive/search#q="Enoch."

12. See Collins, *Dead Sea Scrolls.*

13. Daniel Assefa, "The Biblical Canon of the Ethiopian Orthodox Tawahedo Church," in *The Oxford Handbook of the Bible in Orthodox Christianity,* ed. Eugen J. Pentiuc (New York: Oxford University Press, 2022), 211–26; David Kessler, *The Falashas: A Short History of the Ethiopian Jews,* 3rd ed. (New York: Frank Cass, 1996), 67.

14. Emanuel Tov, *Textual Criticism of the Hebrew Bible* (Minneapolis: Fortress Press, 2001), 269; Sven Fockner, "Reopening the Discussion: Another Contextual Look at the Sons of God," *Journal for the Study of the Old Testament* 32, no. 4 (2008): 435–56, doi.org/10.1177/0309089208092140; Michael S. Heiser, "Deuteronomy 32:8 and the Sons of God," *Bibliotheca Sacra* 158 (2001): 71–72.

15. Martin G. Abegg Jr., Peter Flint, and Eugene Ulrich, *The Dead Sea Scrolls Bible: The Oldest Known Bible Translated for the First Time into English* (San Francisco: Harper, 1999), 159; Jewish Publication Society of America, *The Holy Scriptures According to the Masoretic Text* (Philadelphia, 1917), jps.org/wp -content/uploads/2015/10/Tanakh1917.pdf.

16. Abegg, Flint, and Ulrich, *Dead Sea Scrolls Bible,* 506; Peter W. Flint, "Unrolling the Dead Sea Psalms Scrolls," in *The Oxford Handbook of the Psalms,* ed. William P. Brown (Oxford: Oxford University Press, 2014), 243, doi.org/10 .1093/oxfordhb/9780199783335.013.015.

17. Timothy Michael Law, *When God Spoke Greek: The Septuagint and the Making of the Christian Bible* (Oxford: Oxford University Press, 2013), 49.

18. Ibid., 62; Albert Pietersma and Benjamin G. Wright, eds., *A New English Translation of the Septuagint* (Oxford: Oxford University Press, 2007), vii; William P. Brown. "The Psalms: An Overview," in Brown, *Oxford Handbook of the Psalms,* 3, doi.org/10.1093/oxfordhb/9780199783335.013.001.

19. Law, *When God Spoke Greek,* 63, 72.

20. Karen H. Jobes and Moisés Silva, *Invitation to the Septuagint* (Grand Rapids: Baker Academic, 2015), 161–62.

21. Michael Heiser, "Deuteronomy 32:8 and the Sons of God," LBTS Faculty Publications and Presentations (2001), 279. See also Alexandria Frisch, *The Danielic Discourse on Empire in Second Temple Literature* (Boston: Brill, 2016), 140; "Deuteronomion," in Pietersma and Wright, *New English Translation of the Septuagint,* ccat.sas.upenn.edu/nets/edition/05-deut-nets.pdf.

22. Chanoch Albeck, ed., *Mishnah: Six Orders* (Jerusalem: Bialik, 1955–59).

23. Maxine Grossman, "Lost Books of the Bible," in *The Oxford Dictionary of the Jewish Religion,* ed. Adele Berlin, 2nd ed. (Oxford: Oxford University Press, 2011); Geoffrey Khan, *A Short Introduction to the Tiberian Masoretic Bible and Its Reading Tradition* (Piscataway, N.J.: Gorgias Press, 2013).
24. Bart D. Ehrman, *Forged: Writing in the Name of God: Why the Bible's Authors Are Not Who We Think They Are* (New York: HarperOne, 2011), 300; Annette Y. Reed. "Pseudepigraphy, Authorship, and the Reception of 'the Bible' in Late Antiquity," in *The Reception and Interpretation of the Bible in Late Antiquity: Proceedings of the Montréal Colloquium in Honor of Charles Kannengiesser,* ed. Lorenzo DiTommaso and Lucian Turcescu (Leiden: Brill, 2008), 467–90; Stephen Greenblatt, *The Rise and Fall of Adam and Eve* (New York: W. W. Norton, 2017), 68; Dale C. Allison Jr., *Testament of Abraham* (Berlin: Walter De Gruyter, 2013), vii.
25. Grossman, "Lost Books of the Bible."
26. See, for example, Tzvi Freeman, "How Did the Torah Exist Before It Happened?," Chabad.org, www.chabad.org/library/article_cdo/aid/110124/jewish/How-Did-the-Torah-Exist-Before-it-Happened.htm.
27. Seth Schwartz, *Imperialism and Jewish Society, 200 B.C.E. to 640 C.E.* (Princeton, N.J.: Princeton University Press, 2001); Gottfried Reeg and Dagmar Börner-Klein, "Synagogue," in *Religion Past and Present,* ed. Hans Dieter Betz et al. (Leiden: Brill, 2006–12), dx.doi.org/10.1163/1877-5888_rpp_COM_025027; Kimmy Caplan, "Bet Midrash," in Betz et al., *Religion Past and Present,* dx.doi.org/10.1163/1877-5888_rpp_SIM_01883.
28. "Tractate Soferim," in *The William Davidson Talmud* (Jerusalem: Koren, 2017), www.sefaria.org/Tractate_Soferim?tab=contents.
29. "Tractate Eiruvin," in *Babylonian Talmud,* chap. 13a, halakhah.com/pdf/moed/Eiruvin.pdf.
30. B. Barry Levy, *Fixing God's Torah: The Accuracy of the Hebrew Bible Text in Jewish Law* (Oxford: Oxford University Press, 2001); Alfred J. Kolatch, *This Is the Torah* (New York: Jonathan David, 1988); "Tractate Soferim."
31. Raphael Patai, *The Children of Noah: Jewish Seafaring in Ancient Times* (Princeton, N.J.: Princeton University Press, 1998), benyehuda.org/read/30739.
32. Shaye Cohen, Robert Goldenberg, and Hayim Lapin, eds., *The Oxford Annotated Mishnah* (Oxford: Oxford University Press, 2022), 1.
33. Mayer I. Gruber, "The Mishnah as Oral Torah: A Reconsideration," *Journal for the Study of Judaism in the Persian, Hellenistic, and Roman Period* 15 (1984): 112–22.
34. Adin Steinsaltz, *The Essential Talmud* (New York: Basic Books, 2006), 3.
35. Ibid.
36. Elizabeth A. Harris, "For Jewish Sabbath, Elevators Do All the Work," *New York Times,* March 5, 2012, www.nytimes.com/2012/03/06/nyregion/on-jewish-sabbath-elevators-that-do-all-the-work.html.
37. Jon Clarine, "Digitalization Is Revolutionizing Elevator Services," *TKE blog,* June 2022, blog.tkelevator.com/digitalization-is-revolutionizing-elevator-services-jon-clarine-shares-how-and-why/.
38. See, for example, "Tractate Megillah," in *Babylonian Talmud,* chap. 16b; "Rashi on Genesis 45:14," in *Pentateuch with Targum Onkelos, Haphtaroth, and Prayers for Sabbath and Rashi's Commentary,* ed. and trans. M. Rosenbaum and A. M. Silbermann in collaboration with A. Blashki and L. Joseph (London:

Shapiro, Vallentine, 1933), www.sefaria.org/Rashi_on_Genesis.45.14?lang=
bi&with=Talmud&lang2=en.

39. For the Talmudic origin of such beliefs, see "Tractate Shabbat," in *Babylonian Talmud,* chap. 119b. For present-day variations on this theme, see, for example, midrasha.biu.ac.il/node/2192.

40. Bart D. Ehrman, *Lost Christianities: The Battles for Scripture and the Faiths We Never Knew* (Oxford: Oxford University Press, 2003); Frederick Bird, "Early Christianity as an Unorganized Ecumenical Religious Movement," in *Handbook of Early Christianity: Social Science Approaches,* ed. Anthony J. Blasi, Jean Duhaime, and Paul-André Turcotte (Walnut Creek, Calif.: AltaMira Press, 2002), 225–46.

41. Konrad Schmid, "Immanuel," in Betz et al., *Religion Past and Present.*

42. Ehrman, *Lost Christianities,* xiv; Sarah Parkhouse, "Identity, Death, and Ascension in the First Apocalypse of James and the Gospel of John," *Harvard Theological Review* 114, no. 1 (2021): 51–71; Gregory T. Armstrong, "Abraham," in *Encyclopedia of Early Christianity,* ed. Everett Ferguson (New York: Routledge, 1999), 7–8; John J. Collins, "Apocalyptic Literature," in ibid., 73–74.

43. Ehrman, *Lost Christianities,* xi-xii.

44. Ibid., xii; J. K. Elliott, ed., *The Apocryphal New Testament: A Collection of Apocryphal Christian Literature in an English Translation* (Oxford: Oxford University Press, 1993), 231–302.

45. Ibid., 543–46; Ehrman, *Lost Christianities;* Andrew Louth, ed., *Early Christian Writings: The Apostolic Fathers* (New York: Penguin Classics, 1987).

46. *The Festal Epistles of St. Athanasius, Bishop of Alexandria* (Oxford: John Henry Parker, 1854), 137–39.

47. Ehrman, *Lost Christianities,* 231.

48. Daria Pezzoli-Olgiati et al., "Canon," in Betz et al., *Religion Past and Present;* David Salter Williams, "Reconsidering Marcion's Gospel," *Journal of Biblical Literature* 108, no. 3 (1989): 477–96.

49. Ashish J. Naidu, *Transformed in Christ: Christology and the Christian Life in John Chrysostom* (Eugene, Ore.: Pickwick Publications, 2012), 77.

50. Bruce M. Metzger, *The Canon of the New Testament: Its Origin, Development, and Significance* (Oxford: Clarendon Press, 1987), 219–20.

51. Metzger, *Canon of the New Testament,* 176, 223–24; Christopher Sheklian, "Venerating the Saints, Remembering the City: Armenian Memorial Practices and Community Formation in Contemporary Istanbul," in *Armenian Christianity Today: Identity Politics and Popular Practice,* ed. Alexander Agadjanian (Surrey, U.K.: Ashgate, 2014), 157; Bart Ehrman, *Forgery and Counterforgery: The Use of Literary Deceit in Early Christian Polemics* (Oxford: Oxford University Press, 2013), 32. See also Ehrman, *Lost Christianities,* 210–11.

52. Ehrman, *Lost Christianities,* 231.

53. Ibid., 236–38.

54. Ibid., 38; Ehrman, *Forgery and Counter-forgery,* 203; Raymond F. Collins, "Pastoral Epistles," in Betz et al., *Religion Past and Present.*

55. Ariel Sabar, "The Inside Story of a Controversial New Text About Jesus," *Smithsonian Magazine,* Sept. 17, 2012, www.smithsonianmag.com/history/the-inside-story-of-a-controversial-new-text-about-jesus-41078791/.

56. Dennis MacDonald, *The Legend of the Apostle: The Battle for Paul in Story and Canon* (Philadelphia: Westminster Press, 1983), 17; Stephen J. Davis, *The Cult*

of Saint Thecla: A Tradition of Women's Piety in Late Antiquity (Oxford: Oxford University Press, 2001), 6.

57. Davis, *Cult of Saint Thecla.*

58. Knut Willem Ruyter, "Pacifism and Military Service in the Early Church," *CrossCurrents* 32, no. 1 (1982): 54–70; Harold S. Bender, "The Pacifism of the Sixteenth Century Anabaptists," *Church History* 24, no. 2 (1955): 119–31.

59. Michael J. Lewis, *City of Refuge: Separatists and Utopian Town Planning* (Princeton, N.J.: Princeton University Press, 2016), 97.

60. Irene Bueno, "False Prophets and Ravening Wolves: Biblical Exegesis as a Tool Against Heretics in Jacques Fournier's Postilla on Matthew," *Speculum* 89, no. 1 (2014): 35–65.

61. Peter K. Yu, "Of Monks, Medieval Scribes, and Middlemen," *Michigan State Law Review* 2006, no. 1 (2006): 7.

62. Marc Drogin, *Anathema! Medieval Scribes and the History of Book Curses* (Totowa, N.J.: Allanheld, Osmun, 1983), 37.

63. Nicholas Watson, "Censorship and Cultural Change in Late-Medieval England: Vernacular Theology, the Oxford Translation Debate, and Arundel's Constitutions of 1409," *Speculum* 70, no. 4 (1995): 827.

64. David B. Barrett, George Thomas Kurian, and Todd M. Johnson, *World Christian Encyclopedia: A Comparative Survey of Churches and Religions in the Modern World* (Oxford: Oxford University Press, 2001), 12.

65. Eltjo Buringh and Jan Luiten Van Zanden, "Charting the 'Rise of the West': Manuscripts and Printed Books in Europe, a Long-Term Perspective from the Sixth Through Eighteenth Centuries," *Journal of Economic History* 69 (2009): 409–45.

66. In the following discussion of the European witch hunts, I relied primarily on Ronald Hutton, *The Witch: A History of Fear, from Ancient Times to the Present* (New Haven, Conn.: Yale University Press, 2017).

67. Hutton, *Witch.*

68. Ibid. The *Canon Episcopi,* composed in the early tenth century (or perhaps in the late ninth century), became part of canon law. It argued that Satan deludes people to believe in all kinds of fantastical occurrences—for example, that they can fly in the sky—and that believing that these occurrences are real is a sin. This is the exact opposite of the position taken by early modern witch-hunters, who insisted that such things actually happened and doubting their reality is a sin. See also Julian Goodare, "Witches' Flight in Scottish Demonology," in *Demonology and Witch-Hunting in Early Modern Europe,* ed. Julian Goodare, Rita Voltmer, and Liv Helene Willumsen (London: Routledge, 2020), 147–67.

69. Hutton, *Witch;* Richard Kieckhefer, "The First Wave of Trials for Diabolical Witchcraft," in *The Oxford Handbook of Witchcraft in Early Modern Europe and Colonial America,* ed. Brian P. Levack (Oxford: Oxford University Press, 2013), 158–78; Fabrizio Conti, "Notes on the Nature of Beliefs in Witchcraft: Folklore and Classical Culture in Fifteenth Century Mendicant Traditions," *Religions* 10, no. 10 (2019): 576; Chantal Ammann-Doubliez, "La première chasse aux sorciers en Valais (1428–1436?)," in *L'imaginaire du sabbat: Édition critique des textes les plus anciens (1430 c.–1440 c.),* ed. Martine Ostorero et al. (Lausanne: Université de Lausanne, Section d'Histoire, Faculté des Lettres, 1999), 63–98; Nachman Ben-Yehuda, "The European Witch Craze: Still a Sociologist's Perspective," *American Journal of Sociology* 88, no. 6

(1983): 1275–79; Hans Peter Broedel, "Fifteenth-Century Witch Beliefs," in Levack, *Oxford Handbook of Witchcraft.*

70. Hans Broedel, *The "Malleus Maleficarum" and the Construction of Witchcraft: Theology and Popular Belief* (Manchester: Manchester University Press, 2003); Martine Ostorero, "Un lecteur attentif du *Speculum historiale* de Vincent de Beauvais au XVe siècle: L'inquisiteur bourguignon Nicolas Jacquier et la réalité des apparitions démoniaques," *Spicae: Cahiers de l'Atelier Vincent de Beauvais* 3 (2013).

71. This and the following discussions of Kramer and his writings are based primarily on Broedel, *"Malleus Maleficarum" and the Construction of Witchcraft.* See also Tamar Herzig, "The Bestselling Demonologist: Heinrich Institoris's *Malleus Maleficarum,"* in *The Science of Demons: Early Modern Authors Facing Witchcraft and the Devil,* ed. Jan Machielsen (New York: Routledge, 2020), 53–67.

72. Broedel, *"Malleus Maleficarum" and the Construction of Witchcraft,* 178.

73. Jakob Sprenger, *Malleus Maleficarum,* trans. Montague Summers (London: J. Rodker, 1928), 121.

74. Tamar Herzig, "Witches, Saints, and Heretics: Heinrich Kramer's Ties with Italian Women Mystics," *Magic, Ritual, and Witchcraft* 1, no. 1 (2006): 26; André Schnyder, *"Malleus maleficarum" von Heinrich Institoris (alias Kramer) unter Mithilfe Jakob Sprengers aufgrund der dämonologischen Tradition zusammengestellt: Kommentar zur Wiedergabe des Erstdrucks von 1487 (Hain 9238)* (Göppingen: Kümmerle, 1993), 62.

75. Broedel, *"Malleus Maleficarum" and the Construction of Witchcraft,* 7–8.

76. On the link between the print revolution and the European witch-hunt craze, see Charles Zika, *The Appearance of Witchcraft: Print and Visual Culture in Sixteenth-Century Europe* (London: Routledge, 2007); Robert Walinski-Kiehl, "Pamphlets, Propaganda, and Witch-Hunting in Germany, c. 1560–c. 1630," *Reformation* 6, no. 1 (2002): 49–74; Alison Rowlands, *Witchcraft Narratives in Germany: Rothenburg, 1561–1652* (Manchester: Manchester University Press, 2003); Walter Stephens, *Demon Lovers: Witchcraft, Sex, and the Crisis of Belief* (Chicago: University of Chicago Press, 2002); Brian P. Levack, *The Witch-Hunt in Early Modern Europe* (London: Longman, 1987). For a study that downplays the link between print and witch-hunting, see Stuart Clark, *Thinking with Demons: The Idea of Witchcraft in Early Modern Europe* (Oxford: Clarendon Press, 1997).

77. Brian P. Levack, introduction to *Oxford Handbook of Witchcraft,* 1–10n13; Henry Boguet, *An Examen of Witches Drawn from Various Trials of Many of This Sect in the District of Saint Oyan de Joux, Commonly Known as Saint Claude, in the County of Burgundy, Including the Procedure Necessary to a Judge in Trials for Witchcraft,* trans. Montague Summers and E. Allen Ashwin (London: J. Rodker, 1929), xxxii.

78. James Sharpe, *Witchcraft in Early Modern England,* 2nd ed. (New York: Routledge, 2019), 5.

79. Robert S. Walinski-Kiehl, "The Devil's Children: Child Witch-Trials in Early Modern Germany," *Continuity and Change* 11, no. 2 (1996): 171–89; William Monter, "Witchcraft in Iberia," in Levack, *Oxford Handbook of Witchcraft,* 268–82.

80. Sprenger, *Malleus Maleficarum,* 223–24.

81. Michael Kunze, *Highroad to the Stake: A Tale of Witchcraft* (Chicago: University of Chicago Press, 1989), 87.

82. For all details of the case, see ibid. For the execution, see also Robert E. Butts, "De Praestigiis Daemonum: Early Modern Witchcraft: Some Philosophical Reflections," in *Witches, Scientists, Philosophers: Essays and Lectures,* ed. Graham Solomon (Dordrecht: Springer Netherlands, 2000), 14–15.

83. Gareth Medway, *Lure of the Sinister: The Unnatural History of Satanism* (New York: New York University Press, 2001); Broedel, *"Malleus Maleficarum" and the Construction of Witchcraft;* David Pickering, *Cassell's Dictionary of Witchcraft* (London: Cassell, 2003).

84. Gary K. Waite, "Sixteenth-Century Religious Reform and the Witch-Hunts," in Levack, *Oxford Handbook of Witchcraft,* 499.

85. Mark Häberlein and Johannes Staudenmaier, "Bamberg," in *Handbuch kultureller Zentren der Frühen Neuzeit: Städte und Residenzen im alten deutschen Sprachraum,* ed. Wolfgang Adam and Siegrid Westphal (Berlin: De Gruyter, 2013), 57.

86. Birke Griesshammer, *Angeklagt—gemartet—verbrannt: Die Opfer der Hexenverfolgung in Franken* [Accused—martyred—burned: The victims of witch hunts in Franconia] (Erfurt, Germany: Sutton, 2013), 43.

87. Wolfgang Behringer, *Witches and Witch-Hunts: A Global History* (Cambridge, U.K.: Polity Press, 2004), 150; Griesshammer, *Angeklagt—gemartet—verbrannt,* 43; Arnold Scheuerbrandt, *Südwestdeutsche Stadttypen und Städtegruppen bis zum frühen 19. Jahrhundert: Ein Beitrag zur Kulturlandschaftsgeschichte und zur kulturräumlichen Gliederung des nördlichen Baden-Württemberg und seiner Nachbargebiete* (Heidelberg, Germany: Selbstverlag des Geographischen Instituts der Universität, 1972), 383.

88. Robert Rapley, *Witch Hunts: From Salem to Guantanamo Bay* (Montreal: McGill-Queen's University Press, 2007), 22–23.

89. Gustav Henningsen, *The Witches' Advocate: Basque Witchcraft and the Spanish Inquisition, 1609–1614* (Reno: University of Nevada Press, 1980), 304, ix.

90. Arthur Koestler, *The Sleepwalkers: A History of Man's Changing Vision of the Universe* (London: Penguin Books, 2014), 168.

91. Yuval Noah Harari, *Sapiens: A Brief History of Humankind* (New York: Harper, 2015), chap. 14.

92. See, for example, Dan Ariely, *Misbelief: What Makes Rational People Believe Irrational Things* (New York: Harper, 2023), 145.

93. Rebecca J. St. George and Richard C. Fitzpatrick, "The Sense of Self-Motion, Orientation, and Balance Explored by Vestibular Stimulation," *Journal of Physiology* 589, no. 4 (2011): 807–13; Jarett Casale et al., "Physiology, Vestibular System," in *StatPearls* (Treasure Island, Fla.: StatPearls Publishing, 2023).

94. Younghoon Kwon et al., "Blood Pressure Monitoring in Sleep: Time to Wake Up," *Blood Pressure Monitoring* 25, no. 2 (2020): 61–68; Darae Kim and Jong-Won Ha, "Hypertensive Response to Exercise: Mechanisms and Clinical Implication," *Clinical Hypertension* 22, no. 1 (2016): 17.

95. Gianfranco Parati et al., "Blood Pressure Variability: Its Relevance for Cardiovascular Homeostasis and Cardiovascular Diseases," *Hypertension Research* 43, no. 7 (2020): 609–20.

96. "Unitatis redintegratio" (Decree on Ecumenism), Second Vatican Council, Nov. 21, 1964, www.vatican.va/archive/hist_councils/ii_vatican_council /documents/vat-ii_decree_19641121_unitatis-redintegratio_en.html.

97. Rabbi Moses ben Nahman (ca. 1194–1270), Commentary on Deuteronomy 17:11.
98. Ṣaḥīḥ al-Tirmidhī, 2167; Mairaj Syed, "Ijmaʿ," in *The Oxford Handbook of Islamic Law,* ed. Anver M. Emon and Rumee Ahmed (Oxford: Oxford University Press, 2018), 271–98; Iysa A. Bello, "The Development of Ijmāʿ in Islamic Jurisprudence During the Classical Period," in *The Medieval Islamic Controversy Between Philosophy and Orthodoxy: Ijmāʿ and Ta'Wīl in the Conflict Between al-Ghazālī and Ibn Rushd* (Leiden: Brill, 1989), 17–28.
99. "Pastor aeternus," First Vatican Council, July 18, 1870, www.vatican.va /content/pius-ix/en/documents/constitutio-dogmatica-pastor-aeternus-18 -iulii-1870.html; "The Pope Is Never Wrong: A History of Papal Infallibility in the Catholic Church," University of Reading, Jan. 10, 2019, research .reading.ac.uk/research-blog/pope-never-wrong-history-papal-infallibility -catholic-church/; Hermann J. Pottmeyer, "Infallibility," in *Encyclopedia of Christianity Online* (Leiden: Brill, 2011).
100. Rory Carroll, "Pope Says Sorry for Sins of Church," *Guardian,* March 13, 2000, www.theguardian.com/world/2000/mar/13/catholicism.religion.
101. Leyland Cecco, "Pope Francis 'Begs Forgiveness' over Abuse at Church Schools in Canada," *Guardian,* July 26, 2022, www.theguardian.com/world /2022/jul/25/pope-francis-apologizes-for-abuse-at-church-schools-on-visit -to-canada.
102. On institutional church sexism, see April D. DeConick, *Holy Misogyny: Why the Sex and Gender Conflicts in the Early Church Still Matter* (New York: Continuum, 2011); Jack Holland, *A Brief History of Misogyny: The World's Oldest Prejudice* (London: Robinson, 2006), chaps. 3, 4, and 8; Elisabeth Schüssler Fiorenza, *In Memory of Her: A Feminist Theological Reconstruction of Christian Origins* (New York: Crossroad, 1994). On antisemitism, see Robert Michael, *Holy Hatred: Christianity, Antisemitism, and the Holocaust* (New York: Palgrave Macmillan, 2006), 17–19; Robert Michael, *A History of Catholic Antisemitism: The Dark Side of the Church* (New York: Palgrave Macmillan, 2008); James Carroll, *Constantine's Sword: The Church and the Jews* (Boston: Houghton Mifflin, 2002), 91–93. On intolerance in the Gospels, see Gerd Lüdemann, *Intolerance and the Gospel: Selected Texts from the New Testament* (Amherst, N.Y.: Prometheus Books, 2007); Graham Stanton and Guy G. Stroumsa, eds., *Tolerance and Intolerance in Early Judaism and Christianity* (Cambridge, U.K.: Cambridge University Press, 1998), esp. 124–31.
103. Edward Peters, ed., *Heresy and Authority in Medieval Europe* (Philadelphia: University of Pennsylvania Press, 2011), chap. 6.
104. Diana Hayes, "Reflections on Slavery," in *Change in Official Catholic Moral Teaching,* ed. Charles E. Curran (New York: Paulist Press, 1998), 67.
105. Associated Press, "Pope Francis Suggests Gay Couples Could Be Blessed in Vatican Reversal," *Guardian,* Oct. 3, 2023, www.theguardian.com/world /2023/oct/03/pope-francis-suggests-gay-couples-could-be-blessed-in -vatican-reversal.
106. Robert Rynasiewicz, "Newton's Views on Space, Time, and Motion," in *Stanford Encyclopedia of Philosophy,* ed. Edward N. Zalta, Spring 2022 (Palo Alto, Calif.: Metaphysics Research Lab, Stanford University, 2022).
107. See, for example, Sandra Harding, ed., *The Postcolonial Science and Technology Studies Reader* (Durham, N.C.: Duke University Press, 2011); Agustín Fuentes et al., "AAPA Statement on Race and Racism," *American Journal of Physi-*

cal Anthropology 169, no. 3 (2019): 400–402; Michael L. Blakey, "Understanding Racism in Physical (Biological) Anthropology," *American Journal of Physical Anthropology* 175, no. 2 (2021): 316–25; Allan M. Brandt, "Racism and Research: The Case of the Tuskegee Syphilis Study," *Hastings Center Report* 8, no. 6 (1978): 21–29; Alison Bashford, "'Is White Australia Possible?': Race, Colonialism, and Tropical Medicine," *Ethnic and Racial Studies* 23, no. 2 (2000): 248–71; Eric Ehrenreich, *The Nazi Ancestral Proof: Genealogy, Racial Science, and the Final Solution* (Bloomington: Indiana University Press, 2007).

108. Jack Drescher, "Out of DSM: Depathologizing Homosexuality," *Behavioral Sciences* 5, no. 4 (2015): 565–75; Sarah Baughey-Gill, "When Gay Was Not Okay with the APA: A Historical Overview of Homosexuality and Its Status as Mental Disorder," *Occam's Razor* 1 (2011): 13.

109. Shaena Montanari, "Debate Remains over Changes in DSM-5 a Decade On," *Spectrum*, May 31, 2023.

110. Ian Fisher and Rachel Donadio, "Benedict XVI, First Modern Pope to Resign, Dies at 95," *New York Times*, Dec. 31, 2022, www.nytimes.com/2022/12 /31/world/europe/benedict-xvi-dead.html; "Chief Rabbinate Rejects Mixed Male-Female Prayer at Western Wall," *Israel Hayom*, June 19, 2017, www .israelhayom.co.il/article/484687; Saeid Golkar, "Iran After Khamenei: Prospects for Political Change," *Middle East Policy* 26, no. 1 (2019): 75–88.

111. See, for example, Kathleen Stock, *Material Girls: Why Reality Matters for Feminism* (London: Fleet, 2021), for her ordeal brought about by criticizing current mainstream opinions in gender studies; and Klaus Taschwer, *The Case of Paul Kammerer: The Most Controversial Biologist of His Time*, trans. Michal Schwartz (Montreal: Bunim & Bannigan, 2019), for the accusations made against Paul Kammerer regarding his experiments that seemed to contradict the contemporary orthodoxy regarding inheritance.

112. D. Shechtman et al., "Metallic Phase with Long-Range Orientational Order and No Translational Symmetry," *Physical Review Letters* 53 (1984): 1951–54.

113. For accounts of the discovery of quasicrystals and accompanying controversy, see Alok Jha, "Dan Shechtman: 'Linus Pauling Said I Was Talking Nonsense,'" *Guardian*, Jan. 6, 2013, www.theguardian.com/science/2013/jan/06 /dan-shechtman-nobel-prize-chemistry-interview; Nobel Prize, "A Remarkable Mosaic of Atoms," Oct. 5, 2011, www.nobelprize.org/prizes/chemistry /2011/press-release/; Denis Gratias and Marianne Quiquandon, "Discovery of Quasicrystals: The Early Days," *Comptes Rendus Physique* 20, no. 7–8 (2019): 803–16; Dan Shechtman, "The Discovery of Quasi-Periodic Materials," Lindau Nobel Laureate Meetings, July 5, 2012, mediatheque.lindau -nobel.org/recordings/31562/the-discovery-of-quasi-periodic-materials -2012.

114. Patrick Lannin and Veronica Ek, "Ridiculed Crystal Work Wins Nobel for Israeli," Reuters, Oct. 6, 2011, www.reuters.com/article/idUSTRE7941EP/.

115. Vadim Birstein, *The Perversion of Knowledge: The True Story of Soviet Science* (Boulder, Colo.: Westview Press, 2001).

116. Ibid., 209–41, 394, 401, 402, 428.

117. Ibid., 247–55, 270–76; Nikolai Krementsov, "A 'Second Front' in Soviet Genetics: The International Dimension of the Lysenko Controversy, 1944– 1947," *Journal of the History of Biology* 29, no. 2 (1996): 229–50.

CHAPTER 5: DECISIONS

1. For an in-depth discussion of information flows in authoritarian networks, see Jeremy L. Wallace, *Seeking Truth and Hiding Facts: Information, Ideology, and Authoritarianism in China* (Oxford: Oxford University Press, 2022).

2. Fergus Millar, *The Emperor in the Roman World, 31 BC–AD 337* (Ithaca, N.Y.: Cornell University Press, 1977); Richard J. A. Talbert, *The Senate of Imperial Rome* (Princeton, N.J.: Princeton University Press, 2022); J. A. Crook, "Augustus: Power, Authority, Achievement," in *The Cambridge Ancient History*, vol. 10, *The Augustan Empire, 43 BC–AD 69*, ed. Alan K. Bowman, Andrew Lintott, and Edward Champlin (Cambridge, U.K.: Cambridge University Press, 1996), 113–46.

3. Peter H. Solomon, *Soviet Criminal Justice Under Stalin* (Cambridge, U.K.: Cambridge University Press, 1996); Stephen Kotkin, *Stalin: Waiting for Hitler, 1929–1941* (New York: Penguin Press, 2017), 330–33, 371–73, 477–80.

4. Jenny White, "Democracy Is Like a Tram," Turkey Institute, July 14, 2016, www.turkeyinstitute.org.uk/commentary/democracy-like-tram/.

5. Müller, *What Is Populism?*; Masha Gessen, *The Future Is History: How Totalitarianism Reclaimed Russia* (New York: Riverhead Books, 2017); Steven Levitsky and Daniel Ziblatt, *How Democracies Die* (New York: Crown, 2018); Timothy Snyder, *The Road to Unfreedom: Russia, Europe, America* (New York: Crown, 2018); Gideon Rachman, *The Age of the Strongman: How the Cult of the Leader Threatens Democracy Around the World* (New York: Other Press, 2022).

6. H.J.Res.114–107th Congress (2001–2002): Authorization for Use of Military Force Against Iraq Resolution of 2002, Congress.gov, Oct. 16, 2002, www.congress.gov/bill/107th-congress/house-joint-resolution/114.

7. Frank Newport, "Seventy-Two Percent of Americans Support War Against Iraq," Gallup, March 24, 2003, news.gallup.com/poll/8038/SeventyTwo-Percent-Americans-Support-War-Against-Iraq.aspx.

8. "Poll: Iraq War Based on Falsehoods," UPI, Aug. 20, 2004, www.upi.com/Top_News/2004/08/20/Poll-Iraq-war-based-on-falsehoods/75591093019554/.

9. James Eaden and David Renton, *The Communist Party of Great Britain Since 1920* (London: Palgrave, 2002), 96; Ian Beesley, *The Official History of the Cabinet Secretaries* (London: Routledge, 2017), 47.

10. Müller, *What Is Populism?*, 34.

11. Ibid., 3.

12. Ibid., 3–4, 20–22.

13. Ralph Hassig and Kongdan Oh, *The Hidden People of North Korea: Everyday Life in the Hermit Kingdom* (Lanham, Md.: Rowman & Littlefield, 2015); Seol Song Ah, "Inside North Korea's Supreme People's Assembly," *Guardian*, April 22, 2014, www.theguardian.com/world/2014/apr/22/inside-north-koreas-supreme-peoples-assembly.

14. Andrei Lankov, *The Real North Korea: Life and Politics in the Failed Stalinist Utopia* (Oxford: Oxford University Press, 2013).

15. Graeber and Wengrow, *Dawn of Everything*, chaps. 2–5.

16. Ibid., chaps. 3–5; Bellah, *Religion in Human Evolution*, 117–209; Pierre Clastres, *Society Against the State: Essays in Political Anthropology* (New York: Zone Books, 1988).

17. Michael L. Ross, *The Oil Curse: How Petroleum Wealth Shapes the Development of Nations* (Princeton, N.J.: Princeton University Press, 2013); Leif Wenar, *Blood Oil: Tyrants, Violence, and the Rules That Run the World* (Oxford: Oxford University Press, 2015); Karen Dawisha, *Putin's Kleptocracy: Who Owns Russia?* (New York: Simon & Schuster, 2014).

18. Graeber and Wengrow, *Dawn of Everything,* chaps. 3–5; Eric Alden Smith and Brian F. Codding, "Ecological Variation and Institutionalized Inequality in Hunter-Gatherer Societies," *Proceedings of the National Academy of Sciences* 118, no. 13 (2021).

19. James Woodburn, "Egalitarian Societies," *Man* 17, no. 3 (1982): 431–51.

20. Graeber and Wengrow, *Dawn of Everything,* chaps. 3–5; Bellah, *Religion in Human Evolution,* chaps. 3–5. For a discussion of information flows among the Kope—a tribe in Papua New Guinea of about five thousand people subsisting in part by hunting and foraging and in part by farming—see Madden, Bryson, and Palimi, "Information Behavior in Pre-literate Societies."

21. For the claim that Mesopotamian city-states like Uruk were occasionally democratic, see Graeber and Wengrow, *Dawn of Everything.*

22. John Thorley, *Athenian Democracy* (London: Routledge, 2005), 74; Nancy Evans, *Civic Rites: Democracy and Religion in Ancient Athens* (Berkeley: University of California Press, 2010), 16.

23. Thorley, *Athenian Democracy;* Evans, *Civic Rites,* 79.

24. Millar, *Emperor in the Roman World;* Talbert, *Senate of Imperial Rome.*

25. Kyle Harper, *The Fate of Rome: Climate, Disease, and the End of an Empire* (Princeton, N.J.: Princeton University Press, 2017), 30–31; Walter Scheidel, "Demography," in *The Cambridge Economic History of the Greco-Roman World,* ed. Ian Morris, Richard P. Saller, and Walter Scheidel (Cambridge, U.K.: Cambridge University Press, 2007), 38–86.

26. Vladimir G. Lukonin, "Political, Social, and Administrative Institutions, Taxes, and Trade," in *The Cambridge History of Iran: Seleucid Parthian,* vol. 3, *The Seleucid, Parthian, and Sasanid Periods,* ed. Ehsan Yarshater (Cambridge, U.K.: Cambridge University Press, 1983), 681–746; Gene R. Garthwaite, *The Persians* (Malden, Mass.: Wiley-Blackwell, 2005).

27. It was 390 BCE according to the traditional Varronian chronology, but 387 or 386 BCE is more likely. See Tim Cornell, *The Beginnings of Rome: Italy and Rome from the Bronze Age to the Punic Wars (c. 1000–264 B.C.)* (London: Routledge, 1995), 313–14. The details of this episode are given in Livy, *History of Rome,* 5:34–6:1, and Plutarch, *Camillus,* 17–31. For a discussion of the role of dictator, see Andrew Lintott, *The Constitution of the Roman Republic* (Oxford: Oxford University Press, 2003), and Hannah J. Swithinbank, "Dictator," in *The Encyclopedia of Ancient History,* ed. Roger S. Bagnall et al. (Malden, Mass.: John Wiley & Sons, 2012).

28. Harper, *Fate of Rome,* 30–31; Scheidel, "Demography."

29. Rein Taagepera, "Size and Duration of Empires: Growth-Decline Curves, 600 B.C. to 600 A.D.," *Social Science History* 3, no. 3/4 (1979): 115–38.

30. William V. Harris, *Ancient Literacy* (Cambridge, Mass.: Harvard University Press, 1989), 141, 267.

31. Theodore P. Lianos, "Aristotle on Population Size," *History of Economic Ideas* 24, no. 2 (2016): 11–26; Plato B. Jowett, "Plato on Population and the State," *Population and Development Review* 12, no. 4 (1986): 781–98; Theodore Lia-

nos, "Population and Steady-State Economy in Plato and Aristotle," *Journal of Population and Sustainability* 7, no. 1 (2023): 123–38.

32. See Gregory S. Aldrete and Alicia Aldrete, "Power to the People: Systems of Government," in *The Long Shadow of Antiquity: What Have the Greeks and Romans Done for Us?* (London: Continuum, 2012). See also Eeva-Maria Viitanen and Laura Nissin, "Campaigning for Votes in Ancient Pompeii: Contextualizing Electoral Programmata," in *Writing Matters: Presenting and Perceiving Monumental Inscriptions in Antiquity and the Middle Ages*, ed. Irene Berti et al. (Berlin: De Gruyter, 2017), 117–44; Willem Jongman, *The Economy and Society of Pompeii* (Leiden: Brill, 2023).

33. Aldrete and Aldrete, *Long Shadow of Antiquity*, 129–66.

34. Roger Bartlett, *A History of Russia* (Houndsmills, U.K.: Palgrave, 2005), 98–99; David Moon, "Peasants and Agriculture," in *The Cambridge History of Russia*, ed. Dominic Lieven (Cambridge, U.K.: Cambridge University Press, 2006), 369–93; Richard Pipes, *Russia Under the Old Regime*, 2nd ed. (London: Penguin, 1995), 18; Peter Toumanoff, "The Development of the Peasant Commune in Russia," *Journal of Economic History* 41, no. 1 (1981): 179–84; William G. Rosenberg, "Review of *Understanding Peasant Russia*," *Comparative Studies in Society and History* 35, no. 4 (1993): 840–49. But for the dangers of idealizing these communes as democratic models, see T. K. Dennison and A. W. Carus, "The Invention of the Russian Rural Commune: Haxthausen and the Evidence," *Historical Journal* 46, no. 3 (2003): 561–82.

35. Andrew Wilson, "City Sizes and Urbanization in the Roman Empire," in *Settlement, Urbanization, and Population*, ed. Alan Bowman and Andrew Wilson (New York: Oxford University Press), 171–72.

36. This is a rough estimate. Scholars lack detailed population data for early modern Poland and work on the assumption that about half the Polish population were adults and half of the adults male. Regarding *szlachta* population, Urszula Augustyniak estimates it at 8–10 percent of the total population in the second half of the eighteenth century. See Jacek Jedruch, *Constitutions, Elections, and Legislatures of Poland, 1493–1977: A Guide to Their History* (Washington, D.C.: University Press of America, 1982), 448–49; Urszula Augustyniak, *Historia Polski, 1572–1795* (Warsaw: Wydawnictwo Naukowe PWN, 2008), 253, 256; Norman Davies, *God's Playground: A History of Poland*, vol. 1, *The Origins to 1795* (New York: Columbia University Press, 1981), 214–15; Aleksander Gella, *Development of Class Structure in Eastern Europe: Poland and Her Southern Neighbors* (Albany: State University of New York Press, 1989), 13; Felicia Roşu, *Elective Monarchy in Transylvania and Poland-Lithuania, 1569–1587* (New York: Oxford University Press, 2017), 20.

37. Augustyniak, *Historia Polski*, 537–38; Roşu, *Elective Monarchy in Transylvania and Poland-Lithuania*, 149n29. Some sources give much higher figures, around 40,000–50,000. See Robert Bideleux and Ian Jeffries, *A History of Eastern Europe: Crisis and Change* (New York: Routledge, 2007), 177, and W. F. Reddaway et al., eds., *Cambridge History of Poland: From the Origins to Sobieski* (Cambridge, U.K.: Cambridge University Press, 1971), 371.

38. Davies, *God's Playground*; Roşu, *Elective Monarchy in Transylvania and Poland-Lithuania*; Jedruch, *Constitutions, Elections, and Legislatures of Poland*.

39. Davies, *God's Playground*, 190.

40. Peter J. Taylor, "Ten Years That Shook the World? The United Provinces as

First Hegemonic State," *Sociological Perspectives* 37, no. 1 (1994): 25–46, doi .org/10.2307/1389408; Jonathan Israel, *The Dutch Republic: Its Rise, Greatness, and Fall, 1477–1806* (Oxford: Clarendon Press, 1995).

41. For discussions of the democratic characteristics of the early modern Netherlands, see Maarten Prak, *The Dutch Republic in the Seventeenth Century*, trans. Diane Webb (Cambridge, U.K.: Cambridge University Press, 2023); J. L. Price, *Holland and the Dutch Republic in the Seventeenth Century: The Politics of Particularism* (Oxford: Clarendon Press, 1994); Catherine Secretan, "'True Freedom' and the Dutch Tradition of Republicanism," *Republics of Letters: A Journal for the Study of Knowledge, Politics, and the Arts* 2, no. 1 (2010): 82–92; Henk te Velde, "The Emergence of the Netherlands as a 'Democratic' Country," *Journal of Modern European History* 17, no. 2 (2019): 161–70; Maarten F. Van Dijck, "Democracy and Civil Society in the Early Modern Period: The Rise of Three Types of Civil Societies in the Spanish Netherlands and the Dutch Republic," *Social Science History* 41, no. 1 (2017): 59–81; Remieg Aerts, "Civil Society or Democracy? A Dutch Paradox," *BMGN: Low Countries Historical Review* 125 (2010): 209–36.

42. Michiel van Groesen, "Reading Newspapers in the Dutch Golden Age," *Media History* 22, no. 3–4 (2016): 334–52, doi.org/10.1080/13688804.2016 .1229121; Arthur der Weduwen, *Dutch and Flemish Newspapers of the Seventeenth Century, 1618–1700* (Leiden: Brill, 2017), 181–259; "Courante," Gemeente Amsterdam Stadsarchief, April 23, 2019, www.amsterdam.nl /stadsarchief/stukken/historie/courante/.

43. van Groesen, "Reading Newspapers in the Dutch Golden Age." Newspapers appeared around the same time also in Strasbourg, Basel, Frankfurt, Hamburg, and various other European cities.

44. Jürgen Habermas, *The Structural Transformation of the Public Sphere: An Inquiry into a Category of Bourgeois Society*, trans. Thomas Burger (Cambridge, U.K.: Polity Press, 1989); Benedict Anderson, *Imagined Communities: Reflections on the Origin and Spread of Nationalism* (London: Verso, 2006), 24–25; Andrew Pettegree, *The Invention of News: How the World Came to Know About Itself* (New Haven, Conn.: Yale University Press, 2014).

45. In 1828, there were 863 newspapers printing about sixty-eight million copies a year. See William A. Dill, *Growth of Newspapers in the United States* (Lawrence: University of Kansas Department of Journalism, 1928), 11–15. See also Paul E. Ried, "The First and Fifth Boylston Professors: A View of Two Worlds," *Quarterly Journal of Speech* 74, no. 2 (1988): 229–40, doi.org/10.1080 /00335638809383838; Lynn Hudson Parsons, *The Birth of Modern Politics: Andrew Jackson, John Quincy Adams, and the Election of 1828* (New York: Oxford University Press, 2009), 134–35.

46. Parsons, *Birth of Modern Politics*, 90–107; H. G. Good, "To the Future Biographers of John Quincy Adams," *Scientific Monthly* 39, no. 3 (1934): 247–51, www.jstor.org/stable/15715; Robert V. Remini, *Martin Van Buren and the Making of the Democratic Party* (New York: Columbia University Press, 1959); Charles N. Edel, *Nation Builder: John Quincy Adams and the Grand Strategy of the Republic* (Cambridge, Mass.: Harvard University Press, 2014).

47. Alexander Saxton, "Problems of Class and Race in the Origins of the Mass Circulation Press," *American Quarterly* 36, no. 2 (Summer 1984): 211–34.

48. "Presidential Election of 1824: A Resource Guide," Library of Congress, accessed Jan. 1, 2024, guides.loc.gov/presidential-election-1824/; "Bicentennial

Edition: Historical Statistics of the United States, Colonial Times to 1970," U.S. Census Bureau, Sept. 1975, accessed Dec. 30, 2023, www.census.gov /library/publications/1975/compendia/hist_stats_colonial-1970.html; Charles Tilly, *Democracy* (Cambridge, U.K.: Cambridge University Press, 2007), 97–98. For information on the number of eligible voters in 1824, see Jerry L. Mashaw, *Creating the Administrative Constitution: The Lost One Hundred Years of American Administrative Law* (New Haven, Conn.: Yale University Press, 2012), 148; Ronald P. Formisano, *For the People: American Populist Movements from the Revolution to the 1850s* (Chapel Hill: University of North Carolina Press, 2008), 142. Note that the percentages represent estimates, depending on how exactly one defines adulthood.

49. Colin Rallings and Michael Thrasher, *British Electoral Facts, 1832–2012* (Hull: Biteback, 2012), 87; John A. Phillips, *The Great Reform Bill in the Boroughs* (Oxford: Clarendon Press, 1992), 29–30; Edward Hicks, "Uncontested Elections: Where and Why Do They Take Place?," House of Commons Library, April 30, 2019, commonslibrary.parliament.uk/uncontested-elections -where-and-why-do-they-take-place/. The U.K. census information comes from *Abstract of the Answers and Returns Made Pursuant to an Act: Passed in the Eleventh Year of the Reign of His Majesty King George IV* (London: House of Commons, 1833), xii. Available to read here: www.google.co.uk/books /edition/_/zQFDAAAAcAAJ?hl=en&gbpv=0. Pre-1841 census information is available at 1841census.co.uk/pre-1841-census-information/.

50. "Census for 1820," U.S. Census Bureau, accessed Dec. 30, 2023, www.census .gov/library/publications/1821/dec/1820a.html.

51. For various views about the democratic nature of the early United States, see Danielle Allen, "Democracy vs. Republic," in *Democracies in America*, ed. Berton Emerson and Gregory Laski (New York: Oxford University Press, 2022), 17–23; Daniel Walker Howe, *What Hath God Wrought: The Transformation of America, 1815–1848* (New York: Oxford University Press, 2007).

52. "The Heroes of July," *New York Times*, Nov. 20, 1863, www.nytimes.com/1863 /11/20/archives/the-heroes-of-july-a-solemn-and-imposing-event -dedication-of-the.html.

53. Abraham Lincoln and William H. Lambert, "The Gettysburg Address. When Written, How Received, Its True Form," *Pennsylvania Magazine of History and Biography* 33, no. 4 (1909): 385–408, www.jstor.org/stable /20085482; Ronald F. Reid, "Newspaper Response to the Gettysburg Addresses," *Quarterly Journal of Speech* 53, no. 1 (1967): 50–60.

54. William Hanchett, "Abraham Lincoln and Father Abraham," *North American Review* 251, no. 2 (1966): 10–13, www.jstor.org/stable/25116343; Benjamin P. Thomas, *Abraham Lincoln: A Biography* (Carbondale: Southern Illinois University Press, 2008), 403.

55. Martin Pengelly, "Pennsylvania Newspaper Retracts 1863 Criticism of Gettysburg Address," *Guardian*, Nov. 16, 2013, www.theguardian.com/world /2013/nov/16/gettysburg-address-retraction-newspaper-lincoln.

56. "Poll Shows 4th Debate Had Largest Audience," *New York Times*, Oct. 22, 1960, www.nytimes.com/1960/10/22/archives/poll-shows-4th-debate-had -largest-audience.html; Lionel C. Barrow Jr., "Factors Related to Attention to the First Kennedy-Nixon Debate," *Journal of Broadcasting* 5, no. 3 (1961): 229–38, doi.org/10.1080/088381561093859691961; Vito N. Silvestri, "Television's Interface with Kennedy, Nixon, and Trump: Two Politicians and One

TV Celebrity," *American Behavioral Scientist* 63, no. 7 (2019): 971–1001, doi .org/10.1177/0002764218784992. U.S. population in the census of 1960 was 179,323,175. See "1960 Census of Population: Advance Reports, Final Population Counts," U.S. Census Bureau, Nov. 15, 1960, www.census.gov/library /publications/1960/dec/population-pc-a1.html.

57. "National Turnout Rates, 1789–Present," U.S. Elections Project, accessed Jan. 2, 2024, www.electproject.org/national-1789-present; Renalia DuBose, "Voter Suppression: A Recent Phenomenon or an American Legacy?," *University of Baltimore Law Review* 50, no. 2 (2021), article 2.

58. Much of the following discussion of totalitarianism relies on classical studies of the phenomenon: Hannah Arendt, *The Origins of Totalitarianism* (New York: Harcourt, 1973); Carl Joachim Friedrich and Zbigniew Brzezinski, *Totalitarian Dictatorship and Autocracy* (Cambridge, Mass.: Harvard University Press, 1965); Karl R. Popper, *The Open Society and Its Enemies* (Princeton, N.J.: Princeton University Press, 1945); Juan José Linz, *Totalitarian and Authoritarian Regimes* (Boulder, Colo.: Lynne Rienner, 1975). I have also referred to more recent interpretations, notably Gessen, *Future Is History,* and Marlies Glasius, "What Authoritarianism Is . . . and Is Not: A Practice Perspective," *International Affairs* 94, no. 3 (2018): 515–33.

59. Vasily Rudich, *Political Dissidence Under Nero* (London: Routledge, 1993), xxx.

60. See, for example, Tacitus, *Annals,* 14.60. See also John F. Drinkwater, *Nero: Emperor and Court* (Cambridge, U.K.: Cambridge University Press, 2019); T. E. J. Wiedemann, "Tiberius to Nero," in Bowman, Champlin, and Lintott, *Cambridge Ancient History,* 198–255.

61. Carlos F. Noreña, "Nero's Imperial Administration," in *The Cambridge Companion to the Age of Nero,* ed. Shadi Bartsch, Kirk Freudenburg, and Cedric Littlewood (Cambridge, U.K.: Cambridge University Press, 2017), 48–62.

62. The figure includes both legionnaires and auxiliaries. See Nigel Pollard, "The Roman Army," in *A Companion to the Roman Empire,* ed. David Potter (Malden, Mass.: Blackwell, 2010), 206–27; Noreña, "Nero's Imperial Administration," 51.

63. Fik Meijer, *Emperors Don't Die in Bed* (London: Routledge, 2004); Joseph Homer Saleh, "Statistical Reliability Analysis for a Most Dangerous Occupation: Roman Emperor," *Palgrave Communications* 5, no. 155 (2019), doi.org /10.1057/s41599-019-0366-y; Francois Retief and Louise Cilliers, "Causes of Death Among the Caesars (27 BC–AD 476)," *Acta Theologica* 26, no. 2 (2010), www.doi.org/10.4314/actat.v26i2.52565.

64. Millar, *Emperor in the Roman World.* See also Peter Eich, "Center and Periphery: Administrative Communication in Roman Imperial Times," in *Rome, a City and Its Empire in Perspective: The Impact of the Roman World Through Fergus Millar's Research,* ed. Stéphane Benoist (Leiden: Brill, 2012), 85–108; Benjamin Kelly, *Petitions, Litigation, and Social Control in Roman Egypt* (New York: Oxford University Press, 2011); Harry Sidebottom, *The Mad Emperor: Heliogabalus and the Decadence of Rome* (London: Oneworld, 2023).

65. Paul Cartledge, *The Spartans: The World of the Warrior-Heroes of Ancient Greece, from Utopia to Crisis and Collapse* (New York: Vintage Books, 2004); Stephen Hodkinson, "Sparta: An Exceptional Domination of State over Society?," in *A Companion to Sparta,* ed. Anton Powell (Hoboken, N.J.: Wiley-Blackwell, 2017), 29–57; Anton Powell, "Sparta: Reconstructing History

from Secrecy, Lies, and Myth," in Powell, *Companion to Sparta*, 1–28; Michael Whitby, "Two Shadows: Images of Spartans and Helots," in *The Shadow of Sparta*, ed. Anton Powell and Stephen Hodkinson (London: Routledge, 2002), 87–126; M. G. L. Cooley, ed., *Sparta*, 2nd ed. (Cambridge, U.K.: Cambridge University Press, 2023), 146–225; Sean R. Jensen and Thomas J. Figueira, "Peloponnesian League," in Bagnall et al., *Encyclopedia of Ancient History;* D. M. Lewis, "Sparta as Victor," in *The Cambridge Ancient History*, ed. D. M. Lewis et al. (Cambridge, U.K.: Cambridge University Press, 1994), 24–44.

66. Mark Edward Lewis, *The Early Chinese Empires: Qin and Han* (Cambridge, Mass.: Harvard University Press, 2010), 109.

67. Fu, *China's Legalists*, 6, 12, 23, 28.

68. Xinzhong Yao, *An Introduction to Confucianism* (Cambridge, U.K.: Cambridge University Press, 2000), 55, 187–213; Chad Hansen, "Daoism," in *The Stanford Encyclopedia of Philosophy*, ed. Edward N. Zalta, Spring 2020, accessed Jan. 5, 2025, plato.stanford.edu/cgi-bin/encyclopedia/archinfo.cgi?entry=daoism.

69. Sima Qian, Raymond Dawson, and K. E. Brashier, *The First Emperor: Selections from the Historical Records* (Oxford: Oxford University Press, 2007), 74–75; Lewis, *Early Chinese Empires;* Frances Wood, *China's First Emperor and His Terra-Cotta Warriors* (New York: St. Martin's Press, 2008), 81–82; Sarah Allan, *Buried Ideas: Legends of Abdication and Ideal Government in Early Chinese Bamboo-Slip Manuscripts* (Albany: State University of New York Press, 2015), 22; Anthony J. Barbieri-Low, *The Many Lives of the First Emperor of China* (Seattle: University of Washington Press, 2022).

70. For this account of both the Qin and the Han Empires, see Lewis, *Early Chinese Empires*, chaps. 1–3; Julie M. Segraves, "China: Han Empire," in *The Oxford Companion to Archaeology*, vol. 1, ed. Neil Asher Silberman (New York: Oxford University Press, 2012); Robin D. S. Yates, "Social Status in the Ch'in: Evidence from the Yun-Men Legal Documents. Part One: Commoners," *Harvard Journal of Asiatic Studies* 47, no. 1 (1987): 197–237; Robin D. S. Yates, "State Control of Bureaucrats Under the Qin: Techniques and Procedures," *Early China* 20 (1995): 331–65; Ernest Caldwell, *Writing Chinese Laws: The Form and Function of Legal Statutes Found in the Qin Shuihudi Corpus* (London: Routledge, 2018); Anthony François Paulus Hulsewé, *Remnants of Ch'in Law: An Annotated Translation of the Ch'in Legal and Administrative Rules of the 3rd century BC Discovered in Yün-meng Prefecture, Hu-pei Province, in 1975* (Leiden: Brill, 1975); Sima Qian, *Records of the Grand Historian*, trans. Burton Watson (New York: Columbia University Press, 1993); Shang, *Book of Lord Shang;* Yuri Pines, "China, Imperial: 1. Qin Dynasty, 221–207 BCE," in *The Encyclopedia of Empire*, ed. N. Dalziel and John M. MacKenzie (Hoboken, N.J.: Wiley, 2016), doi.org/10.1002/9781118455074.wbeoe112; Hsing I-tien, "Qin-Han Census and Tax and Corvée Administration: Notes on Newly Discovered Materials," in *Birth of an Empire: The State of Qin Revisited*, ed. Yuri Pines et al. (Berkeley: University of California Press, 2014), 155–86; Charles Sanft, *Communication and Cooperation in Early Imperial China: Publicizing the Qin Dynasty* (Albany: State University of New York Press, 2014).

71. Kotkin, *Stalin*, 604.

72. McMeekin, *Stalin's War*, 220.

73. Thomas Henry Rigby, *Communist Party Membership in the U.S.S.R.* (Princeton, N.J.: Princeton University Press, 1968), 52.

74. Iu. A. Poliakov, ed., *Vsesoiuznaia perepis naseleniia, 1937 G.* (Institut istorii SSSR, 1991), 250. For the number of informants, ten million is given for 1951 in Jonathan Brent and Victor Naumov, *Stalin's Last Crime: The Plot Against the Jewish Doctors, 1948–1953* (New York: HarperCollins, 2003), 106.

75. Kotkin, *Stalin*, 888.

76. Stephan Wolf, *Hauptabteilung I: NVA und Grenztruppen* (Berlin: Bundesbeauftragte für die Stasi-Unterlagen, 2005); Dennis Deletant, "The Securitate Legacy in Romania," in *Security Intelligence Services in New Democracies: The Czech Republic, Slovakia, and Romania*, ed. Kieran Williams (London: Palgrave, 2001), 163.

77. Kotkin, *Stalin*, 378.

78. Ibid., 481.

79. Robert Conquest, *The Great Terror: Stalin's Purges of the Thirties* (New York: Collier, 1973), 632.

80. Survey of biographies in N. V. Petrov and K. V. Skorkin, *Kto rukovodil NKVD 1934–1941: Spravochnik* (Moscow: Zvenia, 1999), 80–464.

81. Julia Boyd, *A Village in the Third Reich: How Ordinary Lives Were Transformed by the Rise of Fascism* (New York: Pegasus Books, 2023), 75–84.

82. David Shearer, *Policing Stalin's Socialism: Repression and Social Order in the Soviet Union, 1924–1953* (New Haven, Conn.: Yale University Press, 2009), 133; Stephen Kotkin, *Magnetic Mountain: Stalinism as a Civilization* (Berkeley: University of California Press, 1995).

83. Robert William Davies, Mark Harrison, and S. G. Wheatcroft, eds., *The Economic Transformation of the Soviet Union, 1913–1945* (Cambridge, U.K.: Cambridge University Press, 1993), 63–91; Orlando Figes, *The Whisperers: Private Life in Stalin's Russia* (New York: Picador, 2007), 50.

84. Kotkin, *Stalin*, 16, 75; R. W. Davies and Stephen G. Wheatcroft, *The Years of Hunger: Soviet Agriculture, 1931–1933* (New York: Palgrave Macmillan, 2004), 447.

85. Davies and Wheatcroft, *Years of Hunger*, 446–48.

86. Kotkin, *Stalin*, 129; Figes, *Whisperers*, 98.

87. Figes, *Whisperers*, 85.

88. Kotkin, *Stalin*, 29, 42; Lynne Viola, *Unknown Gulag: The Lost World of Stalin's Peasant Settlements* (New York: Oxford University Press, 2007), 30.

89. On the historical context and significance of Stalin's speech, see Lynne Viola, "The Role of the OGPU in Dekulakization, Mass Deportations, and Special Resettlement in 1930," *Carl Beck Papers* 1406 (2000): 2–7; Kotkin, *Stalin*, 34–36.

90. As of January 1930, Soviet authorities aimed to finish collectivization (and with that dekulakization) in the key grain-producing regions by no later than the spring of 1931 and in the less important regions by no later than the spring of 1932. See Viola, *Unknown Gulag*, 21.

91. Ibid., 2 (description of commission); V. P. Danilov, ed., *Tragediia sovetskoi derevni: Kollektivizatsiia i raskulachivanie: Dokumenty i materialy, 1927–1939* (Moscow: ROSSPEN, 1999), 2:123–26 (draft resolution by commission stating 3–5 percent goal). For earlier estimates of kulaks, see Moshe Lewin, *Russian Peasants and Soviet Power: A Study of Collectivization* (New York: Norton,

1975), 71–78; Nikolai Shmelev and Vladimir Popov, *The Turning Point: Revitalizing the Soviet Economy* (New York: Doubleday, 1989), 48–49.

92. This decree is available in English in Lynne Viola et al., eds., *The War Against the Peasantry, 1927–1930: The Tragedy of the Soviet Countryside* (New Haven, Conn.: Yale University Press, 2005), 228–34.

93. Viola, *Unknown Gulag,* 22–24; James Hughes, *Stalinism in a Russian Province: Collectivization and Dekulakization in Siberia* (New York: Palgrave, 1996), 145–46, 239–40nn32 and 38, 151–53; Robert Conquest, *The Harvest of Sorrow: Soviet Collectivization and the Terror-Famine* (Oxford: Oxford University Press, 1986), 129; Figes, *Whisperers,* 87–88. On the inflation of numbers, see Figes, *Whisperers,* 87, and Hughes, *Stalinism in a Russian Province,* 153.

94. Conquest, *Harvest of Sorrow,* 129–31; Kotkin, *Stalin,* 74–75; Viola et al., *War Against the Peasantry,* 220–21; Lynne Viola, "The Second Coming: Class Enemies in the Soviet Countryside, 1927–1935," in *Stalinist Terror: New Perspectives,* ed. John Arch Getty and Roberta Thompson Manning (Cambridge, U.K.: Cambridge University Press, 1993), 65–98; Figes, *Whisperers,* 86–87; Sheila Fitzpatrick, *Stalin's Peasants: Resistance and Survival in the Russian Village After Collectivization* (New York: Oxford University Press, 1994), 55; Hughes, *Stalinism in a Russian Province,* 145–57, 239–40; Viola et al., *War Against the Peasantry,* 230–31, 240.

95. Figes, *Whisperers,* 88. Two hundred eighty-eight households lay within this rural soviet's jurisdiction. See *Naselennye punkty Ural'skoi oblasti,* vol. 7, *Kurganskii okrug* (Sverdlovsk, 1928), 70, elib.uraic.ru/bitstream/123456789/12391/1/0016895.pdf. A quota of 17 households from this rural soviet would have amounted to 5.9 percent of its households.

96. Kotkin, *Stalin,* 75. Some authors submit numbers as high as ten million peasants forced from their homes. See, for example, Norman M. Naimark, *Genocide: A World History* (New York: Oxford University Press, 2016), 87; Figes, *Whisperers,* 33.

97. Conquest, *Harvest of Sorrow,* 124–41; Fitzgerald, *Stalin's Peasants,* 123.

98. Figes, *Whisperers,* 142; Conquest, *Harvest of Sorrow,* 283–84; Viola, *Unknown Gulag,* 170–78.

99. Figes, *Whisperers,* 145–47.

100. Ibid., 122–29; Fitzpatrick, *Stalin's Peasants,* 255–56.

101. Conquest, *Harvest of Sorrow,* 295. The Reuters report from May 21, 1934, which Conquest cites, is available at archive.org/stream/NewsUK1996UKEnglish/May%2022%201996%2C%20The%20Times%2C%20%2365586%2C%20UK%20%28en%29_djvu.txt.

102. Robert W. Thurston, "Social Dimensions of Stalinist Rule: Humor and Terror in the USSR, 1935–1941," *Journal of Social History* 24, no. 3 (1991): 544.

103. Figes, *Whisperers,* xxxi.

104. I. S. Robinson, *Henry IV of Germany, 1056–1106* (Cambridge, U.K.: Cambridge University Press, 2009), 143–70; Uta-Renate Blumenthal, "Canossa and Royal Ideology in 1077: Two Unknown Manuscripts of *De penitentia regis Salomonis,*" *Manuscripta* 22, no. 2 (1978): 91–96.

105. Thomas F. X. Noble, "Iconoclasm, Images, and the West," in *A Companion to Byzantine Iconoclasm,* ed. Mike Humphreys (Leiden: Brill, 2021), 538–70; Marie-France Auzépy, "State of Emergency (700–850)," in *The Cambridge History of the Byzantine Empire, c. 500–1492,* ed. Jonathan Shepard (Cam-

bridge, U.K.: Cambridge University Press, 2010), 249–91; Mike Humphreys, introduction to *A Companion to Byzantine Iconoclasm,* ed. Mike Humphreys (Leiden: Brill, 2021), 1–106.

106. Theophanes, *Chronographia,* AM 6211, cited in Roman Cholij, *Theodore the Stoudite: The Ordering of Holiness* (New York: Oxford University Press, 2002), 12.

107. Peter Brown, "Introduction: Christendom, c. 600," in *The Cambridge History of Christianity,* vol. 3, *Early Medieval Christianities, c. 600–c. 1100,* ed. Thomas F. X. Noble and Julia M. H. Smith (Cambridge, U.K.: Cambridge University Press, 2008), 1–20; Miri Rubin and Walter Simons, introduction to *The Cambridge History of Christianity,* vol. 4, *Christianity in Western Europe, c. 1100–c. 1500,* ed. Miri Rubin and Walter Simons (Cambridge, U.K.: Cambridge University Press, 2009); Kevin Madigan, *Medieval Christianity: A New History* (New Haven, Conn.: Yale University Press, 2015), 80–94.

108. See, for example, Piotr Górecki, "Parishes, Tithes, and Society in Earlier Medieval Poland, c. 1100–c. 1250," *Transactions of the American Philosophical Society* 83, no. 2 (1993): i–146.

109. Marilyn J. Matelski, *Vatican Radio: Propagation by the Airwaves* (Westport, Conn.: Praeger, 1995); Raffaella Perin, *The Popes on Air: The History of Vatican Radio from Its Origins to World War II* (New York: Fordham University Press, 2024).

110. Jaroslav Hašek, *The Good Soldier Švejk,* trans. Cecil Parrott (London: Penguin, 1973), 258–62, 280.

111. Serhii Plokhy, *Atoms and Ashes: A Global History of Nuclear Disaster* (New York: W. W. Norton, 2022); Olga Bertelsen, "Secrecy and the Disinformation Campaign Surrounding Chernobyl," *International Journal of Intelligence and CounterIntelligence* 35, no. 2 (2022): 292–317; Edward Geist, "Political Fallout: The Failure of Emergency Management at Chernobyl," *Slavic Review* 74, no. 1 (2015): 104–26; "Das Reaktorunglück in Tschernobyl wird bekannt," *SWR Kultur,* April 28, 1986, www.swr.de/swr2/wissen/archivradio /das-reaktorunglueck-in-tschernobyl-wird-bekannt-100.html.

112. J. Samuel Walker, *Three Mile Island: A Nuclear Crisis in Historical Perspective* (Berkeley: University of California Press, 2004), 78–84; Plokhy, *Atoms and Ashes;* Edward J. Walsh, "Three Mile Island: Meltdown of Democracy?," *Bulletin of the Atomic Scientists* 39, no. 3 (1983): 57–60; Natasha Zaretsky, *Radiation Nation: Three Mile Island and the Political Transformation of the 1970s* (New York: Columbia University Press, 2018); U.S. President's Commission on the Accident at Three Mile, *Report of the President's Commission on the Accident at Three Mile Island: The Need for Change, the Legacy of TMI* (Washington, D.C.: U.S. Government Printing Office, 1979).

113. Christopher Carothers, "Taking Authoritarian Anti-corruption Reform Seriously," *Perspectives on Politics* 20, no. 1 (2022): 69–85; Kaunain Rahman, "An Overview of Corruption and Anti-corruption in Saudi Arabia," Transparency International, Jan. 23, 2020, knowledgehub.transparency.org/assets/uploads /helpdesk/Country-profile-Saudi-Arabia-2020__PR.pdf; Andrew Wedeman, "Xi Jinping's Tiger Hunt: Anti-corruption Campaign or Factional Purge?," *Modern China Studies* 24, no. 2 (2017): 35–94; Jiangnan Zhu and Dong Zhang, "Weapons of the Powerful: Authoritarian Elite Competition and Politicized Anticorruption in China," *Comparative Political Studies* 50, no. 9 (2017): 1186–220.

114. Valerii Soifer, *Lysenko and the Tragedy of Soviet Science* (New Brunswick, N.J.: Rutgers University Press, 1994), 294; Jan Sapp, *Genesis: The Evolution of Biology* (New York: Oxford University Press, 2002), 173; John Maynard Smith, "Molecules Are Not Enough," *London Review of Books*, Feb. 6, 1986, www.lrb .co.uk/the-paper/v08/n02/john-maynard-smith/molecules-are-not-enough; Jenny Leigh Smith, *Works in Progress: Plans and Realities on Soviet Farms, 1930–1963* (New Haven, Conn.: Yale University Press, 2014), 215; Robert L. Paarlberg, *Food Trade and Foreign Policy: India, the Soviet Union, and the United States* (Ithaca, N.Y.: Cornell University Press, 1985), 66–88; Eugene Keefe and Raymond Zickel, eds., *The Soviet Union: A Country Study* (Washington, D.C.: Library of Congress Federal Research Division, 1991), 532; Alec Nove, *An Economic History of the USSR, 1917–1991* (London: Penguin, 1992), 412; Sam Kean, "The Soviet Era's Deadliest Scientist Is Regaining Popularity in Russia," *Atlantic*, Dec. 19, 2017, www.theatlantic.com/science /archive/2017/12/trofim-lysenko-soviet-union-russia/548786/.

115. David E. Murphy, *What Stalin Knew: The Enigma of Barbarossa* (New Haven, Conn.: Yale University Press, 2005), 194–260; S. V. Stepashin, ed., *Organy gosudarstvennoi bezopasnosti SSSR v Velikoi Otvechestvennoi voine: Sbornik dokumentov* [The organs of state security of the USSR in the Great Patriotic War: A collection of documents], vol. 2, book 2 (Moscow: Rus', 2000), 219; A. Artizov et al., eds., *Reabilitatsiia: Kak eto bylo. Dokumenty Prezidiuma TsK KPSS i drugie materialy* [Rehabilitation: How it was. Documents of the Presidium of the CC CPSU and other materials] (Moscow: Mezhdunarodnyi Fond "Demokratiia," 2000), 1:164–66; K. Simonov, *Glazami cheloveka moego pokolennia. Razmyshleniia o I. V. Staline* [Through the eyes of a person of my generation. Reflections on I.V. Stalin] (Moscow: Kniga, 1990), 378–79; Montefiore, *Stalin*, 305–6; David M. Glantz, *Colossus Reborn: The Red Army at War, 1941–1943* (Lawrence: University Press of Kansas, 2005), 715n133.

116. McMeekin, *Stalin's War*, 295.

117. Ibid., 302–16.

118. Ibid., 319.

119. Figes, *Whisperers*, 383; McMeekin, *Stalin's War*, 96, 451; Catherine Merridale, *Ivan's War: Life and Death in the Red Army, 1939–1945* (New York: Metropolitan, 2006); Roger Reese, *Why Stalin's Soldiers Fought: The Red Army's Military Effectiveness in World War II* (Lawrence: University Press of Kansas, 2011); David M. Glantz, *Stumbling Colossus: The Red Army on the Eve of World War* (Lawrence: University Press of Kansas, 1998); Glantz, *Colossus Reborn*; Alexander Hill, *The Red Army and the Second World War* (Cambridge, U.K.: Cambridge University Press, 2017); Ben Shepherd, *Hitler's Soldiers: The German Army in the Third Reich* (New Haven, Conn.: Yale University Press, 2016), 114–15.

120. Evan Mawdsley, *Thunder in the East: The Nazi-Soviet War, 1941–1945*, 2nd ed. (London: Bloomsbury, 2016), 208–9; Geoffrey Roberts, *Stalin's Wars: From World War to Cold War, 1939–1953* (New Haven, Conn.: Yale University Press, 2006), 133–34; Merridale, *Ivan's War*, 140–59; Glantz, *Stumbling Colossus*, 33.

121. Montefiore, *Stalin*, 486–88; Roy Medvedev, *Let History Judge: The Origins and Consequences of Stalinism* (New York: Knopf, 1972), 469.

122. Joshua Rubenstein, *The Last Days of Stalin* (New Haven, Conn.: Yale University Press, 2016); Brent and Naumov, *Stalin's Last Crime*; Elena Zubkova, *Russia After the War: Hopes, Illusions, and Disappointments, 1945–1957* (Ar-

monk, N.Y.: M. E. Sharpe, 1998), 137–38, 223nn21–25; Figes, *Whisperers*, 521.

123. Robert Service, *Stalin: A Biography* (Cambridge, Mass.: Harvard University Press, 2005), 571–80; Montefiore, *Stalin*, 566–77, 640; Oleg V. Khlevniuk, *Stalin: New Biography of a Dictator* (New Haven, Conn.: Yale University Press, 2015), 1–6, 33, 36, 92, 142–44, 189–90, 196–97, 250, 309–14; Zhores Medvedev and Roy Medvedev, *Unknown Stalin: His Life, Death, and Legacy* (New York: Overlook Press, 2005), 19–35.

124. Arthur Marwick, *The Sixties: Cultural Revolution in Britain, France, Italy, and the United States, c. 1958–c. 1974* (London: Bloomsbury Reader, 1998); Peter B. Levy, *The Great Uprising: Race Riots in Urban America During the 1960s* (Cambridge, U.K.: Cambridge University Press, 2018).

125. For a fascinating and insightful study of this and previous "chip wars," see Chris Miller, *Chip War: The Fight for the World's Most Critical Technology* (New York: Scribner, 2022), 43.

126. Victor Yasmann, "Grappling with the Computer Revolution," in *Soviet/East European Survey, 1984–1985: Selected Research and Analysis from Radio Free Europe/Radio Liberty*, ed. Vojtech Mastny (Durham, N.C.: Duke University Press, 1986), 266–72.

CHAPTER 6: THE NEW MEMBERS

1. Alan Turing, "Intelligent Machinery," in *The Essential Turing*, ed. B. Jack Copeland (New York: Oxford University Press, 2004), 395–432.

2. Alan Turing, "Computing Machinery and Intelligence," *Mind* 59, no. 236 (1950): 433–60.

3. Alexis Madrigal, "How Checkers Was Solved," *Atlantic*, July 19, 2017, www.theatlantic.com/technology/archive/2017/07/marion-tinsley-checkers/534111/.

4. Richard Rhodes, *The Making of the Atomic Bomb* (New York: Simon & Schuster, 1986), 711.

5. Levin Brinkmann et al., "Machine Culture," *Nature Human Behavior* 7 (2023): 1855–68.

6. Max Fisher, *The Chaos Machine: The Inside Story of How Social Media Rewired Our Minds and Our World* (New York: Little, Brown, 2022).

7. The following discussion relies on Thant Myint-U, *The Hidden History of Burma: Race, Capitalism, and the Crisis of Democracy in the 21st Century* (New York: W. W. Norton, 2020); Habiburahman, *First, They Erased Our Name: A Rohingya Speaks*, with Sophie Ansel (London: Scribe, 2019); Amnesty International, *The Social Atrocity: Meta and the Right to Remedy for the Rohingya* (London: Amnesty International, 2022), www.amnesty.org/en/documents/asa16/5933/2022/en/; Christina Fink, "Dangerous Speech, Anti-Muslim Violence, and Facebook in Myanmar," *Journal of International Affairs* 71, no. 1.5 (2018): 43–52; Naved Bakali, "Islamophobia in Myanmar: The Rohingya Genocide and the 'War on Terror,'" *Race and Class* 62, no. 4 (2021): 1–19; Ali Siddiquee, "The Portrayal of the Rohingya Genocide and Refugee Crisis in the Age of Post-truth Politics," *Asian Journal of Comparative Politics* 5, no. 2 (2019): 89–103; Neriah Yue, "The 'Weaponization' of Facebook in Myanmar: A Case for Corporate Criminal Liability," *Hastings Law Journal* 71, no. 3 (2020): 813–44; Jennifer Whitten-Woodring et al., "Poison If You

Don't Know How to Use It: Facebook, Democracy, and Human Rights in Myanmar," *International Journal of Press/Politics* 25, no. 3 (2020): 1–19.

8. See Thant, "Unfinished Nation," in *Hidden History of Burma*. See also Amnesty International, "Briefing: Attacks by the Arakan Rohingya Salvation Army (ARSA) on Hindus in Northern Rakhine State," May 22, 2018, www .amnesty.org/en/documents/asa16/8454/2018/en/; Amnesty International, "'We Will Destroy Everything': Military Responsibility for Crimes Against Humanity in Rakhine State," June 27, 2018, www.amnesty.org/en/documents /asa16/8630/2018/en/; Anthony Ware and Costas Laoutides, *Myanmar's "Rohingya" Conflict* (New York: Oxford University Press, 2018), 14–53.

9. Thant, *Hidden History of Burma*; Ware and Laoutides, *Myanmar's "Rohingya" Conflict*, 6; Anthony Ware and Costas Laoutides, "Myanmar's 'Rohingya' Conflict: Misconceptions and Complexity," *Asian Affairs* 50, no. 1 (2019): 60–79; UNHCR, "Bangladesh Rohingya Emergency," accessed Feb. 13, 2024, www.unhcr.org/ph/campaigns/rohingya-emergency; Mohshin Habib et al., *Forced Migration of Rohingya: The Untold Experience* (Ontario: Ontario International Development Agency, 2018), 69; Annekathryn Goodman and Iftkher Mahmood, "The Rohingya Refugee Crisis of Bangladesh: Gender Based Violence and the Humanitarian Response," *Open Journal of Political Science* 9, no. 3 (2019): 490–501.

10. Thant, *Hidden History of Burma*, 165.

11. Amnesty International, *Social Atrocity*, 45.

12. Thant, *Hidden History of Burma*, 166.

13. Kumar Ramakrishna, "Understanding Myanmar's Buddhist Extremists: Some Preliminary Musings," *New England Journal of Public Policy* 32, no. 2 (2020), article 4; Ronan Lee, *Myanmar's Rohingya Genocide: Identity, History, and Hate Speech* (London: Bloomsbury, 2021), 89; Sheera Frenkel, "This Is What Happens When Millions of People Suddenly Get the Internet," *BuzzFeed News*, Nov. 20, 2016, www.buzzfeednews.com/article/sheerafrenkel /fake-news-spreads-trump-around-the-world; Megan Specia and Paul Mozur, "A War of Words Puts Facebook at the Center of Myanmar's Rohingya Crisis," *New York Times*, Oct. 27, 2017, www.nytimes.com/2017/10 /27/world/asia/myanmar-government-facebook-rohingya.html.

14. Amnesty International, *Social Atrocity*, 7.

15. Tom Miles, "U.N. Investigators Cite Facebook Role in Myanmar Crisis," Reuters, March 13, 2018, www.reuters.com/article/idUSKCN1GO2Q4/.

16. Amnesty International, *Social Atrocity*, 8.

17. John Clifford Holt, *Myanmar's Buddhist-Muslim Crisis: Rohingya, Arakanese, and Burmese Narratives of Siege and Fear* (Honolulu: University of Hawaii Press, 2019), 241–43; Kyaw Phone Kyaw, "The Healing of Meiktila," *Frontier Myanmar*, April 21, 2016, www.frontiermyanmar.net/en/the-healing-of-meiktila/.

18. On the cultural power of recommendation algorithms, see also Brinkmann et al., "Machine Culture"; Jessica Su, Aneesh Sharma, and Sharad Goel, "The Effect of Recommendations on Network Structure," in *Proceedings of the 25th International Conference on World Wide Web* (Geneva: International World Wide Web Conferences Steering Committee, 2016), 1157–67; Zhepeng Li, Xiao Fang, and Olivia R. Liu Sheng, "A Survey of Link Recommendation for Social Networks: Methods, Theoretical Foundations, and Future Research Directions," *ACM Transactions on Management Information Systems* 9, no. 1 (2018): 1–26.

19. Amnesty International, *Social Atrocity*, 47.

20. Ibid., 46.

21. Ibid., 38–49. See also Zeynep Tufekci, "Algorithmic Harms Beyond Facebook and Google: Emergent Challenges of Computational Agency," *Colorado Technology Law Journal* 13 (2015): 203–18; Janna Anderson and Lee Rainie, "The Future of Truth and Misinformation Online," Pew Research Center, Oct. 19, 2017, www.pewresearch.org/internet/2017/10/19/the-future-of-truth-and-misinformation-online/; Ro'ee Levy, "Social Media, News Consumption, and Polarization: Evidence from a Field Experiment," *American Economic Review* 111, no. 3 (2021): 831–70; William J. Brady, Ana P. Gantman, and Jay J. Van Bavel, "Attentional Capture Helps Explain Why Moral and Emotional Content Go Viral," *Journal of Experimental Psychology: General* 149, no. 4 (2020): 746–56.

22. Yue Zhang et al., "Siren's Song in the AI Ocean: A Survey on Hallucination in Large Language Models" (preprint, submitted in 2023), arxiv.org/abs/2309 .01219; Jordan Pearson, "Researchers Demonstrate AI 'Supply Chain' Disinfo Attack with 'PoisonGPT,'" *Vice*, July 13, 2023, www.vice.com/en/article /xgwgn4/researchers-demonstrate-ai-supply-chain-disinfo-attack-with -poisongpt.

23. František Baluška and Michael Levin, "On Having No Head: Cognition Throughout Biological Systems," *Frontiers in Psychology* 7 (2016), article 902.

24. For a much deeper discussion of consciousness and decision making in humans, see Mark Solms, *The Hidden Spring: A Journey to the Source of Consciousness* (London: Profile Books, 2021).

25. For an in-depth discussion of consciousness and intelligence in humans and AI, see Yuval Noah Harari, *Homo Deus* (New York: Harper, 2017), chaps. 3, 10; Yuval Noah Harari, *21 Lessons for the 21st Century* (New York: Spiegel & Grau, 2018), chap. 3; Yuval Noah Harari, "The Politics of Consciousness," in Aviva Berkovich-Ohana et al. (eds.), *Perspectives on Consciousness: Highlighting Subjective Experience* (Cambridge, Mass.: MIT Press, 2025 [forthcoming]), chap. 7; Patrick Butlin et al., "Consciousness in Artificial Intelligence: Insights from the Science of Consciousness" (preprint, submitted in 2023), arxiv.org/abs/2308.08708.

26. OpenAI, "GPT-4 System Card," March 23, 2023, 14, cdn.openai.com/papers /gpt-4-system-card.pdf.

27. Ibid., 15–16.

28. See Harari, *Homo Deus*, chaps. 3, 10; Harari, "The Politics of Consciousness."

29. For real-life examples, see Jamie Condliffe, "Algorithms Probably Caused a Flash Crash of the British Pound," *MIT Technology Review*, Oct. 7, 2016, www .technologyreview.com/2016/10/07/244656/algorithms-probably-caused -a-flash-crash-of-the-british-pound/; Bruce Lee, "Fake Eli Lilly Twitter Account Claims Insulin Is Free, Stock Falls 4.37%," *Forbes*, Nov. 12, 2022, www .forbes.com/sites/brucelee/2022/11/12/fake-eli-lilly-twitter-account-claims -insulin-is-free-stock-falls-43/?sh=61308fb541a3.

30. Jenna Greene, "Will ChatGPT Make Lawyers Obsolete? (Hint: Be Afraid)," Reuters, Dec. 10, 2022, www.reuters.com/legal/transactional/will -chatgpt-make-lawyers-obsolete-hint-be-afraid-2022-12-09/; Chloe Xiang, "ChatGPT Can Do a Corporate Lobbyist's Job, Study Determines," *Vice*, Jan. 5, 2023, www.vice.com/en/article/3admm8/chatgpt-can-do-a-corporate -lobbyists-job-study-determines; Jules Ioannidis et al., "Gracenote.ai: Legal

Generative AI for Regulatory Compliance," SSRN, June 19, 2023, ssrn.com /abstract=4494272; Damien Charlotin, "Large Language Models and the Future of Law," SSRN, Aug. 22, 2023, ssrn.com/abstract=4548258; Daniel Martin Katz et al., "GPT-4 Passes the Bar Exam," SSRN, March 15, 2023, ssrn.com/abstract=4389233. Though see also Eric Martínez, "Re-evaluating GPT-4's Bar Exam Performance," SSRN, May 8, 2023, ssrn.com/abstract= 4441311.

31. Brinkmann et al., "Machine Culture."
32. Julia Carrie Wong, "Facebook Restricts More Than 10,000 QAnon and US Militia Groups," *Guardian*, Aug. 19, 2020, www.theguardian.com/us-news /2020/aug/19/facebook-qanon-us-militia-groups-restrictions.
33. "FBI Chief Says Five QAnon Conspiracy Advocates Arrested for Jan 6 U.S. Capitol Attack," Reuters, April 15, 2021, www.reuters.com/world/us/fbi -chief-says-five-qanon-conspiracy-advocates-arrested-jan-6-us-capitol -attack-2021-04-14/.
34. "Canadian Man Faces Weapons Charges in Attack on PM Trudeau's Home," Al Jazeera, July 7, 2020, www.aljazeera.com/news/2020/7/7/canadian-man -faces-weapons-charges-in-attack-on-pm-trudeaus-home. See also Mack Lamoureux, "A Fringe Far-Right Group Keeps Trying to Citizen Arrest Justin Trudeau," *Vice*, July 28, 2020, www.vice.com/en/article/dyzwpy/a-fringe -far-right-group-keeps-trying-to-citizen-arrest-justin-trudeau.
35. "Rémy Daillet: Conspiracist Charged over Alleged French Coup Plot," BBC, Oct. 28, 2021, www.bbc.com/news/world-europe-59075902; "Rémy Daillet: Far-Right 'Coup Plot' in France Enlisted Army Officers," *Times*, Oct. 28, 2021, www.thetimes.co.uk/article/remy-daillet-far-right-coup-plot-france -army-officers-qanon-ds22j6g05.
36. Mia Bloom and Sophia Moskalenko, *Pastels and Pedophiles: Inside the Mind of QAnon* (Stanford, Calif.: Stanford University Press, 2021), 2.
37. John Bowden, "QAnon-Promoter Marjorie Taylor Greene Endorses Kelly Loeffler in Georgia Senate Bid," *Hill*, Oct. 15, 2020, thehill.com/homenews /campaign/521196-qanon-promoter-marjorie-taylor-greene-endorses-kelly -loeffler-in-ga-senate/.
38. Camila Domonoske, "QAnon Supporter Who Made Bigoted Videos Wins Ga. Primary, Likely Heading to Congress," NPR, Aug. 12, 2020, www.npr .org/2020/08/12/901628541/qanon-supporter-who-made-bigoted-videos -wins-ga-primary-likely-heading-to-congre.
39. Nitasha Tiku, "The Google Engineer Who Thinks the Company's AI Has Come to Life," *Washington Post*, June 11, 2022, www.washingtonpost.com /technology/2022/06/11/google-ai-lamda-blake-lemoine/.
40. Matthew Weaver, "AI Chatbot 'Encouraged' Man Who Planned to Kill Queen, Court Told," *Guardian*, July 6, 2023, www.theguardian.com/uk-news /2023/jul/06/ai-chatbot-encouraged-man-who-planned-to-kill-queen-court -told; PA Media, Rachel Hall, and Nadeem Badshah, "Man Who Broke into Windsor Castle with Crossbow to Kill Queen Jailed for Nine Years," *Guardian*, Oct. 5, 2023, www.theguardian.com/uk-news/2023/oct/05/man -who-broke-into-windsor-castle-with-crossbow-to-kill-queen-jailed-for -nine-years; William Hague, "The Real Threat of AI Is Fostering Extremism," *Times*, Oct. 30, 2023, www.thetimes.co.uk/article/the-real-threat-of-ai -is-fostering-extremism-jn3cw9rd3.
41. Marcus du Sautoy, *The Creativity Code: Art and Innovation in the Age of AI*

(Cambridge, Mass.: Belknap Press of Harvard University Press, 2019); Brinkmann et al., "Machine Culture."

42. Martin Abadi and David G. Andersen, "Learning to Protect Communications with Adversarial Neural Cryptography," arXiv, Oct. 21, 2016, arXiv .1610.06918.

43. Robert Kissell, *Algorithmic Trading Methods: Applications Using Advanced Statistics, Optimization, and Machine Learning Technique* (London: Academic Press, 2021); Anna-Louise Jackson, "A Basic Guide to Forex Trading," *Forbes,* March 17, 2023, www.forbes.com/adviser/investing/what-is-forex-trading/; Bank of International Settlements, "Triennial Central Bank Survey: OTC Foreign Exchange Turnover in April 2022," Oct. 27, 2022, www.bis.org /statistics/rpfx22_fx.pdf.

44. Jaime Sevilla et al., "Compute Trends Across Three Eras of Machine Learning," *2022 International Joint Conference on Neural Networks (IJCNN)*, IEEE, Sept. 30, 2022, doi.10.1109/IJCNN55064.2022.9891914; Bengio et al., "Managing Extreme AI Risks Amid Rapid Progress."

45. Kwang W. Jeon, *The Biology of Amoeba* (London: Academic Press, 1973).

46. International Energy Agency, "Data Centers and Data Transmission Networks," last update July 11, 2023, accessed Dec. 27, 2023, www.iea.org/ energy-system/buildings/data-centers-and-data-transmission-networks; Jacob Roundy, "Assess the Environmental Impact of Data Centers," TechTarget, July 12, 2023, www.techtarget.com/searchdatacenter/feature/Assess-the -environmental-impact-of-data-centers; Alex de Vries, "The Growing Energy Footprint of Artificial Intelligence," *Joule* 7, no. 10 (2023): 2191–94, doi .org/10.1016/j.joule.2023.09.004; Javier Felipe Andreu, Alicia Valero Delgado, and Jorge Torrubia Torralba, "Big Data on a Dead Planet: The Digital Transition's Neglected Environmental Impacts," The Left in the European Parliament, Nov. 15, 2022, left.eu/issues/publications/big-data-on-a-dead -planet-the-digital-transitions-neglected-environmental-impacts/. On water requirements, see Shannon Osaka, "A New Front in the Water Wars: Your Internet Use," *Washington Post,* April 25, 2023, www.washingtonpost.com /climate-environment/2023/04/25/data-centers-drought-water-use/.

47. Shoshana Zuboff, *The Age of Surveillance Capitalism: The Fight for a Human Future at the New Frontier of Power* (New York: PublicAffairs, 2018); Mejias and Couldry, *Data Grab;* Brian Huseman (Amazon vice president) to Chris Coons (U.S. senator), June 28, 2019, www.coons.senate.gov/imo/media/doc /Amazon%20Senator%20Coons__Response%20Letter_6.28.19%5B3%5D .pdf.

48. "Tech Companies Spend More Than €100 Million a Year on EU Digital Lobbying," Euronews, Sept. 11, 2023, www.euronews.com/my-europe/2023 /09/11/tech-companies-spend-more-than-100-million-a-year-on-eu-digital -lobbying; Emily Birnbaum, "Tech Giants Broke Their Spending Records on Lobbying Last Year," Bloomberg, Feb. 1, 2023, www.bloomberg.com/news /articles/2023-02-01/amazon-apple-microsoft-report-record-lobbying -spending-in-2022.

49. Marko Köthenbürger, "Taxation of Digital Platforms," in *Tax by Design for the Netherlands,* ed. Sijbren Cnossen and Bas Jacobs (New York: Oxford University Press, 2022), 178.

50. Omri Marian, "Taxing Data," *BYU Law Review* 47 (2021); Viktor Mayer-Schönberger and Thomas Ramge, *Reinventing Capitalism in the Age of Big*

Data (New York: Basic Books, 2018); Jathan Sadowski, *Too Smart: How Digital Capitalism Is Extracting Data, Controlling Our Lives, and Taking Over the World* (Cambridge, Mass.: MIT Press, 2020); Douglas Laney, "Unlock Tangible Benefits by Valuing Intangible Data Assets," *Forbes*, March 9, 2023, www.forbes.com/sites/douglaslaney/2023/03/09/unlock -tangible-benefits-by-valuing-intangible-data-assets/?sh=47f6750b1152; Ziva Rubinstein, "Taxing Big Data: A Proposal to Benefit Society for the Use of Private Information," *Fordham Intellectual Property, Media, and Entertainment Law* 31, no. 4 (2021): 1199, ir.lawnet.fordham.edu/iplj/vol31 /iss4/6; M. Fleckenstein, A. Obaidi, and N. Tryfona, "A Review of Data Valuation Approaches and Building and Scoring a Data Valuation Model," *Harvard Data Science Review* 5, no. 1 (2023), doi.org/10.1162/99608f92 .c18db966.

51. Andrew Leonard, "How Taiwan's Unlikely Digital Minister Hacked the Pandemic," *Wired*, July 23, 2020, www.wired.com/story/how-taiwans-unlikely -digital-minister-hacked-the-pandemic/.

52. Yasmann, "Grappling with the Computer Revolution"; James L. Hoot, "Computing in the Soviet Union," *Computing Teacher*, May 1987; William H. Luers, "The U.S. and Eastern Europe," *Foreign Affairs* 65, no. 5 (Summer 1987): 989–90; Slava Gerovitch, "How the Computer Got Its Revenge on the Soviet Union," *Nautilus*, April 2, 2015, nautil.us/how-the-computer-got -its-revenge-on-the-soviet-union-235368/; Benjamin Peters, "The Soviet InterNyet," *Eon*, Oct. 17, 2016, eon.co/essays/how-the-soviets-invented-the -internet-and-why-it-didnt-work; Benjamin Peters, *How Not to Network a Nation: The Uneasy History of the Soviet Internet* (Cambridge, Mass.: MIT Press, 2016).

53. Fred Turner, *From Counterculture to Cyberculture: Stewart Brand, the Whole Earth Network, and the Rise of Digital Utopianism* (Chicago: University of Chicago Press, 2010).

54. Paul Freiberger and Michael Swaine, *Fire in the Valley: The Making of the Personal Computer*, 2nd ed. (New York: McGraw-Hill, 2000), 263–65; Laine Nooney, *The Apple II Age: How the Computer Became Personal* (Chicago: University of Chicago Press, 2023), 57.

55. Nicholas J. Schlosser, *Cold War on the Airwaves: The Radio Propaganda War Against East Germany* (Champaign: University of Illinois Press, 2015), esp. chap. 5, "The East German Campaign Against RIAS," 107–34; Alfredo Thiermann, "Radio Activities," *Thresholds* 45 (2017): 194–210, doi.org/10 .1162/THLD_a_00018.

CHAPTER 7: RELENTLESS

1. Paul Kenyon, *Children of the Night: The Strange and Epic Story of Modern Romania* (London: Apollo, 2021), 353–54.

2. Ibid., 356.

3. Ibid., 373–74.

4. Ibid., 357.

5. Ibid.

6. Ibid.

7. Deletant, "Securitate Legacy in Romania," 198.

8. Marc Brysbaert, "How Many Words Do We Read per Minute? A Review

and Meta-analysis of Reading Rate," *Journal of Memory and Language* 109 (Dec. 2019), article 104047, doi.org/10.1016/j.jml.2019.104047.

9. Alex Hughes, "ChatGPT: Everything You Need to Know About OpenAI's GPT-4 Tool," BBC Science Focus, Sept. 26, 2023, www.sciencefocus.com /future-technology/gpt-3; Stephen McAleese, "Retrospective on 'GPT-4 Predictions' After the Release of GPT-4," *LessWrong*, March 18, 2023, www .lesswrong.com/posts/iQx2eeHKLwgBYdWPZ/retrospective-on-gpt -4-predictions-after-the-release-of-gpt; Jonathan Vanian and Kif Leswing, "ChatGPT and Generative AI Are Booming, but the Costs Can Be Extraor-dinary," CNBC, March 13, 2023, www.cnbc.com/2023/03/13/chatgpt-and -generative-ai-are-booming-but-at-a-very-expensive-price.html.

10. Christian Grothoff and Jens Purup, "The NSA's SKYNET Program May Be Killing Thousands of Innocent People," *Ars Technica*, Feb. 16, 2016, arstech nica.co.uk/security/2016/02/the-nsas-skynet-program-may-be-killing -thousands-of-innocent-people/.

11. Jennifer Gibson, "Death by Data: Drones, Kill Lists, and Algorithms," in *Remote Warfare: Interdisciplinary Perspectives*, ed. Alasdair McKay, Abigail Watson, and Megan Karlshøj-Pedersen (Bristol: E-International Relations, 2021), www.e-ir.info/publication/remote-warfare-interdisciplinary-perspectives/; Vasja Badalič, "The Metadata Driven Killing Apparatus: Big Data Analytics, the Target Selection Process, and the Threat to International Humanitarian Law," *Critical Military Studies* 9, no. 4 (2023): 1–21, doi.org/10.1080/23337486 .2023.2170539.

12. Catherine E. Richards et al., "Rewards, Risks, and Responsible Deployment of Artificial Intelligence in Water Systems," *Nature Water* 1 (2023): 422–32, doi.org/10.1038/s44221-023-00069-6.

13. John S. Brownstein et al., "Advances in Artificial Intelligence for Infectious-Disease Surveillance," *New England Journal of Medicine* 388, no. 17 (2023): 1597–607, doi.org/10.1056/NEJMra2119215; Vignesh A. Arasu et al., "Comparison of Mammography AI Algorithms with a Clinical Risk Model for 5-Year Breast Cancer Risk Prediction: An Observational Study," *Radiology* 307, no. 5 (2023), article 222733, doi.org/10.1148/radiol.222733; Alexander V. Eriksen, Sören Möller, and Jesper Ryg, "Use of GPT-4 to Diagnose Complex Clinical Cases," *NEJM AI* 1, no. 1 (2023), doi.org/10.1056 /AIp2300031.

14. Ashley Belanger, "AI Tool Used to Spot Child Abuse Allegedly Targets Parents with Disabilities," *Ars Technica*, Feb. 1, 2023, arstechnica.com/tech-policy /2023/01/doj-probes-ai-tool-thats-allegedly-biased-against families-with -disabilities/.

15. Yegor Tkachenko and Kamel Jedidi, "A Megastudy on the Predictability of Personal Information from Facial Images: Disentangling Demographic and Non-demographic Signals," *Scientific Reports* 13 (2023), article 21073, doi.org /10.1038/s41598-023-42054-9; Jacob Leon Kröger, Otto Hans-Martin Lutz, and Florian Müller, "What Does Your Gaze Reveal About You? On the Privacy Implications of Eye Tracking," in *Privacy and Identity Management. Data for Better Living: AI and Privacy*, ed. Michael Friedewald et al. (Cham: Springer International, 2020), 226–41, doi.org/10.1007/978-3-030-42504 -3_15; N. Arun, P. Maheswaravenkatesh, and T. Jayasankar, "Facial Micro Emotion Detection and Classification Using Swarm Intelligence Based

Modified Convolutional Network," *Expert Systems with Applications* 233 (2023), article 120947, doi.org/10.1016/j.eswa.2023.120947; Vasileios Skaramagkas et al., "Review of Eye Tracking Metrics Involved in Emotional and Cognitive Processes," *IEEE Reviews in Biomedical Engineering* 16 (2023): 260–77, doi.org/10.1109/RBME.2021.3066072.

16. Isaacson, *Elon Musk,* chap. 65, "Neuralink, 2017–2020," and chap. 89, "Miracles: Neuralink, November 2021"; Rachel Levy, "Musk's Neuralink Faces Federal Probe, Employee Backlash over Animal Tests," Reuters, Dec. 6, 2023, www.reuters.com/technology/musks-neuralink-faces-federal-probe -employee-backlash-over-animal-tests-2022-12-05/; Elon Musk and Neuralink, "An Integrated Brain-Machine Interface Platform with Thousands of Channels," *Journal of Medical Research* 21, no. 10 (2019), doi.org/10.2196 /16194; Emily Waltz, "Neuralink Barrels into Human Tests Despite Fraud Claims," *IEEE Spectrum,* Dec. 6, 2023, spectrum.ieee.org/neuralink-human -trials; Aswin Chari et al., "Brain-Machine Interfaces: The Role of the Neurosurgeon," *World Neurosurgery* 146 (Feb. 2021): 140–47, doi.org/10.1016/j .wneu.2020.11.028; Kenny Torrella, "Neuralink Shows What Happens When You Bring 'Move Fast and Break Things' to Animal Research," *Vox,* Dec. 11, 2023, www.vox.com/future-perfect/2022/12/11/23500157 /neuralink-animal-testing-elon-musk-usda-probe.

17. Jerry Tang et al., "Semantic Reconstruction of Continuous Language from Non-invasive Brain Recordings," *Nature Neuroscience* 26 (2023): 858–66, doi .org/10.1038/s41593-023-01304-9.

18. Anne Manning, "Human Brain Seems Impossible to Map. What If We Started with Mice?," *Harvard Gazette,* Sept. 26, 2023, news.harvard.edu /gazette/story/2023/09/human-brain-too-big-to-map-so-theyre-starting -with-mice/; Michał Januszewski, "Google Research Embarks on Effort to Map a Mouse Brain," Google Research, Sept. 26, 2023, blog.research.google /2023/09/google-research-embarks-on-effort-to.html?utm_source=substack &utm_medium=email; Tim Blakely and Michał Januszewski, "A Browsable Petascale Reconstruction of the Human Cortex," Google Research, June 1, 2021, blog.research.google/2021/06/a-browsable-petascale-reconstruction -of.html.

19. This may change as technology develops. An Ohio State University research report published on June 2, 2022, claimed that brain scans can accurately predict whether people were politically conservative or liberal. Seo Eun Yang et al., "Functional Connectivity Signatures of Political Ideology," *PNAS Nexus* 1, no. 3 (July 2022): 1–11, doi.org/10.1093/pnasnexus/pgac066. See also Petter Törnberg, "ChatGPT-4 Outperforms Experts and Crowd Workers in Annotating Political Twitter Messages with Zero-Shot Learning," arXiv, doi .org/10.48550/arXiv.2304.06588; Michal Kosinski, "Facial Recognition Technology Can Expose Political Orientation from Naturalistic Facial Images," *Scientific Reports* 11 (2021), article 100, doi.org/10.1038/s41598-020 -79310-1; Tang et al., "Semantic Reconstruction of Continuous Language."

20. Algorithms are already able to identify and predict human emotions without biometric surveillance. See, for example, Sam Machkovech, "Report: Facebook Helped Advertisers Target Teens Who Feel 'Worthless,'" *Ars Technica,* May 1, 2017, arstechnica.com/information-technology/2017/05 /facebook-helped-advertisers-target-teens-who-feel-worthless/; Alexander

Spangher, "How Does This Article Make You Feel?," Open NYT, Medium, Nov. 1, 2018, open.nytimes.com/how-does-this-article-make-you-feel -4684e5e9c47.

21. Amnesty International, "Automated Apartheid: How Facial Recognition Fragments, Segregates, and Controls Palestinians in the OPT," May 2, 2023, 42–43, www.amnesty.org/en/documents/mde15/6701/2023/en/; Tal Shef, "Re'ayon im Sasi Elya, rosh ma'arach ha-cyber bashabak" [Interview with Sasi Elya, head of the Shin Bet's cyber unit], *Yediot Ahronot,* Nov. 27, 2020, www .yediot.co.il/articles/0,7340,L-5851340,00.html; Human Rights Watch, *China's Algorithms of Repression: Reverse Engineering a Xinjiang Police Mass Surveillance App* (New York: Human Rights Watch, 2019), 9, www.hrw.org /sites/default/files/report_pdf/china0519_web5.pdf; United Nations Office of the High Commissioner for Human Rights (OHCHR), "OHCHR Assessment of Human Rights Concerns in the Xinjiang Uyghur Autonomous Region," Aug. 31, 2022, www.ohchr.org/sites/default/files/documents /countries/2022-08-31/22-08-31-final-assesment.pdf; Geoffrey Cain, *The Perfect Police State: An Undercover Odyssey into China's Terrifying Surveillance Dystopia of the Future* (New York: Public Affairs, 2021); Michael Quinn, "Realities of Life in Kashmir," Amnesty International Blog, July 12, 2023, https:// www.amnesty.org.uk/blogs/country-specialists/realities-life-kashmir; PTI, "AI-based facial recognition system inaugurated in J-K's Kishtwar," The Print, December 9, 2023, https://theprint.in/india/ai-based-facial-recognition -system-inaugurated-in-j-ks-kishtwar/1879576/; Max Koshelev, "How Crimea Became a Testing Ground for Russia's Surveillance Technology," Hromadske, 15 September 2017, https://hromadske.ua/en/posts/how-crimea -became-a-testing-ground-for-russias-surveillance-technology; Council of Europe, "Human rights situation in the Autonomous Republic of Crimea and the City of Sevastopol, Ukraine," 31 August 2023, 10–18, https://rm.coe .int/CoERMPublicCommonSearchServices/DisplayDCTMContent ?documentId=0900001680ac6e10; Shaun Walker and Pjotr Sauer, "'The Fight Is Continuing': A Decade of Russian Rule Has Not Silenced Ukrainian Voices in Crimea," *The Guardian,* 12 March 2024, https://www.theguardian .com/world/2024/mar/14/crimea-annexation-10-years-russia-ukraine; Melissa Villa-Nicholas, *Data Borders: How Silicon Valley is Building an Industry around Immigrants* (Oakland: University of California Press, 2023); Petra Molnar, *The Walls Have Eyes: Surviving Migration in the Age of Artificial Intelligence* (New York: The New Press, 2024); Asfandyar Mir and Dylan Moore, "Drones, Surveillance, and Violence: Theory and Evidence from a US Drone Program," *International Studies Quarterly* 63, no. 4 (2019): 846–862; Patrick Keenan, "Drones and Civilians: Emerging Evidence of the Terrorizing Effects of the U.S. Drone Programs," *Santa Clara Journal of International Law* 20, no. 1 (2021): 1–47; Trevor McCrisken, "Eyes and Ear in the Sky—Drones and Mass Surveillance," in *In the Name of Security—Secrecy, Surveillance and Journalism,* eds. Johan Lidberg and Denis Muller (London: Anthem Press, 2018), 139–158.

22. Giorgio Agamben, *State of Exception,* trans. Kevin Attell (Chicago: University of Chicago Press, 2005).

23. L. Shchyrakova and Y. Merkis, "Fear and loathing in Belarus," *Index on Censorship* 50 (2021): 24-26, https://doi.org/10.1177/03064220211012282; Anastasiya Astapova, "In Search for Truth: Surveillance Rumors and Vernacular

Panopticon in Belarus," *Journal of American Folklore* 130, no. 517 (2017): 276–304; R. Hervouet, "A Political Ethnography of Rural Communities under an Authoritarian Regime: The Case of Belarus," *Bulletin of Sociological Methodology/Bulletin de Méthodologie Sociologique* 141, no. 1 (2019): 85–112, https://doi.org/10.1177/0759106318812790; Allen Munoriyarwa, "When Watchdogs Fight Back: Resisting State Surveillance in Everyday Investigative Reporting Practices among Zimbabwean Journalists," *Journal of Eastern African Studies* 15, no. 3 (2021): 421–441; Allen Munoriyarwa, "The Militarization of Digital Surveillance in Post-Coup Zimbabwe: 'Just Don't Tell Them What We Do,'" *Security Dialogue* 53, no. 5 (2022): 456–474.

24. International Civil Aviation Organization, "ePassport Basics," https://www.icao.int/Security/FAL/PKD/Pages/ePassport-Basics.aspx.

25. Paul Bischoff, "Facial Recognition Technology (FRT): Which Countries Use It?," Comparitech, January 24, 2022, https://www.comparitech.com/blog/vpn-privacy/facial-recognition-statistics/.

26. Bischoff, "Facial Recognition Technology (FRT): Which Countries Use It?," Comparitech; "Surveillance Cities: Who Has the Most CCTV Cameras in the World?," Surfshark, https://surfshark.com/surveillance-cities; Liza Lin and Newley Purnell, "A World With a Billion Cameras Watching You Is Just Around the Corner," *The Wall Street Journal*, December 6, 2019, https://www.wsj.com/articles/a-billion-surveillance-cameras-forecast-to-be-watching-within-two-years-11575565402.

27. Drew Harwell and Craig Timberg, "How America's Surveillance Networks Helped the FBI Catch the Capitol Mob," *The Washington Post*, April 2, 2021, https://www.washingtonpost.com/technology/2021/04/02/capitol-siege-arrests-technology-fbi-privacy/; "Retired NYPD Officer Thomas Webster, Republican Committeeman Philip Grillo Arrested for Alleged Roles in Capitol Riot," CBS News, February 23, 2021, https://www.cbsnews.com/newyork/news/retired-nypd-officer-thomas-webster-queens-republican-group-leader-philip-grillo-arrested-for-alleged-roles-in-capitol-riot/.

28. Zhang Yang, "Police Using AI to Trace Long-Missing Children," China Daily, June 4, 2019, http://www.chinadaily.com.cn/a/201906/04/WS5cf5c8a8a310519142700e2f.html; Zhongkai Zhang, "AI Reunites Families! Four Children Missing for 10 Years Found at Once," Xinhua Daily Telegraph, June 14, 2019, http://www.xinhuanet.com/politics/2019-06/14/c_1124620736.htm; Chang Qu, "Hunan Man Reunites with Son Abducted 22 Years Ago," QQ, June 25, 2023, https://new.qq.com/rain/a/20230625A005UX00; Phoebe Zhang, "AI Reunites Son with Family but Raises Questions in China about Ethics, Privacy," *South China Morning Post*, December 10, 2023, https://www.scmp.com/news/china/article/3244377/ai-reunites-son-family-raises-questions-china-about-ethics-privacy; Ding Rui, "In Hebei, AI Tech Reunites Abducted Son With Family After 25 Years," Sixth Tone, December 4, 2023, https://www.sixthtone.com/news/1014206; Ding-Chau Wang et al., "Development of a Face Prediction System for Missing Children in a Smart City Safety Network," *Electronics* 11, no. 9 (2022): Article 1440, https://doi.org/10.3390/electronics11091440; M. R. Sowmya et al., "AI-Assisted Search for Missing Children," *2022 IEEE 2nd Mysore Sub Section International Conference* (Mysuru: IEEE, 2022), 1–6.

29. Jesper Lund, "Danish DPA Approves Automated Facial Recognition," EDRI, June 19, 2019, https://edri.org/danish-dpaapproves-automated-facial

-recognition; Sidsel Overgaard, "A Soccer Team in Denmark Is Using Facial Recognition to Stop Unruly Fans," NPR, October 21, 2019, https://www.npr .org/2019/10/21/770280447/a-soccer-team-in-denmark-is-using-facial -recognition-to-stop-unruly-fans; Yan Luo and Rui Guo, "Facial Recognition in China: Current Status, Comparative Approach and the Road Ahead," *Journal of Law and Social Change* 25, no. 2 (2021): 153–179.

30. Rachel George, "The AI Assault on Women: What Iran's Tech Enabled Morality Laws Indicate for Women's Rights Movements," Council on Foreign Relations online, December 7, 2023, https://www.cfr.org/blog/ai-assault -women-what-irans-tech-enabled-morality-laws-indicate-womens-rights -movements; Khari Johnson, "Iran Says Face Recognition Will ID Women Breaking Hijab Laws," *Wired*, January 10, 2023, https://www.wired.com /story/iran-says-face-recognition-will-id-women-breaking-hijab-laws/.

31. Johnson, "Iran Says Face Recognition Will ID Women Breaking Hijab Laws," *Wired*.

32. Farnaz Fassihi, "An Innocent and Ordinary Young Woman," *The New York Times*, September 16, 2022, https://www.nytimes.com/2023/09/16/world /middleeast/mahsa-amini-iran-protests-hijab-profile.html; Weronika Strzyzynska, "Iranian Woman Dies 'After Being Beaten by Morality Police' over Hijab Law," *The Guardian*, September 16, 2022, https://www.theguardian .com/global-development/2022/sep/16/iranian-woman-dies-after-being -beaten-by-morality-police-over-hijab-law.

33. "Iran: Doubling Down on Punishments Against Women and Girls Defying Discriminatory Veiling Laws," Amnesty International, July 26, 2023, https:// www.amnesty.org/en/documents/mde13/7041/2023/en/; "One Year Protest Report: At Least 551 Killed and 22 Suspicious Deaths," Iran Human Rights, September 15, 2023, https://iranhr.net/en/articles/6200/; Jon Gambrell, "Iran Says 22,000 Arrested in Protests Pardoned by Top Leader," AP News, March 13, 2023, https://apnews.com/article/iran-protests-arrested-pardons -mahsa-amini-ac3c45c6bcc883900ff1b1e83f85df95.

34. "Iran: Doubling Down on Punishments Against Women and Girls Defying Discriminatory Veiling Laws," Amnesty International.

35. Ibid.

36. Ibid.

37. "Iran: International Community Must Stand with Women and Girls Suffering Intensifying Oppression," Amnesty International, 26 July 2023, https:// www.amnesty.org/en/latest/news/2023/07/iran-international-community -must-stand-with-women-and-girls-suffering-intensifying-oppression/; "Iran: Doubling Down on Punishments Against Women and Girls Defying Discriminatory Veiling Laws," Amnesty International.

38. Johnson, "Iran Says Face Recognition Will ID Women Breaking Hijab Laws," *Wired*.

39. "Iran: Doubling Down on Punishments Against Women and Girls Defying Discriminatory Veiling Laws," Amnesty International.

40. "Iran: Doubling Down on Punishments Against Women and Girls Defying Discriminatory Veiling Laws," Amnesty International; Shadi Sadr, "Iran's Hijab and Chastity Bill Underscores the Need to Codify Gender Apartheid," Just Security, April 11, 2024, https://www.justsecurity.org/94504/iran-hijab -bill-gender-apartheid/; Tara Subramaniam, Adam Pourahmadi and Mostafa

Salem, "Iranian Women Face 10 Years in Jail for Inappropriate Dress after 'Hijab Bill' Approved," CNN, September 21, 2023, https://edition.cnn.com /2023/09/21/middleeast/iran-hijab-law-parliament-jail-intl-hnk/index .html; "Iran's Parliament Passes a Stricter Headscarf Law Days after Protest Anniversary," AP News, September 21, 2023, https://apnews.com/article /iran-hijab-women-politics-protests-6e07fae990369a58cb162eb6c5a7ab2a ?utm_source=copy&utm_medium=share.

41. Christopher Parsons et al., "The Predator in Your Pocket: A Multidisciplinary Assessment of the Stalkerware Application Industry," Citizen Lab, Research report 119, June 2019, citizenlab.ca/docs/stalkerware-holistic.pdf; Lorenzo Franceschi-Bicchierai and Joseph Cox, "Inside the 'Stalkerware' Surveillance Market, Where Ordinary People Tap Each Other's Phones," *Vice,* April 18, 2017, www.vice.com/en/article/53vm7n/inside-stalkerware-surveillance -market-flexispy-retina-x.

42. Mejias and Couldry, *Data Grab,* 90–94.

43. Ibid., 156–58.

44. Zuboff, *Age of Surveillance Capitalism.*

45. Rafael Bravo, Sara Catalán, and José M. Pina, "Gamification in Tourism and Hospitality Review Platforms: How to R.A.M.P. Up Users' Motivation to Create Content," *International Journal of Hospitality Management* 99 (2021), article 103064, doi.org/10.1016/j.ijhm.2021.103064; Davide Proserpio and Giorgos Zervas, "Study: Replying to Customer Reviews Results in Better Ratings," *Harvard Business Review,* Feb. 14, 2018, hbr.org/2018/02/study -replying-to-customer-reviews-results-in-better-ratings.

46. Linda Kinstler, "How Tripadvisor Changed Travel," *Guardian,* Aug. 17, 2018, www.theguardian.com/news/2018/aug/17/how-tripadvisor-changed-travel.

47. Alex J. Wood and Vili Lehdonvirta, "Platforms Disrupting Reputation: Precarity and Recognition Struggles in the Remote Gig Economy," *Sociology* 57, no. 5 (2023): 999–1016, doi.org/10.1177/00380385221126804.

48. Michael J. Sandel, *What Money Can't Buy: The Moral Limits of Markets* (London: Penguin Books, 2013).

49. On the medieval "reputation market," see Maurice Hugh Keen, *Chivalry* (London: Folio Society, 2010), and Georges Duby, *William Marshal: The Flower of Chivalry* (New York: Pantheon Books, 1985).

50. Zeyi Yang, "China Just Announced a New Social Credit Law. Here's What It Means," *MIT Technology Review,* Nov. 22, 2022, www.technologyreview.com /2022/11/22/1063605/china-announced-a-new-social-credit-law-what -does-it-mean/.

51. Will Storr, *The Status Game: On Human Life and How to Play It* (London: HarperCollins, 2021); Jason Manning, *Suicide: The Social Causes of Self-Destruction* (Charlottesville: University of Virginia Press, 2020).

52. Frans B. M. de Waal, *Chimpanzee Politics: Power and Sex Among Apes* (Baltimore: Johns Hopkins University Press, 1998); Frans B. M. de Waal, *Our Inner Ape: A Leading Primatologist Explains Why We Are Who We Are* (New York: Riverhead Books, 2006); Sapolsky, *Behave;* Victoria Wobber et al., "Differential Changes in Steroid Hormones Before Competition in Bonobos and Chimpanzees," *Proceedings of the National Academy of Sciences* 107, no. 28 (2010): 12457–62, doi.org/10.1073/pnas.1007411107; Sonia A. Cavigelli and Michael J. Caruso, "Sex, Social Status, and Physiological Stress in Pri-

mates: The Importance of Social and Glucocorticoid Dynamics," *Philosophical Transactions of the Royal Society B: Biological Sciences* 370, no. 1669 (2015): 1–13, doi.org/10.1098/rstb.2014.0103.

CHAPTER 8: FALLIBLE

1. Nathan Larson, *Aleksandr Solzhenitsyn and the Modern Russo-Jewish Question* (Stuttgart: Ibidem Press, 2005), 16.
2. Aleksandr Solzhenitsyn, *The Gulag Archipelago, 1918–1956: An Experiment in Literary Investigation, I–II* (New York: Harper & Row, 1973), 69–70.
3. Gessen, Homo Sovieticus, in *Future Is History,* chap. 4; Gulnaz Sharafutdinova, *The Afterlife of the "Soviet Man": Rethinking Homo Sovieticus* (London: Bloomsbury Academic, 2023), 37.
4. Fisher, *Chaos Machine,* 110–11.
5. Jack Nicas, "YouTube Tops 1 Billion Hours of Video a Day, on Pace to Eclipse TV," *Wall Street Journal,* Feb. 27, 2017, www.wsj.com/articles/youtube-tops-1-billion-hours-of-video-a-day-on-pace-to-eclipse-tv-1488220851.
6. Fisher, *Chaos Machine;* Ariely, *Misbelief,* 262–63.
7. Fisher, *Chaos Machine,* 266–77.
8. Ibid., 276–77.
9. Ibid., 270.
10. Emine Saner, "YouTube's Susan Wojcicki: 'Where's the Line of Free Speech— Are You Removing Voices That Should Be Heard?,'" *Guardian,* Aug. 10, 2011, www.theguardian.com/technology/2019/aug/10/youtube-susan-wojcicki-ceo-where-line-removing-voices-heard.
11. Dan Milmo, "Frances Haugen: 'I Never Wanted to Be a Whistleblower. But Lives Were in Danger,'" *Guardian,* Oct. 24, 2021, www.theguardian.com/technology/2021/oct/24/frances-haugen-i-never-wanted-to-be-a-whistleblower-but-lives-were-in-danger.
12. Amnesty International, *Social Atrocity,* 44.
13. Ibid., 38.
14. Ibid., 42.
15. Ibid., 34.
16. "Facebook Ban of Racial Slur Sparks Debate in Burma," *Irrawaddy,* May 31, 2017, www.irrawaddy.com/news/burma/facebook-ban-of-racial-slur-sparks-debate-in-burma.html.
17. Amnesty International, *Social Atrocity,* 34.
18. Karen Hao, "How Facebook and Google Fund Global Misinformation," *MIT Technology Review,* Nov. 20, 2021, www.technologyreview.com/2021/11/20/1039076/facebook-google-disinformation-clickbait/.
19. Hayley Tsukayama, "Facebook's Changing Its News Feed. How Will It Affect What You See?," *Washington Post,* Jan. 12, 2018, www.washingtonpost.com/news/the-switch/wp/2018/01/12/facebooks-changing-its-news-feed-how-will-it-affect-what-you-see/; Jonah Bromwich and Matthew Haag, "Facebook Is Changing. What Does That Mean to Your News Feed?," *New York Times,* Jan. 12, 2018, www.nytimes.com/2018/01/12/technology/facebook-news-feed-changes.html; Jason A. Gallo and Clare Y. Cho, "Social Media: Misinformation and Content Moderation Issues for Congress," Congressional Research Service Report R46662, Jan. 27, 2021, 11n67, crsreports

.congress.gov/product/pdf/R/R46662; Keach Hagey and Jeff Horwitz, "Facebook Tried to Make Its Platform a Healthier Place. It Got Angrier Instead," *Wall Street Journal*, Sept. 15, 2021, www.wsj.com/articles/facebook-algorithm -change-zuckerberg-11631654215; "YouTube Doesn't Know Where Its Own Line Is," *Wired*, March 2, 2010, www.wired.com/story/youtube-content -moderation-inconsistent/; Ben Popken, "As Algorithms Take Over, YouTube's Recommendations Highlight a Human Problem," NBC News, April 19, 2018, www.nbcnews.com/tech/social-media/algorithms-take-over -youtube-s-recommendations-highlight-human-problem-n867596; Paul Lewis, "'Fiction Is Outperforming Reality': How YouTube's Algorithm Distorts Truth," *Guardian*, Feb. 2, 2018, www.theguardian.com/technology/2018 /feb/02/how-youtubes-algorithm-distorts-truth.

20. M. A. Thomas, "Machine Learning Applications for Cybersecurity," *Cyber Defense Review* 8, no. 1 (Spring 2023): 87–102, www.jstor.org/stable /48730574.

21. Allan House and Cathy Brennan, eds., *Social Media and Mental Health* (Cambridge, U.K.: Cambridge University Press, 2023); Gohar Feroz Khan, Bobby Swar, and Sang Kon Lee, "Social Media Risks and Benefits: A Public Sector Perspective," *Social Science Computer Review* 32, no. 5 (2014): 606–27, doi.org /10.1177/089443931452.

22. Vanya Eftimova Bellinger, *Marie von Clausewitz: The Woman Behind the Making of "On War"* (Oxford: Oxford University Press, 2016); Donald J. Stoker, *Clausewitz: His Life and Work* (Oxford: Oxford University Press, 2014), 1–2, 256.

23. Stoker, *Clausewitz*, 35.

24. John G. Gagliardo, *Reich and Nation: The Holy Roman Empire as Idea and Reality, 1763–1806* (Bloomington: Indiana University Press, 1980), 4–5.

25. Todd Smith, "Army's Long-Awaited Iraq War Study Finds Iran Was the Only Winner in a Conflict That Holds Many Lessons for Future Wars," *Army Times*, Jan. 18, 2019, www.armytimes.com/news/your-army/2019/01/18 /armys-long-awaited-iraq-war-study-finds-iran-was-the-only-winner-in -a-conflict-that-holds-many-lessons-for-future-wars/. One of the authors of the study, as well as a colleague, recently provided a summary to *Time*. See Frank Sobchak and Matthew Zais, "How Iran Won the Iraq War," *Time*, March 22, 2023, time.com/6265077/how-iran-won-the-iraq-war/.

26. Nick Bostrom, *Superintelligence: Paths, Dangers, Strategies* (Oxford: Oxford University Press, 2014), 122–25.

27. Brian Christian, *The Alignment Problem: Machine Learning and Human Values* (New York: W. W. Norton, 2022), 9–10.

28. Amnesty International, *Social Atrocity*, 34–37.

29. Andrew Roberts, *Napoleon the Great* (London: Allen Lane, 2014), 5.

30. Ibid., 14–15.

31. Ibid., 9, 14.

32. Ibid., 29–40.

33. Philip Dwyer, *Napoleon: The Path to Power, 1769–1799* (London: Bloomsbury, 2014), 668; David G. Chandler, *The Campaigns of Napoleon* (New York: Macmillan, 1966), 1:3.

34. Maria E. Kronfeldner, *The Routledge Handbook of Dehumanization* (London: Routledge, 2021); David Livingstone Smith, *On Inhumanity: Dehumaniza-*

tion and How to Resist It (New York: Oxford University Press, 2020); David Livingstone Smith, *Less Than Human: Why We Demean, Enslave, and Exterminate Others* (New York: St. Martin's Press, 2011).

35. Smith, *On Inhumanity,* 139–42.

36. International Crisis Group, "Myanmar's Rohingya Crisis Enters a Dangerous New Phase," Dec. 7, 2017, www.crisisgroup.org/asia/southeast-asia/myanmar/292-myanmars-rohingya-crisis-enters-dangerous-new-phase.

37. Bettina Stangneth, *Eichmann Before Jerusalem: The Unexamined Life of a Mass Murderer* (New York: Alfred A. Knopf, 2014), 217–18.

38. Emily Washburn, "What to Know About Effective Altruism—Championed by Musk, Bankman-Fried, and Silicon Valley Giants," *Forbes,* March 8, 2023, www.forbes.com/sites/emilywashburn/2023/03/08/what-to-know-about-effective-altruism-championed-by-musk-bankman-fried-and-silicon-valley-giants/; Alana Semuels, "How Silicon Valley Has Disrupted Philanthropy," *Atlantic,* July 25, 2018, www.theatlantic.com/technology/archive/2018/07/how-silicon-valley-has-disrupted-philanthropy/565997/; Timnit Gebru, "Effective Altruism Is Pushing a Dangerous Brand of 'AI Safety,'" *Wired,* Nov. 30, 2022, www.wired.com/story/effective-altruism-artificial-intelligence-sam-bankman-fried/; Gideon Lewis-Kraus, "The Reluctant Prophet of Effective Altruism," *New Yorker,* Aug. 8, 2022, www.newyorker.com/magazine/2022/08/15/the-reluctant-prophet-of-effective-altruism.

39. Alan Soble, "Kant and Sexual Perversion," *Monist* 86, no. 1 (2003): 55–89, www.jstor.org/stable/27903806. See also Matthew C. Altman, "Kant on Sex and Marriage: The Implications for the Same-Sex Marriage Debate," *Kant-Studien* 101, no. 3 (2010): 332; Lara Denis, "Kant on the Wrongness of 'Unnatural' Sex," *History of Philosophy Quarterly* 16, no. 2 (April 1999): 225–48, www.jstor.org/stable/40602706.

40. Geoffrey J. Giles, "The Persecution of Gay Men and Lesbians During the Third Reich," in *The Routledge History of the Holocaust,* ed. Jonathan C. Friedman (London: Routledge, 2010), 385–96; Melanie Murphy, "Homosexuality and the Law in the Third Reich," in *Nazi Law: From Nuremberg to Nuremberg,* ed. John J. Michalczyk (London: Bloomsbury Academic, 2018), 110–24; Michael Schwartz, ed., *Homosexuelle im Nationalsozialismus: Neue Forschungsperspektiven zu Lebenssituationen von lesbischen, schwulen, bi-, trans- und intersexuellen Menschen 1933 bis 1945* (Munich: De Gruyter Oldenbourg, 2014).

41. Jeremy Bentham, "Offenses Against One's Self," ed. Louis Crompton, *Journal of Homosexuality* 3, no. 4 (1978): 389–406; Jeremy Bentham, "Jeremy Bentham's Essay on Paederasty," ed. Louis Crompton, *Journal of Homosexuality* 4, no. 1 (1978): 91–107.

42. Olga Yakusheva et al., "Lives Saved and Lost in the First Six Months of the US COVID-19 Pandemic: A Retrospective Cost-Benefit Analysis," *PLOS ONE* 17, no. 1 (2022), article e0261759.

43. Bitna Kim and Meghan Royle, "Domestic Violence in the Context of the COVID-19 Pandemic: A Synthesis of Systematic Reviews," *Trauma, Violence, and Abuse* 25, no. 1 (2024): 476–93; Lis Bates et al., "Domestic Homicides and Suspected Victim Suicides During the Covid-19 Pandemic 2020–2021," U.K. Home Office, Aug. 25, 2021, assets.publishing.service.gov.uk/media/6124ef66d3bf7f63a90687ac/Domestic_homicides_and_suspected_victim_suicides_during_the_Covid-19_Pandemic_2020-2021

.pdf; Benedetta Barchielli et al., "When 'Stay at Home' Can Be Dangerous: Data on Domestic Violence in Italy During COVID-19 Lockdown," *International Journal of Environmental Research and Public Health* 18, no. 17 (2021), article 8948.

44. Jingxuan Zhao et al., "Changes in Cancer-Related Mortality During the COVID-19 Pandemic in the United States," *Journal of Clinical Oncology* 40, no. 16 (2022): 6581; Abdul Rahman Jazieh et al., "Impact of the COVID-19 Pandemic on Cancer Care: A Global Collaborative Study," *JCO Global Oncology* 6 (2020): 1428–38; Camille Maringe et al., "The Impact of the COVID-19 Pandemic on Cancer Deaths due to Delays in Diagnosis in England, UK: A National, Population-Based, Modelling Study," *Lancet Oncology* 21, no. 8 (2020): 1023–34; Allini Mafra da Costa et al., "Impact of COVID-19 Pandemic on Cancer-Related Hospitalizations in Brazil," *Cancer Control* 28 (2021): article 10732748211038736; Talía Malagón et al., "Predicted Long-Term Impact of COVID-19 Pandemic-Related Care Delays on Cancer Mortality in Canada," *International Journal of Cancer* 150, no. 8 (2022): 1244–54.

45. Chalmers, *Reality+*.

46. Pokémon GO, "Heads Up!," press release, Sept. 7, 2016, pokemongolive.com /en/post/headsup/.

47. Brian Fung, "Here's What We Know About Google's Mysterious Search Engine," *Washington Post*, Aug. 28, 2018, www.washingtonpost.com/technology /2018/08/28/heres-what-we-really-know-about-googles-mysterious-search -engine/; Geoffrey A. Fowler, "AI Is Changing Google Search: What the I/O Announcement Means for You," *Washington Post*, May 10, 2023, www .washingtonpost.com/technology/2023/05/10/google-search-ai-io-2023/; Jillian D'Onfro, "Google Is Making a Giant Change This Week That Could Crush Millions of Small Businesses," *Business Insider*, April 20, 2015, www .businessinsider.com/google-mobilegeddon-2015-4.

48. SearchSEO, "Can I Improve My Search Ranking with a Traffic Bot," accessed Jan. 11, 2024, www.searchseo.io/blog/improve-ranking-with-traffic -bot; Daniel E. Rose, "Why Is Web Search So Hard . . . to Evaluate?," *Journal of Web Engineering* 3, no. 3–4 (2004): 171–81.

49. Javier Pastor-Galindo, Felix Gomez Marmol, and Gregorio Martínez Pérez, "Profiling Users and Bots in Twitter Through Social Media Analysis," *Information Sciences* 613 (2022): 161–83; Timothy Graham and Katherine M. FitzGerald, "Bots, Fake News, and Election Conspiracies: Disinformation During the Republican Primary Debate and the Trump Interview," Digital Media Research Center, Queensland University of Technology (2023), eprints .qut.edu.au/242533/; Josh Taylor, "Bots on X Worse Than Ever According to Analysis of 1M Tweets During First Republican Primary Debate," *Guardian*, Sept. 9, 2023, www.theguardian.com/technology/2023/sep/09/x-twitter-bots -republican-primary-debate-tweets-increase; Stefan Wojcik et al., "Bots in the Twittersphere," Pew Research Center, April 9, 2018, www.pewresearch .org/internet/2018/04/09/bots-in-the-twittersphere/; Jack Nicas, "Why Can't the Social Networks Stop Fake Accounts?," *New York Times*, Dec. 8, 2020, www.nytimes.com/2020/12/08/technology/why-cant-the-social-networks -stop-fake-accounts.html.

50. Sari Nusseibeh, *What Is a Palestinian State Worth?* (Cambridge, Mass.: Harvard University Press, 2011), 48.

51. Michael Lewis, *The Big Short: Inside the Doomsday Machine* (New York: W. W. Norton, 2010); Marcin Wojtowicz, "CDOs and the Financial Crisis: Credit Ratings and Fair Premia," *Journal of Banking and Finance* 39 (2014): 1–13; Robert A. Jarrow, "The Role of ABS, CDS, and CDOs in the Credit Crisis and the Economy," *Rethinking the Financial Crisis* 202 (2011): 210–35; Bilal Aziz Poswal, "Financial Innovations: Role of CDOs, CDS, and Securitization During the US Financial Crisis 2007–2009," *Ecorfan Journal* 3, no. 6 (2012): 125–39.

52. *Citizens United v. FEC*, 558 U.S. 310 (2010), supreme.justia.com/cases /federal/us/558/310/; Amy B. Wang, "Senate Republicans Block Bill to Require Disclosure of 'Dark Money' Donors," *Washington Post*, Sept. 22, 2022, www.washingtonpost.com/politics/2022/09/22/senate-republicans -campaign-finance/.

53. Vincent Bakpetu Thompson, *The Making of the African Diaspora in the Americas, 1441–1900* (London: Longman, 1987); Mark M. Smith and Robert L. Paquette, eds., *The Oxford Handbook of Slavery in the Americas* (New York: Oxford University Press, 2010); John H. Moore, ed., *The Encyclopedia of Race and Racism* (New York: Macmillan Reference USA, 2008); Jack D. Forbes, "The Evolution of the Term Mulatto: A Chapter in Black–Native American Relations," *Journal of Ethnic Studies* 10, no. 2 (1982): 45–66; April J. Mayes, *The Mulatto Republic: Class, Race, and Dominican National Identity* (Gainesville: University Press of Florida, 2014); Irene Diggs, "Color in Colonial Spanish America," *Journal of Negro History* 38, no. 4 (1953): 403–27.

54. Sasha Costanza-Chock, *Design Justice: Community-Led Practices to Build the Worlds We Need* (Cambridge, Mass.: MIT Press, 2020); D'Ignazio and Klein, *Data Feminism*; Ruha Benjamin, *Race After Technology: Abolitionist Tools for the New Jim Code* (Cambridge, U.K.: Polity Press, 2019); Virginia Eubanks, *Automating Inequality: How High-Tech Tools Profile, Police, and Punish the Poor* (New York: St. Martin's Press, 2018); Wendy Hui Kyong Chun, *Discriminating Data: Correlation, Neighborhoods, and the New Politics of Recognition* (Cambridge, Mass.: MIT Press, 2021).

55. Peter Lee, "Learning from Tay's Introduction," Microsoft Official Blog, March 25, 2016, blogs.microsoft.com/blog/2016/03/25/learning-tays -introduction/; Alex Hern, "Microsoft Scrambles to Limit PR Damage over Abusive AI Bot Tay," *Guardian*, March 24, 2016, www.theguardian.com /technology/2016/mar/24/microsoft-scrambles-limit-pr-damage-over -abusive-ai-bot-tay; "Microsoft Pulls Robot After It Tweets 'Hitler Was Right I Hate the Jews,'" *Haaretz*, March 24, 2016, www.haaretz.com/science -and-health/2016-03-24/ty-article/microsoft-pulls-robot-after-it-tweets -hitler-was-right-i-hate-the-jews/0000017f-dede-d856-a37f-ffde9a9c0000; Elle Hunt, "Tay, Microsoft's AI Chatbot, Gets a Crash Course in Racism from Twitter," *Guardian*, March 24, 2016, www.theguardian.com/technology /2016/mar/24/tay-microsofts-ai-chatbot-gets-a-crash-course-in-racism -from-twitter.

56. Morgan Klaus Scheuerman, Madeleine Pape, and Alex Hanna, "Auto-essentialization: Gender in Automated Facial Analysis as Extended Colonial Project," *Big Data and Society* 8, no. 2 (2021), article 20539517211053712.

57. D'Ignazio and Klein, *Data Feminism*, 29–30.

58. Yoni Wilkenfeld, "Can Chess Survive Artificial Intelligence?," *New Atlantis* 58 (2019): 37.

59. Ibid.
60. Matthew Hutson, "How Researchers Are Teaching AI to Learn Like a Child," *Science*, May 24, 2018, www.science.org/content/article/how-researchers-are-teaching-ai-learn-child; Oliwia Koteluk et al., "How Do Machines Learn? Artificial Intelligence as a New Era in Medicine," *Journal of Personalized Medicine* 11 (2021), article 32; Mohsen Soori, Behrooz Arezoo, and Roza Dastres, "Artificial Intelligence, Machine Learning, and Deep Learning in Advanced Robotics: A Review," *Cognitive Robotics* 3 (2023): 54–70.
61. Christian, *Alignment Problem*, 31; D'Ignazio and Klein, *Data Feminism*, 29–30.
62. Christian, *Alignment Problem*, 32; Joy Buolamwini and Timnit Gebru, "Gender Shades: Intersectional Accuracy Disparities in Commercial Gender Classification," in *Proceedings of the 1st Conference on Fairness, Accountability, and Transparency, PMLR* 81 (2018): 77–91.
63. Lee, "Learning from Tay's Introduction."
64. D'Ignazio and Klein, *Data Feminism*, 28; Jeffrey Dastin, "Insight—Amazon Scraps Secret AI Recruiting Tool That Showed Bias Against Women," Reuters, Oct. 11, 2018, www.reuters.com/article/idUSKCN1MK0AG/.
65. Christianne Corbett and Catherine Hill, *Solving the Equation: The Variables for Women's Success in Engineering and Computing* (Washington, D.C.: American Association of University Women, 2015), 47–54.
66. D'Ignazio and Klein, *Data Feminism*.
67. Meghan O'Gieblyn, *God, Human, Animal, Machine: Technology, Metaphor, and the Search for Meaning* (New York: Anchor, 2022), 197–216.
68. Brinkmann et al., "Machine Culture."
69. Suleyman, *Coming Wave*, 164.
70. Brinkmann et al., "Machine Culture"; Bengio et al., "Managing Extreme AI Risks Amid Rapid Progress."

CHAPTER 9: DEMOCRACIES

1. Andreessen, "Why AI Will Save the World"; Kurzweil, *The Singularity Is Nearer*.
2. Laurie Laybourn-Langton, Lesley Rankin, and Darren Baxter, *This Is a Crisis: Facing Up to the Age of Environmental Breakdown*, Institute for Public Policy Research, Feb. 1, 2019, 12, www.jstor.org/stable/resrep21894.5.
3. Kenneth L. Hacker and Jan van Dijk, eds., *Digital Democracy: Issues of Theory and Practice* (New York: Sage, 2000); Anthony G. Wilhelm, *Democracy in the Digital Age: Challenges to Political Life in Cyberspace* (London: Routledge, 2002); Elaine C. Kamarck and Joseph S. Nye, eds., *Governance.com: Democracy in the Information Age* (London: Rowman & Littlefield, 2004); Zizi Papacharissi, *A Private Sphere: Democracy in a Digital Age* (Cambridge, U.K.: Polity, 2010); Costa Vayenas, *Democracy in the Digital Age* (Cambridge, U.K.: Arena Books, 2017); Giancarlo Vilella, *E-democracy: On Participation in the Digital Age* (Baden-Baden: Nomos, 2019); Volker Boehme-Nessler, *Digitising Democracy: On Reinventing Democracy in the Digital Era—a Legal, Political, and Psychological Perspective* (Berlin: Springer Nature, 2020); Sokratis Katsikas and Vasilios Zorkadis, *E-democracy: Safeguarding Democracy and Human Rights in the Digital Age* (Berlin: Springer International, 2020).

4. Thomas Reuters Popular Law, "Psychotherapist-Patient Privilege," uk .practicallaw.thomsonreuters.com/6-522-3158; U.S. Department of Health and Human Services, "Minimum Necessary Requirement," www.hhs.gov /hipaa/for-professionals/privacy/guidance/minimum-necessary-requirement /index.html; European Association for Psychotherapy, "EAP Statement on the Legal Position of Psychotherapy in Europe," January 2021, available at www.europsyche.org/app/uploads/2021/04/Legal-Position-of -Psychotherapy-in-Europe-2021-Final.pdf.

5. Marshall Allen, "Health Insurers Are Vacuuming Up Details About You— and It Could Raise Your Rates," ProPublica, July 17, 2018, www.propublica .org/article/health-insurers-are-vacuuming-up-details-about-you-and-it -could-raise-your-rates.

6. Jannik Luboeinski and Christian Tetzlaff, "Organization and Priming of Long-Term Memory Representations with Two-Phase Plasticity," *Cognitive Computation* 15, no. 4 (2023): 1211–30.

7. Muhammad Imran Razzak, Muhammad Imran, and Guandong Xu, "Big Data Analytics for Preventive Medicine," *Neural Computing and Applications* 32 (2020): 4417–51; Gaurav Laroia et al., "A Unified Health Algorithm That Teaches Itself to Improve Health Outcomes for Every Individual: How Far into the Future Is It?," *Digital Health* 8 (2022), article 20552076221074126.

8. Nicholas H. Dimsdale, Nicholas Horsewood, and Arthur Van Riel, "Unemployment in Interwar Germany: An Analysis of the Labor Market, 1927–1936," *Journal of Economic History* 66, no. 3 (2006): 778–808.

9. Hubert Dreyfus, *What Computers Can't Do* (New York: Harper and Row, 1972). See also Brett Karlan, "Human Achievement and Artificial Intelligence," *Ethics and Information Technology* 25 (2023), article 40, doi.org/10 .1007/s10676-023-09713-x; Francis Mechner, "Chess as a Behavioral Model for Cognitive Skill Research: Review of Blindfold Chess by Eliot Hearst and John Knott," *Journal of Experimental Analysis Behavior* 94, no. 3 (Nov. 2010): 373–86, doi:10.1901/jeab.2010.94-373; Gerd Gigerenzer, *How to Stay Smart in a Smart World: Why Human Intelligence Still Beats Algorithms* (Cambridge, Mass.: MIT Press, 2022), 21.

10. Eda Ergin et al., "Can Artificial Intelligence and Robotic Nurses Replace Operating Room Nurses? The Quasi-experimental Research," *Journal of Robotic Surgery* 17, no. 4 (2023): 1847–55; Nancy Robert, "How Artificial Intelligence Is Changing Nursing," *Nursing Management* 50, no. 9 (2019): 30–39; Aprianto Daniel Pailaha, "The Impact and Issues of Artificial Intelligence in Nursing Science and Healthcare Settings," *SAGE Open Nursing* 9 (2023), article 23779608231196847.

11. Erik Cambria et al., "Seven Pillars for the Future of Artificial Intelligence," *IEEE Intelligent Systems* 38 (Nov.–Dec. 2023): 62–69; Marcus du Sautoy, *The Creativity Code: Art and Innovation in the Age of AI* (Cambridge, Mass.: Belknap Press of Harvard University Press, 2019); Brinkmann et al., "Machine Culture."

12. On how humans recognize emotions, see Tony W. Buchanan, David Bibas, and Ralph Adolphs, "Associations Between Feeling and Judging the Emotions of Happiness and Fear: Findings from a Large-Scale Field Experiment," *PLOS ONE* 5, no. 5 (2010), article 10640, doi.org/10.1371/journal .pone.0010640; Ralph Adolphs, "Neural Systems for Recognizing Emotion," *Current Opinion in Neurobiology* 12, no. 2 (2002): 169–77; Albert Newen,

Anna Welpinghus, and Georg Juckel, "Emotion Recognition as Pattern Recognition: The Relevance of Perception," *Mind and Language* 30, no. 2 (2015): 187–208; Joel Aronoff, "How We Recognize Angry and Happy Emotion in People, Places, and Things," *Cross-Cultural Research* 40, no. 1 (2006): 83–105. On AI and emotion recognition, see Smith K. Khare et al., "Emotion Recognition and Artificial Intelligence: A Systematic Review (2014–2023) and Research Recommendations," *Information Fusion* 102 (2024), article 102019, doi .org/10.1016/j.inffus.2023.102019.

13. Zohar Elyoseph et al., "ChatGPT Outperforms Humans in Emotional Awareness Evaluations," *Frontiers in Psychology* 14 (2023), article 1199058.

14. John W. Ayers et al., "Comparing Physician and Artificial Intelligence Chatbot Responses to Patient Questions Posted to a Public Social Media Forum," *JAMA Internal Medicine* 183, no. 6 (2023): 589–96, jamanetwork.com/journals /jamainternalmedicine/article-abstract/2804309.

15. Seung Hwan Lee et al., "Forgiving Sports Celebrities with Ethical Transgressions: The Role of Parasocial Relationships, Ethical Intent, and Regulatory Focus Mindset," *Journal of Global Sport Management* 3, no. 2 (2018): 124–45.

16. Karlan, "Human Achievement and Artificial Intelligence."

17. Harari, *Homo Deus,* chap. 3.

18. Edmund Burke, *Revolutionary Writings: Reflections on the Revolution in France and the First Letter on a Regicide Peace* (Cambridge, U.K.: Cambridge University Press, 2014); F. A. Hayek, *The Road to Serfdom* (London: Routledge, 2001); F. A. Hayek, *The Constitution of Liberty: The Definitive Edition* (London: Routledge, 2020); Jonathan Haidt, *The Righteous Mind: Why Good People Are Divided by Politics and Religion* (London: Vintage, 2012); Yoram Hazony, *Conservatism: A Rediscovery* (New York: Simon & Schuster, 2022); Peter Whitewood, *The Red Army and the Great Terror: Stalin's Purge of the Soviet Military* (Lawrence: University Press of Kansas, 2015).

19. Hazony, *Conservatism,* 3.

20. Bureau of Labor Statistics, "Historical Statistics of the United States, Colonial Times to 1970, Part I," *Series D 85–86 Unemployment: 1890–1970* (1975), 135; Curtis J. Simon, "The Supply Price of Labor During the Great Depression," *Journal of Economic History* 61, no. 4 (2001): 877–903; Vernon T. Clover, "Employees' Share of National Income, 1929–1941," *Fort Hays Kansas State College Studies: Economics Series* 1 (1943): 194; Stanley Lebergott, "Labor Force, Employment, and Unemployment, 1929–39: Estimating Methods," *Monthly Labor Review* 67, no. 1 (1948): 51; Robert Roy Nathan, *National Income, 1929–36, of the United States* (Washington, D.C.: U.S. Government Printing Office, 1939), 15 (table 3).

21. David M. Kennedy, "What the New Deal Did," *Political Science Quarterly* 124, no. 2 (2009): 251–68.

22. William E. Leuchtenburg, *In the Shadow of FDR: From Harry Truman to Barack Obama* (Ithaca, N.Y.: Cornell University Press, 2011), 48–49.

23. Suleyman, *Coming Wave.*

24. Michael L. Birzer and Richard B. Ellis, "Debunking the Myth That All Is Well in the Home of *Brown v. Topeka Board of Education:* A Study of Perceived Discrimination," *Journal of Black Studies* 36, no. 6 (2006): 793–814.

25. United States Supreme Court, *Brown v. Board of Education,* May 17, 1954, available at: www.archives.gov/milestone-documents/brown-v-board-of -education#transcript.

26. "*State v. Loomis:* Wisconsin Supreme Court Requires Warning Before Use of Algorithmic Risk Assessments in Sentencing," *Harvard Law Review* 130 (2017): 1530–37.

27. Rebecca Wexler, "When a Computer Program Keeps You in Jail: How Computers Are Harming Criminal Justice," *New York Times,* June 13, 2017, www .nytimes.com/2017/06/13/opinion/how-computers-are-harming-criminal -justice.html; Ed Yong, "A Popular Algorithm Is No Better at Predicting Crimes Than Random People," *Atlantic,* Jan. 17, 2018, www.theatlantic.com /technology/archive/2018/01/equivant-compas-algorithm/550646/.

28. Mitch Smith, "In Wisconsin, a Backlash Against Using Data to Foretell Defendants' Futures," *New York Times,* June 22, 2016, www.nytimes.com/2016 /06/23/us/backlash-in-wisconsin-against-using-data-to-foretell-defendants -futures.html.

29. Eric Holder, "Speech Presented at the National Association of Criminal Defense Lawyers 57th Annual Meeting and 13th State Criminal Justice Network Conference, Philadelphia, PA," *Federal Sentencing Reporter* 27, no. 4 (2015): 252–55; Sonja B. Starr, "Evidence-Based Sentencing and the Scientific Rationalization of Discrimination," *Stanford Law Review* 66, no. 4 (2014): 803–72; Cecelia Klingele, "The Promises and Perils of Evidence-Based Corrections," *Notre Dame Law Review* 91, no. 2 (2015): 537–84; Jennifer L. Skeem and Jennifer Eno Louden, "Assessment of Evidence on the Quality of the Correctional Offender Management Profiling for Alternative Sanctions (COMPAS)," Center for Public Policy Research, Dec. 26, 2007, cpb-us-e2.wpmucdn.com/sites.uci.edu/dist/0/1149/files/2013/06/CDCR -Skeem-EnoLouden-COMPASeval-SECONDREVISION-final-Dec-28 -07.pdf; Julia Dressel and Hany Farid, "The Accuracy, Fairness, and Limits of Predicting Recidivism," *Science Advances* 4, no. 1 (2018), article eaao5580; Julia Angwin et al., "Machine Bias," ProPublica, May 23, 2016, www .propublica.org/article/machine-bias-risk-assessments-in-criminal -sentencing. However, see also Sam Corbett-Davies et al., "A Computer Program Used for Bail and Sentencing Decisions Was Labeled Biased Against Blacks: It's Actually Not That Clear," *Washington Post,* Oct. 17, 2016, www .washingtonpost.com/news/monkey-cage/wp/2016/10/17/can-an -algorithm-be-racist-our-analysis-is-more-cautious-than-propublicas.

30. "*State v. Loomis:* Wisconsin Supreme Court Requires Warning Before Use of Algorithmic Risk Assessments in Sentencing."

31. Seena Fazel et al., "The Predictive Performance of Criminal Risk Assessment Tools Used at Sentencing: Systematic Review of Validation Studies," *Journal of Criminal Justice* 81 (2022), article 101902; Jay Singh et al., "International Perspectives on the Practical Application of Violence Risk Assessment: A Global Survey of 44 Countries," *International Journal of Forensic Mental Health* 13, no. 3 (2014): 193–206; Melissa Hamilton and Pamela Ugwudike, "A 'Black Box' AI System Has Been Influencing Criminal Justice Decisions for over Two Decades—It's Time to Open It Up," *The Conversation,* July 26, 2023, theconversation.com/a-black-box-ai-system-has-been-influencing -criminal-justice-decisions-for-over-two-decades-its-time-to-open-it-up -200594; Federal Bureau of Prisons, "PATTERN Risk Assessment," accessed Jan. 11, 2024, www.bop.gov/inmates/fsa/pattern.jsp.

32. Manish Raghavan et al., "Mitigating Bias in Algorithmic Hiring: Evaluating Claims and Practices," in *Proceedings of the 2020 Conference on Fairness, Ac-*

countability, and Transparency (2020): 469–81; Nicol Turner Lee and Saman-
tha Lai, "Why New York City Is Cracking Down on AI in Hiring," Brookings
Institution, Dec. 20, 2021, www.brookings.edu/articles/why-new-york-city
-is-cracking-down-on-ai-in-hiring/; Sian Townson, "AI Can Make Bank
Loans More Fair," *Harvard Business Review,* Nov. 6, 2020, hbr.org/2020/11
/ai-can-make-bank-loans-more-fair; Robert Bartlett et al., "Consumer-
Lending Discrimination in the FinTech Era," *Journal of Financial Economics*
143, no. 1 (2022): 30–56; Mugahed A. Al-Antari, "Artificial Intelligence for
Medical Diagnostics—Existing and Future AI Technology!," *Diagnostics* 13,
no. 4 (2023), article 688; Thomas Davenport and Ravi Kalakota, "The Potential for Artificial Intelligence in Healthcare," *Future Healthcare Journal* 6,
no. 2 (2019): 94–98.

33. European Commission, "Can I Be Subject to Automated Individual Decision-
Making, Including Profiling?," accessed Jan. 11, 2024, commission.europa.eu
/law/law-topic/data-protection/reform/rights-citizens/my-rights/can-i-be
-subject-automated-individual-decision-making-including-profiling_en.

34. Suleyman, *Coming Wave,* 54.

35. Brinkmann et al., "Machine Culture."

36. Suleyman, *Coming Wave,* 80. See also Tilman Räuker et al., "Toward Transparent AI: A Survey on Interpreting the Inner Structures of Deep Neural
Networks," *2023 IEEE Conference on Secure and Trustworthy Machine Learning (SaTML),* Feb. 2023, 464–83, doi:10.1109/SaTML54575.2023.00039.

37. Adele Atkinson, Chiara Monticone, and Flore-Anne Messi, *OECD/
INFE International Survey of Adult Financial Literacy Competencies* (Paris:
OECD, 2016), web-archive.oecd.org/2018-12-10/417183-OECD-INFE
-International-Survey-of-Adult-Financial-Literacy-Competencies.pdf.

38. DODS, "Parliamentary Perceptions of the Banking System," July 2014, posi-
tivemoney.org/wp-content/uploads/2014/08/Positive-Money-Dods
-Monitoring-Poll-of-MPs.pdf.

39. Jacob Feldman, "The Simplicity Principle in Human Concept Learning,"
Current Directions in Psychological Science 12, no. 6 (2003): 227–32; Bethany
Kilcrease, *Falsehood and Fallacy: How to Think, Read, and Write in the Twenty-
First Century* (Toronto: University of Toronto Press, 2021), 115; Christina N.
Lessov-Schlaggar, Joshua B. Rubin, and Bradley L. Schlaggar, "The Fallacy of
Univariate Solutions to Complex Systems Problems," *Frontiers in Neurosci-
ence* 10 (2016), article 267.

40. D'Ignazio and Klein, *Data Feminism,* 54.

41. Tobias Berg et al., "On the Rise of FinTechs: Credit Scoring Using Digital
Footprints," *Review of Financial Studies* 33, no. 7 (2020): 2845–97, doi.org/10
.1093/rfs/hhz099.

42. Ibid.; Lin Ma et al., "A New Aspect on P2P Online Lending Default Prediction Using Meta-level Phone Usage Data in China," *Decision Support Systems*
111 (2018): 60–71; Li Yuan, "Want a Loan in China? Keep Your Phone
Charged," *Wall Street Journal,* April 6, 2017, www.wsj.com/articles/want
-a-loan-in-china-keep-your-phone-charged-1491474250.

43. Brinkmann et al., "Machine Culture."

44. Jesse S. Summers, "*Post Hoc Ergo Propter Hoc:* Some Benefits of Rationalization," *Philosophical Explorations* 20, no. 1 (2017): 21–36; Richard E. Nisbett
and Timothy D. Wilson, "Telling More Than We Can Know: Verbal Reports
on Mental Processes," *Psychological Review* 84, no. 3 (1977): 231; Daniel M.

Wegner and Thalia Wheatley, "Apparent Mental Causation: Sources of the Experience of Will," *American Psychologist* 54, no. 7 (1999): 480–92; Benjamin Libet, "Do We Have Free Will?," *Journal of Consciousness Studies* 6, no. 8–9 (1999): 47–57; Jonathan Haidt, "The Emotional Dog and Its Rational Tail: A Social Intuitionist Approach to Moral Judgment," *Psychological Review* 108, no. 4 (2001): 814–34; Joshua D. Greene, "The Secret Joke of Kant's Soul," *Moral Psychology* 3 (2008): 35–79; William Hirstein, ed., *Confabulation: Views from Neuroscience, Psychiatry, Psychology, and Philosophy* (New York: Oxford University Press, 2009); Michael Gazzaniga, *Who's in Charge? Free Will and the Science of the Brain* (London: Robinson, 2012); Fiery Cushman and Joshua Greene, "The Philosopher in the Theater," in *The Social Psychology of Morality: Exploring the Causes of Good and Evil,* ed. Mario Mikulincer and Phillip R. Shaver (Washington, D.C.: APA Press, 2011), 33–50.

45. Shai Danziger, Jonathan Levav, and Liora Avnaim-Pesso, "Extraneous Factors in Judicial Decisions," *Proceedings of the National Academy of Sciences* 108, no. 17 (2011): 6889–92; Keren Weinshall-Margel and John Shapard, "Overlooked Factors in the Analysis of Parole Decisions," *Proceedings of the National Academy of Sciences* 108, no. 42 (2011), article E833.

46. Julia Dressel and Hany Farid, "The Accuracy, Fairness, and Limits of Predicting Recidivism," *Science Advances* 4, no. 1 (2018), article eaao5580; Klingele, "Promises and Perils of Evidence-Based Corrections"; Alexander M. Holsinger et al., "A Rejoinder to Dressel and Farid: New Study Finds Computer Algorithm Is More Accurate Than Humans at Predicting Arrest and as Good as a Group of 20 Lay Experts," *Federal Probation* 82 (2018): 50–55; D'Ignazio and Klein, *Data Feminism,* 53–54.

47. The EU Artificial Intelligence Act, European Commission, April 21, 2021, artificialintelligenceact.eu/the-act/. The act says, "The following artificial intelligence practices shall be prohibited: . . . (c) the placing on the market, putting into service or use of AI systems by public authorities or on their behalf for the evaluation or classification of the trustworthiness of natural persons over a certain period of time based on their social behavior or known or predicted personal or personality characteristics, with the social score leading to either or both of the following: (i) detrimental or unfavorable treatment of certain natural persons or whole groups thereof in social contexts which are unrelated to the contexts in which the data was originally generated or collected; (ii) detrimental or unfavorable treatment of certain natural persons or whole groups thereof that is unjustified or disproportionate to their social behavior or its gravity" (43).

48. Alessandro Bessi and Emilio Ferrara, "Social Bots Distort the 2016 U.S. Presidential Election Online Discussion," *First Monday* 21, no. 11 (2016): 1–14.

49. Luca Luceri, Felipe Cardoso, and Silvia Giordano, "Down the Bot Hole: Actionable Insights from a One-Year Analysis of Bot Activity on Twitter," *First Monday* 26, no. 3 (2021), firstmonday.org/ojs/index.php/fm/article/download /11441/10079.

50. David F. Carr, "Bots Likely Not a Big Part of Twitter's Audience—but Tweet a Lot," *Similarweb Blog,* Sept. 8, 2022, www.similarweb.com/blog/insights /social-media-news/twitter-bot-research-news/; "Estimating Twitter's Bot-Free Monetizable Daily Active Users (mDAU)," *Similarweb Blog,* Sept. 8, 2022, www.similarweb.com/blog/insights/social-media-news/twitter-bot -research/.

51. Giovanni Spitale, Nikola Biller-Andorno, and Federico Germani, "AI Model GPT-3 (Dis)informs Us Better Than Humans," *Science Advances* 9, no. 26 (2023), doi.org/10.1126/sciadv.adh1850.

52. Daniel C. Dennett, "The Problem with Counterfeit People," *Atlantic*, May 16, 2023, www.theatlantic.com/technology/archive/2023/05/problem-counterfeit-people/674075/.

53. See, for example, Hannes Kleineke, "The Prosecution of Counterfeiting in Lancastrian England," in *Medieval Merchants and Money: Essays in Honor of James L. Bolton*, ed. Martin Allen and Matthew Davies (London: University of London Press, 2016), 213–26; Susan L'Engle, "Justice in the Margins: Punishment in Medieval Toulouse," *Viator* 33 (2002): 133–65; Trevor Dean, *Crime in Medieval Europe, 1200–1550* (London: Routledge, 2014).

54. Dennett, "Problem with Counterfeit People."

55. Mariam Orabi et al., "Detection of Bots in Social Media: A Systematic Review," *Information Processing and Management* 57, no. 4 (2020), article 102250; Aaron J. Moss et al., "Bots or Inattentive Humans? Identifying Sources of Low-Quality Data in Online Platforms" (preprint, submitted 2021), osf.io/preprints/psyarxiv/wr8ds; Max Weiss, "Deepfake Bot Submissions to Federal Public Comment Websites Cannot Be Distinguished from Human Submissions," *Technology Science*, Dec. 17, 2019; Adrian Rauchfleisch and Jonas Kaiser, "The False Positive Problem of Automatic Bot Detection in Social Science Research," *PLOS ONE* 15, no. 10 (2020), article e0241045; Giovanni C. Santia, Munif Ishad Mujib, and Jake Ryland Williams, "Detecting Social Bots on Facebook in an Information Veracity Context," *Proceedings of the International AAAI Conference on Web and Social Media* 13 (2019): 463–72.

56. Drew DeSilver, "The Polarization in Today's Congress Has Roots That Go Back Decades," Pew Research Center, March 10, 2022, www.pewresearch.org/short-reads/2022/03/10/the-polarization-in-todays-congress-has-roots-that-go-back-decades/; Lee Drutman, "Why Bipartisanship in the Senate Is Dying," FiveThirtyEight, Sept. 27, 2021, fivethirtyeight.com/features/why-bipartisanship-in-the-senate-is-dying/.

57. Gregory A. Caldeira, "Neither the Purse nor the Sword: Dynamics of Public Confidence in the Supreme Court," *American Political Science Review* 80, no. 4 (1986): 1209–26, doi.org/10.2307/1960864.

CHAPTER 10: TOTALITARIANISM

1. See, for example, the otherwise excellent and insightful Zuboff, *Age of Surveillance Capitalism*; Fisher, *Chaos Machine*; Christian, *Alignment Problem*; D'Ignazio and Klein, *Data Feminism*; Costanza-Chock, *Design Justice*. Kai-Fu Lee, *AI Superpowers: China, Silicon Valley, and the New World Order* (New York: Houghton Mifflin, 2018), is an outstanding counterexample. See also Mark Coeckelbergh, *AI Ethics* (Cambridge, Mass.: MIT Press, 2020).

2. The Varieties of Democracy Institute at the University of Gothenburg estimated that in 2022, 72 percent of the world's population (5.7 billion people) lived under authoritarian or totalitarian regimes. See V-Dem Institute, *Defiance in the Face of Autocratization* (2023), v-dem.net/documents/29/V-dem_democracyreport2023_lowres.pdf.

3. Chicago Tribune Staff, "McDonald's: 60 Years, Billions Served," *Chicago Tri-*

bune, April 15, 2015, www.chicagotribune.com/business/chi-mcdonalds-60 -years-20150415-story.html.

4. Alphabet, "2022 Alphabet Annual Report," 2023, abc.xyz/assets/d4/4f /a48b94d548d0b2fdc029a95e8c63/2022-alphabet-annual-report.pdf; Statcounter, "Search Engine Market Share Worldwide—December 2023," accessed Jan. 12, 2024, gs.statcounter.com/search-engine-market-share; Jason Wise, "How Many People Use Search Engines in 2024?," Earthweb, Nov. 16, 2023, earthweb.com/search-engine-users/.

5. Google Search, "How Google Search Organizes Information," accessed Jan. 12, 2024, www.google.com/search/howsearchworks/how-search-works /organizing-information/; Statcounter, "Browser Market Share Worldwide," accessed Jan. 12, 2024, gs.statcounter.com/search-engine-market-share.

6. Parliamentary Counsel Office of New Zealand, "Privacy Act 2020," Dec. 6, 2023, www.legislation.govt.nz/act/public/2020/0031/latest/LMS23223.html; Jessie Yeung, "China's Sitting on a Goldmine of Genetic Data—and It Doesn't Want to Share," CNN, Aug. 12, 2023, edition.cnn.com/2023/08/11 /china/china-human-genetic-resources-regulations-intl-hnk-dst/index .html.

7. Dionysis Zindros, "The Illusion of Blockchain Democracy: One Coin Equals One Vote," Nesta Foundation, Sept. 14, 2020, www.nesta.org.uk /report/illusion-blockchain-democracy-one-coin-equals-one-vote/; Lukas Schädler, Michael Lustenberger, and Florian Spychiger, "Analyzing Decision-Making in Blockchain Governance," *Frontiers in Blockchain* 23, no. 6 (2023); PricewaterhouseCoopers, "Estonia—the Digital Republic Secured by Blockchain," 2019, www.pwc.com/gx/en/services/legal/tech/assets /estonia-the-digital-republic-secured-by-blockchain.pdf; Bryan Daugherty, "Why Governments Need to Embrace Blockchain Technology," *Evening Standard,* May 31, 2023, www.standard.co.uk/business/government -blockchain-technology-business-b1080774.html.

8. Cassius Dio, *Roman History,* book 78.

9. Adrastos Omissi, "*Damnatio Memoriae* or *Creatio Memoriae*? Memory Sanctions as Creative Processes in the Fourth Century AD," *Cambridge Classical Journal* 62 (2016): 170–99.

10. David King, *The Commissar Vanishes: The Falsification of Photographs and Art in Stalin's Russia* (New York: Henry Holt, 1997); Herman Ermolaev, *Censorship in Soviet Literature, 1917–1991* (Lanham, Md.: Rowman & Littlefield, 1997), 56, 59, 62, 67–68; Denis Skopin, *Photography and Political Repressions in Stalin's Russia: Defacing the Enemy* (New York: Routledge, 2022); Figes, *Whisperers,* 298.

11. Amnesty International Public Statement, EUR 46/7017/2023, "Russia: Under the 'Eye of Sauron': Persecution of Critics of the Aggression Against Ukraine," July 20, 2023, 2, www.amnesty.org/en/documents/eur46/7017 /2023/en/.

12. Sandra Bingham, *The Praetorian Guard: A History of Rome's Elite Special Forces* (London: I. B. Tauris, 2013).

13. Tacitus, *Annals,* book 4.41.

14. Ibid., book 6.50.

15. Albert Einstein et al., "The Russell-Einstein Manifesto [1955]," *Impact of Science on Society—Unesco* 26, no. 12 (1976): 15–16.

CHAPTER 11: THE SILICON CURTAIN

1. Suleyman, *Coming Wave,* 12–13, 173–77, 207–13; Emily H. Soice et al., "Can Large Language Models Democratize Access to Dual-Use Biotechnology?" (preprint, submitted 2023), doi.org/10.48550/arXiv.2306.03809; Sepideh Jahangiri et al., "Viral and Non-viral Gene Therapy Using 3D (Bio) Printing," *Journal of Gene Medicine* 24, no. 12 (2022), article e3458; Tommaso Zandrini et al., "Breaking the Resolution Limits of 3D Bioprinting: Future Opportunities and Present Challenges," *Trends in Biotechnology* 41, no. 5 (2023): 604–14.

2. "China's Foreign Minister Visits Tonga After Pacific Islands Delay Regional Pact," Reuters, May 31, 2022, www.reuters.com/world/asia-pacific/chinas -foreign-minister-visits-tonga-after-pacific-islands-delay-regional -pact-2022-05-31/; David Wroe, "China Eyes Vanuatu Military Base in Plan with Global Ramifications," *Sydney Morning Herald,* April 9, 2018, www .smh.com.au/politics/federal/china-eyes-vanuatu-military-base-in-plan -with-global-ramifications-20180409-p4z8j9.html; Kirsty Needham, "China Seeks Pacific Islands Policing, Security Cooperation—Document," Reuters, May 25, 2022, www.reuters.com/world/asia-pacific/exclusive-china-seeks -pacific-islands-policing-security-cooperation-document-2022-05-25/; Australia Department of Foreign Affairs and Trade, "Australia-Tuvalu Fale-pili Union," accessed Jan. 12, 2024, www.dfat.gov.au/geo/tuvalu/australia -tuvalu-falepili-union; Joel Atkinson, "Why Tuvalu Still Chooses Taiwan," East Asia Forum, Oct. 24, 2022, www.eastasiaforum.org/2022/10/24/why -tuvalu-still-chooses-taiwan/.

3. Thomas G. Otte and Keith Neilson, eds., *Railways and International Politics: Paths of Empire, 1848–1945* (London: Routledge, 2012); Matthew Alexander Scott, "Transcontinentalism: Technology, Geopolitics, and the Baghdad and Cape-Cairo Railway Projects, c. 1880–1930" (PhD diss., Newcastle University, 2018).

4. Kevin Kelly, "The Three Breakthroughs That Have Finally Unleashed AI on the World," *Wired,* Oct. 27, 2014, www.wired.com/2014/10/future-of -artificial-intelligence/.

5. "From Not Working to Neural Networking," *Economist,* June 23, 2016, www .economist.com/special-report/2016/06/23/from-not-working-to-neural -networking.

6. Liat Clark, "Google's Artificial Brain Learns to Find Cat Videos," *Wired,* June 26, 2012, www.wired.com/2012/06/google-x-neural-network/; Jason Johnson, "This Deep Learning AI Generated Thousands of Creepy Cat Pictures," *Vice,* July 14, 2017, www.vice.com/en/article/a3dn9j/this-deep -learning-ai-generated-thousands-of-creepy-cat-pictures.

7. Amnesty International, "Automated Apartheid: How Facial Recognition Fragments, Segregates, and Controls Palestinians in the OPT," May 2, 2023, 42–43, www.amnesty.org/en/documents/mde15/6701/2023/en/.

8. The paper that described the development and architecture of AlexNet has, by 2023, been cited more than 120,000 times, which makes it one of the most influential academic articles in modern history: Alex Krizhevsky, Ilya Sutskever, and Geoffrey E. Hinton, "Imagenet Classification with Deep Convolutional Neural Networks," *Advances in Neural Information Processing Systems* 25

(2012). See also Mohammed Zahangir Alom et al., "The History Began from AlexNet: A Comprehensive Survey on Deep Learning Approaches" (preprint, submitted 2018), doi.org/10.48550/arXiv.1803.01164.

9. David Lai, *Learning from the Stones: A Go Approach to Mastering China's Strategic Concept, Shi* (Carlisle, Pa.: U.S. Army War College, Strategic Studies Institute, 2004); Zhongqi Pan, "*Guanxi, Weiqi,* and Chinese Strategic Thinking," *Chinese Political Science Review* 1 (2016): 303–21; Timothy J. Demy, James Giordano, and Gina Granados Palmer, "Chess vs Go—Strategic Strength, Gamecraft, and China," *National Defense,* July 8, 2021, www.nationaldefensemagazine.org/articles/2021/7/8/chess-vs-go---strategic-strength-gamecraft-and-china; David Vergun, "Ancient Game Used to Understand U.S.-China Strategy," U.S. Army, May 25, 2016, www.army.mil/article/168505/ancient_game_used_to_understand_u_s_china_strategy; "No Go," *Economist,* May 19, 2011, www.economist.com/books-and-arts/2011/05/19/no-go.

10. Suleyman, *Coming Wave,* 84.

11. Ibid.; Lee, *AI Superpowers;* Shyi-Min Lu, "The CCP's Development of Artificial Intelligence: Impact on Future Operations," *Journal of Social and Political Sciences* 4, no. 1 (2021): 93–105; Daitian Li, Tony W. Tong, and Yangao Xiao, "Is China Emerging as the Global Leader in AI?," *Harvard Business Review,* Feb. 18, 2021, hbr.org/2021/02/is-china-emerging-as-the-global-leader-in-ai; Robyn Mak, "Chinese AI Arrives by Stealth, Not with a Bang," Reuters, July 28, 2023, www.reuters.com/breakingviews/chinese-ai-arrives-by-stealth-not-with-bang-2023-07-28/.

12. "'Whoever Leads in AI Will Rule the World': Putin to Russian Children on Knowledge Day," Russia Today, Sept. 1, 2017, www.rt.com/news/401731-ai-rule-world-putin/; Ministry of External Affairs, "Prime Minister's Statement on the Subject 'Creating a Shared Future in a Fractured World' in the World Economic Forum (January 23, 2018)," Jan. 23, 2018, www.mea.gov.in/Speeches-Statements.htm?dtl/29378/Prime+Ministers+Keynote+Speech+at+Plenary+Session+of+World+Economic+Forum+Davos+January+23+2018.

13. Trump White House, "Executive Order on Maintaining American Leadership in AI," Feb. 11, 2019, trumpwhitehouse.archives.gov/ai/; Cade Metz, "Trump Signs Executive Order Promoting Artificial Intelligence," *New York Times,* Feb. 11, 2019, www.nytimes.com/2019/02/11/business/ai-artificial-intelligence-trump.html.

14. For a general discussion of data colonialism, see also Mejias and Couldry, *Data Grab.*

15. Conor Murray, "Here's What Happened When This Massive Country Banned TikTok," *Forbes,* March 23, 2023, www.forbes.com/sites/conormurray/2023/03/23/heres-what-happened-when-this-massive-country-banned-tiktok/; "India Bans TikTok, WeChat, and Dozens More Chinese Apps," BBC, June 29, 2020, www.bbc.com/news/technology-53225720.

16. Seung Min Kim, "White House: No More TikTok on Gov't Devices Within 30 Days," Associated Press, Feb. 28, 2023, apnews.com/article/technology-politics-united-states-government-ap-top-news-business-95491774cf8f0fe3e2b9634658a22e56; Stacy Liberatore, "Leaked Audio of More Than 80 TikTok Meetings Reveal China-Based Employees Are Accessing US User Data, New Report Claims," *Daily Mail,* June 17, 2022, www.dailymail.co.uk/sciencetech/article-10928485/Leaked-audio-80-TikTok-meetings-reveal

-China-based-employees-accessing-user-data.html; Dan Milmo, "TikTok's Ties to China: Why Concerns over Your Data Are Here to Stay," *Guardian,* Nov. 7, 2022, www.theguardian.com/technology/2022/nov/07/tiktoks-china -bytedance-data-concerns; James Clayton, "TikTok: Chinese App May Be Banned in US, Says Pompeo," BBC, July 7, 2020, www.bbc.com/news /technology-53319955.

17. Tess McClure, "New Zealand MPs Warned Not to Use TikTok over Fears China Could Access Data," *Guardian,* Aug. 2, 2022, www.theguardian.com /world/2022/aug/02/new-zealand-mps-warned-not-to-use-tiktok-over -fears-china-could-access-data; Milmo, "TikTok's Ties to China."

18. Akram Beniamin, "Cotton, Finance, and Business Networks in a Globalized World: The Case of Egypt During the First Half of the Twentieth Century" (PhD diss., University of Reading, 2019); Lars Sandberg, "Movements in the Quality of British Cotton Textile Exports, 1815–1913," *Journal of Economic History* 28, no. 1 (1968): 1–27; James Hagan and Andrew Wells, "The British and Rubber in Malaya, c. 1890–1940," in *The Past Is Before Us: Proceedings of the Ninth National Labor History Conference* (Sydney: University of Sydney, 2005), 143–50; John H. Drabble, "The Plantation Rubber Industry in Malaya up to 1922," *Journal of the Malaysian Branch of the Royal Asiatic Society* 40, no. 1 (1967): 52–77.

19. Paul Erdkamp, *The Grain Market in the Roman Empire: A Social, Political, and Economic Study* (Cambridge, U.K.: Cambridge University Press, 2005); Eli J. S. Weaverdyck, "Institutions and Economic Relations in the Roman Empire: Consumption, Supply, and Coordination," in *Handbook of Ancient Afro-Eurasian Economies,* vol. 2, *Local, Regional, and Imperial Economies,* ed. Sitta von Reden (Berlin: De Gruyter, 2022), 647–94; Colin Adams, *Land Transport in Roman Egypt: A Study of Economics and Administration in a Roman Province* (New York: Oxford University Press, 2007).

20. Palash Ghosh, "Amazon Is Now America's Biggest Apparel Retailer, Here's Why Walmart Can't Keep Up," *Forbes,* March 17, 2021, www.forbes.com /sites/palashghosh/2021/03/17/amazon-is-now-americas-biggest-apparel -retailer-heres-why-walmart-cant-keep-up/; Don-Alvin Adegeest, "Amazon's U.S. Marketshare of Clothing Soars to 14.6 Percent," Fashion United, March 15, 2022, fashionunited.com/news/retail/amazon-s-u-s-marketshare -of-clothing-soars-to-14-6-percent/2022031546520.

21. Invest Pakistan, "Textile Sector Brief," accessed Jan. 12, 2024, invest.gov.pk /textile; Morder Intelligence, "Bangladesh Textile Manufacturing Industry Size & Share Analysis—Growth Trends & Forecasts (2023–2028)," accessed Jan. 12, 2024, www.mordorintelligence.com/industry-reports/bangladesh -textile-manufacturing-industry-study-market.

22. Daron Acemoglu and Simon Johnson, *Power and Progress: Our 1000-Year Struggle over Technology and Prosperity* (Cambridge, Mass.: MIT Press, 2023).

23. PricewaterhouseCoopers, "Global Artificial Intelligence Study: Sizing the Prize," 2017, www.pwc.com/gx/en/issues/data-and-analytics/publications /artificial-intelligence-study.html.

24. Matt Sheehan, "China's AI Regulations and How They Get Made," Carnegie Endowment for International Peace, July 10, 2023, carnegieendowment.org /2023/07/10/china-s-ai-regulations-and-how-they-get-made-pub-90117; Daria Impiombato, Yvonne Lau, and Luisa Gyhn, "Examining Chinese Citi-

zens' Views on State Surveillance," *Strategist*, Oct. 12, 2023, www.aspistrategist
.org.au/examining-chinese-citizens-views-on-state-surveillance/; Strittmat-
ter, *We Have Been Harmonized*; Cain, *Perfect Police State*.

25. Zuboff, *Age of Surveillance Capitalism*; PHQ Team, "Survey: Americans Divided on Social Credit System," PrivacyHQ, 2022, privacyhq.com/news
/social-credit-how-do-i-stack-up/.

26. Lee, *AI Superpowers*.

27. Miller, *Chip War*; Robin Emmott, "U.S. Renews Pressure on Europe to Ditch
Huawei in New Networks," Reuters, Sept. 29, 2020, www.reuters.com/article
/us-usa-huawei-tech-europe-idUSKBN26K2MY/.

28. "President Trump Halts Broadcom Takeover of Qualcomm," Reuters,
March 13, 2018, www.reuters.com/article/us-qualcomm-m-a-broadcom
-merger/president-trump-halts-broadcom-takeover-of-qualcomm
-idUSKCN1GO1Q4/; Trump White House, "Presidential Order Regarding
the Proposed Takeover of Qualcomm Incorporated by Broadcom Limited,"
March 12, 2018, trumpwhitehouse.archives.gov/presidential-actions/presi
dential-order-regarding-proposed-takeover-qualcomm-incorporated
-broadcom-limited/; David McLaughlin and Saleha Mohsin, "Trump's Message in Blocking Broadcom Deal: U.S. Tech Not for Sale," Bloomberg,
March 13, 2018, www.bloomberg.com/politics/articles/2018-03-13/trump
-s-message-with-broadcom-block-u-s-tech-not-for-sale#xj4y7vzkg.

29. Suleyman, *Coming Wave*, 168; Stephen Nellis, Karen Freifeld, and Alexandra
Alper, "U.S. Aims to Hobble China's Chip Industry with Sweeping New Ex-
port Rules," Reuters, Oct. 10, 2022, www.reuters.com/technology/us-aims
-hobble-chinas-chip-industry-with-sweeping-new-export-rules-2022-10
-07/; Alexandra Alper, Karen Freifeld, and Stephen Nellis, "Biden Cuts
China Off from More Nvidia Chips, Expands Curbs to Other Countries,"
Oct. 18, 2023, www.reuters.com/technology/biden-cut-china-off-more
-nvidia-chips-expand-curbs-more-countries-2023-10-17/; Ann Cao, "US
Citizens at Chinese Chip Firms Caught in the Middle of Tech War After
New Export Restrictions," *South China Morning Post*, Oct. 11, 2022, www
.scmp.com/tech/tech-war/article/3195609/us-citizens-chinese-chip-firms
-caught-middle-tech-war-after-new.

30. Miller, *Chip War*.

31. Mark A. Lemley, "The Splinternet," *Duke Law Journal* 70 (2020): 1397–427.

32. Simcha Paull Raphael, *Jewish Views of the Afterlife*, 2nd ed. (Plymouth, U.K.:
Rowman & Littlefield, 2019); Claudia Seltzer, *Resurrection of the Body in
Early Judaism and Early Christianity: Doctrine, Community, and Self-Definition*
(Leiden: Brill, 2021).

33. Tertullian is quoted in Gerald O'Collins and Mario Farrugia, *Catholicism: The
Story of Catholic Christianity* (New York: Oxford University Press, 2015), 272.
For the quotations from the catechism, see *Catechism of the Catholic Church*,
2nd ed. (Vatican City: Libreria Editrice Vaticana, 1997), 265.

34. Bart D. Ehrman, *Heaven and Hell: A History of the Afterlife* (New York: Simon
& Schuster, 2021); Dale B. Martin, *The Corinthian Body* (New Haven, Conn.:
Yale University Press, 1999); Seltzer, *Resurrection of the Body*.

35. Thomas McDermott, "Antony's Life of St. Simeon Stylites: A Translation of
and Commentary on an Early Latin Version of the Greek Text" (master's
thesis, Creighton University, 1969); Robert Doran, *The Lives of Simeon Stylites*
(Kalamazoo, Mich.: Cistercian Publications, 1992).

36. Martin Luther, "An Introduction to St. Paul's Letter to the Romans," trans. Rev. Robert E. Smith, in *Vermischte Deutsche Schriften*, ed. Johann K. Irmischer (Erlangen: Heyder and Zimmer, 1854), 124–25, www.projectwittenberg.org/pub/resources/text/wittenberg/luther/luther-faith.txt.

37. Lemley, "Splinternet."

38. Ronen Bergman, Aaron Krolik, and Paul Mozur, "In Cyberattacks, Iran Shows Signs of Improved Hacking Capabilities," *New York Times*, Oct. 31, 2023, www.nytimes.com/2023/10/31/world/middleeast/iran-israel-cyberattacks.html.

39. For a fictional exploration of this idea by Admiral James Stavridis, NATO Supreme Allied Commander Europe from 2009 to 2013, see Elliot Ackerman and James Stavridis, *2034: A Novel of the Next World War* (New York: Penguin Press, 2022).

40. James D. Morrow, "A Twist of Truth: A Reexamination of the Effects of Arms Races on the Occurrence of War," *Journal of Conflict Resolution* 33, no. 3 (1989): 500–529.

41. See, for example, President of Russia, "Meeting with State Duma Leaders and Party Faction Heads," July 7, 2022, en.kremlin.ru/events/president/news/68836; President of Russia, "Valdai International Discussion Club Meeting," Oct. 5, 2023, en.kremlin.ru/events/president/news/72444; Donald J. Trump, "Remarks by President Trump to the 74th Session of the United Nations General Assembly," Sept. 24, 2019, trumpwhitehouse.archives.gov/briefings-statements/remarks-president-trump-74th-session-united-nations-general-assembly/; Jair Bolsonaro, "Speech by Brazil's President Jair Bolsonaro at the Opening of the 74th United Nations General Assembly—New York," Ministério das Relações Exteriores, Sept. 24, 2019, www.gov.br/mre/en/content-centers/speeches-articles-and-interviews/president-of-the-federative-republic-of-brazil/speeches/speech-by-brazil-s-president-jair-bolsonaro-at-the-opening-of-the-74th-united-nations-general-assembly-new-york-september-24-2019-photo-alan-santos-pr; Cabinet Office of the Prime Minister, "Speech by Prime Minister Viktor Orbán at the Opening of CPAC Texas," Aug. 4, 2022, 2015-2022.miniszterelnok.hu/speech-by-prime-minister-viktor-orban-at-the-opening-of-cpac-texas/; Geert Wilders, "Speech by Geert Wilders at the 'Europe of Nations and Freedom' Conference," Gatestone Institute, Jan. 22, 2017, www.gatestoneinstitute.org/9812/geert-wilders-koblenz-enf.

42. Marine Le Pen, "Discours de Marine Le Pen, (Front National), après le 2e tour des Régionales," Hénin-Beaumont, Dec. 6, 2015, www.youtube.com/watch?v=Dv7Us46gL8c.

43. Trump White House, "President Trump: 'We Have Rejected Globalism and Embraced Patriotism,'" Aug. 7, 2020, trumpwhitehouse.archives.gov/articles/president-trump-we-have-rejected-globalism-and-embraced-patriotism/.

44. Bengio et al., "Managing Extreme AI Risks Amid Rapid Progress."

45. John Mearsheimer, *The Tragedy of Great Power Politics* (New York: W. W. Norton, 2001), 21. See also Hans J. Morgenthau, *Politics Among Nations: The Struggle for Power and Peace* (New York: Alfred A. Knopf, 1949).

46. de Waal, *Our Inner Ape*.

47. Douglas Zook, "Tropical Rainforests as Dynamic Symbiospheres of Life," *Symbiosis* 51 (2010): 27–36; Aparajita Das and Ajit Varma, "Symbiosis: The Art of Living," in *Symbiotic Fungi: Principles and Practice*, ed. Ajit Varma and

Amit C. Kharkwal (Heidelberg: Springer, 2009), 1–28. See also de Waal, *Our Inner Ape;* Frans de Waal et al., *Primates and Philosophers: How Morality Evolved* (Princeton, N.J.: Princeton University Press, 2009); Frans de Waal, "Putting the Altruism Back into Altruism: The Evolution of Empathy," *Annual Review of Psychology* 59 (2008): 279–300.

48. Isabelle Crevecour et al., "New Insights on Interpersonal Violence in the Late Pleistocene Based on the Nile Valley Cemetery of Jebel Sahaba," *Nature Scientific Reports* 11 (2021), article 9991, doi.org/10.1038/s41598-021-89386-y; Marc Kissel and Nam C. Kim, "The Emergence of Human Warfare: Current Perspectives," *Yearbook of Physical Anthropology* 168, no. S67 (2019): 141–63; Luke Glowacki, "Myths About the Evolution of War: Apes, Foragers, and the Stories We Tell" (preprint, submitted in 2023), doi.org/10.32942/X2JC71.

49. Steven Pinker, *The Better Angels of Our Nature: Why Violence Has Declined* (New York: Viking, 2011); Gat, *War in Human Civilization,* 130–31; Joshua S. Goldstein, *Winning the War on War: The Decline of Armed Conflict Worldwide* (New York: Dutton, 2011); Harari, *21 Lessons for the 21st Century,* chap. 11; Azar Gat, "Is War Declining—and Why?," *Journal of Peace Research* 50, no. 2 (2012): 149–57; Michael Spagat and Stijn van Weezel, "The Decline of War Since 1950: New Evidence," in *Lewis Fry Richardson: His Intellectual Legacy and Influence in the Social Sciences,* ed. Nils Petter Gleditsch (Cham: Springer, 2020), 129–42; Michael Mann, "Have Wars and Violence Declined?," *Theory and Society* 47 (2018): 37–60.

50. The original Chinese quotations can be found in Chen Xiang, *Guling xiansheng wenji,* accessed Feb. 15, 2024, read.nlc.cn/OutOpenBook/OpenObjectBook?aid=892&bid=41448.0; Cai Xiang, *Caizhonghuigong wenji,* Feb. 15, 2024, ctext.org/library.pl?if=gb&file=127799&page=185&remap=gb; Li Tao, *Xu zizhi tongjian changbian* (Beijing: Zhonghua Shuju, 1985), 9:2928.

51. Emma Dench, *Empire and Political Cultures in the Roman World* (Cambridge, U.K.: Cambridge University Press, 2018), 79–80; Keith Hopkins, "The Political Economy of the Roman Empire," in *The Dynamics of Ancient Empires: State Power from Assyria to Byzantium,* ed. Ian Morris and Walter Scheidel (New York: Oxford University Press, 2009), 194; Walter Scheidel, "State Revenue and Expenditure in the Han and Roman Empires," in *State Power in Ancient China and Rome,* ed. Walter Scheidel (New York: Oxford University Press, 2015), 159; Paul Erdkamp, introduction to *A Companion to the Roman Army,* ed. Paul Erdkamp (Hoboken, N.J.: Blackwell, 2007), 2.

52. Suraiya Faroqhi, "Part II: Crisis and Change, 1590–1699," in *An Economic and Social History of the Ottoman Empire,* vol. 2, *1600–1914,* ed. Halil Inalcik and Donald Quataert (Cambridge, U.K.: Cambridge University Press, 1994), 542.

53. Jari Eloranta, "National Defense," in *The Oxford Encyclopedia of Economic History,* ed. Joel Mokyr (Oxford: Oxford University Press, 2003), 30–31.

54. Jari Eloranta, "Cliometric Approaches to War," in *Handbook of Cliometrics,* ed. Claude Diebolt and Michael Haupert (Heidelberg: Springer, 2014), 1–22.

55. Ibid.

56. Jari Eloranta, "The World Wars," in *An Economist's Guide to Economic History,* ed. Matthias Blum and Christopher L. Colvin (Cham: Palgrave, 2018), 263.

57. James H. Noren, "The Controversy over Western Measures of Soviet Defense Expenditures," *Post-Soviet Affairs* 11, no. 3 (1995): 238–76.

58. For relevant statistics on military expenditure as a percentage of government expenditure, see SIPRI, "SIPRI Military Expenditure Database," accessed Feb. 14, 2024, www.sipri.org/databases/milex. For data on U.S. military expenditures as a percentage of government expenditure, see also "Department of Defense," accessed Feb. 14, 2024, www.usaspending.gov/agency /department-of-defense?fy=2024.

59. World Health Organization, "Domestic General Government Health Expenditure (GGHE-D) as Percentage of General Government Expenditure (GGE) (%)," WHO Data, accessed Feb. 15, 2024, data.who.int/indicators/i /B9C6C79; World Bank, "Domestic General Government Health Expenditure (% of General Government Expenditure)," April 7, 2023, data.worldbank .org/indicator/SH.XPD.GHED.GE.ZS.

60. For data on recent conflict trends, see ACLED, "ACLED Conflict Index," Jan. 2024, acleddata.com/conflict-index/. See also Anna Marie Obermeier and Siri Aas Rustad, "Conflict Trends: A Global Overview, 1946–2022," PRIO, 2023, www.prio.org/publications/13513.

61. SIPRI fact sheet, April 2023, www.sipri.org/sites/default/files/2023-04/2304 _fs_milex_2022.pdf. "World military expenditure rose by 3.7 percent in real terms in 2022, to reach a record high of $2240 billion. Global spending grew by 19 percent over the decade 2013–22 and has risen every year since 2015." Nan Tian et al., "Trends in World Military Expenditure, 2022," SIPRI, April 2023, www.sipri.org/publications/2023/sipri-fact-sheets/trends-world -military-expenditure-2022; Dan Sabbagh, "Global Defense Spending Rises 9% to Record $2.2Tn," *Guardian*, Feb. 13, 2024, www.theguardian.com /world/2024/feb/13/global-defense-spending-rises-9-per-cent-to-record -22tn-dollars.

62. On the difficulties of estimating the exact number, see Erik Andermo and Martin Kragh, "Secrecy and Military Expenditures in the Russian Budget," *Post-Soviet Affairs* 36, no. 4 (2020): 1–26; "Russia's Secret Spending Hides over $110 Billion in 2023 Budget," Bloomberg, Sept. 29, 2022, www .bloomberg.com/news/articles/2022-09-29/russia-s-secret-spending-hides -over-110-billion-in-2023-budget?leadSource=uverify%20wall. For other estimates of Russia's military expenditures, see Julian Cooper, "Another Budget for a Country at War: Military Expenditure in Russia's Federal Budget for 2024 and Beyond," SIPRI, Dec. 2023, www.sipri.org/sites/default/files/2023 -12/sipriinsights_2312_11_russian_milex_for_2024_0.pdf; Alexander Marrow, "Putin Approves Big Military Spending Hike for Russia's Budget," Reuters, Nov. 28, 2023, www.reuters.com/world/europe/putin-approves-big -military-spending-hikes-russias-budget-2023-11-27/.

63. Sabbagh, "Global Defense Spending Rises 9% to Record $2.2Tn."

64. On Putin's various forays into the field of history, see Björn Alexander Düben, "Revising History and 'Gathering the Russian Lands': Vladimir Putin and Ukrainian Nationhood," *LSE Public Policy Review* 3, no. 1 (2023), article 4; Vladimir Putin, "Article by Vladimir Putin 'On the Historical Unity of Russians and Ukrainians,'" President of Russia, July 12, 2021, en.kremlin.ru /events/president/news/66181. Western views of Putin's article are surveyed in Peter Dickinson, "Putin's New Ukraine Essay Reveals Imperial Ambitions," Atlantic Council, July 15, 2021, www.atlanticcouncil.org/blogs /ukrainealert/putins-new-ukraine-essay-reflects-imperial-ambitions/; Timothy D. Snyder, "How to Think About War in Ukraine," *Thinking About . . . ,*

Jan. 18, 2022, snyder.substack.com/p/how-to-think-about-war-in-ukraine. For examples of specialists who think Putin truly believes this historical narrative, see Ivan Krastev, "Putin Lives in Historic Analogies and Metaphors," *Spiegel International,* March 17, 2022, www.spiegel.de/international/world /ivan-krastev-on-russia-s-invasion-of-ukraine-putin-lives-in-historic -analogies-and-metaphors-a-1d043090-1111-4829-be90-c20fd5786288; Serhii Plokhii, "Interview with Serhii Plokhy: 'Russia's War Against Ukraine: Empires Don't Die Overnight,'" *Forum for Ukrainian Studies,* Sept. 26, 2022, ukrainian-studies.ca/2022/09/26/interview-with-serhii-plokhy-russias-war -against-ukraine-empires-dont-die-overnight/.

65. Adam Gabbatt and Andrew Roth, "Putin Tells Tucker Carlson the US 'Needs to Stop Supplying Weapons' to Ukraine," *Guardian,* Feb. 9, 2024, www .theguardian.com/world/2024/feb/08/vladimir-putin-tucker-carlson -interview.

EPILOGUE

1. Yuval Noah Harari, "Strategy and Supply in Fourteenth-Century Western European Invasion Campaigns," *Journal of Military History* 64, no. 2 (April 2000): 297–334; Yuval Noah Harari, *The Ultimate Experience: Battlefield Revelations and the Making of Modern War Culture, 1450–2000* (Houndmills, U.K.: Palgrave Macmillan, 2008).

2. Thant, *Hidden History of Burma,* 74.

3. Ben Caspit, *The Netanyahu Years,* trans. Ora Cummings (New York: St. Martin's Press, 2017), 323–24; Ruth Eglash, "Netanyahu Once Gave Obama a Lecture. Now He's Using It to Boost His Election Campaign," *Washington Post,* March 28, 2019, www.washingtonpost.com/world/2019/03/28 /netanyahu-once-gave-obama-lecture-now-hes-using-it-boost-his-election -campaign/.

4. Jennifer Larson, *Understanding Greek Religion* (London: Routledge, 2016), 194; Harvey Whitehouse, *Inheritance: The Evolutionary Origins of the Modern World* (London: Hutchinson, 2024), 113.

Index

religion (*cont.*)
  errors and, 70
  human abuse of power and, xiii
  incentive structures and, 111–12
  inconsistency and, 71–72
  infallibility and, 69, 71–73, 103, 106–7
  intersubjective realities and, 22, 27, 287
  memory and, 23–24, 43, 44
  nations and, 33
  personal revelations and, 71–72
  populism and, xxvii, xxviii
  self-correcting mechanisms and, 35–36, 104,
    106–7, 108–9
  social credit systems and, 291–92
  social order and, 36, 71
  stories and, 19, 22–24, 38, 416n19
  totalitarianism and, 173–76
  truth-order balance and, 38
  utilitarianism and, 283, 284
  See also Christianity; holy books; Judaism;
    religious institutions
religious institutions, 72–73, 76–77, 80, 81, 88,
  91, 173–76
  See also Catholic Church
Replika, 211
Republic (Plato), 34, 410–11n21
reputation market, 251–52, 253
rigidity/pliability, 314–16
robots, 218, 316–17
Rohingya massacre (Myanmar), 195–200
  alignment problem and, 272
  alternative views and, 197–98
  computer network goals and, 199, 259, 265
  computers as independent agents and, 197,
    198–200
  culpability for, 199–200
  deontology and, 278–79
  error-enhancing mechanisms and, 265
  misinformation/disinformation and, 195,
    196
  self-correcting mechanisms and, 264
  tech company culpability and, 199, 200, 219,
    220, 263
Roman Empire
  autocracy vs. totalitarianism and, 154–55,
    156
  centralization of power and, 118–19,
    356–58, 372–73
  damnatio memoriae, 351
  democracy and, 139, 141, 142, 143–44
  infallibility and, 119
  military spending, 390
  self-correcting mechanisms and, 151–52
Romania, 65–67, 231–33, 234, 236, 424n52
romantic triangles, 60

Roosevelt, Franklin D., 33, 325
Rousseau, Jean-Jacque, 102
Royal Society of London for Improving
  Natural Knowledge, 102
Russell, Bertrand, 359–60
Russell-Einstein Manifesto (1955), 359–60
Russia
  AI development and, 369
  democracy as autocratic tool and, 122, 123,
    134
  doublespeak and, 352–53
  Silicon Curtain and, 375
  social media banning, 371
  Ukraine invasion, 353, 392–93
  See also Tsarist Russia
Rwanda genocide (1994), 60, 197
Rychagov, Pavel, 180–81

Said, Edward, xxv
Salazar Frías, Alonso de, 101
Sayadaw U Vithuddha, 197–98
science
  bureaucracy and, 51–52
  collaboration and, xxvii
  compartmentalization and, 51–54
  cooperation and, 32, 33
  dissent and, 113–15, 180
  majority rule and, 127
  Nazism and, 38
  populism on, 133
  religion and, 16
  self-correcting mechanisms and, 103–5,
    110–15
  skeptical empiricism and, xxvi–xxvii
  skeptical views of, xxv, xxvi
  Soviet collectivization and, 166, 168
scientific revolution, 92, 101, 102–3
Second Council of Lyon (1274), 379
Sedol, Lee, 332, 333, 368
Sejanus, Lucius Aelius, 356–58
self-correcting mechanisms, 103–17
  absence in autocracies, 117, 119, 179–80,
    358–60
  algorithms as, 336–38
  ancient world, 156
  civil rights and, 124
  computer-based network fallibility and, 301
  computer network goals and, 274–75
  decentralization and, 312–13
  democracy and, 117, 119, 120–22, 123,
    124–25, 128, 147, 151
  denial of, 109
  dissent and, 113–16, 432n111
  elections and, 121–22, 126
  as essential, 402–4

ABOUT THE AUTHOR

Professor YUVAL NOAH HARARI is a historian, a philosopher, and the bestselling author of *Sapiens: A Brief History of Humankind, Homo Deus: A Brief History of Tomorrow, 21 Lessons for the 21st Century,* and the series *Sapiens: A Graphic History* and *Unstoppable Us.* He is considered one of the world's most influential public intellectuals working today. Born in Israel in 1976, Harari received his PhD from the University of Oxford in 2002 and is currently a lecturer in the Department of History at the Hebrew University of Jerusalem. He cofounded the social impact company Sapienship, focused on education and media, with his husband, Itzik Yahav.

ABOUT THE TYPE

This book was set in Caslon, a typeface first designed in 1722 by William Caslon (1692–1766). Its widespread use by most English printers in the early eighteenth century soon supplanted the Dutch typefaces that had formerly prevailed. The roman is considered a "work-horse" typeface due to its pleasant, open appearance, while the italic is exceedingly decorative.